BANKING AND EMPIRE IN IRAN

The History of The British Bank
of the Middle East

VOLUME 1

BANKING AND EMPIRE IN IRAN

The History of The British Bank
of the Middle East

VOLUME 1

GEOFFREY JONES

Business History Unit, London School of Economics and Political Science

Research by

FRANCES BOSTOCK, GRIGORI GERENSTEIN
JUDITH NICHOL

The right of the
University of Cambridge
to print and sell
all manner of books
was granted by
Henry VIII in 1534.
The University has printed
and published continuously
since 1584.

CAMBRIDGE UNIVERSITY PRESS

CAMBRIDGE

LONDON   NEW YORK   NEW ROCHELLE
MELBOURNE   SYDNEY

Published by the Press Syndicate of the University of Cambridge
The Pitt Building, Trumpington Street, Cambridge CB2 1RP
32 East 57th Street, New York, NY 10022, USA
10 Stamford Road, Oakleigh, Melbourne 3166, Australia

First published 1986

Printed in Great Britain at the University Press, Cambridge

British Library cataloguing in publication data
Jones, Geoffrey
Banking and Empire in Iran
(The history of The British Bank of the Middle East)
Vol. 1
1. The British Bank of the Middle East – History
I. Title. II. Series
332.1′2′0955 HG 3270.2.A8B7

Library of Congress cataloguing in publication data
Jones, Geoffrey.
Banking and empire in Iran
Bibliography: v. 1, p.
1. British Bank of the Middle East – History.
2. Banks and banking, British – Iran.
3. Banks and banking, British – Near East.
I. Bostock, Frances. II. Gerenstein, Grigori. III. Nichol, Judith.
IV. Title.
HG3270.2.A8B755 1986 332.1′5′0955 85–31359
ISBN 0 521 32322 3

CE

CONTENTS

TABLES

ILLUSTRATIONS

xi

The Hongkong and Shanghai Banking Corporation is indebted to Mr William L. S. Barratt for his assistance in making available a number of the bank notes of The Imperial Bank of Persia which are reproduced in this book.

To Frances

FOREWORD

The HongkongBank Group has long since grown into an institution of global proportions but I feel that we should not forget our more modest origins.

It was the British more than anyone else who pioneered overseas banking and Dr Geoffrey Jones has shown us in this, the first of two volumes of The History of The British Bank of the Middle East, something of the pioneering spirit of that Bank in its early years as The Imperial Bank of Persia.

The British Bank of the Middle East became a member of The Hongkong-Bank Group in 1960. However, its particular expertise and character, which have grown from so many years of experience since its foundation in 1889, continue to make it a powerful force in the Middle East where the 'BBME' has long been a household name.

When HongkongBank commissioned Dr Geoffrey Jones to write The History of The British Bank of the Middle East, I was anxious that it should be researched independently of the Bank from several archival sources and be a thorough, academic business history. In particular, I did not want a history reflecting a partisan line. What was wanted was a history which, to make it credible, would show the Bank's failings and weaknesses as well as its hopes and strengths. I congratulate Dr Jones and his dedicated research assistants for keeping to this mandate and giving us what I feel is a most readable, accurate and important contribution to banking and business history.

In Volume 1, Dr Jones lets us see not only the triumphs and trials of The Imperial Bank of Persia as it pioneered modern banking in Iran, but also how so often it was drawn into the intricacies of international diplomacy and had to cope with much more than just the day to day problems of routine commercial banking. In 1952 the Bank made the painful decision to withdraw from Iran where for so long it had had its roots and Chief Office. However, Volume 2, *Banking and Oil*, which will be published later in 1986, will describe how by then the Bank was already expanding throughout the Arabian Gulf, showing once again that it had lost nothing of its pioneering spirit by being the first bank in Kuwait, Dubai and Oman.

As the Arabian Gulf itself was transformed by its new oil wealth, and as the Bank's business grew, it was increasingly evident that The British Bank of the Middle East remained a medium sized bank with a modest capitalisation. It was inevitable that, sooner or later, it would have to merge with a larger organisation. We are all happy that, when it came, the marriage was with The Hongkong and Shanghai Banking Corporation.

Today, HongkongBank is one of the largest banks in the world. We look at our past and our origins with pride and no little gratitude for the good fortune we have enjoyed. We also look to the future with the confidence we have always had and we still have plenty of the pioneering spirit which is so evident in this history.

We must not forget that behind past successes there lies the dedication and personal lives of the staff. The staff, both local and expatriate, are not forgotten by Dr Jones in this history, and I think it is fitting to regard this book as a tribute to the men who founded this Bank, established its business and kept it going, often through very difficult times, to make The British Bank of the Middle East what it is today.

1 Queen's Road Central   M G R SANDBERG
Hong Kong

PREFACE

In April 1982 the Hongkong Bank asked me to write a history of The British Bank of the Middle East, or BBME, a member of the Hongkong Bank Group since 1960. I was offered full access to the Bank's confidential archives, and a promise that I would be allowed to write a scholarly and objective study. This promise has keen kept. Although this History was sponsored by the Hongkong Bank, the views expressed in it are mine and there has been no censorship. This is a business history, warts and all. Banks have rarely allowed business historians free access to their records, especially for the twentieth century. It is to be hoped that the Hongkong Bank's example will be followed by others.

This book tells the history of the BBME before 1952. The Bank's name changed several times between its foundation in 1889 and 1952. Originally it was The Imperial Bank of Persia. In 1935 it became The Imperial Bank of Iran, and in 1949 The British Bank of Iran and the Middle East. The present name was adopted in 1952. The common factor behind the changing names was that until the 1940s the Bank's primary area of business was Iran, where it occupied a special and unique place. This book focuses on the Bank's history in that country. A second volume will examine the Bank's remarkable diversification into the Arab world after 1940.

It must be emphasised that this is a history of a bank. It is not a study of British diplomacy in Iran. Nor is it an examination of modern Iranian political and economic history. I have tried to place the Bank's history in a wider political and economic context, but inevitably this context has often been painted with a broad brush. I hope diplomatic historians, and specialists in Iranian history, will forgive my, at times, cavalier treatment of their work. Equally, banking historians must excuse my frequent focus on political and diplomatic matters. The Imperial Bank was, as this History makes clear, a political bank, and its significance cannot be understood by a narrow concentration on purely banking business. A business history cannot, and should not, say everything about its institution. It is the historian's role to select the themes and issues which he believes to be important.

My greatest debt in the writing of this book is to my researchers. Without their help, I could not have penetrated the voluminous archives of the Bank and the British government. Frances Bostock was a tower of strength to the Project. Her dedication, enthusiasm and hard work have made a fundamental contribution, while her humour and kindness have preserved her colleagues' sanity at a time when the complexities of Middle East banking seemed to overwhelm us. Grigori Gerenstein took time off his career as a writer to research Russian policy in Iran, and stayed to make himself an expert on banking under Reza Shah. Judith Nichol researched the sections on India and Iraq, and enlivened our work with stories of the social lives of the Bank's staff. The work and ideas of these three researchers permeates the History. I should also like to thank a number of individuals who have made contributions to the Project for shorter periods, especially Shirley Keeble, Judy Slinn and Nuala Zahedieh.

Current and former staff of the BBME and their wives have provided an unfailing source of guidance and help. I would particularly like to mention, for their contribution to this volume: P. E. H. Alexander, K. Bradford, G. A. Calver, A. Crowe, A. H. Ebtehaj, H. Evans, J. L. A. Francis, J. D. Hammond, E. S. Jenkins, F. H. Johnson, C. D. Lunn, A. Macqueen, P. Mason, K. R. H. Murray, the late T. Sheahan, Mrs M. W. Sinclair, T. M. Tagg, and C. F. Warr. The memories of many of these people have been recorded in a separate Oral History Project, directed by Christopher Cook. The transcripts are stored in the Archives of the Hongkong Bank Group, and I have drawn on them in the chapters in this History dealing with the period after the First World War. I have, except in a few instances, left the extracts unedited, in order to preserve the original flavour of the recollections.

A special mention needs to be made of the contribution of J. L. A. Francis. While still in service with the Bank he played a key role in the administration of the History Project, and in introducing the historian to retired members of staff. After his retirement in 1983, he retained his interest in the History, and read and commented upon every draft which was produced. No one could have been more helpful.

I have received the greatest assistance and co-operation from the staff of the Hongkong Bank in London and Hong Kong. The Chairman, M. G. R. Sandberg, has read and commented upon draft chapters of the History. P. E. Hutson has read each chapter, and his helpful criticisms have helped to reduce my errors. The Controller of Group Archives, S. W. Muirhead, has not only undertaken some herculean administrative tasks concerning the Project, but read the History in its various stages of development. Only he and I know how much work this has involved. Margaret Lee, also in Group Archives, has searched Hong Kong for materials relevant to BBME's story.

In London, Alex Cheeseman, P. Holness, G. Plastow and Pat Roberts have all helped the Project in many and varied ways.

Among academic colleagues, a number have helped me greatly in the preparation of this History. Professor F. H. H. King of the University of Hong Kong has interrupted his own research on the Hongkong Bank to guide, criticise and even, once or twice, praise my work. Catherine and David King have at various times subjected my drafts to their critical attention. Professor Leslie Pressnell has read each chapter and given me the benefit of his formidable knowledge of finance and banking. Dr Paul Luft, of the University of Durham, has helped correct some of my misapprehensions regarding Iranian history, and together with J. L. A. Francis, guided me through the problem of Persian transliteration. I would also like to thank Mrs Bates for allowing the publication of several of her father's photographs, and Dr Luft and Dr R. I. Lawless for arranging the reproduction of them.

In this History Persian words have been transliterated following, in general, the rules established for modern Persian. However, in the cases of well-known place names I have left the spelling in the form known to most English-speakers. I have done the same with personal names. Diacritical signs have been omitted. Persia became officially known as Iran in the 1930s. There is no elegant way of dealing with this change. I have used Persia in the first seven chapters of this book, dealing with the period up to the 1930s, and Iran in the remaining five chapters. Many British people continued to refer to Persia long after 1935, and when I have quoted directly I have not changed such references to Iran.

A penultimate and heartfelt word of thanks must go to the generations of typists who have turned my scrawl into a typescript. Beverly Chandler, Susan Crawshaw, Penny Ewles, Rachel Harry, Joan Lynas, Gail Martin, and Eve Mason have all had this task inflicted upon them. They have typed and retyped drafts, corrected my grammar and generally cheered me up. Their efforts have been very appreciated.

The final word of thanks goes to my wife, Frances. She has initiated me into some of the mysteries of accountancy, criticised draft chapters, made the tea, and understood when, as has been the norm over the last three years, her husband seemed to put the History before all else.

Despite the great assistance I have received from colleagues and friends, final responsibility for this book and the judgements expressed in it remain with the author.

London
April 1985

GEOFFREY JONES

INTRODUCTION

This is the first volume of a two-volume History of The British Bank of the Middle East, from its foundation in London in 1889, under the name of The Imperial Bank of Persia, until the present day.

The Imperial Bank of Persia was one of many overseas banks established in Britain in the second half of the nineteenth century. By 1914 there were some 18 British-owned banks doing business in the Empire (known as the 'Imperial Banks'), and a further 24 (known as the 'International Banks') banking in foreign countries.[1] The Imperial Bank was at best a medium-sized overseas bank, never matching the size, and prestige of, say, the mighty Hongkong and Shanghai Banking Corporation (known hereafter as the Hongkong Bank). Before 1940 the Bank largely conducted business in Persia, or Iran as that country became officially known in 1935. After 1940 the Bank developed an extensive branch network in the Arabic-speaking countries of the Middle East, a metamorphosis which culminated when it left Iran in 1952 and symbolised by its adoption of the new name, The British Bank of the Middle East (or BBME). In terms of British overseas banks, however, BBME remained medium-sized, and in 1960 it merged with the Hongkong Bank.

The significance of this History for British business history lies not in the overall size of the Bank, but in the fact that BBME has maintained an extensive historical archive, and that the Hongkong Bank has invited an independent historian to write an objective and scholarly account of BBME's development. The history of British overseas banking has hardly begun to be written. With some exceptions, most overseas banks have had their histories written by novelists or retirees.[2] This History will, it is hoped, shed light not only on this particular bank, but also on the history of the whole of British overseas banking activity. Moreover, business history is notoriously biased towards the study of the large and successful firm or bank. This study of a smaller institution, and one whose history was not one of continuous expansion and success, will help to compensate this situation.

This History is not simply a contribution to British business and banking history. BBME was a small fish in a large pool of British overseas banks, but the Bank's significance in the Middle East was altogether different. The Bank was, and still is, a major force in Middle East banking. In country after country it pioneered modern banking. In Persia between 1889 and 1928 the Imperial Bank was the de facto state bank, with sole note issuing authority. After 1940 the Bank introduced modern banking to the Arabian Gulf states, being, for instance, the first and only bank in Kuwait between 1941 and 1952, in Dubai between 1946 and 1963, and in Oman between 1948 and 1968. BBME staff saw, and the Bank participated in, the transformation of these states into some of the richest countries in the world in the space of a few decades. The Bank may have been a minor player in the story of British overseas banking, but it had a starring role in the twentieth-century economic history of several Middle Eastern countries.

The British Bank of the Middle East has to be seen as both a British and a Middle Eastern institution. It was in one sense thoroughly British; its Board, management, senior staff and banking methods were solidly British. Yet it was also in Persia, and later on in various Arab countries, an agent in the economic development, and in a real sense a national institution, of those countries. The dual identity of the Bank will be a recurring theme of this History.

Part 1

FOUNDATION AND GROWTH

1

THE FOUNDATION OF THE BANK

1.1 SETTING

The British Bank of the Middle East is the direct descendant of the Imperial Bank of Persia, a British bank formed in 1889 with a Royal Charter granted by Queen Victoria and a Concession from the Persian government making it the state bank of Persia.

The origins of the Bank are found in events and negotiations which stretch back for 17 years before 1889. As befitted an institution with a dual identity, British and Middle Eastern, a colourful assembly of politicians and entrepreneurs in both Britain and Persia were parties to this extended story. The number of interests involved, and the diversity of their aims, help to explain why it took so long to achieve anything concrete. So, too, does the fact that the common denominator between these various British and Persian interests was a conviction that the construction of railways in Persia held the key to achieving their diverse goals. It was a considerable irony that the end result of nearly two decades of negotiations was not a railway, but a bank.

The story of the Imperial Bank's foundation is long and tortuous, moving from Persia to Britain and back again. It is a story worth following, however, for much about the Imperial Bank's early history cannot be understood without an appreciation of the strange circumstances which led to its birth.

1.2 GENESIS: THE REUTER CONCESSION OF 1872

The history of the Imperial Bank's foundation begins in the early 1870s, and with two men, one famous, and one long forgotten. The forgotten figure was Mirza Hoseyn Khan, Sepahsalar Moshir od-Doule, a Persian reformer remembered now only by historians of nineteenth-century Persia. The famous figure was Baron Julius de Reuter, a European whose surname is still a household word thanks to the News Agency which he founded.

In 1870 the Shah of Persia, Naser od-Din, appointed Mirza Hoseyn Khan

3

Map 1 Persia, showing branches of the Bank in 1913

in quick succession to the offices of Minister of Justice, Minister of War and, in November 1871, Prime Minister. (See Appendix 8 for an explanation of Persian names in this period.) Mirza Hoseyn Khan had already established a reputation as a reformer. As Persian Minister to Istanbul in the 1860s he had strongly advocated reforming measures in the despatches home,[1] and in his new position of power he determined to put his reforms into practice.

Although a Bank history is not the place for a detailed examination of the politics and economics of late nineteenth-century Persia, a brief thumbnail sketch is necessary to indicate the problems faced by Mirza Hoseyn Khan.

The case for reform in Persia in 1870 was overwhelming. Persia at this time was, as a recent economic historian has observed, 'one of the most backward countries in the world'.[2] The country was extremely large, its 630 000 square miles being equal to the combined area of the Ten members (in 1985) of the European Economic Community (see Map 1, which depicts Persia in this period and gives the location of the Bank's branches before the First World War). Reliable statistics on Persia in this period are conspicuous by their absence, but there is a consensus amongst writers on the subject that most of the population, which may have increased from five million in 1800 to ten million in 1914, was extremely poor, ravaged by disease and dependent for its livelihood on an agricultural sector subject to periodic famines. Statistics on agricultural production are non-existent for the nineteenth century, but it does seem that cash crops such as silk, cotton and opium expanded their production severalfold during the middle decades of the century. However, an outbreak of silkworm disease in 1864 badly dislocated silk production, and in 1869 and 1870 a drought crippled agriculture in much of the country. The silkworm disease hit the country's major export. In the early 1860s Persia exported more than 20 000 bales of silk a year, but by 1870 this figure had dropped by 75%.[3] When Mirza Hoseyn Khan came to power his country's agriculture was in crisis.

Other aspects of the Persian economy were also in an unhealthy condition. In past centuries traditional Persian handicrafts had reached a considerable level of sophistication, but during the nineteenth century many traditional crafts fared badly against the competition of cheap machine-made European goods. It was a similar story in Asian countries, such as India, and as elsewhere the picture was not one of unrelieved decline. Improvements in international transport and the completion of the Suez Canal in 1869 opened new market opportunities in Europe for traditional crafts. During the last decade of the century, for example, both foreign capitalists and Persian merchants began to establish workshops and factories to supply Persian carpets to meet growing demand in Europe and the United States, but in 1870 this trend had hardly begun.[4] There was no modern factory industry in Persia in 1870, and as late as 1914 fewer than 2000 Persians were employed in factories.

The reports of foreign consuls in Persia provide patchy evidence on the country's balance of payments. Persia was probably running a deficit by 1870. In the first half of the century visible exports may have covered imports, but from the early 1860s there seems to have been a deficit as Persia imported increasing quantities of textiles, sugar and tea, while silk exports fell. In 1864 imports were estimated at £1.8 million and exports at £600 000. In 1871 imports were estimated to be under £800 000 and exports only £340 000. Almost nothing is known about the invisible items in Persia's balance of payments, such as the expenditure of foreign pilgrims visiting the Persian holy city of Mashad and Persian pilgrims visiting holy places of the Shia sect of

Islam in neighbouring Turkish territory. Widespread contemporary evidence of specie leaving the country, however, has been used to suggest that there was an overall balance of payments deficit.[5]

The Persian currency system, about which much will be said in later chapters, also manifested signs of weakness, although in 1870 some of the worst problems had yet to appear. The exchange value of the Kran, the standard monetary unit in Persia, fell by 50% compared to Sterling between 1800 and 1850, and it fell by a further 50% between 1850 and 1880. Before 1870 the main reason for this depreciation was the debasement of the currency by successive governments. After 1870 the situation was complicated by a fall in the world price of silver relative to gold. Persia, like most countries except Britain and Portugal before 1870, used both gold and silver to settle its international accounts. But from 1871, when Imperial Germany went on to the gold standard, there was a fairly rapid move by most countries away from silver. From the early 1870s, this demonetisation of silver together with the discovery of large new deposits of silver in Nevada and various other factors, caused silver to depreciate against gold. Although Persia remained nominally bimetallic, most of its limited gold reserves drained away during the next 20 years and its currency increasingly became silver only. Persian currency began weakening against Sterling from around 1875, but it was not until the early 1890s that a really sharp fall occurred.[6] The silver problem, as it came to be called, was to have a considerable impact on the early life of the Imperial Bank, and will be discussed in greater detail in the next chapters.

The administrative structure inherited by Mirza Hoseyn Khan was also visibly in need of reform. The Qajar dynasty of Shahs, which had ruled Persia since the 1790s, had restored internal peace within the country after decades of unrest, and constructed the framework of a centralised state, but the administration rested on weak foundations. All posts in the state bureaucracy were sold, or 'farmed' as the practice was called, a policy which in the long term severely circumscribed the government's revenue-raising capabilities. One estimate is that tax collectors kept three times as much of the tax receipts as ultimately reached the government.[7] Similarly the sale of posts in the Army rendered that institution useless. By common consent Persia had the worst standing army in the world. There had been hopes of reform after Naser od-Din became Shah in 1848. A reforming Prime Minister, Amir Kabir, had established a technical college at the capital, Tehran. But he was soon assassinated for his pains, and by 1870 little or nothing had been achieved.

Mirza Hoseyn Khan and others who sought to reform their country, knew that the economic condition of Persia and its ramshackle administration had serious implications for national sovereignty. Persia's misfortune was its location between the Asiatic Empire of the Russian Tsar and the Indian

Empire of the British Queen. Throughout the nineteenth century Russia steadily expanded its power and influence among the Muslim nations to the north of the Persian Empire. In 1801 Russia had annexed the Persian province of Georgia. Persia had gone to war to recover its lost territory, and as a result lost most of the rest of her Caucasus provinces, including Baku. A further war between 1826 and 1828 led to another humiliating Persian defeat. The Treaty of Turkomanchai in 1828 resulted in the loss of more Persian territory in the Caucasus region. After 1828 there was no further Russian acquisition of Persian territory west of the Caspian, and Russian attention focused instead on the Central Asian Khanates and nomads east of the Caspian. In the second half of the century, the Russian military made large advances in this region, and by the early 1870s they had occupied the three Central Asian Khanates of Khokand, Bukhara, and Khiva.[8]

The British government watched the Russian advance in the second half of the century with increasing alarm. The approach of the Russians was seen as having extremely serious implications for Britain's position in India, the jewel of the British Empire: 'Were it not for our possessing India', Lord Salisbury, Conservative Prime Minister and Foreign Secretary in the late nineteenth century observed, 'we should trouble ourselves but little about Persia.'[9] The British were uncertain about the motivation of the Russian advance, but as Anglo–Russian rivalry was an almost constant feature of the entire nineteenth century most observers ascribed the worst motives to the Tsar and his generals. It was widely suspected that Russia's long-term aim was a warm-water port on the Gulf, from which it could challenge British control of India.

No clear policy had emerged in the British government by 1870 in response to the Russian advance in Central Asia. Some British officials in India argued for 'masterly inactivity', a policy of monitoring the Russian advance, but avoiding a precipitate reaction. In England, the Liberals led by Gladstone were associated with this view. A rival school recommended 'mischievous activity', a policy of using the states between India and the advancing Russians – namely Persia and Afghanistan – as outposts in India's defence. Conservatives such as Disraeli and Lord Salisbury supported this approach, although these party divisions were not rigid.[10]

During this period two main threads were discernible in British diplomatic policy towards Persia. The first was to try and reach an agreement with Russia to guarantee the frontiers, including those of Persia, in the region. The second policy was the buffer principle. This involved encouraging reform in Persia, and the improvement of the economy and communications, with the hope that Persia could be turned into an effective barrier against further Russian advance. This British aim coincided with the plans of the Persian reformers, but there was little trust between the two parties. Although most

Persians loathed and feared the Tsarist government, British motives were
also suspect. Few wished to see Persia follow the fate of India. On the other
side, most Britons doubted the Persian ability for reform. 'The Shah is about
as likely to undertake a genuinely great public work as he is to turn
Protestant', G. N. Curzon (the future Lord Curzon, Viceroy of India
1899–1905, British Foreign Secretary 1919–24, and author of the masterly
work *Persia and the Persian Question*), observed when he returned from his
travels in Persia.[11]

Persia in 1870 was already the uncomfortable host for British and
Russian diplomatic and commercial rivalry and intrigue: 'Turkestan, Afghanistan, Transcaspia, Persia', Curzon wrote, 'to many these words breathe
only a sense of utter remoteness or a memory of strange vicissitudes and of
moribund romance. To me, I confess, they are pieces on a chessboard upon
which is being played out a game for the dominion of the world.'[12]

Mirza Hoseyn Khan had no wish for his country to be reduced to a
British or a Russian pawn. On assuming power as Prime Minister he
launched a series of judicial and legislative reforms, attempted to improve
the state of the Army, and strove to make the revenue system more
effective.[13] He aimed to improve trade and reverse the decline of Persia's
handicrafts. For him and other Persian reformers railways were seen as
holding the key to success. Railways were a symbol of modernisation in the
nineteenth century, the equivalent to the international airport of the 1980s.
The world's leading industrial nation, Britain, had led the way in railway
construction earlier in the century, and it seemed that railways and modernisation were an inseparable duo. Persian reformers observed that some
Middle Eastern countries had already begun railway construction. Egypt
had its first railway in 1853, followed by Turkey in 1867. Railways seemed
a panacea for the country's ills. The expansion of cash crop production, and
therefore exports, and the development of modern industry were visibly
handicapped by Persia's poor internal transport system. Sea transportation
was of limited value. The Gulf ports were separated from access to the
Persian highlands by natural barriers and hostile groups of population. The
country's only navigable river, the Karun from the Gulf, was closed to
foreigners for commerce by the Persian government until 1888. There were
virtually no roads in Persia, and therefore no wheeled vehicles. The fastest
means of transport was by *chapar*, a system of riding horses in stages which
enabled some 60–100 miles to be covered daily. Goods had to travel by
mule or camel caravan, a very slow process. Railways seemed to offer a
quick breakthrough out of this situation. 'The establishment of a railroad in
Iran', the Persian Consul in Tiflis, the capital of Russian Caucasus, wrote
in 1864, 'will in three years revolutionise the country, bring order and

civilisation to the state and nation, and be the greatest source of power. In one word, Iran will become a paradise.'[14]

The diagnosis complete, there only remained the question of how the treatment could be implemented. As the Persian government had neither the technology nor the capital to construct railways, the obvious answer was to look abroad. During the 1860s Persian governments made a number of *ad hoc* attempts to attract foreign capitalists to Persia to finance and build railways. Various French, German and British capitalists, including Siemens Brothers and a director of Britain's South Eastern Railway, had been offered tempting terms or 'concessions' to bring railways to Persia, but none of the schemes had come to fruition.[15] It was in the same spirit that, in 1870, the Persian Minister in London, Mo'in al-Molk, approached Julius de Reuter, with a proposal that he should negotiate a large concession, involving among other things the construction of a railway in Persia.

Julius de Reuter was 54 years old when he met Mo'in al-Molk. He was the founder of the most famous News Agency in the world at that time. He had been born Israel Beer Josophat in Germany in 1816, and had changed his name to Paul Julius de Reuter in 1844 on becoming a Christian. De Reuter began operating a commercial news service in Paris in 1848, but this had not been a great success and he moved to England in 1851, becoming a British subject six years later. In 1851 a telegraph cable was laid between England and France, and de Reuter took this opportunity to build a highly successful news service supplying brokers and merchants in London and Paris with the opening and closing prices of the two Stock Exchanges. The news agency developed, and the founding of many provincial newspapers in England in the 1850s provided a wide market for news for de Reuter's agents in foreign countries. In 1871 de Reuter's efforts were rewarded with the award of a Barony from the Duke of Saxe-Coburg-Gotha, with the name of Paul Julius, Baron von Reuter.[16]

The Persian Minister clearly regarded de Reuter as a successful, prosperous and well-connected British capitalist who might bring a railway concession scheme to fruition. It is less clear why de Reuter should have been attracted by the Persian proposal. He was already past 50 and had achieved great financial success. His name was a household word in Britain and elsewhere. As the owner of a news agency, he would not have been ignorant of the difficult economic and political conditions in Persia. What had he to gain from building railways in Persia? The answer seems to have been the opportunity the scheme presented for a further, even more spectacular, entrepreneurial coup. 'Though entirely foreign to the field which had engaged his activities in past years', Henry Collins, who was to be appointed de Reuter's Agent in Tehran in 1873, later explained, 'the prospect of being able to achieve a second and still greater triumph during his lifetime was not without its attractions.'[17]

In early 1872 de Reuter, his appetite for 'a second and still greater triumph' whetted, despatched a Monsieur Cotte to Tehran to undertake further negotiations. Cotte negotiated directly with Mirza Hoseyn Khan and within a few months they had reached an agreement. The later famous Reuter Concession was signed in Tehran on 25 July 1872. Its terms were wide-ranging, later being described by Curzon as 'the most complete and extraordinary surrender of the entire industrial resources of a kingdom into foreign hands that has probably ever been dreamed of, much less accomplished, in history'.[18]

The core of the Concession concerned railways.[19] De Reuter was granted 'for a period of 70 years the exclusive and definitive concession of a line of railway extending from the Caspian Sea to the Persian Gulf', with the right to build any branch lines and a variety of provisions designed to assist railway construction, such as the right to import necessary construction materials into Persia duty free. A penalty clause obliged de Reuter to deposit £40 000 at the Bank of England which would be given to the Persian government if railway construction had not started within fifteen months. The Persian government was to receive 20% of the net returns on the operation of the railway, and 15% on the net profits of every mine, and had the right to take the Mining Rights Company over after 70 years.

The remainder of the Concession granted de Reuter extensive privileges over the exploitation of Persia's natural resources, including most minerals, water supplies and forests, and stipulated how the Concession was to be financed. De Reuter was to issue a £6 million capital in shares, on which the Persian government guaranteed 5% per annum interest and 2% sinking fund contributions, but only after a railway line from Rasht to Esfahan had been completed, and if the Concessionaires had sufficiently reorganised the revenue system to generate sufficient funds to cover the interest payments. De Reuter was also granted the administration, or *Regie*, of the Customs for 20 years, but for the first five years he would have to pay the government the sums paid to it by the previous customs contractors plus a yearly premium of £20 000.

Almost as an afterthought, Article 20 of the 24-article Concession gave de Reuter the first option should 'the Persian government in the future … decide upon granting permission to start a Bank or any establishment of credit'. This article was the origin of the Imperial Bank of Persia.

The Reuter Concession provoked at the time, and has continued to provoke, a wide range of reactions. Liberal historians and later Persian nationalists have regarded it as a betrayal of Persia by the Qajar dynasty.

'Thus without any pressure having been exercised by foreign powers, without the slightest interference from the British legation', Firuz Kazemzadeh in his standard study of *Russia and Britain in Persia 1864–1914* has written, 'the King of Kings, the Shadow of God, gave away practically the entire resources of his impoverished and misgoverned nation to a greedy business manipulator of dubious reputation.'[20]

Such an interpretation is most unfair. Bribes did exchange hands during the Concession negotiations. De Reuter later claimed he had spent £180 000 to get the Concession signed. However this should not obscure the serious purpose of Mirza Hoseyn Khan. Few negotiations in Persia were held without an exchange of financial favours. That was how business was conducted in Persia, and it would be myopic to dwell on the bribes and ignore the more serious aims of the Persian government. Surviving Persian government documents make it clear that Mirza Hoseyn Khan regarded the Reuter Concession as the easiest, and perhaps the only, way to get a railway in Persia,[21] and close reading of the terms of the Concession shows that its terms were far less onerous than its critics have suggested. If it had been implemented, Persia would have acquired over the next 70 years a railway network, a mining industry and a modern irrigation system, as well as perhaps a bank and western-style factories. In return for this, the Persian government was not required to find any capital – the foreigners themselves were burdened with the task of making the country's revenue-raising system work more efficiently – and would have taken quite a large share of any profits that were to be made. Even if the whole Concession flopped, the government would have received £40 000 caution money to assist its finances. A committee of Persian ministers, asked by the Shah to review the Concession, admitted that Persia had given a great deal away, but rightly concluded that de Reuter had largely secured the right to exploit 'unemployed resources which up to now have conferred no benefit on the government and, should they remain in our hands, will after this confer no benefit either'.[22] The Reuter Concession may have been naive, but it cannot be dismissed as a self-inflicted rape of Persia by a corrupt government.

Nor can de Reuter be regarded as a 'greedy business manipulator'. The available evidence suggests that he was completely serious in his intention to carry out the terms of the Concession.[23] During the autumn of 1872 he approached Hugh Matheson, one of the most enterprising figures in Britain's commercial world at that time, in an attempt to raise the initial capital necessary to start the works.

Hugh Mackay Matheson had been born in Edinburgh in 1821. In 1843 he was invited by his wealthy uncle, James Matheson, to join the Hong Kong firm of Jardine, Matheson and Company. Hugh Matheson, however, disliked

Jardine Matheson's involvement in the opium trade, and preferred to join the London correspondents of the Hong Kong firm. In 1847 this firm went bankrupt, but in the following year it was reconstituted as Matheson and Company, with Hugh Matheson in charge of the business. He soon turned it into one of the leading merchant houses in London. The firm diversified from importing China silk and tea on behalf of Jardine Matheson to the export of Lancashire cotton piece-goods to China, and in the 1850s it began importing into Britain a range of Indian commodities. During the 1860s Matheson became involved in an ever wider range of schemes, including the construction of railways and cotton mills in China in alliance with Jardine Matheson. These entreprenurial schemes were combined with a Presbyterian religious fervour, and a deep commitment to missionary work. Indeed, in classic Victorian fashion, business and religion were almost one for Matheson. He was convinced that, in the last resort, only the acceptance of Christian values would 'raise' the Eastern countries in the 'scale' of human civilisation.[24]

Matheson was attracted by de Reuter's scheme. He was about to become involved in launching a company to exploit iron ore mines at Rio Tinto in Spain, and subsequently became the first chairman of the Rio Tinto Company, the ancestor of the present day Rio Tinto Zinc Corporation. To such a man de Reuter's schemes looked practical, potentially lucrative, and likely to be of benefit to Persia. In December 1872 Matheson wrote excitedly to a friend that he was 'entering upon what may prove a considerable undertaking along with Baron Reuter, in the matter of Public works of all kinds for Persia, under a concession which he has obtained of a very remarkable kind from the Shah and his government'. Although Matheson foresaw 'great difficulties ... in the excessively bad character of the official people in that miserable country', he had high hopes that de Reuter would achieve some good for the country. 'It will be something', he observed, 'if we can raise it on the scale of civilisation, indeed in developing its rich resources hitherto scarcely touched in modern times.'[25] Over the next 20 years Matheson, and through him Jardine Matheson, retained an interest in de Reuter's schemes.

1.3 STALEMATE 1873–88

The hopes and ambitions of Mirza Hoseyn Khan, de Reuter and Matheson were never realised. The Reuter Concession stirred up a storm of opposition outside and inside Persia. Its fate was effectively sealed when it became entangled with Anglo–Russian diplomatic rivalry in Persia.

Both the British and the Russian governments disliked the Concession. The Foreign Office in Britain resented the fact that they had never been consulted during the Concession negotiations, and practically every feature of the Concession raised objections and suspicions in official quarters. De Reuter was not only a capitalist – and British diplomats' reluctance in the nineteenth century to dirty their hands by supporting British commercial interests was notorious – he had a foreign-sounding name, and he was also of Jewish extraction. Few British officials had any faith in Persian ability to set their house in order. As a result, they felt in their bones that a concession such as de Reuter's was doomed to failure, and that they would be dragged into the sordid consequences if British investors were involved.[26] Moreover, on political grounds the Foreign Office did not want a north–south railway in Persia, as it could only increase the danger of Russia getting closer to a warm water port. The implications for the defence of India were most unwelcome.

On 12 September 1872 de Reuter applied for official British diplomatic support for his Concession, pointing to the spread of the Russian railway network toward the Caspian Sea and the consequent vital political importance of a British-owned railway project in Persia.[27] The Foreign Office was not impressed, taking over a month to reply that they could not 'bind themselves officially' to protect his interests.[28] In their private views, officials were scathing of de Reuter and his schemes, though they felt a need to humour him in case, being an 'unreliable foreigner', he auctioned off his Concession to the Russians.[29]

The attitude of most British diplomats was summed up in a despatch to London by the British Minister in Tehran, after the cancellation of the Concession. He observed that 'as a Commercial Speculation' the Concession was 'in its entirety ... an impracticable one', promoted by 'speculators' who would abandon the Company as soon as they had made a quick profit, and who would leave the resulting losses to fall on 'women of limited income and minors in the hands of trustees, seduced into investment by the fallacious hope of a high rate of interest for their capital'.[30]

While British diplomats remained unhelpful and suspicious, de Reuter faced positive opposition from the Russian government. The Russians believed, quite erroneously, that the Reuter Concession had been engineered by the British government as a means of checking Russian influence.[31] Russian displeasure was forcibly expressed as soon as they heard of the agreement. 'Though they do not yet know the articles and conditions of the agreement', Mirza Hoseyn Khan wrote to the Shah of Russian reaction, 'they are enumerating its shortcomings and dangers.'[32]

Russian opposition, however, was not effective until the Shah arrived at the Tsar's very doorstep. In the spring of 1873 the Shah went on his first tour to Europe. This move was seen by Mirza Hoseyn Khan as an important aspect of his westernising policy, designed both to impress on the Shah's mind the need for reform and to establish closer links with the European countries.[33]

The Shah's large retinue first visited Russia. During the Shah's stay in Moscow, Mirza Hoseyn Khan, irritated by her scheming, despatched the Shah's favourite wife, Anis od-Doule, home. This move, which turned her into an inveterate opponent and centre of opposition to his administration back in Persia, was to be his undoing.[34] Meanwhile, during the Shah's stay at St Petersburg, the Russian capital, extreme pressure was put on him to cancel the Reuter Concession and, if possible, substitute that concession with one to a Russian subject. After leaving Russia, the Shah travelled through Germany and Belgium and reached London on 18 June 1873. Although Queen Victoria invested him with the Order of the Garter, British ministers were not prepared to offer Persia firm guarantees against Russian aggression, nor did they express firm support for the Reuter Concession.[35]

The Shah's party returned home, after another politically uncomfortable passage through Russia, and landed at Enzeli on 7 September 1873. Naser od-Din immediately learned that some 80 leading government officials had taken sanctuary, or *bast*, in the palace of Anis od-Doule and were demanding the dismissal of Mirza Hoseyn Khan. This was a traditional form of political protest in the country. As the Shah moved towards Rasht the protests against his Prime Minister grew. At the court, ministers and bureaucrats threatened by Mirza Hoseyn Khan's reforms united in a campaign against him, using the Reuter Concession as a prime excuse to urge his dismissal. The Reuter Concession had also raised the ire of part of the *ulama*, or religious leaders. The *ulama* were a powerful force in nineteenth-century Persia. They were financially self-sufficient and therefore independent of the government as they directly collected religious taxes, and they controlled education, and most forms of judicial and legal activity and social and charitable services. Often as venal as the bureaucracy, the *ulama* nevertheless had strong popular support, and could be relied upon to raise opposition to any perceived threats against Islam.[36] De Reuter's railway was regarded in such a light. Fears were expressed that foreigners would pour into Persia and undermine Islam, and the *ulama* organised public demonstrations against Mirza Hoseyn Khan and his scheme.[37]

The Russians encouraged this opposition, although to what degree is not known. Their virulent opposition to de Reuter had, however, already been made clear to the Shah, and no doubt greatly weakened any resolve on his part to oppose it. On 9 September Mirza Hoseyn Khan was dismissed. The Shah reinstated him the following day, relieved him of his post again on 11 September, and then appointed him Governor of Rasht. Although he was later to regain influence, the crisis seems to have exercised a marked effect on him. After September 1873, Mirza Hoseyn Khan no longer followed a uniformly pro-British policy. Moreover, although he continued to urge reform, he lost his reputation for honesty. The Shah, too, seems to have lost much of the interest he had in reform.[38]

These political developments had disastrous consequences for de Reuter's schemes. Soon after the Concession's ratification by the Shah on 25 July 1872, de Reuter appointed Henry Collins, the Manager of the Reuter News Agency's Eastern branches, as his special representative in Persia. After gathering together a staff, Collins left England for Persia early in February 1873, and after the long journey to Persia through Russia, reached Tehran.[39]

Collins faced difficulties from the start. The day before he reached Tehran in May the Shah left for Enzeli to begin his European tour, and Mirza Hoseyn Khan, though he welcomed Collins to Tehran, left to follow the Shah soon afterwards. As a result, the Minister of Public Works, a relatively minor state official, was put in charge of assisting Collins. Nevertheless, Collins began to pursue his task energetically, and a survey of the country from Rasht to Tehran was undertaken. By September 1873 he had recruited 1000 construction workers, the first consignment of rails and equipment was on its way from Britain, and a few miles of earthworks prepared. By November, however, the Shah and Mirza Hoseyn Khan, back in favour but without an official position, were discussing with the British Minister in Tehran the cancellation of the Reuter Concession, on the grounds that the articles which provided for the commencement of the railway line within 15 months of the signing of the contract, had not been implemented.[40] On 10 November the Tehran *Gazette* announced its cancellation. For some months Collins continued to proceed with the work, but in the spring of 1874 the labourers were dismissed and the professional staff left for Europe.[41]

De Reuter made representations for assistance to the British Foreign Office. He was coolly received. Lord Derby, the Foreign Secretary, observed privately that even though the cancellation of the Concession involved 'considerable hardship to Baron Reuter', the Persian government 'has done wisely in cancelling the contract'.[42] De Reuter spent the next 15 years trying to get somebody to assist him to get the cancellation of his Concession reversed, or at least some compensation for the cancellation. In 1878 he relinquished control of his News Agency to his son Herbert, and devoted himself full-time to this matter, but it was a further decade before any significant progress was made.

The British government remained coolly aloof from de Reuter, being moved to action only when the existence of the Concession could be used in the diplomatic contest against Russia. The Reuter Concession was used, for example, to torpedo a rival Russian concession. In the autumn of 1873 Baron von Falkenhagen, a retired Russian general, who had built railways in Transcaucasia, was encouraged by the Russian government to seek a concession for the construction of a railway from the Russian border at Julfa to Tabriz, and intensive Russian diplomatic pressure was exerted on the Shah to grant him a concession.[43]

The Persian government, well aware of the political overtones of the proposed concession, appealed for British help to resist it. The prior claim of the Reuter Concession provided excellent grounds to oppose Falkenhagen, and the Foreign Office was transformed into an enthusiastic supporter of de Reuter's claims. The British Minister in Tehran was instructed to intervene officially on de Reuter's behalf. Although Falkenhagen probably got to the stage of signing a draft contract with the Persian government, the threat of continued British opposition led the Russian government to abandon the whole scheme.[44]

As soon as the Falkenhagen concession was defeated, the British government lost its enthusiasm for de Reuter. The Legation offered no more assistance. In October 1875 a frustrated Collins left Tehran. De Reuter was left with his claim for £1 million compensation (which included his expenses of £200 000 and financial favours of £180 000), together with a further £40 000 in caution money locked up in the Bank of England.[45]

In two years, 1877 and 1885, de Reuter's hopes of a breakthrough were raised, only to be subsequently dashed. After Collins' withdrawal from Tehran, de Reuter attempted to modify his concession in directions that would both make it more acceptable to the Persians, and attract sustained diplomatic support from the British government. In November 1875 he proposed to the British Foreign Secretary a revised scheme whereby in return for writing off his claims under the old Concession, de Reuter offered to reach a new agreement with the Persian government. The construction of a railway remained at the heart of his plans, but to lessen any British political fears he suggested the line should run 'from the Turco–Persian frontier near Baghdad, or from some other point on the West or South West of Persia to Isfahan, to be carried via Kermanshah or such other route as may hereafter prove most feasible'. He continued to seek rights over 'the working of certain mines and forests', and, interestingly for this History, included in his proposed revised concession the right to establish a 'Bank under special guarantees from the Persian Government'.[46]

De Reuter's proposal found slightly more favour with the Foreign Office than his original Concession, perhaps because the new railway route would facilitate British trade with Persia. On 19 August 1876 de Reuter received a letter from the Foreign Office promising the Legation's 'unofficial support' for a 'modified Concession' which would 'embrace the construction of a line of railway from Schuster to Tehran by way of Ispahan'.[47] Collins was despatched to Tehran in early 1877 to put the revised concession proposal before the Shah, but before he reached his destination the Russo–Turkish war broke out, and the Shah refused to enter into discussions as long as the conflict continued. As the British Legation continued to offer nothing but 'unofficial support', Collins could achieve little, and in the summer of 1878 he once again left Tehran.

Over the next few years several negotiations for railway schemes were discussed between de Reuter and the Persian government, but no progress was made until 1885 when Anglo–Russian relations reached a new low. On 24 January 1885 de Reuter wrote to the British Foreign Secretary with a renewed request for diplomatic support. If the Foreign Office still refused to support him, de Reuter proposed the formation of 'an International Company for carrying out the concession in its entirety'.[48] It was an opportune moment, for the Russian advance into Central Asia, which had been a matter of concern to British governments for years, reached crisis point when Russian troops occupied the Penjdeh oasis, claimed by the Afghans, at the end of March 1885. Gladstone, the Prime Minister, contemplated declaring war on Russia during the crisis. The Reuter Concession became, once again, a political issue. In May and June of 1885 his case was discussed by the Cabinet. De Reuter continued to push for government support, offering, in return for adequate compensation, to transfer all his rights to the government. Alternately, he pressed for support for his proposed international company.[49]

De Reuter's discussions with the British government continued after the fall of the Liberal government and the arrival of a new Conservative one, headed by Lord Salisbury. By August 1885 de Reuter's plans for an international company had crystallised into the idea of forming a 'Compagnie universalle des chemins de fer de Perse', with an international Board of administration. He claimed that Prince Bismarck, the German Chancellor, supported this concept, and also that the Rothschilds, the famous banking family, were interested in the scheme. De Reuter pushed the Russian menace as his most potent bargaining weapon. His international company, he informed the British government, would form 'a valuable bulwark against the aggression of Russia'.[50]

This proposal was discussed at the highest levels of the British government, and found considerable support. The Penjdeh incident had, it seemed, finally shifted the balance of opinion in the British government. The Secretary of State for War favoured the inflow of British and German captial into Persia as a 'check to Russian ambition', while the Secretary of State for India argued that 'any arrangement under which the integrity of Persia might become an object of material solicitude to Germany so as to lead her to join with England in guaranteeing it could not fail to be of the utmost advantage to Indian interests'.[51]

The London house of the Rothschilds were duly sounded out on the practicability of de Reuter's new proposals. They advised that the international scheme was unlikely to be successfully floated with the public without a government guarantee of the Concession and of the integrity of Persia, together with the creation of an army officered by Britons and Germans who could effectively police the collection of the customs receipts.[52] By August Lord Salisbury was prepared to contemplate such measures, if Germany would act jointly with Britain.[53] In September de Reuter's schemes were sent to the British Ambassador in Berlin with instructions to place them before Bismarck. De Reuter had never been nearer success, but the Germans refused to be drawn into the Persian embroglio. Bismarck replied to the British request, declining to become involved in Persian affairs.[54] Salisbury was not interested in de Reuter's scheme except as a means of involving Germans in Persia in order to counterbalance the Russians, and so the discussions with de Reuter ended.

The next two years were bleak ones for de Reuter. Russian economic and political power in Persia grew. During the 1880s Russian trade in Persia expanded. The value of Russian exports to Persia grew from 3.6 million Roubles in 1883 to 10.9 million in 1890.[55] (£1 was approximately equal to 9.4 Roubles in this period). British diplomatic influence in Tehran declined. In 1885 the Legation was taken over by the *Chargé d'Affaires*, Arthur Nicolson, who virtually abandoned any attempt to oppose Russian power. Britain, Nicolson observed, should not waste her 'energies in endeavouring to counteract Russian influence on the Central Government at Tehran'.[56] The Foreign Office continued to propose to the Persian government the need for a railway, and to support de Reuter's claims for 'adequate compensation in some form or other', but little that was positive was achieved in these years.[57]

In contrast to Nicolson, in 1887 the Russian government appointed an ambitious and ruthless diplomat, Prince Nicholas Dolgurukov, to represent them in Tehran. He rapidly extended Russian influence. In September 1887, in a major coup, he secured from the Shah an agreement 'not to give orders or permission to construct railways or waterways to companies of foreign nations before consulting with his Majesty the Emperor'.[58] Russia had effectively secured a veto on future railway schemes in the country. De Reuter was never further from achieving his goals.

1.4 A NEW CONCESSION

Within a year the situation had been transformed. In October 1888 de Reuter's son, George, and his old associate Monsieur Cotte arrived in Tehran, and in January 1889 they signed a concession giving them the right to establish a bank with unique privileges. This section explains why there was a breakthrough from the long period of stalemate, and why the breakthrough took the form of a bank, rather than a railway, concession.

At this stage a new Persian character assumes an important role in the story. Malkam Khan was the son of an Armenian convert to Islam. While working in the Persian diplomatic service, he became involved in the reform movement. In the late 1850s he wrote a series of essays on the need for reform, and in 1860 formed a loose society, which had certain freemasonry features, called the *faramushkhaneh*, where reformers would meet. This move led to his banishment to Ottoman territory in the following year. There he came into contact with Mirza Hoseyn Khan, who was then Chief of the Persian Mission to Istanbul, and with the latter's assistance he was given a series of diplomatic appointments in the Ottoman Empire. He held these posts throughout the 1860s, except for a period of suspension at the end of the decade, during which he secured Ottoman citizenship. When Mirza Hoseyn Khan was appointed to the Persian government in 1870, Malkam Khan was soon recalled from Istanbul to act as his special adviser.

On his recall to Tehran, Malkam Khan became involved in the negotiations for the Reuter Concession. In early 1873 he was sent as Ambassador to Britain, to arrange the details of the Shah's visit and bring the Reuter negotiations to a final conclusion.[59] After ratification of the Concession, Mirza Hoseyn Khan had insisted on appending to the agreement an article whereby no work could be undertaken until details had been agreed by both sides and set out in a *cahier des charges* or set of estimates. Malkam Khan was apparently placed in charge of this *cahier*. De Reuter experienced a prolonged and unsatisfactory period of negotiations with him. Malkam Khan claimed that he held title to a fourth of the Concession, and it was not until July 1873, after he had received some financial consideration, that the negotiations for a *cahier* were successfully concluded.[60]

Malkam Khan has been the subject of much controversy. Many have praised him for his role as one of Persia's leading reformers, a precursor of the Persian revolution, and a literary genius. Others have seen him as a crook and pedlar of fraudulent concessions.[61] He is best seen as a mixture of all these things and the key to understanding him would appear to lie in the recognition that, in the context of late nineteenth-century Persia, these various categories were far from mutually exclusive.

Malkam Khan remained as Ambassador to Britain between the cancellation of the Reuter Concession and 1889, and indeed between 1873 and his death in 1908 he only returned to Persia for two brief periods. Almost as soon as the Concession was cancelled, he began promoting new concessions. In December 1873 he wrote to Mirza Hoseyn Khan, recently reappointed as

Foreign Minister, offering to arrange for the construction of a railway and the establishment of a bank in Persia, 'the necessary condition for Iran's existence'.[62] During 1885 he had discussions with Lord Salisbury about the need to construct roads and railways in Persia.[63] At some stage in, or before, 1888 de Reuter secured Malkam Khan's services in support of his claim for a concession. According to the testimony of Malkam Khan in October 1889, de Reuter had paid him £20 000 in return for his withdrawing his claims to a concession. In addition, the formation of a bank was to be 'the signal' for a further payment of £30 000.[64] The accuracy of these figures cannot be ascertained, but it seems certain that by the time George de Reuter reached Tehran Malkam Khan had helped to clear his path with the Persian government.

Although the evidence is fragmentary, it also seems clear that de Reuter had secured the assistance by 1888 of the Shah's French doctor, Dr Tholozon. Tholozon had himself been behind several concession schemes in the 1870s, and he acted as consultant to the Shah on a wide range of matters from freemasonry to the economy.[65] In April 1895 he wrote to George de Reuter and reminded him, in passing, of

the part I played and the action which I took, with success – with you – in the formation of the Imperial Bank of Persia in 1888. I saw in this the only means of delivering your father of the heavy burden of his first contract with Persia.[66]

It is far less clear what direct role, if any, was played in the 1888 negotiations by the new British Minister to Tehran, Sir Henry Drummond Wolff. Wolff, a career diplomat who had important connections in both politics and the City, was appointed by Lord Salisbury at the end of 1887. Wolff's brief from Lord Salisbury was in two parts. Firstly, he was to come to some sort of agreement with Russia whereby Britain and Russia would end their rivalry, encourage reform and recognise each other's respective positions. Secondly, he was to bolster Persia immediately by devices such as the promotion of trade, the improvement of internal security, and the introduction of western capital.[67]

Wolff set about his task energetically in April 1888 after his arrival in Tehran. His first achievement was to secure from the Shah a declaration of the inviolability of the property rights of his subjects. His second move came in October 1888, when the Shah agreed to open the Karun river to all commercial ships. The *quid pro quo*, and the reason for the Shah's acquiescence in this policy, was a guarantee that 'in the event of any power making an attack without just cause or provocation on Persia...' the British government would '...take such steps as may in their judgement be best calculated to prevent any infringement of the integrity of Persia'.[68] The opening of the Karun was widely regarded as a victory for Britain at the expense of the Russians. De Reuter, increasingly anxious to get his money back, toyed with exploiting Russian resentment by making an offer, through the Russian Ambassador in London, 'to undertake the construction of a railway from the shores of the Caspian Sea, at points which the Russian Government would indicate, to Tehran', but his idea was not taken up.[69]

The concession which George de Reuter was to secure, and which provided the basis on which the Imperial Bank of Persia was founded, has commonly been seen as a further *coup* by Drummond Wolff,[70] but this view is misleading. Drummond Wolff was taken by surprise by George de Reuter's arrival in Persia. He first heard of it on October 15 through the arrival at the Legation of a letter addressed to 'Mr. George Reuter'. Later on the same day he received news from a French diplomat that 'he had travelled with a son or grandson of Baron Reuter who would reach Teheran shortly'.[71] The following day the Russian *Chargé d'Affaires*, who had also heard the rumour about de Reuter's son, told Drummond Wolff that the Russian government would find the revival of de Reuter's claims 'very distasteful'.[72]

Wolff did see George de Reuter and Cotte as soon as they arrived in Tehran. He offered them his support, but he did not offer to negotiate the concession for them.[73] Nor was his direct assistance required, for he sensed that Julius de Reuter had prepared the ground well. 'I do not know', Wolff reported to Salisbury, 'whether Baron George de Reuter's journey to Persia was or was not suggested or encouraged from this side. There has been a rapidity of decision on the part of the Shah and his Ministers which looks as though the arrival of the mission had been previously considered.'[74]

Wolff, therefore, lent no special support to the new negotiations. It suited his general strategy if a modern banking system in British hands could be established in Persia, but by the time of George de Reuter's arrival such a bank had already been established. In the summer of 1888 the New Oriental Bank Corporation Ltd established a branch in Tehran, becoming Persia's first modern bank. The New Oriental Bank Corporation had been established in July 1884 out of the ashes of the Oriental Bank Corporation, a British Eastern exchange bank founded in 1845 which had built a wide international branch network and business before crashing in 1884.[75] The successor bank rapidly re-established the branch network, and by the time of its arrival in Tehran it boasted branches in Bombay, Colombo, Hong Kong, Singapore, Yokohama, Aden and elsewhere. In August 1888 the bank rented a large building in Artillery Square, in central Tehran. The business seems to have got off to a quick start, and the bank became involved in the transmission of taxes from the provinces to Tehran, in making local advances, and it established agencies in various provincial cities, such as Bushire. The New Oriental Bank Corporation seems to have met no opposition from the Persian government, but Drummond Wolff supported it when required and was well pleased with its progress.[76]

George de Reuter's and Cotte's negotiations with the Shah and his favourite minister Amin os-Soltan, proceeded rapidly, assisted by Malkam Khan's arrangements, the support of Dr Tholozon, Drummond Wolff's discreet backing, and, no doubt, various gifts. George de Reuter's aim was still to secure the entire range of business promised by the original Concession to his father, especially the exclusive right to construct railways. By November, however, he had come to believe that the best means of securing this aim was through the revival of Article 20 of the 1872 Concession, the foundation of a bank. The logic was quite simple. The Shah had promised Prince Dolgurokov not to give a concession for the construction of railways or waterways 'to companies of foreign nations' without Russian permission. However, a national bank would be a Persian and not a foreign institution. 'Being thus a national institution objections might be avoided,' Drummond Wolff reported to Lord Salisbury on 8 November, 1888, 'while the original privileges granted to the Baron might be maintained.'[77] This strategy found particular favour with the Shah, eager as ever to extricate himself from Russian clutches. 'The Shah seems to think', Drummond Wolff wrote to Salisbury on 28 November, 1888, 'that the construction of railways by a national institution will not come within the restrictions of his engagements to the Emperor of Russia.'[78]

The idea of founding a bank, therefore, was still seen as late as November 1888 as a means to secure the primary end of a railway concession. To emphasise the point, during December and January 1889 Julius de Reuter continued to insist that something should be said in any new concession about railways. On 12 December George de Reuter told Drummond Wolff that his father would 'not accept the Bank Concession without the Karun Railway'.[79] Drummond Wolff considered that this idea was a non-starter, in view of the Persian agreement with Russia about railway concessions, and continued to stress that there 'would probably be no difficulty as to the Bank when once formed as a national institution, getting the railway'.[80]

De Reuter was still adamant on 28 January that any concession should contain 'one clause giving the right of priority in the construction of all railways and public works on equal terms with those offered by others'.[81] Two days later, however, the combined pressures of Russian opposition and Drummond Wolff's recommendations to compromise finally forced de Reuter to abandon his claims. On 30 January 1889 George de Reuter, Amin os-Soltan and the Persian Minister of Foreign Affairs, Qavam od-Doule, signed the concession which founded the Imperial Bank of Persia, but which carefully omitted the magic word 'railway'.

The Imperial Bank's Concession, which was for 60 years, is printed in full in Appendix 1 at the end of this volume. In brief, the Concession entitled de Reuter to form 'a State Bank in the Persian Empire', with a head office in Tehran. It was to have an authorised capital of £4 million, but the bank could open for business once £1 million had been raised. The Imperial Bank was given the exclusive right of note issue in Persia, subject to certain regulations, and it was exempted 'from every kind of tax or duty'. In return for these privileges, the Imperial Bank was obliged to lend the Persian government £40 000 at 6% per annum interest for ten years, the debt and interest to be repaid out of the government's share of the Bank's annual net profits (which was to be 6%, or £4000, whichever was the larger). The Bank was also to provide further loans to the government, on agreed terms. As for de Reuter, in return for renouncing all the rights of his 1872 Concession, he was to get his £40 000 caution money back one day after the new bank was formed. However, some flavour of the original Concession was retained in the new one, for Articles 11–13 of the 1889 Concession granted de Reuter a monopoly over a wide range of natural resources in Persia, subject only to the provision that mining operations had to begin within ten years. Three Appendices were attached to the new Concession over the following days to tidy up various administrative details.

There were yet further delays. The Shah departed from Tehran for another, and what proved to be his last, visit to Europe before all the formalities of the Concession had been completed. George de Reuter had to set off to St Petersburg in hot pursuit of the royal party to extract a declaration from the Shah that projected articles of association of the bank were in accordance with the terms of the Concession.[82]

Additional complications arose when the question of giving the Imperial Bank an appropriate corporate identity in Britain was discussed. By June 1889 Julius de Reuter had produced an outline plan for the shape of the new bank, which he intended should be a British-registered joint stock company with limited liability. Closer examination of the relevant Joint Stock Act, however, revealed that a bank with the right of note issue was excluded from the privileges of limited liability as regards its note issue. De Reuter judged that it would be hard to find buyers for shares of the proposed bank with its shareholders unprotected in this respect, and on 21 June he wrote to Lord Salisbury to suggest what seemed the only solution – that the new bank should be granted a Royal Charter.[83]

The request ran in the face of the whole trend of the British government's policy on overseas banks. Banks formed in England and Wales before 1858 did not have the privilege of limited liability. It was still possible, however, to obtain a qualified form of limited liability by means of a Royal Charter, and this was the method used by the many banks established from the 1830s to operate in British colonies and with London Head Offices, in order to give their shareholders limited liability. The British Treasury, in return, exercised supervision over such banks' affairs and particularly over note-issuing activities. Some 25 British 'imperial' banks were granted such Royal Charters between the 1830s and the 1860s.[84] The Oriental Bank Corporation had received one in 1851. The Hongkong Bank also obtained a Charter when it was founded in 1865, though as its founders wished the Head Office to be in Hong Kong it was not a Royal Charter but a special ordinance of the Hong Kong Legislature. However, the privilege of limited liability was extended to any banking company of seven persons or more by an Act of 1858 and the consolidating Companies Act of 1862, and after this legislation the practice of granting Royal Charters soon ceased. Banks found the restrictions imposed on their activities by such Charters irksome. The Treasury disliked regulatory duties over, and possible responsibility for, commercial banks. As a result, not a single Royal Charter had been granted to a bank since 1864.[85]

The Treasury was highly reluctant to break convention for the sake of de Reuter's proposed bank, and it was at this stage that the Foreign Office played its most important role in the formation of the Imperial Bank by pleading that 'special political reasons' required the granting of a Royal Charter in this unique instance. 'The collapse of this concession', the Foreign Office confided to its Treasury colleagues in a letter sent on 2 July, 'would, on political grounds, be a serious evil.' After sketching the Russian threat in Persia, the Foreign Office made it clear that, like de Reuter, it regarded the new bank as a means to achieve more important ends.

If communications with the sea and with India by railway can be established, the difficulties in the way of a Russian subjugation will be largely increased ... On this account it becomes a matter of capital importance to encourage the creation of the commercial machinery by which undertakings of this kind can be carried out. The accumulation of money in Persia is only possible through the medium of a successful banking system, and in the face of the diplomatic conditions which exist, it is not probable that the necessary communications will ever be established with the sea, and with other countries, except by the action of native enterprise, nominally at least supported by native resources.[86]

The Treasury did not resist the cry of 'national interest'. It did, however, insist on modifications to the original Concession to bring it more in line with standard practice before they would recommend the Crown to grant a Charter.[87] As a result of this pressure, de Reuter was obliged to make a number of modifications which were agreed by the Shah on 27 July, in Brighton, where his European tour had taken him, and which were incorporated in an Appendix 4 to the Concession. This is printed in full at the end of this volume, but essentially the Treasury secured changes in a number of areas which were all to have, as will be explained in later chapters, a significant bearing on the Bank's later history. The Bank's note issuing rights were constrained. The Treasury was particularly watchful of the note issuing powers of overseas banks since, in the wake of the Oriental Bank's collapse in 1884, the Governor of the British Colony of Ceylon had felt obliged to guarantee that bank's note issue in his territory. Persia was not a British colony, but the Treasury nevertheless felt one could not be too careful. The Concession required the Bank to hold a metallic reserve equal to at least half of the note issue in its first two years of operation, and one-third thereafter. Appendix 4 further required that the difference between the metallic reserve and the note circulation was not to exceed the Bank's paid-up capital. The Bank's powers to lend to the Persian government were more strictly defined, and the total amount of such loans limited to one-third of paid-up capital. The Treasury also found the combination of banking and mining unacceptable. Appendix 4 precluded the Bank from undertaking mining, obliging it to cede its privileges to another concessionaire after undertaking initial prospecting work.

The way was now open for a Royal Charter to be granted. The Charter, dated 2 September 1889, is printed in full in Appendix 2 at the end of this volume. It incorporated the essential points of the Concession, but it also introduced a further significant restraint on the proposed Bank. The Concession had given the Bank powers to establish branches in Persia 'and abroad'. The Charter, however, limited the Bank to undertaking 'the business of a banker in Persia, but not elsewhere, save and except that they may carry on by or through agencies such financial operations as being commenced in Persia have to be continued elsewhere, or being commenced elsewhere have to be continued in Persia'. This clause was destined to cause difficulties for the Imperial Bank in future years. The Charter also emphasised the British nature of the Bank. The proposed bank was to 'have a domicile in England and also have a board of directors in London', and more than 50% of the issued capital was to be 'issued in the United Kingdom'. (In contrast, Article 2 of the Concession had envisaged the share issue should be opened in five European capitals, plus Tehran.) A deed of settlement was to 'provide for the Bank remaining British in character, for its being regulated by a body of directors in the United Kingdom, (and) for the majority of the directors being British subjects'.

The Bank's Concession made the Bank a Persian national institution. The Royal Charter made it a thoroughly British banking institution. The dual identity was to prove a difficult legacy.

1.5 THE CITY DIMENSION

The story now moves from the corridors of Whitehall and the intricacies of Persian politics to the City of London. If de Reuter was to turn his Persian concession into a British bank, he needed the assistance of the City. By the time the Royal Charter was granted he had, in fact, already taken this matter in hand.

On 3 August Julius de Reuter reached an agreement, designed to turn his proposed Bank into a reality, with two important City institutions, J. Henry Schröder & Co. and David Sassoon & Co., and a firm of city stockbrokers, Walpole Greenwell & Co. The agreements provided for the formation of a bank with £1 million capital, divided into 100 000 £10 shares. 200 of these shares were designated 'Founders Shares', whose holders were to be entitled, 'after payment of a cumulative dividend at the rate of eight per cent per annum' on the paid-up share capital and after making adequate provisions for reserves, to an additional dividend 'in proportion to the shares for the time being held by them respectively to one half of the surplus divisible profits'. As soon as £250 000 had been subscribed to the Company, de Reuter was to receive £200 000 in cash to cover his expenses. J. H. Schröder were to receive £60 000 of this sum, and in return agreed to undertake the formation of the bank and the issue of its shares. Finally, de Reuter was allocated 100 of the Founders Shares, Sassoons 20, J. H. Schröder 58 and Walpole Greenwell 22. The successful achievement of a Royal Charter on 2 September, led to a revision of the original agreement on 4 September. The cumulative dividend was raised to 10% and, in a flush of optimism after the granting of the Charter, it was resolved to issue the shares at a £2 per share premium. De Reuter was to receive the £200 000 from the premium.[88]

Much remains unclear about how de Reuter found his backers in the City. J. Henry Schröder was an acceptance house, or what came to be called a merchant bank, with strong German connections which had been established in London in 1804. It grew rapidly over the century, and by 1889 was one of London's leading merchant banks. Its business connections, however, were largely with the United States and Continental Europe, and Persian matters were clearly out of its normal ambit. De Reuter's German background may have provided the connection with the firm. J. H. Schröder had also participated in the issue of North American railway stocks, and as there was still an expectation that the Imperial Bank's foundation would be followed by Persian railway schemes this may have provided a link.[89] Or perhaps J. H. Schröder simply saw the opportunity for good business, for the firm was guaranteed £60 000 to cover its costs and profits provided the share issue was successful. Walpole Greenwell & Co.'s involvement can probably also be explained in such terms.

The Sassoons' interest in the Imperial Bank of Persia is clearer. The Sassoons were an Iraqi Jewish trading family, who had moved to Bombay in the 1830s to get away from racial harassment. In Bombay, the firm of David Sassoon & Co. built up a flourishing trade, selling English textiles to Persia and Iraq, and in exchange importing craft goods from these countries for re-export to England. The firm's fortunes were made by taking the lead in the trade between Bombay and China after China had been forced to open its ports to British merchants in the early 1840s. Sassoons were extensively involved in the opium trade, becoming the largest dealer sending Indian opium to China.[90] In 1858 a member of the family moved to London, and London soon emerged as the centre of the trade house's management. The death of the founder in 1864 led to a split in the firm, with the eldest son, Abdullah (Sir Albert), inheriting the business and a more energetic son, Elias David, leaving to form his own firm in Bombay in 1867.[91]

David Sassoon & Co. retained contacts in Persia and the Ottoman Empire, in addition to the firm's activity in Bombay and China. At least until the late nineteenth century, many of the firm's staff were recruited from amongst the Jewish communities of Baghdad, Bombay and Persia. Sir Albert (knighted 1872, baronet in 1880) spoke Persian. It was, therefore, appropriate as well as symbolic of the family's arrival in English high society, that he was chosen to be one of the Shah's main hosts when he visited England in July 1889.[92] It seems that Drummond Wolff, who returned to England just ahead of his visit, made contact with both the Rothschilds and the Sassoons to pave the way for a successful visit, as well as to enlist their support for the various commercial schemes then being considered. It also seems likely that the Russian Minister in London secured assurance from Baron Nathaniel Rothschild that he would not participate in financing de Reuter's venture. The Sassoons, however, appear to have been attracted by it.[93]

The formation of a bank in Persia would have been seen as a good business opportunity by Sir Albert. Such a bank could be expected to facilitate his firm's trade in the region. Earlier, in China, Sassoons' desire for a reliable banking service had led them to become co-founders of the Hongkong Bank in 1865. Arthur Sassoon, a brother of Sir Albert, was on the original Board of the Hongkong Bank, and that bank's first premises in Queen's Road Central, Hong Kong, were originally rented from David Sassoon & Co. and then purchased from them. Although David Sassoon & Co. had banking activities in India and China, the company preferred trade to finance and left the initiatives in banking and finance to the Hongkong Bank once it was founded.[94] Sir Albert clearly had similar plans for Persia, where his firm also did some banking but seems to have preferred to sponsor a separate bank, of which his brother Reuben was to be a founder.

The granting of the Royal Charter, and the final agreement between de Reuter and his associates in the City, meant that the formation of the Imperial Bank could proceed and nine directors were appointed. Two of the four founders were represented on the Board. George de Reuter took one seat.

David Sassoon & Co. nominated Edward Sassoon, a son of Sir Albert, and S. Ezekiel, a member of the firm whose family was intermarried with the Sassoons, for two more seats. Walpole Greenwell and, at this stage, J. H. Schröder were not represented.

William Keswick was chosen to be Chairman of the new Bank. He was a former Chairman of the Hongkong Bank (1880–1), became a member of its London Consultative Committee in 1890, and was also a former Chairman of Jardine, Matheson & Company. In both connections Keswick would have come into contact with de Reuter's scheme, through Hugh Matheson's long-standing involvement and the Hongkong Bank's close contacts with David Sassoon & Co. Moreover, Keswick became Chairman during 1889 of a new investment company, the Trust and Loan Company of China, Japan and the Straits Ltd (known as the 'China Trust'), which, in the words of its Prospectus, aimed to promote investment in 'all kinds of public works, railroads, telegraphs, docks, waterworks' in China.[95] The parallel between this and the hopes for the Imperial Bank were clear. Keswick's appointment as Chairman of Imperial Bank indicated the solidity of purpose behind the enterprise, and also placed the Bank's origins firmly in the context of the surge of interest in 'developing' countries such as China and Persia at that moment.

Keswick was joined on the Board by David McLean, one of the Hongkong Bank's leading Managers during its first 25 years. McLean had been offered the Chief Managership of the Hongkong Bank three times, and had three times refused it.[96] He had acquired a formidable experience in Eastern silver and exchange affairs, and this knowledge and his general banking expertise was clearly a major asset for the Imperial Bank. On joining the Imperial Bank's Board he had just retired from the London Managership of the Hongkong Bank, and joined the London Committee of that Bank. He was also, like Keswick, a director of the China Trust.

The second banker on the Imperial Bank's Board was Geoffrey Glyn, the eldest son of Pascoe Glyn, senior partner of the London banking firm of Glyn, Mills, Currie & Co. Glyn Mills, a leading private bank which had taken joint stock status in 1885, had a unique personality in the nineteenth-century City. They were the only City bank of the period to show a continuous interest in transport and industrial concerns. They were particularly active in the finance of foreign railways, and came to be known as the 'Railway Bank'.[97] They were also active in promotion of overseas banks, including the Ottoman Bank in 1856, the London and Brazilian Bank in 1862 and the Anglo-Austrian Bank in 1864.[98] Pascoe Glyn had been connected with the incorporation of the Australian merchant banking house of Dalgety in 1884, and during the 1890s became Chairman of the London and Brazilian Bank.

Glyn Mills, with their experience in floating loans for foreign railways and their involvement in overseas banks, held obvious attractions for the Imperial Bank, and in addition to Geoffrey Glyn's directorship, they were appointed the Imperial Bank's London bankers.

Also appointed to the Board were two representatives of merchant houses. H. D. Stewart came from Stewart, Thompson and Co., a Manchester cotton firm. His appointment reflected hopes that the Bank would become involved in the finance of the export of British cotton piece goods to Persia. A. P. H. Hotz was a partner of I. C. P. Hotz, a Dutch trading firm based in Bushire. In the mid-nineteenth century, this firm had qualified for British consular protection for their activities by registering their local offices in England, and they subsequently came to be regarded as British to all intents and purposes.[99] The firm were primarily import–export merchants, dealing in piece goods, opium and assorted commodities, with a wide network of agents in southern Persia likely to prove useful to the Imperial Bank.

The final director, Sir Lepel Griffin, came from the public service rather than commerce. His appointment reflected the Bank's founders' need for expertise in facing the political problems which could be expected to arise for a British bank operating in Persia. Griffin's career had been in the Indian Civil Service. He seems to have been regarded as a brilliant young man, but as the years passed his reputation for flamboyancy and instability grew and kept him out of top posts. He retired in 1889 when he was passed over for an Indian Governorship, and he clearly resolved to embark on a new business career for, in addition to joining the Imperial Bank's Board, he also became head of a small oil syndicate in Burma.[100]

The business interests represented on the Imperial Bank's Board provide an insight into how the Bank was envisaged at the time of its foundation. Representatives of trading concerns in Persia and the Gulf had been brought together with men with substantial Eastern banking and financial experience. And several of the parties had a particular interest in railway promotion and other types of 'development'. The Imperial Bank was not to be just a regional traders' bank: it was to lead to greater things.

1.6 THE IMPERIAL BANK OF PERSIA IS FOUNDED

The assembly of a Board of Directors, and the completion of arrangements for the Imperial Bank's flotation, enabled the final stages of the formation of the Bank, in both Persia and Britain, to be undertaken.

In Persia, General A. Houtum Schindler was appointed the fledgling Bank's 'Adviser' in Tehran in September. Schindler, like de Reuter himself, was a naturalised British subject of German origin. By 1889 he had lived in

Persia for over two decades, being employed by the Indo–European Telegraph Company, the Persian Telegraphic Service, and also apparently by the
Shah's Army. He acquired a formidable knowledge of many aspects of
Persian history, politics and economy, which he later displayed to the full in a
wide-ranging entry on Persia published in the ninth and eleventh editions of
the *Encyclopaedia Britannica* in the 1900s. Already by 1889 he had become, in
Curzon's words, 'a sort of *deus ex machina* required to assist in the solution of
most Persian problems'.[101]

Schindler's talents were well-appreciated by Drummond Wolff, who
attempted to secure his services for the British Legation. He was pre-empted,
however, by de Reuter. By early March 1889 it was known that Schindler was
working for de Reuter.[102] In the previous month he had already sent de Reuter
a report on Persia's economic prospects, which was obviously intended for
publication and was in fact summarised in the Imperial Bank's Prospectus. In
this letter Schindler waxed lyrical on the opportunities for a bank in Persia,
and the many investment opportunities for Europeans in Persian industry and
minerals. 'It is my honest opinion', he concluded, 'that the concession which
His Majesty the Shah has granted you [de Reuter] for the establishment of a
National Persian Bank is a great step in the right direction, and with the
establishment of this bank a new era of prosperity and progress will
commence for Persia, and Europeans will be enabled to find new fields for the
profitable investment of their capital.'[103] Schindler subsequently co-operated
with George de Reuter in the post-Concession negotiations in Tehran, and
his appointment as the Bank's Adviser, therefore, only confirmed his *de facto*
position.

Meanwhile, on 20 September the Prospectus of the Imperial Bank
appeared in London. The issue was underwritten by J. Henry Schröder and
David Sassoon & Co. 200 Founders Shares and 33 250 Ordinary Shares
were already subscribed, but the Prospectus offered the remaining Ordinary
Shares for sale at £12, including the £2 premium. Significantly, the Prospectus focused on the mining rights granted in the Concession. It was noted
that the Bank would not work the mines itself, 'but sub-concessions will from
time to time be granted upon terms which it is expected will be productive of
large returns to the Bank'. The actual banking concession was also mentioned, but the implication was that, valuable as it was, it would be the mines
that would make the investors' fortunes. 'The immense value of the privileges
by the Concession to this institution, with the object of developing the great
but hitherto neglected resources of Persia', the Prospectus observed, 'can
hardly be overrated.'

The Subscription List was opened on 24 September, and the issue was an
enormous success. 'So great was the confidence in the undertaking', wrote

Curzon, 'that, within a few hours of the date of issue, the capital, amounting to £1 000 000, was subscribed fifteen times over.'[104] The first dealings in the shares took place in a burst of excitement, and shares were sold at a premium of about £5 over the £12 issue price.[105] The Concession had made provision for the Persian government, or Persian subjects, to acquire up to 20% of the called up capital, and an attempt was made to offer shares to the Persian government, but they were given little notice and reacted slowly. On 19 September Schindler in Tehran had telegraphed the Amin os-Soltan, who was away from the city, offering to sell to the Persian government one-fifth of the share capital. The Amin os-Soltan, however, took nearly two weeks to reply. The reply, when it came on 2 October 1889, reported the Amin os-Soltan's 'inability to give a definite reply till after the safe arrival of the Imperial Camp at Tehran'.[106] By that time all the shares had been subscribed. The Sassoons may have acquired 30% or more of the shares, although the use of nominees and family members to hold shares makes an exact figure impossible to obtain.

The successful share issue meant that Julius de Reuter finally recovered his expenses from the 1872 Concession negotiations. On 15 October he received from the Imperial Bank the £200 000 from the premium on the share issue (£60 000 of which was paid to Schröders) and on 19 November he received a further £40 000 from the Imperial Bank, representing the return of his original caution money. De Reuter had still not got a railway, but a bank and his expenses were clearly an improvement on nothing.

Meanwhile, the path was clear for the new bank to start business. In December 1889 Joseph Rabino, the man chosen to be the first Chief Manager of the Imperial Bank of Persia, arrived in Tehran. He had to find staff and premises, and begin from scratch the conversion of the privileges of the Concession into a practical reality in Persia. It would not have been, in the best circumstances, an easy job. Even in his worst nightmares, however, Rabino could scarcely have imagined that within four years of his arrival the mining rights of the Concession and all hopes of building railways would have come to naught and his bank forced to rely on banking to make a profit; that a world silver crisis would have caused a sharp depreciation of Persia's currency and the writing-down of the Bank's capital; that a scandal involving Malkam Khan and widespread popular agitation against foreign concessions would have wrecked Persia's international credit standing for two decades; that Russian interests would have founded a rival bank to the Imperial Bank; and that the Bank's keen supporter, Drummond Wolff, would have had a nervous breakdown and left Persia. If Rabino had guessed what lay ahead, he might have left Tehran just as fast as the appalling Persian transport system could have carried him.

2

SURVIVAL AGAINST THE ODDS 1889–95

On 27 September 1889 the Board of the Imperial Bank of Persia resolved to offer the post of Chief Manager to Joseph Rabino, the Manager of the Cairo branch of Crédit Lyonnais, the large French bank. On 1 October Rabino telegraphed his acceptance to the Chairman of the Bank, and on 15 October he left Egypt for London and then Persia.[1] For the next 18 years Rabino was the main force behind the Imperial Bank's development, and the architect of its survival.

Rabino was a short, stout man, with a glass eye; a man of strong character, substantial intelligence and considerable ego. A man whose dignity could be offended rather easily. Much about his life before he joined the Imperial Bank remains unknown, and the information we do have rests largely on his own short autobiography written in 1915. Even his nationality has been a matter of dispute. He has been variously described as a Frenchman, an Italian, and a 'Levantine'. In fact, he was born at 97 Wardour Street, in the Soho district of central London, on 23 March 1843, of an Italian father, Giovanni Rabino, and an English mother, Sophia, née Tully. His father had left Italy some time before and had eventually settled in London, where he worked as a tailor. Rabino was educated in England and France, and started work at the age of 16, holding a series of junior clerical positions with a bookbinder and several merchants. In 1870 he began his banking career by joining Crédit Lyonnais in Paris. He was sent back to London almost at once to open an Agency. He successfully accomplished this task, and was also married in London in 1871. He briefly left the Crédit Lyonnais during the 1870s, but rejoined them as an Inspector in Lyons. This led in 1881 to an appointment in Alexandria, as Sub-Manager, and he spent the next eight years in Egypt.[2]

Rabino's service in Egypt in the 1880s was a useful preparation for some of the problems he was to face in Persia. He was involved in reforming the

Egyptian silver currency, being awarded an Egyptian honour and 200 Egyptian pounds for his efforts. He seems to have established cordial relations with the British political establishment in Egypt, and Sir Evelyn Baring, the British Consul in that country, acted as one of his referees for the Chief Managership of the Imperial Bank. Rabino's work on the Egyptian currency also brought him to the attention of overseas banking circles in London, and he wrote articles on the subject for learned and banking journals in Britain.[3]

Rabino seems to have come to the notice of the Imperial Bank's Board through Julius de Reuter. In 1889 de Reuter had asked Dr Tholozon, the Shah's doctor and de Reuter's ally in gaining the 1889 Concession, to travel from Paris to London to consult about Rabino, whom – Tholozon later recalled, 'we both thought . . . was the best man for this important position'.[4] Rabino was undoubtedly better qualified than many British bankers for establishing the Imperial Bank in Persia. He had long experience of Egypt and unlike most Victorian Englishmen, he was an accomplished linguist. He was completely fluent in French, the official language of the Persian Court, and he also spoke German and Italian. In addition, Rabino's contact with official circles in Egypt gave him experience of the high-level governmental and diplomatic circles in which he would be required to move in Tehran.

There is little evidence why Rabino wanted the job. It was a promotion from being a branch Manager to running a whole bank, and he had apparently been passed over by the Crédit Lyonnais for the post of Chief Manager in Egypt. But it was clearly also an enormous gamble for a 46-year-old man with a wife and family. Rabino later wrote that he 'applied for the post of Chief Manager, very much as [he] would have bought a lottery ticket'.[5]

Having won the lottery, Rabino travelled to Persia via Russia and the Ottoman Empire. By the end of December he was established as Chief Manager in Tehran. His immediate tasks were to recruit staff, establish branches and build a banking business in Persia.

2.2 STAFF RECRUITMENT

When Rabino arrived in Tehran he inherited one member of staff, General Schindler, the Bank's Adviser. He was able to bring with him, however, three other Europeans from Egypt. These were Duke Baker, formerly Manager of the Alexandria branch of the Anglo–Egyptian Bank who was recruited to be the Deputy Manager, W. D. van Lennep, the son of friends of the Rabino family who had worked for the firm of E. Mallinson & Co. in Alexandria, who was to be Chief Correspondent, and W. Giglio, who was the General Clerk. Arriving simultaneously with this party came D. F. Putt, a former branch

Manager of the Bank of Liverpool Ltd, who was recruited by the London Office of the Imperial Bank to be Accountant in Tehran.

The evolution of the Imperial Bank's staff recruitment policies will be discussed in later chapters, but it needs to be observed immediately that recruitment of senior staff, who by the conventions of the age had to be male Europeans and not Persians, was a considerable problem. The Imperial Bank was far from alone in this difficulty, and many other British overseas banks found it hard to find men with the appropriate qualifications when they first started.[6] Staff shortages were a major constraint on the pace of a bank's expansion. In the Imperial Bank's case, Rabino and his Board did not see eye to eye on the definition of 'appropriate' staff. The Chief Manager was anxious to build up a cadre of senior staff as rapidly as possible, in order to get the initiation of a branch network under way. He wanted men with some overseas experience and a gift for languages, and he would take any European who had these qualifications. The Board, however, were insistent that *real* Britishers, preferably with experience in domestic banking, should be employed, and the number of non-British staff kept to an absolute minimum. As a result, there was constant tension between London and Rabino over the calibre of recruits sent to Persia. Rabino did not consider that familiarity with British banking practice was of great relevance in the Persian context. He argued that knowledge of the mechanism of foreign exchanges, of the finance of trade, and an ability to conduct the Bank's business in the local language were more valuable skills for a provincial Bank Manager. 'I want a thoroughly trustworthy man or rather two thus,' Rabino wrote to London in January 1890, 'who know languages, can turn their hand to anything in banking and act independently.'[7]

The Board generally overruled Rabino's views on staff. Although a British Consul in Persia complained that the Bank employed too many 'cheap and nasty foreigners instead of Englishmen',[8] Rabino was mostly supplied with young and relatively inexperienced recruits from Britain. In addition, for reasons which will be explained in Chapter 5, staff turnover was high. As a result, in the early years Rabino faced a continual shortage of senior men.

2.3 BUILDING A BRANCH NETWORK

Rabino was eager to build a branch network in Persia. He considered such a step the essential prerequisite if the Imperial Bank was to establish an effective presence in Persia, and indispensable if the Bank was to distribute its notes throughout the country.

Table 2.1 shows that Rabino's strategy was, at least to some extent, implemented. The Bank had eight branches in Persia by 1895, and it had also

Table 2.1. *Branches and agencies of Imperial Bank 1889–95*

Branches in Persia	
Location	Date opened
Chief Office, Tehran	December 1889
Tabriz	April 1890
Bushire	April 1890
Esfahan	June 1890
Mashad	April 1891
Shiraz	May 1891
Yazd	May 1893
Rasht	May 1893

Location	Agencies outside Persia Date opened	Date closed
Baghdad	May 1890	February 1894
Bombay	May 1891	March 1900
Basra	July 1891	February 1894
Calcutta	May 1892	December 1894

established agencies in the neighbouring territory of the Ottoman Empire and in British India.

The first branch to be established was Chief Office in Tehran. As soon as Rabino arrived there, he set up a temporary office in a building later occupied by the Russian Bank in Persia. The first few months were difficult ones. Rabino later described these early days as being 'hard, mortal hard, ... We got beds somehow and improvised some sort of apartments with petroleum stoves to keep us warm, for the snow was heavy on the ground.'[9]

The situation, however, was much improved by the purchase of the business of the New Oriental Bank Corporation, which, it will be remembered, had established a branch in Tehran in 1888. The Imperial Bank's Concession made the Corporation's position untenable and as it had an extremely large international branch network – a policy which was to contribute to its collapse in 1892 – the Corporation's directors resolved to extricate themselves from Persia on the best terms available. Negotiations were under way in London by September 1889. The Corporation's initial request for £60 000 for its Persian assets was rejected, but on 15 April 1890 an agreement was finally reached between the two parties. The Imperial Bank secured 'the entire business established and carried on by the Corporation in Persia' in return for £20 000.[10]

The purchase of the Corporation brought with it their handsome building in Artillery Square in central Tehran. The Imperial Bank took over the building in April 1890, renting it, as the Corporation had done, from Mirza Ali Khan, Amin od-Doule. The Square was one of the principal centres of life in the city. Along two sides of it stood the Shah's artillery and in the centre was a garden. The Bank occupied the entire eastern side. In front of the Bank there was a large puddle, known as the Lake of the Bank-e Shahi (the Imperial Bank was known in Persia as the 'Bank-e Shahi', or the Shah's Bank). In winter this was a very sizeable pool, but in summer it almost vanished.[11] This prominent and centrally located building was well-suited to be the Headquarters of a Bank which aspired to be a national institution.

In the meantime, Rabino had moved quickly to establish the first provincial branches. Tabriz, the commercial centre of northern Persia and the capital of Azerbaijan, the country's richest province, was an obvious location and in April 1890 a branch was opened. Bushire, the largest Persian port on the Gulf, was the next town where the Bank opened. The New Oriental Bank Corporation had established a branch there during 1889, and the Imperial Bank acquired this branch, together with its Manager, when it bought the Corporation's business in Persia. A branch at Esfahan was also opened. This town was attractive not only because of its location on one of the great Persian trade arteries from Bushire on the Gulf to the north, but also because it was the seat of government of the Shah's eldest son, the Zell os-Soltan, who was pro-British in his political sympathies.

In addition, the Imperial Bank established a number of 'agencies' in Persia. These were at Kermanshah, Mashad, Rasht and Shiraz. The use of the terms 'branch' and 'agency' by British overseas banks was rather ambiguous in this period. The Imperial Bank in the early 1890s seems to have regarded a branch as an office where there was a European Manager conducting a full range of banking business, including note issue. An agency, in contrast, consisted of a local merchant who collected the Bank's bills on its behalf. Confusingly, the Bank's Annual Report in the first few years listed branches and agencies together, thereby giving an exaggerated impression of the Bank's growth.

In early 1891 the Mashad and Shiraz agencies were converted into branches, and British officers sent to both towns. Shiraz was intended to complement the branch at Bushire. The problem with Bushire was that all imports and exports were in transit only. The main distribution centres were Shiraz, Esfahan, Yazd and further north. It was decided, therefore, to open in Shiraz, and to place Bushire under the control of the new branch. No new branches were opened in 1892, but in May 1893 branches at Yazd and Rasht were opened. The establishment of these branches brought to an end the first phase of the Bank's branch expansion. Apart from the extension of the Bazaar office in Tehran into a virtual branch in the late 1890s, there were to be no new branches until one at Kermanshah was established in 1902.

The Imperial Bank also established agencies in Baghdad, Basra, Bombay and Calcutta. The unhappy stories of these ventures will be related later in this chapter. Here it will suffice merely to note that although these offices were known as agencies – under the Bank's Charter it was only allowed to open agencies outside Persia – they were managed by Europeans and conducted a full range of banking business apart from the issue of notes.

Working out an appropriate relationship between Chief Office and the branches took time. Branch Managers inevitably exercised considerable freedom in their day-to-day business, and communication difficulties meant that their activities could only be supervised in the most general sense by Rabino in Tehran. From the beginning of 1893 all branch Managers were required to compile a half-yearly 'Report on Progress', which was sent both to Rabino and London. Although the contents of this Report varied greatly between Managers, all of them supplied both statistics and opinions on the development of the branch's business.

Much about the Bank's administrative structure was still haphazard by 1895. Rabino in the early 1890s was fully occupied with the more immediate problems of ensuring that the Bank survived from one day to the next. Moreover, he was temperamentally more interested in negotiations with the Persian government and British diplomats than in building administrative structures. From this point of view, it was unfortunate that the position of Deputy Manager was left unfilled after D. Baker resigned from the Bank in 1892. Right up to his departure from the Bank in 1908, Rabino never had sufficient assistance at a senior level to free him to focus his mind for any length of time on administration.

2.4 THE BOARD AND LONDON OFFICE

Tehran was the Chief Office of the Imperial Bank, and Rabino was the Chief Manager. Yet during Rabino's Chief Managership considerable executive power was retained in London. The Board kept a close watch on Rabino's activities, and tried to legislate on all important aspects of Bank policy, including senior staff appointments, lending policies and the allocation of capital to branches. This procedure was not unique to the Imperial Bank, and seems to have been the norm for British overseas banks of the period.[12] In August 1893 the Board's control over the Persian business was increased when it was decided to establish a small committee to examine the Reports on Progress made by each branch. This development was the result of an initiative by Henry Coke, the Manager of the London office of David Sassoon

& Co., who joined the Bank's Board in September 1892 as a representative of that firm in place of S. Ezekiel. Coke had his view that the Imperial Bank had an 'inadequate and unsatisfactory' administration written into the Board minutes. His solution was the establishment of a small committee of three directors to form an Audit Committee to 'examine all returns and accounts from Teheran and the branches and Agencies of the Bank and to report thereon to the Board'.[13] By the time of the first meeting on 30 August 1893, the Audit Committee had been renamed the Inspection Committee, and it soon acquired an influential role in the Bank's policy-making.

There were some changes in the composition of the Imperial Bank's Board between 1890 and 1895. In 1892, as already mentioned, Henry Coke replaced S. Ezekiel on the Bank's Board. In December 1893 H. D. Stewart, a shadowy figure, resigned, followed by A. P. H. Hotz, after allegations of conflict of interest had arisen regarding the relationship between his firm and the Bank.[14] In 1893 General Sir Thomas E. Gordon joined the Board. The 60-year-old Gordon was half Spanish and half Scottish, and an identical twin. He and his twin brother, John, had entered the British Army on the same day in 1849, and had achieved their promotion to the rank of General on the same day after notable military careers. In 1889 Thomas was appointed Oriental and Military Secretary to the British Legation in Tehran, and in 1891 he became Military Attache. He brought to the Bank's Board recent knowledge of Persia and a number of high-level contacts in that country. The final Board change came in January 1895, when Geoffrey Glyn resigned from the Board and was replaced by George Stielow, a representative of J. Henry Schröder & Co.

The Board was supported by a small staff in London Office. London Office was initially established in temporary premises in Winchester House, 100 Old Broad Street in the City of London, but in the New Year in 1890 it moved to permanent offices at 14 Austin Friars. This office was rather small, a description which fits all the Bank's subsequent London premises until it moved to 99 Bishopsgate in 1976, but at least in March 1893 electric lighting was installed to relieve the gloom.

The most senior official in London Office was the Secretary. After having a temporary Secretary during the period of its formation, in October 1889 the Board appointed the 42-year-old George Newell, formerly with the London Office of the Comptoir National d'Escompte de Paris, to the post. He was to retain that position, which he combined with that of Manager of the London Branch after this post was created in 1898, until his retirement in 1917. Newell, the Board's faithful servant, was an opaque figure with apparently little significance in policy-making. His successor as London Manager concluded that Newell had always appeared 'so busy' because 'his great aim was to avoid if possible going straight to the point *if* it necessitated accepting any responsibility by being decisive'.[15]

2.5 THE PERFORMANCE OF THE BANK 1889–1895

How did the Imperial Bank fare during its first six years of existence? During this period the main source for assessing the Bank's performance is its published balance sheet. Appendices 3, 4 and 5 at the end of this volume give, on an annual basis, the main items of the Bank's balance sheet, the size of shareholders' funds and of published profits. This section will confine itself to indicating the main trends as shown in these published figures, leaving a more detailed look at the business for later in the chapter. Incidentally, it is worth noting in this context the Bank's strange year-end, 20 September, which the Imperial Bank seems to have shared with no other British bank. The date was chosen, according to the first Directors' Report, because it was the Persian half-year, and it was also the anniversary of the Bank's foundation.

The picture as presented in the Bank's balance sheet was an unprepossessing one. After a strong start the Bank clearly experienced difficulties. Deposits peaked in 1892, and over the following three years they fell lower than when the Bank started. The Bank's holding of cash in 1895 was down 73% from 1891, and investments fell by 65% over the same period. The one bright spot was the note issue, which grew from nothing to £94 000 in 1894, but even this fell by almost a quarter in the following year. The overall balance sheet total was 20% lower in 1895 than in 1890.

The Bank's shareholders' funds told a similar story. In 1895 the Bank wrote down its £1 million capital by a third, reducing it to £650 000. The overall size of shareholders' funds was 40% lower in 1895 than in 1890.

The Bank's published profits also fell away between 1890 and 1895. In later years it is known that transfers were made to and from inner reserves before the Bank's net profit was arrived at, and so the 'real' level of profits was different from the published figure. It is not impossible that such transfers were being made in this period, but as no figures survive there is no alternative but to treat the published figures as 'real' profits. These published profits peaked in 1892, and then dwindled. In both 1894 and 1895 they were 60% lower than the 1892 level. Falling profits were translated into falling dividends. In the first year, 10/4d (i.e. old shillings and pence) was paid on each £10 share. In each of the following three years 10/- was paid, but in 1894 no dividend was paid at all. In 1895 7/- per share was paid.

The Imperial Bank's performance between 1890 and 1895 was, therefore, rather less than meteoric. Nevertheless, as the rest of this chapter will argue, in the difficult circumstances faced by the Bank in Persia, it performed rather better than its balance sheet would suggest, even if there were some self-inflicted wounds. Moreover, the Imperial Bank's performance needs to be kept in perspective. The first half of the 1890s was a period of crisis for British overseas banking in which mere survival was an achievement for a bank.

There were several contributory factors to this general crisis. In 1890 Baring Brothers, which was one of the two most prominent British merchant banks (the other being Rothschilds), nearly collapsed after becoming incautiously involved in Argentine loan issues. The house was saved by a guarantee fund organised by the Bank of England, a rescue in which Glyn, Mills, Currie & Co. played a leading role. The Baring Crisis, however, shook the City and confidence in overseas lending crumbled for a decade.[16] A further blow came from Australia, where a number of bank collapses in the early 1890s culminated in a major crisis in 1893, when dozens of local and British overseas banks in Australia collapsed.[17]

Meanwhile British overseas banks in the East were buffeted by sharp falls in the gold price of silver in the early 1890s (see later in this chapter). The New Oriental Bank Corporation collapsed in 1892, partly because of the 'silver problem' and partly through sheer bad management.[18] In 1892 The Chartered Mercantile Bank of India, London and China got into difficulties, and had to write-down its capital. The Bank reincorporated, without its Royal Charter, as The Mercantile Bank of India, Ltd. Even the Hongkong Bank, to an extent sheltered from the silver problem as its balance sheet was in silver-based Hong Kong Dollars, experienced considerable difficulties in the early 1890s.[19]

The Imperial Bank of Persia did not exist in a vacuum. It was buffeted by the same pressures that hit other British overseas banks, notably the 'silver problem', and it felt the shock waves of the Baring and Australian banking crises. It was not an ideal time for a new bank to be launched.

2.6 BANKING IN PERSIA

Quite apart from surviving adverse global circumstances, the Imperial Bank after its foundation faced the daunting task of introducing modern banking to Persia. Rather surprisingly, Rabino found this the least of his worries, and most of the Imperial Bank's early difficulties arose when it strayed from Persian banking into other activities.

Until the establishment of the Tehran branch of the New Oriental Bank Corporation in 1888, no modern bank existed in Persia. This did not mean, however, that credit institutions did not exist. Large merchants often offered banking services, and indigenous bankers, or *sarrafs*, were widespread.[20] The function of these *sarrafs* varied between cities, but as a rule they were concerned with short-term advances and seasonal lending to agriculture. Most *sarrafs* were petty money lenders, but in Tehran and a few other cities a number of them had considerable resources and influence. Despite the Islamic prohibition against taking interest, it was the universal practice to charge interest on loans. It is impossible to generalise on interest rates, except to say that they were 'high' compared with contemporary European levels, being known to have reached 100% per annum or more. Interest rates were a function of the risks of lending and, as many loans would have been of a short-term 'emergency' nature, these high rates may not have seemed so crippling as at first sight.

Persians, therefore, were not unfamiliar with the basic concepts of banking and interest when the Imperial Bank opened, but a wide gulf existed between the business practices of Victorian Britain and of Qajar Persia. The nature of the savings and capital markets in the two countries was also radically different. There was no long-term capital market in Persia. Moreover, Persians, like all undeveloped agricultural communities, tended to hoard savings to deal with harvest fluctuations. Political uncertainty, and lack of investment opportunities, also encouraged hoarding. Both Persians and British bankers had much to learn about one another.

What kind of banking did the Imperial Bank establish in Persia? 'Our real business', Rabino explained to the Tabriz Manager in March 1893, 'is to borrow money from Mohammed to lend it to Hussein and consequently all our efforts tend towards obtaining deposits and pushing the circulation of our notes.'[21]

Rabino's words describe the essence of the routine banking business established by the Imperial Bank in the early 1890s, which followed the lines of conventional British overseas banking practice. The first principle of such banking was to establish a local deposit base and use these deposits to fund the banking activities of each branch. In an ideal situation, shareholders' equity was not to be used to work the local business, but would remain in London safe from any exchange risk and as a last-resort guarantee of the business. 'My ideal', Rabino wrote, 'would be an English bank worked with Persian money.'[22]

But how was this 'Persian money' to be attracted? In the long term Rabino looked longingly towards the large savings believed to be hoarded, but he was not a utopian, and he continually stressed that Persians were unlikely to change age-old savings patterns overnight. His initial strategy was to secure large deposits from a few key notables. This made considerable sense in a country with a very unequal wealth distribution. The Shah's money was an obvious target, and Rabino worked hard to secure some of it. In April 1891 the Shah, to Rabino's delight, did make a deposit with the Bank. In the following October the Zell os-Soltan, the Shah's eldest son, also deposited £20 000 and in the next month one of the Shah's wives paid in £10 000.[23]

Rabino was anxious to encourage long-term deposits rather than deposits at call or short notice which might be withdrawn from the Bank with little warning. However, there was initially no clear policy towards the various types of accounts. The Bank, anxious to attract funds, paid interest on at least some deposits at call, and this remained a regular practice.[24] The ideal remained money deposited for a fixed amount of time, preferably 12 months, on which a fixed rate of interest was given. In practice, however, Rabino learned to be flexible on time periods. Important personages, like the Zell os-Soltan, were usually allowed to withdraw money at any time from their allegedly 'fixed' deposits. In so far as Persians hoarded money in case they needed it in the event of some political or other emergency, Rabino had little choice but to adopt this line if the Bank was to become established as an alternative to hoarding.

The Bank's deposits in Persia peaked in terms of Sterling in 1892, at £291 555. They subsequently fell away to £187 349 in 1895. These figures were lower than the Bank's total deposits, which included deposits in London and in the agencies outside Persia. The Bank's Persian deposits were in Krans, the local monetary unit, and their apparent fall after 1892 largely reflected the depreciation of the Kran against Sterling. The Bank converted its year-end balance sheet into Sterling using an 'adjustment rate', each branch having its own rate until the end of the century. Appendix 6 gives the Bank's adjustment rates throughout its time in Persia, together with an alternative series for the Kran–Sterling exchange rate derived from other sources. Using the Bank's adjustment rate – and all conversions will use this rate unless otherwise stated – the Bank's deposits rose from 6.8 million Krans (£209 061) in 1891 to 11.2 million Krans (£228 705) in 1894, before falling to 9.8 million Krans in 1895.

Behind the national figures there were marked regional fluctuations. In August 1894, 50% of Persian deposits originated from Chief Office in Tehran, and 19% from Tabriz branch. Mashad, Esfahan and Yazd branches had attracted only insignificant amounts by 1894.

In order to acquire both fixed assets and initial working capital, local deposits were supplemented by importing silver from Britain. The transportation of bullion to Persia was extremely difficult, while the minting of bullion into coin once it was in Persia presented a further set of obstacles. The Mint was run by the government in a highly unsatisfactory fashion. Rabino considered it to be 'the abomination of desolation'.[25] The Mintmaster was corrupt, and the Mint's machinery so antiquated that it kept breaking down.

Moreover, the Bank, despite its status and rights under the Concession, did not have sole access to the Mint, but had to share its poor facilities with merchants and other enterprises. Some of the Bank's capital was also imported in the form of gold bullion, to be used as security against which to borrow silver or to purchase silver within the country.

The importation of silver into Persia fluctuated with the exchanges. Between mid-1889 and mid-1890, when the Kran temporarily rose in exchange value against Sterling, Rabino was very reluctant to import silver. By late 1891, however, falling silver prices prompted him to import more of it. 'Provided only silver does not run up', he noted in May 1891, 'we shall be able to import more capital to the general advantage.'[26] By November 1891 Tehran had imported about £500 000.

Initially, the Bank allocated funds as required to the various branches. In December 1892, however, the Board decided that there should be a fixed apportionment of capital between branches and agencies, reflecting their relative business importance. Tehran received the largest amount – £390 000 – followed by the Indian agencies, which received £230 000. The other offices received smaller amounts, ranging from £85 000 for Tabriz to £25 000 for Mashad.[27] Not all of each branch's capital, however, was converted into local currency and physically located at that branch; some might be retained in the branch's account in London. Alternatively, the branch could overdraw in London to the extent of the undrawn allocated capital.

In addition to their allocated capital and deposits, the issue of bank notes also provided resources for branches. Bank notes essentially represented an interest-free loan to a bank, and they also gave a bank considerable prestige. In Persia they were the most visible display of the Imperial Bank's status as the national bank. The Bank gave considerable thought to the design of its banknotes, striving for a high standard both as a safeguard against forgery and to ensure that the Bank's notes made a favourable impression in Persia.

Notes were printed in denominations of 1, 2, 3, 4, 10, 20, 50, 100, 500, and 1000 Tomans, although the 1000 Toman note was not put in circulation. Tomans were a unit of account – one being equal to ten Krans – and never appear to have been used as a circulating coin. Persian currency, therefore, came to consist of Imperial Bank notes in Tomans and silver coins in Krans. Each note had a Persian inscription with the Persian Imperial insignia of the Lion and the Sun on one side, and an English inscription with the Shah's portrait on the other.

The issue of the Imperial Bank's notes did not proceed smoothly. An immediate problem was that the Imperial Bank was not the first institution to issue notes. The New Oriental Bank Corporation had done so when it opened branches in Persia, and in February 1890 the Board ordered Rabino to secure the withdrawal of those notes, but the potential threat of competing note issues was removed when the Corporation's business in Persia was acquired in April.

A second problem concerned the place at which notes should be payable. Under the terms of the Concession the Bank was liable for encashment of the notes in Tehran as well as at the branch of issue. From the beginning Rabino insisted that this policy had to be changed and that notes should only be payable at the branch of issue. He pointed to the difficulties in the way of transporting specie from one branch to another, the requirement that the Bank in its first two years should have at least a 50% reserve of specie against the issue of notes, and the Bank's liability to pay silver coin for its notes on demand. Tehran, Rabino argued, was as vulnerable as any branch to being overwhelmed by a huge flood of notes. Moreover, he argued, fluctuations in the value of coins between towns would be likely to prompt merchants of a town where coin was lower in value than in Tehran to send their notes to the capital for encashment.[28] In September 1890 the Board agreed to cancel the option for the encashment in Tehran of notes issued at the branches.[29] It subsequently became the Bank's practice to accept notes at branches other than the one of issue, but at a discount.

The first consignment of the Imperial Bank's notes, some 3000 notes with a value of £22 000 in Sterling, arrived in Tehran on 5 May 1890. Issuing the notes was a laborious and time-consuming task. They had to be signed and checked, and stamped by the Bank's High Commissioner, the Persian official appointed in accordance with Article 4 of the Concession to watch over the Bank's affairs. It was not until all this preliminary work had been completed that the really difficult business could begin of persuading the public to accept the notes as a medium of exchange.

The note issue, therefore, grew slowly. The troubles of 1891 associated with the Tobacco Concession (see below) hindered their acceptance, and there were several attempts to boycott the Bank's notes. Predictably, it proved much easier to expand note circulation in Tehran than in the provinces. In August 1894 53% of the Bank's note issue was issued from Chief Office. The other main centre was the southern branches of Shiraz and Bushire, which accounted for a further 30% of the note issue. In contrast to the situation with deposits, Managers in Tabriz – as well as the other northern branches – found it hard to expand their note issue. Thus although the Bank's note circulation grew during these early years, reaching 4.7 million Krans in 1894 before falling to 3.8 million in 1895, the pace of growth did not fulfil the Bank's initial expectations.

To summarise, the Bank's branches in Persia were put in funds by transfers from London, local deposits, and by their note issue. How was this money used? Like other British overseas banks, the core of Imperial Bank's business – at least in theory – was exchange operations and the provision of short-term trade finance. Later chapters will go into greater detail on the Imperial Bank's business, but although the surviving records for the early 1890s are sparse, the main outlines of the Bank's activities can be sketched.

The Bank developed a business in both internal and external exchange. Persia in the late nineteenth century offered considerable scope for internal exchange operations. The movement of funds from one place to another was extremely difficult in a country so devoid of efficient communications. Yet the seasonal nature of Persian agriculture made movements of funds inevitable. 'From June to September', Rabino explained in a paper read to the Institute of Bankers in London, 'the opium crop absorbs all the floating capital of the provinces, of which Isfahan and Yezd are the centres; the money goes into the villages, to the great inconvenience of those towns.'[30]

The Bank was also active in external exchange operations, though this was a complicated business. Foreign exchange dealings in the 1890s contained a large element of guesswork about future exchange rate movements. Persian exchanges, as a writer as late as 1917 observed, were 'confusing and difficult to follow intelligibly'.[31] The Persian exchange rate was to an extent dependent on the course of imports and exports, that is, to supply and demand in those sectors but other influences also had a marked effect: the Russian Rouble affected exchange in the north, while the Indian Rupee had its own effect in the south. In addition, the external value of the Kran was in the long term linked to movements in the gold price of silver on the London market, although over the short term movements in the price of silver could bear little relation to the rate of exchange in Persia. Persian exchange operations, therefore, were far from straightforward in the early years of the Bank. They were, as Rabino told London, 'a dangerous thing'.[32]

Even more dangerous, especially from the point of view of the Board in London, was local lending. The item of 'Bills Discounted, Loans and Advances' which appeared on the Bank's balance sheet covered a range of business. There was some lending to government. And, despite allegations from some later writers that the Imperial Bank 'discriminated against Persians in giving credit',[33] Rabino undertook lending to Persian merchants and traders from the beginning. There was little alternative, as the few expatriate firms in Persia generated little business, especially as several of them performed quasi-banking operations themselves. Nevertheless lending money to Persians did run straight into the problem of the different British and Persian business mores. By the late nineteenth century English banking orthodoxy was that the legitimate business of a bank was short-term, self-liquidating advances. Advances were to be made against security, and the long-term investment, or 'lock up' of funds as it was known by contemporaries, was to be avoided at all costs. The traditional Persian credit system stood in complete contrast. When a bill of exchange or loan repayment was overdue, the creditor often granted an extension and raised the interest rate. As the initial interest rate was usually over 20%, it could soar to 60% or more. At this sort of interest level, the debt might be written off after a final payment of interest, which, added to what had already been recovered, equalled the original indebtedness plus a reasonable profit.[34]

The Board of the Imperial Bank were determined that the Imperial Bank should operate in Persia on English banking principles. 'We must get the Persians into our way of doing business', Newell wrote to Rabino in November 1893, 'otherwise the Bank had better close. It will take a little time no doubt, but they will appreciate us the more afterwards...'.[35] Rabino considered such views naive. 'As to introducing English business customs into Persia', he replied to Newell, 'neither I nor any man on earth can do so and any expectation of success in this direction can only lead to disappointment.'[36]

There was nothing unique about the different perspectives of Rabino and his Board. In Australia, South America and elsewhere, British bankers discovered that, if they were to do business, they might have to lend on the strangest security, or on none at all, and that generally the strict rules of banking orthodoxy had to bend to the realities of doing business in foreign countries. The problem was how far the rules should be bent. Almost invariably, Boards in London pressed for British banking norms to be observed, while Managers overseas pleaded the realities of life.[37] The near-catastrophe of the Baring Crisis in 1890 served to strengthen the resolve of Boards in the City to enforce orthodoxy in overseas banking and financial matters.[38] The survival of a bank could depend, to an extent at least, on the compromise reached between the two sides. British overseas banks that attempted either to maintain too strict an orthodox policy, or alternatively to follow completely local customs, were the most vulnerable to failure.

During the 1890s and the 1900s, then, there were frequent conflicts between Rabino and London on the issue of local lending. London attempted to lay down a framework of rules for such operations, pressing not only for all loans to be made against good security but even attempting to make the Persian branches consult London on all loans and advances before they were made, a particularly impractical policy as such consultations would have involved at least a month-long delay.[39] Rabino insisted that the Board's demands for cast-iron security for each loan were unnecessary, arguing that bad debts were actually rather rare. He regarded the interest paid by borrowers, usually 12%, as a valuable source of income, and he also stressed the institutional difficulties in the way of strictly enforcing the repayment of debts. 'You who live in a country with perfectly organised institutions', he observed to Newell, 'cannot understand what it is to work a banking business without any means of coercion at command.'[40]

Rabino's assurances did not prevent the Board becoming steadily more worried about 'loans, advances and discounts' during the early 1890s. Quite apart from the general atmosphere of caution in London generated by the Baring Crisis and the Australian banking collapse, business conditions in Persia looked unstable to London. The Sterling–Kran exchange rate was, as will be discussed below, a matter of grave concern. A series of natural disasters caused bad harvests and these led to a rising level of advances which were not repaid on time, which were known in the language of the time as 'outstandings'. In 1892 a cholera epidemic swept through Persia, killing thousands, including two British and one Armenian member of staff of the Tehran branch. The epidemic restricted the movement of goods and led to the closure of bazaars. Among other things, this badly affected the importers of Manchester piece goods, and caused many of them to delay repayments.[41] Further difficulties were caused by price fluctuations for Persia's cash crops, of which opium was one of the most important. By 1892, the Shiraz branch of the Bank was involved in financing the opium trade, acting as middlemen between the opium houses, notably David Sassoon & Co., and the local growers of the crop. Yet the next two years were extremely difficult ones for this region, with falling world opium prices, warring tribesmen devastating the country, harvest failure due to locusts, and floods in December 1893. It was hardly surprising that borrowers fell behind in their repayments.

Overall, however, the Bank's lending policies seem to have been successful given that they were new to Persia. Despite considerable difficulties in recovering overdue debts, most overdue loans and advances were eventually recovered.

A more difficult problem than bad debts, at least in the Bank's early days and on occasion later, was finding sufficient outlet for its funds. During 1891 this was a particularly difficult, although not surprising problem. The depressed conditions in parts of Persia and considerable political unrest did not encourage merchants to borrow from the Bank, while the Bank for its part had of necessity to be selective in lending as it built up information on customers. Nevertheless the slow pace of the Bank's business expansion stimulated calls in some quarters for drastic action. A. P. H. Hotz, one of the original Board members, wrote to the Chairman as early as May 1891 calling for the Bank's capital to be reduced, on the grounds that there was 'no doubt that the capital of the Bank is too large for its requirements'.[42] Rabino, however, fiercely resisted this pressure, and by the end of 1891 it had died down as he developed more uses for funds. Within a year he was reporting that the Bank's funds in Persia were 'employed up to the hilt'.[43]

2.7 SCANDALS, CONCESSIONS AND THE PERSIAN LOAN OF 1892

Rabino's achievements in attracting deposits, launching the note issue and establishing a lending business seem all the more noteworthy when it is remembered that the early 1890s saw an upsurge of anti-western agitation in Persia, which at times looked like threatening the Imperial Bank and which did lead to the collapse of Persia's international credit rating.

The problems were sparked off by two concessions which the Shah had granted or negotiated during his stay in Britain in 1889. The first was a very vague document, which the Shah had signed even though the nature of business to be undertaken and the name of the concessionaire had been left blank. The document was handed to Malkam Khan for copying and transmission to Tehran. By the time it reached Persia the word 'Roulette' had been inserted in it. Meanwhile, Malkam Khan promoted a company in London, known as the Persian Investment Corporation, to exploit this and other concessions. The firm's Board included Malkam Khan's brother and a director of the New Oriental Bank Corporation, and its prospectus, advertised on 2 December 1889, listed a wide range of objectives, including 'all kinds of financial and banking business'.

Events soon turned sour. Persian officials immediately objected, on religious grounds, to the promotion of gambling in the country. Drummond Wolff, the British Minister in Tehran, was also extremely alarmed at the dubious nature of the venture. The British government's legal advisers ruled that the Persian Investment Corporation's activities fell foul of British gambling laws. On 5 December 1889 the Shah telegraphed Malkam Khan cancelling the concession. Despite this news, Malkam Khan sold the concession to the Persian Investment Corporation for £20 000, the New Oriental Bank Corporation advancing the sum.

It was not long before Malkam Khan's behaviour became known to both the Persian government and his British business partners. The Shah, on learning what had happened, dismissed Malkam Khan from his post as Ambassador in London. Meanwhile the Persian Investment Corporation, which had been informed on 17 December 1889 by the British government that the concession was illegal, attempted to sue Malkam Khan and obtain some compensation from the Persian government. Despite his loss of diplomatic immunity, however, Malkam Khan managed to side-step the legal action taken against him by his partners. Remarkably, within a year of the whole unsavoury incident, he had established a reputation as a major *emigré* critic of the corrupt practices of the Persian government.[44]

This debacle, which became known as the 'Lottery Scandal', was extensively reported in *The Times* and elsewhere, and did nothing to inspire confidence in Persia among British investors and capitalists. The New Oriental Bank Corporation had its £20 000 loan listed as one of its many bad debts when it went bankrupt in the summer of 1892.

There was worse to come. During the Shah's visit to Britain Drummond Wolff had introduced him to a Major Gerald F. Talbot. There were discussions about the granting of concessions to Talbot for the buying, selling and manufacturing of tobacco in Persia, and in March 1890 he secured a concession on these lines from the Shah. Talbot was granted a 50-year monopoly, or 'Regie', over the production, sale and export of Persia's entire tobacco crop. In return he was required to pay £15 000 to the Persian Treasury whether he benefited or lost by the business. In addition, after all expenses pertaining to the business had been deducted, and after paying a 5% dividend on capital to the proprietors, the Persian government was to receive a quarter of the net annual profits.[45] Over the following year Talbot organised a syndicate to exploit his concession, and in early 1891 the Imperial Tobacco Corporation of Persia was launched with a capital of £650 000.

Talbot's concession, like the Reuter Concession, has been widely criticised. 'Thousands of tobacco merchants and peddlers were virtually sold to a foreign company', one historian has observed, 'and suddenly found their business confiscated in fact if not in law.'[46] Yet, while not overlooking undoubted injustices, the Tobacco Concession needs to be seen within the context of the Persian government's attempts to improve the state's financial base. The government was anxious to tap the funds being generated by the marked expansion in agricultural exports in the late nineteenth century. The Tobacco Concession offered the government an apparently easy means to achieve this goal, without undertaking any strenuous reforms of its own creaking bureaucracy. There was also nothing unique about the Persian Tobacco Regie. Many countries taxed widely used commodities such as tobacco and salt and both their sale and the collection of the tax were often made a monopoly for which private business people were allowed to bid. The Ottoman government in 1883 had granted a tobacco monopoly in its territory to a European consortium, the *Regie des Tabacs*, as part of the settlement of a financial crisis.

In the spring of 1891 J. J. Ornstein, the representative appointed by the Imperial Tobacco Corporation to organise its business, arrived in Persia. Ornstein had been deputy director of customs in Egypt, but despite their

shared Egyptian experience he and Rabino were soon in conflict. The Bank
had expected to finance the establishment of the Tobacco Regie but
arrangements did not proceed smoothly. The Corporation imported
£100 000 of silver into Persia and arranged a minting contract directly with
the Mintmaster. Characteristically, the Mintmaster was unable to fulfill his
obligations and in August 1891 the Imperial Tobacco Corporation was
obliged to turn to the Imperial Bank for a loan to meet its cash requirements.
Very large sums – of between £150 000 and £300 000 – were mentioned, but
no progress was made chiefly because of the Bank's insistence on good
security for any advance.[47]

By this time opposition to the Tobacco Concession in Persia was building
up. After the grant of the Concession there had been some sporadic protests.
Tobacco served as an ideal focus for popular discontent since, as almost
everyone in Persia smoked, there were few people who were not affected in
some way by the tobacco monopoly. During the autumn of 1891, when the
tobacco was being harvested and the Corporation began exercising its
powers, there was an upsurge of opposition. Merchants who perceived a
threat to their trade, the *ulama* who loathed western influence of any kind, and
reformers who saw the Tobacco Concession as a symbol of Qajar corruption
and the sale of Persia to foreign interests, all became involved in protests.
They were joined by the Russians, who could usually be relied upon to
support any anti-British movement. Tabriz was a centre of disturbances, and
in September 1891 the Persian government was forced to stop the Tobacco
Corporation's activities in Azerbaijan. This success inspired agitation in other
towns.[48] There were riots in Shiraz, and in Mashad where extra guards had to
be posted around the Bank. The situation was made worse, from the British
point of view, by the fact that Drummond Wolff had left Persia in early 1891
because of a nervous breakdown, and British diplomatic affairs over the
following crucial months were in the hands of a junior *Chargé d'Affaires*.

By the middle of 1891 the Bank had been drawn into the growing chaos.
The furore over the Tobacco Concession stimulated opposition against all
other foreign concessions, including the Imperial Bank.[49] Rabino greatly
resented this threat to the Imperial Bank, as he felt scant sympathy for the
Tobacco Corporation. He considered that they had handled the situation
with little tact. Ornstein, he wrote to Newell, 'has alarmed and irritated the
population by invading the country with hundreds of Europeans posting many
of them in spots where no European was ever seen, besides ordering tobacco
merchants to stop business'.[50]

At the end of 1891 the agitation against the Tobacco Concession came to a
head. In December a letter from Mirza Hassan Shirazi, a leader of the
Persian Shias, requested all Persians to stop smoking until the Concession

was abolished. The Persian government attempted to prevaricate but by January the agitation proved overwhelming. The new British Minister, who had arrived in Tehran in November 1891, Sir Frank Lascelles, advised the Shah to compromise.[51] Finally, on 4 January 1892, the Shah promulgated a decree ending the Tobacco Monopoly.

The cancellation of the Tobacco Concession had widespread repercussions. It dramatically illustrated the potential power of opposition to the Shah, and may have led to long-term changes in the nature of the reform movement. Before 1890 Britain was seen by many reformers as a major source of support. After 1890, the reform movement, under the influence of the *ulama*, became more anti-foreign, and also anti-Shah.[52] Internationally, the chief effect of the cancellation of the Tobacco Concession was a further deterioration in Persia's credit rating on the capital markets.

However, the most important consequence of the Tobacco Concession's cancellation for the Imperial Bank was that it forced Persia to borrow abroad. Persia was very late amongst Middle Eastern countries in acquiring a foreign debt. The Ottomans had taken their first foreign loan in 1854, and further large borrowings followed at regular intervals. By the early 1900s service charges on the loans had reached over 30% of total Ottoman government revenue. Egypt, Tunisia and Morocco floated their first foreign loans in the 1860s. There were common pressures in all these countries which prompted them to resort to foreign borrowing. On the one hand, antiquated and corrupt administrations limited governments' revenue-raising capacity. On the other hand, the rising cost of military expenditure and a high propensity to consume on the part of monarchs and bureaucrats created a demand for more and more funds.[53]

The cancellation of the Tobacco Concession forced Persia to join the ranks of Middle East borrowers. The Tobacco Corporation were determined to secure full compensation for damages and loss of profits. After long negotiations, and some Foreign Office mediation between the two parties, the Persian government agreed in March 1892 to offer the Corporation £350 000, payable over ten years at an interest rate of 5% per annum, together with an additional £150 000 as payment for all assets of the Corporation save for cash. Alternatively, the Persian government were prepared to pay a lump sum of £500 000. After pressure from the Foreign Office, the Corporation agreed in principle to this latter arrangement.[54]

The only unresolved problem was that the Persian government did not have £500 000. Some thought was given to forming an international company to raise the sum, but this proved abortive,[55] and on Sir Frank Lascelles' advice, the Persian government asked the Imperial Bank to arrange a loan of £500 000 in order to settle the Tobacco Corporation's claims. Rabino welcomed the idea in principle, believing that promoting a loan for the Persian government could greatly enhance the Bank's power in Persia, but agreeing terms proved to be a long and tiresome business.

The negotiations fell into two distinct periods. During the first period in March and early April there was much talk and no action. The Board of the Imperial Bank, though sharing Rabino's general enthusiasm for a loan, sought as security a first charge on all the Gulf customs' receipts. These revenues, derived largely from British trade, formed one of the most regular sources of income for the Persian government, and therefore offered an obvious and attractive security. The Bank's directors also tried to use the loan negotiations as a way of finding money for their road concession which – as will be seen below – was in increasing difficulties. These considerations led the Bank to propose on 17 March a loan of £750 000, to be used both to compensate the Tobacco Corporation and pay for the construction of the Bank's road, but the Persians refused to consider borrowing more than £500 000.[56]

The tone of the negotiations was completely changed when, on 18 April, it became known to the Foreign Office and the Imperial Bank that Russian interests had offered Persia a loan. The Amin os-Soltan sent a message to the British Minister to the effect that the Russian Minister had offered £500 000 at 6%.[57] Although no one was quite sure if the Persians were simply using the threat of a Russian loan as a bargaining counter, the danger of the Russians gaining a hold over the Persian government galvanised the Foreign Office into action. Before the Russian loan offer Foreign Office policy was limited essentially to support for the Corporation's claims for compensation. Afterwards, the Foreign Office's chief goal was that any loan should be British, and the specific claims of the Corporation became very much a secondary consideration.

The Imperial Bank's Chairman, Keswick, was called to the Foreign Office, and persuaded to reconsider his Bank's terms. It was agreed that the Bank would try to raise a loan at 6% and at 96 or 97, on the security of monthly instalments from the Southern customs.[58] The Bank initially insisted that the loan would have to be for £530 000 in order to cover the costs of issue, but on 27 April the Board put forward a new proposal. As the market for Persian government securities was hardly at its best after the events of the previous two years, the Board reckoned that it was unlikely that a loan could be successfully floated. They suggested, therefore, that the Bank should underwrite £250 000 of the loan and the Tobacco Corporation do the same. The Corporation would also be obliged to pay the Bank £15 000 to cover the expenses of the issue.[59]

The Foreign Office, under constant pressure from the threat of a Russian loan, now moved to clinch a deal between the Persian government and the Imperial Bank. On 5 May Keswick was called to the Foreign Office. He was told that the Shah had been told of the 'disfavour' of the British government if he accepted a Russian loan, and he had therefore declined the loan. At the same time, the Bank was asked to 'take the matter up and with the aid of the British Legation obtain in connection with the Loan the position of Agents for Persia in London and conclude an agreement with the Shah on the terms offered by Russia'.[60] Keswick agreed. Foreign Office pressure worked because it suited both sides. The Persian government needed to find funds from somewhere to compensate the Corporation, and few Persians wanted to expand the Tsar's influence in their country. The Bank was as anxious as the Foreign Office not to see a Russian loan. The losers were the Tobacco Corporation, now in liquidation, who were left out of the arrangements.

On 15 May an agreement was duly signed by the Shah and Amin os-Soltan, on behalf of the Persian government, and Joseph Rabino on behalf of the Imperial Bank. The Persian government placed at the Bank's disposal £500 000 in bonds bearing 6% interest. This sum was redeemable by 40 yearly instalments of £12 500 and a 'sinking fund' to cover interest payments. The payments were to be secured on the customs of the Gulf ports of Bushire, Bandar Abbas, Lingah and the town of Shiraz.[61]

The importance of the 1892 Loan in the Bank's history can hardly be over-estimated. It considerably assisted Rabino's task of establishing the Bank as a permanent fixture in Persia. The loan negotiations were also the first time that the Bank had been used as a political instrument by the British government, a role which was to grow over the following three decades.

Meanwhile the Imperial Bank was left to sort out an arrangement with the Tobacco Corporation. The Foreign Office were interested that any Persian loan should be in British hands, but left the Bank and the Corporation to fight out between them the details of how the indemnity was to be paid. It was not until 3 September that an agreement was finally in view. The Imperial Bank was to issue the £500 000 Loan to the public at 95, charging the Corporation £10 000 for expenses, and underwriting £150 000 of the Loan at 90. The Corporation was to underwrite the remaining £350 000. The Bank was to pay the Corporation in cash half of £150 000, less expenses, after the Loan was issued.[62]

Meanwhile the Persian government had managed to improve its financial situation despite the cancellation of the Corporation's concession. In 1891 a Société du Tombac had been formed in Constantinople, on the initiative of Sir Edgar Vincent of the Imperial Ottoman Bank and with substantial French capital, to secure a monopoly of Persia's tobacco export trade, a great proportion of which went to the Ottoman Empire. In October 1891 it had made a formal agreement with the Imperial Tobacco Corporation. The Société du Tombac was not overwhelmed by the protests against the Corporation, and early in October 1892 the Shah indeed granted it a monopoly over Persia's tobacco exports in return for £450 000 paid over 25 years.[63]

The subscription lists for the Loan were opened on Monday 17 October 1892 and closed at 4.00 p.m. on the following Tuesday. The issue was as poorly received as everyone had feared. Only 164 out of the 5000 bonds issued were applied for by and allotted to the public, raising £15 580. Both the Corporation and the Bank were naturally far from pleased about the outcome. For the three years after 1894 the Bank's auditors insisted on noting in their certificate on the balance sheet that the Persian government 6% Loan bonds, taken at 90, were unsaleable at that price, although the directors in their reports for these years pointed out that they regarded the bonds as a satisfactory investment, and small sales were made. The Stock Exchange did not share this assessment, and consistently refused to quote the bonds. Whenever the question of the 1892 Loan obtaining a quotation was raised, the parties involved in the Lottery Concession, including the liquidators of the New Oriental Bank Corporation, raised opposition on the grounds that they had received no compensation for the Concession's cancellation.

On balance, however, the 1892 Loan was a major political gain for the Bank, and it did not prove a bad investment. In 1899 the Bank still held £122 100 of the Loan, but in the following year the Loan was to be redeemed at par.

2.8 THE RUSSIAN DIMENSION

In addition to the lottery scandal and tobacco riots, the Imperial Bank faced further complications in the early 1890s through the creation of a rival Russian bank.

The Russian Bank had its origins in the activities of two entrepreneurial brothers, Lazar and Yakov Poliakov. During the late 1880s the Poliakovs had contemplated building railways in Persia, including one from Rasht to Tehran.[64] The scheme had not attracted support from the Russian Foreign Ministry, and – in direct parallel with de Reuter's case – they ended up with a bank instead. In 1890 Yakov Poliakov obtained a concession for 75 years to set up a bank in Persia. The bank, known as the Lending Company of Persia (*Ssudnoe Obshchestov Persii*), or the Société des Prêts, was planned on a much smaller scale than the Imperial Bank. Its capital was fixed at 5 million Francs, and it was conceived as a loan company, granting small loans on any security except real estate. It also had the right to run auctions. The Shah was to get

10% of the Bank's profits and he was also paid an annual 10 000 Kran fee for giving it the privilege of holding auctions.[65]

In addition to the Société des Prêts, the Poliakovs launched a variety of other commercial ventures in Persia. In 1892 they opened a branch in Tehran of another bank with which they were connected, the International Commercial Bank of Moscow. They also founded an insurance and transport company, began the construction of a match factory, and acquired 75% of the equity of a Belgium company which had been established to run a horse-tramway in Tehran. In 1893 Lazar Poliakov obtained a concession to build a road from the Caspian coast to Kazvin, and in 1895 further on to Tehran.[66]

In the early 1890s, the relationship between the Imperial Bank and the Poliakov bank in Persia was good. Rabino found the Société des Prêts a positive asset to his Bank. The Russian Bank, he wrote to Newell in December 1891, 'does us no kind of harm and rather acts as a foil to the Bank'.[67] The Société des Prêts assisted the growth of the Imperial Bank's note issue because it asked to be paid in notes. Moreover, the Russian banks eased exchange dealings, as remittances to Britain could be directed through Russia. From the Poliakovs' point of view, however, banking in Persia proved a risky and unremunerative business. The Russians experienced the same kind of problems in securing the repayment of loans as the Imperial Bank, and they were also hard hit by the currency depreciation of the early 1890s. As a result, by 1893 the Société des Prêts had been reduced to little more than a glorified and unprofitable pawn shop.

At this stage the Russian government intervened in the Russian Bank's affairs. The Russian government, like the British, was well aware of the value of commerce for furthering political aims, and evolved a policy of 'rouble imperialism',[68] aimed both at encouraging Russian enterprises and discouraging British ones. It was unfortunate for British commercial interests that as Russian government policy became more assertive in this respect, British government interest in Persia waned. A Liberal government replaced Lord Salisbury and the Conservatives in the summer of 1892. The new government attached less importance to Persia, and showed little faith in the Persian government's ability to reform its 'decadence'. During the rest of the 1890s, despite Lord Salisbury's return to power in 1895, British diplomacy in Persia lacked the clarity of purpose it had achieved in the opening years of the decade.[69] In contrast, Russian policy in Persia was given a considerable sense of direction by the appointment of the powerful Count Sergei Witte as Minister of Finance. Soon after his appointment Witte raised the question of expanding Russian trade with its 'Asiatic' neighbours, on the grounds that they both served as markets for Russian products and that Russian trade influence was 'most closely associated with her political influence'.[70] As a result, a Special Committee on Trade with Asiatic Countries was created with representatives from the Ministries of Finance, War and Foreign Affairs.

In early 1894 the subject of the Russian banks in Persia, which were by then on the verge of liquidation, was taken up by Witte. In April 1894 he decided that the Russian State Bank should purchase Poliakov's Société des Prêts. Political circumstances made it rather awkward for the Russian government to establish a branch of the Russian State Bank in Persia, but the purchase of the Société des Prêts meant that Witte could achieve the same goal while maintaining the fiction that the Bank was a private Russian venture. By 1 May an agreement had been reached with the Poliakovs. Yakov Poliakov's shares in the Bank were purchased for 1 875 000 Roubles (around £200 000). From May 1894 the Bank, now known as the Lending Bank of Persia (*Ssusdnyi Bank Persii*) or the Banque des Prêts, was in effect a branch of the Russian State Bank, although it retained the guise of a private bank. On 16 April 1894 the Bank's aims were defined by a meeting of the Finance Committee of the Russian government. The Bank was, the Committee ordered, 'to promote the development of active Russian trade in Persia and the sale of Russian products, to circulate among the Persian population Russian banknotes and to assist the ousting of English products from Persia'.[71]

The details of this development were not, of course, officially known either to the Imperial Bank or the British government. However, rumours flourished, fuelled by 'leaks' from the Tehran Manager of the Banque des Prêts.[72] Although Rabino was unaware of the full extent of the Russian government's involvement in the Banque des Prêts, and that Bank's policy brief, he was sufficiently informed of events to express fears that the Imperial Bank now faced a more powerful and dangerous competitor than had hitherto been the case.[73]

After 1894 it became clear that Rabino's fears were justified. The pawnbroking business was transformed, with the aid of regular injections of Russian government cash, into a potentially powerful financial institution. However, the Imperial Bank did not feel the full force of competition from the Russian Bank until the early 1900s when, after a series of ineffectual political appointments as managers, a tough and professional financier took over.

2.9 MINES AND ROADS

The Imperial Bank's prospectus made it clear that although the Bank's promoters considered some money could be made from banking in Persia, their hopes of making a fortune were focussed on the development of Persia's mineral resources and, although this was left unsaid, on building railways. As already observed, the Imperial Bank was not to be just a bank: its banking business was to lead to greater things. It was unfortunate, therefore, that although Rabino did manage to establish a viable banking business, the Imperial Bank's ventures into mines and transportation were financial disasters.

The Bank's Concession had granted it monopoly rights over most of Persia's mineral resources. However, Appendix 4 of the Imperial Bank's Concession had specified, at the insistence of the British Treasury, that although the Bank could conduct initial prospecting work it had subsequently to sell its mining rights to another party.

As a result, early in 1890 the Bank formed a separate company to develop its mining rights, the Persian Bank Mining Rights Corporation. Three of the Bank's directors were also directors of the Mining Rights Corporation. Sir Lepel Griffin became the Chairman, and he was joined on the Board by George de Reuter and S. Ezekiel. The other three directors were Frederick Sassoon, uncle of Edward Sassoon and a former Hongkong Bank Chairman, W. D. Duff Bruce, an engineer recruited by Keswick, and George Curzon. Curzon had approached Edward Sassoon in March 1890 to see if he could have a place on the Board of the Imperial Bank. Sassoon could not, or would not, offer him such a position, and as compensation offered him a directorship of the Mining Rights Corporation.[74]

The Prospectus for the Corporation appeared in April 1890. J. Henry Schröder and D. Sassoon & Co. acted as underwriters for the issue. The Prospectus outlined the wide-ranging mining rights which were to be purchased from the Imperial Bank. The working capital to be raised by the share issue, the Prospectus argued, would 'be amply sufficient to explore the whole mineral resources of the Empire, [and] to develop and work such of the mines as the Company may deem it expedient to work themselves'. Substantial profits were forecast, especially from the subsequent sale of 'mining rights to subsidiary Companies'.

The capital of the Mining Rights Corporation was to be £1 million. This was issued as 70 000 preferred ordinary shares of £5 each, and 130 000 ordinary shares of £5 each. The ordinary shares were all allotted to the Imperial Bank in part payment for its mining rights. In addition, the Imperial Bank received in cash another £150 000 raised from the issue of the preferred ordinary shares. Only £3/10/- of each £5 preferred ordinary share was actually called up, raising £245 000. After the payment to the Bank, therefore, the Mining Rights Corporation was left with a working capital of a mere £95 000.

General Schindler was placed in charge of the mining business. He was appointed Inspector General of Mines in March 1890, and after the formation of the Mining Rights Corporation his salary was shared between the Bank and the Corporation. His instructions from London were wide-ranging. 'In copper, cobalt asbestos mercury and nickel I think, be our best chances of success', Lepel Griffin advised him in February 1891, 'with coal in a few favoured situations and petroleum near the coast.'[75] To assist him in the herculean task of initiating such a broadly based mining venture, the Corporation recruited three mining engineers. G. H. Liddell was appointed Chief Mining Engineer, with two Assistants, Charles Henderson and J. Hadkinson.

Liddell and Henderson tackled the north of Persia. Liddell was soon writing pessimistic reports about the area's mineral resources. He had been led to believe that he would begin mining operations soon after he reached Persia. Instead, he found himself travelling in great discomfort in search of apparently non-existent riches. By February 1891 he had, as he complained to Keswick, seen nothing of the 'immense deposits' described in the Prospectus.[76] This letter led to his, and Henderson's dismissal.[77] His successor, W. Ferguson, an expert in Central African goldfields, was a complete contrast. He was greatly optimistic about prospects in Persia, but unfortunately his views rested on his imagination rather than on reality. A small number of mining operations were, however, launched.

The situation was rather similar in the south. The Mining Rights Corporation acquired from I.C.P. Hotz a small oil concession area at Daliki, but neither I.C.P. Hotz nor the Corporation could find any oil. There was, too, some drilling on Qushm Island, but this had to be abandoned when work was interrupted by rioters and a boat was burned. The Corporation also attempted, with little success, to begin the exploitation of the red ochre deposits at Hormuz in the Gulf and borax deposits at Sirjan in the Kerman district (see Map 2 for the location of these ventures).

As early as 1891 Lepel Griffin began urging Schindler to obtain 'as quickly as possible some definite results ... we have not earned one shilling towards our dividend'.[78] Nevertheless, in the absence of definite results, he was still prepared to persevere, commenting in October 1892 that 'non-success hitherto was no excuse for not continuing our efforts'.[79] In March 1893 a geologist, James Mactear, was sent out from London to investigate the Corporation's failure. His report, written after six months, made dismal reading. Ferguson's excessive optimism was exposed, and his management severely criticised. Expensive mining machinery had been conveyed at enormous costs to quite unsuitable spots. Mactear concluded that the only hope for success was further large cash injections.[80]

Events came to a head after the manager in charge of the Sirjan borax works was arrested by the provincial Governor after protesting at illegal

Tehran—Qum Road constructed by Bank;
Qum—Soltanabad Road constructed by Persian
Transport Company;
Esfahan—Ahwaz (Bakhtiari) Road constructed
by Lynch Bros
■ Borax deposits
▲ Red ochre (iron ore) deposits
⌐ ⌐ Kerman Mining Syndicate Concession
⋈ Oil exploration areas

PERSIA

• Tehran
• Qum
• Soltanabad

• Esfahan
Shuster
⋈ • Masjed e Soleyman
Ahwaz

• Kerman
■ • Sirjan

⋈ • Daliki

▲ Hormuz Isle
Qushm Isle

0 miles 200
0 km 300

Map 2 Mines and roads in Persia before 1914

duties imposed on borax. He was dragged off to prison by the legs and placed
in stocks with an iron collar round his neck.[81] This proved to be the final
straw, and in January 1894 it was decided to put the Mining Rights
Corporation into voluntary liquidation.

The whole affair had been a fiasco. Although the uproar against foreign·
enterprises caused by the Tobacco Concession had not helped the Mining
Rights Corporation, it seems clear that the main problem was the hopelessly
unrealistic overall strategy devised in London which was badly implemented
by incompetent management in Persia. Remarkably little thought had been
given to the difficulties of undertaking widespread mining operations in a
country so lacking in basic infrastructure as Persia. The absence of roads
made the transportation of plant and machinery an expensive operation, and
costs were forced up by the Corporation's strategy of prospecting all over the
country.

The fact that the Corporation had only itself to blame for its demise did not prevent it from claiming compensation from the Persian government for the failure of the venture. Lepel Griffin appealed for Foreign Office assistance to secure this compensation, but he received no support for, in the words of an Under-Secretary, his 'preposterous claim'.[82]

The liquidation of the Corporation did not cause a financial loss to the Imperial Bank. By January 1894 only £2400 of the Corporation's £94 500 working capital remained, but this capital had been provided by the share issue and not by the Bank. Although the Bank was left with 130 000 ordinary shares in the Corporation with a nominal value of £650 000, which were now worthless and were written off in the 1894 balance sheet, it had not paid money for these shares, and had actually received £150 000 in cash for its mining rights. This money was used to establish the Bank's reserves. The real damage was to the Imperial Bank's prestige. 'The Road and Mines are looked upon by everyone from the Shah downwards', Rabino had written to Newell in December 1893, 'as departments of the Bank.'[83] The fiasco was not a good advertisement for the Bank's efficiency. In addition, the hopes of great financial gain to be secured from the mining rights lay in ruins.

Arguably, the Mining Rights Corporation might have avoided complete collapse if the Imperial Bank's plans to improve the transport system in Persia had come to fruition. Unfortunately, these plans were also unsuccessful, and this time the Bank itself could not avoid large financial losses.

When the Bank's Concession had been signed on 30 January 1889 all the parties concerned were still interested, probably primarily interested, in building railways. It was hoped that the Imperial Bank, as a Persian national institution, could escape from the Shah's agreement with the Tsar that no railways were to be built by foreign enterprises in Persia without Russian permission. This scheme, however, never succeeded. In March 1889 the Russian government pressured the Shah into agreeing to a five-year moratorium on the construction of all railways. In November 1890, under Russian pressure, Naser od-Din Shah agreed to a ten-year restriction.[84] Yet the Imperial Bank was less depressed by this news than might have been thought, for by that date it had become involved in the promotion of an alternative to railways. 'The prohibition of railway construction', Lepel Griffin observed in November 1890, 'much increases the financial value of the road concession.'[85]

In 1889 the Persian Minister of Justice and of Commerce, Yahya Khan, Mo'tamed ol-Molk (brother of Mirza Hoseyn Khan), had been granted a 60-year concession for the construction of a road from Ahwaz to Tehran, together with a road going from Borujerd to Esfahan, and for the operation of a regular passenger and freight transport service along these roads. For a variety of reasons the Imperial Bank became involved in this concession. Drummond Wolff expressed a 'vehement desire to see the Bank inaugurate its operations by a project of unquestioned advantage to the economic progress of the Empire'.[86] Moreover Rabino recognised that the mining company was unlikely to succeed unless transport could be improved. 'Bear in mind the Mining Concession *is worth nothing without the road*' (the emphasis being his).[87]

In January 1890 the Imperial Bank acquired the road concession. The contractual arrangements were complicated because the original concession had contained a clause prohibiting its transfer to another party. Mo'tamed ol-Molk, therefore, transferred his concession to the Bank as security for an advance made to him by the Bank at 8% interest.[88] The legality of this transfer was questioned from the beginning. The Bank's lawyers advised that Mo'tamed ol-Molk had no power to deal with any rights under the concession beyond his own lifetime – he was in fact to die in January 1892 – and that the concession and its transfer raised so many problems that it would be impossible for the Bank to float a company in London to work the road concession.[89] This legal opinion did not prevent the Bank from proceeding with its road schemes. Indeed, in the autumn of 1890 the Bank considered acquiring a further road concession, this time from Tehran to Tabriz. The likely cost of this venture, and the Foreign Office's preference for a southern road to the Gulf rather than any road which might facilitate Russian access to the capital led to this idea being dropped.[90]

It was decided to start the construction of the southern road from Tehran, and work on the Tehran to Qum section started in early 1890 (see Map 2 for the alignment of the road). A road engineer was recruited in February 1890, and he was joined later in the year by other staff. In April 1891 an English veterinary surgeon joined the team, bringing with him 45 horses from Kurdistan ready to undertake the transport service when the road was finished.

The road venture was poorly managed from the start. The enterprise was run as a department of the Imperial Bank. General Schindler was in nominal charge but, as he was also running the Mining Rights Corporation, and acting as the Bank's Inspector, his management was of necessity sometimes very nominal indeed. Costs rose daily. Schindler had originally estimated that a Tehran to Ahwaz road could be constructed at a cost of £20 per mile, and that £100 000 would cover the entire building of the road and the purchase of all necessary equipment to launch the transport service. By the end of 1890, however, the projected costs had risen to £200 per mile for what was, after all, only a good cart road.[91] A. P. H. Hotz visited the road in May 1891, and was highly critical of its management. His solution was straight-forward. 'I have no doubt', he wrote, 'that the delay in taking the work in hand energetically is caused by the delay in forming a Road and Transport Company'.[92]

Such a solution was quite impossible. Apart from the general suspicion of the London money market about Persian investments, the Bank's advisers continued to maintain that the terms of the transfer of the road concession made a public flotation impossible.[93] Various other expedients were tried. It was suggested to the Persian government in January 1892 that they might subsidise the road, but no assistance was forthcoming from that direction. A little later the Foreign Office was sounded out, to see if it would give the Bank a subsidy. Their response was equally cool.[94] The matter also became entangled with the Persian loan negotiations. The Bank suggested that the proposed loan should be big enough to provide capital for the road. This idea, too, was unsuccessful. It was thought that the limitation of the construction of the road to the Tehran–Qum section might increase the venture's attractiveness, but the proposition could not remove the legal doubts and the general scepticism about the profitability of building any road in Persia.

Meanwhile, the pressure on the Imperial Bank of rising construction costs was increased by the chronic failure to generate any revenue. In June 1891 the Persian government had granted the Bank permission to levy tolls on the completed Tehran–Qum section of the road. The various difficulties involved in collecting these tolls, however, led to a decision to postpone their collection until the spring of 1892.

By November 1892 the Bank had spent some £88 000 on the Persian road, and it had already been decided that enough was enough.[95] The Bank's Charter, in any case, forbade the Bank to carry on the working of the road concession itself for an extended period. As in the case of the Mining Rights Corporation, it was hoped that the Persian government would compensate the Bank for the failure of the venture. In November 1892 A. P. H. Hotz had travelled to Persia with instructions to obtain repayment from the Persian government for all the money the Bank had spent on the road, together with interest at 8%.[96] Hotz, however, made no progress with the Persian authorities. He became side-tracked by a plan to sell off some shares in the road to rich Persian investors. Rabino was not impressed by the scheme. 'The idea that the Bank will simply get rid of the road and get back its expenditure', he observed to Newell in March 1893, 'is I am sorry to say an absolute delusion.'[97]

The failure of the Hotz mission left the Board with no choice but to carry on the struggle, but their main emphasis by this period was simply to reduce expenditure as much as possible. In November 1893 the Bank's cart and carriage traffic on the Tehran–Qum road was discontinued. Schindler was instructed to devote all his time to the road enterprise, and warned that his future in the Bank was dependent on an improvement in the road situation.[98]

By this time the Bank had tried, and failed, to secure funds from almost every possible source to help with the road enterprise, including the Foreign Office, the Persian government and private Persian investors. In desperation, one further and unlikely group were approached, the Russians. In the autumn of 1893 George de Reuter and Yakov Poliakov, who possessed a concession to build a road between Tehran and Rasht, began discussions about the possible amalgamation of the two ventures. There was an intermediary between the two parties in the shape of Reuben de Gubbay, who was son-in-law of Poliakov and whose father was a partner in David Sassoon & Co.[99]

Poliakov proposed that the two concessions should be amalgamated into an international company with a capital of £400 000 raised in France, Belgium, Russia and Britain, and that this company should construct a rough unmetalled road from Rasht to Tehran and onwards to Mohammarah (Khorramshahr).[100] After some hesitation, and a far from enthusiastic response to the idea from the Foreign Office, the Board decided to proceed with the plan, which also came to include the ailing Mining Corporation. By May 1894, however, the Russian government had begun to insist that any new company should be Russian rather than international, and it may have been this factor which caused the negotiations to peter out during June 1894.[101]

One curious by-product of the whole affair was a misconception that the Russians were going to buy not merely the mining rights and road concessions but the Imperial Bank of Persia itself. During August 1894 the British *Chargé d'Affaires* in Tehran reported that the Russian State Bank was about to buy up the Bank.[102] Moreover, Count Witte, during his discussions with fellow Ministers, supported his case for the Russian government to acquire the Poliakov bank in April 1894 by revealing that the Imperial Bank's directors had offered their bank for sale to Poliakov, 'except the mineral exploiting company'.[103] Both the British *Chargé d'Affaires* and Witte were incorrectly informed. The Imperial Bank of Persia was never on sale to the Russians.

The Bank remained burdened with its roads until the 1900s, and it had little choice but to continue to oversee the working of the Tehran–Qum section. Schindler was dismissed in May 1894, leaving him with some bitterness. 'I found', he wrote to Curzon in February 1895, 'that a board of Directors in London, and particularly that of the Imperial Bank of Persia, is generally a very unpleasant institution to deal with.'[104] Meanwhile the Bank at the end of 1894 wrote off against reserves the £88 000 spent on the road.

The loss of an eleventh of the Bank's issued capital in this way was to be a contributory factor in the decision to write down its capital by a third in 1895.

2.10 DIVERSION IN THE OTTOMAN EMPIRE

In May 1890 the Imperial Bank of Persia opened an agency, run by a British officer, in Baghdad, and in July of the following year an agency was opened in Basra. These two towns were to become the principal cities of the state of Iraq after the First World War, but before 1914 they and their surrounding territories formed part of the far-flung Ottoman Empire. The Imperial Bank was the first Western bank to open in both places.

Baghdad and Basra held obvious attractions for the Imperial Bank. Basra was the largest port in the Gulf. It had a large export trade in dates, wool, wheat and barley, commodities which were grown or produced in its hinterland, and it also handled substantial imports of cotton piece goods and other manufactures from British India, Britain and elsewhere. Much of this trade was in the hands of British trading companies such as Lynch Brothers and I.C.P. Hotz. Basra's trade was closely linked with Persia's, as many goods imported at Basra were transported to Baghdad, Khanaqin and on to Kermanshah and other Persian destinations. The volume of trade along this route expanded in the late nineteenth century. In addition to these trade connections, many Persian pilgrims visited Shia holy places in this part of the Ottoman Empire.[105] The business potential offered by these connections seemed additionally attractive because it was virgin banking territory. Although the Imperial Ottoman Bank, which had been founded with British and French capital in 1856 as the state bank of the Ottoman Empire, had established a wide branch network by 1890, it had yet to reach Baghdad and Basra.

The short history of the Baghdad and Basra agencies can be characterised as a period of initial hope followed by growing despondency. The initial optimism was fuelled by the fact that the new Baghdad agency reported small profits soon after its foundation. There was an atmosphere of expansion. Basra agency was opened in July 1891. During 1891 A. P. H. Hotz urged his fellow directors on the Imperial Bank's Board to consider opening also in Istanbul, the Ottoman capital. Hotz urged that there were strong trade links between Baghdad and Istanbul, and that the Imperial Bank of Persia should establish itself firmly in the finance of this trade before the Imperial Ottoman Bank moved to capture it.[106]

During 1892, however, London and Chief Office in Tehran began to receive bad news about the Ottoman agencies. Managers found it hard to expand business turnover. The large European trading companies seemed unwilling to give much business to the Bank. The exception was the firm of I.C.P Hotz, due no doubt to the presence of A. P. H. Hotz on the Imperial Bank's Board, but even this firm was not above using the Basra agency as a means of disposing of dubious trade bills.[107] The Bank found it hard to establish contacts with sound local merchants, and bad debts began to mount on the loans that were made.[108] Moreover, the accounts of the British Consulates also eluded the Bank.[109]

Much about the Imperial Bank's agencies remains unclear, but the explanation of their unsatisfactory performance seems to lie in a combination of ill fortune and poor management. It was unfortunate, to explore the first category of explanation, that before the Imperial Bank had had time to build up a good business the Imperial Ottoman Bank which was in a strong position because of its long presence in the Ottoman Empire and its possession of government accounts, opened a branch in Baghdad. The opening of the Imperial Ottoman's branch in that city in December 1892 was followed by the dwindling of the Imperial Bank's business.[110] Fluctuations in the silver exchange rate caused exchange losses. Again, Managers found it hard to recruit appropriate local clerical staff, and the weakness in this sphere hindered the development of the agencies. And the agencies were practically finished off by an outbreak of cholera in the summer of 1893, which closed down the port of Basra and badly damaged Baghdad's commercial life.[111]

On the other hand, the Imperial Bank was not simply a victim of circumstances outside its control. The agencies did not receive a great deal of support from Chief Office. Rabino regarded the Baghdad and Basra ventures as unwelcome diversions from the main task of building a bank in Persia.[112] The agencies were poorly managed. Baghdad saw the worst management failure. It transpired during 1893 that the books of the agencies were in complete chaos, and the reports on business sent to London had been largely fictitious.[113]

By the autumn of 1893 the unwholesome combination of strong competition, bad debts, the cholera epidemic and poor management had convinced the Board that the Ottoman agencies had to be closed. In addition, there were growing fears that the Imperial Ottoman Bank would establish branches in Persia. In September 1893, therefore, the Imperial Bank signed an agreement with the Imperial Ottoman Bank designed to extricate itself from the unsuccessful agencies, and defuse the danger of competition to its Persian business. The Imperial Ottoman Bank agreed to take over the assets and liabilities of the Imperial Bank in Baghdad and Basra, although the Imperial Bank was left to sort out 'certain engagements and liabilities'. The Imperial Ottoman Bank also agreed not to open any agencies or branches in Persia, and to use the Imperial Bank exclusively as their correspondents in that country. In turn the Imperial Bank made the same commitment regarding Baghdad and Basra provinces.[114]

Under the terms of the agreement the Imperial Bank of Persia was due to close its agencies on 30 September 1893. However, their accounts were so inexact, and the level of bad debts so high, that it was not until February 1894 that the Imperial Ottoman Bank would accept the handover of the agencies. A young officer, S. F. Rogers, who joined the Bank in 1892 and was to retire from it in 1930 as London Manager, had to be sent to Baghdad in December 1894 to sort out the continuing chaotic legacy, and he remained at that melancholy duty until October 1895.

The inglorious episode of the Ottoman agencies offered costly support to Rabino's thesis that, with the poor communications existing and the inability to provide regular inspection facilities, it was more profitable to focus on Persian banking than undertake more peripheral activities. It would appear that all of the £60 000 capital allocated to the agencies in 1892 was lost. In fact, some £70 000 was set aside by the Imperial Bank in an account held by the Imperial Ottoman Bank to cover the liabilities of the Baghdad and Basra agencies. Not only was all of this sum used up, but in 1896 the Imperial Bank had to make a final additional payment of £2000.[115] Further, in the 1895 accounts another £12 000 was written off as a 'loss on exchange' to cover the costs of closing the agencies.[116] Total losses carried by the Baghdad and Basra agencies, therefore, may well have been at least £84 000.

2.11 SILVER, INDIA AND THE REDUCTION OF CAPITAL IN 1894

The previous two sections have helped to explain some of the features of the performance of the Imperial Bank which were highlighted in Section 2.5. The losses on roads and in the Ottoman Empire were clearly factors in the decline of the Bank's profits after 1892 and the withering of shareholders' funds. However, the most important element in the story has as yet only been referred to obliquely. This was the 'silver problem'.

The world price of silver had been gradually depreciating against gold in the two decades before the Imperial Bank was founded. The exchange value of the silver-based Kran followed the general movement of silver on world markets, although it was also subject to special influences.[117] The overall trend of depreciation, however, masked periodic fluctuations. During the last half of 1887 and the first half of 1888, for example, the world price of silver had stabilised, and in September 1889 silver prices actually began to increase. This development was closely related to the apparent success in the United States of the so-called silver lobby, which led to the passing by Congress of the Sherman Silver Purchase Act of 1890; this required the United States Treasury to purchase a fixed amount of silver at pre-depreciation prices. By September 1890 world silver prices were higher than for 13 years. Thereafter prices fell. By the middle of 1892 world silver prices had fallen to their lowest hitherto seen. In the following year the downward trend was reinforced by the repeal of the Sherman Act and by the Government of India's drastic measures to strengthen the Rupee. The Indian policy was to check the fall of the currency and then to raise the value of the Rupee to a level – 16 pence – at which it might be stabilised. This involved closing the Mints to the free coinage of silver, and linking the Rupee to Sterling. In these conditions, silver prices continued to fall, with little pause, into the early years of the new century.

The depreciation of silver had a most unfortunate effect on Eastern banks, such as the Imperial Bank of Persia, whose balance sheets were in Sterling (on the gold standard), but whose main business was in silver-based currencies. The fall in the exchange value of the Kran resulted in a depreciation of the Sterling value of the Imperial Bank's assets in Persia. 'The great fall which has taken place in the value of silver since the Bank was established has affected the Capital', the directors reported on the annual balance sheet presented to the shareholders in December 1893, 'and were it necessary to recall all funds, at present rates, there would be a deficiency of about £200 000.'

The problems stemming from silver depreciation were brought to a head by the question of dividends. On the 1893 balance sheet the auditors recommended that dividend payments should be restricted until a reserve had been provided 'to meet the loss of capital due to the fall in silver'. When the Board took legal advice, however, the legality of paying any dividend at all was questioned. On 4 December 1893 the Bank's solicitors advised that if it was known 'that the assets of a Company have become permanently depreciated no dividend can properly be paid until the capital of the Company is intact, and (that) the directors incur serious personal responsibility if a dividend is paid practically out of capital'.[118] It was clear that something had to be done if the Bank wished to declare a dividend, and it was important to declare a dividend because the Bank's shares were dropping in value. By February 1894 they had reached £3/10/-, or a quarter of their price when the Bank had been floated. On 6 December 1893 the Board decided that the £1 million capital of the Bank had to be written down, and the Bank settled on a 35% reduction to £650 000.

It took a considerable time to effect this reduction. A Supplemental Charter had to be obtained from the Treasury, which was far from enthusiastic. When the Chartered Mercantile Bank of India, London and China had needed to write down its capital in 1892, the Treasury had obliged it to reincorporate, without its Royal Charter, under the Companies Act.

Keswick, however, was able to enlist the Foreign Office to support the Imperial Bank's case that it should be allowed to write down its capital and retain its Royal Charter. In the autumn of 1894 Treasury approval was secured, although the Imperial Bank was obliged to accept an unwelcome condition.[119] The Treasury objected strongly to the impact of the capital reduction on the shareholders' reserve liability. It insisted that the Imperial Bank's shareholders had to continue 'to be liable to contribute the full £10 per share in the event of insolvency'.[120] The Bank had perforce to accept this view, and under the terms of the Supplemental Charter, although the par value of each Bank share was reduced from £10 to £6 10/-, the reserve liability of the shareholders remained at £10. The Supplemental Charter was eventually signed on 17 December 1894.

The prolonged negotiations with the Treasury meant that it was not until 1 January 1895 that an extraordinary general meeting of shareholders could be called to approve the Supplemental Charter. The delay meant that the Imperial Bank was unable to declare a dividend for 1894, which was the first and only time during its existence as an independent bank between 1889 and 1960 that it failed to make an annual distribution to shareholders.

In its statements to the British government and shareholders the Board stressed that the capital reduction was made necessary because of the fall in silver. It was emphasised that the Bank's assets in Persia had only depreciated in the sense of their Sterling value. In fact, the 'silver problem' was also used as a convenient umbrella to cover the losses in the Ottoman Empire and on the Persian roads already discussed and even greater losses caused by the Bank's misguided investment policies and the establishment of agencies in India. The Bank's largely self-inflicted problems were severe and brought it close to ruin.

The opening of the Indian agencies and the investment policies were interconnected, but will be discussed separately. David Sassoon & Co. acted as the Bank's correspondents in India during the first year of its existence, but at the beginning of 1891 the Board decided to establish an agency in Bombay. The precise motivation for this step is unclear, but it may have originated with a former colleague and friend of George Newell, Thomas Payn, who worked for the Comptoir National d'Escompte de Paris in India. Payn was active in the discussions on establishing an agency, and was appointed its first Manager. A further stimulus could have come from the Bank of China, Japan and the Straits Ltd. This was the former Trust and Loan Company of China, Japan and the Straits which had adopted its new name in January 1891. William Keswick remained Chairman, and David McLean a director, of both the Imperial Bank and the Bank of China, Japan and the Straits. The connections between the two institutions were, at this stage, close, with the Imperial Bank making the Bank of China, Japan and the Straits several large loans, including one of £100 000 for two years in January 1891.[121] It was not surprising, therefore, that it was decided that the new Bombay agency should be jointly run by the two banks.

In May 1891 the agency opened for business. Payn developed a business in trade bills, of which at least a portion were concerned with Indian trade with Persia, exchange and the buying and selling of Government of India securities. Business at first seems to have gone well, and Bombay agency recorded a profit of nearly £12 000 in the period up to March 1892. In May 1892 another joint agency with the Bank of China, Japan and the Straits was opened in Calcutta. Payn moved to this city, and ran both agencies from there, clearly having little regard for the 'very troublesome Persian business' undertaken by Bombay.[122] At the end of 1892 the Indian agencies were allocated a capital of £230 000 by the Board, second only to Chief Office's allocation of £390 000.

During 1893 the business of the Indian agencies took a sharp turn for the worse, as the exchanges went through a period of crisis culminating in the closure of the Indian Mints. In the year ending September 1893 the Indian agencies recorded a loss of £11 600. Payn's solution was speculative dealings in Council Bills.[123] The full repercussions of this policy had not emerged when, in December 1893, Payn accepted the post of London Manager of the Bank of China, Japan and the Straits and left the Indian agencies.

After Payn's departure Bombay and Calcutta were run by separate Managers. They both seemed to have indulged in substantial speculative buying and selling of government paper, and in May 1894 Newell issued forceful instructions for this risky activity to be reduced.[124] His warnings were not heeded, and the Indian agencies recorded a £22 000 loss in September 1894. Calcutta was closed at the end of the year. During 1895 Bombay, which was wholly owned by the Imperial Bank after the liquidation of the Bank of China at the end of 1894 (see below), engaged in further speculative transactions.[125] At the end of 1895 £89 096 was written off due to losses on Indian exchange operations.

Over the next few years Bombay's business became more stable, and it seems that the agency concentrated on 'genuine' trade finance rather than speculation. However, profits were measured in hundreds rather than thousands of pounds, and at the end of the decade a further flurry of speculation occurred. In March 1899 the agency made an exchange loss of £2000 after the Manager had purchased Sterling in the expectation that the rate would go one way and it went the other.[126] This was the final straw, and in March 1900 Bombay agency was closed.

The Bank's investment policies contained a strong element of speculation in Government of India securities. As early as November 1889 S. Ezekiel raised on the Bank's Board the 'propriety of buying silver in anticipation of an advance in its value consequent upon the probable legislation in the USA'.[127] The spurt in silver prices encouraged the Bank to make large purchases of Government of India paper, and by September 1890 some £60 000 was held.

Despite the fall in silver prices after the middle of 1890, the Bank continued to purchase Government of India securities at a rapid pace. The September 1891 balance sheet recorded that all the Bank's investments, which reached £377 361, were in this form. The Board maintained a strong belief that silver prices would recover, a belief reinforced by advice to that effect from Thomas Payn in India. The Bank was, therefore, badly caught in early 1892 when silver prices fell sharply. In September 1892 £50 000 had to be written off the Reserve Fund to cover the loss on the depreciation of Government of India securities. The Bank was left with Government of India securities valued at £230 294. By this time shareholders were beginning publicly to complain about their Bank's investment policies. One shareholder at the Ordinary General Meeting in December 1892 argued that the Bank should have invested in safe Consols rather than in paper 'subject to great fluctuations', and Keswick was obliged to concede that, although Rupee investments had seemed a good idea at the time, it had become a 'very unpleasant matter' that so many of the Bank's funds were invested in this fashion.

1893 was a low point. The Bank of China, Japan and the Straits hovered on the brink of collapse, an indication that Keswick and McLean had clearly misread the silver exchanges in the early 1890s. In March 1893 this bank used up all its reserves, and thereafter passed through growing difficulties culminating in liquidation in December 1894 (and eventual reconstruction as the Bank of China and Japan Ltd). In 1894 Keswick and McLean were both asked to resign from the London Consultative Committee of the Hongkong Bank before the 1893 Annual Report of the Bank of China came out. The Imperial Bank, which had lent money to the Bank of China, Japan and the Straits, was forced to seek large loans from its London bankers, Glyn, Mills, Currie & Co. By the beginning of 1893 it owed them £200 000, and during January it was obliged to borrow another £125 000 for three months at 4% interest against the security of the 1892 Persian Loan bonds.[128] The Australian banking crisis raised fears that the big banks in the London market would call in their loans, and retain their funds,[129] and the closure of the Indian Mints increased the danger of a crisis of confidence. During August

Glyn, Mills, Currie & Co. would lend the Imperial Bank no more than £50 000, and then only for one month. Meanwhile, losses continued to mount on Government of India securities, and this dangerous situation seems to have finally forced the Board to get out of Rupee securities. In September 1893 the Bank's Rupee investments still totalled £234 176, but in October the Bank's Inspection Committee sternly minuted that: 'Taking into consideration the very large interest the Bank has in Silver, the Committee think it is undesirable for the Bank in London to enter into large operations in rupee paper.'[130] Indian investments were subsequently run-down, with further losses,[131] but by September 1894 the item had disappeared from the balance sheet.

Thus, although the depreciation of silver did indeed strain the Imperial Bank's balance sheet, it was ill-advised investment policies which had brought the Bank to crisis point. In mitigation, it must be observed that the fall in silver was so unprecedented that one must not judge too harshly those caught up in the situation. Nevertheless, it is clear that the Bank's capital write-down covered a multitude of sins.

2.12 THE SURVIVAL OF THE BANK

The years 1893 to 1895 were the nadir of the Imperial Bank's fortunes. The initial balance sheet growth had ceased. The price of the Bank's shares declined. No dividends were paid in 1894, and by September 1895 shareholders' funds were 40% lower than their original level.

Yet, in retrospect, it can be seen that the Imperial Bank's sheer survival was a significant achievement. Overseas banking had been shaken by the Baring Crisis and the Australian banking failures. Other Eastern banks, such as the New Oriental Bank Corporation, had collapsed. The Bank of China, Japan and the Straits Ltd. lay in semi-ruins. The Imperial Bank's survival was the more remarkable given the difficulties of doing business in Persia, especially during the upheavals of the Tobacco Concession, and the scale of the Bank's 'self-imposed' losses, arising from the poorly managed Ottoman and Indian agencies, the Persian road fiasco and ill-advised investment policies.

The key to the Imperial Bank's survival was its successful construction of a viable banking business in Persia. 'Persia alone kept the flag flying', Rabino reflected of this period in his autobiography, and with much justification.[132] Deposits had been collected, advances made and exchange business negotiated. The 1892 Loan had marked the Bank's acceptance as the Persian government's banker. Joseph Rabino had himself played the essential role in this achievement. 'Mr. Rabino', A. P. H. Hotz wrote to Keswick in May 1891, 'lives solely for the Bank and the almost immediate success which we have had here is due in a very great measure to his hard work and tact.'[133] By 1894 he looked irreplaceable. If the Bank were to dismiss Rabino, the British *Chargé* in Tehran reflected in June 1894, it would 'be the coup de grace of the Bank, and it might as well put up the shutters next day'.[134]

3

RECOVERY AND CONFLICT 1896–1908

In August 1908 Joseph Rabino left Tehran for the last time, in semi-disgrace with the Bank he had served since 1889. However, the Imperial Bank did not, as the British *Chargé* had predicted in 1894, put up the shutters on the day after his departure. Rabino had left a legacy of a well-established and respectable bank, which could survive him. A central theme of this chapter is the recovery of the Imperial Bank from the hazardous period of the early 1890s.

The Bank's balance sheet between 1896 and 1908 supports the thesis of recovery, albeit a slow one. The evidence from the balance sheet is not always easy to interpret in this period. The level of 'Bills Payable', for example, fluctuated widely, but as this item was used for 'endorsements and adjustments' and to accommodate inner reserves, the significance of these movements can be doubted. However, the main trends in the Bank's business can be followed. Deposits continued to fall after 1895, reaching a low of £179 581 in 1899. They rose sharply in 1900, and a strong spurt after 1904 took them to £607 937 in 1908, an increase of 170% over 1896. The note issue also grew from £82 203 in 1896 to £526 479 in 1905, an expansion only interrupted in 1897 when it slumped to £38 000. After 1905 the note issue declined, and in 1908 stood at £430 435. There was no increase in the Bank's lending. After growing in the mid-1890s, loans, advances and bills discounted fell to £643 966 in 1899, and there were further falls until 1903 when they reached £494 096, their lowest level in the Bank's history. By 1908 they had recovered to £1 168 115, almost identical to 1896 and a lower figure than in 1890. As a ratio of deposits and the note issue, advances fell from 385% in 1896 to 86% in 1903, before rising to 112% in 1908.

The Bank's investments grew by 217% between 1896 and 1907, and there was a significant change in their composition. During the second half of the 1890s the Bank's investments were almost entirely in the 1892 Persian

73

Government Loan. In 1896 the Bank's balance sheet still carried an endorsement from the auditors that this investment had 'no saleable value' at the figure at which it had been acquired. This qualification was dropped in 1897. Following the redemption of the Loan by the Persian government in 1900, the Bank acquired a more conventional portfolio of British and Colonial government and London and county stocks. The Bank reduced its investment portfolio by 50% in 1908, strengthening its cash ratio as Persia weathered a revolution.

The recovery of the Bank was also reflected in the growth of shareholders' funds. The capital write down reduced them to a low ebb in 1895. They grew slowly in the late 1890s, and more substantially after 1902 to reach £876 494 in 1908, an increase of 17% over 1896.

In fact, the Imperial Bank's reserves were higher than these figures suggested, because of the existence of inner reserves. The use of inner, undisclosed or 'secret' reserves by British banks and companies was widespread in the nineteenth century. Inner reserves, which exist whenever there is an understatement of an asset or an overstatement of a liability, were created in a variety of ways, including conservative accounting policies, the provision of insufficient detail on balance sheets, and sometimes the total omission of items from them. Businessmen supported their existence on a number of grounds, including the need to retain adequate funds within a business rather than pay out excessively large dividends. Bankers argued that hidden reserves were essential, as they enabled banks to smooth fluctuations in results, and thereby avoid crises of confidence, and so protect the interests of depositors. In fact, inner reserves were widely used by bankers not only as profit equalisation accounts, but also to conceal losses through bad debts. It was not until the inter-war years that inner reserves began to be criticised. The Companies Act of 1948 prohibited their use by most companies, but not banks, and only in 1969 did British clearing banks begin to make full disclosure of their profits and reserves. The Imperial Bank of Persia was a non-disclosing bank, a practice which its successors maintained.

It is unknown at what stage the Imperial Bank established its inner reserves, but it may be safely assumed that the directors would have seen it as a matter of priority. By the early 1900s there are scattered references concerning transfers to and from profits to inner reserves, but the sums involved are not known until 1905. Appendix 4, at the end of this volume, gives the level of the Bank's inner reserves thereafter. By 1908 they stood at £46 051. There is no indication for this period what percentage of this sum was allocated to meet specific contingencies, and what percentage constituted in effect additional shareholders' funds.

Turning to profits, the Imperial Bank's published profits recovered from

Table 3.1. *Published profits and transfers to inner reserves 1906–08*

Year end (20 September)	(£ Sterling) Published net profits	Transfers (to) or from profits
1906	59 930	(10 000)
1907	67 262	25 000
1908	55 279	10 000

the doldrums of 1894 and 1895 to reach £40 616 in 1896. Thereafter they fluctuated, falling again in the late 1890s and generally rising after the turn of the century. It was not until 1907 that its profits for that year of £67 262 surpassed the level of 1892. However, the transfers to and from inner reserves before the net profit figure was struck mean that published figures provide only a partial clue to the Bank's performance. Table 3.1 shows the extent of these transfers after they became known in 1906. The profit equalisation function of the inner reserves is evident. In 1906 £10 000 was transferred from them in order to support published profits, which otherwise would have been lower by that amount. Conversely, in 1907 and 1908 the Bank's 'real profits' were higher than the published figure, because substantial sums were transferred to inner reserves.

The smoothing of profits by the use of inner reserves enabled the Bank, among other things, to pay shareholders regular dividends with no untoward fluctuations. Dividends of 7/- were paid between 1896 and 1903, and this was increased to 8/- between 1904 and 1908. The Stock Exchange's assessment of the Bank slowly improved as one result of this reliable performance. In 1895 the market value of the Bank's shares had stood at around £3/10/-. Ten years later they reached their par value of £6/10/-.

Taken as a whole, therefore, the Bank's performance between 1896 and 1908 was one of slow growth, quickening after the turn of the century. Shareholders' funds had expanded; an inner reserve had been built up; and a more respectable investment portfolio acquired. The Bank had been able to pay regular dividends. It must be said that this was a very modest affair, yet it was achieved against the background of harsh political and economic circumstances.

In 1896 Naser od-Din Shah was assassinated. He was succeeded as Shah by his son, Mozaffar od-Din, under whose reign the conflicts in the Qajar political system came to a head. The regime's financial system hovered on the brink of collapse. Two large Russian loans in 1900 and 1902 were followed by an increasing dependence on Russian and British funds. During 1906 a tide of protest engulfed the government, and the Shah was forced to grant his people a representative assembly. As to the Persian economy, although the last years of the nineteenth century were relatively prosperous, the opening years of the new century were more difficult. The political crisis disrupted economic activity. Moreover, Persia was hit by a series of natural disasters, including a ferocious outbreak of cholera in 1904, a hail storm which destroyed 50% of the silk crop of Gilan in the same year, and a locust plague in Khorasan which caused harvest failures and famine.

Yet if recovery, and recovery once again against unfavourable odds, provides one theme of this chapter, conflict at a variety of levels provides the other. The Imperial Bank in the period 1896–1908 was often placed in an uncomfortable position by the conflicting loyalties inherent in its foundation. The Bank was the state bank of Persia, and played a significant role in the Qajar attempts to strengthen the country's financial administration and improve the condition of the government's finances. Yet the Bank was also a British institution, and by the 1900s was functioning as an agent of the British government in the diplomatic struggle against Russian influence in Persia. These two roles could not always be performed in harmony. Moreover, there were further complexities. The further requirement for the Bank to function as a commercial institution, dependent for its survival on earning sufficient profits to satisfy its shareholders, often conflicted with these other two roles.

These conflicts were reflected by conflicts within the Bank. Joseph Rabino steered the Bank in Persia through the various crises of the period. He grew in stature as one of the most informed and influential Europeans in Tehran, the confidant of the Persian government and the British Legation. He knew Persia, and how to make things work in that country. Yet his perspective and that of the Imperial Bank's Board in London remained quite different. They wanted a British bank run on British lines. Rabino had to run a bank on the spot, with conditions as they were rather than as the Board desired them to be. This tension ran throughout Rabino's period as Chief Manager, and it was to lead to his downfall.

There were some changes in the personnel, but not in the overall attitudes of the Imperial Bank's Board. In 1899 William Keswick resigned as Chairman, although he remained as a director until his death in 1912. Keswick had just been elected to Parliament as Unionist member for Epsom, and he gave the pressure of Parliamentary duties as his reason for resigning.[1] He had also, despite the unfortunate experience of the Bank of China, Japan and the Straits, become involved in ambitious new development schemes for China. In May 1898 the Hongkong Bank and Keswick's firm, Jardine, Matheson and Company, jointly established the British and Chinese Corporation. William Keswick was the Corporation's first Chairman, and the new venture was soon actively involved in Chinese railway concessions.[2] Almost certainly, Keswick resolved to give his attention to the twin glittering prizes of Chinese railways and British political life in preference to the less glamorous affairs of the Imperial Bank. Sir Lepel Griffin was elected Chairman in Keswick's place, and he retained this position until his death in March 1908.

There were several departures from the Board. Edward Sassoon resigned in December 1896. His firm was disappointed by the Imperial Bank's modest performance, and in his letter of resignation he criticised the proliferation of branches, on the understandable grounds that the Bank did not possess sufficient managerial and personnel talent to support it.[3] In 1902 George Stielow died, and in the following year David McLean left the Board because of ill-health.

The replacements to these men possessed considerable weight. In 1903 Sir George S. Mackenzie joined the Board. He was senior partner of Gray Paul, one of a number of firms affiliated to the British India Steam Navigation Company. Gray Paul not only acted as agents for this company at the Gulf ports, but also for the Ellerman and Bucknall Shipping Line which provided a direct link between Britain and the Gulf.[4] Mackenzie had long experience of commercial conditions in Persia which was of obvious benefit to the Bank's Board.

The most significant new appointment in 1903, however, strengthened the Imperial Bank's connections with the Hongkong Bank, which were broken at director level after Keswick and McLean had resigned from the London Committee of that bank in 1894. The old links were re-formed by the appointment of Sir Thomas Jackson to the Imperial Bank's Board. Sir Thomas Jackson was one of the most respected and longest serving Chief Managers of the Hongkong Bank, who had finally left Hong Kong in 1902 after serving three separate terms as Chief Manager between 1876 and 1902. Jackson's appointment was a *coup* for the Imperial Bank, as he brought both unrivalled banking experience and considerable prestige to the Bank. When Sir Lepel Griffin died in 1908, Jackson was elected Chairman, and he served in that post until his own death in December 1915.

In March 1908 Jackson invited another former Hongkong Bank man, V. A. Caesar Hawkins, to join the Board.[5] Hawkins had been Chief Inspector of the Hongkong Bank, but had resigned in 1907, possibly because he felt he stood no further chance of promotion. As we shall see later, immediately after his appointment to the Board, Hawkins was sent to Persia on a mission which made full use of his Inspector's talents. He was to remain on the Board until September 1939.

The new faces on the Board, however, did not resolve the problem of the conflicting perspectives of Rabino in Tehran and his Board in the City of London.

3.2 THE STATE BANK OF PERSIA

The Imperial Bank's Concession made it the state bank of Persia, and Rabino was eager that the Bank should perform and develop this role. He considered that the provision of banking services to the Persian government would not only be profitable, but would also strengthen the Bank's overall position in the country. The worsening financial position of the Persian government and its defective bureaucracy offered plenty of scope, or even the necessity, for the Bank to act in this capacity. However, these factors also made government business, especially in the Board's eyes, fraught with danger.

During 1895 the Bank's relationship with the Persian government had deteriorated. The government had fallen behind in its interest payments on the 1892 Loan, and also on its repayments of advances from the Bank. The problem was that the Bank's Concession only permitted it to lend to the Persian government an amount equivalent to one-third of its paid-up capital (or £216 666), and if this sum was exceeded there was a danger that the Bank's auditors would block the payment of dividends. Despite sustained pressure on the Persian government, the level of government borrowings at the end of April 1896 stood at £220 370 (10 467 575 Krans).[6]

On 1 May 1896 the fate of the Bank's advances, and of Persia itself, was thrown into the balance when Naser od-Din was assassinated. There had never been a peaceful transfer of power in the history of the Qajar dynasty, and foreign observers had long predicted a breakdown of order if and when the Shah died. The situation was saved, however, by Ali Asghar, Amin os-Soltan, the Sadre-e A'zam (Prime Minister), who moved quickly to secure British and Russian support for the Shah's son, Mozaffar od-Din (the Valiahd or Crown Prince), who was living in Tabriz.[7]

The Imperial Bank played an important role in assisting this peaceful succession. Rabino reacted immediately to the Prime Minister's requests for money to support the new Shah. 'Bank guard double and well supplied', he telegraphed to London on the day of the assassination, 'have opened a credit in favour of HIH Valiahd by order of Sadr Azam.'[8] The day after the assassination, Rabino, despite a serious run on the Bank in Tehran, allowed the Prime Minister one million Krans to pay the army, thereby ensuring public security, and a further 500 000 Krans to cover the cost of Mozaffar od-Din's journey from Tabriz to Tehran. The Board approved Rabino's initial action, and supported his subsequent decision taken on the urgent recommendation of the British Minister to allow the new Shah to draw an additional 1.5 million Krans from the Tabriz branch.[9]

Rabino's support for the new government in the critical days of early May strengthened the Imperial Bank's position as the state bank of Persia, and enhanced its public image. After 1896 the Bank assumed an important role in the Persian government's attempts to improve its financial administration. The Bank was helped in this capacity by the arrival in 1898 of three Belgian civil servants, of whom the most important was Joseph Naus, to run the customs administration. Although Naus, the Director of Customs who later became Minister of Customs and Posts, and virtual finance minister, has been regarded by some historians as a 'Russian tool', and this was certainly the opinion of many British diplomats, he developed in fact a good relationship with Rabino and worked in close harmony with the Imperial Bank.[10] Naus was concerned to do his job of reforming the Persian government's customs, and he was glad to work with the Imperial Bank – or the Russian Bank – if this assisted his overall strategy. Unfortunately, despite considerable effort, he and Rabino could do little to stem the growing financial crisis facing the Persian government.

The following sections look at the Imperial Bank's role in currency matters; as revenue collector and paymaster for the government; and as provider of funds.

Notes and coinage

The Imperial Bank's primary involvement in the Persian currency stemmed from the note issuing monopoly in its Concession. The expansion of the note issue before 1905, and its subsequent fall, have already been noted. As there were only marginal exchange rate fluctuations between 1896 and 1908, the balance sheet figures can be taken as representing movements of the note issue in Krans. (Exchange rates are given in Appendix 6.) Tehran's note issue continued to be the largest, representing 72% of the total in 1900, while outside the capital the southern branches generally had larger issues than the northern ones.

Rabino worked hard to expand the note issue, but there were a number of obstacles to the rapid spread of the Bank's notes. As the notes became more generally acceptable so they were hoarded alongside, or even instead of, coin. Moreover, the Bank's laborious procedures for signing notes imposed a physical constraint on the number that could be issued. In the early 1890s the Chief Manager, the Cashier and the Persian High Commissioner of the Bank were all required to sign every note. 'I have signed nearly 60 000 notes a great part during the last 6 weeks', Rabino complained to Newell in April 1896, 'you are fortunate in not knowing what that means.'[11] It was not until December 1896 that the Board allowed the use of a stamped signature by the Chief Manager for the smaller denomination 1, 2 and 3 Toman notes.

The activities of opponents and enemies of the Bank also slowed down the spread of the note issue. The Bank faced a series of runs on its notes, when they were presented in bulk for repayment. The most serious attack came in 1897, and this accounted for a 54% decline in the note issue shown in the balance sheet for that year. The run started in Tehran on 27 August, and lasted for over a fortnight. Both Rabino and outside observers regarded the affair as exceptionally serious.[12] It was orchestrated by a group of merchants and *sarrafs*, with probable Russian involvement. During the 1900s the Russian Bank also organised runs against the Imperial Bank's note issue, although by this period the note issue was widely enough accepted and the Bank's cash reserves so adequate that there was little difficulty in overcoming these Russian challenges. Further difficulties were caused by the circulation of *bijacks*, the cash orders issued by local trading companies which in many regions functioned as *de facto* bank notes. After 1897 the Bank made regular complaints to the Persian government and the British Legation in an effort to stop their circulation.[13] However, there was little the Persian government could or would do, especially as its authority was very limited in outlying provinces.

The spread of the note issue was also dependent on the Imperial Bank's access to silver coinage. The Bank's Charter specified that a reserve of at least one-third of the note issue must be kept in coin, and in practice the danger of runs led the Bank to keep a reserve of about two-thirds. Rabino never forgot that if the Bank was unable to meet its note issue in coin on demand, the Concession would be cancelled. Yet because of the inadequacies of the Persian government's Mint, whose administration was farmed, as well as the problem of hoarding, coins were often in short supply.

In these circumstances the right of the Bank to import silver and have it coined at the Mint was of major importance. In July 1896 Rabino, in the afterglow of the Bank's support for the accession of the new Shah, achieved a major *coup* by securing silver import and coinage contracts from the government. The Bank agreed to import £100 000 of silver, with an option of £200 000 more, whilst the Mint was required to take this silver and coin it 'as soon as delivered to the exclusion of all other coinage operations'.[14] Similar contracts were made in May 1897, November 1898, February 1899 and November 1899. These silver contracts were extremely important to the Bank, which was guaranteed access to the silver coinage it required to cover its note issue. The business was also profitable. The Bank purchased silver in London and shipped it to Persia, selling it to the Mint which paid in coin. Profits were made both through the initial exchange operation and from the negotiation of a favourable contract with the Mint in terms of the weight of silver sold and the number of Krans paid. Between 1900 and 1902 the Bank made total profits of £47 116 on importing bar silver, or about 35% of total published profits in those years.

This aspect of the Bank's business, however, rarely worked smoothly. There was a series of difficulties with the Mint and the Persians who farmed it, and Rabino never realised his long-term ambition of bringing the Mint under the Bank's control. On several occasions the Bank was left with insufficient coin, and Rabino had to fall back on various stratagems. In December 1896, for example, he used the pretext of it being winter to shorten the Bank's official opening hours in order to limit the time available for customers to demand coin in exchange for notes.

After 1900 the Imperial Bank's virtual monopoly of access to the Mint was broken, and on occasion it looked as if the Bank might actually be excluded altogether. The Russian government in 1901 and 1902 sought to make loans to the Persian government conditional on the exclusion of the Bank from the Mint. However, the threat was averted, with the assistance of Naus, and over the following years the Imperial Bank retained a share of the Mint's time alongside the Russian Bank and various Persian merchants. In addition, the Bank during the 1900s imported bullion as an agent of the government. A commission was earned on such transactions, but as the government was often a slow payer the Bank regularly found its funds locked up in government silver. During 1905 and 1906 the Bank preferred not to import silver on its own account because of exchange fluctuations, but it did import silver on the government's behalf in return for its commission.

The Imperial Bank was also involved in several schemes to reform the coinage system of Persia. Persia's small denomination copper coinage had become increasingly debased and discredited, adding to the inflationary pressures on the economy in the late nineteenth century. Public confidence in copper coins had reached such a low ebb that cardboard tokens were widely used as coin. Rabino was anxious to introduce reforms in this area, and in 1896 the Persian government accepted a Bank proposal to withdraw excess copper coinage from circulation. The Bank was to buy the copper coinage from the public on the government's behalf and store it. The reform seemed to have some success for a while, but within a couple of years the problem was as bad as ever. There was only a limited amount that could be done so long as the Mint was farmed out, and Mint farmers had a vested financial interest in debasing the currency.

In 1899 the Bank and the Persian government reached an agreement on an attempt at reforming the coinage. Under the terms of a contract signed on 18 November 1899, all copper coin was to be demonetised and a new nickel coinage introduced. The Bank agreed to import the nickel coins, which on Naus's insistence were to be minted at the Brussels Mint, and to distribute them throughout the country. H. W. Maclean, the Deputy Chief Manager who negotiated the contract in Rabino's absence on leave, hoped that the contract would 'form a stepping stone towards control of the Mintage',[15] as well as earn the Bank a considerable commission.

The deal, however, turned sour. When the Board saw the contract Maclean had signed they were displeased to discover that it included a clause which, as Lepel Griffin complained to the Foreign Office, 'placed very serious future obligations on the Bank as to later and larger issues of Nickel Currency'.[16] Maclean refused to acknowledge that he had exceeded the Bank's instructions, and resigned in October 1900. The Board, despite their displeasure at the details of the contract, decided to continue with the Bank's involvement. The Bank's position had been weakened by the Russian loan of 1900, and it was felt that a withdrawal from the contract could only weaken it further. The issue of the new nickel coinage began in February 1901, and was a complete success.

Revenue collector and paymaster

Rabino sought to assist the Persian government in its collection of revenues and the disbursement of funds. Both activities were in disarray, and an improvement offered not only profits for the Bank but the hope of improved financial stability for the government. The farming of taxes and customs meant that the central government received only a proportion of total revenue collected. It was commonly asserted in Tehran that customs revenues could have been doubled if the customs had not been farmed. The Amin os-Soltan, Prime Minister until November 1896, and again after 1898, and chief customs farmer in Persia, was rumoured to derive an annual income of £70 000 from the customs revenues.[17] While government revenues leaked to the tax farmers, there were rarely sufficient funds to pay the bureaucracy or army on a regular basis.

The Bank made only limited progress in this area. In 1895, at the insistence of Colonel Kosagovskii, the commander of the Cossack Brigade, the Bank took over the payment of the salaries of the Brigade. However, this was an isolated success for the Bank. The Belgian Minister in Tehran failed in his attempt to insert a clause in the contracts of the Belgian customs administrators that their salaries would also be paid through the Bank.[18]

In addition, Rabino attempted to make the Bank the agent for the encashment of provincial revenues and customs receipts, a business controlled by *sarrafs*. During the short reformist administration, from 1896 to 1898, of Mirza Ali Khan, Amin od-Doule (the man who owned the building in which the Chief Office was located), some progress was made. On 17 May

1897 the Bank signed a customs and revenue contract, under which it agreed to pay out 850 000 Krans a month to government ministries, receiving in return customs and revenue receipts.[19] Although these contracts were renegotiated annually, over the next few years the Bank regularly handled the transfer of provincial customs revenues to the central government. Moreover, in 1898 the negotiations for a loan to the Persian government led to a further development. The Bank took the customs receipts of Bushire and Kermanshah as security for a £50 000 advance and thus assumed responsibility with the Belgian customs officers for the collection and administration of the customs. This arrangement, however, was ended after a year, although it set a precedent for the future.

During the 1900s the Imperial Bank co-operated with Naus's plans to modernise the taxation system of Persia. In 1904, for example, Naus arranged that the *maliyat* tax, essentially a land and property tax paid in both cash and kind, was to be collected directly by provincial governors and paid regularly to agents of the central government's treasury. The Bank was appointed as the depository for these revenues, and in April 1904 Naus opened a new Treasury Account with the Bank for this purpose. However, this reform, like so many, was overwhelmed after 1905 by the spreading administrative and political chaos.

Foreign loans 1897–1900

During the second half of the 1890s the financial situation of the Persian government became critical, and the Imperial Bank found itself in the middle of the crisis. The Bank was involved in highly complicated negotiations aimed at securing a foreign loan for Persia. It is not possible in this History to follow these negotiations in detail, and this section will confine itself to a brief survey of the policies of the four principal actors – the Persian government, the Imperial Bank, and the British and Russian governments – in the events which led up to the Russian Loan of 1900.[20]

The Persian government's aim was simple. It needed to find from somewhere sufficient money to service its existing debts and meet immediate expenditure, while avoiding the political strings which potential foreign lenders sought to attach to their loan offers. Mirza Ali Khan, Amin od-Doule, was inclined to borrow from Britain, or at least from a non-Russian source, and this line was particularly favoured by his Finance Minister, the Oxford educated Naser ol-Molk. The Amin os-Soltan, who returned to power after the Amin od-Doule's fall in July 1898, was more pro-Russian in his inclinations, although he was prepared to consider funds from any source if the terms were right. Both men conducted the loan negotiations with skill, but their freedom of manoeuvre was limited by the pressing financial crisis and the fact that a fundamental reform of the financial system was ruled out.

The Imperial Bank assisted Persian governments to keep functioning by the provision of advances. Between 1890 and May 1898 the Bank advanced the Kran equivalent of around £1 million to the Persian government. This was profitable business for the Bank. It usually charged 12% per annum on Kran advances, and 6% per annum on Sterling loans repayable in England in Sterling. However, the twin problems of the £216 666 lending limit in the Bank's Concession and government 'outstandings' loomed over any enjoyment of profits from interest payments. By January 1898 the Bank's direct advances to the government were very close to the lending limit, and over the next two years delays in repayments led the Bank on several occasions to consider declaring the Persian government to be in default. During 1898 to 1900, therefore, the Bank was of little use to the government in its search for funds, being prepared only to make small temporary advances on the firmest of security.

As the Imperial Bank was unable or unwilling to make further advances, and constantly pressed for the repayment of the advances it had made, the only means whereby the Persian government could raise a large sum of capital was a foreign loan. During these years various Continental syndicates were involved in loan negotiations, and the Imperial Bank tried hard to negotiate a loan through the City. However, it proved difficult to finalise an agreement. Foreign loans were still at a low ebb in the City in the wake of the Baring Crisis and the Australian banking collapse. In so far as some investors continued to place funds abroad, speculative investments in South African and Western Australian gold mining were one of the most popular fields. In addition, the Lottery Concession and the tobacco affair had left Persia with no credit rating. As a result, although the Imperial Bank was most willing to act as an agent for placing a loan on behalf of the Persian government, on a strictly commission basis, when in March 1898 the Bank explored the chances of floating a large loan in the City it became immediately clear that there was no hope of success.[21] The only thing that might coax British investors into Persia appeared to be a British government guarantee or assurance which would prevent a repeat of the lottery and tobacco debacles.

Such a guarantee was hard to elicit. British government policy between 1898 and 1900 was not helpful to Persia's search for external funds. The Foreign Office obstructed non-British loan proposals, especially if they implied non-British control over the customs of the Gulf ports. The British *Chargé d'Affaires* in Tehran protested to the Persian government in the autumn of 1897 when it seemed likely that S. Oppenheim would provide a loan, largely raised in France, pledged on the customs revenue of Gulf ports and Kermanshah.[22] In October 1897 the *Chargé* had secured written assurance from the Persian government that the Southern customs would never be alienated to a 'foreign' (i.e. non-British) power. The Prime Minister and Foreign Secretary, Lord Salisbury, fully appreciated the political importance of foreign loans, and was eager to use the Bank to forward British interests in Persia. But the Treasury resisted the idea of offering guarantees, expressing distrust of the Persian government and distaste for the Imperial Bank, whose high interest charges officials regarded as 'usurious'. Consequently, the Foreign Office could move only slowly towards accepting responsibility for investors in Persia. It was not until June 1898 that the Foreign Office agreed to appoint an administrator to collect customs revenues on which a prospective British loan of £1.25 million was to be secured.[23]

This Foreign Office offer, however, came too late. Amin od-Doule was dismissed on 5 June. Over the following weeks Amin os-Soltan returned to power again, and with his rise came a resurgence of Russian influence at the Shah's court. Despite the fact that the Foreign Office was finally prepared to offer British investors the assurance the Bank had pressed for so urgently, the Amin os-Soltan requested a loan of nearly double the previous amount, which was taken by both the Bank and the Foreign Office to be a polite way of refusing a British loan.

Russian government policy towards Persia was the mirror image of British policy. The Russians also appreciated the links between loans and political influence, and were suspicious for that reason of non-Russian loans to Persia. However, the Russian government in the late 1890s was far more prepared than its British counterpart to make loans itself for political purposes through the state-controlled Lending Bank of Persia, or Banque des Prêts. In the autumn of 1898 the Persian government, under pressure by the Imperial Bank to pay its outstandings by the closing of the Bank's yearly accounts on 20 September, secured a 1.5 million Rouble loan (£159 000) from the Lending Bank of Persia on the security of the customs revenues in the north of Persia and the income from fishing rights in the Caspian Sea.[24] This loan enabled the Persian government to repay £150 000 to the Imperial Bank.

During 1899 various loan proposals were discussed, including parallel British and Russian loans and, towards the end of the year, a large British loan. Throughout 1899 Rabino warned the Bank's Board that a Russian loan was imminent, and in the New Year it finally happened. In January 1900 a loan of 22.5 million Roubles (£2.4 million), at 5% annual interest repayable over 75 years, was announced. The Loan was guaranteed by revenues of all the customs except those of Fars and the Gulf ports. The Persian government used this Russian Loan to repay not only the 1892 Loan at par, but also the whole of its debt to the Bank, which amounted to about 12 million Krans (£233 000). There were a variety of strings attached to the Loan, including a provision that Persia was not to accept a loan from any other country until the Russian Loan had been repaid, as well as a further extension of the agreement not to construct railways.

The Imperial Bank reacted to the Russian Loan with some anger, and more than a little pessimism about the future. 'The joint inaction of the Money Market and the Foreign Office has done England and the Bank great and lasting injury', Lepel Griffin wrote to Rabino in February 1900.[25] Government borrowing, for all the worries about outstandings, had allowed the Bank to earn 12% per annum. The same funds invested in British government securities would have earned only 2.5–4% per annum. And it seemed that there would be no easy way to recapture the lost government business. 'You must accustom yourself to the idea', Rabino advised Newell in April 1900, 'that we are henceforth heavily handicapped and that the preference in financial matters will always be given to the Banque des Prêts.'[26]

3.3 AGENT OF EMPIRE

The aftermath of the Russian Loan

The Russian Loan changed the Imperial Bank's position in Persia. The Bank ceased to be the major source of the government's finance, and instead had to fight to be considered as merely one source of external borrowing. Politically, the Loan greatly increased Russian influence in Persia. British diplomats, in turn, were stung into pursuing more forceful policies, with the Bank being recruited as a front line force in the attempt to re-assert British influence. By 1905 the Russian government had lent nearly 70 million Roubles (£7.5 million) to Persia. By contrast, the British government had lent less than £0.5 million, although in terms of influence Britain managed to re-establish a relatively stronger diplomatic position in the country.

The Russian Loan did not have the baleful effect on the Imperial Bank's commercial fortunes that Rabino and the Board had feared. In fact, the Imperial Bank did rather well from it. The repayment of the 1892 Loan at par provided profits, as the loan had been issued at a discount. Moreover, the professional expertise of the Imperial Bank, and the lack of such expertise by the Russian Bank, meant that neither the Persian nor the Russian governments could dispense with its services. Rabino was particularly astute in securing much of the exchange business involved in the Russian Loan. He moved swiftly on the announcement of the Russian Loan to sell as much exchange as possible in Persia – thus strengthening the Bank's cash position – while buying all the paper he could in Baku. As a result, the Imperial Bank was in a better position than either the Russian bank or the *sarrafs* to transfer funds from Russia to Persia, and about three-quarters of the exchange business on the Russian Loan passed through the Imperial Bank.[27] The considerable profits on this business were largely responsible for an increase of over £11 000 in the Bank's published net profits in 1900, and the Bank also made a transfer to inner reserves, although the amount in question is unknown.[28]

Naus fully recognised the professional expertise of the Imperial Bank, and soon after the Russian Loan was completed he was again passing on Persian government business. He restored the Bank to its position as a lender to the Persian government. By April 1900 the Shah was in need of 2 million Krans (£38 800) to meet partially the expenses of a trip to Europe in the summer, as the Russian Loan was only gradually remitted to Persia. Naus asked the Imperial Bank, and the Bank agreed, to make the Shah an advance of that sum against bullion, which suited the Bank since it implied access to the Mint for coinage.[29] This advance was rapidly paid off as the Russian funds arrived, but in the following year Naus arranged a further advance. In March 1901 the Bank agreed to make an advance of 10 million Krans (£188 700) at 12% per annum interest against the security of a preferential claim on the southern customs, repayable by 36 monthly instalments. This agreement also gave the Bank a contract to import £100 000 of silver for the government, and a Mint contract.[30]

The Anglo-Indian Loans 1903–05

The British Minister in Tehran between 1900 and 1905, Sir Arthur Hardinge, had enthusiastically supported the Bank's advance to the Shah in March 1901, and this was indicative of the more active official British policy in Persia after the Russian Loan. Hardinge was eager to encourage the Bank's lending, believing that the further Persia fell into debt to Britain the more Britain's political influence in the country would increase and Russia's influence diminish. He wanted the Imperial Bank to develop as the equivalent of the Russian Bank, as Britain's 'principal political lever here, indestructible as a British institution',[31] and he even went so far in March 1903 as to argue that the British government should acquire a majority shareholding in the Imperial Bank.

There was never, however, a consensus among Britain's policy makers over Persia in the early 1900s. George, now Lord, Curzon, the Viceroy of India, considered Hardinge too polite in his dealings with the Persian government, and pushed for tougher policies. Persia was not a major preoccupation of the Foreign Office, although Lord Lansdowne, who was appointed Foreign Secretary in 1900, showed more interest in the country than some of his predecessors. There continued to be a divide in British government circles between those who argued that Persia should be strengthened as a buffer state between British India and Russia, and those who felt that Persia was crumbling and that the best that could be hoped for would be to control the south and east regions of the country which were of strategic importance to British India.[32] These divisions meant that official British policy-making continued to be a slow process, and that often ideas were not turned into policies. Hardinge's proposal for the British government to take over the Imperial Bank, for example, was rejected by Foreign Office officials unwilling to be too closely associated with a bank they regarded as 'usurious and somewhat shady'.[33] Nevertheless the overall thrust of British policy in the early 1900s was more active than previously. Government of India money was used to support the Persian government, and Secret Service funds were used to sweeten key personalities in Persian politics.

The Imperial Bank played a major role in this official policy. The process by which the Bank became the channel through which British government money was lent to the Persian government was long and tortuous. During the summer of 1901 negotiations were under way for a further Bank advance of 10 million Krans to the Persian government.[34] However, Anglo-Russian rivalry reached another peak during the summer and autumn of 1901. The granting to William Knox D'Arcy of a comprehensive oil concession on 28 May, which was to give rise to Persia's oil industry, provoked a hostile Russian reaction.[35] In September a Russian advance of 945 000 Roubles (£100 000) was made to the Persian government, and negotiations for a much larger sum began in anticipation of a further European visit by the Shah. In addition, H. W. Maclean, who had been appointed Mint Master by the Persian government after his resignation from the Imperial Bank, was dismissed from his post on Russian insistence in October and replaced by a Belgian. It even seemed for a time that the Russian Bank, now under the aggressive management of E. K. Grube, would acquire a monopoly of access to the Mint.

It was in these conditions that the idea of a British government advance to the Persian government through the Imperial Bank was first mooted. In September 1901 Hardinge suggested that the Government of India might advance £500 000 through the Bank.[36] The great advantage of the proposal was that the Bank, as a Persian institution, was not strictly covered by the provision in the Russian Loan agreement that the Persian government could not borrow from abroad without Russian consent. It proved difficult, however, to get Hardinge's scheme off the ground. Curzon, who had made a similar proposal in May, was interested, but concerned to ensure that any loan was secured by the revenues of the Gulf ports and of Seistan province, thus strengthening British influence in the areas of strategic importance to India.[37] Hardinge's scheme also had outright opponents. The morality of encouraging the Persian government to evade the legal conditions of the Russian Loan was questioned, and on 8 October the whole scheme was ruled out when the Political Committee of the Indian Council rejected the use of Indian funds to avoid establishing a 'mischievous precedent'.[38]

It was another eighteen months before a loan was made on the lines originally suggested by Hardinge. Rabino, Hardinge, and the British, Russian and Persian governments were all involved in the unproductive negotiations in this period, and there were some surprising developments. Early in November 1901 the Russian government itself suggested that the British government might advance money through the Imperial Bank.[39] This led to a reconsideration of the British loan position, and a decision to authorise an advance to Persia of up to £500 000 using Indian funds.[40] But the Russian government had been clearly playing for time. When the British proposal was submitted, the Russians at once raised objections to it, and a second Russian Loan was announced on 20 March 1902. It comprised 10 million Roubles (nearly £1.1 million). Yet, as before, the money was spent almost as soon as the Loan was issued, and by the beginning of the following year Naus was probing the Legation about the possibility of the British government assisting the Bank to make a further loan of between £300 000 and £400 000.[41]

While the Legation, the Foreign Office and the Government of India argued over what political strings could be attached to such a loan, the Persian government made a direct request to the Bank for a loan.[42] The Bank, however, infinitely preferred to lend someone else's money rather than its own, and on 3 April 1903 an agreement was reached with the British government which made this possible. The Government of India agreed to lend up to £500 000 to the Imperial Bank. The money was to be on-lent to the Persian government at a rate of 4% per annum, plus an additional 1% per annum which the Bank was to earn as commission. The principal and interest were to be guaranteed by the British and Indian governments.[43] On 8 April 1903 the Bank signed a loan agreement with the Persian government. The Bank was to provide the Persian government with £200 000 at 5% per annum, and a further £100 000 of the Anglo-Indian money was to be held in reserve to follow up the first advance. The principal source of repayment was to be the royalties due from the Caspian Sea fisheries, followed by the revenues of the postal and telegraph services, followed as a third resort by the customs revenues of Fars and the Gulf.

The Persian government were by now locked in a vicious circle. In order to service their debts they needed to borrow still further. Over £120 000 of the April loan was committed to the repayment and servicing of debts, and by May 1903 Naus was back at the Bank to see if an additional £100 000 loan was possible. In fact it took a further year before the second half of the Anglo–Indian loan was made. The British government's, and more especially Lord Curzon's, desire to attach firm political strings to the loan made the Persians wary and anxious to find accommodation elsewhere. In the meantime, and in expectation of the completion of the Anglo–Indian loan, the Bank advanced the Persian government 3 million Krans (£55 000), and in July 1903 the Russians provided a further loan of 3 million Krans. It was not until September 1904, after many abortive negotiations and further small advances from the Bank, that the British government authorised the issue of the final £100 000 through the Imperial Bank to the Persian government. Under the terms of this loan the payments of interest on both the old and new loans were converted into a single regular annual charge on the Persian government for the next 20 years.

Although the 1904 loan was again made through the agency of the Imperial Bank, the negotiations were conducted directly between the Legation and the Persian government. The Persian government, Hardinge observed, made a direct application to the British government for a loan 'without a reference to the fiction of the Imperial Bank of Persia'.[44] The Bank did not feel offended by its exclusion from the complex diplomatic negotiations. It derived a satisfactory income from the Anglo-Indian loans – estimated by the Bank at £1900 per annum over 20 years – and the Bank also undertook the exchange business on the repayment of the loans and interest.[45]

During 1905 the financial situation of the Persian government continued to deteriorate. The British and Russian governments attached such restrictive political conditions to loan offers that the Persians found them impossible to accept.[46] The Persian government tried to escape from the British and Russian clutches by turning to a 'neutral' third party, a tactic which successive governments were to adopt until the 1950s. In this case Germany was the target. There were discussions about the formation of a German bank in Persia, a process which eventually culminated in the granting of a concession in July 1907.[47] Meanwhile, as the government's finances worsened, the Imperial Bank for a time extended facilities. But in April 1905 the Persian government requested an advance of £150 000, at 8% interest, from the Bank to cover expenses while the Shah made another visit to Europe. Rabino and Hardinge were eager to make the advance, but it would have taken the Bank well above its Concessionary lending limit and in July the Board definitely ruled out such an advance.[48] Despite this ruling the Persian government's overdraft with the Bank edged upwards, and by the autumn of 1905 the Bank was owed about £100 000 above the Concession limit. Repayments were increasingly difficult to extract. A crisis was in the making when the first stirrings of the Constitutional Revolution occurred at the end of the year.

Banking for the Empire

The Imperial Bank's role as agent of Empire in the 1900s was not only limited to acting as the medium through which loans were passed. The Bank was also asked, and sometimes agreed, to open branches for political rather than commercial reasons, and to make loans to politically important individuals.

The British government encouraged the Imperial Bank to open branches in several towns as part of its overall policy of encouraging British commerce, and with it political influence, in Persia. The clearest case was Seistan, which bordered on the Indian province of Baluchistan. The Viceroy, Lord Curzon, countered the possibility of Russia gaining a railway concession which might enter Seistan from the north, via Mashad, by opening up an overland trade route between Quetta and Mashad via Nushki. In January 1901 it was suggested that the Bank should open a branch on this trade route.[49] Seistan's location across the great Persian desert from Tehran, and the absence of any real commercial activity, did not make this an attractive proposition for the Bank, but in May 1903 the Foreign Office offered the Bank a subsidy not exceeding £1500 per annum for five years in order to establish a branch. The subsidy would be reduced by the amount of any net profits made by the branch.[50]

During 1903 a branch was duly opened at Nasratabad in Seistan. Over the next four years it accumulated a total loss of nearly £2800, even after the payment of the subsidy. The Government of India discovered that although it could take the Bank to Seistan, it could not make the Bank do the kind of business it desired. Officials had hoped that the Bank would, in the absence of established merchants in the province, perform mercantile functions in order to develop the commercial life of the region. The Bank, however, concentrated on doing the small amount of exchange business that was available, and making a few advances on the best possible security. By August 1907 the disgruntled British Consul in Seistan had concluded that the Nasratabad branch was an 'empty show' of 'no value whatever' as a political asset.[51]

The British government did not subsidise any other branches of the Imperial Bank. Nevertheless, the Bank was encouraged in other ways to open in various Persian towns. British officials were eager to develop a network of consular officers in Persia, and, with this in mind, in May 1900 the British Legation offered to pay £200 a year towards the salary of a Manager if the Bank opened in Kermanshah, provided the Manager was also appointed a Vice-Consul.[52] The Bank accepted this arrangement and in 1902 a sub-branch at Kermanshah was opened. Rabino's son, Hyacinth, was appointed Manager, against the advice of his father who considered him too inexperienced.[53] Hyacinth Rabino was subsequently appointed a Vice-Consul. The British government also encouraged the Bank to open branches in Kerman and Bandar Abbas, and although it was considered that poor climate and bad communications ruled out Bandar Abbas, in 1904 a sub-branch of Yazd branch was opened at Kerman.

The Imperial Bank was also encouraged by the British government to make various loans to institutions and individuals who might be expected to favour British interests. Hardinge, for instance, was eager to attach Persia's *mullahs* to Britain's cause, and as part of this strategy the Legation in 1903 guaranteed an advance of £1800 by the Bank to the sacred shrine of Mashad.[54] However, the Foreign Office were sparing in using their powers of guarantee, while the Imperial Bank was extremely cautious about making 'political' advances without such guarantees. In February 1904 and August 1905 the Bank refused to accede to Hardinge's requests, which were not accompanied by offers of guarantees, to accommodate Mohammad Ali Mirza, the Valiahd (heir apparent) in Tabriz. The Valiahd had already accumulated large debts with the Bank, and had proved to be an unreliable customer.[55]

Roads and Mines (see Map 2)

The Foreign Office also became involved in the road and mining rights concessions held by the Imperial Bank. In April 1896 Rabino secured a renewal of the road concession for a further 10 years, despite the early difficulties of the venture. Hyacinth Rabino reorganised the Bank's road department, and by the late 1890s the Bank was earning an annual income of between £1000 and £1500 on the Tehran–Qum road.[56] Rabino senior was eager to extend the road, from Qum to Soltanabad and on to Ahwaz, and also from Qum to Esfahan. The Board was not prepared, however, to undertake further capital expenditure on road construction, and there seemed no possibility of raising capital elsewhere. The Legation regarded British-built and managed roads as a most useful way of spreading British influence, but the Foreign Office ruled out any government guarantee for a loan to extend the Bank's road. Instead, British officials sponsored negotiations between the Imperial Bank and Messrs Lynch and Co., the controlling interest in the Euphrates and Tigris Steam Navigation Company, and one of the leading

Gulf trading houses. H. F. B. Lynch, the firm's owner, had recently been asked by the Bakhtiari tribes to build a road through their territories from Ahwaz to Esfahan.[57] The Bank had taken considerable exception to this arrangement, for although it did not have a concession for the Esfahan to Ahwaz route, it claimed first right to the construction of roads in southern Persia.

The Bank's negotiations with Lynch proved unproductive, and in November 1901 the Bank reached an agreement with the Persian government to sell its concession back to them for £20 000. This announcement caused a considerable stir at the Foreign Office, for it was quite likely that the hard-pressed Persian government would re-sell the road concession to the Russians. Foreign Office officials acknowledged, however, that more concrete inducement would be required to persuade the Bank to abandon the chance of realising £20 000 on its forlorn road investment. In January 1902 the Foreign Office offered the Bank, if it stayed in the road business in co-operation with Lynch, an annual subsidy of £500 for five years 'towards covering loss on the road expenditure', together with the firm hope that the Government of India would match this amount.[58] At the same time the Foreign Office offered to increase to £1500 the subsidy they paid to the Euphrates and Tigris Steam Navigation Company to run a steamship on the Karun as far as Ahwaz.[59]

Despite these inducements, the Imperial Bank and Lynch found it hard to reach an agreement. A major stumbling block was that Lynch desired that the Bank should retain some responsibility for the road, while the Bank was anxious to abandon any such role. Finally, in September 1902, agreement was reached for the sale of the road concession to a new transport company, to be known as the Persian Transport Company. The Bank was to get £15 000 cash, plus £10 000 shares in the company.

There were yet further delays. By the beginning of 1903 Lynch had still not signed the agreement, and was voicing a string of complaints about the state of the Bank's road construction and repair. The Foreign Office, convinced by now that the only way to solve the problem was to throw money at it, raised their offer of assistance to the proposed Persian Transport Company to £20 000. This still did not satisfy Lynch, and a new nadir in relationships was reached in September 1903 when he brought a legal action against the Imperial Bank. He claimed that the Bank had painted far too rosy a picture of its road in the negotiations, an allegation which was flatly denied. Ministers and officials did not want the use of British government funds to build roads in Persia to become public knowledge through a court case, and so Lynch was offered a further £2000 to stop his legal action.[60] It was not until 9 April 1904 that the sale of the Bank's concession and road to the Persian Transport

Company was finally completed. The Bank was left as a minority shareholder in the new Company. Its direct involvement in road matters was ended, although one of the three Persian Transport Company directors was also a director of the Bank. As for Persia's roads, the new company completed the Qum to Soltanabad link in the 1900s, and in 1920 began the construction of a road from Qum to Esfahan, though the Persian government abrogated the concession before the work was completed.

The Bank was unable to realise any money from its mining rights. The Persian Bank Mining Rights Corporation, in which the Bank held 130 000 shares, had been in the hands of the liquidators since the mid-1890s. The mining rights shares appeared in the Bank's balance sheet like, as Sir Lepel Griffin put it in March 1901, 'the dead branch of a tree'.[61] This unsatisfactory situation was finally brought to an end on 21 July 1901, when the liquidators closed the books.

3.4 BANKING OPERATIONS

While the Imperial Bank developed its twin roles as state bank and agent of British policy in Persia, the importance of its commercial banking operations also continued.

The Bank maintained the policy of allocating a fixed capital to its branches, although the sum was frequently adjusted. The topic was the occasion of several disputes between Rabino and his Board. During the mid-1890s, in the aftermath of the silver crisis and the writing down of the capital, the Board were reluctant to allow the Persian branches access to further funds. Rabino, anxious to develop the Bank's business in Persia, found this a great inconvenience. At the turn of the century the situation was reversed. The closure of the Bombay agency, together with the repayment of government debts and the 1892 Loan at par, made the Bank more liquid. The Board wanted Rabino to employ the extra funds in Persia. Rabino was now convinced that the Bank was in a position to develop on locally generated resources, and pointed to the possible exchange risks of bringing further Sterling funds to Persia should there be a further sharp depreciation of silver.[62]

Rabino seems to have won his point. There was no substantial increase in the Sterling capital allocated to Persian Branches between 1900 and 1905, the sum fluctuating around £320 000. It was not until 1905 that increases in the Bank's loans and advances, mainly to the Persian government, brought further capital to Persia, and by the beginning of 1908 about £374 000 was being employed.

The Bank's Kran deposits were stagnant until 1900, never exceeding the level reached in 1892 of 10.5 million Krans. Persian deposits represented about 90% of the Bank's total deposits in the second half of the 1890s, and about 96% in the 1900s. The lowest point came in 1899, when they sank to £157 467, or 7.9 million Krans. There was some increase subsequently, and in 1904 they reached £394 262, or 23.3 million Krans. By 1908 they stood at £583 243, or 32.6 million Krans.

The Bank paid interest on many of its deposits. In September 1900, 30% of the Bank's deposits in Persia were fixed, for a certain period, usually six months or a year, on which interest was always paid. Interest also continued to be paid on many deposits at call. In 1900, 76% of total Persian deposits were interest-bearing, and 83% of Tehran's deposits. The Bank generally paid 6% interest per annum on deposits with exceptionally an additional 2% on more valued accounts. Rabino repeatedly argued that higher interest rates would have attracted more deposits, a point that seemed to carry validity during the 1890s, but the Board was adamant that 6% per annum should be the normal ceiling. Once again the perspectives of the two parties were different. The collapse of the Australian banks in the early 1890s was widely ascribed to their borrowing at high rates, and on relatively long term, in London. The Australian disasters were a long-remembered lesson about the dangers of high interest on deposits and, if only for the sake of the Imperial Bank's reputation in the City of London, the Board did not wish their Bank to follow the same path.

After 1900 the Board exercised pressure on Rabino to reduce interest rates, a move linked in part to its desire to use more of the Bank's own capital in Persia and in part to falling British interest rates. Rabino, anxious to build up the Bank's deposit base, resisted this pressure but in 1904 the Board finally secured a reduction in the maximum interest given on deposits to 5%. Rabino's fears were not realised, and over the following years there was a sharp upward movement in the Bank's deposits. The Imperial Bank was undoubtedly helped by the troubles of the Russian Bank, whose position was not improved by Russia's loss of prestige following its defeat in the Russo–Japanese war in 1905. However, the increase in deposits was partly 'illusory'. The 1904 figure was swelled by unusually large credit balances held by the Persian government with the Bank at the close of accounts in September 1904, and after 1905, the deposit figures included a new government silver account. The Bank, as explained above, imported silver as an agent of the Persian government in these years. When the government were unable to pay for their silver, the Bank held the silver on deposit for them until such time as it was paid for. The government silver account totalled £109 196 in 1907, or 21% of total deposits in Persia in that year of £519 791.

The Imperial Bank, when considering the disposition of its resources, always kept at least 20% of them in cash. Chief Office in June 1900, for example, possessed total resources of £520 000, consisting of allocated capital, deposits and notes in circulation. £111 750 of this sum was kept as cash in hand. The Bank's custom of maintaining a coin reserve equal to at least two-thirds of note issue, the danger of runs, and the difficulty of moving coin from one branch to another, all encouraged the retention of substantial funds in cash.

During the 1890s the Bank developed an extensive business in exchange, with Chief Office in Tehran always being the most important centre for this activity. Bills were purchased on London and other European towns, and these funds were used to supply importers with exchange, pay Persian government requirements in Europe, make forward contracts with importers, supply branches with exchange, and import silver for the Mint.

Rabino discouraged speculative buying and selling of exchange, but the autonomy given to branch Managers in the 1890s meant that his injunctions were not always followed. A number of Managers undertook speculative transactions, which Rabino condemned as 'inadmissible in any seriously managed Bank which has to follow the mode and action of a trader and not that of a Stock Exchange manipulator'.[63] It was also a regular occurrence for Managers to take exchange positions detrimental to other branches and to Rabino's overall policy.

Rabino's solution to these problems was centralisation. During the early 1900s the foreign exchange business was largely centralised on Chief Office. Regular profits were earned. The Bank made exchange profits of £3000 in the year ended September 1905, £2900 in 1906, and £6000 in 1907. The Board, however, maintained that larger profits on exchange could have been made, especially in periods when there were substantial fluctuations in the exchange rate. Between 1904 and 1906, the Kran-Sterling rate fluctuated between 64 and 55. The Board regretted that Rabino had failed to profit from these rapid changes, while Rabino for his part pointed out that local circumstances, and the Bank's pre-eminent position in the market, prevented him from being able necessarily to take up the most profitable exchange position. However, there was a growing feeling in London that Rabino's centralisation of exchange operations on Tehran had curbed the powers of individual Managers too much and prevented the exploitation of profitable business in the exchange market. In 1908 one director, V. A. Caesar Hawkins, calculated that the Bank only handled about 6.5% of Persia's foreign trade financing.[64] As the total volume of exchange operations is unknown, the accuracy of this estimate cannot be assessed, but it does serve to underline the point that after nearly 20 years in Persia a great deal of banking business, including exchange, still eluded the

Bank and was in the hands of *sarrafs*, merchants, the European trading firms and the Russians.

While the Board criticised Rabino for being inactive in exchange business, they continued to complain that he was far too free in his use of the Bank's resources in loans and advances. 'However good the advances may be', Newell wrote to Rabino in December 1898, 'we prefer the funds employed in exchange business.'[65] In the mid-1890s London's poor view of local lending was reinforced by a debacle at Shiraz branch. Shiraz appeared to have a profitable local lending business, but during 1895 and 1896, it became clear that some of the lending had been extremely ill-considered. Bills and loans overdue by at least six months had reached 3.5 million Krans (£70 000) in December 1896, with the two worst debtors being an opium exporter and an importer of Manchester piece goods. Almost all of this money seems to have been lost. There were similar difficulties, on a smaller scale, at several other branches. At Esfahan, for example, adulteration of the local opium hit sales to China, leaving the Bank with some bad debts of the opium exporters. The troubles at the Bank's provincial branches were a significant factor in the Bank's low published profits in the late 1890s.

The solution of Rabino and London to these difficulties differed. Rabino concluded that the lesson of Shiraz was the need for more supervision from Tehran over branch Managers, and for branch Managers to have more experience of the country. He proposed various safeguards, including the need for good information, knowledge of the purpose for which an advance was made, and reference to Chief Office for amounts over a certain limit.[66] Rabino also recognised that a more efficient means of collecting bad debts was required, given the Bank's lack of confidence in Persia's legal machinery. He initiated a system of farming out the collection of debts on a commission basis. In 1897, for instance, it was agreed that the Governor of Fars would be granted a commission on debts he recovered, and other branches were authorised to make similar arrangements.[67]

The Board's immediate reaction to the debt crisis at Shiraz was an attempt to prohibit loans and advances as far as possible. During 1896 Managers were under constant pressure not to undertake such business, although Chief Office's lending, much of it 'political', was not curbed. The following year the Board allowed a resumption of loans and advances at most other branches so long as suitable guarantees were secured. At Esfahan, for example, the branch was permitted to make advances on raw opium provided that the arrangements were directly supervised by the Manager, and certificates of quality for the opium were obtained from a recognised expert.[68] But the Board's dislike of local lending was reflected in the declining level of bills discounted, loans and advances shown in the Bank's balance sheet from the late 1890s until 1903. There was some increase in this category of business subsequently, with the overall size of the Bank's bills discounted, loans and advances doubling between 1903 and 1906. The Board had clearly gained confidence about Rabino's risk assessment, and was prepared to see local lending expand. Earnings from interest, including government borrowing, began to exceed those from exchange. However, the political crisis after 1905 was to shatter any consensus between Rabino and his Board on this subject.

The overall pattern of business naturally varied between branches. Chief Office handled most government business. The northern branches of the Bank, such as Tabriz, Mashad and Rasht, were principally involved in financing trade and handling exchange transactions with Russia. The southern branches, Shiraz and Bushire, Esfahan and Yazd, financed trade and arranged exchange between Persia and Britain and British India. The fortunes of individual branches waxed and waned, dependent both on the energy and skill of the Manager and the vitality of the economic life of their surrounding areas. Rasht, for example, was opened as a small sub-branch under an Armenian Manager. In the second half of the 1890s the branch flourished as exports of rice and cotton to Russia from the region expanded. The silk industry of Gilan province also underwent a renaissance, with silk production doubling between 1895 and 1899. The Bank became involved in financing the exports of silk to Europe, and business grew sharply. In 1899 the branch had grown sufficiently for the Armenian to be replaced by a British officer. Rasht's fortunes, however, subsequently declined. A depression in Baku in the early 1900s hit the province's export of rice to Russia, while disease and a devastating hail storm in 1904 ruined the silk crop prospects for a period of years.

The strength of competition to the Imperial Bank also varied from one place to another, and over time. In the late 1890s the Imperial Bank had a cordial relationship with its Russian counterparts. The Lending Bank of Persia, and the Tehran branch of the International Bank of Moscow, placed deposits with the Imperial Bank and the Lending Bank came to the Imperial Bank's assistance during the 1897 run.[69] Moreover, the existence of the Russian banks greatly facilitated exchange operations. But this provided a further area of disagreement with the Board. From London's vantage point, the Russians were a menace, their political ambitions well known, and the Bank's contact with them needed to be kept to a minimum. At the beginning of 1898 Rabino was obliged by the Board to repay the Russian deposits held by the Bank.[70]

Russian competition became more determined after 1900. The Imperial Bank's exchange business was challenged during the period of Russian financial dominance following the 1900 Loan. Moreover, the Lending Bank opened new branches in Tabriz, Mashad and Rasht. The Russian Bank, renamed the Discount and Lending Bank of Persia in 1902, was instructed by the Russian government to boost Russian trade in Persia for political purposes, and to spare no expense in the process.[71] Yet the Imperial Bank was never affected seriously by Russian competition, and by the spring of 1906 the Russian Bank's incautious lending policies had reduced it to insolvency.[72]

It was often local merchants and *sarrafs* who provided the strongest competition for the Imperial Bank. Managers regularly referred to their competitiveness. The willingness of *sarrafs* to lend without the 'security' demanded by British bankers, and cultural ties, were among the factors that gave the indigenous bankers a sizeable share of Persian banking. Generalisations are unwise, however, because the situation differed between towns. Tabriz had some powerful *sarrafs*, and the Armenian merchants, whose exports earned most of the foreign exchange in the city, generally did most of their business with the *sarrafs*. The Tabriz branch of the Imperial Bank attempted during the 1890s to capture some of this business by working through a Persian broker. First one, and in 1900 a second, broker was employed to find business for the Bank and supply information on potential clients, but Tabriz Managers found competing with the *sarrafs* an uphill struggle. At Yazd, a major distribution centre which exported opium and silk and imported green tea and cotton piece goods, Parsee merchants were very strongly entrenched. They generally placed their business with their Parsee co-religionists in Bombay, and the Imperial Bank was only able to secure a small share of the exchange and finance business of the area.

3.5 BRANCHES AND ORGANISATION

The period 1896–1908 saw the gradual expansion of the Imperial Bank's branch network, and an extended debate about the relationship between Chief Office and the branches.

Table 3.2 gives the dates when new branches were opened in Persia between 1896 and 1908. During the second half of the 1890s Rabino actively pressed for the opening of new branches, especially at Hamadan and Kermanshah, but his only achievement was to secure the elevation of Tehran's Bazaar Office, which had been established as a rather *ad hoc* offshoot of Chief Office, to the status of a sub-branch in 1899 with its own European Manager. The Board did not share Rabino's enthusiasm for new branches, and indeed during the mid-1890s considered closing several branches, especially Esfahan, Yazd and Mashad, which had unsatisfactory results.

During the 1900s there was some expansion in the branch network. New branches were opened at Kermanshah in 1902, Nasratabad in 1903 and

Table 3.2. *New branches of Imperial Bank 1896–1908*

Location	Date opened	
Bazaar Office, Tehran	February	1899
Kermanshah	September	1902
Nasratabad	November	1903
Kerman	March	1904

Kerman in 1904. As noted above, there was political pressure from the British government to open in all three places, but only in the case of Nasratabad was an outright subsidy paid. The Board was finally convinced that the two towns offered reasonable business prospects. Kermanshah, for example, was on the trade route between Tehran and Baghdad as well as on the route of the pilgrim trade between Persia and the Shia holy places in the Ottoman Empire.

The relationship between Chief Office and the provincial branches remained unclear. Branch Managers often acted with considerable independence of Rabino. The Board's executive functions re-inforced Managers' independent tendencies by giving the Chief Office the appearance of being *primus inter pares*, rather than the headquarters of the Bank in Persia. Individual Managers had direct access to London, and could appeal against a decision of the Chief Manager, and there were several instances when the Board supported branch Managers against Rabino.

Rabino, a man prone to sensitivity about his status, found this situation most unsatisfactory. He desired a clear brief, which included plainly stated powers of control over branch Managers. The Board, on the other hand, were cagey about defining Rabino's powers, perhaps because of a wish to retain power in their own hands. However, Rabino doggedly pursued a strategy of curbing the independence of the branches, and reducing them to the status of 'sub-branches' of Chief Office. Rasht and Esfahan were reduced to sub-branches at the turn of the century. Kermanshah was opened as a sub-branch of Tehran, and in 1904 Tabriz and Mashad were demoted from full branch to sub-branch status.

Rabino's control over the activities of branches was made particularly difficult by the absence of senior management support for him at Chief Office, and the retarded growth of an Inspection Department. There was no outright replacement for D. Baker after his resignation as Deputy Chief Manager in 1892. L. E. Dalton was appointed as Sub-Manager in Tehran, but his role as Chief Inspector considerably reduced his ability to act as Rabino's deputy. Moreover, between the end of 1895 and 1899 Dalton was almost permanently at Shiraz clearing up the bad debt problem at that branch and then acting as its Manager. In 1899 the situation was improved when the functions of Chief Inspector and Deputy Chief Manager were again separated, and H. W. Maclean, formerly Manager at Tabriz, was appointed to the latter post. But Maclean's resignation in June 1900 over the nickel contract again led to Dalton taking up the dual function. He was appointed as Acting Deputy Chief Manager, as well as Chief Inspector, a post which was confirmed as from 1 January 1903 when he became officially Deputy Chief Manager and Chief Inspector. Dalton acted as Chief Manager when Rabino was in London in 1901 and 1902. It was not until his death in a shooting accident in April 1905 that the functions were again separated, with the Chief Accountant, A. F. Grundy, becoming Deputy Chief Manager and A. F. Churchill, Acting Chief Inspector. The upshot was that for long periods of his Chief Managership, Rabino was personally burdened with the whole range of senior management responsibilities from high-level negotiations with the Persian government to trying to exercise some control over provincial managers, quite apart from the day-to-day administration of the Chief Office.

The growth of an Inspection Department was also very slow. A full inspection of branches had been carried out in 1892 by the Bank's Chief Accountant in London, but a formal Inspection Department was started in Persia on Rabino's return to Tehran after his leave in 1895. L. E. Dalton had been previously described as Inspector of Branches, a role filled in the Bank's earliest years by General Schindler, but the post was a vague one and few branch inspections had been undertaken. The new Inspection Department was, however, a very shoe-string affair. Dalton, as already mentioned, was despatched to Shiraz for four years after 1895. Moreover, the Board proved most reluctant to appoint other officers to the Inspection Department, and especially a travelling inspector who, as Rabino observed, was so essential 'in a country without mechanical means of locomotion and where the distance of branches from Chief Office varies from 200 to 800 miles'.[73] In 1900, after Dalton resumed the roles of Sub-Manager and Chief Inspector, he was finally given an assistant who could carry out the duties of travelling inspector. A further officer was allocated to the Inspection Department in the following year. Dalton's continuing role as Rabino's deputy, however, necessarily reduced his effectiveness as Chief Inspector. When the Board desired an inspection of Chief Office in July 1902 while Rabino was in London, they had to call in an outside inspector from a firm of London auditors, who went out to Persia accompanied by George Newell. The effectiveness of the Inspection Department as a whole was also reduced because Dalton's assistants were regularly sent off to act as Managers when occasion arose. Moreover, the Department experienced an abnormally high death rate. Dalton's death was followed 18 months later by that of his successor, A. F. Churchill, who died of smallpox and pneumonia, rumoured to have been contracted from purchasing old Persian carpets.[74]

3.6 REVOLUTION AND THE FALL OF RABINO

Rabino's relationship with the Board in London was rarely easy. Apart from conflicts on banking strategy and organisation, there were other disagreements. The Board was suspicious of the close relationship he had with the British Legation in Tehran, especially when Sir Arthur Hardinge was British Minister. Rabino, Newell complained in 1902, went to the Legation 'with everything'.[75] Rabino for his part frequently complained about the low quality of the British staff the Board selected for service in Persia.[76] There were disputes between Tehran and London over salaries and wages. Rabino regularly petitioned for salary increases for his staff, especially as the inflation rate rose in many areas of Persia in the 1900s, but the Board was most reluctant to raise anyone's salary.

A rather bizarre event at the end of 1901 led to permanent deterioration in the relationship between Rabino and the Board. Rabino was returning to Persia from London when L. E. Dalton telegraphed him that there had been an apparent leakage of confidential Bank documents to an Austrian concessionaire. On arriving in Tehran Rabino interviewed the Austrian, and was told that the documents had originated from someone on or close to the Board. Rabino, always inclined to impulsive gestures, despatched a peremptory letter to London complaining of this apparent breach of confidence. The Board reacted violently to Rabino's suggestion that someone on the Board could have leaked documents. He was informed that any breach of confidence must have originated in Tehran.[77] In May 1902 Rabino was ordered to appear in person before the Board. Despite his apologies for his hasty reaction before and after reaching London, on 16 July the Board, in an 'adjourned' meeting which was not officially minuted, ordered him to take immediate leave for six months on half-pay, with the question of whether he would ever return to Tehran left open. During his absence the Board ordered an independent inspection of Chief Office's books.

In December 1902 the Board decided that Rabino would be allowed to resume his post, but on strict and, for Rabino, somewhat humiliating conditions. Dalton, his Deputy, was to be consulted on all matters, and to read and initial all correspondence to and from London and between the Chief Office and the Persian government or the British Legation. The administration of Chief Office was to be improved. In addition, Rabino was instructed to have a more distant relationship with the British Legation.[78] Rabino accepted these conditions, and returned to Persia. However, a distinct coolness pervaded the relations between Rabino and the Board thereafter.

It was hardly surprising that tensions between Rabino and London began to mount as political conflict turned into Revolution in Persia. By 1903 there were already signs of growing political and social unrest. At the end of 1905 the punishment of several merchants in the bazaar for having raised the price of sugar led to a major outbreak of discontent. A group of important clergy and merchants took sanctuary (or *bast*), and calls were made for an elected or representative assembly. The government reacted by arresting or exiling some of the protest movement's leaders. Throughout the winter and spring of 1906 the situation deteriorated and the government became progressively weaker, especially after Mozaffar od-Din Shah had a stroke in May. In July a *sayyid*, a man who claimed descent from the Prophet, was killed by the army. This led, on 19 July, to the staging of a giant *bast* in the grounds of the British Legation. By the end of the month an estimated crowd of 14 000 were milling around the Legation's garden. The protest movement had by now many strands, religious and reactionary, secular and radical. After considerable vacillation, on 17 September the Shah signed a regulation for an assembly. Early in October 1906 elections were held, and on 7 October a representative assembly, or Majles, was opened. The adoption of a constitution followed on 30 December. The Shah died a week later, on 8 January 1907.[79]

The main concern of the Imperial Bank in these events was that it had lent a considerable amount of money to a government that seemed to be on the verge of disintegration. By the end of 1905 the Shah was in urgent need of funds, while the Bank had an almost equally urgent desire to achieve the repayment of some of its advances to the government. The government had borrowed from the Bank nearly £100 000 (or 6 million Krans) over the Concessionary limit. The Bank, with some help from the Legation, managed to extract a promissory note for 7 070 000 Krans (£126 250) signed by the Shah and the Prime Minister. In March 1906 this note was renewed, on the security of revenues from the Southern customs. The Bank, however, saw no sign of its money, while the Foreign Office refused to be drawn into a guarantee of the Persian government's debts.[80] Instead, requests for yet further advances multiplied. For instance, in June 1906 Naus, on the expectation that a Russian loan of 20 million Roubles (£2 100 000) would soon be signed, asked the Bank for a temporary advance of 3 million Krans (£53 600).[81]

The Bank was most reluctant to provide further accommodation for the Persian government. The great *bast* in the British Legation led to a collapse of the government's financial machinery. Throughout the disorder and confusion of the summer and autumn of 1906 Rabino struggled in vain to secure the repayment of the Bank's promissory note. The one hope seemed to be a foreign loan. In September 1906 the British and Russian governments began negotiations for a joint loan, agreeing in October on a loan of £400 000 at 7% with a first instalment of half that sum.[82] The British government went so far as to deposit £100 000 with the Imperial Bank ready to pay its half of the loan. In December a further £50 000 was deposited with the Bank in case a loan to the Valiahd became necessary in the event of his father's probable demise.

The Anglo–Russian loan, however, never materialised. The Majles which was increasingly hostile to foreign influence in Persia, refused to sign a loan agreement. Furthermore, they counterproposed that funds should be found by a National Bank to be formed with a capital of 500 million Krans (£9 million) to be raised from the Persian public. However, the scheme for a National Bank failed to get off the ground. The upshot was that the Imperial Bank was left forlornly pleading for its money.

During 1907 the confusion and unrest grew in Persia. In April, the new Shah, Mohammad Ali, summoned back the former Prime Minister, Amin os-Soltan, in an attempt to stem the chaos. By August a scheme had been worked out which would have enabled the government to arrange a foreign loan, but two events on 31 August wrecked the plan. The first was the assassination of Amin os-Soltan. The second was the signing of the Anglo–Russian Convention. The Convention caused consternation among Persians, as well as in the British Legation in Tehran which was not involved in the negotiations, for it divided Persia into spheres of influence. The Russians were allocated the north, Britain the south-east, and the remainder was to be 'neutral' territory. (Map 1 on p. 4 shows the lines of this territorial division).

Persian constitutionalists who had regarded Britain as their natural ally were stunned by Britain's willingness to co-operate with Russia in deciding Persia's fate. The Liberal government in Britain, however, saw the Convention as part of its wider concern to combat the rise of Germany by coming to terms with Russia. Indeed, it could be said that the guarantee of Persia's integrity was of greater long-term importance than her division into spheres of influence. This guarantee served to protect Persia from possible annexation by Russia in the years leading to the First World War. From the Imperial Bank's point of view, however, the Convention diminished the British government's willingness to lend to Persia. Within a week of its signing, the British government withdrew the £150 000 which had been deposited with the Imperial Bank in expectation of a British loan.

The Bank had no hope of any repayment from the Persian government for the rest of the year. As the autumn of 1906 progressed and the Shah and the Majles came increasingly into conflict, the Board had become preoccupied

I Baron Julius de Reuter (by courtesy of Reuters Limited).

II The Seal of The Imperial Bank of Persia.

III An Oil Painting of The Imperial Bank of Persia, Chief Office, Tehran, circa 1930.

IV A contemporary view of Persian Loans.

V A Persian Carpet made for The Imperial Bank of Persia patterned on a note payable at Tabriz office.

VII The redemption of Imperial Bank of Persia notes was restricted to individual branches. As this illustration shows, this was effected by means of an overstamp endorsed on the note either by hand stamping or printing.

VI A very early 1 Toman note of The Imperial Bank of Persia bearing the signature of Joseph Rabino as Chief Manager and payable only at Meshed (Mashad). (approximately two thirds actual size).

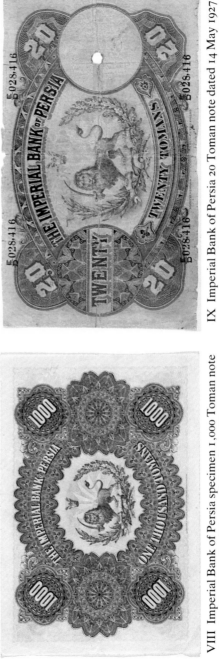

IX Imperial Bank of Persia 20 Toman note dated 14 May 1927 overstamped 'Payable at Abadan only'. The note bears the portrait of Naser od-Din Shah and is signed by V. L. Walter as Chief Accountant. The note was printed by Bradbury Wilkinson & Co Ltd. (approximately half actual size).

VIII Imperial Bank of Persia specimen 1,000 Toman note bearing the portrait of Naser od-Din Shah. The note was printed by Bradbury Wilkinson & Co Ltd. (approximately one third actual size).

X Imperial Bank of Persia 1 Toman note dated 4 August 1924. This is an example of the second series of Imperial Bank of Persia notes. It bears the signature of V. L. Walter as Chief Accountant. The overstamp shows that the note was payable only at Barfrush

XI Imperial Bank of Persia specimen 10 Toman note of the second series bearing the signature of V. L. Walter as Chief Accountant and the portrait of Mozaffar od-Din Shah. (approximately one half actual size).

with the extent of the Persian government's borrowings. A year later the government debt to the Bank had grown slightly, an increase exacerbated in sterling terms by the change in the Kran–Sterling exchange rate from 56 to 50. Total government indebtedness had stood at 21 468 608 Krans, or £383 400 at the end of 1906. By the end of 1907 it was 21 560 500 Krans, or £431 200. As the Bank's Concessionary lending limit was £216 666, the situation was looked upon with the utmost seriousness.

The Board were inclined to blame Rabino for the massive 'lock-up' of funds in government loans, and they did not like the way the debt had inexorably risen during 1906 despite all attempts to reduce it. Moreover, the extent of lending to the Persian government made London very sensitive about Rabino's lending to the private sector. After 1905 old fears about this activity resurfaced.

During 1905 and 1906 Rabino extended loans and advances to private individuals. He was convinced that this was one of the few areas where the Bank could expand its business, and he also wanted to help old customers in temporary need of funds because of the political and economic disturbances of the period. Many richer merchants were owed considerable sums by the government, and they were no more likely to receive payment than was the Imperial Bank. Rabino was by now convinced, probably over-convinced, of his skill at risk assessment of Persian borrowers. The Board, however, instinctively felt that advances should be reduced rather than extended in such disturbed times.

The Chief Manager's position was not strengthened by the disgrace of his son, Hyacinth. During 1906 an inspection of Kermanshah revealed a dismal tale of mismanagement, fraud and sheer bad lending stretching back to the early days of Hyacinth Rabino's tenure as Manager. While Rabino junior had been away on consular duties, he had most unwisely left the branch in the hands of a clever, English-educated, and ultimately dishonest Persian. An extraordinary range of misdemeanours had developed, including even the running of a retail grocery business from the Bank's premises. By the end of 1907 the bad debts at the branch were estimated at £10 000. The worst of the misdemeanours had taken place after Hyacinth had left the branch in 1905, but in July 1907 his father had had to report officially to London that his son's misplaced faith in his Persian assistant had 'led him into neglecting all proper precautions so that his action is the primary cause of the disaster'.[83] Hyacinth Rabino had in fact resigned from the Bank in early 1906, before the Kermanshah affair 'broke', to join the British consular service. Despite this and the fact that it had been London, against the advice of Rabino senior, who had appointed Hyacinth Rabino as Manager of Kermanshah, Hyacinth's disgrace cast further doubts in the Board's eyes on Rabino's abilities.

Table 3.3. *Profits from exchange and interest in Persia 1905–08*

Year end (20 Sept)	Exchange profits		Interest profits	
	Krans (millions)	Sterling equivalent	Krans (millions)	Sterling equivalent
1905	1.8	30 508	3.1	52 542
1906	1.6	28 571	3.4	60 714
1907	3.1	62 000	4.0	80 000
1908	0.6	10 714	3.9	69 643

Meanwhile, his son was written off by Board members in pejorative terms as 'that highly scented geranium'.[84]

As the full extent of the Kermanshah disaster became known, Rabino's policy on advances and loans was increasingly criticised in London. The problem was not the profitability of the business. As Table 3.3 shows, the Bank's profits from interest grew between 1905 and 1907 and surpassed exchange profits in all three years, while in 1908 earnings from interest sustained the Bank when exchange profits slumped. (The relationship between these profits and the final profit figure calculated in London is unclear, although the two moved up and down in tandem.)

Such profits, however, did not reconcile the Board to a policy of lending to the private sector during a revolution, even though non-government advances formed only a small part of the Bank's total lending. In September 1907 the Bank's loans, advances and discounts in Persia amounted to about 57.5 million Krans (£1 150 000). 75% of these loans were to the government, or were government-guaranteed, 9% were to correspondents, and only 16% to merchants and others.[85] Yet the Board regarded these latter advances with great suspicion, particularly when it became clear that one or two names carried undoubtedly high risks.

Rabino's advances to a small group of individuals during 1907 came under the special scrutiny of the Board. Direct advances to the Amin ol-Zarb, perhaps the most important Persian merchant of the period,[86] reached 1 875 000 Krans (£37 500) in March 1907. He had also acted as guarantor of advances for a larger sum, amounting to about 8.4 million Krans (£168 000). In October 1907 an inspection of Chief Office raised considerable doubts about these advances. The inspection by A. O. Wood, who had been appointed Acting Chief Inspector in October 1906 on the death of A. F. Churchill, seemed to reveal that the Bank had been financing the Amin ol-Zarb by accommodation bills. In addition, doubts were cast on the value of the securities deposited against his liability. The Amin ol-Zarb had deposited with the Bank jewels worth 531 550 Krans (£10 630) and title deeds of property worth 7.3 million Krans (£146 000). Moreover, the Amin ol-Zarb's account seemed as if it might be the tip of a very unsatisfactory iceberg.[87]

Wood's reports reinforced the opinion of the Board in London that Rabino's advances had got out of hand. At the end of December 1907 the Board despatched £40 000 in silver from London on Wood's advice that the cash position of Tehran office was dangerously low. Wood's actions infuriated Rabino, as did the Board's immediate inclination to believe Wood's version of the situation rather than the Chief Manager's. In his memoirs, written in 1915, Rabino catalogued the indignities the Board had subjected him to over the years, as well as observing the melancholy fate that awaited the Board's servants:

The Sub-Manager (Mr L E Dalton) was invited to send home private letters by every mail which I was not to see but any of my private letters had to be countersigned by him ... he even showed me a private telegram from the Chairman asking him to draw up a report which the Board could use against me. The Sub-Manager shot himself accidently and died very shortly afterwards. Then a second assistant (Mr Alfred F. Churchill) was sent out whose orders were, evidently, to make my position untenable by continual insubordination and private reports. He died of small-pox. Lastly the present Manager (Mr A. O. Wood) was sent out with similar instructions. Aided by the Accountant (Mr David Brown) he drew up a most insulting and mendacious report on the balance sheet which he declared was false if not fraudulent.[88]

Rabino was particularly annoyed by Wood's allegations about the security of his advances, and by the Board's willingness to accept the opinion of his subordinates. 'The bills I declare to be sound and genuine', he complained to the Chairman in January 1908, have been declared to be 'mere valueless fabrications.'[89] Sir Lepel Griffin's reply did nothing to reassure Rabino as to his position. On 19 February Rabino offered his resignation. This was accepted, but he was told to remain in Tehran until Chief Office's accounts were in order.

Rabino's final six months in Tehran were uncomfortable and sad. One final transaction reduced the Board's opinion of him even further. Under orders from London to reduce the Amin ol-Zarb's debt, Rabino received 800 000 Krans (£14 286) from him, and in return surrendered the property deeds worth 7.3 million Krans. The Board had dismissed these deeds as worthless, 'notes of the Bank of Elegance', but they were nevertheless outraged at his action.[90]

These last months of Rabino's Chief Managership saw disorder reigning in Persia. In June 1908 the Shah used the Cossack Brigade to disperse the Majles. Rebellion broke out in several towns, and especially in Tabriz. As Rabino left Persia in August 1908, the country in which he had lived for nearly 20 years seemed on the brink of inexorable disintegration.

Rabino was never to return to Persia, despite repeated rumours that he would go back. His name was mentioned by the German interests still planning a German bank for Persia, but this scheme was never successful.[91] Rabino was also rumoured to be a potential Manager of the proposed national bank, but such a bank never materialised until 1928. And so Rabino returned to England where he lived in retirement until his death, in London, on 9 September 1919, aged 76.

Rabino had been the single most important figure in the Imperial Bank's establishment and development in Persia. He had guided it through one crisis after another, from the struggle to survive in the early 1890s to the political upheavals of his last few days. When he left Persia the Imperial Bank was still making profits. The contrast with the ruined Russian Bank would have been obvious to everyone in Persia. The Board, however, were in London rather than in Persia, and they saw only an egotistical little man with a foreign sounding name who had 'locked up' their shareholders' funds. There was little gratitude for Rabino's achievements. Sir Thomas Jackson, who succeeded as Chairman after Sir Lepel Griffin's death on 9 March 1908, did observe to the shareholders at the Bank's nineteenth ordinary general meeting that Rabino had devoted 'unwearied attention to the interest of the Bank'. But the Board's private feelings were more revealing. Caesar Hawkins, sent out to Tehran during Rabino's last months, observed that as soon as Rabino's resignation had been made public, British members of the Bank's staff had started to criticise the Chief Manager. 'I think the following remark', Hawkins wrote to Jackson in July 1908, 'is worth recording which was made by one of them – "The IBP is now going to be a white man's bank not a Levantines."'[92] It was a less than generous epitaph to the man without whom the Imperial Bank might never have survived.

4

BANKING FOR GOVERNMENTS 1909–14

4.1 THE BANK UNDER WOOD

Augustus Ottiwell Wood, Rabino's successor as Chief Manager, had joined the Imperial Bank in February 1893 at the age of 28, after previously being employed at the Bombay branch of the New Oriental Bank Corporation.

Wood served in the south of Persia for 13 years after joining the Imperial Bank. Between 1893 and 1898 he was first Accountant, and then Acting Manager at Bushire. In November 1898 he became Manager at Esfahan. But Wood made his real impact so far as London were concerned through his skills as an inspector. In 1906 he inspected the confused affairs of the Shiraz and Bushire branches. His report was favourably received in London, to the extent that he was granted a £100 bonus. Wood was then offered the Managership of the Shiraz branch, but declined it on health grounds as he had had a history of fever in Bushire and did not wish to experience a similar climate again. In October 1906 he was appointed Acting Chief Inspector after the death of A. F. Churchill. It was in this capacity that, in October 1907, Wood had inspected Chief Office and revealed, in the Board's eyes, Rabino's shortcomings. Moreover, Wood seemed the obvious replacement for Rabino, and in June 1908 he was nominated Chief Manager, and assumed this post in August.

Wood developed a good working relationship with London. He had none of Rabino's flamboyant characteristics, and the Board seem to have felt considerably more at ease with his solid and thoroughly English personality. The new Chief Manager's views mirrored those of his Board. He had little faith in Persians or their country. '"Nationalist" and "Constitutionalist"', he observed to Newell about the reform movement in Persia, 'are mere catch words now and are employed to cloak all the rascality that goes on throughout the country.'[1] An underlying assumption that Persians were rascals and rogues, and indeed that non-English speaking peoples in general were unreliable, coloured Wood's policies. The Board felt that they could trust a man with such views, and a measure of their satisfaction was that in 1920, after his retirement in October 1919, he was made a director.

There were considerable changes in the composition of the Board between 1909 and 1914, following the deaths of most of the longest serving directors. George de Reuter died in 1909, Sir George Mackenzie in 1910, William Keswick in 1912, Henry Coke in 1913 and General Sir T. E. Gordon in 1914.

Their replacements came, in a now familiar pattern, from representatives of other British commercial interests in Persia, descendants and associates of original founders of the Bank, and retired civil servants with Indian or Foreign Office experience. W. A. Buchanan, who was elected in 1910 and was to remain a director until his death in 1945, and was a partner in the Gulf trading firms Gray, Paul and Company and Gray, Mackenzie and Company, and was therefore the direct replacement for Sir George Mackenzie. Charles Greenway, also elected in 1910, was Managing Director of the Anglo–Persian Oil Company. This company had been formed after the discovery of large reserves of oil in 1908 at Meydan-e Naftun in south-west Persia, by British interests working on the basis of the concession granted to William Knox D'Arcy in 1901.[2] The Bank and the oil company became the two leading British commercial institutions in Persia. In 1912 another new director arrived when Henry Keswick MP took his deceased father's place, although he resigned in the following year.

In 1913 Sir Hugh Barnes joined the Board. Barnes was in the mould of Sir Lepel Griffin and General Sir T. E. Gordon. He had served with the Indian Civil Service, becoming the Lieutenant Governor of Burma between 1903 and 1905 and a member of the Council of India between 1905 and 1913. He had become a director of Anglo–Persian in 1909. A solid rather than inspiring character – one Foreign Office official described him as 'remarkably dense and slow at the uptake'[3] – Barnes was to be appointed Chairman of the Imperial Bank in 1916 and serve in that capacity until 1937.

Two further directors were appointed in 1914. Frederick D. Sassoon became the second member of his family to sit on the Bank's Board. Also appointed was Lord Inchcape, the Chairman of the British India Steam Navigation Company, and a well-known figure in shipping and eastern affairs. He was also appointed one of the two directors representing the British government on the Board of Anglo–Persian following its purchase of a controlling interest in the Company in 1914.[4]

The change of Chief Manager did nothing to reverse the expansionary trend in the Bank's business which had begun in 1904. The growth in several aspects of the Bank's business continued at a marked pace until 1913. The note issue expanded by 124% between 1908 and 1913, increasing by more in five years than in the previous 13, and reaching £962 419 in 1913. Deposits increased by 49% between 1908 and 1913, and stood at £905 995 in that year. The level of bills discounted, loans and advances remained stagnant. In 1912 they fell to £723 782, and in 1914 stood at £1 127 669, a lower figure than in 1890. The ratio of advances to deposits and note issue showed a further decline, being at a low point of 46% in 1912 before rising to 74% in 1914. The outbreak of the First World War in August 1914, and a fall in the Kran's value against Sterling, meant that the September 1914 balance sheet showed falls in many items, with deposits declining to £695 367 and the note issue to £832 011.

Investments grew by over 200% between 1908, when they had fallen to a low level because of the Bank's need to increase its cash reserves, and 1914. The Imperial Bank's portfolio contained, as it had since 1900, a large amount of British government, Colonial and municipal stocks. However, the 90% increase in investments shown in 1911 was primarily due to the taking of a substantial holding in the new Persian Loan issued in that year, an investment which will be discussed later in this chapter. The Bank also regularly made small investments – between £5000 and £25 000 – in stock issued by, or involving, banks and firms with which it had special connections, and it sometimes underwrote parts of such issues. In the mid-1900s, for example, the Imperial Bank invested in the Chinese government and railway, and Japanese government, loans which the Hongkong Bank managed. Again, small investments, not exceeding £20 000, were made between 1908 and 1914 in South American and Russian municipal and railway loans managed by J. Henry Schröder, for most of which the firm W. Greenwell, one of the four founders of the Imperial Bank in 1889, acted as brokers. The Bank's investments were certainly not confined to loans handled by friends – in 1909 and 1910 there was a spate of purchases of American and Mexican railway stock where no 'special' connection existed – but it definitely had a circle of contacts in the City, the most important of whom were the Hongkong Bank, J. Henry Schröder, and W. Greenwell, in whose loan issues it took a special interest.

Published shareholders' funds grew slowly between 1908 and 1914. In 1914 they stood at £903 358, a 3% growth over 1908. The really striking feature of the pre-War years was the large increase in the Bank's inner reserves, which rose from £46 051 in 1908 to £143 438 in 1914. In 1908 inner reserves amounted to 25% of published reserves, but in 1914 this proportion had risen to 68%. In one year, 1911, internal Bank evidence establishes that £61 192 out of the total inner reserve of £118 117 was provision for doubtful accounts,[5] but the absence of information for other years means it is impossible to be sure whether in general around 50% of the

Table 4.1. *Imperial Bank's profits 1909–14 (£ Sterling)*

	Published net profits	Movement through inner reserves	
Year ending (20 September)	(after transfers to inner reserves)	Transfers from profits	Bad debts recovered (or provided for)
1909	47 985	nil	2041
1910	58 447	49 000	(2580)
1911	64 501	23 000	603
1912	53 538	10 000	518
1913	51 149	nil	(1737)
1914	31 244	20 000	(3647)

inner reserve was unallocated. But it is clear that the Board had a preference, no doubt strengthened by the perceived risks of banking in Persia in this period, to keep large funds available for use at its discretion rather than to apply them to strengthening their published balance sheet.

The growth of the inner reserves indicates that the Bank's profits in these years were higher than its published figures suggested. Table 4.1 shows that this was indeed the case, for substantial transfers to inner reserves were made before the published profit figure was reached. (The table also shows the use of inner reserves to meet bad debts.)

The use of inner reserves to smooth fluctuations in results is again clear. If the Bank's 'real' profits are taken as published profits plus transfers to inner reserves, they were 124% higher in 1910 than in 1909. Yet the published figure showed only a 22% increase. And while the 1914 net profit figure showed a 39% fall over the previous year, 'real profits' as defined above stayed almost the same. In 'real profit' terms, the Bank's fortunes peaked in 1910 and 1911, while profits for 1913 and 1914 were less than 50% of the 1910 level.

Shareholders were rewarded for the Bank's good performance in the two peak years, even if they did not know the dimensions of that performance. A dividend of 8/- per share was paid in 1909, as it had been since 1904, but in 1910 this was increased to 9/- and in 1911 to 10/-. This higher figure was maintained in the two following years, but in 1914 the Bank's determination to make provision against the exigencies of war led to a decision to lower the dividend to 8/-.

The Bank, therefore, had maintained its respectable growth in the pre-War years, and earned higher than usual profits in 1910 and 1911. It must be said that by the standards of the major English clearing banks the Imperial Bank's business remained small indeed. The Midland Bank, for example, expanded its deposits from £67 million in 1908 to £126 million in 1914. But Persia was a very different banking market from England.

Indeed, the political situation in Persia in the six years before the outbreak of the First World War was particularly disturbed. The political pendulum fluctuated sharply. In November 1908 Mohammad Ali Shah issued a Rescript declaring the constitutional system contrary to the laws of Islam. By January 1909 Tabriz, the main centre of opposition, was surrounded by the Shah's forces. Four months later, however, Anglo–Russian pressure forced the Shah to lift the siege. In July revolutionaries from the northern cities and Bakhtiaris from Esfahan stormed Tehran and deposed and exiled the Shah. Mohammad Ali's 12-year-old son, Ahmad, was installed in his father's place under the tutelage of a Regent.

The staff of the Imperial Bank remained calm, and working, in the middle of the Constitutional Revolution, and *sang-froid* prevailed. The Bank stayed open in Tabriz when the city was under siege in the latter half of 1908, despite the closure of the bazaars for three months and a direct hit from a shell on the wall of the Bank's compound. In the following year, when Tehran was under bombardment by the nationalists, the reaction was the same. Wood and his Deputy, S. F. Rogers, slept at the Bank. Wood described the situation in July 1909 in a report to London.

The square is held by a few hundred Persian regulars and nondescripts of sorts who loose off the whole night long just to show they are awake; and what with the bombs and ill directed shells sleep is impossible. Last night both our bedrooms ... were pierced by shrapnel, but we were in bed in a safe place.[6]

In November 1909 a Second Majles opened and an age of reform seemed to have dawned. Foreigners were recruited to plan and implement reforms, a development which culminated in the appointment as Treasurer General of an American, W. Morgan Shuster in May 1911. Shuster established excellent relations with the Majles as he tried to steer an independent course between Britain and Russia, but his stay in Persia was short. In July the former Shah, with the connivance of Russia, landed on the Caspian shore of Persia with an invading army, and caused much disruption until he was driven out again in September. Shuster's deteriorating relations with the Russians caused his dismissal in December 1911 after Russian troops had threatened to occupy Tehran.[7] The Majles was once again dissolved. December 1911 is usually taken as the end of the Constitutional Revolution. It was not, however, the end of Persia's disintegration. Over the next 30 months the power of central government waned, and the provinces gained increasing autonomy. In July 1914 Ahmad Shah was crowned at the age of 17. He was to be the last Qajar ruler.

Internal disintegration was accompanied by growing foreign encroachments on Persia's sovereignty. The Anglo–Russian Convention in 1907 may have prevented the complete dismemberment of Persia, but British and Russian influence in their respective spheres of influence grew steadily in its wake. Azerbaijan province came under the almost complete control of the Russians. In 1912 Russian troops brutally suppressed a rising in Tabriz and bombarded the sacred shrine at Mashad, an action which caused outrage throughout Persia. In the south, British troops landed at Bushire in October 1911 in response to an upsurge of tribal disorder, and before long small detachments were also stationed in Shiraz and Esfahan. It was with such foreign encroachments in view that Shuster published, after his dismissal and return to America, his book called *The Strangling of Persia*.[8]

Yet Persia was not strangled. When the First World War began in August 1914 the country was still independent. This chapter will argue that the Imperial Bank made an important contribution to the survival of Persia's independence.

4.2 THE BANK AS THE STATE BANK

The financial position of Persian governments deteriorated further in the pre-War period. The loss of control over large areas of the country diminished the fiscal base of the central government. Western-owned commercial ventures made little contribution. The Imperial Bank was exempted by its Concession from taxes and customs dues, and paid only a modest sum – averaging £4077 per annum between 1909 and 1914 – for its privilege of note issue. The birth of Persia's oil industry brought no revenue at all. The Anglo–Persian Oil Company constructed a pipeline to take the oil to a refinery at Abadan, and in May 1912 the first cargo of crude oil was exported, but the Persian government's royalties were linked to Anglo–Persian's profits, and the oil company declared no profits before 1915.[9]

Nevertheless the reforms undertaken by foreign advisers had positive effects. The Belgians had brought some order into administration, and Shuster, who had had experience in sorting out the finances of Cuba and the Philippines, continued to work in the same direction during his tenure of office. Shuster's Belgian successor, J. Mornard, maintained this work. However, to some extent the main achievement of the Belgians and Shuster was to give Persian governments an indication of the extent of their financial plight. In 1913 Mornard managed to construct a government 'budget', which showed annual receipts of around £2 million and annual expenditure at £1.6 million. His estimates were recognised to contain a high margin of error, with the revenue figures in particular regarded as optimistic, but the compilation of any kind of statistics was an achievement. Mornard's calculation that about a third of government funds were being consumed by debt servicing and the remainder by 'administration' seems to have been the right order of magnitude.[10]

The Imperial Bank played an important role in the attempts to reform the administration, and an indispensable role in staving off the bankruptcy of the Persian government. 'Under most difficult and complicated circumstances', Shuster wrote to Wood in January 1912 after his dismissal, 'I have ever found a disposition on the part of yourself and other officials of the Imperial Bank to serve the best interests of the Persian government, and to co-operate with the officials of the Persian government in reforming their financial methods and systems.'[11]

The rest of this section will examine the ways in which the Imperial Bank served 'the best interests of the Persian government' by arranging finance, collecting revenues and in currency matters, but it should be observed here that the Bank's support was not consistent. At the behest of the British government, as will be seen later, the Bank declined to assist Mohammad Ali Shah's government. Wood himself had little initial confidence in the succeeding Constitutional government which was formed in the middle of 1909. On the other hand, he was enthusiastic about Shuster, and made considerable efforts to help him. In contrast, Wood's relations with Mornard were initially cool, reflecting his conviction that the Belgians were Russian surrogates. However, familiarity bred a degree of respect and during 1913 the Bank entered another period of close co-operation with the central government.

Financing the government

Persian governments were increasingly forced to borrow to meet their financial requirements before 1914. The government borrowed funds from three different sources – the Imperial Bank, a new loan on the London Stock Exchange, and the British and Russian governments. The Bank was involved, in different ways, in all three types of government borrowing and, as this matter was so important yet has received practically no attention from historians, it will be necessary to explore it in some depth.

The Bank continued to make advances to the Persian government. The outstanding balances of these advances at various dates are shown in Table 4.2. The actual sums owed by the government in fact often rose higher than these figures would suggest, as the Bank would make a determined effort to reduce the level of outstandings before each half-year and year end.

The Imperial Bank's advances, which exceeded the Concessionary lending limit for most years except 1912 and 1913, played an essential role in

Table 4.2. *Imperial Bank advances (outstanding balances) to Persian government 1908–14*

Date	Comment	Balance in Krans	Sterling equivalent	Interest rate per annum
September 1908		27 766 140	495 823	12%
September 1909		34 565 100	628 456	12%
May 1910	Amalgamated loan	33 966 974	617 581	7%
March 1911		36 185 270	663 949	7%
September 1911		38 150 000	700 000	7%
March 1912		3 300 000	60 000	7%
September 1913		9 543 710	173 522	7%
September 1914		12 682 340	211 372	7%

financing the government, which on several occasions was only able to meet pressing obligations because of them. The Bank advances paid some of the Army, and especially the Swedish-officered gendarmerie formed in this period, and thereby ensured that a central government presence was maintained in parts of Persia. Moreover, the Bank's advances enabled Persia to meet sufficient of its debt repayments to the British and Russian governments that they were never either compelled or given an excuse to end Persia's independence. For their part, Persian governments regarded borrowing from the Bank as preferable to borrowing from foreign governments, whose loans carried political conditions, while alternative sources of borrowing within Persia were in short supply in the pre-war period. The fortunes of many larger *sarrafs*, traditional lenders to government, were adversely affected by the political disturbances of the period, while the Russian Bank in the pre-War period was moribund and overwhelmed by a portfolio of bad debts.[12]

However, there was a strong element of symbiosis in the Bank's relationship with government. Lending to the government was valuable business, and between 1909 and 1914 at least 60% of the Bank's total loans, advances and discounts was often allocated to this sector. It was a profitable activity, as long as the government met its interest payments. It was considered safer than lending to Persian merchants, and it also provided the Bank with a lever to expand its influence over government.

During the first two years of Wood's Chief Managership, however, the Bank extended further credit to Persian governments only with the greatest reluctance. This was partly in response to the policy of the British government. The Bank agreed, in February 1909, under Foreign Office pressure, not to lend 'a penny further' to Mohammad Ali Shah.[13] But Wood was also unwilling to assist the subsequent Constitutional government. Between August and December 1909 that government made several urgent requests to the Bank for financial assistance, but met with a cool response. Nevertheless, the government debt to the Bank did rise in this period, as few if any interest payments were met, a factor which explains in large part the Bank's low 'real profits' in 1909.

During the opening months of 1910, however, Wood became more sympathetic when the Persian government proposed a wide-ranging scheme for a rescheduling and consolidation of its debt to the Bank. During the subsequent negotiations the Foreign Office intimated that the 1903–04 Anglo–Indian loans should also be included, and these were duly incorporated into the terms of a Loan Amalgamation agreement signed on 27 May 1910.

Under the terms of this agreement, the Bank's advances to government (except for silver) were amalgamated into a single sum, amounting to the Kran equivalent of £617 581, and the interest rate was reduced from 12% to 7% per annum.[14] Capital and interest were to be redeemed within 15 years, but the government was given the option of liquidating the advance after one year. The £314 282 owed on the 1903–04 Anglo–Indian loans was also to be repaid over 15 years, at 5% per annum interest. (The interest rate differential reflected the difference in currency risk between loans which were to be repaid in Britain, which carried the lower interest, and loans due for repayment in Persia). The great advantage to the Bank of the Loan Amalgamation was that it held the promise of more regular debt repayments. The government was to pay the customs revenues of the Gulf ports into the Bank every month. The Bank was permitted to deduct the money it was owed from these revenues before any other payments were made. The 1903–04 Anglo–Indian loans had taken as security, firstly the revenues from the Caspian Fisheries, then of the posts and telegraphs, and then of the Gulf ports, but under the Amalgamation Agreement the repayments for the Anglo–Indian loans from the Gulf customs revenues were only to be made if there was any surplus left after the Bank had been paid.

During the following months the agreement proved a success. The government met its debt repayments to the Bank, and the resulting surge in interest earnings was an important factor in the rise in 'real profits' in 1910. But a familiar pattern soon reasserted itself. As expenditure outstripped revenue, the government began to seek further accommodation. Wood was now more co-operative, especially in view of the good prospects that a new Sterling Loan would be floated in London for the government (see below). Between December 1910 and March 1911 he advanced nearly 2 million Krans (around £36 700) to the government against the anticipated proceeds

Table 4.3. *Imperial Bank advances for silver importation and minting 1910–14*
(outstanding balances)

Date	Balance in Krans	Sterling equivalent	Interest rate per annum
March 1910	5 113 110	93 000	9%
September 1910	13 985 870	254 288	9%
September 1911	5 068 500	93 000	5%
March 1912	20 350 000	370 000	5%
September 1913	5 861 700	106 576	5%
September 1914	10 510 330	175 000	5%

of the prospective Sterling Loan. Yet by the spring of 1911 another major financial crisis seemed inevitable.

These circumstances help to explain the enthusiasm of Wood for Shuster, and the promise that the state's finances would finally be put on a firmer basis. Shuster's request for an advance of 2.4 million Krans (£45 870) to tide him over while he straightened out the country's finances was readily granted. And within a few months the proceeds of the 1911 Loan enabled Shuster sharply to reduce the government's debt to the Bank. By September 1911 the Bank's advances to the government had reached £700 000. This was practically all paid off as a result of the Sterling Loan, and in March 1912 the Bank's advances to the government had fallen to a mere £60 000.

This was the lowest level of the government's indebtedness to the Bank. By the autumn of 1912 Mornard was pleading for assistance from the Bank. In November and December Wood advanced 1.2 million Krans (£21 820) to pay the salaries of the Swedish gendarmerie. Then, at the beginning of 1913, Mornard agreed to pay a number of tax receipts into the Bank as security against further advances, and on this basis Wood began extending further advances. By 31 August 1914 the government debt exceeded £300 000 but this had been brought down to £211 372 by the time of the Bank's year-end on 20 September.

In addition to these direct Bank advances to the Persian government, the Bank also advanced funds after 1910 against the import of silver, and this too became an important source of government borrowing. The sums involved are shown in Table 4.3.

Between 1908 and 1910 the Bank had continued to import silver for minting in Persia, and it was able to take advantage of favourable market rates to secure good exchange profits on these operations. The Bank calculated that its total profits on the importation of silver between September 1908 and September 1910 amounted to £91 578.[15] In March 1910, however, a new agreement was signed with the Persian government which radically changed the nature of the silver business.[16] The government assumed a monopoly over the import of silver and, for one year, appointed the Imperial Bank as its sole agent. The Bank had in fact suggested such a move on several occasions, and it held the prospects of good profits. Under the initial contract, the Bank was to import some £960 000 of silver, although this could be reduced if exchange rate or silver price fluctuations made the proposition unprofitable. The Bank was to be paid a commission of 0.25% on all silver imported, calculated on the Sterling cost of silver and payable in Krans. The Bank, for its part, agreed to advance, at an interest rate of 9% per annum, the necessary sums for the purchase of silver, up to a limit of £200 000. The Bank was to have a lien on all the silver until it was actually minted as security for the sums advanced.

Over the next four years the Imperial Bank found itself advancing large sums to the Persian government under the terms of the March 1910 and succeeding agreements. Each advance lasted from the time the Bank purchased silver in London until the time when it was repaid in minted silver coin in Persia. Delays in shipping the silver, and backlogs at the Mint, often made this interval a long one and, as Table 4.3 indicates, the Bank's advances against silver were substantial. In early 1912, after the 1911 Sterling Loan had paid off most of the Bank's direct advances, it still had £370 000 advanced to the government for silver purchases.

The only major change in the arrangements agreed in March 1910 came in April 1911, when the Bank signed a further one year silver contract. The Russians had bitterly complained about the granting of the sole silver import agency to the Imperial Bank.[17] The Russian Bank bid for the business, and although the Persian government had no wish to see the Russians involved in silver importation, the existence of competition was used to get the rate of interest charged by the Imperial Bank reduced to 5% per annum, and the overall limit on Bank advances for silver increased to £300 000.

Shuster's period in office gave the Imperial Bank a further opportunity to expand this business. In November 1911 Shuster and Wood signed a ten-year sole agency agreement, to take effect from 22 March 1912. The longer duration of the contract was partly compensated for by a reduction of the Bank's commission on the value of silver imported to 0.125%.[18] This coup was challenged, however, in the new political circumstances following Shuster's dismissal and the disbanding of the Majles. Shuster's right to have signed the ten-year agreement was questioned. The British Minister in Tehran complained that the agreement imposed an unnecessary strain on Anglo–Russian relations.[19] The Russian Bank came up with a draft contract of its own, offering the Persians more favourable terms than the Imperial Bank.[20] In July 1913 the Foreign Office definitely ruled that it would not support the validity of Shuster's agreement, and in a good diplomatic compromise proposed that silver importation should be divided between the Imperial Bank and the Russian Bank.[21] The opinion of the Persian government, which as late as July 1913 had suggested a three-year contract exclusively with the Imperial Bank, was disregarded by Whitehall.[22] The Imperial Bank's Board was not prepared to come into fundamental conflict with the Foreign Office, and agreed to its suggestion so long as it retained its right to import sufficient silver to cover its note issue.

At a meeting on 3 February 1914, attended by Sir Thomas Jackson and several other directors, and representatives of the Russian government and the Russian Bank, it was agreed that the Imperial Bank and the Lending Bank of Persia should share between them the import of silver for the Persian government.[23] The Russian victory, however, was a pyrrhic one. The Russian Bank was in no position to undertake silver importing, and the Russians had not even approached the Persian government on the matter by the time the First World War broke out. The Imperial Bank continued to import silver under the 1911 contract renewed on an annual basis. By September 1914 the Bank had £175 000 advanced to the government on the silver account.

The Persian government's second source of borrowing, leaving aside advances from the Imperial Bank, was the flotation of a new loan on the London market. This was achieved in 1911, and the Bank was again directly involved.

The negotiations which led to the 1911 Loan, like all the pre-War Persian loan negotiations, were tortuous, because of the involvement of a large number of parties, including the Persian government and Majles, the British and Russian governments, the Imperial Bank and various London financial institutions.[24] A Sterling loan floated in London offered the promise of a large injection of funds into Persian government coffers without the political conditions of a British or Russian government loan, but this very fact made those two governments wary of allowing the Persians to arrange such a loan. The British government was eager to see the 'regeneration' of Persia, but was determined that this had to be orchestrated by the British and Russian governments rather than by commercial interests which might open the door to other parties. During the early months of 1910 several attempts by London financiers to raise money for Persia were foiled by pressure from the British and Russian governments. This was unfortunate since in 1910 the London market, in view of the emergence of the new Persian constitutional government, seemed to take a more favourable view on lending to Persia than it had for two decades. The Foreign Office, however, dampened enthusiasm by making it known that, as long as the Persian government remained so heavily indebted to the British and Russian governments and the British and

Russian banks, they would allow no hypothecation of Persian revenues as security for any private advance.

In July 1910 the situation changed. The Foreign Office abandoned all hope of an official Anglo–Russian government loan and there was also a growing danger that an undesirable third party, such as German banking interests, might step in to meet the Persian government's requirements. The Foreign Office therefore gave the green light to the two well-established merchant banks which had expressed an interest in a Persian loan, M. Samuel & Son and Seligmans, an Anglo–American house, to proceed with their loan offers and, at the same time, the Anglo–Persian Oil Company was encouraged to consider floating a loan.

The Imperial Bank remained detached from the subsequent round of loan negotiations, until, on 10 October, the Persian government formally applied to Seligmans for a loan of £1.2 million, secured by a first lien on the Southern customs. The Bank realised, as soon as a serious loan offer was on the cards, that the security it traditionally depended upon in lending to the government was in danger of being hypothecated elsewhere. The Foreign Office and the Bank were in close touch from the moment the Seligman loan proposal was on the table. The Foreign Office immediately expressed reservations about Seligmans' international, and allegedly German, connections and moved quickly to prevent the loan becoming a reality by informing Seligmans that their offer was not in the national interest, and in effect obliging them to withdraw it. As Seligmans were a highly respectable and conservative institution,[25] the Foreign Office resolve to keep Persian government business in hands it knew and trusted was clear. The Foreign Office, therefore, encouraged the Imperial Bank to make a counter offer.[26] Yet the need to obtain a letter of assurance from the Foreign Office, such as had been proposed for the abortive 1898 loan, for insertion in the Prospectus, upholding the proposed loan contract as binding on the Persian government, meant that it was not until 11 November that the Bank was able to make a firm loan offer. The proposal was for a loan of £1 250 000, of which the Persian government was to receive 87.5%, at 5% per annum interest. All the charges were to be paid by the Imperial Bank, including a final settlement of the still outstanding Lottery Syndicate claim.[27]

The Bank's loan offer was a pleasant surprise to the Persian government, as Seligmans had intended to issue a £1.2 million loan at 84 or 85, but as so often there were further complications. The Russian government was insistent that no loan contract could be signed until an agreement had been reached on the amalgamation of Persia's debts to the Russian Bank. It was not until 10 January 1911 that the Persian government signed such an Amalgamation Agreement with the Russian Bank, under which government debts to the Bank were consolidated into a unified sum of 60.5 million Krans (£1 110 000) at 7% interest repayable over 15 years. The assassination of the Persian Finance Minister, opposition in the Majles, and the Coronation celebrations in London for King George V, caused further delays, and it was not until 13 July that the Imperial Bank issued the 1911 Persian government 5% Loan on the London market.

The £1 250 000 Loan was issued on the market at 96.5. It was redeemable at par by means of a cumulative sinking fund of 0.5% per annum starting in 1916 and extending over a period not longer than 50 years. The Persian government had the right to redeem the Loan at any time after 1916 on giving six months' notice. The security for the Loan was to be a first lien on the Gulf customs, subject only to prior charges of £15 714 per annum for three years, and £30 278 per annum from 1913 to 1928, required for the 1903–04 Anglo–Indian loans. All customs receipts were to be paid into the Bank, without deduction except for administration expenses. If customs receipts fell short of the amount required for the service of the Loan and the customs administration, the Persian government bound itself to make up any deficiency from other sources of revenue.

There was no repetition of the 1892 Loan fiasco. W. Greenwell assembled an underwriting list, and a small committee consisting of Caesar Hawkins, Charles Greenway and George Newell arranged the final allotments.[28] The Imperial Bank allotted itself £119 640 of the issue, and during August and October made further purchases to bring its total holding to £332 889. The Bank, therefore, contributed 30% of the funds raised by the Loan, which can in this respect be seen as a refinancing operation under which some of its advances were liquidated, and some transformed into a loan carrying a British government guarantee. The Bank's participation in the 1911 Loan and its silver advances meant that even in March 1912, when its lending to government was ostensibly at a low point, the Bank was in fact exposed to the extent of over £760 000, 47.5% of total annual government expenditure as calculated by Mornard in the following year.

Meanwhile, Greenwell used the Imperial Bank's circle of contacts in the City to place the rest of the issue. The Hongkong Bank took £20 000 of the issue, and the British and Chinese Corporation, the joint venture owned by the Hongkong Bank and Jardine, Matheson and whose chairman was William Keswick, subscribed £25 000. The Chinese Central Railways Company, which was closely linked with the British and Chinese Corporation and for whom the Hongkong Bank acted as agent, took a further £15 000. The Sassoons also participated in the Loan, the firms of David Sassoon and Co. and E. D. Sassoon & Co. taking between them £25 000, while the banking department of Reuters News Agency took a further £20 000. The wider connections of directors were also utilised. The Union Discount Company, of which Sir Thomas Jackson was a director, took £20 000 of bonds. The Bank of West Africa, where Henry Coke was a director, took £15 000. And the British and Foreign General Securities and Investment Trust Limited, whose Chairman was Charles Greenway, took £25 000.

These preparations helped to guarantee that the 1911 Loan was well-received by the Stock Exchange and it was fully taken up. But it made little impression on the Persian government's financial plight. The issue, at 96.5, raised £1 206 250. The Persian government, as agreed, received 87.5% of the Loan's nominal value, or £1 093 750. The difference went to the Bank to meet issuing costs, commission and compensation to the Lottery Syndicate. After paying off the Bank's Amalgamated Loan, the residue was largely committed to equipping and paying for the army despatched to deal with the invasion of Mohammad Ali Shah.[29] By the end of August 1911 the government's proceeds from the Loan had been exhausted.

As a result the Persian government was increasingly obliged to resort to its third source of external borrowing, foreign government loans. Again the Imperial Bank was involved, not as a lender but as the channel through which British government loans were made to Persia. This aspect of Persia's indebtedness has been well-examined by historians, and so it will only be dealt with briefly here.

Between 1906 and 1912 there were prolonged but fruitless negotiations about an Anglo–Russian government advance to Persia. The situation alternated between the Persian government wanting a loan but the British and Russian governments refusing to make one, and the British and Russians offering money, but the Persians refusing to take it because of attached strings. By 1912, however, Persian finances were such that strings had to be accepted. In February an Anglo–Russian advance of £200 000 was offered, on condition that a considerable proportion of the money was earmarked for the Swedish-officered gendarmerie, that the Persian government reached a settlement with Mohammad Ali Shah in order to remove him and his army from Persia, and that Persian ministers generally agreed to follow British and Russian dictates.[30] The Persian government accepted these conditions, and in March the advance was made. Several further advances were made later in the year, and by the end of 1912 the British government had advanced £140 000 to Persia, and the Russians a further £125 000. The interest on all the loans was 7% per annum, and the Imperial Bank received a commission of 1% per annum on the British advances. Table 4.4 lists the British and Russian loans to Persia in this period, including the consolidations of 1910 and 1911 which amalgamated past accumulated loans.

There were further British and Russian advances in 1913, although the

Table 4.4. *Foreign Government Loans 1910–14*[a]

Date	Source	Amount in Sterling	Interest per annum
May 1910	Amalgamated Anglo–Indian Loan	314 282	5%
January 1911	Amalgamated Russian Loan	1 110 000	7%
1912	Britain	140 000	7%
1912	Russia	125 000	7%
1913	Russia	200 000	7%
April 1913	Britain	200 000	7%
May 1913	Britain	100 000	7%
June 1914	Britain	50 000	7%

Note: [a] A proportion of the 'British' Loans was supplied by the Government of India.

political strings extended with each loan. In April 1913 the British and Russian governments agreed to advance a total of £400 000, the British share of the advance specifying that a certain proportion of the loan was to be set aside for the administration of Fars, and for the construction of a new customs house in Bushire.[31] In May 1913 a further British advance of £100 000 was made, specifically for the support of the gendarmerie. The whole amount was deposited with the Imperial Bank in a special account, and it was stipulated that the money could only be used in monthly instalments of £8000.[32] No further British or Russian loans materialised before the outbreak of the First World War, except for £50 000 by Britain in June 1914.

How is the Imperial Bank's role in financing the Persian government to be assessed? On the one hand the Bank, through its advances to the government, its issuing of the 1911 Loan and its role as a channel for official British loans, can be regarded as an instrument in the imperialist 'strangling of Persia'. The surge of borrowing before 1914 brought unprecedented constraints on Persia's sovereignty. On the other hand, however, Persia's situation would have been worse without the Bank. The funds lent, or raised, by the Bank offered a breathing space by keeping the government functioning. The Bank played a role in saving the Persian financial system from falling under the kind of direct foreign control imposed on, say, the Ottoman Empire by their foreign debtors. Persia was never forced to have a Public Debt Administration run by foreigners, and this was partly because the Imperial Bank performed that function in a less obtrusive manner. The British government trusted the Imperial Bank as it did no other 'Persian' institution, and the British authorities were prepared to work through it rather than directly.

Revenue collection

In the years before 1914 the Imperial Bank expanded its role as revenue collector for the Persian government. To some extent governments were obliged to concede this function to the Bank as a *quid pro quo* for advances. But the Bank also possessed a more competent administration than the government, and its participation in revenue collection offered an opportunity to put state finance on a firmer footing.

The first significant development in this direction came in May 1911, when the Persian Finance Ministry suggested that the Bank should finance the government's month-by-month expenditures, on the security of 30 or 60 day bills drawn by provincial governors on the basis of internal revenues.[33] This proposal was implemented by Shuster. In return for advances, Shuster instructed his financial agents in the provinces to pay all revenues into the Bank's branches each week. Shuster had even grander plans for the Imperial Bank. As a large proportion of Persia's internal revenues were collected in kind, and there was believed to be substantial leakage, Shuster proposed that the Bank should take control of the government's wheat stores and sell grain for the government in return for a 10% commission. Wood agreed to this scheme, but it was never implemented because of Shuster's fall.[34]

The departure of Shuster after a mere six-and-a-half months in office halted the Bank's progress in this, and several other fields, but in January 1913 Mornard, as observed in the previous section, requested that, in return for advances, inland revenues should again be paid into the Imperial Bank. Mornard also transferred the tax revenues of the northern provinces, excluding those of Azerbaijan which were in Russian hands, from the Russian Bank to the Imperial Bank, and hypothecated to the Bank the revenues of the southern provinces in return for advances of 300 000 Krans monthly over a six-month period in order to maintain the governor of Kermanshah.[35] By the outbreak of War the Bank's role as a fiscal agent for the Persian government had considerably expanded, although its performance in this capacity was limited by the extent to which central government's influence stretched to the provinces. If a provincial governor was too powerful or independent, central government rarely saw any of the tax revenues.

Notes and coinage

The Bank continued to play an important role in the currency system of Persia. Despite the political disturbances of the period, the note issue reached £962 419 (53 million Krans) in 1913. This paper currency assisted the monetarisation of the Persian economy, as did the Bank's attraction of deposits from funds previously hoarded. In retrospect the growth of the note issue seems rather low, but there were problems stemming from the Bank's position as a commercial institution which need to be taken into account.

The first problem concerned the overall size of the note issue. The Bank was eager to increase note circulation. Notes brought prestige to the branches. The Bank also registered a growing demand for its notes, partly because they were sometimes hoarded in preference to bulky coins. Wood was well aware that if the Bank restricted its note issue too severely there might be a resurgence of the *bijack* problem. But the Bank's enthusiasm for expanding its note issue was constrained by the provisions of its Charter and the demands of prudent banking. The Bank was obliged to maintain a one-third cash reserve against its notes, and the Charter further stipulated that the difference between the cash reserve and the total note issue was not to exceed the paid-up capital (£650 000 after 1895) minus the amount paid for the Concession (£200 000): i.e. £450 000 after 1895. This meant that once the total note issue exceeded £675 000 the Bank was obliged to maintain a 100% cash reserve against the extra notes. Moreover in practice, the Bank for reasons of security maintained even higher cash reserves, some 50% against the first £450 000 and 100% thereafter.

These high cash reserves meant that the Bank could not continue to expand the note issue without detriment to its business. 'Having to hold by Statute Kran for Kran in coin (i.e. against notes issued in excess of £675 000) besides bearing the cost of Issue', the Board's Finance Committee observed, 'it is the reverse of profitable.'[36] By 1914 the Board had come to the conclusion that a £1.2 million ceiling on the note issue was essential. Wood's pleas for flexibility, however, delayed any firm ruling on the subject by the time the First World War broke out.

The second, related problem was the Imperial Bank's insistence, dating from Rabino's early days as Chief Manager, that its notes would only be payable at the branch of issue. All notes were overprinted with 'Payable at ... only', although the Bank often seems to have permitted the encashment of notes at branches other than the issuing one at a discount. It cannot be disputed that the policy limited the impact of the paper currency as an agent in the monetarisation of the economy. 'A bank-note which can only be cashed where it is issued', observed the British consul at Mashad in 1919, 'is not money at all and will never do the work of money.'[37] Yet the Imperial Bank's reluctance to introduce interchangeability was entirely rational. Both the Russian Bank and Persian *sarrafs* had organised runs against the Bank's notes. Communications between branches, and hence their ability to assist one another, remained difficult. Yet if the Bank failed to provide cash for notes at a branch its Concession stipulated that this would constitute an act of bankruptcy, and the Concession would be cancelled.

The Imperial Bank's role in the provision of silver coinage, especially after 1910 when it became the Persian government's sole agent for importing silver, has already been discussed at length. In addition, the Bank's reform of the smaller denomination coins was important in halting the debasement of the coinage, and was thus a further contribution to the monetarisation of the Persian economy. The Bank continued throughout the 1900s to issue and maintain the nickel currency established when the debased copper coinage was withdrawn in 1899. Moreover, in 1910 the Bank agreed to undertake on the government's behalf the withdrawal of pre-1877 ('old') Krans, manufactured when there had been several Mints in Persia producing a coinage of non-uniform weight and content. This exercise continued for several years. In 1911 Shuster arranged that the Bank should withdraw all cracked or badly minted post-1877 ('new') Kran coins from circulation, an arrangement which continued after Shuster's departure.[38] None of these operations was profitable for the Bank, which often had to hold a large quantity of withdrawn coin until it could be reminted.

4.3 AGENT OF EMPIRE

The Imperial Bank continued to have a close relationship with the British government in the period. The most important aspect of this relationship – the use of the Bank to transmit British government loans to Persia, and to administer the Persian loan repayments – would appear firmly to implicate the Bank as an agent in the 'strangling of Persia' by Britain and Russia. The willingness of the Bank to follow Foreign Office dictates about its own policy on advances – as when financial assistance was refused to Mohammad Ali Shah – would appear to confirm the Bank's role as an imperialistic tool.

In fact the Imperial Bank never became a complete instrument of the Foreign Office before 1914, and relations between the two parties were rarely completely harmonious. Diplomats and bankers often held different assessments of political events in Persia. The Bank did not like the Foreign Office's placating stance towards the Russians after the Anglo–Russian Convention. The Foreign Office disapproved of Wood's wholehearted support of Morgan Shuster, while Wood initially disagreed with the Foreign Office's support of Mornard after Shuster's fall. The Bank generally considered that the Foreign Office was far too willing to ask it to sacrifice profits on the nebulous altar of national interest. 'Political considerations', S. F. Rogers, the Bank's Deputy Chief Manager, wrote to Newell in November 1909, 'do not pay our dividends.'[39] The problem was that the political conditions of pre-1914 Persia meant that the Bank had little chance of surviving without the support of the British government. 'You see how we dance to the piping from Downing Street and get more kicks than ha'pence for our trouble', Wood wrote to Newell in November 1910, 'and yet we must maintain in *all* quarters these good relations which are a sine qua non to our best interests.'[40] The diplomats had the best cards. The Bank could only attempt to make the best possible bargain in each situation.

This section looks at a number of areas where the Foreign Office encouraged the Bank to assist or implement official policy. The first of these was the Foreign Office's continued wish for the Bank to provide consular representation in Persian towns. Although the Bank did not like its Managers' time being diverted in this direction, it usually agreed to requests. In May 1913, for example, it allowed the Manager of Hamadan branch to be appointed unpaid vice-consul at Hamadan pending the establishment there of a salaried post.[41]

The Foreign Office also continued to urge the Bank to open branches in areas of strategic importance to Britain. In September 1908 the India Office's £1500 per annum subsidy for maintaining a branch at Nasratabad in Seistan ran out. Notwithstanding Foreign Office pleas, the India Office refused to continue the subsidy, particularly as it had received regular reports that the Bank had been less than energetic in encouraging commerce in the region. But despite the withdrawal of the subsidy the branch remained open, and coincidently in September 1908 it earned for the first time a net profit after the deduction of the subsidy. Over the next few years until 1914 Nasratabad managed to make small profits. Apart from Seistan, the Foreign Office was concerned to close the Gulf region to non-British influences, especially in view of the growing fears of German commercial encroachment. The Legation encouraged the Bank to open in Mohammarah, which it did in 1909, and such other places as Bandar Abbas and Lingah, which it did not.[42]

The Imperial Bank was also prepared to accede to Foreign Office requests to make politically desirable loans, provided such lending was guaranteed by the British government and was commercially feasible or at least was not likely to become a bad debt. One example was a 500 000 Kran (£8333) advance to the Governor of Luristan in June 1914. This was granted at the urgent behest of the British Minister, with the object of preventing Russia from obtaining any stake in an area in which railway development was expected to occur. The British Minister's pressure encouraged the Bank to take various title deeds as collateral security – just the kind of business the Bank usually refused to entertain.[43]

During the 1900s a central aim of British diplomacy in Persia was to encourage British commerce in southern Persia, on the grounds that British political influence would be strengthened in the wake of British business. The British government usually avoided the Russian model of direct subsidisation of commercial interests, but British diplomats played an active role in advising, organising and supporting British commercial interests in the region.[44] The pre-War years saw a resurgence of 'development' schemes in Persia, and the Imperial Bank, despite its burnt fingers over the mines and roads in the 1890s, became involved in various British mining and railway ventures in southern Persia in this period.

Until the spring of 1913 the Bank acted as the agent for the main British business concerns involved in southern Persia in their dealings with the Persian government. A. O. Wood represented the Anglo–Persian Oil Company and the Persian Railways Syndicate (see below), while his deputy, D. Brown, looked after the interests of the Kerman Mining Syndicate (formed in 1912 to develop mining around Kerman), and of F. Strick and Co., who were attempting to exploit red ochre deposits in the Gulf. There was also a considerable interlocking at director level between the Bank and the British companies in southern Persia. General Sir T. E. Gordon was one of the three directors of the Persian Transport Company. Charles Greenway's appointment to the Bank's Board in 1910 linked it to the oil company and when the Persian Railways Syndicate was established in the following year Greenway was its Chairman and Caesar Hawkins a director.

The Imperial Bank played an important role in the revived British hopes to build railways in Persia. Between 1890 and 1910 the sterilising agreement between Russia and Persia had blocked any railway construction. The British government was not unhappy about this situation, as it was feared that Persian railways would open up India to possible attack. However after 1910, when the sterilising agreement came to an end, the British government adopted a policy of 'earmarking' options and attempting to influence the alignment of any projected railway. This view lay behind the British government's acquiescence in the formation in 1911 of an Anglo–French–Russian syndicate, the Société International du Chemin de Fer Transpersan, to build railways in Persia. The Bank contributed £742 of this company's total capital, but little progress was made in securing an option from the Persians.

The Bank, however, was soon offered the opportunity to secure a more substantial stake in Persian railways. Persian governments were, with justification, extremely suspicious of the intention of the British and Russian governments as regards railway projects. In December 1910 the Minister of Finance informed Wood that railway concessions were only to be given to Persians, although foreign capital for the construction of any project was welcomed.[45] Wood immediately suggested that the Imperial Bank was ideally qualified, as a Persian institution, to hold a railway concession, and in the following May the Foreign Office agreed to leave the way clear for the Imperial Bank in this field.[46]

As a result, in August 1911 the Bank sponsored the formation of the

Persian Railways Syndicate Ltd. The Foreign Office supported the Syndicate, as a means of strengthening British influence in the south of Persia, even though British policy remained contented to see no railways actually constructed.[47] The Bank and its partners saw the venture as a promising business proposition. The subscribers to the shares of the new company were a roll-call of the main British banking and commercial interests in Persia. The Imperial Bank took £2500 of the £15 000 capital, held in the names of directors. Other shares were held by directors and representatives of the Anglo–Persian Oil Co., F. Strick and Co., the Persian Transport Co., Lynch and Co., Gray Paul, Ellerman Shipping Lines, and the British India Steam Navigation Co. The major 'outsider', probably introduced by Greenway, was Lord Cowdray, the owner of the large contracting firm of S. Pearson & Son and of a growing integrated oil business centred on large oilfields in Mexico.[48]

The Persian Railways Syndicate, like everything in Persia at this time, was slow to get started. Shuster's dismissal and the dissolving of the Majles threw negotiations with the Persian government into confusion. It was not until the end of 1912 that talks between Wood, representing the Syndicate, and the Persian government were resumed. The Foreign Office gave their support to Wood, especially after the Russian government secured a concession for a Tabriz–Julfa railway in February 1913.[49] It was in these circumstances that the Foreign Office made the granting of a further British government loan conditional upon progress in the railway negotiations, and the April 1913 Loan (see above, p. 124) only materialised when a promise to that effect was extracted. On 3 March the Persian government granted the Syndicate a two-year option for the construction of a 300 km railway due north from Mohammarah to Khorramabad.

This alignment reflected a major Foreign Office concern that the railway line being built through the Ottoman Empire to Baghdad by German interests would be extended to Tehran via Kermanshah and Hamadan. If this came to pass, the penetration of German goods into the Persian market could well have been facilitated at the expense of British goods arriving from the Gulf. A British-owned railway from Mohammarah to Khorramabad would be tactically of great benefit as it could open up a new trade route and undercut any Baghdad to Tehran route, on which goods in transit would be liable to Ottoman duties.[50] However, the Syndicate's terms from the Persian government were somewhat unsatisfactory. In contrast to the firm Russian concession in the north-west the Syndicate was only given an option. Moreover, it was understood that a joint survey would be made by the Syndicate and the Persian government. When the survey was complete, the Persian government would be free either to grant the Syndicate a concession or to commission it to construct a state-owned railway.[51]

On this rather unsatisfactory note, the Bank's direct involvement with the

railway negotiations ceased. In the spring of 1913 H. W. Maclean, the former
Deputy Chief Manager of the Imperial Bank, arrived in Tehran to represent
the interests of Anglo–Persian and the various British railway and mining
syndicates on a full-time basis. In 1914 the Bank raised its shareholding, still
in directors' names, in the Persian Railways Syndicate to £5000 out of an
enlarged capital of £30 000, but it no longer exercised any direct managerial
function. The Syndicate continued in existence until 1939, but it never built
any railways.

The Imperial Bank, therefore, actively co-operated with the Foreign
Office's strategy of encouraging British-financed railways and other development projects in southern Persia. Yet it always regarded such schemes as
commercial propositions, and was by no means simply an instrument of
British diplomacy. Indeed, the most noteworthy aspect of the Bank's business
in this respect was its willingness, in contrast to the stereotyped image of
British overseas banks, to promote infrastructure investment through roads,
mines and railways. The relative failure of these schemes reflected not the
Bank's lack of interest in 'development' schemes, but the complexity of the
political and economic situation in Persia, and the diplomatic conflict of
Britain and Russia in that country.

4.4 BRANCHES AND ORGANISATION

During Wood's Chief Managership the senior management structure of the
Bank seemed stronger and more stable than in Rabino's time. Wood seems
to have delegated responsibility more readily than his predecessor to his
Deputy Chief Managers – S. F. Rogers between 1908 and 1910 and David
Brown thereafter. Both men had the ability to exercise responsibility, but
Wood's policy also arose because – as his successor as Chief Manager later
alleged – he was far from accomplished in a number of areas of the Bank's
business, including exchange banking.[52] Nevertheless it was a healthier state
of affairs that the Bank was not so dependent on a single individual in
Tehran.

Wood had the benefit of a more stable Inspection Department than
Rabino. Brown replaced Wood as Chief Inspector in 1908, and when he
moved up the hierarchy in 1910 B. Messervy became Chief Inspector. The
staffing of the Department remained thin, however, with the Chief Inspector
and one Travelling Inspector. The small staff meant that branches were still
not inspected on a regular basis. After Wood's 1907 onslaught, Chief Office
was not inspected again until the 1920s.

Despite the disturbed political conditions in Persia, the branch network
expanded faster under Wood than under Rabino. Table 4.5 gives the dates
when new branches were opened in Persia between 1909 and 1914.

Table 4.5. *New branches of Imperial Bank 1909–14*

Location	Date opened
Hamadan	October 1909
Mohammarah	December 1909
Kazvin	January 1911
Ahwaz	March 1911
Soltanabad	January 1913
Birjand	September 1913
Sabzevar	September 1914

Surprisingly, four of the seven new branches, Hamadan, Kazvin, Soltanabad (later known as Arak) and Sabzevar, were in the Russian-dominated north, an indication of how little the diplomatic division of Persia between Britain and Russia in 1907 affected the Imperial Bank's business. The Board continued to be less enthusiastic than its Chief Manager over expanding the branch network. In 1911, for example, Wood's plans to open branches in a number of northern cities, including Barforush, Nishapur, Shahrud, Bandargez and Quchan, were rejected by the Board.[53] However, the Board's greater trust in Wood, compared with Rabino, encouraged them to be more flexible in allowing new branches to be started. Moreover, by the late 1900s there were more experienced officers available to man such branches.

The prospect of good commercial business, especially in exchange, remained the primary criterion for the opening of a new branch. Hamadan was one of the major trade routes from Baghdad, and was a large distribution centre for imports. The branch at Mohammarah was designed to serve the new oil business of the Anglo–Persian Oil Company. Ahwaz was intended to strengthen the Bank's position in the trade of the Karun region, as well as to service the oilfield. Kazvin was a leading centre for trade with Russia, and on the route from both Tehran and Hamadan to Rasht. Soltanabad was a centre of the growing carpet industry. Birjand in the east was on another important trade route. Sabzevar, between Mashad and the Caspian Sea, was in a cotton and opium growing region. It was believed to offer good trading prospects, especially as the branch of the Russian Bank in the city was known for not being very active.[54] The Bank was sometimes encouraged by the British Legation in Tehran to open in certain centres, such as Mohammarah and Birjand, but it never obliged unless the branch had a chance of becoming profit-making, the only exception being Nasratabad branch. There is no evidence that the British authorities encouraged the Bank's expansion into the Russian sphere of influence in Persia.

The initial results of the new branches were mixed. Hamadan rapidly built up a substantial business in exchange and local bills discounted, but the other branches were slower to develop. In the south, Mohammarah secured the exchange business of the Anglo–Persian Oil Company and some of the business of various European firms such as Gray MacKenzie & Co. and F. Strick & Co., who serviced the oil company. The branch, however, made little progress in the bazaars against the competition of the well-established Jewish *sarrafs* in the town, who had good business connections with Basra and Baghdad, while the Bank's notes found few takers in an area where Turkish Pounds and Indian Rupees were more generally accepted as the medium of exchange. Ahwaz was also slow to develop. The branch took over two years to return a very small profit, and failed initially to live up to expectations because of the slower than expected economic development of the Karun region. Birjand did make profits, but as much of its business had previously been sent to the branch at Nasratabad the main result was to force the latter branch back into unprofitability between 1914 and 1916. In the north, none of the new branches was as successful as Hamadan, although Soltanabad developed an exchange business and engaged in local advances to the carpet industry. Kazvin, on the other hand, made little progress, while Sabzevar's commercial prospects were clouded by Russian objections to the branch.

Wood gradually relaxed Rabino's tightly centralised control over the branches, and the system of turning branches into sub-branches of Tehran with no autonomy in such matters as exchange was reversed. In 1911 Tabriz and Mashad became independent branches again. Both branches performed creditably after their emancipation from Chief Office, assisted by Wood's insistence that branches should regularly share information with one another. After the relative success of Tabriz and Mashad, the Bank converted many sub-branches into independent branches. In March 1913 Esfahan and Hamadan became fully independent, followed by Kermanshah, Kerman and Rasht in September. In March 1914 Soltanabad became independent. The sub-branch system was not totally abandoned, however, and a number of regional groupings of branches were retained or formed. In the south, Bushire remained a sub-branch of Shiraz and Ahwaz a sub-branch of Mohammarah, while Nasratabad and Birjand became sub-branches of Mashad.

4.5 BANKING OPERATIONS

A remarkable feature of the period between 1909 to 1914 was the extent to which the Imperial Bank seemed able to maintain a commercial banking business despite the apparent chaos surrounding it.

In part the explanation lies in the increasing importance of Persian government business to the Imperial Bank and, in so far as the deepening political crisis forced the Persian government to borrow, the Bank was a beneficiary of that crisis. Between 1909 and 1912 around 90% of the Bank's 'new' advances were to the government. The issue of the 1911 Sterling Loan, and the servicing of British government advances, generated more business and profits. Silver purchases often brought large exchange profits, while after 1910 the Bank's role as the government's agent in silver purchases generated commission and interest on advances made to the government for this purpose. The increase in 'real' profit in 1910 and 1911 stemmed largely from developments in government business, namely the 1910 Amalgamated Loan and the 1911 Sterling Loan.

The political disturbances may also have helped the Imperial Bank's commercial business in a paradoxical way. The visible weakness of the Persian government, and its lack of authority outside Tehran, reinforced public confidence in the stability of the Bank, whose branches spanned Persia. The security of the Bank, backed by Sterling capital, attracted deposits. The disorders seem to have inflicted more damage on the Imperial Bank's competitors, notably the Russian Bank, than on itself. These conditions did not, however, encourage the Bank to expand its lending to the private sector.

Moreover, the 'real' economy in Persia may not have been as badly affected by the political crisis as might have been expected. Generalisations about the Persian economy in the pre-War period remain hazardous, but the available figures suggest that Persia's foreign trade was expanding in the 1900s, and this in turn may imply increasing activity in some sectors of the economy. The value of estimated imports rose from £5.5 million in 1901–2 to £10.3 million in 1912–13 and £11.8 million in 1913–14. Estimated exports expanded in the same years from £3.8 million, to £7.9 million and £8.2 million. Persian production and export of cash crops such as grain and rice seem to have expanded. There was a particular growth in carpet exports in the wake of falling transport costs, rising world demand and the advent into the industry of European firms which organised production and controlled quality. By 1913 carpets accounted for 12% of Persia's total exports.[55]

The main pattern of the Bank's commercial business after 1909 followed that of earlier years. Persian business continued to be in part financed by capital allotted to the Persian branches. The allotted capital in Persia was raised at the beginning of 1909 to £400 000, and it reached £417 000 following the opening of the new branch at Mohammarah in December. However, the fall of Shuster, and the decline of safe and profitable lending opportunities, led to the decision to reduce the capital at risk in Persia.[56] In 1912, therefore, the Bank's capital in Persia was reduced to £200 000, at which level it stayed until after the outbreak of the First World War. When necessary, the capital allocation to branches was supplemented by overdrafts with London Office.

The Bank's Kran deposits continued to rise after 1908. They stood at £655 932 (36.1 million Krans) in 1909, and reached £840 128 (46.2 million Krans), their pre-War peak, in 1913, before the outbreak of War reduced them to £628 277 (37.7 million Krans) in September 1914. The overall importance of Chief Office as a source of deposits fell slightly compared to the early 1900s. It contributed about 52% of total Persian deposits at the beginning of 1914.

As in Rabino's era, the Board in London were anxious to reduce the proportion of accounts bearing interest, and to reduce interest rates. Wood had more sympathy for this strategy than Rabino, and it made sense in the years before 1914. The Bank was used as a safe depository during disturbances, and it was not necessary to pay for such funds. The Bank also had problems in employing its funds safely, and this situation was made worse because inter-branch transfers were rendered difficult by the obstacles in the way of the physical movement of *specie*. It took 13 months for one caravan of *specie* to get from Yazd to Tehran. When Bushire required notes from Tehran, they had to be shipped via London! Many branches reduced the number of current accounts on which interest was paid. Rasht, Tabriz and Shiraz seem to have stopped paying interest on such accounts entirely by 1911. In Esfahan, the percentage of interest bearing accounts fell from 72% in early 1909 to 33% in 1912.

The Bank also reduced its interest rates, although there were still many variations for different accounts and between branches. By the beginning of 1913, 3.5% per annum was being paid on most 12-month fixed deposits, as compared to the 5% of Rabino's last years. In contrast, the London Bank Rate had moved in the opposite direction, being around 3.7% per annum in the mid-1900s but rising to around 4% per annum in the period 1911 to 1913. Falling interest rates did not lead to falling deposits, but in 1913 there was the first evidence that there was a threshold below which rates could not be pushed. Several branches, including Tabriz and Esfahan, reduced their fixed deposit interest rate to 3% per annum, and this was followed by a sharp decline in deposits. In Tabriz's case fixed deposits fell by 50% within a year. As business activity increased in many areas in the second half of 1913, and opportunities for lending expanded, the interest paid on fixed deposits increased at most branches to 4% per annum. There was a recognition that the Bank could not allow fixed deposits to fall below a certain, if undefined, level. 'A Bank must have some Fixed Deposits', the Bank's Finance Committee observed in March 1913, 'we cannot live safely on credit alone liable to attack on demand.'[57]

It is possible for one year-end, September 1909, to assemble a breakdown of the 'resources' at the disposal of the Bank's Persian branches, and their disposition. Notes, deposits and allocated capital (plus London Office overdrafts) provided around one-third each of total 'resources' – £1 920 000 (105.6 million Krans) – available to the Bank in Persia. 56% of these resources was lent out in bills discounted, loans and advances, and 33% was kept in cash. The remainder consisted of silver in transit, premises and various miscellaneous items.[58] This pattern of business did not change radically until the outbreak of the War, although the growth of the note issue beyond £675 000 led to a rise in the amount of funds held in cash, while Shuster's repayment of the Bank's advances to government temporarily reduced the total level of loans and advances in 1912.

A more important change came in the direction of the Bank's lending. Lending to the private sector was at a low point between 1909 and 1912. Chief Office accepted practically no new business in this category. During Wood's Chief Managership the Bank came as close as it ever would to restricting its business to government and expatriate firms.

Yet some commercial lending to Persians continued. At the provincial branches, where government business was virtually non-existent, the Bank continued to undertake bill discounting, provided it was strictly limited to short-dated commercial bills. By March 1912, for example, Hamadan's bill discount business was averaging about 2.2 million Krans (£40 000) per annum, and two years later it had risen to 7.7 million Krans (£128 000) per annum. Mashad branch was active in financing the trade of eastern Persia with Russia, working closely with the Russian Transport Bureau. Sometimes the Russian Bureau made advances to merchants against its own receipts; sometimes the Imperial Bank made such advances. The Bank also bought the bills on London of Mashadi merchants of good standing.[59] Although there remained little industry in Persia for the Bank to finance, it did provide facilities for the fast-growing carpet industry.

Even Chief Office never quite abandoned making advances to the private sector, mostly notables and government officials. During Wood's early years as Chief Manager a number of large advances were inherited from Rabino, and these were only slowly liquidated, and in 1913 Wood began making a few advances to notables, several of which were at the behest of the British government. By mid-1914 such advances, largely against title deeds, amounted to 4.3 million Krans (£71 666). The Board remained sceptical. 'It will be interesting to see if the Persian is changing his habits', the Finance Committee minuted in March 1914, 'and if the engagement as to instalments is regularly kept up.'[60]

The Board retained its old preference for exchange business in preference

Table 4.6. *Profits from exchange and interest in Persia 1909–14*

Year end (20 Sept.)	Exchange profits		Interest profits	
	Krans (millions)	Sterling equivalent	Krans (millions)	Sterling equivalent
1909	3.5	63 636	1.7	30 909
1910	3.4	61 818	5.4	98 181
1911	3.7	67 890	2.9	53 211
1912	4.1	74 545	1.9	34 545
1913	4.1	74 545	1.6	29 091
1914	3.6	60 000	2.8	46 666

to advances, and Wood worked hard to put this policy into effect. The abandoning of the policy of centralising exchange business on Chief Office made branch Managers more active in the pursuit of exchange opportunities, as they could see the results of their efforts reflected in their branch results. The situation was helped because branch Managers were more willing to co-operate with one another than in Rabino's time, probably because there had developed a *cadre* of Managers who had spent all or most of their careers with the Bank.

The available figures, which are far from complete, indicate that the Bank's exchange business was growing. Esfahan's foreign exchange turnover grew from £91 397 in the half-year ending September 1908 to £247 000 in the half-year ending March 1914. Over the same period Kermanshah's turnover rose from £29 983 to £243 705, Rasht's from £86 507 to £188 738 and Tabriz's from £129 528 to £548 818. All of this stemmed from commercial exchange operations, as government exchange business passed through Chief Office. However, as Persia's foreign trade was growing in this period, it is unclear whether Wood had significantly expanded the Bank's share of the total available exchange business. The *sarrafs* and the European trading firms appear to have retained a high proportion of Persian exchange business right up to the outbreak of war.

Table 4.6 gives the Bank's profits in Persia from interest and exchange between 1909 and 1914. This table would appear to suggest that, compared to the situation between 1905 and 1908 (see Table 3.3 in Chapter 3), exchange was assuming a greater importance in the Bank's business. Not only were exchange profits for all years except 1910 and 1914 higher than in the 1905–08 period, but exchange profits comfortably exceeded interest profits in every year except 1910, while in the earlier period interest profits had regularly exceeded exchange profits. In this sense the Bank may be regarded as becoming more of an 'exchange bank' in the pre-War years, but as so much of both exchange and interest profits stemmed from government business it might be better described as a 'government bank'.

The Imperial Bank's performance in Persia before 1914 presents a number of paradoxes. The Bank had introduced modern banking into the country, and continued in business despite the political and other challenges it faced. It had established a nationwide branch network, despite the division of the country between Britain and Russia. Yet the impact of the modern banking sector on the Persian economy had been limited. *Sarrafs* and trading companies retained a large proportion of the country's exchange business. The Imperial Bank had provided credit facilities for merchants, often given on an unsecured basis, but the requirements of English banking prudence meant that it did not handle much of the business of the bazaars. The Bank had introduced a paper currency into Persia, but its position as an institution which had to make profits in order to survive meant that the note issue expanded rather slowly, and that its acceptance was reduced by the Bank's requirement that notes were payable at par only at the branch of issue.

From the point of view of British overseas banking, the growth of the Imperial Bank before 1914 had not been spectacular. Taking the very crude measure of total balance sheet size, the Bank had grown by 84% between its foundation and 1913. Other, older established, banks had shown faster growth rates. The balance sheet of the Bank of London and the River Plate, a leading British bank in South America, had grown by 146% and that of the Hongkong Bank by 224% over the same period. Among banks which operated in the Middle East, the Anglo–Egyptian, capitalised at £500 000 in 1913, had grown by 112% and the Imperial Ottoman Bank, capitalised at £5 million in 1913, by 94%.

The striking feature of the Imperial Bank was the range of functions it had undertaken in Persia. It was very far from being simply an exchange bank. As the state bank, it had issued paper currency; it imported silver on behalf of the government; it managed the nickel currency; floated loans on the London market; and participated in attempts to reform the financial administration of the country. The Bank had also acted as the channel for British government lending to Persia. As a retail bank, it had established branches, collected deposits, discounted bills and made advances. The Bank had even been involved in a number of mining and transport projects. The Imperial Bank may have been a 'conservative' institution before 1914, but it was also a highly versatile one.

5

THE BANKERS 1889–1914

The Imperial Bank of Persia was always a small and intimate bank. 'This Bank', one of its directors observed in 1950, 'stands or falls by the efforts, ability and personality of some sixty men.'[1] In the 1900s there were never more than 40 or 50 men on the expatriate staff of the Bank in Persia at any one time. This was less than a third of the number of Europeans serving with the Hongkong Bank in the East at that time.[2] All of the European staff would have recognised each other's names, and probably known much about each other's abilities and personalities, although such was the size of Persia, the difficulties of travel and the absence of local leave, that it was quite possible for men to serve many years without ever meeting in person.

One hundred and seventy-five men joined the overseas staff of the Bank before the First World War, of whom 79 were recruited between 1889 and 1899 and the remainder in the following 15 years. The first generation of bankers were more cosmopolitan in origin than later ones. A comprehensive record of staff birth places and nationalities before 1914 does not exist, but at least five Frenchmen, three Dutchmen, two Germans, one Austrian and one Swiss joined between 1889 and 1899. In addition, there were nine men whom the Board habitually described as 'Levantine', a rather arbitrary category into which people with dark complexions born in the Middle East or even Europe seem to have been placed. At least one man termed 'Levantine', Joseph Rabino, had been born in Britain and had British nationality. The bulk of recruits, however, were British, with Irish and Scots being very well-represented. After 1900 the Bank's recruits were almost entirely British, with only one Frenchman and one Austrian joining between 1900 and 1914.

The Bank before 1914 was a young man's bank. In the 1890s, as the Bank sought to acquire experienced staff, about half of the recruits were aged 25 or over. Many of these left, however, while between 1900 and 1914 80% of the new recruits were under 25. This created difficulties. 'The young fellows sent out', Rabino complained to London in 1893, 'are very fair machines but will require some years experience to be more than that.'[3] The problem was that a small bank could not carry juniors until they gained 'experience', and young men were thrust into positions of responsibility much earlier than in larger and longer established overseas banks. By the mid-1890s, for example, Hongkong Bank men appointed to the post of Accountant would normally have 10–15 years service in the East behind them, and Managers 20 years service. In contrast, in the Imperial Bank a man could reasonably expect to be made an Accountant after three years in Persia, and appointment as an Acting Manager of a branch could follow soon afterwards. Confirmed status as a Manager took longer to acquire. In March 1914 the Bank's Managers had on average to wait eight years from their first arrival in Persia to their appointment as a confirmed Manager.

The possibilities of early promotion must have attracted ambitious and confident young men, but from the point of view of senior management in Tehran the youthfulness of the Bank was a headache. Rabino's correspondence to London was littered with complaints about having to run a bank with insufficient experienced staff, and the Bank's capacity to open new branches, for example, was often restricted by lack of appropriate staff. The problem was still evident after Rabino's departure. 'We are most wanting in senior men', S. F. Rogers wrote to London in 1910, '. . . The fact of our Managers being so young and inexperienced involves a further burden of responsibility on the shoulders of the Management.'[4]

A high staff turnover exacerbated this problem. Between 1889 and 1899, while 79 men joined the Bank's overseas staff, 39 left and four died in service. Between 1900 and 1914 96 joined, but 54 left and seven died. One-fifth of recruits between 1889 and 1899 left even before they were sent overseas, and a further fifth went within their first three years abroad. 'Juniors, after the first three or four years', Rabino observed in 1900, 'do not find the prospects sufficiently tempting to compensate for the many disadvantages they have to put up with and so they seize any opportunity to leave the Bank.'[5]

Low salaries were sometimes stated as one of the 'disadvantages' which caused men to resign. It is hard to generalise on salary levels as it took time for a consistent salary structure to evolve. In the early 1890s there were many anomalies in the salary scale which often, as Rabino observed in 1893, gave 'rise to feelings of sourness'.[6] However, by the 1900s, when the Bank was no longer recruiting senior staff from other banks, salaries began to be standardised. Staff were initially employed on five-year contracts, but by the mid-1890s the Bank had settled on three year contracts, which could be ended on either side by six months' notice or payment of six months' salary in lieu. A junior would be paid £250 during the first year of his contract followed by two annual increments of £25. It was standard practice to mark the end of an officer's first three years by confirming him in the rank of Accountant, and raising his salary a further £25. Further salary increments were tied, in a still far from consistent fashion, to such factors as rank, seniority and posting. Branches, and thereby their Managers' salaries, were graded in order of importance. In 1907 Shiraz and Tabriz headed the list, with Managers paid £650 and £550 per annum respectively, and Kermanshah and Rasht were at the bottom, with Managers paid £400 at both branches.

Rabino himself was engaged in 1889 on £2000 a year. At the end of 1891 he was given an entertainment allowance of £500 a year plus a 2% bonus on annual net profits in Persia. His three-year contract was renewed in 1895 and 1898, and he was then placed on a permanent basis on £3000 per annum, including entertainment allowance and bonus. He remained on that salary for the rest of his time as Chief Manager. A. O. Wood, who was a good deal younger than Rabino, was appointed Chief Manager on a salary of £1500, and this was increased by two increments of £500 to reach £2500 in March 1916.

Salaries were sometimes supplemented by bonuses. These were given to individuals as rewards for good work. A. O. Wood, for example, was granted £100 in 1906 in recognition of his 'excellent work' in inspecting Shiraz and Bushire.[7] The entire expatriate staff at Chief Office were given £200 to share amongst them in recognition of their work during a run on the bank in 1897. And in 1907 and 1910 the Bank's overseas and the local staff received a general bonus of 10% of their salaries.

The Imperial Bank's salaries were generous by the standards of domestic British banks. A young man joining a London office of a clearing bank often started at between £25 to £75 per annum in the late nineteenth century. At the other end of the scale, General Managers of provincial banks in the same period are known to have earned £2000 or £2500 per annum.[8] 'I am rather inclined to think this Bank was an exceptionally lucky find', wrote one man a year after joining the Imperial Bank in 1910 at the age of 22, who had been sent straight out to Persia, 'and even now, I am better off – financially and socially – than the English Bank manager of young experience.'[9]

Comparisons with other overseas banks were not necessarily so favourable. The Bank of New Zealand paid men of eight years' service £120 per annum in the 1890s.[10] On the other hand, the Hongkong Bank's salaries seemed more generous, although the fact that promotion came later in the East than in Persia limits the value of the comparison. In 1897 the Hongkong Bank paid juniors HK$1800 (£200) per annum, Accountants HK$4200–4800 (£460–530), Managers HK$12 000–15 000 (£1320–1650). The salaries of Rabino and Wood do not appear generous in a comparative perspective. In the 1900s the Chief Manager of a large English clearing bank might have received £10 000 per annum, that of a smaller domestic bank perhaps £5000 per annum. In 1901 Thomas Jackson received, as Chief Manager of the Hongkong Bank, almost £13 800.

The cost of living and conditions of service in London, New Zealand, Persia and the Far East were, of course, so different that comparisons of salaries have little meaning. The regular complaints of the Imperial Bank's staff about salaries would suggest that in the conditions of Persia they were not perceived as generous. And as salaries were fixed in Sterling, and paid at the exchange rate of the day, appreciations in the value of the Kran against Sterling were customarily followed by cries of anguish. Staff who expected to eat and drink as they did in Britain seem to have found life in Persia expensive. In 1892 D. Baker, the Bank's Deputy Chief Manager, complained bitterly of the high cost of living in Tehran, with prime English bacon 2/- a pound, Bass beer 1/8d a bottle, 'sound' claret 5/- and champagne 10/-.[11] Baker resigned shortly afterwards. As will become clear later, however, living conditions in Persia, rather than salaries *per se*, were probably the main factor which prompted men to leave the Bank's service.

The high staff turnover was not entirely a matter of resignations. Fifteen men between 1889 and 1914 were either dismissed or did not have their contracts renewed within their first three years of service. General inefficiency was the main reason which led to the non-renewal of contracts, while dismissals were usually a result of 'gross misconduct' of some kind. Six officers, for example, were dismissed from the Bank's service because of excessive drinking: three of these were diagnosed as suffering from actual *delirium tremens*, one from homicidal mania, and another from drug addiction as well. Another officer was dismissed for wild behaviour – he caused several affrays, culminating in picking a fight with a fellow member of staff and giving him a black eye. Another man was dismissed for an undefined 'unnatural offence of a loathsome nature'.

The following two sections review the reasons which led men to join the Imperial Bank, their careers within the Bank, and their lives as Bank officers.

5.2 MOTIVES, CAREER AND TERMS OF SERVICE

The exact reasons which led men to join the Imperial Bank before 1914 have died with them. It can be assumed, however, that many of the reasons which led men later to join the Bank applied before 1914: the wish for adventure, or as a later General Manager put it, 'to know what was on the other side of the mountain';[12] family connections with Persia or the East; the more rapid promotion prospects and the anticipated higher incomes of service overseas. Despite some of the difficulties of life in Persia, the Bank offered a dramatic opportunity to escape from office routine in Britain.

The Bank's recruitment policy initially consisted of a haphazard and urgent search for staff. As was seen in Chapter 2, Rabino recruited a small *cadre* of experienced bankers who had been working in Egypt with him. Other men, such as A. O. Wood, were acquired from the ruined New Oriental Bank Corporation. Several staff were recruited without banking knowledge but with relevant overseas experience or language ability. This category included former employees of other British enterprises in Persia, such as the Imperial Tobacco Corporation and the Indo–European Telegraph Company.

The Board, however, was not happy with the cosmopolitan nature of the staff acquired in this way. The directors never shared Rabino's wish to recruit the best men available with overseas banking experience and foreign languages, regardless of nationality. It wanted a British bank. 'I hope we may soon', the Chairman, William Keswick, observed in 1895, 'get the Bank's staff in Persia composed of men of our own nationality and representative in a truer sense than at present of this country's interests.'[13] As the Board was in direct control of recruitment, Keswick's hope was soon fulfilled. The normal pattern of entry into the Bank's service came to be through joining London Office as a junior, and then proceeding overseas after a period of training. This practically guaranteed that new staff would be British.

Juniors came to the Bank through a variety of routes, of which personal recommendation or family connections were very noticeable. The sons of both Joseph Rabino and General Schindler entered the Bank. There were several pairs of brothers on the staff, including the Wilkinsons, one of whom – Edward – was to become Chief Manager between 1926 and 1934. A number of men were recruited on the personal recommendation of directors, and sometimes of other staff. E. M. Eldrid, appointed in 1893 at the age of 17 and destined to serve the Bank for 63 years, was appointed a junior in London as a result of the recommendation of a fellow junior.

Whatever the avenues of recruitment were, it is evident that by the 1900s the Board had in mind some criteria as to the kind of juniors it required. The Imperial Bank shared with all other British ventures in the East the belief that public school men had the character and upbringing required for service overseas, although the strong Scots and Irish contingent among the staff must have meant that it was far from the preserve of English public school boys. British nationality and background was a prime requisite. There was also a preference for men with some banking, or at least accountancy, experience. 'The Board are convinced', Newell wrote in 1892, 'that it is a mistake to offer appointments to men who have not had previous banking training and who are not conversant with banking methods.'[14] Nevertheless juniors seem to have been taken on without such experience, and 'trained' in London Office. A knowledge of French, the European language generally used in Tehran at the Court and in diplomatic circles before 1914, was regarded as a prerequisite for joining the Bank. These nationality, educational experience and language preferences were rather demanding, and the Board rarely felt satisfied with the available supply of potential recruits. Sir Lepel Griffin blamed the apparent absence of men who could speak modern languages and understand commerce on 'the accursed system ... of teaching at schools and universities Latin and Greek instead of subjects of use and importance'.[15]

Juniors invariably spent some time in London Office after joining the Bank, although the length of time men stayed there varied widely from a few weeks to three or four years, depending on their age and on Persia's need for staff at any particular time. E. M. Eldrid, for example, had to wait four years before he was sent to Persia. By the 1900s it had become rare for a man under the age of 21 to be sent overseas, with only four exceptions to this rule between 1900 and 1914.

While in London Office, juniors learnt the rudiments of the Imperial Bank's practices and business by working in each of the departments. In addition, they were encouraged to take the Institute of Bankers' exams and attended, alongside juniors from other banks such as the Hongkong Bank, the Gilbart Lectures. The value of this 'training' in London Office, however, was a matter of some dispute. Rabino for one had strong opinions. 'London experience', he informed Newell in 1892, 'is practically useless.'[16]

On arrival in Persia a new junior would often be sent to Chief Office in Tehran. Rabino's view was that a man needed three or four years' service in Chief Office to learn the Bank's business before being sent to a provincial branch.[17] However, this was a luxury the Board was unwilling to afford, and most juniors in the 1900s seem to have spent about half that length of time at Tehran before being sent to a branch, usually one of the smaller ones, in the capacity of acting Accountant. Men were sometimes sent direct to the provinces. Whether in Chief Office or in the provinces, junior British officers would find themselves in charge of numerous local clerks, the more senior of which would know a great deal more about the business than themselves. One 22-year-old junior, arriving in Tehran in 1910, found himself, 'Controller and Chief of the Note Issue Dept. with full sole control of a staff of 27 natives ... responsible for the only note circulation in Persia and the new plates now print a facsimile of my signature on every note issued'.[18]

The Imperial Bank encouraged its European staff to learn Persian. This was common practice among the Eastern banks. The Hongkong Bank had a major language programme in Chinese, and paid a gratuity to those who learned Hindustani. The Mercantile Bank of India also encouraged the learning of local languages. In Persia such a policy made the only sense. A bachelor would often find himself the only European in a town, and face total social isolation if he was not even able to make polite conversation in Persian. There were worries, too, that total dependence on local staff for risk assessment could lead to bad debts and losses. Both Rabino and the Board agreed – for once – on the importance of British staff learning Persian. 'If any young man has not within two years made himself a good Persian scholar he should be removed as incompetent', Sir Lepel Griffin wrote to Rabino in 1900, 'and *by good* I do not mean enough Persian to talk to his *Ferash* (i.e. bank messenger) and his groom but competency to hold a conversation on banking business and general subjects with a merchant or gentleman.'[19]

During the 1890s the European staff were constantly urged to learn Persian, and by 1900 language lessons were readily available for them. These were often given by the *mirzas*, or interpreters, employed by the Bank. Gradually, formal incentive schemes were built into the terms of the Bank's service. By 1905 the Bank's junior staff were told that 'knowledge of Persian was a requisite and that promotion would depend on the candidate qualifying himself in that respect'.[20] In 1908 the Bank's first formal examinations in Persian were held, and practically every member of the European staff seems to have taken part.

What is unknown is how many of the Bank's European staff in this period became *really* competent in speaking and understanding Persian. In later periods it is known that, while most British staff achieved some knowledge of Persian or Arabic, business would be normally conducted either in English or through an interpreter. This was probably also the case before 1914. In June 1903 an analysis by L. E. Dalton, then Deputy Chief Manager, of the linguistic knowledge of the European staff put only four officers in Class 1, that is, possessing a fluent reading and writing knowledge of Persian. Thirteen had a Class 2, 'fair working' knowledge, and eight had a Class 3, or nodding acquaintance with the language.[21] Too much weight cannot be put on this survey as it covered only half the European staff and also refrained from assessing the Persian knowledge of the Chief Manager, Rabino. But the small numbers of officers in Class 1, and the fact that the four who were in this category included the sons of Rabino and General Schindler as well as a Dutchman, would suggest that by the early 1900s the British staff had not distinguished themselves as Persian linguists.

The rules for leave, or *furlough* as it was universally known in the Bank, were specified in 1892. Officers were to be given six months' leave on full pay after five years of service abroad. This was rather less generous than the Hongkong Bank, which from 1894 gave one year's leave after five years in the East, with half of the leave on full pay and the remainder on half-pay. But leave in the Imperial Bank was calculated from the date of a man's arrival in, to the date of his departure from, Britain, with the time spent travelling counted as leave on half-pay. In the Hongkong Bank leave was calculated from day of departure from and arrival in an overseas post, and the journey from the East to Britain took a month by ship. The Bank did not pay for travel between Persia and Britain, except for the passage home on the termination of a man's contract. There appears to have been no concept of 'local leave', to be spent within Persia, before 1914. These leave policies and conditions were by no means exceptional, and had many similarities to those operated by similar banks.

The Bank's rules on leave could cause hardship. Many junior officers had problems in raising sufficient money to cover their travelling expenses. Moreover, travelling expenses varied sharply according to the distance of a branch from Rasht, from where most staff left for Britain. Such were the difficulties of travel in Persia that, in 1914, it was calculated that while the travel cost from Rasht to London was £25, it cost £60 to travel from Nasratabad to London and £75 from Kerman to London.[22] It was not until July 1914 that the Bank agreed to pay officers' travelling costs from their branches to Rasht, although still not from Rasht to Britain. The travelling expenses of wives and children were not paid until 1945.

Leave was strictly at the convenience of the Bank. Although there was provision for leave after five years overseas, it was quite usual for individual officers to spend much longer periods in Persia. With only a small staff, officers had to wait until it was convenient from the Bank's viewpoint for them to go on leave. One man who joined in 1906 stayed in Persia for eight years before his first leave: another who joined in 1910 spent ten years in Persia before his first leave.[23]

The Bank provided their staff with access to free medical advice, a very necessary provision in the conditions of pre-1914 Persia. All new appointees to the overseas service had a rigorous medical examination in London, with the Imperial Bank in the 1890s sharing a medical adviser – Dr George Thin, a former Shanghai doctor, of Cavendish Square – with the Hongkong Bank and The Chartered Mercantile Bank (later The Mercantile Bank of India Ltd). In Tehran it retained a medical officer. At the provincial branches the Bank where possible paid a small annual fee to retain the services of a doctor attached to the British Consulate. The Bank was not overgenerous. Wives and families usually had to pay for their own treatment, and while the doctor in Tehran supplied 'ordinary' drugs free of charge, 'extraordinary' drugs had to be paid for by patients.

The Bank believed in celibacy. As in the Hongkong Bank and other Eastern banks, the marriage of young men was discouraged, although as we lack

statistics on the number of Bank officers who married before 1914, and their
age of marriage, one cannot quantify the effects of such policies. It was held
that marriage restricted the mobility of staff. 'There seems to be an epidemic
of marriage setting in amongst our assistants', Sir Lepel Griffin bemoaned in
1903, '... Our staff is already far too much married, and in a country like
Persia it is exceedingly difficult to relieve the distant posts, which is often
necessary, when the only available persons for the change are burdened with a
wife and family.'[24] The other side of the argument, however, was the Bank's
urgent need before 1914 to reduce staff turnover, as well as prevent its men
from succumbing to even worse temptations than marriage, such as drink,
drugs or local women. 'Our young men are not worse than others but they are
not Carthusians', Rabino warned in 1901, 'and their life even in Tehran is
horribly monotonous. The consequences are great temptations and too often
a tendency to drink.'[25]

As a result of these conflicting pressures, the Bank tended to make
draconian regulations against marriage, but then to grant exceptions when the
case seemed deserving. The Board resolved in 1895 that it did 'not approve of
any officer under the rank of manager marrying', and any man who did was to
be dismissed.[26] In practice, however, this ruling came to mean that officers,
under the rank of Manager, had to seek permission from the Board if they
wished to marry, and this was fairly regularly given. In 1903, in a further stand
against marriage, the Board specified that no officer was to marry until he had
a salary of £500 per annum, or if his salary and the income of his fiancée
amounted to this sum. In the case of the latter circumstance written testimony
from an officer's prospective father-in-law was usually required. This basic
salary requirement was large, amounting to that of a senior branch Manager.
Yet the Board continued on occasion to grant exemptions from the ruling,
and other British enterprises in the East had even higher thresholds before a
man could marry. In Burmah Oil before 1914, for example, men were only
permitted to marry after seven years' service and after obtaining a salary of
£800 per annum.[27] And in the Hongkong Bank men were generally permitted
to marry only after ten years service in the East. On the other hand, the
Imperial Bank sometimes used arbitrary criteria, as well as the £500 ruling, to
forbid marriages. In 1915 one man, who had been with the Bank since 1910,
was refused permission to marry not only because his salary was under the
required amount, but because his knowledge of Persian was inadequate.[28]

A further obstacle that had to be crossed before a man could marry was the
Bank's assessment of the suitability of his proposed wife. Bank wives had to be
of a certain social standing, who would not disgrace their husbands in
expatriate society. This again was characteristic of British banks and firms in
the East at this time. The Chief Manager's assessments of the social

suitability of an officer's fiancée carried considerable weight with the Board, and Rabino and Wood shared similar visions of the ideal Bank wife. 'A quiet domesticated and sensible girl', Wood described one lady in 1913 whose marriage to an officer he recommended to the Board.[29] Women were expected to be supportive of their husbands, capable of running households, and sensible, because survival in the trying circumstances of Persia required a great deal of common sense.

The real sparks would fly if a man proposed marriage to a non-British woman. One man eventually won the Board's permission, against A. O. Wood's advice, to marry the daughter of a Russian Colonel stationed in northern Persia. But marriages to Persians and Armenians were definitely regarded as beyond the pale, and men who pursued this course were dismissed. It was held that by such 'native' marriages Europeans lost the respect of the local population, and that it was also socially impossible for their wives to be integrated with the expatriate community. The marriage of one officer to an Armenian lady in 1892 (before the Board's permission to marry had to be sought formally) meant, in Rabino's view, that the man could never work in Chief Office. 'I could not give him quarters', Rabino explained, 'and he would be placed in a very humiliating position.'[30]

Sometimes the Board found its hand forced on the marriage question. W. J. P. Church joined the Bank as a bachelor aged 27 in April 1912, and sailed for Persia at the beginning of May. In the interim he hurriedly married his fiancée, who was recently orphaned and had no close relatives to depend on. The Bank did not find out about the marriage until nearly a year later, when Church requested that his wife be allowed to join him in Persia.[31] The Board were not amused by their discovery, but after discussion resolved on a course of leniency. Church was allowed to stay in the Bank's service, but his wife was not permitted to join him until their combined income reached £500 a year.[32] Church died of blood poisoning in April 1915, when he was earning a salary of £300. His wife never joined him.

There were no pensions in the Imperial Bank before 1914, but like other British overseas banks of the period a Provident Fund was established. The immediate stimulus to the foundation of the Officers' Provident Fund was the death of L. E. Dalton in a shooting accident early in 1905. Two other officers had died during the previous few months, of phthisis and cholera respectively. In June 1905 the Board decided to create the Provident Fund, and the scheme started in the following October.[33]

Under the terms of this Fund, which were in line with general contemporary practice, a deduction of 5% was made monthly from the salaries of all European officers and the salaried staff of London Office. The Bank added a further 5% half-yearly from profits to this sum. This money was placed in special accounts at the Bank, opened in the names of individual officers, on which 5% per annum interest was given. The balance was payable to a man on his retirement or, in the event of death, to his legal personal representative. In January 1912 the Bank's contribution to the Provident Fund was doubled to 10% of the monthly salary of staff, and in 1920 staff contributions were increased to 10% and the Bank's to 20%. The scheme remained in operation on these terms until 1947.

The rules of the Provident Fund encouraged long service with the Bank. In order to qualify for the full balance an officer had to serve 15 years. Otherwise, he received only his contribution plus accrued interest. There were also conditions whereby members could forfeit all interest in the Fund, and the portion so forfeited would accrue for the ultimate benefit of the other members. For example, the Board could dismiss a member of the Fund for ill-health, and in such a case his interest in the Fund would be forfeited.

In addition to the Provident Fund, it became the practice of the Imperial Bank to pay gratuities to long-serving staff. This became normal practice in the interwar years, but given the Bank's starting date there were hardly any qualifying cases before 1914. Joseph Rabino and S. F. Rogers were the only two long-serving men who can be said to have retired, as opposed to being dismissed, resigning, or dying. Rogers received an appointment in London Office rather than a gratuity, while Rabino was given £1500. It was during the First World War that long-serving staff began to retire, and these men were awarded gratuities. Wood received £10 000 in 1919, and Newell £3500 in 1917. The clearest hardship cases before 1914 came from the widows of men who had died in the Bank's service. Almost invariably the Board would grant some money to widows of long-serving staff who made a request for financial assistance, with *ex gratia* payments of £500 being quite common.

5.3 LIFE IN PERSIA

The first task of an officer on appointment to the overseas service of the Bank was to kit himself out. From 1910 staff were given a set of notes on 'The Journey from London to Tehran, and hints on Outfit'.[34] The notes recommended that men should acquire from their tailor a frock coat and a dress suit ('made of thin cloth – and get them very well cut, and with all suits bring extra trousers'); two flannel or tropical tweed suits; two dark suits, two pairs of white flannel trousers ('be careful that the flannel is thoroughly shrunk; Persian laundries have a knack of making flannel shrink to an inconvenient extent'); one Harris tweed travelling Ulster; one light rainproof overcoat; one heavy pair of riding breeches of strong material. Hosiery requirements included white and black dress ties; half-a-dozen tennis shirts; and 24 pairs of socks. A variety of shoes, boots, pumps, tennis shoes and slippers were also on the list, plus a straw panama and silk and felt hats – and a pith helmet if the officer was arriving in Persia between May and September. 200 visiting cards were essential ('as you can't get them printed well here').

Suitably equipped, staff travelled to Persia by a variety of routes. During the 1890s it was common to proceed by rail to Paris, the Orient Express to Istanbul, steamer to Batoum, a rail journey to Baku, steamer to Enzeli and by road to Tehran. Others travelled by rail to Marseilles, and then caught a steamer to Istanbul and proceeded as above. Yet another route was to take a train to Odessa via Berlin, and then cross the Black Sea to Batoum. Finally, there was an option of going by steamer all the way, usually via Bombay to Bushire. During the 1900s two further routes became popular. First, rail to Baku via Flushing, Dresden, Vienna and Rostov. Secondly, by P & O Steamers to Bushire via Marseilles and – sometimes – Muscat.

Journey times, especially in the 1890s, could be a month or more. Snow on the Continent or bad weather on the Caspian often caused long delays, while the difficulties of moving inside Persia were substantial. Wives often travelled between Rasht and Tehran in a *kajareh*, a box-like contraption carried on one side of a mule. 'Two of the *kajareh* are slung on a mule', wrote one officer in 1895 explaining why his wife had vowed never to repeat the experience, 'and along the mountain paths one side must necessarily overhang the precipice, so that the feelings of the occupant, who can only see straight ahead, may be better imagined than described.'[35] Travelling in northern Persia in winter was particularly grim. 'The mud, the snow, the rain, the want of any civilised accommodation, the fatigue of 20 days, perhaps, or more horseriding, the excessive cold, the filth and discomfort everywhere', D. Baker wrote in 1892 describing a journey from Tehran to Tabriz, 'makes a winter journey to Tabriz one of the most severe physical ordeals to which the town bred European can be subjected to.'[36] In the south in the summer there was the opposite problem of unremitting heat. 'I was nearly roasted between Kashan and a place called Sin-Sin', one officer wrote in 1896. 'It was so hot that my stirrup irons burnt my boots! When I reached Sin-Sin I drank 26 cups of tea straight off.'[37] Persian tea cups are small, but even so this was quite a feat!

Men tended to react in extreme ways to their life once they had arrived at their post. Some considered Persia to be the nearest thing to hell on earth, a country, as D. Baker wrote in 1892, 'absolutely destitute of all those things which render life worth living for'.[38] Others adored the place and their new life. 'I like the country, my work, my social position and everything else', a junior wrote home soon after his arrival in 1911 '...you cannot find a more contented youth.'[39]

The largest proportion of the European staff in Persia worked in Tehran.

By 1895 the Chief Office had seven permanent expatriate officers, including the Chief Manager, and 20 years later this figure had grown to 18. In Tehran staff could lead a congenial expatriate life. The city's British population may have reached 150 by 1914, and the social standing of the Bank's officials seems to have been high. Staff at all levels were fully involved in the European social life of the city. This meant, even for juniors, a regular diet of afternoon calls, the leaving of cards, dances and dinners, all activities being conducted in correct and formal dress. 'Invitations to dinner and dances and all that kind of rubbish with married folks are becoming a damned nuisance', complained one newly arrived junior in Tehran in 1911, 'but one must go and smile to the ladies and afterwards keep up the weekly round of afternoon calls.' The people were a 'nice crowd', the young man continued, but he could not help becoming 'fed up with ... sitting on a silk cushion, a cup of tea in one hand and a piece of cake in the other trying to keep up a conversation with a Missioner's daughter.'[40] The Chief Manager and the senior management mixed as equals with the senior levels of the diplomatic corps, attending garden parties and dinners held at the British Legation on special occasions, such as the Queen's birthday. Similarly, the senior staff had social contacts with the highest levels of Persian society. It was not unknown for leading members of government and the more important princes and notables to visit Rabino, and later Wood, in their offices or homes.

It was a different story in the provinces. By the 1900s the most important provincial branches of the Bank had an expatriate Manager and an Accountant, but smaller branches were often only allocated one European. Their life could be lonely and bleak, especially if they were bachelors, and summers at the 'hot' branches were nightmares, with air-conditioning still several decades away. The European communities in the provincial towns were often small and occasionally non-existent, while social contact with the local inhabitants was often difficult.

Mashad seems to have taken a particular toll of the men sent to run the branch. 'A dull and nasty place all round', one man wrote in 1891, '... the feeling of being a prisoner is sometimes maddening.'[41] The local population were said to have been so inimical to Europeans that the Bank's Manager there could only leave his house if he were accompanied by guards.[42] There was a succession of human disasters at the branch. One young officer committed suicide. A successor had to leave because he developed severe mental depression and liver disease. Yet another man developed chronic *delirium tremens*. 'As you know I have been up here for over two years', another officer wrote from Mashad in 1905 begging for an urgent transfer, 'and did you know anything of Mashad you would know what a terrible ordeal that has been'.[43]

Mashad, however, did not hold a monopoly of horrors. Many provincial branches had the same tales of loneliness, hostile climates, and appalling conditions, with a man's physical and mental endurance being tested to the limit. 'Shiraz is a terrible place', wrote one man in 1907, '... Last week I had a sunstroke which nearly killed me. ... This is due to the Bank quarters being 1.5 miles from the offices and in the middle of the day there is no shade whatever.'[44] Bushire, in the opinion of one man, was, 'the worst god forsaken hellfire place in Persia and perhaps even in the world'.[45] Nasratabad in Seistan was cut off by the desert from all the other branches, and had a tiny European population. The branch's first Manager lasted only six months before, 'overcome by the depressing conditions of life', he resigned from the Bank.[46] Political upheavals, such as the tobacco riots in 1892 and the Constitutional Revolution, brought further hazards. Tribal warfare in southern Persia in the years before 1914 caused constant chaos. Travel to Shiraz was often disrupted for months on end.

The Bank took some responsibility for accommodating its European staff. Staff in the provinces were always provided with accommodation, as hotels were non-existent. In Tehran, many juniors were housed inside Chief Office. This splendid building was purchased for £13 700 in 1902 from the owner, the Amin od-Doule. By 1900 about eight single junior officers were housed in it. Married officers, however, had a housing allowance and had to find their own accommodation. The exception to this rule was the Chief Manager. Rabino had built a house in 1890. Conscious of the importance of status in Persia, he had made sure that it looked 'suitable to its purpose and our station'.[47] Wood, however, did not appear to like the house, and in 1911 he purchased another one for 250 000 Krans (£4950).

Outside Tehran, the Bank initially rented both its offices and housing. It was very usual, especially in the early years, for the Manager and the Accountant at provincial branches to share a house. During the 1900s the Bank started to build its own houses for staff. In 1908 Tabriz built new staff quarters and Esfahan bought a ready built house. A Manager's house was constructed at Hamadan in 1911, a building which earned high praise from subsequent Managers. In 1912 new houses were built in Bushire and Kermanshah for both the Managers and the Accountants. Overall, the Bank spent over £60 000 on housing and office accommodation in Persia between 1902 and 1914.

The Bank did something to provide recreational facilities for staff. In 1892 a staff tennis court was constructed in Tehran. In the same year Rabino had a billiard table sent out from London. He envisaged it would be kept in the banking hall, and during working hours, by means of covering it with a wooden lid and a piece of oil cloth, it would be used as a table on which customers could count their money.[48] During the 1890s some books were also sent out from London and in 1897, on Rabino's initiative, a library was established in Chief Office which contained both reference books (on banking, law, Persia, etc.) and a 'recreational and instructional section'.[49] A book collection, substantial at least for Persia at that time, was soon acquired, largely through gifts and donations.

Apart from books, tennis courts or billiard tables provided by the Bank, staff had to make their own recreation. Some had a keen interest in religion. E. M. Eldrid spent much of his time in Kerman preaching with the Church Missionary Society Mission, perhaps under the influence of his fiancée (and later wife) who was a medical missionary. This activity was regarded as most embarrassing by the Bank, and pressure was exerted on Eldrid to calm his evangelistic fervour.[50] Another officer became excessively devoted to Persian culture, and Islam. His habit of dressing in Persian clothes particularly embarrassed the Bank. The officer was eventually dismissed for kidnapping the wife of a Persian Christian and despatching her to Baghdad.[51] He was, however, subsequently hired by the Anglo–Persian Oil Company, and by 1914 had risen to a senior position in their oil-field operations.[52]

More conventional officers devoted themselves to sporting activities. Horses were so cheap that even junior British officers could afford to ride. Hunting foxes and hares, hawking and shooting were very popular among expatriates in Tehran. Polo – a sport which had originated in Persia – was reintroduced to Tehran in 1897 and the Bank fielded its own team against the Indo–European Telegraph Company and the Legation. In 1896 a race track was built at Gulhak, now a suburb of modern Tehran but then still separated from the city, where the British and other Legations had their summer quarters. There was a two-day race meeting each September.[53] In Tehran there were sufficient Bank staff to raise a cricket team, and sufficient other British inhabitants to play against. 'What with riding, tennis, cricket etc. we get plenty of exercise', one man wrote in 1896, '... every Friday from October to about Xmas day and from March to the end of May we have a cricket match in town, and from June to the end of September we have one every Sunday, that being the only day we get sufficient players at Gulahek.'[54] In the winter, skating provided the exercise which tennis and cricket gave through the long summers.

In the provinces, however, team games were often an impossibility, as there were not enough Europeans to make teams. In such places men were more prone to turn to drink. Intemperance was a major problem within the Imperial Bank. The six officers who were dismissed from the Bank's service before 1914 for excessive drinking were only the tip of an unhappy iceberg. As early as 1893 Dr Thin, the Bank's Medical Adviser in London, issued a warning on the subject to the Board after hearing reports of the dimensions of excessive alcohol consumption by Bank staff in Persia.[55] But the Board's strictures had little effect on men isolated in depressing provincial towns. 'The causes of intemperance in Persia', Rabino explained bluntly to London in 1904, 'are the intense monotony of existence particularly in the provinces.'[56]

The Bank's correspondence makes it clear that heavy drinking remained widespread in the Bank, and on occasion this turned into catastrophe. A Manager of Mashad branch in 1898 was found in a state of complete alcoholic stupefaction, his mind wandering, as the result of many months of intoxication.[57] In 1902 another man, overcome by 'the drink fiend', tried to shoot two fellow officers.[58] In 1913 a young man who had become a heavy drinker while in Chief Office, resorted to morphine and cocaine after being appointed Accountant in Esfahan, a branch which traditionally engaged in financing the opium trade. He had to be sent to a sanatorium in London.[59] But the majority of men simply went about their work, using alcohol as and when required to provide solace from 'the intense monotony of existence'. Whisky was the 'oil of joy', wrote one young officer in 1913. 'Mackay Liquor Whiskey, that's the stuff to soothe one's unending thirst, to bury one's nose in, to get quietly tight on. No nasty headaches in the morning and no undue rush to that wonderful bottle of Eno's (the drunkards' drink)...'[60]

The many dangers of living in Persia must have encouraged some men to seek relief in the 'oil of joy'. Diseases such as cholera, smallpox, the plague, malaria and tuberculosis were endemic, and the very low level of sanitary conditions, especially outside Tehran, meant that the likelihood of a European succumbing to at least one of these diseases was high. Eleven European officers died in the Bank's service between 1889 and 1914. Two Europeans, and nine Persian staff, were lost in the cholera epidemic of 1892. The victims were nursed day and night by their colleagues, as there were no nurses. 'The dead and dying were to be seen in every street', D. Baker, the Bank's Deputy Chief Manager, reported to London, 'and uncovered corpses were transported to the burial ground on donkey-back – in fact everywhere for a month death in its most horrible and revolting forms.'[61] Another officer died at Shiraz in the 1904 cholera epidemic, and at Kermanshah customers dropped dead at the Bank's doors.[62] Two British officers died from 'galloping consumption'. Smallpox, malaria and tetanus claimed the lives of three other men. At any one time many of the British staff would be ill with some disease. At Baghdad and Basra in the 1890s in particular, British officers endured fevers almost continuously.

Wives suffered alongside their husbands. The climate and diseases undermined health, and helped to make childbirth more hazardous than usual. Several wives died in childbirth, including the wife of S. F. Rogers at

Yazd in 1899. When the wife of another officer was having her first child at Yazd shortly before the First World War, she reportedly heard the servants saying, 'Oh this woman's sure to die. The last one did.' In fact, the lady in question did recover, 'after seven months in bed', though sadly her young daughter was accidentally burnt to death two years later in Kerman.[63] Bank wives were regularly required to nurse the sick and dying. When the wife of a member of the Chief Office staff contracted smallpox in 1899, Mrs Rabino nursed her through the initial stages of the illness.[64] Happily, the woman survived.

Such conditions can hardly have been an incentive to young ladies to marry Imperial Bank men. Finding a wife could be a huge problem. Meeting and marrying a girl while on leave was necessarily a tense and hurried business, but if a man missed his opportunity it might be five years or more before he had another chance. It was unwise to leave such matters to chance, and young officers in search of a wife often turned to the relatives of colleagues in the Bank, or sometimes in the Legation or the other British commercial ventures in Persia. As a result, distinct 'Bank families' had emerged by 1914. In 1904, for example, one mother hearing of the cholera epidemic in Persia, wrote to Newell to enquire about three of her children. Her son was serving in the Bank, while two daughters were married to Bank men.[65] There were other Bank families. To take just one example, H. L. G. Taylor joined the Bank in 1906. His sister, Dr Elsie Taylor, was the medical missionary who was to marry E. M. Eldrid. Taylor's daughter, Margo, was later to marry into the Bank herself when she became the wife of H. B. Sinclair in 1940.

5.4 THE LOCAL STAFF

The local staff can be the forgotten men of British overseas banks. The written records largely record the words, achievements and problems of the European officers. Yet, at least in the case of the Imperial Bank of Persia, the local staff played an indispensable role in the Bank's survival and growth. Although they worked under expatriate officers, the more senior clerks would have known far more of the Bank's business than the young men sent out from England. Moreover, the loyalty of the local staff during times of crisis, such as the runs on the Bank, the cholera epidemics and the Constitutional Revolution, was amply demonstrated.

Chief Office employed the largest number of local staff. Its size, excluding domestic servants, grew from 24 in August 1891, to 48 in 1903 to 150 in 1911. The provincial branches employed fewer men, although the exact numbers employed at all the branches is not known. In 1897 Tabriz and

Shiraz are known to have had 17 and 16 local staff respectively. Esfahan in 1898 had 24 local staff and 17 *farrashes*.[66]

The most important members of the Bank's local staff were the interpreters, known to the Bank as *mirzas*. Each branch had at least one *mirza*, and Tehran had three in the 1890s. It is tempting, but misleading, to compare the Persian *mirza* with the Chinese *compradore*. In China, the *compradores* working for the Hongkong Bank and the foreign banks introduced Chinese business on a commission basis, guaranteed that business, and employed and guaranteed the Chinese staff. In Persia, the *mirzas* also acted as intermediaries between the foreigners and the indigenous commercial sector, but their intermediary role carried less power and responsibility. They acted as the eyes and ears of Managers in the recruiting of local staff, but the element of formal guarantee of customers and staff was missing, and the Bank directly employed its own local staff. The Imperial Bank's determination that its European staff should learn Persian was one indication that more direct contact between them and their customers was envisaged than in China, and also that as the *mirzas* did not guarantee local business, European officers had more responsibility for the safe employment of Bank funds. *Mirzas* were also often used to give Persian lessons to European staff, a function which *compradores* seem rarely if ever to have undertaken.

In Tehran, the Bank's *mirzas* were employed, in addition to their commercial duties, in liaison with government. The Bank's first Chief *mirza*, Abdol Hasan Khan, acquired a high reputation in this respect, as well as for his business acumen. The Board in London, however, had little faith in the Persian character, and was gravely suspicious of the reliance which Rabino seemed to place on his *mirzas*. 'Such men', Sir Lepel Griffin observed concerning the Chief *mirza*, 'are all bought and sold by the Persian Ministers and will tell you what they are ordered or paid to say'.[67] However, not only were Griffin's views the product more of assumption rather than evidence, it was also impossible to dispense with *mirzas* in relations with government. In April 1899, following instructions from London, Rabino had meetings with the Prime Minister accompanied only by his son, who spoke fluent Persian. This caused grave displeasure. It went against all the acceptable polite formalities. 'On Friday last', Rabino reported, 'the Sadr Azam sent for our Chief *mirza*, expressed his surprise and displeasure at the innovation, informed him in detail of everything that had passed at our three interviews and entrusted him with an important communication for me.'[68]

The Bank's local staff were drawn from a wide variety of nationalities. The *mirzas* were normally Persian, together with the occasional Armenian. In the northern branches, Armenians were the backbone of the Bank's local staff. The majority of Tehran's local staff were also Armenian. In the southern branches, clerks tended to be a mixture of Armenians, Ceylonese, Indians, and Jews.

Suitable local staff, especially for relatively skilled jobs, were often hard to find. Racial stereotypes abounded in the descriptions of recruiting staff. 'The habits, temperament and education of Persians', the Tehran management cried in despair in 1900, 'render it impossible to train them in regular and accurate clerical work.'[69] E. M. Eldrid in 1906 lamented the unemployability of the inhabitants of Kerman. 'The constitutions of those who are not themselves slaves to the opium habit', he observed, 'are apparently affected by the hereditary taint with the result that their instincts of right and wrong seem deadened and even common ambition stifled.'[70] In retrospect, however, it is clear that the Bank's staff problems were no greater, or smaller, than in similar countries where illiteracy was high, and the form of 'work discipline' which had developed in western cultures largely unknown.

As with the European staff, there was little in the way of a salary structure for local staff at first. The average starting salary for clerks in Tehran in the 1890s and early 1900s was between 100 and 150 Krans a month (say, £23–£35 per annum). There was no regular pattern of annual increases, but some rises were granted as a reward for good work. The Board was most reluctant to consider matching rises in the cost of living with salary increases, and Rabino's pleas on this front earned him regular rebukes from London. 'You are a great deal too soft-hearted in your recommendations for increase of salary; especially in the case of the native staff', Sir Lepel Griffin told him in January 1907. '. . . You do not guard with sufficient jealousy the interests of the Bank.'[71]

Local staff received little benefit from the Bank except in the form of wages. There was no free housing and no paid holidays, although staff were allowed the normal public holidays. Local staff were not eligible to join any sort of provident fund. The Bank did, however, offer regular and secure employment of a kind almost non-existent in the Persia of the period. Government service was, by contrast, insecure and dependent on contacts, and a man's career could depend on the ebb and flow of political life.[72] In the Bank, a man would receive regular wages and fair treatment, and prestige for working in the Bank-e Shahi.

A Persian would, however, have no prospect of promotion to management. In this the Imperial Bank's policy was characteristic of all British Eastern exchange banks, although not of banks such as the Imperial Ottoman Bank which did regularly employ non-Europeans as Managers by the late nineteenth century. Before 1914 there is little surviving evidence that local staff resented their non-existent promotion prospects, although various letters suggest that some men at least felt their work was not appreciated. 'I am afraid the Board of directors do not realise that the local staff contribute their fair share to the success and prosperity of the Bank', the chief clerk in Tehran's bill department wrote to Rabino in 1906. '... Our services are untiring and self-sacrificing and the encouragement we have received is very small.'[73]

One case, that of Ismail Bagher, suggests that the more ambitious men may have felt they deserved better. Bagher, who had received some education in Britain, had joined the local staff in 1894. After serving in Tehran, where Rabino considered him 'specially deserving of commendation',[74] he was sent to Mashad where he rapidly became invaluable. By the beginning of 1898, when the Mashad Manager had been rendered completely incapable because of drink, he was in effect running the branch.[75] Bagher seems to have hoped that his hard work and devotion would earn his transfer to the European staff, and he even went to the length of anglicising his name to Baker. The Bank, however, made it explicit that he had no hope of such a promotion, and soon afterwards a decline in the quality of his work began to be noticed.[76] Nemesis came in Kermanshah in the early 1900s. His manager, Hyacinth Rabino, was preoccupied with his duties as vice-consul, and, with no other European officer below him, left Bagher virtually to run the branch. Bagher, soured by the Bank's treatment, began to pursue his own business interests, and, as seen in Chapter 3, bad debts and mayhem followed. Bagher was dismissed. In the interwar years the frustration of another member of the Persian staff – Abol Hassan Ebtehaj – was to lead him to leave the Bank and mastermind a campaign to curb its business in his country.

5.5 LONDON OFFICE

London Office was still very small in 1914, with a permanent staff of four or five, supported by a changing population of juniors awaiting appointment to Persia. George Newell, Secretary and London Manager, presided over the Office, supported after 1910 by S. F. Rogers, the former Deputy Chief Manager in Tehran, who had resigned from the overseas service because of ill-health, as Sub-Manager.

The London staff contained many long-serving men. Newell served from 1889 to December 1917, when he retired aged 70. E. S. Shoebridge joined as an Assistant Accountant in 1896, rose to Chief Cashier, and retired in 1923, again aged 70. S. F. Rogers was, therefore, a comparative youngster when he joined London Office in 1910 aged 43. Even the messengers were long-serving employees. C. Froome joined the Bank in 1889 at the age of 39 and remained in his post until his death in 1913. G. Birkett joined in 1890, at the age of 20, and stayed until he retired in 1935.

Salaries in London were lower than those of the overseas staff, although the duties and lives of the London staff and the men in Persia were so different that it is hard to make comparisons. George Newell's salary on appointment as Secretary was £600 per year. In 1902 this was increased to £1200, and it remained at that level until his retirement. Rogers was appointed Sub-Manager in 1910 on a salary of £700 per annum, £150 less than he had earned as Deputy Chief Manager. These salaries were quite good for the time. In the Hongkong Bank's London Office in the 1900s, the Accountant received £750 per year, and no-one else more than £350. Birkett was paid 17/6d per week in 1890, and when he retired in 1935 he was earning 82/6d per week. In addition to their wages, London Office staff regularly received an annual bonus of 10% on their salaries in the early 1900s and 5% between 1905 and 1910, when the remaining 5% was allocated to the Officers' Provident Fund. In contrast, overseas staff, as was remarked above, were only paid a general bonus twice, in 1907 and 1910. No one received a bonus between 1910 and the outbreak of the War.

London Office was located in small, cramped offices in the City. The premises were initially located in temporary offices at 100 Old Broad Street. In 1896 the Bank moved from 14 Austin Friars to ground floor and basement premises at 25 Abchurch Lane, and remained at this location until 1924. (London Office was to return to Abchurch Lane, but this time Nos. 19–22, between 1970 and 1975). Just before the First World War the offices were renovated. A Boardroom was created; a book lift was installed; a heating system was put in, with hot-water radiators fuelled from a boiler in the basement; and electric lighting was fitted.

But, to later eyes at least, London Office remained a musty place. Everything was written by hand, with the single typewriter in the office reserved for outgoing letters. G. W. Kelbe, who joined the Bank aged 29 in 1889 as the Bank's Accountant, and retired in 1927, regarded the noise of a typewriter as incompatible with the dignity of a banking hall. The typist, therefore, had to work in the Boardroom. On days when the Board met, usually once a week, no typing was permitted until the directors had left. All letters were press-copied by the two messengers. The office was naturally an exclusively male preserve, until the exigencies of War drove the Bank to employing women. In 1915 Miss Jessie Thomsett, the Bank's first female employee, was appointed a correspondence clerk on a weekly salary. Several women followed in her footsteps, including Miss M. Owen who came in November 1917. Miss Owen has left a vivid impression of the office, its atmosphere and staff. E. S. Shoebridge, she later recalled 'was a man of small stature, wore high, stiff collars that thrust into his neck and played the organ at his local Church twice on Sundays. His cheeks glowed with the apple red of an illustrated Pickwick. His small daily float of cash was contained in a japanned cash box which stood below the counter where he worked. There was no till; no separate drawer for cash.'[77]

Even this cosy Dickensian world, however, could not insulate itself from the crisis which was to engulf Europe and the Middle East. Chapter 6 must turn to the story of the Imperial Bank during the First World War.

Part 2

THE BANK 1914–39

6

THE BANK AT WAR 1914–18

6.1 THE WAR AND THE BANK'S PERFORMANCE

The Imperial Bank of Persia was no stranger to crisis, but the First World War presented it with the severest challenges yet. Persia became a battleground for the British, Russian, Ottoman and German armies and agents. The Bank's branches were looted; its note issue almost collapsed; and by the end of the War the Persian economy was dislocated and famine widespread. The Bank faced unprecedented demands on its resources to assist the finance of Allied forces in Persia. Yet it proved itself, once again, to have the capacity to survive in the face of adversity. The greatest casualty of the War was the Bank's dual identity, British and Persian. The requirements of the British war effort were placed firmly above those of the Persian government, or Persian business. There was no real alternative to such a choice, for apart from the natural sympathies of its British staff, the Bank was subjected to British government dictates, while Persia and its government all but disintegrated. The Bank made good profits in the second half of the War. But its very explicit role as the agent of Empire, a role which was to expand even further in the immediate post-War years, was not to place it in a good position to resist nationalist critics of its position during the 1920s.

The Bank's fortunes were so closely tied to the First World War that it is necessary to begin by briefly reviewing the War's impact on Persia.[1] Persia tried to stay out of the conflict, despite sympathy in many quarters for Germany, the enemy of Russia and, of course, Britain. On 1 November 1914 Persia declared its neutrality, but given its geographical position and military weakness there was little chance this would be respected. During the winter the Ottomans invaded Azerbaijan, where Russian troops had been stationed for some years, and in January 1915 Tabriz was briefly occupied. Although Russian troops subsequently relieved that city, strong Ottoman Forces remained in the province until the spring. German agents, especially the formidable Captain Wassmuss, were also active. Wassmuss had been

German Consul at Bushire before the War, and on the outbreak of hostilities he returned to Persia to use his contacts among the tribal leaders in the south to encourage anti-British activities.[2] As these foreign influences on Persia increased, Persian politics became highly unstable, with 16 changes of Cabinet between 1914 and 1918, although there was a greater continuity in personnel in government than this turnover would suggest.[3]

During 1915 British and Russian policy came close to disaster. Ottoman troops reinvaded the north, and by the end of the year they had occupied Kermanshah, Soltanabad and Hamadan. In the south, Wassmuss organised a tribal revolt against British influence. Shiraz was occupied, and Esfahan, Yazd and Kerman evacuated by their British communities. In March Britain and Russia reached a secret agreement which went even further than the 1907 Convention in dividing up Persia. Russia was to be allowed 'full liberty of action' in the north of the country, while the former neutral zone was allocated to British 'influence'.[4] Although the existence of this treaty was unknown in Persia, in August the Persian government decided to join the Germans and Ottomans. However, before any formal alliance could be forged Russian troops moved south, almost reaching Tehran in November. Most of the government and Majles fled to Qum, and later to Kermanshah where a provisional government was formed. The Shah, however, was persuaded by the Allied Ministers to stay in Tehran, and on 25 December a new Cabinet was installed led by the pro-British notable Farman Farma.[5] The provisional government was forced to retreat to Ottoman territory, and reached Berlin in 1917.

The following year, 1916, began better for the Allies. By March the Ottomans had been driven out of most of Persia. A new government formed in that month, headed by Sepahdar Azam, agreed in April to allow Britain and Russia to recruit troops in Persia, and to put Persian finances under Allied control. In return Persia was to receive an Allied subsidy. In June, however, Ottoman forces entered Persia again, and by the following month Kermanshah, Soltanabad and Hamadan had been reoccupied. The government of Sepahdar Azam fell in August, and the agreement with the Allies was renounced.[6] The new Prime Minister claimed that the document containing the Allied agreement had gone missing, 'a peculiarly Persian bit of chicanery', as one recent historian has observed, 'that illustrates the foolishness to which Anglo–Iranian relations so often aspired'.[7] Despite the collapse of Sepahdar Azam's agreement, however, a small British military mission under Sir Percy Sykes recruited local troops, and between March and November 1916 this force, which became known as the South Persia Rifles, marched from Bandar Abbas through Kerman, Yazd and Esfahan to Shiraz, driving out German agents and their local supporters.

During 1917 the Persian situation was further complicated by the collapse of Russian power in Persia following the overthrow of the Tsar in March, and the subsequent Bolshevik Revolution in October. By the autumn the Russian Army in Persia had begun to disintegrate, and in January 1918 Lenin's government renounced all agreements which had restricted Persia's sovereignty. The secret Anglo–Russian treaty of March 1915 was published in Moscow, and denounced.

The main British concern became to fill the vacuum left by the Russian withdrawal, and further British and Indian troops were despatched. Prominent among these was a small military mission under Major General L. C. Dunsterville, which was sent to Persia with the objective of holding the southern Caucasus against the Ottomans.[8] 'Dunsterforce', however, got no further than Enzeli in February 1918, from where it was forced to retreat by nationalist Jangalis (literally, jungle dwellers) who, under the leadership of Kuchek Khan, had captured most of Gilan province over the previous year. Over the following months Jangalis, Dunsterforce, anti-Bolshevik Russian officers and German agents were in conflict. But by November 1918, when the war in Europe ended, the Jangalis had been forced to sue for peace, and British troops controlled almost all of Persia.

The Imperial Bank, therefore, found itself in the midst of almost constant turmoil which affected practically all of Persia at one time or another. Its fortunes in Persia continued to be directed by A. O. Wood, who remained Chief Manager throughout the War. Wood was not an ideal occupant for this post during the War. At a time when the Bank's role as agent of Empire assumed new and blatant proportions, Wood's impatience, dislike and disdain for Persia and Persians sharpened the contrast between the ideal and the reality of the Imperial Bank's claims to be the state bank of the country. 'I have always done my best to assist the Persian government and will continue to do so', he wrote to the British Minister in Tehran in September 1914, 'but you will readily understand that even with the very best of goodwill it is difficult if not impossible at times to help so corrupt a people as we have to deal with out here.'[9] Condescending and xenophobic in a peculiarly British way, Wood earned few admirers among Persians of any hue.

Nor did Wood's talents as a banker compensate for any failure as a diplomat. When James McMurray succeeded Wood as Chief Manager in 1919, he painted a bleak picture of Wood's performance, arguing that most of the work had been done by the Deputy Manager, Brown, and the Chief Accountant, Edward Wilkinson. 'A.O.W. was a mere cypher', McMurray wrote to Rogers in 1919:

and from what I saw when I came here must have been all the time since he became C.M. You know as well as I do that he had not the most elementary knowledge of

Exchange. . . . He got one copy of the telegrams, No. 2 a copy and Wilkinson a copy. He initialled them at such a rate that made it quite certain he didn't read them. Offers were accepted and made by W. and A.O.W. never knew what happened. . . . All he did was to attend to staff matters and write you a confidential letter occasionally the contents of which, including Staff changes etc., were the products of E.W.'s brain.[10]

A man's comments on his predecessor are often jaundiced, but there is sufficient evidence to believe that McMurray's picture of Wood was not too unfair.

In London there were several changes on the Board. Sir Thomas Jackson died on 21 December 1915. Sir Hugh Barnes succeeded him as Chairman, a post which he was to hold until 1937. In 1917 Frederick Sassoon also died and two more directors resigned because of pressure of other commitments, Lord Inchcape in 1915 and Charles Greenway in 1918. The new appointments came from familiar sources. The Hongkong Bank connection was retained by the appointment in 1916 of H. E. R. Hunter. He had been on the staff of the Hongkong Bank between 1881 and 1912, and its Acting Chief Manager in 1906. In June 1917 D. Gubbay replaced Frederick Sassoon as the representative of David Sassoon & Co. In the same month Col. Sir A. Henry McMahon, a former colleague of Barnes in the Indian Civil Service, joined the Board. In April 1918 E. A. Chettle took Greenway's place. Chettle, like Greenway was a partner in the Indian managing agents Shaw, Wallace & Co., and he was also a director of Strick, Scott and Co., the firm which managed the Anglo–Persian Oil Company's operations in Persia.[11] Chettle was the last infusion of new blood for 20 years, for the four directors appointed between 1919 and 1938 were all former members of the Imperial Bank's staff.

'War, it is said, is good for banking', reflected the *Statist* journal in 1919 after examining wartime developments in British banking.[12] This generalisation holds a particular truth for the Imperial Bank. Both the First and Second World Wars were periods of growth and good profits for it. This growth stemmed largely, although not entirely, from the Bank's role in financing British government requirements in Persia. Agent of Empire was a more lucrative role than being state bank.

The Bank's balance sheet grew by 150% between 1914 and 1918, or double the increase between 1889 and 1914. This expansion, however, disguised a fall in 1915 and 1916, followed by rapid growth in the last two years of the War. The Bank's deposits expanded by £695 368 in 1914 to £1 789 369 in 1918, an increase of 157%. The note issue, on the other hand, slumped from £832 012 in 1914 to £180 002 two years later, and even in 1918 it only stood at £667 153 or 20% lower than in 1914. Bills discounted, loans and advances increased only slowly from £1 127 669 to £1 209 787 in

Table 6.1. *Imperial Bank profits 1914–18 (£ Sterling)*

Year ending (20 September)	Published net profits	Movements through inner reserves			
		Losses debited to inner reserves	Transfers (to) or from profits	Bad debts recovered (or provided for)	Transfer from published reserves
1914	31 244	—	20 000	(3647)	—
1915	25 749	(118 725)	(10 000)	(4343)	60 000
1916	50 170	—	—	(2920)	—
1917	79 962	—	24 000	1186	—
1918	78 149	—	205 000	7	—

1917, and then moved sharply upwards to £1 996 275 in 1918. The Bank's investments fell from £631 842 to £429 201 between 1914 and 1916, and by 1918 had soared to £3 518 293. The overall pattern was one of difficulty or decline in the first two years of the War, and very marked expansion in the final year.

This picture is reinforced by movements in shareholders' funds of the Bank. Total published shareholders' funds fell after 1914, and did not regain the 1914 level until 1918, when they stood at £922 388. The inner reserves also fell by a half between 1914 and 1915, and in 1916 there was a further small fall which reduced the reserves to £67 449. However, after a recovery in 1917 inner reserves increased to £297 642 in 1918, making them, for the first time, larger than the Bank's published reserves.

The Imperial Bank's published profits fell in 1915, but doubled in 1916, increased again in 1917 and reached £78 149 in 1918. The 1917 and 1918 net profits were the highest yet shown by the Bank. However, as Table 6.1 makes clear, the use of inner reserves meant that the published figures glossed over a far more uneven pattern.

The year 1915 emerges as particularly bad. £10 000 was transferred from the inner reserves to support the published profits, and £60 000 moved from published to inner reserves. The £118 725 'loss' in 1915 was debited to inner reserves.[13] £68 519 of this figure was caused by a writing down of investments. The War witnessed a fall in the price of most securities on the London market, and many banks had to write down their investments to a more realistic level. The Bank's large holding of the 1911 Persian Loan was particularly hard hit by the fall in security prices. At the outbreak of War the Bank held £344 640 of the stock. This was written down by £55 941 in 1915 and £21 509 in 1916.

In addition, £29 444 of the 1915 loss comprised a write-down of the Bank's Persian assets as a response to a fall in the value of the Kran against

Sterling. The remaining £20 762 was lost on an overbought position in Roubles, which was part of a serious and wider misreading of the exchange markets. In anticipation of a strong demand for exchange in London and India, Wood built up a large Sterling overbought position – amounting to £255 000 in March 1915 – and he similarly made large purchases of Roubles. However, events did not turn out as expected. The Russian government forbade certain exports to Persia during the spring, and the Rouble–Kran exchange rate moved against Wood. There was no upsurge in trade between Persia and Britain and India, and in April there was a run on the Bank's notes which forced Wood to draw on his overbought position to replenish his depleted treasury at rates which were lower than when the position had been built up. Chief Office alone made a foreign exchange loss of £40 430 in the half-year ending September 1915, and this does not seem to have included the £20 762 loss on Roubles the Bank chose to debit to inner reserves. Interestingly, Wilkinson was away in Mashad during the period that the exchange losses were made, leaving Wood presumably to make his own decisions on exchange.

Profits recovered after 1915. In 1917 they were sufficient to make a £24 000 transfer to inner reserves. The following year was a bumper one with a £205 000 transfer to inner reserves before establishing the figure for net profit. Shareholders were, as usual, cushioned from the losses and sheltered from the high profits. Dividends were 6/- in 1915, 7/- in 1916 and 8/- for both 1917 and 1918.

It must be said at this stage that the balance sheet figures, even when movements in inner reserves are taken into account, provide only an approximate indication of the Imperial Bank's performance during the War. From September 1916 portions of profits were retained in Persia rather than remitted to Britain, and used to write off debts and build up reserves. In September 1916 less than half of total Persian profits were remitted to London, with the remainder being retained in Persia as provision for bad debts and allocated to a local contingency account.[14] In March 1917 the Bank boosted its capital in Persia to £497 195 by crediting £261 640 of its half-yearly profits to its capital account there.[15] It would appear safe to conclude that the Bank's profits for 1917 and 1918 were higher than shown in Table 6.1, and that the Bank used high wartime profits not only to remit substantial sums to London but also to strengthen its 'balance sheet' in Persia. This policy was to become a matter of contention between the Bank and the Persian government during the 1920s.

A further caveat concerns exchange rates and the terms used by the Bank to describe its Persian business on its Sterling balance sheet. In 1915 Krans began to appreciate against Sterling, and by the end of that year this appreciation was considerable. This was in part a reflection of a world-wide rise in the price of silver – some 85% during the War – which increased the value of all the silver-based currencies.[16] Other influences included the absence of inflation in Persia, a sharp depreciation in the Rouble against the Kran, and a shortage of Krans caused by the demands of the military forces in Persia.

The Bank's response to this exchange situation was determined by a number of factors. There was a concern that the wartime rise in the value of the Kran should not inflate the size of the balance sheet to such a level that there would be a dramatic decline after the end of the War. After 1915, therefore, the Bank adjusted its balance sheet at an exchange rate which was lower than the actual rate. By 1918 the average exchange rate was 25.5, although there were sharp fluctuations which could be 10% in a week. The Bank, however, adjusted its balance sheet at the rate of 55 Krans to the £1. (See Appendix 6 for the exchange rates in this period.) This had the effect of understating its Persian assets and liabilities in Sterling terms.

Different considerations, however, affected the rate at which the Bank wished to remit profits to Britain. In the last years of the War this rate was substantially different from the balance sheet adjustment rate. In 1917 and 1918 the Bank adjusted its balance sheet at 55 Krans, but remitted profits at 25 and 20 respectively. In arriving at its profit adjustment rate, particular consideration was given to the Bank's exchange position. In September 1916 (in contrast to the previous year) the Bank had a £261 640 oversold position, and insufficient funds to cover it. It was decided, therefore, to remit profits at a rate lower than the actual rate. This underestimated the Bank's profits in Sterling terms, but had the desired effect of keeping funds in Krans.[17] During 1917 and 1918, however, the Bank had large overbought positions in Sterling, and the Bank adjusted its profits at a higher exchange rate than the prevailing one. This overestimated the Bank's profits in Sterling terms, but covered the exchange position.

The following sections examine the impact of the War on the Bank, its relations with the British and Persian governments, and the Bank's banking business.

6.2 THE BANK AT WAR

'I hardly think that banking has ever been carried on under circumstances of such peril and difficulty', Sir Percy Sykes later wrote of the Imperial Bank's role in wartime Persia, 'nor perhaps has it ever rendered greater services.'[18]

The 'peril and difficulty' can be easily documented. By the end of 1916 twelve of the Bank's British staff in Persia had enlisted with the Bank's permission, and at least three others had resigned without permission to join the Army. Three of the former Bank staff became officers in Sykes' South Persia Rifles where – as Sykes told the Bank's AGM in 1919 – they 'greatly distinguished themselves'. Other men acted unofficially for the British forces in Persia, as consuls or sources of intelligence. The Kermanshah manager, R. Dewar-Durie, particularly distinguished himself in this respect. He played a notable role in intelligence gathering. In December 1916, the Legation warned Wood that if Dewar-Durie ceased his special work 'the whole of our intelligence service, to which the Russians attach great importance, will collapse'.[19] In 1918 Dewar-Durie was a member of a British military mission sent into the Caucasus. He was captured by the Bolsheviks and held for several months.

The provincial branches regularly acted as billets for British troops. General Dunsterville made his Hamadan headquarters at the home of the Bank Manager, James McMurray. 'Throughout all the varying fortunes of the force in North Persia', he later wrote, 'the Bank House at Hamadan stands out as a landmark, a never-failing refuge for the weary, a centre of genial hospitality and a focus of all political news.'[20] McMurray also turned his branch into a famine relief centre when fighting, bad weather and speculation caused major food shortages in northern Persia in 1918.[21] McMurray and Dewar-Durie were both awarded OBEs for their wartime services by the British government.

The Bank's branches were inevitably caught up in the fighting in Persia. During 1915 Ottoman troops and pro-German tribesmen in the south caused many of the branches to close. At the beginning of 1915 Tabriz and Ahwaz were forced to close. By the end of the year Kermanshah, Shiraz, Esfahan, Hamadan, Soltanabad, Kerman and Yazd had closed. Sometimes Managers had sufficient notice to remove their treasuries and books: at other times they simply had to flee. At Shiraz in November 1915, the Manager, M. Ferguson and his Accountant, F. A. Ayrton, were arrested by pro-German Swedish-led gendarmerie. The two bankers were held prisoner with other male members of the British community by tribesmen demanding conditions from the British government. Meanwhile the women were escorted to Bushire, with Mrs Ferguson assuming a prominent role in maintaining morale, and subsequently campaigning for months to get her husband released. 'The ladies, inspired by Mrs Ferguson', Sykes later wrote, '. . . never showed the slightest nervousness, even when insulted by a raging mob at Kazerun, and their behaviour under very trying circumstances was a credit to our race.'[22]

Some Managers were luckier than Ferguson. In December 1915 A. H. Wright found his Yazd branch surrounded by tribal contingents with German leaders, who took possession of it. The Germans, however, were courteous.

Wright was able to get a receipt for all the cash they removed from his treasury; he was allowed 20 000 Krans to get him to Tehran; and he was permitted to stay in the city until he had collected debts.[23]

In early 1916 Hamadan, Soltanabad and Kermanshah were reopened as the Russians pushed back the Ottomans, but by the summer the Ottomans had returned and the Bank's British staff had once again to flee. This time, however, they were not taken by surprise and were able to rescue books and treasuries. These branches did not reopen until May 1917. Kerman, Yazd, Esfahan and Shiraz were all able to reopen when the South Persia Rifles reached the towns. Their Managers were all in the van of Sykes' forces.

At the end of 1917 the Jangalis seized control of Rasht and for three weeks the Bank Manager, R. S. Oakshott, was held captive in the jungle, and for a further two months he was under house arrest. Oakshott eventually contrived to escape to Russian lines. Russian troops subsequently occupied Rasht, and on 13 July Oakshott reopened the branch. A week later, however, Jangali forces attacked the city, and the Bank house was defended for some hours by Oakshott, three British officers, three soldiers and a box of Mills bombs, before relief arrived.[24]

Inevitably there was considerable damage to the Bank's property and premises. The Manager's home at Hamadan was used by the Ottomans as the Army headquarters during 1916 and 1917, and most removable fittings had vanished by the time they left. Hamadan and Esfahan had large amounts of cash looted, and Yazd lost around 1.5 million Krans of notes.

The Bank considered that the Persian government should indemnify it against these losses, as the government had undertaken in the 1889 Concession to protect the Bank's property.[25] The Persian government, however, had neither the ability – nor the inclination – to oblige the Bank. There was some discussion whether the British government could either indemnify the Bank or lend the money to the Persians for such a purpose, but though Foreign Office officials regarded the Bank as 'an important political asset', the Treasury would not allocate government funds to compensate it.[26] In September 1917 the Bank wrote off its losses against its Persian profits before they were remitted to London, but pursued its claims for compensation from the Persian government. By July 1919 the claim stood at 11.2 million Krans (£204 000).[27] This matter was to continue, unresolved, throughout the 1920s.

The withdrawal of men to fight in the War and the lack of new recruits meant inevitable staff shortages, and by the later years of the War branch closures were on the agenda. Sabzevar was closed in September 1917, by which time the Bank's Manager was the only European in the town. Soltanabad, twice occupied by the Germans, was closed in September 1918, though only until staff shortages eased. On the other hand, small temporary offices were opened in Zanjan – located between Tabriz and Kazvin – and Baku in Russia towards the end of 1918 at the request of the British authorities to serve the British Army. They were always conceived as being temporary.[28] Bandar Abbas branch, however, which opened in December 1918, was regarded as permanent. A decision had been taken to open there before the War, but the outbreak had prevented the opening. By 1918 the British Army had banking requirements in the city, but it also seemed likely that the port's commercial business would expand.

6.3 THE NOTE ISSUE IN CRISIS

The sharp wartime decline in the Imperial Bank's note issue has already been observed. Converting Sterling into Krans at the Bank's adjustment rate, the note issue slumped from 49.9 million Krans in 1914 to 13.1 million in 1915 and only 11.3 million in 1916, before recovering to reach 36.7 million Krans in 1918.

The large fall in 1915 was due to a series of runs on the Bank, especially in Tehran. News of the outbreak of War in Europe caused a 10% fall in Tehran's note issue within a month, as confidence in the Imperial Bank waned and German agents began spreading rumours against it. During November there was a further run on the Bank, with Tehran's note issue falling 30% over the month. The simmering crisis finally turned into a large-scale run on the Bank in April 1915. On 26 April the resignation of the Persian Cabinet caused a run which came, in Wood's words, 'like a thunder-clap'.[29] It could hardly have come at a worse time. Tehran's ratio of cash to immediate liabilities had fallen from 64% in September 1914 to 36% in February 1915 and to 20% by March 1915. This situation was directly related to the large overbought position Wood had created, at the expense of the Bank's liquidity. To make matters worse, communications with the provincial branches were at one of their periodic low points, so Chief Office could expect little immediate help from that quarter.

The Bank was, as the Finance Committee later put it, in a 'truly dangerous' position.[30] Wood appealed for assistance from the British Minister, Charles Marling. There was no time for consultation with the Foreign Office. Marling, with the aid of the Russians, secured the appointment of a new Cabinet, and on 28 April an emergency decree was passed by the Majles to assist the Bank. Under the terms of the decree, for 60 days the Bank in Tehran was required to pay a daily total of only 100 000 Krans in silver against its notes. Above this amount, the Bank was authorised, when paying out notes, to include only ten Krans of such sums in silver currency. Perhaps the most surprising feature of the deal was that Marling, in order to get the Persian government's approval for the law, guaranteed on behalf of the British government if necessary to repay in silver any notes remaining in circulation at the end of the 60 days.[31] After discussion with Wood, Marling estimated that on the worst possible scenario the British government could find itself with a bill for £200 000 under this arrangement. It was agreed, retrospectively, that the Bank would place its holding of the 1911 Persian Loan with the British government as security for this guarantee.

The law of 28 April served its purpose in slowing the outflow of silver from the Chief Office. It took longer, however, to restore confidence in the Bank's notes. On 4 May Marling reported that they still seemed to be 'thoroughly discredited, and only accepted by speculators at a considerable discount'.[32] The discount was about 30% for some weeks. Persian Cabinet Ministers allegedly made a tidy profit by demanding silver daily from the Bank, buying notes in the bazaar at a discount and then encashing them at the Bank at their face value.[33] However, by 26 June, when the temporary law expired, confidence seems to have been restored, and the Bank had sufficient funds to resume payment of notes in coin if required.

The Bank's note issue was never again in such grave danger as in the first half of 1915. Particular branches experienced occasional runs, and the occupation of branches by enemy forces had an inevitable impact on note issues. Tehran's average note circulation was still in decline – though a slow one – during the second half of 1915 and the first half of 1916, and only began to recover in the second half of that year. In the north, the note issue at Mashad declined by 80% and at Hamadan by 93% in the two years after September 1916. Overall, however, by 1917 the note issue was recovering in towns not occupied or under enemy attack.

6.4 THE PERSIAN GOVERNMENT IN CRISIS

The immediate pre-War years had seen the Persian government acquire a growing external debt. The outbreak of War, and the disasters that befell Persia, pushed the precarious state finances to the brink, and beyond. Mornard had resigned in frustration in 1914 on the eve of the Shah's coronation, and during the first year of the War many of the Belgian officials who had manned provincial Treasury offices seemed to have left the country. As the central government's power waned, many provincial revenues seem not to have reached Tehran.

Wood had no sympathy for the succession of Persian governments, of either the pro-Allied or pro-German variety, formed during the War. Prudent banking would of necessity have dictated a policy of caution in a

Table 6.2 *Imperial Bank advances (outstanding balances) to Persian government 1914–18*

Date	Balance in Krans	Sterling equivalent at adjustment rate	Interest rate
September 1914	12 682 340	211 372	7%
September 1915	17 189 270	272 845	7%
September 1916	16 989 470	269 674	9%
September 1917	11 607 220	211 040	9%
December 1917	8 500 000	154 545	9%
July 1918	1 948 580	35 429	9%

country which had turned into a battlefield and where the administration was disintegrating. Moreover, as will be seen below, the British government exercised a tight control over the Bank's policies towards the Persian government. But Wood's distaste for, and distrust of, Persians was also much in evidence, attitudes which sat oddly with his position as chief representative of the state bank. Table 6.2 shows the Bank's lending to the Persian government during the First World War. (The British government's lending to Persia, which was passed through the Bank, is discussed in the following section.) The Persian government's debt to the Imperial Bank edged upwards during 1915, and then began to decline. This was in line with the Bank's policy not only to restrict any new advances to the government, but also to secure the repayment of most of its existing advances.

In September 1914 the Persian government made its first request for an advance of around £100 000. The Bank, after consulting the Foreign Office, refused the request.[34] Instead, Wood moved arbitrarily to ensure that some of the government's debt was repaid. In 1913 Mornard had agreed that the government's inland revenues should be paid into the Bank. Wood decided not to pass them on to the Persian government, but to retain them for use to reduce the government debt.[35] When Wood, in the following February, allowed the government an advance, it was against the inland revenue receipts.[36] These early manoeuvres set the tone for the Bank's relationship with the government during the War.

In January 1916 Wood raised the interest on the government debt, excluding silver advances, from 7% per annum to 9% per annum. The Board had suggested an increase to 8%, but Wood recommended the higher level.[37] When the pro-British government of Farman Farma complained that it was hardly opportune for the state bank to raise interest rates at a time when the government was in dire financial straits, Wood responded with a curt lesson in market forces. 'Owing to the War and the present deplorable state of the country', he wrote to the Minister of Finance, 'the Bank finds that it can employ its money more profitably than locking it up at 7% per annum. If the rate of 9% is not suitable, the remedy is too obvious to mention.'[38] Although the Bank had a perfect right to raise interest rates, Wood's bluntness must have added offence to an already difficult situation.

In March 1916 Wood took his firm line even further with the equally pro-British government of Sepahdar Azam. Under the terms of the 1910 Amalgamation Advance and the 1911 Loan, the Bank had a lien on the Gulf or Southern customs receipts, which were paid into the Bank. In March Wood decided that if there were any surplus on the revenues after the lien had been deducted, he would apply it to reduction of government's debt with the Bank. The use of these revenues led to a fall in government debt by September 1916, and to much larger falls in subsequent years as Persian imports from India increased, bringing a rise in Southern customs receipts.[39]

Successive Persian governments deeply resented Wood's policy, making a series of requests to be allowed to receive at least part of the surplus of the Gulf customs in cash.[40] Wood would not budge, however, and he was often supported by the British Legation which did not wish the Persian government to have an independent source of funds outside its control.[41] In December 1917 the Persian government demanded 6 million Krans, which they said the Bank owed them, and claimed – erroneously – that the Bank had used the customs revenues for the payment of its claim for looted property. Various compromise proposals were suggested but failed to materialise. Finally in December 1917, wishing to placate the current Cabinet, the British Minister in Tehran proposed that the Persian government should be allowed to retain half the surplus Gulf customs receipts.[42] The Bank agreed to the Legation's suggestion but it was not until July 1918 that the Persian government could bring itself to accept the compromise proposal. By then the government debt was less than 2 million Krans. By December 1918 it was 'practically non-existent'.[43]

The Imperial Bank also continued after 1914 to advance funds to the Persian government as part of the silver import business. In September 1914 the outstanding balance was 10 510 300 Krans (£175 172) at 5% interest. The patchy evidence does not, however, allow a picture of the size of the Bank's silver advances in the War years to be reconstructed.

Since March 1910 the Bank had been sole agent for importing silver for the government. The War, however, disrupted traditional sources of supply, just as the Bank could have done with more silver being minted. Not only did world silver prices move upwards, but shortages of cargo space made the despatch of silver to Persia a difficult problem. Nevertheless during 1915 and 1916 the Bank imported substantial amounts of silver. In 1915 at least

£100 000 of silver was brought into Persia by the Bank and minted, and in the following year a total of £666 000 silver was imported. These silver imports were the primary factor in the large oversold position the Bank had acquired by September 1916.

A wide net had to be cast for sources of supply. In early 1916 the Bank imported £70 000 of silver from Shanghai via Vladivostok, and the Russian government also supplied a further £150 000 of Chinese silver.[44] Silver was also imported from Britain via Archangel and Baku in the summer months, and Bushire and Ahwaz in the winter. By the end of 1917, however, the revolutions in Russia had disrupted supply lines through that country, while a world-wide shortage made it hard to find silver anywhere. Nevertheless during 1917 at least £300 000 of silver was imported into Persia.

Politics caused further difficulties in the silver situation. The Imperial Bank had agreed before the War to allow the Russian Bank a joint role as silver importer to the Persian government. This agreement, however, was never implemented, and as the War progressed the Russian government began to make vocal complaints on this score. The Imperial Bank countered that the Russian Bank did not have the resources to undertake silver importation, but this did not prevent Foreign Office pressure on the Bank to reach an agreement with Britain's Russian allies.[45] However, the lack of an effective government in Persia for much of 1915 did not provide opportune circumstances for negotiating a silver agreement and it was not until 23 October 1916 that a five-year contract was signed, which made the British and Russian Banks joint agents for the Persian government's silver imports. At the insistence of the Russians, an interest rate of 7% per annum on advances against silver was charged.[46] There is little evidence, however, that the Russian Bank was able to take advantage of the contract, and within a year it was – like the Tsarist government – on the brink of collapse.

6.5 'ONE OF OUR MAIN PROPS AND ASSETS'

The Imperial Bank's role as agent of Empire had always been influential before 1914. During the War it became paramount. The Bank's resources were largely devoted to meeting the requirements of the British government in Persia. The Bank, in the words of one Foreign Office official in January 1916, served as one of Britain's 'main props and assets in Persia'.[47] The Bank's contribution was in two stages. It acted as the channel through which increasingly large sums of British government money were sent to Persia, and it found the local currency which was required to make those funds of use in the country.

British government spending in Persia took four different forms. Firstly, the British government, after an initial period of difficulty, maintained and extended its pre-War policy of financing the Persian government. During the first months of the War the British government was unwilling to extend such financial assistance to the Persian government, or allow the Bank to provide any help. 'The situation in Persia', the Foreign Office informed the Bank in September 1914, 'is scarcely one to warrant any advance by HMG in view of the absence of any adequate supervision over the finances and of the Persian Government's many outstanding liabilities.'[48] The pro-German and anti-Russian sympathies of Persia were well-known, and not liked in London. The British government was, however, prepared to preserve Persian credit in London by paying the November 1914 coupon due on the 1911 Loan. A default on this stock, and a subsequent total collapse in its value, would have wiped out half of the Imperial Bank's investment portfolio, as well as carrying unforeseen consequences for City confidence in overseas loans. Moreover, there was a danger that Persia's shaky neutrality might have toppled over into active support of Germany.

In June 1915 the Allied governments began considering stronger support for the tottering Persian regime. The British and Russian Ministries in Tehran formulated a plan whereby they would pay to the Persian government part of the Gulf and Northern customs receipts which were allocated to the repayment and service of their debts. This was called a 'moratorium'.[49] The constant political shifts in Tehran and some delays on the Russian side meant that it was not until October 1915 that a 'moratorium' agreement was reached by the three parties. Britain and Russia were to provide £30 000 a month for the Persian government, in equal shares, although in fact Britain ended up by supplying the whole amount with the promise of eventual repayment from Russia.[50] No interest rate was mentioned in the agreement, but British officials seem to have assumed that 7% per annum would be charged. The monthly advance was also to be backdated to the previous March, representing a payment of £240 000. The agreement was in fact a straight loan rather than a 'moratorium', with the money being paid directly by Britain rather than from customs receipts, but its original name was retained as a device to obviate reference to the Majles, where neither the Persian Cabinet nor the Allies wanted to provoke opposition from nationalist deputies. This subterfuge added to the general confusion surrounding the moratorium loans, and it is clear that British officials only partially understood what they were doing. 'In obscuring the issue to deceive the Majlis', one historian has commented, 'the British also confused themselves.'[51]

The Bank's role, as before 1914, was to act as the channel through which British government funds reached the Persian government. The Bank was allowed to make exchange profits on remitting funds to Persia. The 'moratorium' advances were used as a political lever, switched on and off when required to assist the overall British policy of maintaining, in Marling's words, 'a strictly neutral Persia, but not a hostile Persia'.[52] The payment of the retrospective £240 000 was delayed by a prolonged debate between Britain and Russia about the form of financial control that should be imposed upon Persia as a *quid pro quo*. It was not until April 1916 that the Persian government headed by Sepahdar Azam agreed to a commission of control over the country's finances – and to the British and Russians being able to recruit troops in Persia – in return for the £240 000. A seconded official from the Imperial Bank was nominated to serve on the commission, alongside a representative from the Russian Bank, two Persian notables and, as President, one of the remaining Belgian advisers.[53] The arrangement collapsed following the fall of the Sepahdar Azam government in August 1916, but although the Persian representatives resigned, the commission of control remained nominally in existence. The retroactive moratorium money remained frozen in a special account held by the Imperial Bank, being used only to pay the salaries of the non-Persian commissioners.

Nevertheless, between March 1916 and April 1917 £420 000 was paid to the Persian government, through the Imperial Bank, under the moratorium arrangements. After April 1917 the moratorium payments ceased, being either refused by the Persian government because of fear for its sovereignty, or not given by the British government because they disapproved of Persian policies.[54]

In August 1918 a new system of British government financing of the Persian government came into being. The new advances were in Krans, and were to be repaid in Krans. They were supplied to the Imperial Bank by the British government at a provisional exchange rate of 30 – a level imposed after an acrimonious dispute between the Bank and the British Treasury during 1918 described below. The Bank, therefore, no longer had any opportunity to make exchange profits, but it was given a guaranteed profit margin on the operation. Between 15 August and 24 December the Bank provided the Persian government with 127 419 345 Krans under this arrangement. Against this it was paid £4 268 552 by the British government. 'There would be no Persian finance', one Foreign Office official observed in November 1918, 'except for the fact that the Persian government lives on British subsidies and on British loans which are never repaid.'[55]

The second form of British government spending in Persia was military. The Bank was the channel through which all funds for British and Indian troops in Persia were passed. In the south, this meant finding funds to finance the South Persia Rifles. 'I do not say that we were unreasonable', Sir Percy Sykes later recalled of the demands of the South Persia Rifles on the Bank's

Shiraz branch and its Manager, M. Ferguson, 'but I think our demands were extremely stiff at times, and yet Mr Ferguson always managed to find what we wanted – namely, money.'[56] A similar role was played in financing Dunsterforce in the north.[57] In the first eight months of 1918 the Bank provided the Kran equivalent of £1.6 million for Dunsterville's troops. Towards the autumn of 1918 British military costs escalated as Russian troops withdrew from Persia and British and Indian troops took their place.

The British government also undertook substantial 'political' spending in Persia, again through the Imperial Bank. This category included a wide range of expenditure, from the cost of the Legation in Tehran, and the various consuls, to advances to prominent Persian politicians and, by 1918, to famine relief and bread subsidies. This 'political' expenditure seems to have averaged about 7.5 million Krans per month by the autumn of 1918. Overall, by November 1918 British government military and 'political' requirements in Persia seem to have reached some 65 million Krans per month, or £2.4 million at the annual average exchange rate.[58]

The fourth area of British government expenditure came to be the support of Russian forces in Persia. From the early months of the War the Imperial Bank was involved in the finance of the Russian troops, the Russian Legation and the Cossack Brigade in Persia, as the Russian Bank was unable to provide sufficient Krans to meet their requirements. The Imperial Bank was one of the few institutions in Persia which would buy Roubles, as the wartime decline in Russian exports to Persia created little interest in the currency in the bazaar. A system was evolved whereby Roubles and Rouble bills and drafts were collected by the Bank in Persia, despatched to Russia, and the accumulated Rouble balances sold on the London market through the London County and Westminster Bank. Sir Thomas Jackson was a director of this latter bank, which had also been the Hongkong Bank's London bankers since 1866. In June 1915 the Imperial Bank's business with the London County and Westminster Bank had reached such a level that it was decided to open an account with them, so they joined Glyn, Mills, Currie and Co. as the Imperial Bank's London bankers. Overall, between 1 March and April 1916 the Bank had bought and remitted through Russia over 5 million Roubles.[59]

The Russian Revolution in 1917 disrupted these arrangements, and during that year the Bank's role in financing the Russian troops expanded. As Roubles depreciated in value at an increasing rate, the Bank made large purchases of the Russian currency 'in order to prevent panic and the complete collapse of exchange'.[60] It was not, however, a role which the Bank could sustain for long. An interim arrangement was made whereby the Imperial Bank bought up Rouble notes on behalf of the Russian government to the extent of 2 million Roubles per week. The Bank was paid in Sterling in London for this operation. Finally, in October 1917 an arrangement was made whereby Russian forces were financed by direct advances in Krans in exchange for Sterling, without the intermediate purchase of Rouble notes. The Russian government undertook to place at the Bank's disposal in London the Sterling equivalent of 15.6 million Krans a month for Russian forces in Persia.[61] All the money actually came from the British Treasury. A Financial Board of Control was established in Hamadan, under J. McMurray, to adminster the funds. Between October 1917 and May 1918, when British financing of Russian troops ceased, some 60 million Krans were advanced to them through the Imperial Bank.

The British government, therefore, had a large demand for local currency to finance its various operations in Persia. It was the Imperial Bank's task to find these funds. There were a number of ways in which Krans could be found. The note issue could have been expanded, but the runs in the first year of the War and the Bank's obligation to retain cash reserves did not make this an attractive option. Moreover, the demand for Krans was so huge that any reasonable expansion of the note issue would not have begun to do any good. Silver could and was imported and minted, but the wartime problems in silver importation have already been outlined. The Bank was left with generating Krans through the normal trade and exchange business.

This was by no means easy. Imports from Europe fell off during the War, with the result that the Bank found little demand for its Sterling in Persia. On the other hand, imports from India, especially of sugar and tea, did expand during the War, creating a demand for Rupee exchange. By the end of 1916 the Bank had come to 'practically depend upon sales on India to enable us to finance the situation throughout Persia'.[62] Rupee exchange was sold against local currency to Persian importers of Indian goods. The Bank purchased its Rupees through buying Government of India Council Bills – drafts sold in London for Sterling which could be cashed at state treasuries in India for Rupees – and by buying Rupee drafts from the South Persia Rifles and other British forces in Persia. It would appear to have been a fairly lucrative operation, but by no means easy since Rupee exchange was not always available in the amounts needed by the Bank, but it was successfully carried out and the situation never arose when the Bank could not supply the Kran requirements of the British government.

Success, however, was no guarantee of immunity from criticism. By 1916, as the value of the Kran rose against Sterling, the British government began complaining about a situation which increased the Sterling cost of its Persian operations. In the south of Persia, Government of India officials were particularly outspoken in blaming the Bank for the rising Kran exchange rate, and for being too slow to provide them with local currency.[63] There were several instances when the Bank's specie was commandeered by British Forces, and Sir Percy Sykes even requested permission at one stage during 1916 to coin Krans in India, claiming that the expenses of the South Persia Rifles could be halved.[64] His scheme was not taken up.

Further evidence of a lack of sympathy for the Bank among British India officials came in January 1917, when the India Office which was in any case rationing its offer of Council Bills because of a surplus of Sterling, excluded the Imperial Bank from applying for any of them. Foreign Office intervention subsequently helped the Bank to secure a weekly 0.7 million Rupee allocation of Council Bills, but suspicion about the Bank's policies lingered in some quarters of the Government of India.[65] In December 1917 the weekly allotment of Council Bills to the Imperial Bank was reduced to 0.5 million Rupees.

During July 1918 the British Treasury began complaining that the Imperial Bank's rates for Krans supplied to the British government were too high. The Treasury was convinced that differences in Kran–Sterling and Kran–Rupee exchange rates between the Bank's branches indicated that something was seriously amiss.[66] S. F. Rogers, who had taken over as London Manager and Secretary from George Newell in December 1917, attempted to explain the difficulties of Persian banking. 'The cost of transference of funds in specie or otherwise to points where they are called for', he wrote to the Treasury, 'and the difficulties involved in a country totally devoid of railways, and served only by unprotected and dangerous trade routes where quick transport is impossible, must affect very materially their values in the different centres.'[67]

The British government seemed less than convinced. On 12 August, the Treasury – insisting that the current exchange rate was 'unduly and unnecessarily low' – informed the Bank that future British government requirements in Krans would be paid for at the rate of 30 Krans to the £, subject to subsequent adjustment to the actual rate paid, with a 1% commission on the selling rate of Rupee and Sterling drafts. Moreover, the Bank was told to use 'its commanding position in the market' to keep the rate at 30.[68] The Imperial Bank was far from happy about this dictat, and on 6 September Sir Hugh Barnes, H. E. R. Hunter and S. F. Rogers attended a conference to discuss it with Treasury and India Office officials. The Treasury representatives included John Maynard Keynes, who was later to transform the discipline of economics, and the Imperial Bank came in for some heavy criticism from that source. He claimed that the Bank was making 5% or more margins in exchange transactions with the British government, which 'were excessive to use a mild term', and even threatened to ask another bank to open in Persia to handle the government account.[69] However, in a private meeting between Keynes and Barnes after the conference, the Bank was given a concession. The Bank was still allowed a 1% commission only on all Rupee sales, but given 0.5 Kran per £1 for Sterling sales, which amounted in effect to a 2% commission.[70]

These new arrangements lasted until the spring of 1919. The Bank could no longer make exchange profits on its transactions for the British government, but equally the government accepted responsibility for exchange risks. The August agreement was followed by proposals to match more closely the government's demand for Krans and the Bank's supply of them. One of the problems faced by the Bank throughout the War was that the Army was unable or unwilling to provide regular estimates of their currency requirements. In November 1918, rather late in the day, machinery began to be established to give the Bank a better indication of what was expected of it.[71]

6.6 THE COMMERCIAL BANKING SCENE

During the War the Bank focused increasingly on British government business, and its role as commercial banker to the private sector dwindled. This in part reflected the diminished opportunities and increased risks of doing business in wartime Persia. The value of Persian imports fell by 5% between 1914 and 1918, and the value of Persian exports (including oil) fell by 68%.[72] Imports of Manchester cotton piecegoods and exports of carpets seem to have been particularly badly affected. The Bank also took a deliberate decision to reduce its exposure to Persian business, and this policy was reinforced by the incessant demands on the Bank's resources by the British government. By August 1918 the British government was demanding that the Bank's Persian resources should be 'almost entirely reserved for their services'.[73]

The Bank's deposits in Persia reached their lowest point in 1916, when they stood at £560 336 (35.3 million Krans). In 1917 they increased to £952 617 (52.4 million Krans), and in 1918 they reached £1 412 958 (77.7 million Krans).

The patchiness of surviving data makes it hard to reach firm conclusions about the Bank's deposits, but it would seem that the surge in the second half of the War can be largely ascribed to military accounts and the British government's finance of the Persian government. The Bank found it hard to hold on to fixed deposits from the private sector, as uncertainty led to hoarding and commercial activity declined. The Bank's interest rate on 12 month fixed deposits was increased from 4.0 to 4.5% in early 1915 and to 6% by September 1916. Interest was paid on a growing number of current accounts, despite the Bank's longstanding dislike of that practice. In September 1914 Chief Office paid interest on 25% of its total deposits. Two years later this proportion had risen to 57%. By the end of 1917 Shiraz branch was paying 3% per annum interest on some current accounts and as much as 12% on fixed deposits in an effort to attract deposits.

Funds attracted to the Bank were virtually entirely used to meet its obligation to the British government rather than to finance commercial business. The Bank willingly financed imports to the greatest extent possible – because this was its main way of raising Krans – but was very loathe to extend credit for this purpose. 'The Bank is fairly hard put to it to supply the requirements of the British, Indian, Russian and Persian Governments', one of its Managers explained in March 1917, '... even without these heavy calls on its resources, it would naturally curtail its loans and discounts to the general public in the present lamentable condition of Persia.'[74] The Bank's strategy during the War was, as with the Persian government, to recover debts and restrict new lending. By 1915 Chief Office was practically refusing to undertake any new business.[75] This policy was enthusiastically supported by the Board in London. In September 1917, for example, Caesar Hawkins – the Chairman of the Finance Committee – expressed his delight that Shiraz's lending business had drastically fallen, 'especially as exchange gives higher profits'.[76]

Much of the growth of the Bank's loans, bills discounted and advances between 1917 and 1918 was due to financing military expenditure. Hamadan's loans, bills and advances, for example, increased from 800 000 Krans in March 1916 to 7 190 590 Krans in March 1918, and this was almost entirely because of British government spending.

The Bank's surge in profits in the last years of the War was directly related to its role in financing the British government expenditure in Persia. The British government's loans to the Persian government, the finance of the British and Russian troops and the import of silver, all created good business.

Despite the hardships and difficulties, therefore, the First World War was a profitable experience for the Imperial Bank. The Bank had also performed valuable services for the British government, a role symbolised by the award of OBEs to two Managers and the CBE to Wood. Yet within Persia the Bank had won few admirers. 'My predecessor was a persona grata with the Persian government, but not elsewhere', Wood reflected in 1916, 'and since his departure the situation is now exactly reversed.'[77]

The 1920s were to show the danger of this position.

7

'LORD CURZON'S BANK OF PERSIA' 1919–28

During the War the Imperial Bank, when forced to choose between its dual British and Persian identities, had made the only practical decision. It had functioned as one of the British government's 'main props and assets' in Persia. At the end of 1918, however, it remained to be seen whether the Bank would maintain this role in peacetime.

In fact, during the early post-War years British diplomatic policy towards Persia, directed by the Foreign Secretary, Lord Curzon, was at its most assertive and the Imperial Bank was under unprecedented pressure to follow official British policy. Precisely at this time the old Qajar regime finally collapsed. In February 1921 the government was toppled by a coup, the military support for which came from the Cossack Division commanded by Reza Khan. Over the following years Reza Khan consolidated his power, and at the end of 1925 the last Qajar ruler, Ahmad Shah, was deposed and Reza Khan proclaimed Shah.

The new nationalist government, which reversed the erosion of central government authority in Persia, was in a better position than its predecessor to make its views felt about the conflicting loyalties of an expatriate state bank. In August 1922 Reza Khan remarked bitterly that the Imperial Bank of Persia might be more aptly entitled 'Lord Curzon's Bank of Persia'.[1] Five years later the Persian government resolved the problem of the Imperial Bank's dual identity by creating its own state bank, Bank Melli. Thereafter there could be no doubt that the Imperial Bank was a British bank, operating in Persia.

There were several changes of Chief Manager in this period. As early as 1917 Wood had intimated his desire to retire from the Bank's service in the spring of 1919, when he would have completed 30 years service in the East.[2] The Board were reluctant to lose his services, but at the end of the War he firmly resolved to retire no later than October 1919. There was a consensus that his successor should be David Brown, his Deputy Manager. James

184

McMurray, who had joined the Bank in 1897 and acquired an excellent reputation at Hamadan during the War through his work in providing funds for the Allied Forces, was favoured to be Deputy.[3] All seemed set fair for a smooth hand-over when, on 13 July 1919, Brown suddenly dropped dead of a heart attack.

The Bank's plans were thrown into disarray. Wood and the Board agreed that McMurray was the right man for the Chief Managership, but problems arose over the post of Deputy: both McMurray and Wood recommended Edward Wilkinson. He had practically run the Bank's exchange operations during the War, and his qualifications for the position were strong. The Board, however, regarded Wilkinson as quite unsuitable. Not only was he a 'Levantine', but his brother – W. J. Wilkinson – had been asked to resign following the discovery of his total mismanagement of the Soltanabad branch during the War. The Board's candidate was E. M. Eldrid, and, despite the opinion of both Wood and McMurray, he was appointed Deputy Chief Manager in August.[4] Eldrid promptly turned the job down, apparently partly because his wife disliked Tehran's social life and partly because, in his own words to McMurray, 'he funked the responsibility'.[5] He was also 'war weary' after a difficult tour of duty in Rasht during the Jangali rebellion. Eldrid's move left the Board with little choice but to appoint Wilkinson.

McMurray took over from Wood on 21 September 1919, with Wilkinson as his Deputy. Both men seem to have been good technical bankers. In addition, McMurray possessed a determined and independent personality, which was to lead him into taking a more independent policy line than Wood with both the Board and the Foreign Office. He was also more adroit than his predecessor in his relations with Persian politicians, and he was able to minimise the damage done to the Bank by British foreign policy at this period.

In early 1925 McMurray indicated his desire, because of ill-health, to retire. The Board's personal antipathy towards Wilkinson seemed as strong as ever, but no other obvious candidate stood out and McMurray strongly supported his candidature. In November 1925 Wilkinson took over from McMurray, with F. Hale as Deputy Chief Manager. Wilkinson seemed to lack some of his predecessor's social skills. C. F. Warr, who was a junior in the 1920s, remembered him in these terms:

He was a bachelor, and he always gave me the impression that he had a little chip on his shoulder but I was told he was a Levantine.... He was always very nice and he used to go out on the town fairly regularly and we always heard that he had a lady friend tucked away discreetly.[6]

On the other hand, Wilkinson made a good impression on the Bank's Persian staff. A. H. Ebtehaj, who joined the local staff of the Bank in 1920, and will figure largely in this History, later recalled of Wilkinson:

He was a very courteous man, very kindly and cultured. He spoke French very well, this is how he got on with Persian officialdom, most of the people he came in contact with maybe didn't speak English but they spoke French . . . I had social contacts with him and he used to invite me to his house to his parties. . . .[7]

Wilkinson's appointment almost exactly coincided with the proclamation of Reza Khan as Shah, and it was to be his misfortune to be Chief Manager when the consequences of acting as 'Lord Curzon's Bank' came home to roost.

At Board level little changed during the 1920s. The Bank's Board began to assume the unchangeable and introspective character which was to be its most noticeable feature in the interwar years. H. E. R. Hunter died in 1923. The new appointments to the Board were, in a pattern quite different from before 1914, former Bank staff. The first was A. O. Wood, who was the first member of the Bank's staff to be offered a seat on the Board. He accepted the offer in January 1920, but a month later withdrew his acceptance as he was going abroad. He eventually joined the Board in June 1920. His tenure was short, however, for in December 1921 he was found dead, of natural causes, on a train at Doncaster. In 1926 S. F. Rogers, the London Manager between 1917 and 1930, was appointed a director, and in 1928 he was joined by McMurray.

The post-War decade was one of growth for the Imperial Bank. The balance sheet total reached a new peak in September 1919, at £10 076 809. It declined over the next few years, but began moving upwards in 1922 and reached £14 332 495 in March 1928. (In 1924 the Bank abandoned its peculiar year-end date of 20 September, and shifted to 20 March, which was more appropriate for both the British fiscal year and the Persian financial year – Persian New Year, Nouruz, is on 21 March.) The Bank's deposits, which had stood at £2 830 065 in 1919, continued to grow, and amounted to £7 804 441 in 1928. The note issue soared to £1 109 202 in 1919, fell by 40% in the following year, and then climbed steadily to £2 527 471 in 1928. 1919 also saw bills discounted, loans and advances at a high point of £3 241 933. These fell by 54% in 1920 but, after a period of stagnation, climbed to £4 661 199 in 1928.

The Bank quickly re-established a strongly liquid position after the strains imposed by the War. In 1919 the Bank's cash reserves were still at a low level, with a ratio of cash to total assets of only 21%. By 1920 this ratio had doubled and thereafter it stayed at higher levels, standing at 36% in 1928. Lending ratios, on the other hand, fell from their immediate post-War peak as Persia, like much of the rest of the world, passed through a period of deflation. In 1919 the ratio of loans, bills and advances to deposits and note issue was 82%, but this fell to 45% in 1920, and it was at the same level in 1928.

Table 7.1. *Imperial Bank Profits 1919–28* (£ Sterling)

Year ending	Published net profits	Movements through inner reserves	
		Transfers (to) or from profits	Bad debts recovered (or provided for)
20 September 1919	75 421	101 000	200
20 September 1920	76 242	(36 000)	146
20 September 1921	82 904	203 850	—
20 September 1922	86 766	246 000	(200)
20 September 1923	85 924	192 000	—
20 March 1924	49 908	80 000	—
20 March 1925	85 014	90 000	—
20 March 1926	129 402	143 621	—
20 March 1927	135 367	134 841	—
20 March 1928	135 312	(70 070)	—

The level of the Bank's investments fluctuated over the period. It fell sharply in 1920 and 1921 from a peak in 1919, and then rose. In 1919 it was inflated by a large holding of National War Bonds, which were disposed of during the 1920s, and £1 million in British Treasury Bonds. However, in 1920 depreciation wiped around £160 000 off the value of the Bank's investments, which were written down accordingly in March 1921. In 1928 British government stock formed by far the largest component of the Bank's investments, either as Treasury Bonds or in the form of Consolidated or Conversion Loans. The Bank's holding of the Persian 1911 Sterling Loan – with a nominal value of £303 120 and a market value of £148 220 in 1928 – remained the largest non-British government security.

The 1920s saw a marked strengthening of the Bank's reserves. Published shareholders' funds grew by 35% between 1919 and 1928, from £952 809 to £1 289 646. The most noticeable growth, however, was inner reserves. They expanded by 360% between 1919 and 1928, despite large payments of Excess Profits Duty in 1919, 1920 and 1921. By 1928 inner reserves stood at £1 123 464, or more than double the Bank's published reserve account. The 1920s also saw an accretion of the inner reserve accounts. Before 1921 the Bank's biggest inner reserve was the Contingency Account, with only a few thousand pounds in the Officers' Guarantee Fund (the exact sums are unknown until 1925; an estimate has been made for the period 1919 to 1925 and included in the inner reserve figures given in Appendix 4). However, in 1921 a Corporation Tax Reserve Fund was started, and in 1925 an Income Tax Reserve Fund. An insurance underwriting account was also started in 1924. In most cases these new inner reserves were created by transfers from the Contingency Account, and in 1928 this still represented 87% of total inner reserves.

The Imperial Bank's published profits, and transfers to and from inner reserves before the published figure was reached, are shown in Table 7.1.

The published profit figures support the picture of expansion shown by the balance sheet and the growth of shareholders' funds. They edged slowly upwards after the War, reaching a plateau between 1922 and 1925 (leaving aside the aberration caused by the change of the year-end in 1924 and the resulting six-month year accounting period), before rising to a higher plateau between 1926 and 1928. As usual, however, the published figures were influenced by movements through the inner reserves. Profits before such transfers peaked in the periods 1921–23 and 1926–27, when in all five years they exceeded £270 000. On the other hand, 1920 and 1928 emerge as poor years, when the Bank had to make transfers from inner reserves to support published profits. As usual, dividend payments did not reflect the Bank's poor or good years. They were 8/- between 1919 and 1921, rose to 9/- until 1925 (except for 5/- in the 1924 half-year accounting period), 10/- in 1926, and increased to 11/- in 1927 and 1928.

As during the War, however, the Bank's balance sheet cannot be said to give a complete picture of the Bank's performance and worth. In the matter of reserves, for example, the Bank's contingency reserve account established in Persia in 1916, in which all provisions for bad and doubtful accounts were made, remained in existence in the 1920s. Again, in 1922 Chief Office opened a special deposit account in London Office by transferring £1.4 million from its current account, thereby reducing its large overbought position. This special deposit seems to have performed 'quasi-inner reserve' functions. In September 1923, for example, £300 000 from this special deposit was re-transferred back to Persia, increasing Chief Office's profits by the £182 000 exchange profit made on the transfer.[8]

Further problems in interpreting the Bank's balance sheet are caused by the exchange rate. The Bank continued the wartime practice of adjusting its balance sheet at one exchange rate – 55 Krans to the £1 throughout the period – and remitting profits to Britain at another rate. The profit adjustment rate reached 10 Krans to the £ in 1920, rose to 58.75 in September 1923, and then declined to 40 in March 1928. In the immediate post-War years the Bank adjusted its profits at a much higher exchange rate than the prevailing one. This enabled the Bank to take maximum advantage of its large overbought position in Sterling. The amount of profit the Persian branches remitted to Britain, and the adjustment rate at which it was remitted, was decided by the Bank in line with its requirements. In the immediate post-War period, for example, the Bank had no wish to pay more Excess Profit Duty in

Table 7.2. *Imperial Bank advances to British government in Persia 1918–21*

Period	Total advances (million Krans)	Destination (%)		
		Persian government subsidy	British military	British legation
December 1918 – March 1919	46	23	71	6
April 1919 – March 1920	143	29	65	6
April 1920 – September 1920	114	18	75	7
October 1920 – March 1921	53	6	88	6
April 1921 – September 1921	16	0	92	8

Britain than it had to, and therefore the overseas branches only remitted sufficient profits to cover the essential allocations necessary to arrive at desired balance sheet figures. An exchange between London Office and Chief Office in 1921 illustrates the point. 'Before fixing adjusting rate', Chief Office telegraphed London in August 1921, 'please telegraph approximate amount you require us to remit at 20 September.' The reply was £400 000 for the year-end. An adjustment rate of 18 was therefore arrived at.[9] 'At the end of each year', C. F. Warr, Assistant Chief Accountant in the late 1920s, subsequently recalled: 'London Office used to tell the Chief Office how much profit they wanted remitted from Persia.'[10]

The upshot from these considerations is that the Imperial Bank's profit and balance sheet figures continued to contain a highly subjective element, and too much weight cannot be placed on any particular figure without consideration of the circumstances in which it was derived. The following sections leave the grey area of figures to consider the Bank's relations with the British and Persian governments.

7.2 BRITISH PAWN OR STATE BANK? 1919–24

The British military and political presence in Persia remained strong after the end of the War, and the Bank continued to handle the British government's financial requirements. As during the War, the Bank made advances to cover the military and political requirements of the British government in Persia. The British government's subsidy to the Persian government was also paid until October 1920. An estimate of the large sums involved, and the destination of the advances, is given in Table 7.2.

The British government seems to have lost track of the amount of money it had lent to the Persian government. In February 1921 one estimate of the total amount owed to Britain was between £7 and £8 million, including arrears of interest,[11] but the size of the debt in Sterling was naturally vulnerable to the Sterling/Kran exchange rate used in the calculation and this figure – which seems over large – cannot be taken as authoritative.

The Bank's advances on behalf of the British government continued to be plagued by disputes about the terms. In August 1918 the Bank had agreed to make advances in Krans against Sterling supplied to it by the British government at a provisional exchange rate of 30, with a later adjustment to the actual rate. In April 1919 this arrangement was replaced by an agreement under which Kran advances on behalf of the British government were repaid at once on telegraphic advice, at the current rate of exchange plus a commission to the Bank of 1%. By September 1919, however, allegations were in the air that the Bank had taken advantage of differences between the Sterling and Rupee exchange rates in Persia to make a large profit at the British government's expense.[12] It was not until April 1920 that the Treasury conceded, after a long and detailed explanation by the Imperial Bank of its exchange operations, that the Bank 'did not make any profit from the difference between the Kran–Sterling and Kran–Rupee exchange'.[13]

The Bank's difficulties with the Treasury, however, were small compared to the difficulties in which it was placed by Lord Curzon, the British Foreign Secretary between 1919 and 1924. At the end of the War British forces dominated Persia. Curzon was determined to maintain that position by turning Persia into a virtual British protectorate, a link between Mesopotamia, which had been mandated to the British after the War, and British India. Britain, he wrote in August 1919, could not allow Persia to become 'a hotbed of misrule, enemy intrigue, financial chaos and political disorder'.[14] The apparent triumph of this policy was the Anglo–Persian Agreement signed on 9 August 1919. It provided for the reorganisation of the Persian Army and finances under British control, British assistance in the construction of railways and roads, and the revision of the customs tariff in Britain's favour. The 1907 Anglo–Russian Convention was to be abrogated – a step already taken by the new Soviet government – and Persia was promised a British loan of £2 million at 7% per annum interest.[15]

Under the terms of the Agreement a British financial mission, headed by Sydney Armitage-Smith, and a British military mission, headed by Major General W. E. R. Dickson, arrived in Persia in early 1920. Armitage-Smith's main achievement was to arbitrate in a dispute between the Persian government and the Anglo–Persian Oil Company concerning the royalty payments due to the government under the D'Arcy Concession, an issue over which the Bank and the government were also to clash in later years. The outcome was an alteration, favourable to the Persians, of the basis on which royalties were to be calculated, and a payment by the oil company of £1 million in respect of past royalties.[16] The military mission's main accomplishment was the replacement of Russian by Persian officers in the Cossack Brigade, which led to the rise of Reza Khan, 'an almost illiterate soldier who had risen from the ranks'.[17]

However, Curzon's Agreement and the British missions were soon in deep difficulties. The 1919 Agreement caused violent opposition in Persia. It was not helped by the methods British officials had used to get it signed. Not only was the Agreement negotiated in great secrecy, but it soon became known that three Persian ministers involved – Vosuq od-Doule (the Prime Minister), Prince Firuz, Nosrat od-Doule (Minister of Foreign Affairs) and Akbar Mirza, Sarem od-Doule (Minister of Finance) – had received a £131 000 payment, ostensibly as an 'advance' against the £2 million promised in the Agreement. The money was paid through the Imperial Bank, where Wood referred to it simply as 'bakshish'.[18] This interpretation was reinforced when, in February 1920, Akbar Mirza attempted to persuade McMurray to make false entries in the Bank's books to disguise the payment or, when McMurray refused, at least to provide him with an alternative explanation for the money.[19]

As no Majles was sitting, the 1919 Agreement was never formally ratified. Moreover, during 1919 and 1920 Persian reaction to it became more hostile. Newspapers attacked the Agreement, and there were demonstrations against it. This surge of nationalism was combined with a growth of separatist movements in several provinces. In May 1920, Bolshevik troops landed at Enzeli in pursuit of White Russian Forces. They also acted in support of a revived Jangali movement, under Kuchek Khan, which had acquired strong pro-Bolshevik views.[20] At the same time, the British government, concerned about the cost of its military operations and British public opinion, decided to withdraw British Forces from the north of Persia by the following year, falling back if necessary on the south-west of Persia to protect Britain's oil interests.[21] The Bank was, initially, badly affected by these events. The disorder and unrest caused the Rasht branch to close in July 1920. By the following January Mashad and Tabriz had also been forced to close. The Bolshevik threat caused McMurray to make contingency plans to send Chief Office's books and surplus cash further south, although the Bank was resolved to stay as long as possible. 'We should not like to fail Persian Government at vital moment', Sir Hugh Barnes telegraphed McMurray in January, 'if presence of bank in Tehran can help to avert disintegration.'[22]

It was in fact the Persians themselves who prevented the disintegration. During the opening months of 1921 a small group of nationalists in Tehran and Reza Khan, newly appointed Commander of the Cossack Division, planned a coup, almost certainly with support from certain British military commanders.[23] On 21 February Reza Khan and his Cossacks entered Tehran and seized power. Reza Khan was subsequently appointed Minister of War, and he remained in this post in the five Cabinets formed between the coup and October 1923, when he became Prime Minister. These Cabinets all showed a new independence and determination. Within months of the coup the Anglo–Persian Agreement had been rejected. A Treaty of Friendship had been made with the Soviet Union which led to the withdrawal of Soviet forces from the north. And Reza Khan's forces began to re-establish the authority of the central government throughout the country.[24]

McMurray welcomed the February 1921 coup as 'the best hope of Persia for some time and possibly the last hope'.[25] He was eager to assist any government whose policy was directed towards re-establishing order and central control in Persia, as such a policy could only benefit the Bank's business. By the end of 1921 the Bank had been able to reopen Tabriz, Mashad and Rasht, although McMurray was prudent enough to staff these branches with bachelors until it was clear that the restoration of order was more or less permanent.

Unfortunately the Bank's relative enthusiasm for the post-coup Persian governments was not matched by that of British officials and of Lord Curzon in particular, and the Bank soon found itself under pressure to refuse advances to governments considered unsatisfactory. Curzon was especially annoyed by the Persian government's pursuit of closer ties with the United States as a third force between Britain and the Soviet Union. A Persian representative was sent to Washington in the middle of 1921 to discuss the question of an oil concession and the participation of the United States in the provision of technical advice and assistance and the provision of a loan. Standard Oil of New Jersey in fact negotiated an oil concession in the north of Persia, which was ratified by the Majles in November 1921.

In Tehran, McMurray resisted separate attempts by the Foreign Office and Armitage-Smith for the Bank 'to lend itself as a weapon to be used against the Government'.[26] While McMurray fulminated against Curzon's 'hopelessly biased' and 'unreasonable' views, even the Bank's Board in London objected to direct Foreign Office pressure to cease all lending. 'For the Bank', Sir Hugh Barnes told the Foreign Office, 'it is no light matter to incur the active hostility of the Persian Government and people, as is likely to be the case if the Board act as desired.'[27] As the Persian government was asking for advances against its own oil royalties which were paid into the Bank's London Office, the Bank's position was felt to be particularly vulnerable. Moreover, McMurray argued that the way to keep the Americans out of Persia was to advance money to the Persian government, rather than more or less to deliver them into the hands of the Americans by forbidding the Bank to make loans.[28]

McMurray was more prepared to act independently than Wood had been. In December 1921 a telegram from Sir Hugh Barnes after he had had an interview with Lord Curzon, ordering McMurray to make no more advances to the Persian government, crossed with a telegram from the Chief Manager saying he had authorised an advance of up to 2 million Krans to meet the urgent immediate needs of the Army.[29] The advance went ahead. Over the next few months McMurray also did his best to limit the damage being done to the Bank by the Foreign Office's policies. On the one hand, he tried to modify British government policies through influencing the Legation, where he was privileged to see all the Foreign Office's secret telegrams to their Minister. McMurray's position was strengthened at the end of 1921 by the arrival of a new British Minister, Sir Percy Loraine, who took a more conciliatory approach to the Persian situation. On the other hand, he was able to retain a friendly relationship with Persian ministers and Reza Khan, in part by blaming the Bank's inability to make advances on 'certain individuals in the Government and Parliament'.[30]

In May 1922 the Foreign Office, after consultation with Sir Percy Loraine, ended their embargo on advances by the Bank.[31] By early July the Bank had advanced 5 million Krans to Reza Khan, with the Bank taking customs receipts as security. Unfortunately, this news produced a ruling from the Foreign Office that advances against such security were not allowable, on the grounds of the British government's prior claim over all receipts from the Persian customs as security for its advances over the previous ten years.[32] The Foreign Office's argument rested on the grounds that the British government's wartime loans to the Persian government were to be considered part of the £2 million Loan to be advanced under the 1919 Anglo–Persian Agreement, against which the British government claimed a lien on all Persia's customs and indeed any other sources of funds.[33] As the Anglo–Persian Agreement had never been ratified by the Majles, and the British government's claims never accepted by the Persian government, the Foreign Office's case was not a strong one. It was not until September 1922, however, that the Foreign Office permitted the Bank to go ahead with further advances against customs receipts, on the basis of a strange formula whereby the prior right of the British government to the customs receipts was recognised *should* the Persian government recognise their claims.[34]

The Bank's lending to the Persian government on a substantial scale was resumed after September 1922; the sums involved will be discussed in the following section. The Foreign Office, however, continued to exercise pressure on the Bank, perhaps less in the expectation of recovering the loans to Persia than in the desire to retain control over available securities so that British influence could be maintained. In May 1923, for example, Loraine suggested that the Bank should delay a 15 million Kran advance against oil revenues it was preparing until the Persian government offered to meet some of the British claims.[35] On this occasion the Board decided to stand firm and go ahead with the advance, explaining 'that the thin edge of the wedge was again being inserted to use us as a political pawn'.[36] But in 1924 the Bank found itself obliged to follow Foreign Office dictates on a much larger matter. In May the Bank, on learning that American interests were believed to be negotiating a $10 million loan to the Persian government against security of oil royalties or customs revenues, counter-proposed the idea of a £2 million loan to be floated by the Bank in London.[37] The Foreign Office refused to support the proposal, announcing that it would have the 'strongest objection' to any such loan unless practically all of it was 'set apart for the purpose of liquidating a large part of the Persian government's indebtedness to His Majesty's Government'.[38] The Bank could not proceed against such a ruling, and the proposed loan was dropped. In fact an American loan never materialised; neither did any Persian payment to the British government.

In retrospect, the Imperial Bank probably made the best of the exceptionally difficult situation in which it was placed in the early 1920s. It was impossible for it, as a British bank, to ignore Foreign Office policies, especially in the light of the long relationship between the two parties since 1889. 'The traditions of the Bank bind us more or less to study the wishes of the Foreign Office', Rogers advised McMurray in October 1921, 'and it is indispensable that we should be guided by them in matters where our interests diverge.'[39] Moreover, the Bank still benefited from the Foreign Office's assistance, as it had before the War. In early 1920, for example, the Foreign Office, believing that 'a single bank gave [the British government] a firmer hold over Persian finance', dissuaded the Eastern Bank from opening a branch in Persia.[40] In 1921 the Foreign Office also intervened on the Bank's behalf with the Treasury, when – as will be seen in Chapter 9 – the Bank wished to amend its Charter so as to convert its agencies in Bombay, Baghdad and Basra into branches.

Given this situation, the Imperial Bank had put up strong resistance to being reduced to the status of a 'political pawn'. McMurray's independence, his sympathy for the Persian governments after 1921 and the Bank's obvious willingness to help them except when the British authorities expressly forbade it, must have limited the bad feeling created in the Persian government by the behaviour of their state bank. But Reza Khan was particularly affected by the Bank's inability to lend, for as Minister of War he was often hard put to find the pay for his troops. Reza Khan's annoyance was visible. In February 1922 he sent McMurray a message threatening that the Imperial Bank would no longer be recognised as the state bank but would be regarded as an ordinary foreign commercial concern.[41] And it was in August of the same year he was heard to speak bitterly of 'Lord Curzon's Bank of Persia'.[42] As will be seen, relations between the Bank and the Persian government improved during the mid-1920s, but it is hard not to draw the conclusion that the assault on the Imperial Bank's position later in the decade was conditioned, in part at least, by the reinforced awareness that, when forced to choose, the Imperial Bank was a British rather than a Persian institution.

7.3 THE BANK AND REZA KHAN

Reza Khan's power had continued to grow after his appointment as Prime Minister in 1923. In 1924 the Sheikh of Mohammarah, who was the de facto ruler of the south-western province of Arabistan (now known as Khusistan) and a protégé of the British, rebelled against the central government, but was defeated by Reza Khan's army. This removed the last major source of opposition to the new regime. In 1923 Ahmad Shah was persuaded to return to Europe, where he had been on and off since the end of the War, and in October 1925 he was formally deposed by the Majles. During December a specially convened assembly proclaimed Reza Khan as Shah, and he was crowned in April of the following year.

Reza Khan's policies focused on the desire to modernise Persia, and to free it from the kind of colonial dependence which Lord Curzon had sought to impose. He was assisted by a new generation of nationalist politicians such as Abdol Hoseyn Teymurtash, Minister of Court between 1925 and 1932, and Ali Akbar Davar, Minister of Public Works 1925–26 and Minister of Justice between 1927 and 1933. During the 1920s the policy of employing the nationals of 'neutral' countries to assist Persia's modernisation was also expanded. Swedes returned to train the army, Italians came to advise the navy, and Frenchmen to undertake legal and public health reforms.[43] From the Bank's standpoint, however, the most important aspect of these policies was the arrival of an American Financial Mission in autumn 1922. Morgan Shuster had been the Persian government's first choice for head of the Mission, but as he was unavailable Dr A. C. Millspaugh was appointed Financial Adviser, a title which he changed after his arrival to Administrator General of Persia's Finances.[44] Millspaugh, who was appointed under a private contract so that his work should not involve the United States government, brought a team of Americans with him. The Mission was soon engaged on schemes for a major reorganisation of government finances, and in particular for an increase in the government's tax yield by organising more effective collection of revenues.[45]

McMurray was able, despite the efforts of the British Foreign Office, to establish a good business and social relationship with Reza Khan. During 1923, while still Minister of War, Reza Khan entrusted the whole of his Ministry's financial affairs to the Bank.[46] Moreover, by early 1925 it is evident that Reza Khan, by now Prime Minister, was in the habit of dining with the McMurrays.[47] When Reza Khan adopted the family name of Pahlavi for his new dynasty, the Bank obliged the Persian ruler by changing its telegraphic address from Pahlavi to Bactria. Only after the new telegraphic address had been publicly announced was its unfortunate similarity to the word 'bacteria' noticed by the Bank.[48]

Perhaps a symbolic highpoint of the relationship with Reza Khan came during the new Shah's Coronation festivities in late April and early May 1926. Chief Office was illuminated for the occasion, and special receptions and dinners held at the Bank. Wilkinson, who had replaced McMurray as Chief Manager several months previously, seemed specially favoured. 'On the evening of the dinner at the Palace', he wrote to London, 'the Prime Minister surrounded by the Cabinet, who were all standing at the entrance to the Throne room, received me very cordially and audibly thanked the Bank for so effectively decorating and illuminating its facade.'[49] Wilkinson was also the only non-diplomatic corps guest – not even Millspaugh was there – to be invited to Reza Khan's reception at his summer palace.

The Bank's relationship with Millspaugh was, initially at least, also good. McMurray was delighted that the Americans seemed set to undertake drastic reforms in Persia's financial affairs, and was prepared to give Millspaugh his full support.[50] The Bank's opinion of Millspaugh went even higher when, from the beginning of 1923, Millspaugh began to centralise government revenue and expenditure on the Bank. The Imperial Bank had already started collecting the Northern customs receipts following liquidation of the Russian Bank. This role was now formalised. Between March 1921 and March 1926 at least 90% of the Government's total customs receipts seem to have passed through the Bank.[51] Moreover, the Bank was also used to remit all other provincial revenues – such as the posts and telegraphs, the sugar and tea monopolies and road tax – to Tehran. In the year ending March 1924 provincial revenues handled by the Bank totalled 123.9 million Krans. By 1928 this figure had grown to 278 million Krans. A series of banking agreements in 1924, 1925 and 1926 confirmed the Imperial Bank's central role as the government's banker.

The Imperial Bank also undertook substantial lending to the Persian government in the 1920s. 'It must always be remembered', S. F. Rogers reminded Wilkinson in July 1926, that the government were the Bank's 'best customers'.[52] Table 7.3 gives the government's debt to the Bank at selected year and half-year ends between 1919 and 1928.[53]

Table 7.3. *Imperial Bank advances to the Persian government 1919–28*

Date	Total advances (Krans)	Alimentation advances (Krans)	Interest Rate	Sterling overdraft (£ Sterling)	Interest Rate
		(Cumulative balances)			
March 1919	5 500 000	—	9%	—	—
September 1920	18 189 097	—	9%	—	—
September 1921	8 471 044	1 502 000	9%	402 515	9%
March 1922	4 561 285	2 252 187	9%	49 929	9%
September 1922	12 025 500	3 495 134	7%	150 000	7%
September 1923	29 270 940	9 785 350	7%	700 000	7%
March 1924	21 460 580	10 465 250	7%	700 000	7%
September 1924	8 307 890	2 147 810	7%	900 000	7%
March 1925	22 131 370	1 078 280	9%	631 732	9%
March 1926	27 581 880	22 418 840	7%	—	
March 1927	n.a.	18 900 000	6%	—	
March 1928	8 258 560	5 616 310	6%	—	

Note: na = not available.

The Persian government's debt to the Imperial Bank had been reduced to practically nothing by the end of the First World War. By March 1919, however, advances totalling 5.5 million Krans had been made, largely to enable the government to purchase grain supplies. By September 1920 McMurray had lent further sums, again mainly for grain purchases, all of which were on the security of customs receipts. The subsequent Foreign Office embargo on lending was reflected in the fall of the Bank's advances, but by September 1922 government debt had started to climb again. McMurray seems to have pursued a very independent line in these years, often informing London after rather than before advances were made.[54]

A large proportion of the Imperial Bank's advances to the Persian government continued to be on account of the purchase of grain, and were made to the Alimentation Service of the Ministry of Finance. This had been established towards the end of the War to control supplies of grain. It regulated the price of grain purchases from landowners as well as the terms of the sale of grain to bakers, and it controlled the transport of grain. Following the arrival of Millspaugh the Service was placed under the control of an American, Colonel McCormack. The Bank's advances played an important and sometimes critical role in the Alimentation Service's functioning. A particular crisis point was the autumn of 1925, when the Bank was called on to provide large facilities because of a serious grain shortage. In addition to its ordinary business, the Bank was also requested to act as intermediary for the purchase of lorries in India, Iraq and Britain. The operation seems to have been both time-consuming and unremunerative, although C. F. Warr, who found himself in Chief Office's Telegraph Department at that time, found it a welcome break from routine duties of a junior:

Night after night the man who was in charge of telegrams and I who was his assistant used to have voluminous telegrams to send all over the Middle East, to Bombay, Calcutta, Beirut, Baghdad, even to France and Belgium: anyone who had a second-hand lorry that was free, would then buy it and send it back to Persia quickly, and it was quite exciting actually.[55]

Further advances to the Persian government were made by the Bank for particular purposes. During 1924, for example, the Bank advanced £200 000 to the government for the purchase of silver. There were no further silver advances, however. Instead, the Bank either imported silver on its own account and sold it to the Mint, or, after 1925 when Tehran Mint could not cope with the throughput of bar silver, purchased silver in Britain, had it minted in Birmingham and then shipped to Persia. The Bank was also asked to collect cracked and defective coin, and return it to Tehran for re-minting. This operation sometimes involved the Bank in advancing to the government, as it had to buy the defective coin from the public and then hold it until it was re-minted. By September 1928 the Bank had collected 112.2 million Krans of defective coin on the government's behalf.

In addition to Kran advances, the Bank also made large Sterling advances to the Persian government against its oil royalties. These royalties were paid into the Bank in London each December and – together with the customs receipts – were Persia's most reliable source of revenue.[56] From 1924 Kran advances were increasingly secured by oil royalties and in 1925 the Bank made Kran advances against oil royalties rather than against customs receipts. Repayments were made against regular revenues collected. Between 1923 and 1925 the Bank's Sterling advances often reached £700 000, and in September 1924 they stood at £900 000, a substantial sum in view of the limit imposed by the Bank's Concession. Each December, however, Anglo–Persian's royalty payment allowed the Sterling advances to be substantially reduced. By 1926 the Persian government's improved administration had enabled it to pay off the Sterling overdraft.

Until the middle of 1922 the Bank charged interest at 9% per annum on both its Sterling and Kran advances. However, the Bank eventually responded to a fall in British Bank Rate from 6% in June 1921 to 3% in July 1922 by reducing the rate to 7%. When Bank Rate rose again 12 months later, the Bank retained its existing interest rate as a special gesture 'to assist the Persian government' while Millspaugh's reorganisation was in progress.[57] In October 1924 the Bank specified a formal connection between its interest rate and British Bank Rate – its interest rate was to change by 1% for every 0.5% change in Bank Rate.[58] The Bank's interest rate fluctuated with Bank Rate for two years, and reached 9% in December 1925 following a rise in Bank Rate to 5%. However, Britain's return to the gold standard in April 1925 made such a connection less clear, and the Bank's policy became more flexible. In February 1926 McMurray reduced the rate to 6% even though there was no change in British interest rates. Moreover, when interest rates rose to 9% in 1925, the Bank continued to charge the Alimentation Service only 7%, because the money was needed to finance essential food supplies.[59]

The Imperial Bank felt pride in the assistance it had provided for Reza Khan and for the Millspaugh Mission. Sir Hugh Barnes related to the Bank's shareholders in December 1923 how the Bank had shouldered its 'share of responsibility' for the reforms in progress.[60] Privately McMurray attributed Millspaugh's achievements to the Bank's assistance. 'It is our money that has made what success [Millspaugh] has achieved possible', McMurray observed in May 1924, '...Without our assistance his career here would have been a very short one.'[61]

It came, therefore, as an unpleasant surprise when relations with the American administration began to deteriorate. A sour note had entered the relationship during 1924, when Millspaugh had been distinctly discouraging to the Bank's idea of raising a loan in Britain, and seemed to favour an American loan.[62] During 1925 the relationship between Millspaugh and the Bank worsened. The Millspaugh Mission had become unpopular in Persia, and the renewal of the Americans' initial three year contracts had seemed for a time in doubt. When the contracts were renewed early in 1925, McMurray believed that Millspaugh was determined to justify his position as an employee of the Persian government by demonstrating his independence from the Bank. For whatever reason, in the space of a few months the Bank faced questions from the Americans on how their royalties to the government were paid; its claim for wartime looted branches – now standing at 8.6 million Krans – was again rejected; and the charges the Bank made for transferring government revenues were questioned. McMurray's response was to withhold a 15 million Kran advance due to be paid to the government.[63]

At this stage McMurray's good relationship with Reza Khan was used to good effect. After Millspaugh had accused the Bank of deliberately making trouble for the government on the eve of Persian New Year, McMurray was able to present his case directly to Reza Khan. When Millspaugh subsequently sent McMurray an angry complaint about his negotiating directly with the Prime Minister, McMurray promptly passed the letter on to Reza

Khan. 'Millspaugh', McMurray later observed, 'must have had a bad few minutes with the Prime Minister' as a result.[64] McMurray gathered that Reza Khan did not have a very high opinion of Millspaugh.

Over the following years the Bank continued to work with Millspaugh. However, the Bank's private opinion of him deteriorated, especially after Wilkinson became Chief Manager. Talking to Millspaugh, Wilkinson wrote in 1927, was 'just as if one were talking to a piece of wood', he was 'a man of outstanding incapacity, narrow-mindedness, obstinacy and stupidity.'[65]

This seems to have been the general consensus of opinion in the British community in Persia. Anglo–Persian's representative in Tehran summed up Millspaugh as 'a BF' (bloody fool), and members of the Legation appeared to share this opinion.[66]

In addition to this deterioration in personal relationships, several issues of major significance for the Bank were raised by Millspaugh in the last months of his Mission. Potentially the most serious was the move to create a national bank, which will be discussed later in this chapter. In January 1927 Millspaugh also formally raised with Wilkinson the question of how the Bank's royalty payments were calculated, and whether the books had been properly audited. Wilkinson dismissed the matter as a 'try on' by Millspaugh, but in fact it was a subject on which the Bank was highly vulnerable.[67] The Bank's published net profit figures were, at best, a subjective assessment of the Bank's performance, and the retention of a share of Persian profits in Persia after 1916 had made the Bank's Sterling balance sheet figures even more distant from reality. In April the Board was sufficiently concerned to ask the Bank's auditors to investigate the definition of the Bank's net profits. By the end of 1927 the Bank's lawyers were also involved, and it had become clear that the Bank's position was a weak one.[68]

Despite these problems, however, in November 1927 Wilkinson was able to sign a further annual banking agreement with the Persian government, which effectively maintained the Bank's exclusive right to government business.[69] This was to be the last such agreement.

7.4 BANKING IN PERSIA

In 1919 the Imperial Bank had 18 branches in Persia. By March 1928 this number had risen to 24 and, with the addition of a further branch in 1929, the Bank's branch network in Persia reached its peak. Table 7.4 lists changes in the Bank's branch network between 1919 and 1928. These new branches were small and often opened at the behest of either the British or Persian governments. British government pressure on the Bank focused on Seistan, which bordered on British India. The Bank was requested from this source to

1 William Keswick (Chairman 1889–99).   2 Sir Lepel Griffin (Chairman 1899–1908).

3 Sir Thomas Jackson (Chairman 1908–15).

4 Sir Hugh Barnes (Chairman 1915–37).

5 Colonel Sir A. Henry McMahon (Chairman 1937–45).

6 Lord Kennet (Chairman 1945–52; 1953–55).

7 Chief Office Staff, 1890. Left to right standing: S. Ferguson, W. Giglio, A. Churchill, D. F. Putt (far right). Left to right sitting: A. C. Grandjean, A. Houtom Schindler, the Persian High Commissioner, Joseph Rabino, D. Baker (half profile only).

8 A. O. Wood
(Chief Manager 1908–19).

9 J. McMurray
(Chief Manager 1919–25).

10 E. Wilkinson
(Chief Manager 1925–34).

11 O. A. Butters
(Chief Manager 1934–39).

12 V. L. Walter
(Chief Manager 1939–48).

13 L. C. Payne
(Chief Manager 1948–52).

14 David McLean (Director, Imperial Bank of Persia 1889–1903).

15 S. F. Rogers (London Manager and Secretary 1918–30;
Director 1926–36).

16 Naser od-Din (Shah 1848–96).

17 Mozaffar od-Din (Shah 1896–1907).

18 Mohammad Ali (Shah 1907–09).

19 Staff of the Shiraz branch in the 1890s, L. E. Dalton (Manager) sitting in the centre.

20 Staff of Basra branch in 1891. Manager, J. Fowler, sitting, right.

21 Bank juniors in 1890s, back row, E. M. Eldrid (far left), E. C. Dalton (far right); front row, A. O. Wood (far right).

22 Local Staff in Tabriz, 1909, left to right sitting, Mirza Mehdi Khan, Mokhtar Khan, Mirza Pasha Khan; standing left to right, Arshavir Chilingarjan, Suren Aftandiljan.

Table 7.4. *Opening and closing of Imperial Bank branches 1919–28*

Branch	Opened	Closed	Re-opened
Shushtar	1921	September 1923	
Birjand		March 1922	September 1925
Duzdab	April 1922		
Barforush	May 1923		
Meyden-e Naftun	June 1923		
Borujerd	February 1926		
Pahlavi (formerly Enzeli)	August 1926		
Abadan	September 1926		

open at Duzdab, the railhead of the Quetta–Nushki railway, in order to develop trade between India and Eastern Persia. In 1925 the Bank was encouraged to reopen Birjand, which it had closed as a *quid pro quo* for opening Duzdab.[70]

The Persian government also encouraged the Bank to open branches. For example, it wanted a branch at Meydan-e Naftun (later known as Masjed-e Soleyman) where Anglo–Persian's oil wells were located, in order to control a smuggling trade in Krans. Although Anglo–Persian's business was already done with Ahwaz branch, and the opening at Meydan-e Naftun rendered the recently opened branch at Shushtar unprofitable, the Bank obliged.[71] In September 1926 the Bank also opened a full branch at Abadan, where a once weekly agency had been operated spasmodically throughout the 1920s. In addition, the Persian government also encouraged the Bank to open at Barforush,[72] probably to facilitate revenue collection in the region.

None of the new branches proved themselves great commercial successes, and by 1927 the Bank's enthusiasm for expansion was distinctly jaded. 'We are more or less surfeited with Branches', S. F. Rogers remarked, 'that have been opened at the instigation of either the Persian government or our own, which don't pay.'[73]

The Bank's note issue continued to be an important feature of its business. The vast increase in 1919 seems to have resulted from the continuing demand from the British Army, combined with the arrival of a large batch of new notes in Persia. These were originally intended to replace notes damaged during the War, but were issued before some of the damaged notes were recalled. The political difficulties in 1920 and 1921, and the closure of three of the Bank's northern branches, in large measure explains the fall in the note issue in 1920.

During 1922 the Bank decided that there should be a new note issue altogether.[74] Over the following two years designs were made. The printing contract was divided between two British securities' engravers, Bradbury Wilkinson and Co. who engraved the first issue, and Waterlow and Sons Ltd. Bradbury Wilkinson printed the 2, 20, 50 and 100 Toman notes, while Waterlow and Sons engraved the 1, 5 and 10 Toman notes. For the first time, the Imperial Bank's notes were watermarked.

The new notes were issued in Tehran from 15 December 1924, and at the provincial branches as soon as possible thereafter. F. H. Johnson, who had gone to Persia as a junior in 1923, was in Tehran when the new notes were issued:

All the old notes were being called in and the new notes were being issued. I went into the Note Department, which meant helping to withdraw all the old notes which had to be put in trays, and then when there were sufficient, I remember a Persian Government Official came along and we had an Imperial bonfire. A couple of farashes – bank messengers – would with forks throw the notes up and down until they were burnt. They all had to be burnt and then this old boy from the Ministry of Finance had to sign a certificate saying these notes had been destroyed. He also had to sit around while new notes were stamped by a machine.[75]

The growth of the note issue during the 1920s, improved communications in Persia, and the increasing needs of Persian trade and industry, drew attention to the fact that the Bank's notes were legally only payable at the branch of issue. Although the Bank's branches had been accustomed to cashing notes other than their own, a premium continued to be charged. At Manager level suggestions began to be made that the system should be changed. In 1924, for example, one Manager suggested that the time was right for an expansion in the note issue of the Karun valley, especially as Anglo–Persian had proposed making more of their payments in Krans than in Rupees. But to expand the note issue effectively, he argued, it would be necessary for the notes issued by the Bank's branch on the oilfields to be made encashable at par at Ahwaz and other branches such as Mohamma-rah.[76] This novel suggestion, however, found no favour at more senior levels of the Bank, which waited until it was forced by the government to make the reform at the end of the 1920s.

The Bank's deposits in Persia expanded considerably in the 1920s, growing from 120 million Krans (£2 181 818) in September 1919 to 272 million Krans (£4 945 454) in March 1928. In 1928 Chief Office accounted for 80% of total Persian deposits, and much of the growth of the 1920s was due to the Bank's receipt of government revenues and the larger credit balances held in government accounts. In March 1928 around 90% of Chief Office's deposits were in the 49 government accounts held by the branch.[77] As before 1914, the Bank paid interest on many of its deposits. In March 1928 38% of the Bank's Persian deposits were interest-bearing current accounts (held almost entirely for the government) and 36% interest-bearing fixed deposits, with only 20% in interest-free current accounts (and the residue in various sundry and unclaimed forms).

The Bank's wartime concentration of resources on the financing of British military requirements declined in 1920 and 1921. During the 1920s Persian government business replaced these as the main recipient of Bank loans and the bulk of Chief Office's activity was focused on government business. Tehran Bazaar Office and the branches, however, contrived to maintain a commercial business, which was conducted on very similar lines to the period before 1914. C. F. Warr remembers that the Bank had three categories of customer. These were:

Ordinary merchants, bazaar merchants, who had a trade arrangement themselves and amongst their friends interprovincial. And that I think was, at that time, the bulk of our advances. There was also what was described by an unsympathetic manager in London as 'the impecunious nobility' to whom Wilkinson and Walter used to lend money. And sometimes they went bad, and sometimes they didn't. Eventually most of them paid it up, but they had very high regards for a good living, some of these big Persians, they were a very educated and a very cultural race. And third, of course, there were commercial concerns. There weren't any real companies; there were two, or three, chiefly foreign firms. There was the Oriental Carpet Manufacturers, there was Gray MacKenzie and the Mesapotamia–Persia Corporation, or Mespers as it was called, and there were one or two German firms, carpet manufacturers.[78]

The provincial branches, as before the War, financed trade in their regions. Finance of the opium trade, for example, was a major part of the business of the branches at Shiraz, Esfahan and Bushire. In 1927 the total lending of these three branches amounted to 19 million Krans (£380 000), and around 80% of this was lent to the opium trade.[79]

The opium trade was not without its dangers. In 1920 Shiraz branch made a one million Kran (£18 200) loss when, having expanded its lending during the post-War boom, it found itself the victim of forgeries in forward contracts. There was also international pressure on Persia to control and limit the opium trade. An Opium Commission visited Persia for this purpose in 1926. Yet Persia's opium trade continued to flourish in the 1920s, and the Imperial Bank viewed it as some of its safest business. 'In spite of the international commissions', reflected an Inspector visiting Bushire branch in 1927, 'the Oriental will generally find some way of satisfying his tastes, and I consider the business to be a good trade risk.'[80]

A particular feature of this trade liked by the Bank was that the Persian exporter received payment before the opium left Persia. In the late 1920s opium was exported through Bushire to a number of destinations. Some was exported to Singapore, which had turned to Persia as a source of supply after India had embargoed opium exports, and this was done under British government licence, payment being made by means of documentary credits opened through the Bank's Bombay branch. The Persian exporter received 90% of his payment on such licensed shipments before they left Persia. There were also 'unlicensed' shipments by Japanese steamers, taking their cargo to China, and the Persian exporter would receive full payment on shipment.

Branches located on active trade routes, such as Mashad, Rasht, Hamadan, Tabriz and Kermanshah, financed the movements of commodities in their areas. Mashad and Rasht financed Persian exports to the Soviet Union, mainly cotton and wool from Mashad, and rice, cotton and dried fruits from Rasht. The northern branches worked closely with the Soviet trade monopolies set up after the Bolshevik Revolution, especially the Russian Cotton Committee which controlled imports of cotton into the Soviet Union. Hamadan financed the import and export trade on the route to Baghdad, principally the import of Manchester piece goods. Some branches specialised in the finance of a single type of business – such as the carpet trade in Soltanabad and Kerman. The carpet trade in Persia was of particular interest to the Bank as it was largely in the hands of European firms who organised the production and export of the carpets. Favoured customers, such as Oriental Carpet Manufacturers, were offered overdrafts of up to £35 000 without security.[81] By the mid-1920s, however, the Persian industry began to be hit by competition in American markets from India and China.

The Bank's biggest single loss in Persia came from Rasht branch's involvement in forged Canadian Dollar notes. The story began innocently. The Bank's northern branches were used in the early 1920s to being presented with foreign currency notes, originating in Russia, which had been acquired in trade with Russia. As soon as such notes were received, they were sent to London and sold by the Bank. The same procedure was adopted when Canadian notes began appearing in Rasht in early 1924. Rasht's first purchase of these notes was in June 1924. They were duly sent to London, sold, shipped off to Canada and accepted by the Imperial Bank of Canada, the state bank. It was not until March 1925, after further transactions of this nature, that a consignment of $82 000 notes was suddenly refused encashment and declared to be counterfeit by the Canadian authorities.[82]

This development left the Imperial Bank in an extremely awkward position. The Bank ended up with forged notes to the value of $275 800 in its possession. Some consideration was given to suing the Imperial Bank of Canada on the grounds that their apparently negligent checking procedures in 1924 had caused the Imperial Bank of Persia greater losses than was necessary. It was eventually concluded, however, that such an action was unlikely to succeed, perhaps because of the difficulty of proving that the first batch of notes had been in fact forgeries. By March 1926 the Bank's total losses on the Canadian notes exceeded £51 379.[83]

With the exception of this unfortunate incident, the Imperial Bank's business in Persia after the War was very straightforward. 'The banking in Persia', C. F. Warr recalled, 'was really child's play. It was nothing more than lending money and hoping you'd get it back. There was no art or any mystique about it.'[84] The Persian interpreter at each branch of the Bank handled relations with the bazaar. In Ahwaz in 1927, Warr later recalled, this man

used to go around the Bazaar, and he used to talk to the customers. In the main they had confidence in him and they would tell him what they knew, and I think he got it from word of mouth and interviews, not official ones just casual picking up gossip and things like that, and seeing what the man's business was. Occasionally going round to his shop to see whether he had any goods in it and things like that.[85]

If the interpreter recommended a customers' business to his British Manager, the Manager would consult the branches' Information List, which set the credit limit for each merchant, and then make a decision on the proposal.

As the state bank and the only bank in most of Persia, Managers felt no need to 'market' their services. They waited for customers to come to them. 'In those days', Warr recalled, 'there was no business propaganda. You sat behind your desk and the people came to you.'[86] 'People came to the Bank', F. H. Johnson remembered of his period at Bushire in the 1920s, '... You never went out in Bushire. I don't think I ever went out ... to a merchant's house, or for that matter any Persian's house.'[87]

7.5 THE ONSET OF COMPETITION

In spite of its apparent monopoly, the Imperial Bank had always faced some competition in Persia. The Russian Bank had provided some competition throughout the period before 1914, and, more importantly, Persian *sarrafs* had retained a strong position in the bazaars. Nonetheless, the Imperial Bank's role as the government's bank, its note issue and its nationwide branch network made it by far the strongest credit institution in Persia. The 1920s saw the beginnings of a change in the situation with the appearance in Persia of other foreign banks and, most fatally, a locally owned bank in 1928.

The Imperial Bank's response to the onset of competition was understandable but maladroit. On the one hand, potential competitors were looked upon with the greatest disdain. It was seen as beyond belief that anyone could rival the exemplary service offered by the Imperial Bank. 'I don't think that any Government in the world', Rogers observed to Wilkinson in July 1926, 'is blessed with a more accommodating Banker than the Shah's Government by the IBP.'[88] On the other hand, potential competitors were regarded with great apprehension, and the Bank's policies toward them were on occasion hostile and petulant.

The first competitor to arrive was the Imperial Ottoman Bank. The Imperial Bank had broken its long standing agreement with the Imperial Ottoman when it had opened branches in Basra and Baghdad during the War, a story which will be told in Chapter 9, and in 1919 the Imperial Ottoman responded by opening a branch in Hamadan. By 1922 it also had branches in Tehran and Kermanshah, and agents in Soltanabad and elsewhere. The Imperial Bank cut its margins where it was faced with competition from the Imperial Ottoman, and this seems to have been successful in meeting the competition from the new arrival.[89] By September 1925 the Imperial Ottoman were said to be operating 'in a minor degree only'.[90] Little but contempt was felt for that bank. 'The few of their Syrian employees I have seen', Wilkinson wrote in 1927, 'we would not touch with a barge pole and almost the same may be said of their English staff.'[91] Nevertheless a working relationship was established between the two banks.

A Russian bank also reappeared in Persia in the 1920s. In 1921 the assets of the pre-war Russian Bank had been given to the Persians by the Soviet government. All Russian loans to the Persian government had also been cancelled. In 1924, however, the Soviets established a new bank in Persia, the Banque Russo–Persane. By September it had seven branches, including a head office in Tehran, and was causing the Imperial Bank 'no small concern'.[92] However, by the following year the Soviet bank seems to have reduced its competitive thrust, and by 1925 cordial and co-operative relations had been established between the two parties.

The most serious threat to the Imperial Bank came from the moves to establish a locally owned bank. It is impossible to date the origins of this idea. During the Constitutional Revolution there had been calls for a national bank, but nothing had materialised. During the early 1920s the Imperial Bank's subordination to the British Foreign Office had, as already observed, caused much criticism inside Persia. In this period the Bank's privileged position, and its role in the exchange markets, seem to have been widely criticised. 'The Persian Government', the British Minister in Tehran, H. Norman, reported in April 1921, 'have an abiding impression that in general [the Bank] takes unfair advantage of its position as the State Bank of Persia and practically the only Bank in the country and this impression is shared by the public, both native and foreign.' Norman reported that the Persian Prime Minister was anxious to establish 'another bank'.[93]

In January 1922 the Imperial Bank learnt of the possibility that the Russian Bank would be reconstructed under the aegis of the Persian Ministry of

Finance, as the 'Bank of Persia'. The Imperial Bank made immediate and repeated protests to the Foreign Office on the grounds that this was an infringement of its Concession and that the similarity of names between the two institutions was unacceptable.[94] This bank was not successful, however, and its main interest is in showing the Imperial Bank's hostility to any challenge to its position from a local bank.

In 1925 and 1926 several small financial institutions were established by the Persian government. In 1925 the Pahlavi Army Bank was started, funded with the resources of the Army retirement fund to handle the accounts of the military. In 1926 the Civil Service Pensions Fund was used in a similar way to set up the State Mortgage Institution which dealt with small commercial operations, and in the same year a state pawn-broking establishment was founded. None of these institutions worried the Imperial Bank as they were not seen as providing direct competition. On the other hand, the Bank was not prepared to offer them much assistance. When, in December 1925, Reza Khan requested an advance from the Imperial Bank of 2 million Krans for the Pahlavi Bank, against his personal guarantee, the Bank refused to make the loan.[95]

There were occasional alarms in the mid-1920s that the Persian government planned to create its own state bank.[96] During 1924 and 1925 Millspaugh and the American Mission seemed to be strongly in favour of the idea. It was not, however, until the second half of 1926 that the rumours began to turn into reality. In August 1926 Wilkinson asked Millspaugh what was happening and was informed that there were plans to form an Agricultural and Industrial Bank.[97] At first Wilkinson was not alarmed, as it appeared that the proposed bank would limit itself to advancing to landowners and to financing public works. But within weeks it was clear that plans were afoot to create a 'state bank'.[98]

The Imperial Bank's reaction was uncomprehending and bitter. Millspaugh was seen as the originator of the scheme, which was regarded as 'a stab in the back' after all the help the Bank had extended to him. 'This may be American methods of appreciation of favours rendered', Rogers observed, 'but they are distinctly UnBritish.'[99] When in November 1926 the Bill for the establishment of the National Bank was published, Wilkinson was almost lost for words about the 'stupid' proposal. 'This extraordinary project', he wrote to London, 'gives one a good idea of Mr Millspaugh's mentality and of his ability as an economist.'[100]

In May 1927 the Bill for the new National Bank was approved by the Majles, despite the Imperial Bank's protest that the measure would contravene Article 1 of its own Concession under which it alone had the right of founding a state bank in Persia.[101] The new bank was authorised to accept deposits and to lend money for the purpose of assisting trade, industry and agriculture. Within the Imperial Bank, little but contempt and hostility was felt for the project. In July 1927 an Assistant Under Secretary at the Foreign Office, Lancelot Oliphant, met one of the Bank's directors after the Bank's AGM. 'Henceforth', Oliphant was told, the Bank was 'going to fight the Persians without gloves.' Oliphant considered that they might indeed 'succeed in making things extremely unpleasant for the Persian Government'.[102] Within a few years, however, it was to become clear that it was the Persians who had taken off the gloves.

8

THE BANK AND THE NEW IRAN 1928-39

8.1 THE OLD BANK AND THE NEW IRAN

In the 1930s Persia changed. In 1935 Reza Shah insisted that his country should henceforth be known as Iran rather than under its 'foreign' name.[1] In Iran, factories were built, roads constructed, and the Trans-Iranian railway completed. Electricity reached all the major cities. A university was established in Tehran. Women were forbidden to wear the Islamic veil. The Bank changed its name to The Imperial Bank of Iran in 1935, but in other respects its response to the new Iran was retarded. The Bank, especially the Board in London, felt little sympathy with the new developments, and considerable resentment at the sustained campaign against its position in the country. The conflict between the old Bank and the new Iran forms the central thesis of this chapter.

It is important to keep the Imperial Bank's experiences in perspective. The 1930s were not a good decade for banks. There were major banking crises in Continental Europe and the United States. International trade dwindled as the prices of many primary products tumbled. Tariffs were erected and exchange controls devised all over the world, even by such traditional free trade countries as Britain and much of its Empire. The traditional exchange and trade finance business of the British overseas banks was buffeted by these developments and they did not fare well. The Anglo–South American Bank, a leading overseas bank, almost collapsed in 1931, was saved by a Bank of England rescue package, but continued in a state of crisis until it was merged into a more stable institution in 1936.[2] Most of the Eastern exchange banks, such as the Hongkong Bank, the Eastern Bank and the Mercantile Bank of India, were forced to cut dividends and reduce overheads during the 1930s.

The struggle to adapt to the new Iran weighed heavily with the two Chief Managers of the period, Wilkinson and O. A. Butters. The Board's confidence in Wilkinson waned in the early 1930s. Faced with the Iranian government's onslaught on the Bank after 1928, most of his time was spent on negotiations with the government rather than banking or staff matters. He remained aloof from his British staff, and seems to have been unable to delegate responsibility. His Deputy Manager, W. J. d'Alton, complained that he ran the Bank like a 'one man band'.[3] Wilkinson's power waned as the Imperial Bank's plight worsened. His recommendation in 1931 that d'Alton should run the Bank while he was on leave was rejected, and the Board insisted instead on O. A. Butters, then Chief Inspector.[4] In early 1934 Sir Hugh Barnes bluntly suggested to Wilkinson that he should retire. The Chief Manager was most unwilling to do any such thing, but the Board was insistent.[5] In October 1934, therefore, the 55-year-old Wilkinson left Tehran on leave, and retired formally in April 1935 at the end of his leave. He died suddenly in June 1937.

Wilkinson's successor, O. A. Butters, was appointed Acting Chief Manager in September 1934. He had been Chief Inspector since 1930, and perhaps because he was thoroughly British rather than a 'Levantine' he enjoyed a more cordial relationship with London Office than Wilkinson. He was a 'robust and ruddy Scot',[6] who was able to instil more confidence in the Bank's British staff than his predecessor. 'He was more sociable perhaps', C. F. Warr later remembered, comparing Butters with Wilkinson. 'He was more approachable, because he had a very charming wife, and I think he inspired a bit more confidence in me anyway than Wilkinson did.'[7] He also seemed more concerned to involve his senior colleagues – the Deputy Managers (R. S. Oakshott from 1935 to 1937, and V. L. Walter from 1937 to 1939) and the Chief Inspector (T. Sheahan between 1935 and 1946) – with decision-making. Nevertheless, Butters' last years as Chief Manager were also plagued by conflict with the Iranian government, and he was obliged to relinquish his post in July 1939 some time before he would have wished.[8]

The composition of the Bank's Board between 1928 and 1939 changed little, with one conspicuous exception. Sir Hugh Barnes remained as Chairman until December 1937 when he resigned aged 84. Despite his considerable age he remained as a director. His successor was Col. Sir A. Henry McMahon, who was 75 in 1938. Two directors died: David Gubbay in 1928 and S. F. Rogers in 1936, and one director retired, E. A. Chettle in 1933. There was little attempt to infuse fresh blood. E. M. Eldrid, another member of the Bank's staff, joined the Board in 1934. By the 1930s, therefore, the Bank's Board had come to consist of a group of aged and long-serving directors appointed from outside the Bank, plus a group of long-serving former Bank staff. They must have resembled more an assembly of Old Testament prophets than the Board of a bank whose business was threatened by an assertive nationalistic government. One of the aged directors was W. A. Buchanan, born in 1858, and something of a legend. 'I'd

Table 8.1. *The Imperial Bank's Board in March 1936*

Director	Age	Date joined Board	Background
Sir Hugh Barnes	83	1913	Indian Civil Service
V. A. Caesar Hawkins	76	1908	Hongkong Bank
W. A. Buchanan	78	1910	Gray, Mackenzie
Col. Sir. A. H. McMahon	74	1917	Indian Civil Service
S. F. Rogers	70	1926	Ex-staff (joined 1892)
J. McMurray	59	1928	Ex-staff (joined 1897)
E. M. Eldrid	60	1934	Ex-staff (joined 1893)

only been in the bank about a week or two', one man who joined London Office in 1943 later remembered, 'when there was a board meeting and I remember a terrible kafuffle ... and into the cul de sac at Telegraph Street drove a large car ... and then a most extraordinary scene took place because the messengers opened the double doors back and an old man with a long beard came shuffling in supported on one side by his chauffeur and on the other by his nurse and this I was told was the famous Mr. Buchanan.'[9] Table 8.1 shows the Board's composition in March 1936

The seven members of the Board had a combined age of 500, and an average age of 71, in March 1936. Age did bring experience, of course, but the long association of all the directors with the Imperial Bank, either as staff or on the Board, was not conducive to policy changes. The Board in London exercised a conservative influence on the Bank's policies. This was certainly the opinion of informed contemporaries, including the British Minister in Tehran, Sir Robert Clive. 'There is no doubt that the board of the bank', he wrote in 1930, 'have for some years past been far too conservative in their policy – I might even say reactionary – and, if it is not too presumptuous on my part to express an opinion on the constitution of the board, I am convinced that the introduction of a little new blood could only be an advantage.'[10]

It must have been an overdue recognition that the Bank needed younger blood which led to the invitation to Lord Kennet to join the Board in November 1937. Kennet, who was to play a leading role in transforming the Imperial Bank after he became Chairman in 1945, was quite different from his fellow directors. He was a man of distinction and wide experience, with close connections with the political and financial establishment. Born Edward Hilton Young in 1879, he had been educated at Eton and Trinity College, Cambridge, where he had been president of the Union and taken a First Class degree in the Natural Sciences Tripos. He subsequently qualified as a barrister, but chose to pursue a career in financial journalism, becoming

Assistant Editor of *The Economist* between 1908 and 1910 and City Editor of the *Morning Post* between 1910 and 1914. He had a distinguished war record in the Royal Navy, winning the DSO and Croix de Guerre, but losing his right arm at Zeebrugge in 1918. In 1922 he married Kathleen, widow of Captain Scott of the Antarctic. He was Liberal MP for Norwich between 1915 and 1923, and again 1924–29, and Conservative MP for Sevenoaks between 1929 and 1935. His political career led him into government. He was Financial Secretary to the Treasury 1921–22, Secretary of the Overseas Trade Department in 1931 and a notable Minister of Health between 1931 and 1935. In 1935 he was given a baronetcy.

During the 1920s and 1930s Kennet had acquired some knowledge of international finance and currency matters, and of the Middle East, and it was this connection which provided the Bank's interest in him, and his in them. He had served as Chairman of the Royal Commission on Indian Currency and Finance in 1926, had been British Delegate to the League of Nations in 1926, 1927, 1928 and 1932, and was a member of British Financial Missions to Iraq in 1925 and 1930. In the latter capacity he had supported the granting of independence to Iraq, and called, in 1930, for Britain to continue to be interested 'in the economic development of the country, and by assisting it with our resources'.[11] Kennet's impact on the Bank before 1939 was, however, strictly limited, and the institution showed little evidence of innovative or original men at its helm. The story was one of reaction to adverse circumstances: to the creation of the Bank Melli, to the loss of the note issue, and the exchange and trade controls which radically diminished the Imperial Bank's business. The Bank survived, as it had done in previous periods of adversity, but by 1939 its long-term future looked far from rosy.

8.2 THE BANK'S PERFORMANCE 1928–39

The Imperial Bank's balance sheets after 1928 told a sorry, if not hopeless, tale. There was visibly a major trauma after 1928. The Bank's balance sheet total fell by 50% between 1928 and 1932, from £14 332 495 to £7 060 454. Deposits fell by 67% over the same period, to reach £2 555 647, the lowest figure since 1918. The note issue fell by 67%, and disappeared in 1933. The Bank's lending and trade finance activities were clearly greatly disrupted, with an 81% fall in bills discounted, loans and advances and a 65% fall in bills receivable over the five year period. The ratio of bills discounted, loans and advances to deposits and note issue fell from 45% in 1928 to 21% in 1932. Despite some growth in the second half of the 1930s, even by 1939 deposits were 57% lower, and bills discounted, loans and advances 54% lower, than in 1928.

This substantial shrinkage of the Bank's business was not experienced by the other leading Eastern exchange banks, even though in some years in the 1930s many of these banks saw the size of their business remain constant or even decline. But by 1939, for example, the Hongkong Bank's deposits were 53% higher than their 1928 level, Eastern Bank's deposits were 21% higher, and the Mercantile Bank of India had increased its deposits by 7%.

Movements in the Imperial Bank's shareholders' funds present a more optimistic picture. Published shareholders' funds increased from £1 189 646 in 1928 to £1 866 930 in 1939, a growth of 57%. The Bank added to the published reserves in every year until 1937, when they reached £750 000 and stayed at that level until 1939. In addition, in 1937 the Bank increased its capital to £1 million, regaining the size it had been forced to abandon in 1895. This was achieved by using the Bank's £200 000 compensation for the loss of its note issue, which had sat uncomfortably on the balance sheet since 1931, together with a £150 000 transfer from inner reserves.

Inner reserves grew more slowly than published shareholders' funds, increasing from £1 123 464 in 1928 to £1 449 995 in 1939. In this troubled period the Bank showed a preference for strengthening its public shop window. The inner reserves continued to consist of a number of separate funds in the 1930s. Large amounts – over £100 000 for most of the 1930s and reaching over £140 000 in 1938 – were held in an Exchange Reserve Account. This was created in 1929, and in the following year credited with the £95 519 the Bank made when it returned its capital to Britain from Iran in February 1930 (see below). The largest inner reserve, however, remained the Contingency Account. There continued to be substantial transfers to and from profits to the Contingency Account, and this account was also used to 'maintain' the value of the Bank's investments. In October 1931, for example, £300 000 was transferred from Contingencies to help meet the reduction in the book value of the Bank's investments. In May 1934 £127 167 was returned from investments to Contingencies.

Table 8.2 shows the profits of the Imperial Bank. After 1928 it is possible to investigate in more depth the nature of the Bank's profits. The table shows the Bank's calculation of its 'real' profits, the amount left after deducting tax, superannuation payments and (before 1932) royalties to the Iranian government, and the subsequent transfers which were made before the published profit figure was reached.

The Bank's 'smoothing' of profits in its published figures is shown clearly. Published profits showed a steady decline down to 1935, a recovery in 1936 and 1937, a decline in 1938 and a recovery in 1939. The movements in 'real' profits, after tax and royaties had been deducted, were quite different. A large sum was earned in 1929, after which 'real' profits slumped in 1930 and 1931.

Table 8.2. *Imperial Bank's profits 1928–39* (£ Sterling)

Year end (20 March)	'Real' profits	'Real' profits after tax, superannuation and royalties[a]	Transfers (to) or from profits	Bad debts recovered (or provided for)	Published net profit
1928	186 066	140 429	(70 000)	(75 117)	135 312
1929	664 579	432 020	271 900	(18 104)	125 955[b]
1930	244 225	160 102	—	(35 823)	124 279
1931	130 504	103 348	—	(10 334)	93 013
1932	157 956	117 956	—	(29 762)	88 194
1933	258 234	215 734	150 000	20 068	85 802
1934	180 696	140 696	65 000	1472	77 169
1935	114 695	64 695	—	11 065	75 760
1936	110 978	75 978	—	(192)	75 786
1937	151 811	74 811	—	2618	77 430
1938	184 555	115 555	43 400	6181	65 974
1939	122 533	47 783	(8754)	11 635	68 172[c]

Notes:

[a] Royalties to the Iranian government were £8637 in 1928, £116 164 in 1929, £17 954 in 1930 and £756 in 1931.

[b] In 1929 an item of £16 060 for 'furniture' was also debited from profits before the net profit figure was struck.

[c] In 1939 the Bank's published profit figure ceased to reflect the fact that tax on dividends had already been deducted, so the published profit figure of £92 922 for that year is not strictly comparable with previous years. For this table, therefore, the tax which in that year amounted to £24 750 has been deducted from the published profit figure.

There was some recovery in 1932 and 1933, but in the following year a downturn set in and the years 1935–37 saw profits at a very depressed level. There was a recovery in 1938, before a new low was reached in 1939. Transfers to and from inner reserves played an important role in the smoothing process. In 1929 and 1933 profit 'peaks' were reduced by large transfers to the inner reserves, and smaller transfers were made in 1934 and 1938. In 1939, on the other hand, a sum was transferred from inner reserves to profit. In three years (1935, 1937 and 1939) published profits exceeded 'real' post-tax profits, while for the rest of the period such profits exceeded published ones.

The overall picture presented by the Bank's profitability suggests an apparent paradox which will need explanation. While the balance sheet showed that the Bank's business declined sharply after 1928 down to 1934, and subsequently recovered, the 'real' profit figures indicate that the Bank's fortunes reached their nadir in the period 1935–39, with 1938 providing the only relief from the gloom.

Table 8.3. *The sources of the Imperial Bank's profits 1928–39 (£ Sterling)*

Year end (20 March)	London Office	Iranian branches	Iraq and Bombay	Adjustment items	'Real' profits before tax, etc.[e]
1928	72 935	108 633	4468	—	186 066
1929	55 176	607 457	1946	—	664 579
1930	89 238	104 860	7324	42 803[a]	244 225
1931	143 676	(6295)	(6877)	—	130 504
1932	144 075	12 797	1084	—	157 956
1933	269 496	(5419)	(5843)	—	258 234
1934	190 212	(11 146)	1630	—	180 696
1935	91 891	(17 739)	8917[b]	31 626[c]	114 695
1936	100 149	1733	9096	—	110 978
1937	104 424	35 755	11 612	—	151 811
1938	83 122	63 906	16 810	20 717[d]	184,555
1939	92 307	25 090	5136	—	122 533
Totals	1 436 701	919 632	55 303	95 146	2 506 832

Notes:
[a] £10 000 overprovision for premises tax. £32 803 interest on defective coinage.
[b] Iraq branches only from 1935.
[c] £23 793 Old Note Settlement; £7 833 unclaimed balances
[d] Sale of premises
[e] Minor adjustments mean that the figures in this column do not exactly equal the sum of the figures in the other columns.

Shareholders, however, continued to be insulated from the consequences of both troughs and peaks. Betweeen 1928 and 1939 the Imperial Bank remained a steady dividend payer. The dividends increased from 10/- per share in 1928 to 11/- in the following year and 13/- in 1930, at which level they stayed until the War. The Bank's share price never fell below par over the period, and in fact remained constant. In this respect the Imperial Bank's steady but sure record contrasted with most of the other Eastern exchange banks. Both the Mercantile Bank of India and the Eastern Bank cut their dividends in 1931, and their share prices fell sharply in the early 1930s. The Hongkong Bank also cut dividends in the 1930s, and its London share price fell from £143 per share in December 1928 to £87 in December 1938.

The next section examines in more detail the sources of the Imperial Bank's profits between 1928 and 1939.

8.3 A RENTIER BANK

One of the most striking features of the Imperial Bank between 1928 and 1939 was how little money it made from overseas banking in most years. This

Table 8.4. *London Office profits 1928–39 (£ Sterling)*

Year end (20 March)	Income from investments	Net profits on investment sold	Charges	London profit
1928	119 150	7998	57 949	72 935
1929	119 217	211	67 673	55 176
1930	138 217	13 298	64 945	89 238
1931	153 457	47 326	63 658	143 676
1932	165 835	34 445	58 608	144 075
1933	173 105	150 454	55 811	269 496
1934	143 079	95 667	53 491	190 212
1935	129 327	18 830	58 137	91 891
1936	137 223	13 518	53 579	100 149
1937	127 709	23 510	49 870	104 424
1938	122 751	4447	47 006	83 121
1939	135 455	2027	49 645	92 307

is shown in Table 8.3. Between 1928 and 1939 the Iranian branches contributed 37% of the Bank's 'real' profits, the Iraqi branches and Bombay 2%, and London Office 57%. This overall statistic, however, does not capture London Office's importance, because 66% of the Iranian profits were made in one year, 1929. Between 1931 and 1939 London's profits exceeded those of the overseas branches in every year. In four years – 1931, 1933, 1934 and 1935 – the Bank made a loss from its overseas banking.

After 1931, therefore, the Imperial Bank's main source of profit was the income from investments managed by London Office. Table 8.4 shows the main components of London's profits (excluding small adjustment items), the charges of the London Office, and the overall profit. The two primary sources of London's income were interest from investments and redemption of investments. The Bank's investment portfolio was a conservative one. In the early 1930s it consisted largely of British and Indian government stock. Towards the end of the period there was some diversification into colonial and local government stock – and a holding of a 4.5% Iraq Government loan – but the basic pattern remained. With Bank Rate in London at 2% between June 1932 and August 1939, the Imperial Bank's investment portfolio provided a stable but low-yield. In two years, 1933 and 1934, when the Bank made no profits from its overseas branches, it also made large sales of investments, the sums realised being largely taken into the inner reserves. Some £86 100 of the 1911 Persian government Loan was sold over those two years.

The Imperial Bank's dependence on income from Sterling investments to supplement its poor trading performance in the 1930s was not unique. The

Hongkong Bank seems to have been in the same position, although it would have earned higher returns than the Imperial Bank because it was not subject to deduction of British income tax on certain British investments so long as they were held in the books of its Hong Kong Head Office rather than in its London Office. One Hongkong Bank Chief Manager in the 1930s observed to a branch Manager that the Bank would make more money by closing his branch and investing the released funds in a Post Office savings account.[12] The same point can be made for the whole of the Imperial Bank after 1929.

The next section turns to the Bank in Iran, and focuses on the critical period between 1928 and 1933.

8.4 COMPETITION AND CRISIS 1928–33

In the years 1928–33 the storm that had been threatening foreign enterprise in Iran since Reza Shah's rise to power finally broke. In May 1928 Iran abolished the capitulations and extraterritorial privileges held by foreigners. In December 1928 the Iranian Prime Minister told the Majles that 'the old concessionaries might, if they wished to count on the full support of the Persian government ... find it advisable to consider some revision of their concessions'.[13] The Anglo–Persian Oil Company had already begun talks on revising their concession, but although long and tortuous, they were unproductive and in November 1932 their concession was unilaterally cancelled by the Shah.[14]

The Imperial Bank could not, and did not, escape the wave of attacks on foreign enterprise in Iran. Press criticism against the Bank grew in intensity. 'The conviction these people seem to have that we are bleeding their country white', Wilkinson reported to London in October 1928, 'is getting stronger every day.'[15] The Bank, however, did little to ameliorate such feelings. When the capitulatory regime was abolished in May the Bank, fearing new uncertainties in the legal safeguards provided for foreigners in Iran, restricted credit considerably, causing an outcry. It was prudent, but in the circumstances, untactful banking.

The opening of the Bank Melli in September 1928 was not well received by the Imperial Bank. In May a German, Dr Kurt Lindenblatt, arrived in Tehran to manage the new bank. At first sight Wilkinson found him pleasant enough. Both he and Prince Firuz, the Minister of Finance, consulted Wilkinson about the prospective bank, and both assured Wilkinson that they did not wish to compete with the Imperial Bank but only to work in close cooperation with it.[16] S. F. Rogers, in London, advised Wilkinson to have no truck with the scheme. 'It is no part of your duty to assist them', he advised the Chief Manager, 'and I hope your conversations with them will be as nebulous as you can make them.'[17] By July Wilkinson had in fact revised his initially good opinion of Lindenblatt, considering him to be 'a snake in the grass'.[18] Bank Melli soon began to challenge the Imperial Bank's business. By March 1929 it had 15 branches, and as the new bank's representation grew in Iran, so government funds were transferred to it from the Imperial Bank. Moreover, the Imperial Bank was soon convinced that direct pressure was being put on its customers to go to the new bank. 'We have not to do with ordinary competition but with the pressure that can be exercised by Persian government officials on their nationals, where conditions are equal, to do their business with the National Bank.'[19] The Imperial Bank also found its local staff being poached by the new bank, an 'unpardonable thing' in Wilkinson's view.[20]

The loss of accounts and of staff to the new bank were naturally resented by the Imperial Bank, but the Imperial Bank also felt a deep and underlying distaste for Bank Melli. This was partly because of dislike for Lindenblatt and the other Germans in the management of the bank. However, there was also great disdain for the constitution of the Iranian bank. 'It is outside the functions of a Government Bank', the Imperial Bank fulminated, 'to interest themselves in financing the overseas trade of the country. This was debarred from the operations of all the Presidency Banks in India, and we know of no other country where a State Bank interests itself in such matters.'[21] The Bank Melli was regarded as an unwholesome and unfair breach of banking orthodoxy – and for that reason for a time it was predicted it would fail – and no effort was made to co-operate with it. The Bank deliberately offered very high rates when it was asked by the Bank Melli to act as its correspondents in London and elsewhere.[22] The Midland Bank accepted that role instead. The Imperial Bank also refused to reach any agreement with the Bank Melli on foreign exchange rates.

The Imperial Bank's attitudes, rooted in British banking practice and on British views of 'fair play', failed to take into account the new environment of Reza Shah's Iran. The government was not interested in banking orthodoxy, nor in fair play. It wanted a national bank to succeed, at any cost. The government's motivation in this, as in other aspects of its economic pro-gramme, was political, even psychological, rather than purely economic or financial. The Imperial Bank's petulant policies only served to intensify opposition to the foreign institution. It was a point which British diplomats grasped quicker than the Bank. 'The Imperial Bank', the British Minister in Tehran reflected in April 1930, 'had been very short sighted in their attitude towards the National Bank. They began by treating this new bank with undisguised contempt.'[23]

The Bank pursued a similarly unco-operative policy to the general economic programme of Reza Shah. By 1928 the government was giving serious consideration to the adoption of the gold standard in Iran. Iran had suffered for years from fluctuations in the price of silver, and, in addition, the gold standard was seen as a recipe for economic success. Britain, which had abandoned the gold standard during the First World War, had triumphantly returned to it in 1925. In December 1928 Wilkinson was asked by the Iranian government to suggest schemes to put Iran on the gold standard.[24] The Bank, however, was concerned about the implications of such a step on its note issue, and moved at a snail's pace over the following year. It was not until July 1929 that the advice of a Bank of England director, Sir Basil Blackett, was requested, but his advice had not been transmitted to the Iranian government by 1930, when events overtook the Bank and Iran.[25]

During 1928 the Bank's Concession and its methods of doing business began to come under criticism. The Bank's note issue was the first target. During the autumn newspapers began demanding that the Bank's notes should be payable at all its branches without a discount, and in December Abdol Hoseyn Teymurtash, the Minister at Court, made this an official request.[26] In a pattern which became familiar Wilkinson advised compromise. But the Bank's Board in London insisted on a firm policy of resistance to the government's 'stupid proposals whereby they can get our Notes paid anywhere'.[27] By September 1929, however, the Imperial Bank had been forced to concede the point, after the Bank Melli had begun encashing notes at par at all its branches. In addition, the Bank found its freedom to issue notes restricted. During early 1929 the Iranian government agreed to allow the sealing of 30 million Krans (£59 000) of new bank notes, but only if an equivalent number of old notes were withdrawn from circulation. The Bank's freedom to decide the size of the note issue was thus effectively curbed.[28] Nevertheless the Bank found itself publicly condemned by Prince Firuz for deliberately withholding notes.

The question of the royalties the Imperial Bank paid the Iranian government also came to a head in the late 1920s. In November 1928 J. McMurray had been invited to join the Bank's Board, and within two weeks he had been sent to Tehran to negotiate a settlement with the Iranian government over their claim for lost revenue. It was hoped that the Bank's counter claim for looted branches would balance out the claim for royalties, and that the government would call it 'quits'.[29] It was a forlorn hope, however, and McMurray eventually agreed to pay £87 304 as supplementary royalties owed to the government since 1890. The Bank's claim for compensation was left unsettled, and eventually abandoned in 1935 when it agreed to pay a further £30 000 to the government for royalties.

By April 1929 a letter of protest to the Iranian government was being drafted by the Board in London. The Bank's protest covered the whole gamut of issues, from calls for curbs on the Bank Melli, to complaints about the restrictions on the note issue, to the claim for compensation for the looted branches.[30] The assistance of the British Legation was requested, and on 10 July Sir Robert Clive and Wilkinson handed Teymurtash a letter of protest signed by Sir Robert. It was a muted affair, however. Both the Foreign Office and the British Legation were reluctant to cause a major diplomatic crisis over the Bank's complaints. After disputing the Imperial Bank's claims that its rights as state bank had been infringed by the Bank Melli, and rejecting once again the Bank's claims over looted property, Teymurtash persuaded Sir Robert to take his letter with him when he left. The Bank had distinct feelings of a very unsatisfactory anti-climax. 'Personally, I feel profoundly disappointed', S. F. Rogers wrote to Wilkinson, 'that the Minister did not leave the letter with Teymourtache *and register* our formal protest. We now stand officially as if nothing had been done at all.'[31] Over the next few months, however, direct pressure on the Bank relaxed following the dismissal of the Iranian Finance Minister, Prince Firuz, and the temporary eclipse of Teymurtash under an associated cloud.[32]

Another crisis was, however, developing on the foreign exchange markets. After 1928 the external value of the Iranian Kran sharply depreciated. The average annual exchange rate fell from 48 Krans to the pound in 1928 to 63.5 in 1930. The primary factor in the decline of the Kran was a world wide depreciation of silver. The gold price of bar silver fell from 28 pence per ounce in May 1928 to 20 pence in January 1930. The situation was exacerbated, however, by the Iranian government's decision in 1928 as part of the scheme to put the country on the gold standard, and to retain in Britain its Sterling income from oil royalties. These royalties, which amounted to £1.44 million in 1929, had previously been credited to the Iranian government in Sterling in London and remitted to Iran as required. The fact that the Iranian government kept its large credit balances in London with banks other than the Imperial Bank helped to increase the British Bank's hostility to Iranian policies.[33] Further pressure was placed on the Iranian currency by the foreign purchases of the government's Railway Syndicate, which spent around £2 million abroad between 1928 and 1930. Finally, still further pressure was put on the currency by the world-wide fall in primary commodity prices, which caused a deterioration in Iran's terms of trade.

During the last months of 1928 and beginning of 1929 the Imperial Bank faced huge demands for Sterling exchange. Between September 1928 and March 1929 £1 million was sold to the Railway Administration, plus £500 000 to the Russian Bank and £175 000 to the Bank Melli for the import of silver. As a result, the Bank's overbought position fell from £2.5 million in September

1928 to under £700 000 in March 1929. These large sales of Sterling exchange, combined with the sharp fall in the Kran exchange rate, resulted in the huge profits the Bank earned in Iran in 1929.

The situation became less satisfactory in the following year. By the autumn of 1929, the Bank Melli and the Imperial Bank were in active competition for increasingly scarce foreign exchange. The scarcity was intensified by a collapse in carpet exports to the United States following the Wall Street crash. By 15 October the Imperial Bank's overbought position had fallen to £570 000 and the Board were becoming seriously concerned. 'We have always in our minds looked upon our Capital in Persia', Rogers wrote to Wilkinson on 17 October, 'as being theoretically in London in the form of an overbought exchange position.'[34] The Imperial Bank by the end of October was desperately short of exchange, and a strategy of outbidding the Bank Melli seemed the only answer if the Bank's customers were to have their requirements met. 'You should strenuously go into the Market and bid for Exchange sufficient to provide for the necessary cover', London wrote to Wilkinson on 31 October 1929, 'irrespective of the rate to which Exchange would be ultimately forced.'[35] As the Kran fell to 60 against the pound, Wilkinson privately blamed the Bank's policies for the speed of the depreciation, and in particular the Board's belief that 'even a moderate oversold position' was 'the end of the world'.[36]

The Bank's remittances to Britain added to the strain on the Iranian currency. The £605 000 profit remittance in March 1929 was followed, later in the year, by a decision to reduce the Bank's commitments in Iran by concentrating all reserves and capital in London. On 23 October the Board decided to remove the £557 195 of Sterling capital allocated to Iran from the Bank's overbought position, and place it in a Special Account. Wilkinson's overbought position was, however, reinforced by £60 000 transferred from the Iraqi branches. On 14 January 1930 the Special Account was closed, and the £557 195 formally transferred to London's books.[37] An additional £95 519 was transferred at the same time representing profit made on adjusting the capital when it was transferred to Britain, and this was placed in the Exchange Reserve Account. There were also transfers to London of miscellaneous reserve accounts held in Tehran – £32 802 in November 1929 from an interest abeyance account, and £30 881 in early 1930 from a suspense account. 'The transfer of these colossal sums we have made to London', Wilkinson observed to Rogers in December 1929, '... has completely dislocated our position vis-à-vis exchange.'[38]

As protests from importers grew, and Teymurtash re-established his political position, the Iranian government began to consider moves to stop the collapsing exchange rate. In the middle of December Teymurtash asked

Wilkinson and Lindenblatt to co-operate to stabilise the currency. Wilkinson suggested that government funds should be used to support the rate, at which point the Iranian Minister commented 'that if the Government were to risk its money, it might just as well make exchange a Government monopoly'.[39] The Bank, however, was in no mood to assist the Iranian government, even if it had had the power to do so, and the Board continued to press throughout January for Wilkinson to follow the downward course of silver and maintain the depreciation of the Kran. By 27 January 1930 Sterling was being quoted by the Imperial Bank at 70.

Nemesis followed. On 2 February Wilkinson heard that the Iranian government had under consideration measures to halt the depreciation of the Kran, including the introduction of a gold standard and exchange controls. The Bank was left out in the cold, unconsulted by the government.[40] Rumours grew and by 13 February Wilkinson had to report that it seemed the 'entire control of exchange' would be given to the Bank Melli.[41]

On 24 February a Foreign Exchange Bill was presented to the Majles, and by 1 March it was law. The new Act decreed that exchange rates were to be fixed, forbade the import of silver and the export of gold, and obliged all sellers of foreign exchange to offer it first either to the government or the bank appointed by the government. The buying rate was fixed at 59.5 and the selling rate at 60, or much higher than the market rate which had fallen to over 70. For several days it seemed that the Imperial Bank's exchange business would cease completely as the Bank Melli was the government's appointed bank, but on 6 March, Wilkinson agreed to an arrangement under which the Imperial Bank undertook to sell to the Bank Melli 50% of the foreign exchange it purchased.[42] The Imperial Bank was, therefore, allowed to continue dealing in foreign exchange.

One impact of the new law was on the Bank's adjustment rates. In 1929, after consultations with the British Inland Revenue, the Bank had agreed to abandon the fixed balance sheet adjustment rate of 55 it had used since 1917, and to convert its assets and liabilities into Sterling at the rate of exchange ruling on 20 March. The introduction of exchange controls in Iran in 1930 meant that, henceforth, the Imperial Bank's adjustment rate was fixed to the official buying rate for Sterling on 20 March of each year. The practice of having a separate profit adjustment rate was also abandoned.

On 21 March 1930 the government announced that Iran would go onto the gold standard. The new exchange controls caused an immediate decline in the Bank's business and, even though it could continue dealing in foreign exchange, profits were drastically curbed. Meanwhile the Bank Melli, aided by the Iranian government and by its 50% share of the foreign exchange purchases of all the other banks, was able to supply foreign exchange to its clients, and use its resources as a bargaining ploy to win merchants' accounts.[43]

There seemed only one glimmer of hope for the Imperial Bank. The Iranian government was anxious to assume the right to issue bank notes, and on 25 February Teymurtash had suggested to Wilkinson that the note issue should be given up in exchange for an interest-free loan from the Iranian government of £650 000 until the Bank's Concession expired.[44] It now seemed that the only course was to use the note issue to secure a relaxation of the controls on the Bank's exchange business. 'In our Note Concession,' Wilkinson wrote in 15 March, 'we have a weapon which could bring the Persian Government – mad as it is – to its senses.'[45] Within a few days S. F. Rogers, who had just handed over as London Manager to E. M. Eldrid, arrived in Tehran to negotiate such an arrangement.

Rogers' first call was on Sir Robert Clive, but his pleas for assistance from the Legation were not warmly received as Clive was convinced that the Bank had been too intransigent in its policies towards the Iranian government. He advised Rogers that Teymurtash considered the Bank 'reactionary and unhelpful', and recommended that Rogers should meet the Minister carrying 'a memorandum couched in conciliatory terms'.[46]

Rogers had his first meeting with Teymurtash on 31 March. The Minister made clear that his government 'was determined to shake the country out of its state of lethargy', and that 'a State bank which was not a State bank in name only' had an important role to play in this process. Later in the interview, however, the Minister expressed again his desire to take control of the note issue, and he agreed that if the Bank relinquished this privilege, the obligation to give half its exchange purchases to the Bank Melli would be lifted.[47] Rogers began detailed negotiations with Lindenblatt on these lines. However, his attempt to secure £1 million compensation for the loss of the note issue was not taken seriously by the Iranian government. For the first time in the Bank's history there were serious thoughts of withdrawing from Iran. On 11 April the Board resolved that Rogers was to press for the repeal of the 50% exchange requirement, then ask the government 'either for the sale of our Note Concession, or, if they preferred it, we were willing to consider a cash offer to cancel the whole Concession and retire from Persia'.[48]

Over the following fortnight further negotiations were undertaken, and on 21 April Teymurtash gave Rogers his final conditions. The Bank was offered an interest-free loan of £350 000 for the 19 years until its Concession expired, in exchange for the surrender of the note issue. As a *quid pro quo*, the 50% exchange requirement was to be dropped; the Bank's exemption from Iranian taxation retained; the post of Iranian High Commissioner would be abolished; the royalty of 6% of net profits would be abolished; and there were promises of a share in the government business. Rogers' complaints that Teymurtash was 'not playing the game' were brusquely swept aside. 'The Concession had been obtained in consideration for a miserable loan of £40 000', Teymurtash told Rogers, 'but how much Baron de Reuter paid in bribes he couldn't say, but he had had to deal in those days with people still living in the jungle who were easily persuaded with a little gold for their pressing needs. Times had changed and they could not be expected to respect such a contract in these enlightened days.' The Bank, Rogers informed Sir Hugh Barnes, had no alternative but 'to take or leave' the Iranian offer.[49]

The Board took it, although instead of the loan the Board asked for a cash equivalent of £200 000. This was agreed, and an exchange of letters and a new appendix to the Bank's Concession cemented the new arrangements.

Appendix No. 5 to the Bank's Concession (which is reprinted in Appendix No. 1 at the end of this volume), was signed on 13 May 1930. Under its terms the Bank relinquished its note issue in return for £200 000. The 6% royalty and the post of High Commissioner were abolished. The Bank was authorised to accept mortgages on immovable property, and permitted to hold such property as security against advances for a period of up to one year. An arbitration procedure was established, with the League of Nations appointed as the arbitrator of last resort. In addition, on 13 May the Minister of Finance wrote to the Imperial Bank promising it a share in government revenues, and the business of purchasing the gold and silver bullion in Britain destined for the coinage of the new currency.[50] Finally, a memorandum of collaboration was signed between the Imperial Bank and the Bank Melli, in which the two banks agreed to reveal to each other their weekly purchases and sales of exchange, and to decide on the allocation of foreign exchange. Each bank was to retain 75% of its purchases, with the remainder pooled and shared equally between the Imperial Bank and the Bank Melli.

Over the following three years the consequences of the May 1930 agreements were worked out. The Imperial Bank was scheduled to have withdrawn its note issue by 20 June 1931, but by December 1930 it had become clear to the Iranian government that it had insufficient time in which to introduce a new currency. In December Teymurtash asked the Bank to postpone its withdrawal of notes. The Bank's Board considered that some financial compensation was appropriate if they were to oblige the Iranians, but fear of further foreign exchange restrictions eventually led them to agree in March 1931 to an extension.[51] The withdrawal of the Bank's notes, therefore, did not commence until 21 June 1932, and was complete on 20 September 1932. In March 1932 a new Rial currency was introduced, with one Rial equivalent to one Kran. 'The privilege we have been enjoying since our advent into this country, 44 years ago,' Wilkinson observed, 'of exercising independent control over the money market will be lost to us, and will perforce hamper our earning capacity.'[52] The new note issue was backed initially by a 100% metallic cover, which was soon modified to 60%. Even at this level the reserve was more rigorous than in most countries, and an indication of the financial conservatism noticeable in the government's economic policies.

The May 1930 agreements had promised the Imperial Bank a share in government business, which it had largely lost to the Bank Melli. Moreover, the Bank's grip on the Southern customs receipts – which had been paid into its Gulf branches in accordance with the conditions of the 1911 Loan – had been challenged. These customs receipts, which had been credited to the government account in Tehran at the Bank's public buying rate on the Gulf branches where the receipts were paid in, had provided a profitable business. After March 1930, however, the Iranian government had taken over the excess receipts – after allowing for the sum required for service of the 1911 Loan – at the place of origin.

On 2 July 1930 the Imperial Bank and Bank Melli entered into an agreement which reversed this trend. The Imperial Bank was to be given a half share with Bank Melli of the customs receipts paid into Mashad, the tax revenues paid into Rasht, and the revenues of government sugar and tea monopolies paid into Kermanshah. There was the same arrangement for the Southern customs receipts, but the old system whereby the Bank transferred the receipts to Tehran was restored, though on a commission of 1 per mil on the amounts transferred. Government credit balances were to earn 1% per annum credit interest. This agreement remained in force, with some modifications, including the transfer of revenues at par, throughout the 1930s. It meant that the Imperial Bank retained the prestige pertaining to the receipt of government revenue, and government funds also helped the cash position of branches.[53]

The Iranian government's policy of exchange controls was not a success. The fixed exchange rate and the free market rate continued to diverge, providing an open invitation for speculation and evasion of official regulations. A variety of measures were undertaken to enforce the exchange controls, but they were largely ineffective due to the problems of enforcement.

The laws did have the effect, however, of drastically reducing the Imperial Bank's foreign exchange turnover. In March 1931 the Bank made a loss on its Iranian business and, although a small profit was made in 1932, further losses were made in 1933 and 1934.

In 1931 a tougher series of exchange restrictions were introduced. In April a Foreign Trade Monopoly Law was passed, designed to reduce imports, promote exports and facilitate barter agreements with countries such as the Soviet Union. Among other provisions, state monopolies were established to import 'necessities' such as sugar, tea and piece goods. From the Imperial Bank's viewpoint, the worst feature of the legislation was that it appeared exporters had to sell all their exchange to the Bank Melli. This would have effectively ended the Bank's exchange business altogether. Wilkinson, 'simply fuming with rage', wondered 'whether there is a Persian in existence who has ever kept to his word'.[54]

The Bank responded with its now usual letters of protest to the Persian government and the Foreign Office.[55] However, O. A. Butters, who was acting Chief Manager while Wilkinson was on leave, recognised the futility of insisting on the Bank's formal rights, and a more indirect approach was adopted. Abol Hassan Ebtehaj, the Bank's Iranian officer in charge of relations with the government, was despatched to see Teymurtash to tell him of the Bank's wish to 'work in harmony with him and the Persian government'.[56] Teymurtash advised that if the Bank was patient and did not insist on its rights, such a course would be rewarded, and on 11 September the Imperial Bank was duly appointed an authorised bank, alongside the Bank Melli, with permission to purchase foreign exchange from exporters.

Thereafter the pressure on the Imperial Bank from the Iranian government relaxed. There were two major factors. First, the government's economic programme ran into increasing difficulties, and, consequently, in March 1932 several policies were reversed. The government's attempt to go onto the gold standard was abandoned. At the same time the exchange control laws, which had been widely evaded, were partially relaxed. Under the new arrangements, exporters were still obliged to sell their exchange to either the Bank Melli or the Imperial Bank. But the banks were allowed to sell this exchange at their own discretion, subject to a number of guidelines. The exchange derived from 80% of the proceeds of commodities exported under a monopoly, for example, had to be allotted to the import of certain high priority goods, such as machinery. In July 1932 the Board felt sufficient confidence in Iran to give Wilkinson permission to overdraw in London by £100 000 if he could not secure sufficient deposits to maintain his business, and in 1934 this sum was formally allocated to Iran as 'capital'.

The second event which assisted the Imperial Bank was the temporary eclipse of the Bank Melli. The Imperial Bank had never liked or trusted Lindenblatt, but by December 1931 Wilkinson was hearing strong rumours that the Bank Melli had undertaken much ill-advised lending and that it would 'not be long before the fat is in the fire'.[57] Within a few months the Shah had established a commission of inquiry into the bank's affairs. In June 1932 Lindenblatt left the country to consult his doctor, and in September his

German deputy fled to Beirut, where he committed suicide while in detention. When Lindenblatt returned to Iran, there were allegations that Teymurtash had been involved in dubious procedures and deals at the Bank Melli, including exchange speculation. The actual reasons behind the allegations against the Court Minister were more complex, and included the Shah's paranoid fear of any potential rival. Teymurtash was arrested in January 1933, tried and convicted on fraud and other charges in March, and died in prison in October.[58]

Corruption and incompetence took its toll on the Bank Melli's business. The bank declared an 8.7 million Rial (nearly £900 000) loss for the year ending March 1932, and public confidence in the new institution was undermined to the benefit of the Imperial Bank. In September 1932 Wilkinson observed that his Bank had gained considerably from the 'regrettable occurrences' at the Bank Melli and had recovered its position as 'the most popular bank in Persia'.[59] By March 1933 Wilkinson was in a buoyant mood. 'The business of the country, which at one time under Nationalistic fervour, combined with certain pressure, tended to flow from us, is now steadily returning to us. . . . The unfortunate happenings in the National Bank of Persia have shown them very clearly that it is safer to stay with old friends.'[60] There were other reasons for optimism too. The Iranian government's dispute with the Anglo–Persian Oil Company was amicably resolved in April 1933, after League of Nations arbitration, and on terms which were not unfavourable to the British company.[61] Perhaps, after all, British firms could survive in Reza Shah's Iran.

Yet the Imperial Bank found it hard to make profits under the new system. The whole thrust of the government's economic programme was towards import-substitution, a policy which could not help but damage a bank that had financed much of Iran's import trade. Government trade monopolies gave their business to the Bank Melli. Fixed exchange rates ruled out large exchange profits. The loss of government accounts obliged the Bank to 'buy' funds from the Bank Melli and Bank Pahlavi, to maintain its business. After returning a small profit in 1932, losses mounted in 1933 and 1934. Wilkinson paid the price for the situation in 1934, when he was obliged to stand down in favour of O. A. Butters.

8.5 THE BANK AND THE IRANIAN INDUSTRIALISATION DRIVE

During the 1930s Reza Shah's industrial development programme got seriously underway. At its centre lay the construction between 1927 and 1938 of the 1394 kilometre Trans-Iranian railway. The railway ran from Bandar Shah on the Caspian Sea to Bandar Shahpur on the Gulf. The railway primarily served a strategic and nationalistic purpose rather than a purely economic one. The route avoided major cities, except Tehran and Ahwaz, which made little commercial sense, while severe gradients made it impossible to transport heavy machinery. It has been estimated that an equivalent road would only have cost 1 to 1.5% of the £30 million spent on the railway. One recent writer has castigated it as 'an unmitigated economic folly'.[62] There was also substantial investment in road transport, with at least 14 000 miles of road being constructed between 1923 and 1938.[63] The overall impact of the Shah's transport programme was drastically to reduce travel times in the country.

Progress was made, too, in industrial promotion. Reza Shah was determined to modernise his country, and to free it from foreign influence. Moreover, the need for industrialisation was made pressing by the falling prices for Iranian exports, which led to a deficit in the balance of payments. A programme of state-led import-substitution was, therefore, initiated, on similar lines to that pursued by Turkey and, on a much grander scale, Stalin's Russia, in the same period. The government's policies of exchange and import controls and the establishment of state factories were not a recipe for the optimum use of available resources, especially given the shortcomings of the government bureaucracy, but nevertheless substantial growth was achieved. Between 1934 and 1938, in particular, there was a large increase in manufacturing industry, with the number of workers employed in that sector increasing by 250% over the four years. The private sector was encouraged by tax exemptions, preferences and cheap credit from the Agricultural and Industrial Bank. Expansion was especially noteworthy in the sugar, cotton and woollen textiles, match and cement industries. There was more limited, but still noticeable, growth in chemicals, soap, oil processing, glass production, and beer and wines, all industries in which the private sector was predominant. The Shah, immensely proud of Iran's achievements, held exhibitions of Iran's industrial and agricultural products in Tehran in several years in the 1930s.[64] In the light of Iran's past economic history, Reza Shah's achievements during the 1930s were indeed substantial.

Considerable emphasis was placed on the fact that this growth was financed by the Iranians themselves. Offers of foreign loans were turned down, and with oil revenues largely allocated to military purposes by the mid-1930s, the cost of the development programme rested on taxes, mainly on consumption, together with an increase in the money supply.

The Imperial Bank was largely, although not entirely, on the sidelines during this first phase of Iranian industrialisation. The Bank did provide, at least after 1935, the short-term facilities required by the foreign contractors employed on government projects, especially railway construction. However the Bank, and more particularly the Board in London, refused to become involved in longer term investment projects. In 1933, for example, the Bank received a request for a 30 million Rial (£291 262) loan, guaranteed by the government, from the Tobacco Monopoly. This government agency had been established in 1932, and needed the funds for construction work inside the country and the purchase of machinery overseas, probably in Britain. The request may have come to the Imperial Bank because of the Bank Melli's internal problems in that year. Wilkinson suggested a 10 million Rial loan over two years to finance a less ambitious scheme.[65] In putting the proposal to London Wilkinson emphasised the political gains to the Bank. 'It would increase the popularity of the Bank in the eyes of the Government', he observed, 'if we could see our way to dissipate the firm view the Authorities hold that our main concern in Persia is to safeguard our own interests, and never to lend a hand in any direction which may help the country to progress.'[66]

Wilkinson's case, however, did not impress the Board. In a tradition which stretched back to the 1890s, while the Chief Manager pleaded political and commercial realities, the Board took its stand on the principles of British banking. 'It is contrary to the tenets of British Banking', Wilkinson was informed by the Board when he pressed the Tobacco Monopoly's request, 'to acquire blocks of bonds or shares in industrial concerns, or to lock up capital in long term advances to them.' This view was reinforced by an understandable resentment about the Imperial Bank's recent treatment, and a feeling that the Iranians should live with the consequences of their actions. 'There can be no just cause for complaint that we safeguard our own interests', Wilkinson was told, 'it is a duty both to our shareholders and the Persian public, ... Thinking Persians must realise that we have not the resources we possessed when holding the Note Concession.'[67] The Board, therefore, refused to lend to the Tobacco Monopoly, or to the telephone company which made a similar request in the same period. This remained the Bank's policy for the remainder of the 1930s, despite later attempts by both Wilkinson and Butters to elicit a change of heart from the Board. This attitude was, of course, that of British bankers generally, but it is hard to avoid the conclusion that a more flexible approach could have been reconciled with the requirements of banking prudence, and that both business opportunities and the opportunity to re-establish a working relationship with the government were lost by such policies.

The Imperial Bank provided few facilities for the Iranian government during the industrialisation drive. After 1928 government debt to the Bank was rapidly run down. This is shown in Table 8.5.

By September 1930 the Iranian government's debt to the Imperial Bank

Table 8.5. *Imperial Bank advances to the Iranian government 1928–30*

Date	Outstanding balance (Krans)	Sterling equivalent
20 March 1928	8 258 560	150 156
20 March 1929	14 302 810	280 447
20 March 1930	266 490	4479
20 September 1930	nil	nil

had been completely liquidated, depriving the Bank of its regular source of income from this source. During 1935, however, the Bank Melli approached the Imperial Bank about the provision of overdraft facilities, and on 11 June it formally requested an overdraft of up to £500 000 over 12 months at 3% interest per annum. The industrialisation drive was clearly running into a foreign exchange constraint, a familiar problem in such a situation. The Board were willing to grant the overdraft, but requested a government guarantee. It was at this stage that difficulties arose, because it soon emerged that the government was most unwilling to make a public statement that the Bank Melli was seeking funds from the Imperial Bank. Various expedients were attempted. Bank Melli, for example, offered an undertaking marked and signed 'Note et pris connaissance' by the Prime Minister and the Minister of Finance.

The Board, however, remained firm that it wanted a government guarantee, and on 24 July decided that such a guarantee would need to be confirmed by the Majles. The Board took its stand on a clause in the Iranian Constitution which stipulated that state loans could only be contracted with the approval of the Majles. Walter argued that the Majles guarantee was politically impossible, and that it would not only be useless to insist upon it, but 'would be regarded as an insult which would seriously damage the future interests of the IBI'.[68] The Board, however, would not be moved, and broke off negotiations with the Bank Melli. The Bank Melli Governor, General Amir Khosrovi and the Iranian government were furious. The Prime Minister sent Butters a message that if relations between Britain and Iran 'were not as they ought to be, it was because of incidents such as this'.[69]

Later in 1935 the Iranian government also attempted to persuade the Imperial Bank to remit more capital to Iran to assist the industrialisation programme. In December General Khosrovi offered to get the government's guarantee, 'but without confirmation of the Majlis', that any fresh capital the Bank remitted to Iran could be returned after two years at the same rate as it had been brought out. He also offered the Bank up to 100 million Rials (£1.5 million) business from the government's syndicates, at a 6% interest rate and

Table 8.6. *Imperial Bank advances and risks to ECC and government companies 1936–39 (outstanding balances) (£ Sterling)*

Date	Total advances to ECC	Advances to govt. companies	Credits and guarantees to govt. companies	Public credits against ECC permits
20 November 1936	104 193	66 428	416 905	150 029
20 March 1937	395 862	150 000	235 409	34 186
20 March 1938	292 372	—	29 753	51 968
20 March 1939	146 650	—	192 167	2390

with a guarantee against bad debts.[70] The Bank, however, refused to oblige, and over the following months, as pressure against the external value of the Rial mounted, relations between the Bank and the Iranian government again deteriorated. 'During the week the General has shown a very unfriendly attitude to us', Butters reported on 18 February, '...hinting that he considered we were responsible for rates going up.'[71]

On 1 March 1936 a new exchange control regime was introduced. An Exchange Control Commission (ECC) was created, whose permission was required for all transactions in foreign exchange. Exporters were obliged to sell all their exchange to an authorised bank.

The new law was the most serious threat yet to the Imperial Bank's business. Failure to be designated an authorised bank would have prevented it from dealing in foreign exchange. Moreover, the ECC had the power to block the remittance of the Bank's profits from Iran. Butters acted quickly, for there was no time to consult London.[72] By 3 March he had reached an agreement with the Iranian government. The Bank was designated an authorised bank, and allowed to remit the Sterling equivalent of its profits once a year to London. In return, however, the Bank was forced to undertake lending to the government and its companies. The ECC was to cover any excess foreign exchange sales over purchases, or purchases over sales, but if sales exceeded purchases the Bank agreed to allow the ECC a Sterling overdraft of up to £300 000. At the same time the Bank agreed overdraft facilities of up to a further £300 000 for companies in which the government owned at least 50% of the share capital. Interest on these Sterling advances was to be paid once a year in Rials.

Butters' agreement saved the Bank, and was recognised by the Board as the only practical option. The provision of facilities for government organisations was unavoidable in a situation where government monopolies controlled a large proportion of trade. The new agreement opened the door for the Imperial Bank to secure some of the business which had previously gone to the Bank Melli. Table 8.6 gives the advances and other 'risks' undertaken by the Bank on the Iranian government's behalf between 1936 and 1939.

It can be seen that the Bank undertook a considerable amount of business under the March 1936 agreement. The interest earned on advances helped the recovery in Bank profits between 1936 and 1938. In 1937 the Bank raised its lending limit to the Iranians to £700 000. The Iranian government also kept its side of the bargain, and the Bank was duly permitted to remit its 1936–37 profit in September 1937. In April 1938 the Bank also won the right to payment in Sterling of interest on its foreign exchange advances to the ECC.[73]

Another crisis was, however, brewing. The cost of the government's development programmes, combined with considerable military spending, was affecting most of the economy. Inflation was growing as a result of government's rapid expansion of money supply. A wholesale price index standing at 100 in 1928 had reached 165 in 1936, and 201 in 1938. The strain was reflected in the gap between the official exchange rate, pegged at a buying rate of 80 Rials to the pound, and the market exchange rate, which had reached 160 Rials by 1938.

In November 1938 the Iranian government, now in increasing need of financial resources, asked the Bank for an unsecured loan of £400 000 repayable in monthly instalments of £50 000. The Bank had received permission in July 1938 to remit only £35 000 of its £63 000 profit for the year ending March 1938. In these circumstances the Board refused the loan request. On 4 December the Minister of Finance responded with a ruling that the Bank was only to be permitted to remit to Britain profits earned on foreign exchange transactions, and would not be permitted to realise in Sterling any profit made from the utilisation of public deposits. Nor was the Bank to be allowed any Sterling to provide for remittances to Britain of its British staff, nor to provide for any requirements from Britain for such things as office supplies.[74] 'On the face of it', London Office concluded, 'the result would seem to indicate say £5000 a year to meet requirements of say £50 000 a year exclusive of any net profit.'[75] A further turn of the screw on the Bank came on 26 December, when the ECC informed it that for most commodities, except government requirements, it could only sell exchange to the extent of its purchases. The effect on the Imperial Bank's business was dramatic. With the exception of some business with the Anglo–Iranian

Oil Company, the Imperial Bank 'almost ceased to be a foreign exchange Bank'.[76]

The first half of 1939, therefore, was one of crisis for the Imperial Bank. It was being virtually blackmailed to lend to the Iranian government, and it had little freedom of manoeuvre. The Bank's attempts to modify the Iranian proposals ran into a stone wall. There was talk, once again, of liquidating the Bank. However, Lord Kennet advised patience. 'We owe our difficulties to the characteristics of a regime which', he wrote in December 1938, 'is of recent growth in Persia. We do not know how long it will last.' Kennet also raised the question of how well the Bank was represented in Tehran. 'Butters', he observed, 'seems to me not to have succeeded in keeping us in touch with the realities of the position [in Tehran], and I have rather got the impression that he does not understand them very well himself, and is not perhaps now very strongly interested in the future. I gather that Walters (sic) is a better man.'[77] Kennet's advice, even though he was the new boy on the Board, seems to have carried weight, and in the New Year Butters was asked to make way for Walter.

By May Butters, who was convinced that the Bank had to agree to the government's demands, feared that its status as an authorised bank would be revoked unless the Bank gave in.[78] On 17 May the Board authorised him to sign the agreement the Iranians requested. On 6 July, therefore, Butters signed an agreement lending the Iranian government £400 000, conditional upon immediate remittance of the remainder of the 1938 profit. The Bank's remittable profits were henceforth limited to its foreign exchange operations. The government also removed the December 1938 restrictions on the Bank's right to sell exchange.

The day Butters signed the agreement he also handed over the Chief Managership to V. L. Walter, and he left Tehran for London two days later. On 12 July the Bank was allowed to remit to Britain the balance of its 1938 profit.

8.6 THE REDUCTION OF THE BRANCH NETWORK

Between 1928 and 1939 the Imperial Bank's branch network was substantially reduced. This is shown in Table 8.7. In 1929 the Bank's branch network had peaked, with 25 branches in Iran, plus three in Iraq and one in Bombay. By 1939 13 of the Iranian branches had been closed, together with one Iraqi branch and the Bombay office. Map 3 shows the location of the expanded Iranian branch network at the end of the 1920s, while Map 4 shows the reduced number of branches in Iran by the end of the 1930s.

The period began with the opening of a new branch at Dezful in December 1928. The town, located in the south-west of Iran on the Karun, was

Table 8.7. *Opening and closing of Imperial Bank branches in Iran 1928–39*

Branch	Date opened	Date closed
Dezful	December 1928	November 1931
Nasratabad	—	April 1930
Masjed-e Soleyman	—	October 1931
Kazvin	—	October 1931
Birjand	—	October 1931
Barforush	—	November 1931
Borujerd	—	November 1931
Bandar Abbas	—	June 1933
Pahlavi	—	January 1936
Kerman	—	September 1936
Yazd	—	March 1939
Zahedan (formerly Duzdab)	—	March 1939
Abadan	—	March 1939

expected to receive the Trans-Iranian railway within two years, and it was hoped that it would develop as a trading centre. The new branch, however, got off to an inauspicious start. The Manager found the town's business 'disappointingly small and insufficient to pay the expenses of the Bank'. Conditions were further disturbed by surrounding tribesmen who made regular raids, mostly for animals, on the environs of the town.[79] The branch was never a success, and was closed in 1931.

In 1930 the first branch closures began. The Bank had expanded into many small towns where, under the best of conditions, it would have been hard to operate much business. As it was, the onset of the depression and the appearance of Bank Melli branches all over the country made the Imperial bank's small branches an obvious target for closure. The first branch to close was Nasratabad in 1930. Throughout the 1920s the Bank had wanted to close the branch, but had deferred to the wishes of the Foreign Office and India Office. F. H. Johnson had been appointed Manager at the branch in February 1929, and had found it a dispiriting experience:

One just sat there. There was nothing doing. Absolutely no business whatsoever. A few odd Sikhs came in. Literally you could go day after day with nothing happening whatsoever.[80]

Johnson recommended the closure of the branch, and it was duly closed in April 1930.

By 1931 the Bank was actively seeking cost reductions wherever it could. Alongside staff reductions, the Bank decided on a programme of branch closures. Six small branches were closed in 1931. In 1933 Bandar Abbas was also closed, after losing 'money year by year'.[81]

Map 3 Iranian branches of the Bank in 1929

By the mid-1930s the system of exchange controls and trade monopolies increasingly centralised business in Tehran, leaving many of the provincial branches with little to do. Further branch closures were, therefore, made. Pahlavi and Kerman were closed in 1936. The Bank's difficulties in Iran in early 1939 led to decisions to close three more branches. Both Yazd and Zahedan had seen their foreign exchange business disappear, and in addition the opening of Bank Melli branches in the two towns had reduced their share of any remaining business. In Abadan, too, the oil company had given a share of its business to the Bank Melli, rendering unviable the Imperial Bank's branch which had opened in that town in 1937.

8.7 BANKING IN IRAN

The Imperial Bank's business dwindled after 1928. In that year the Imperial Bank had held almost all bank deposits and advances in Iran. The Ottoman

Bank (the title 'Imperial' was dropped in 1925) and the Russian Bank then held only small market shares, while the Pahlavi Bank at that stage still confined its activities to army banking and military accounts. In just over a decade this situation had been transformed. By 1939 the Bank held only 9% of bank deposits in Iran, and claimed a mere 6% of bank advances.[82] 'The total credit facilities accorded by the Imperial Bank of Iran', V. L. Walter, Butters' successor as Chief Manager, observed in 1941, 'constitute nowadays only a small fraction of the credit requirements of the country.' The Bank's business, he continued, was 'not keeping pace with developments in the country'.[83]

The appearance of competition, as has already been discussed, was the primary cause of the collapse in the Imperial Bank's relatively strong position. The Bank Melli was the leading competitor, despite the scandals of its early years. That bank's branch network expanded from 15 in 1929 to 30 in 1933 and 51 by 1943. Its first Iranian Governor, General Khosrovi, who was appointed in 1934, was energetic and capable, and Bank Melli soon acquired a reputation as perhaps the most efficient Iranian business organisation. It had an undoubted appeal as a national institution, and its position as the governments' banker gave it the funds and prestige to expand its activities. Bank Melli also made a determined effort to penetrate areas the Imperial Bank had never explored. It attempted, for example, to attract small savings, and in 1939 its activities in this direction were increased by the formation of a separate National Savings Bank. It also, on occasion, charged low interest rates to stimulate private investment.[84]

In addition to Bank Melli, other banking and financial institutions grew in this period. The Pahlavi Bank was formed into a limited company to undertake general banking in 1928. In 1930 Bank Melli formed an agricultural section, and this evolved into an independent Agricultural and Industrial Bank in 1933: by 1940 it had 40 branches. In 1939 the Mortgage Bank of Iran was formed as another offshoot of Bank Melli.

Table 8.8 shows the main trends in the Imperial Bank's deposits and lending in Iran between 1928 and 1939. The 66% fall in deposits between 1928 and 1932 is a noticeable feature of this table. The great reduction in government accounts was the primary factor in this decline. A fall in the percentage of interest-bearing accounts, from 80% of deposits in 1928 to only 19% in 1930 and 43% in 1932, was also attributable to this factor. The 1930 figure for interest-bearing accounts was particularly depressed because of a large balance held at the Imperial Bank by Bank Melli interest-free. Similarly, the Bank Melli's acquisition of government accounts helps to explain the speed at which its overall deposit size overtook that of the Imperial Bank. In 1930 Bank Melli deposits already exceeded those of the Imperial

Map 4 Iranian branches of the Bank in 1938

Bank and had reached 256 million Krans. By 1934 they had climbed to 867 million Rials, and by 1940 2188 million Rials. For a time the Imperial Bank believed that private customers at least would stay with the Bank. 'The Persian has confidence in the Imperial Bank of Persia', Sir Robert Clive explained to the Foreign Office in 1929 after a discussion with the Bank's staff, '. . . He has as yet no confidence in the National Bank and would in any case hesitate to place his money on deposit in an institution under Government control. He could never be sure that the Shah or the Government did not have access to the state of his private account.'[85] Such hopes, however, soon proved illusory.

The upturn in the Bank's deposits between 1935 and 1938 was largely due to the sums held by it to the credit of the ECC's accounts. In addition contractors employed on government projects provided considerable deposits, with large sums being held for contractors who had completed their work

Table 8.8. *Imperial Bank deposits and lending in Iran 1928–39*
(thousand Krans until 1931; Rials thereafter)

Year end (20 March)	Deposits	Bills discounted, loans and advances
1928	272 802	105 290
1929	195 375	98 845
1930	154 897	75 461
1931	118 478	58 546
1932	93 482	56 777
1933	132 884	64 498
1934	129 970	76 546
1935	115 283	81 388
1936	156 356	128 084
1937	179 915	204 881
1938	206 403	193 754
1939	178 156	140 375

and were awaiting the ECC's permission to remit their funds abroad. The subsequent withdrawal of the large deposits by the ECC caused 'an acute shortage of working funds' in the Bank after March 1938, forcing it to restrict credit.[86]

Turning to bills discounted, loans and advances, the fall in the Imperial Bank's business after 1928 is clear. By 1932 such lending had fallen by 46% compared to the 1928 level. This decline had two main causes. The first was the loss of advances to the Iranian government, all of which had been liquidated by September 1930. Secondly, however, the Bank adopted a deliberate policy of restricting credit following the fall in deposits and the decision to repatriate its capital to Britain. The loss of the note issue had the same effect. 'In preparation for the withdrawal of our Notes our cash resources before 20 March must be such as to make our position unassailable', Wilkinson wrote in October 1930, '... It will ... be necessary to reduce our inland risks by at least 30% and confine our advances to 31 days and for 1st class business only.'[87]

The Bank's lending began to increase after 1933, and grew particularly in 1936, 1937 and 1938. Much of this lending was to contractors engaged on the development projects of the government, especially the Trans-Iranian railway, but also various harbour and port schemes. Thus the Bank, whose nineteenth century founders had so hoped would build railways in Iran, belatedly and rather indirectly became involved in such a project.

Table 8.9 shows the growth and subsequent decline of these advances. These advances, usually for 12 months, were made to a group of around ten

Table 8.9. *Imperial Bank advances to contractors on Iranian government projects 1935–39* (thousand Rials)

Date	Balance outstanding
1935	10 907
1936	30 191
1937	63 634
1938	64 326
1939	32 375

European firms, including one British engineering firm, Richard Costain Ltd. They carried interest rates of 5–6% in 1936, rising to 7–8% by early 1939, and were regarded by the Bank as 'very profitable'.[88] They were also very secure, as most of the advances carried the guarantees of leading banks such as Barclays, Lloyds and Hambros. Advances without a banker's guarantee carried higher interest rates than those with them. The provision of facilities was also used as a lever to persuade the contractors to give their foreign exchange business in Iran to the Imperial Bank.[89] The contracting business, together with the provision of facilities for the ECC and government companies was responsible for the recovery of the Bank's profits after 1936.

Nevertheless, despite this business with contractors, the Imperial Bank had found its market share of bank lending drastically reduced by 1939. A contributory factor in this situation had been the loss of many of the Bank's best local staff. The story of the Bank's obstinate refusal to promote Iranians to the level of European officers, and of the subsequent resignation of Abol Hassan Ebtehaj, is told in Chapter 10. Ebtehaj, however, was only part of a trend that left the Bank denuded of its best local staff. 'The defection of many of our best men', V. L. Walter observed in September 1939, 'has left the standard in Chief Office lower than it should be.'[90]

Business at the provincial branches was largely static. Government restrictions, trade depression and the presence of the Bank Melli all contributed to this situation. Hamadan's role as a large distribution centre, for example, fell away during the 1930s and most of the remaining trade in piece goods, tea and sugar went to the Bank Melli. Occasionally new opportunities arose. Shiraz branch by the late 1930s was providing facilities for recently constructed cotton spinning mills in the locality. The Bank also benefited from the vagaries of Bank Melli policy. At Khorramshahr, for example, in late 1937 and early 1938, Bank Melli began 'giving unlimited credit to all merchants at low rates of interest', and as a result made large inroads into the Imperial Bank's business. But after March 1938 'the giving of unlimited credit was abandoned and business with foreigners ceased entirely'.[91] Over the next year, as a result, the Imperial Bank branch was able to develop a good business in providing facilities to the Iraqi Jewish merchants in the city.

For the most part, however, the Bank's provincial branches had few opportunities for expansion. In most places co-operative relations existed between the Imperial Bank and Bank Melli managers, and often by the late 1930s a comfortable duopoly seems to have been established. There was an air of calm among the Imperial Bank's staff, even as their Bank steadily lost market share. Life at the provincial branches was peaceful. At Bandar Abbas, before the branch was closed in 1933, the Bank owned a donkey. F. H. Johnson, who was at the branch in 1930, later recalled the daily routine of the branch, and its donkey:

It was one of those large Bahrain donkeys which used to arrive duly saddled at the house or office. The Manager, in shorts and a topee, then rode this animal accompanied by a ferrash or messenger at the double ... you'd trot to the bank. And I suppose it was a mile away. And this man with the Bank code in his case ran. And when you got to the Bank you got off there in a dignified manner. One never worked in the afternoon. The donkey returned home at full gallop, the Bank Manager trying to retain some kind of dignity.[92]

Young officers, such as Angus Macqueen who had arrived in Persia in 1934, found their lives rather static. 'There was nothing we were doing during these years', Macqueen later recalled, 'that put any strain on one's own ability or intelligence.' Thoughts turned elsewhere. While in Esfahan in 1937 Macqueen remembered talking with a colleague, T. M. Tagg, about the Bank's future:

we would discuss at times why doesn't this Bank expand somewhere. Even though both of us enjoyed living in Persia, enjoyed our life in Isfahan, why weren't we in places like Beirut now, and seeing more of international banking.[93]

Nine years later Tagg opened the Imperial Bank's new Beirut branch.

In 1939, however, the Bank's expansion outside Iran was no more than a topic of speculation among young British officers frustrated by the decade of contraction which they had experienced. The Imperial Bank had lost its status as state bank; it had lost the note issue; and its comparative importance in Iranian banking had been much reduced. For most of the 1930s the Bank had only paid its dividends from the income of its Sterling investments. The balance of power between the Bank and the Iranian government had shifted, in the government's favour. By 1939 it seemed clear that the Bank could only survive in Iran on the sufferance of the Iranian government.

So far as these events were a reflection of the nationalist resurgence of Reza Shah, and of Iran's recovery of full sovereignty, the Bank's problems and relative decline could be regarded as unavoidable. Nevertheless the Bank's response to its circumstances was not satisfactory. Guided by an aged and conservative Board, its policies were reactionary rather than progressive, backward looking rather than coming to terms with the new realities. Reza Shah's government was sometimes wasteful, incompetent and corrupt, but it was the government of Iran. It is hard not to conclude that with more flexible policies, on the lines put forward on occasion by the Bank's own Chief Managers in Tehran, the Imperial Bank could, at least for an extended period, have secured a more satisfactory niche in the new Iran.

Map 5 Iraqi branches of the Bank in the late 1920s

9

IRAQ AND INDIA 1915–45

During the First World War and over the following decade the Imperial Bank reopened agencies and branches in Mesopotamia (or Iraq, as the country became known during the 1920s) and India, where the Bank had had such an undistinguished career in the 1890s. Table 9.1 gives the dates of opening, and closing, of the new offices (see Map 5 for the location of the Iraq branches in the late 1920s).

The Bank's decision to return to Mesopotamia and India stemmed in both cases from the peculiar circumstances of the First World War, and the economic boom which briefly followed the War all over the world. As Chapter 6 demonstrated, the Bank's profits had soared in Iran in 1917 and 1918. Optimism was in the air. Unfortunately, the optimism was soon dented. Economic and political changes during the 1920s removed or diminished the *raisons d'être* for the new branches. But while the Bank in Iraq managed to build up a viable banking business – to such an extent that during part of the 1930s it was the only part of the Bank's overseas business making a profit – the branch in Bombay floundered, and was eventually closed.

The Bank returned to Mesopotamia in the wake of the British Indian Army. In November 1914 the Turks were driven out of Basra and over the following years they were gradually removed from the surrounding areas. In 1917 Baghdad was captured by the British. Mosul was overrun the day after the Allies signed the Armistice with Turkey. In April 1920 the San Remo Conference made Mesopotamia a British Mandated Territory. In the following year the British installed Faisal, a son of the King Hussein who had led the Arab revolt of 1916–18, as King.[1] A British Indian-style administration was introduced, and Indian currency replaced the former Turkish monetary system.

The original stimulus to reopen in Basra, where an agency of the Imperial Bank started operations in February 1915, was the chance of securing the

243

244

Iraq and India 1915–45

Table 9.1. *Imperial Bank branches in Iraq and India 1915–45*

Branch	Date opened	Date closed
Iraq		
Basra	February 1915	1964
Baghdad	June 1918	1964
Kirkuk	February 1926	September 1929
Khanaqin	January 1928	March 1929
India		
Bombay	June 1919	31 August 1934

Note: The Basra and Baghdad branches were officially agencies until 1923. The Bombay branch was described as an agency until 1922.

account of the British forces and occupation authorities. In 1915 Sir Percy Cox, the Chief Political Officer with the British Forces and later the Civil Commissioner for Mesopotamia, made hints to the Bank that they might be given the account of the British Administration.[2] In fact this business, as will be explained below, ended up with a rival bank, but Chief Office and London sensed that there were also longer-term business opportunities in the country. A Basra branch would be an asset in helping Mohammarah branch to finance the Karun trade. The strong trade links between Mesopotamia and Iran, especially the Basra–Baghdad–Kermanshah route which many Iranian imports from Europe travelled, seemed to offer the prospects of good business for the Imperial Bank once the War had finished. It was the desire to strengthen the Bank's participation in this trade which led to the opening of an agency in Baghdad in 1918.[3] The likelihood that Mesopotamia would be under a British administration for some time further boosted the Bank's confidence that it could build a profitable business in the country.

The only obstacle to the Imperial Bank's plans was the agreement with the Imperial Ottoman Bank in 1893, under which that bank had become the Imperial Bank's correspondent in Mesopotamia. Relations between the two banks had not been entirely smooth before 1914, and were disrupted by the outbreak of the War when the Imperial Ottoman's Basra branch had been temporarily closed by the British authorities as an 'enemy' concern. When the Imperial Bank's Basra agency opened, the Imperial Ottoman Bank took legal action against the Imperial Bank for a breach of the 1893 agreement, but the case was subsequently dropped.

Wartime developments also stimulated the Imperial Bank to consider reopening at Bombay. As in Mesopotamia, the Imperial Bank had operated through correspondents after closing its Bombay branch in 1900. The National Bank of India had undertaken this role between 1900 and 1906, when the business was given to the Hongkong Bank, apparently because they offered more generous rates and because the National Bank was thought to be dilatory in promoting the Imperial Bank's business.[4] In 1910 Wood raised with London the possibility of reopening in Bombay, but this idea was not well received on account of the Bank's 'most unfortunate' experience in Bombay in previous years.[5] The War, however, revived ideas of opening in India. India's exports boomed after 1916 in response to wartime requirements. Wood became convinced that India's trade was set on a course of long-term expansion, and that trade between the sub-continent and Iran would share this growth. In December 1916 E. C. Dalton was despatched to Bombay to investigate the prospects for opening a branch.[6]

It was to be another two-and-a-half years before a branch in Bombay was established. Staff shortages were acute during the War, and men could not be spared permanently from the other branches. This constraint relaxed as the War drew to its conclusion. Meanwhile, the case for opening in India was strengthened by the existence of the new agencies in Mesopotamia. Not only was that territory now in the Indian currency system, but the Imperial Bank's major rival in Baghdad and Basra, the Eastern Bank, had branches in Bombay and Calcutta which were believed to be of considerable assistance in exchange business between India and Mesopotamia.[7] In December 1918 Dalton, and a British Accountant recently released from the Army, left London for Bombay, and on 23 June 1919 the new Bombay agency opened for business.

The Imperial Bank's new ventures, however, soon met legal complications. Clause 2 of the Imperial Bank's Charter prohibited the Bank from opening *branches* outside Iran although it was permitted to appoint *agents* elsewhere provided their business was strictly related to Iran. This was why the new Mesopotamian and Bombay operations had been called 'agencies', even though their activities were identical to those of a 'branch', except that they did not have any note issuing function. Unfortunately this convenient semantic compromise was challenged in Bombay. A block of flats for the use of Bank staff was purchased, but it came together with a sitting tenant who refused to leave. When the Bank sought advice from its solicitor, it was informed that if it went to court its whole legal position in India might be questioned and especially its right, as an agency, to own land and property. The Bank's Chief Inspector, who was despatched to Bombay, advised that the only way out was a change in the Bank's Charter to enable it to open branches outside Iran.[8]

On 28 July 1921 the Imperial Bank applied to the British Treasury for permission to convert agencies into branches in 'Mesopotamia, India and elsewhere'.[9] S. F. Rogers, the London Manager, was far from convinced that such a change in the Bank's Charter would be allowed. He feared that the Bank would be forced to close down its new agencies, an outcome which he anxiously sought to avoid not only because he saw opportunities for considerable profits in Bombay and Mesopotamia, but also because he was concerned about the Imperial Bank's long-term future in a politically unstable Iran. He proposed, therefore, the creation of a new, wholly owned subsidiary bank, to be known as the Bank of Mesopotamia and India, which could legally operate in both countries. Should a 'political debacle' occur in Iran, Rogers noted, 'the subsidiary concern could take [the Imperial Bank's] place as a revenue-earning asset'.[10]

Rogers' imaginative scheme never needed to be implemented. Sir Hugh Barnes gained the sympathetic ear of the Foreign Office,[11] and that Ministry's intercessions with the Treasury were successful. In May 1922 the Treasury gave the Imperial Bank permission to open branches in India and Iraq, although not the wider brief for which the Bank had originally asked.[12] On 24 July the Bank was granted a revised Charter incorporating this change. Only the permission of the relevant local administrations remained to be secured. On 4 September the India Office gave the Bank permission to establish a branch, and the Bombay agency was promptly renamed a branch.[13] It took longer to secure permission in Iraq, where both the Colonial Office in London and the Iraqi authorities had a say in the decision, and it was not until November 1923 that the Imperial Bank were allowed to turn the Baghdad and Basra agencies into branches.

The legal obstacles had been removed. The Bank now faced the task of building a successful business.

9.2 THE BANK IN IRAQ 1915–45

Iraq's political system passed through several stages in the three decades after the Imperial Bank returned to Basra. The removal of Turkish authority was followed by the period of the British Mandate. During the 1920s Iraqi governments assumed increasing responsibility from the British authorities, and in 1932 Iraq became a fully independent state. Independence was followed by political instability, especially after the death of King Faisal in 1933. The 1930s saw a number of massacres of minority groups, and in 1936 there was an unsuccessful Army coup.[14] From the Bank's point of view, however, the main point was that no government with strong nationalist aspirations equivalent to Reza Shah's emerged in interwar Iraq, and its business was largely untrammelled by government legislation.

Political independence was followed by financial independence. Indian Rupees provided the currency between 1915 and 1932, but after April 1932

Iraq issued its own currency, regulated by an Iraq Currency Board established in London. The Iraqi Dinar (ID) was at par with the British pound. Iraqi governments made no attempt to emulate the Iranian policies of exchange control which caused so many difficulties for the Imperial Bank in the 1930s in Iran.

Although reliable national income and other economic data are not available for interwar Iraq, it is clear that the structure of the economy changed only marginally over the period. Iraq remained primarily an agricultural country. Dates, barley, wool and wheat comprised 56% of Iraq's exports in 1912–13, and 57% in 1933–39.[15] In the classic pattern of a less developed country, Iraq largely exported agricultural products in return for consumer goods, which usually comprised about two-thirds of the country's imports. During the 1920s the economy was aided by the heavy spending of the British Occupation Forces – amounting to £7.9 million between 1922 and 1924 – and by the Iranian transit trade through Iraq, whose gross value may have been as much as £7.5 million in 1924.[16] Both these items virtually disappeared in the 1930s. On the other hand the introduction of tariffs from the late 1920s encouraged some industrialisation through import-substitution. Iraq's first modern textile factory opened in 1926, and the first cigarette factory in 1929. The impact of these new consumer goods industries was small compared to Reza Shah's industrialisation drive, and during the 1930s falling world agricultural prices hit the Iraqi economy.

The most promising area of the Iraqi economy in the interwar years was oil. The D'Arcy Concession in 1901 had covered the so-called 'Transferred Territories', an area in Iraq which had been transferred from Iran to Turkey in 1913–14. Oil in commercial quantities was found in this region by the Anglo–Persian Oil Company at Naft Khanna in 1923. The bulk of Iraq was covered by an oil concession held by the Turkish Petroleum Company (renamed the Iraq Petroleum Company (IPC) in 1929), which was jointly owned by British, American and French oil majors.[17] In October 1927 IPC found a huge oilfield at Baba Gurgur, north of Kirkuk. Commercial oil production began in the 1930s, and in 1937 oil supplied 10% of Iraq's exports. However this first Arab oil boom was a muted affair. IPC was not encouraged to expand production by the glut in world oil markets of the period. By 1940 Iraq's annual production of 20 million barrels of oil was dwarfed by Iran's 66 million barrels, and total world production of 2150 million barrels, although oil revenues were of value to the Iraq government in alleviating the effects of the 1930s' depression.[18]

The political and economic conditions of interwar Iraq, therefore, had some marked dissimilarities from Iran. The Imperial Bank's position in the two countries was also different. In Iran the Imperial Bank had a virtual monopoly during the 1920s until the foundation of the Bank Melli in 1928, and even after 1928 the Imperial Bank's leading position was only slowly eroded. In Iraq the Imperial Bank faced competition from two other European banks from the start, although no local commercial bank existed until 1941. The Ottoman Bank (the title Imperial was dropped in 1925) had a long-established presence in the country, and as a result good business connections. An even stronger competitor was the Eastern Bank. The Eastern Bank had been founded in 1909 by E. D. Sassoon and Co., and had moved quickly to establish branches in India and, in 1912, it opened a branch in Mesopotamia. During the War the British Army in Mesopotamia appointed this bank as its bankers, apparently deciding against the Imperial Bank because they suspected it might introduce Krans into the country and so threaten the newly established Indian currency.[19] The Eastern Bank kept the British Administration accounts after the end of the War, and its services were retained by the independent Iraqi government of the 1930s. The large government funds at its disposal gave the Eastern Bank a considerable advantage over its competitors. On the other hand, the Imperial Bank was free of the ambiguities of its dual identity in Iran, and was able to function purely as a British commercial bank in Iraq.

Banking in Iraq was a competitive, sometimes cut-throat affair, quite unlike the experience of the Imperial Bank in Iran, especially in the 1920s. Only in 1927 in Basra, and a year later in Baghdad, did the three European banks conclude rates agreements aimed at curbing internecine competition. These agreements broke down in both cities in 1933, and it was not until 1935 that more permanent and wide-ranging agreements were reached by the three banks to regulate the opening of credits, the discounting of bills and interest rates on deposits.

The Imperial Bank's Iraqi offices derived their resources from capital remitted from London, advances from other branches and locally collected deposits. Until 1918 the agencies were run with overdrafts from London Office. In 1919 Baghdad and Basra were allocated their own capital of Rupees 400 000 and Rupees 200 000 (£30 000 and £15 000) respectively, and by 1930 this had been increased to Rupees 800 000 and Rupees 300 000 (£60 000 and £22 500). In addition, Chief Office in Tehran from 1922 gave overdraft facilities to the two branches. In 1931 fears of currency instability prior to the introduction of the Iraqi Dinar led the Imperial Bank to withdraw its capital entirely from Iraq. In 1938, however, a Banking Law was passed by the Iraqi Parliament which stipulated that banks should retain capital in Iraq equivalent to at least one-seventh of their deposits. The Act does not seem to have been enforced, but nevertheless the Bank reallocated a capital of ID 54 000 (par with Sterling) to Baghdad and Basra. By August 1943 this had

Table 9.2. *Imperial Bank deposits and advances in Baghdad and Basra at selected dates, 1922–45 (£ Sterling)*

Date (March)	Deposits	Loans and advances	Exchange Rate
1922	750 000	481 250	Rs16=£1
1925	579 926	289 963	Rs13.45=£1
1927	915 229	495 124	Rs13.33=£1
1931	517 629	120 030	Rs13.33=£1
1933	323 085	118 039	1ID=£1
1935	541 603	192 974	1ID=£1
1939	320 577	300 128	1ID=£1
1941	859 532	434 312	1ID=£1
1944	5 124 578	164 232	1ID=£1
1945	4 463 193	181 808	1ID=£1

been increased to ID 150 000, but there were no further increases during the War.

Table 9.2 gives the main trends in the Imperial Bank's business in Iraq in terms of deposits and loans and advances at selected dates between 1922 and 1945. These sums were naturally in local currency, but they are given here in Sterling in order to allow an easier comparison between the 1920s, when the Rupee was in use, and the 1930s, when the Iraqi Dinar was in use.

The story of the Imperial Bank's deposits is a straightforward one. Deposits soared during the post-War boom in Iraq, peaking in 1922. There was a decline thereafter and, with the exception of 1927, the 1922 level of deposits was not regained until 1941. Deposits fell away particularly sharply in Baghdad. For most of the interwar period Basra had a stronger deposit base than Baghdad, but Baghdad had more funds engaged in loans and advances. Baghdad had 64% of the two branches' combined deposits in 1922, but this had fallen to 47% in 1927 and only 34% by 1933. Thereafter the proportion tended to rise, and it was around 60% or more after 1939.

A decline in deposits is not prima facie evidence of poor showing for a bank, as deposits are only valuable if profitable lending opportunities exist, but the share of total deposits in a country might be used to give some indication of a bank's relative importance. Figure 1 shows the Imperial Bank's share of Iraqi deposits between 1936, when such figures became available, and 1945.

The Imperial Bank held around 20% of deposits in the late 1930s, and a rather higher percentage after 1940. As the Bank held hardly any government funds, it can be concluded that it had achieved a very respectable market share in its new country. From the view point of the Imperial Bank's total

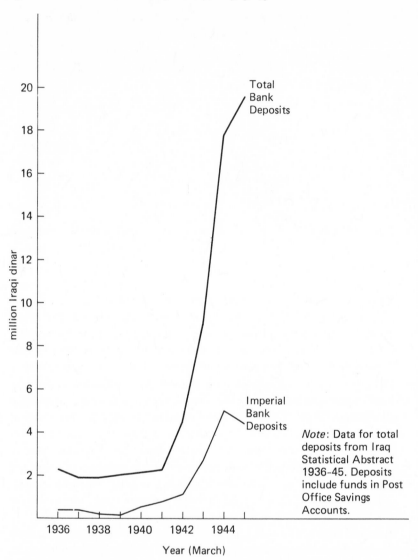

Fig. 1 Imperial Bank deposits and total bank deposits in Iraq 1936–45

business, Iraq contributed 12% of the Bank's deposits in 1936, and 25% in 1944.

The decline in deposits at Baghdad after 1922 was initially a consequence of the trade recession that set in after the post-War boom. The branch was further hit by the progressive decline of British military spending as the 1920s progressed. In 1921 the branch secured the RAF account, and with it numerous personal accounts from officers, and kept it until the Second World War by providing special attention for this valued customer. In 1922 the Bank opened a small sub-office two days a week at Hinaideh on the RAF station near Baghdad, and this provided retail banking facilities for officers. A British junior and a couple of the local staff would drive to the RAF station. One man who was a junior in Baghdad later remembered the routine:

We'd arrive I suppose about half past ten or eleven o' clock. The RAF flyers had completed their flying because they took off round about six in the morning to fly during the best part of the day, before the very high temperatures caused the turbulence that always happens over the desert. So they had finished their day's labours by the time we arrived and invariably after getting the little office set up, there was very little banking to be done except cashing their cheques and receiving Mess funds, so one adjourned quite often to the Mess and listened to the stories of the parties the night before and the parties that might be taking place.[20]

When the RAF moved their main base to Habbaniya, also near to Baghdad, the Bank followed with a sub-office opened in November 1936. This account, however, was a not a major source of deposits from the mid-1920s until the immediate pre-War period when British military spending in Iraq began to rise. The decline in the Iranian transit trade after 1930, which will be discussed below, caused a further decline in deposits.

In Basra the Imperial Bank had to compete harder for its deposits. In 1928 40% of Baghdad's deposits bore interest. All of these were fixed deposits. This proportion subsequently declined to 5% in 1936 and 6% in 1939, as difficult trading conditions made many Baghdadi merchants prefer to keep their funds liquid. In contrast, at Basra interest was paid on some current accounts from the early 1920s, and in 1928 90% of Basra's deposits were interest-bearing, 70% in 1936 and 43% in 1939. Basra's wealth was in agriculture, and bank deposits in the city were subject to considerable seasonal fluctuations, with the size of current accounts in any year being closely tied to the success, or otherwise, of the date harvest. In the early 1920s Basra branch secured some deposits by supplying the Anglo–Persian Oil Company with the Rupees the oil company required to pay its workers at the Abadan oil refinery, although this arrangement ended when the Bank opened a branch at Abadan in 1926. Basra also had the only major government account held by the Bank, the Basra Port Directorate, which managed the port of Basra from the early 1920s. In 1926 the Port Revenue Fund, designed for building new port offices, was placed on fixed deposit with the Imperial Bank. In 1931 the Bank handled the finance of a scheme, organised by Anglo–Persian to dredge a sand bar which crossed the entrance into Basra port. Although in order to retain the account the Imperial Bank had to offer generous terms including interest on current account balances over a certain sum, the Port account bolstered Basra's deposits when falling date prices hit the local economy in the early 1930s.

After the opening of the Mesopotamian branches, the Imperial Bank's Managers faced the problem of deciding who and what to lend to in a country with which they were not familiar. There was the daunting task of getting to know customers and assessing their worth, and these problems were exacerbated because the region was Arabic rather than Persian-speaking. In September 1923 the Basra Manager described the linguistic talents of the staff of his branch:

> 3 Europeans none of whom speaks either Arabic or Persian; 5 cashiers who speak Arabic and Persian but neither speak nor write English; 6 Indians who do not speak Arabic but who are the mainstay of the clerical work of the office; 6 local clerks all of whom speak Arabic and four of whom read Arabic but three of whom are juniors; one interpreter who is inexperienced and tactless.[21]

Ignorance of local conditions and language meant that initially a local broker had to be employed to bring in business. In the circumstances mistakes were bound to occur, and in the early days of Basra branch they did.

Until the end of the First World War the Basra Managers managed the branch along conservative lines, lending only to a few known customers and content to take second place behind the Eastern Bank. However, the trade boom after the end of the War was seen as a means of extending the branch's clientele, and the branch rapidly increased its lending to the bazaar in the form of temporary advances and bill discounting. Most of this lending was on an unsecured basis. Customers considered it an insult to be asked for security, and in any case the Bank did not want the main security that could be offered, which was property. There were dangers in such business, which was disliked in Chief Office and London, and when a trade recession set in after 1922 the vulnerability of the branch's lending was revealed. Bad debt provisions of nearly £54 000 had to be made between 1922 and 1924. Pressure was exerted on Managers from Chief Office to confine their lending to reliable firms, with the large expatriate firms a top priority. After another attempt at business expansion in the bazaars in 1926–27 – during which bad debts of £11 000 were incurred – this was the policy adopted.

It was on appropriately conservative lines that Basra branch became involved in the finance of date exports. The Shatt-al-Arab was the home of the greatest date plantations in the world, with miles of date gardens concentrated in a narrow strip between the river and the desert. There were some 6000 date producers around Basra, who sold their produce each year either to larger producers or to export merchants. The export of dates was largely in the hands of a few large European firms, such as African and

Eastern Company, Strick, Scott and Co. and Andrew Weir and Co., and it was these firms with which the Bank did business.

The finance of date exports was a skilled affair. Climatic variations made growing dates precarious, and the crop was afflicted by various diseases in the interwar years. A considerable familiarity with date crops was required from managers at Basra. One officer in particular developed a special expertise in this area. Harold Evans (or 'Haji' as he was widely known in the Bank, though he was not a Moslem and never went to Mecca) was Accountant at Basra between 1923 and 1927, and Manager 1934–41 and 1944–45. He became a figure of importance in Basra society, regularly dining in the evening with merchants and holding an annual cocktail party. By such means Evans, quite apart from leading a pleasant social life, acquired a detailed knowledge of Basra commercial life and his customers' affairs. He was a regular visitor to the date gardens, and became expert at assessing the quality and types of dates. A continual worry for the Bank was the overstocking of the date market, either due to bumper crops or low prices, which could have left the Bank with dates on their hands if their clients had been unable to sell them. There was a need for particular caution during the 1930s when date prices weakened, and in several years – such as 1933 – there were also crop failures. Although the quantity of date exports rose from 141 000 tons in 1926–32 to 164 000 tons in 1933–39, the value of these exports fell from £972 000 per annum to £917 000 per annum between the two periods. The main brunt of the price reductions fell on the growers rather than the exporters,[22] but the careful lending policies of Evans and the other Basra Managers resulted in the branch's record being almost clear of bad debts in the 1930s.

During the 1920s Basra contributed about one-third of the loans and advances shown in Table 9.2. But this proportion fell as low as 4% in 1933, when the date crop failed. By 1939 it was back at one-third, and in 1944 it reached 50%. Because of cautious lending during the 1930s, as well as the seasonal nature of its business, Basra branch often had considerable surplus funds at its disposal, which were lent to Baghdad or Bombay branches or to London after the Iraq Dinar was established, and on which large amounts of interest were earned.

The Imperial Bank, like the other banks in Iraq, adhered to standard British banking practice in that lending was confined to short-term, self-liquidating finance. As in Iran, the Bank would not consider lending to the agricultural sector *per se*. The seasonal fluctuations in Iraqi agriculture and the problem of security for loans made this policy a sensible one for a commercial bank, and all of the banks in Iraq followed the same line. The banks similarly avoided long-term investment in the nascent industrial sector. In Iraq, as in other Middle Eastern countries, the government moved to fill this gap. In 1936 the Iraqi government founded the Agricultural and Industrial Bank, but its ID 0.5 million capital was moderate and its pre-War achievements were limited.

Baghdad's business developed on different lines from that of Basra, a reflection of the different functions the two cities performed in the Iraqi economy. While Basra was the exporting centre of Iraq, Baghdad was the centre of the import business. Although European firms such as Strick, Scott and Co. and David Sassoon and Co. handled a substantial share of Iraq's imports, there were also many local import merchants. In 1936 there were 51 tea importers in Iraq, and 167 importers of textile piece goods.[23] The Iranian transit trade was the backbone of the branch's business in the 1920s, as had been anticipated when the Baghdad agency was opened. The Bank financed the greater part of the trade along the Basra–Baghdad–Kermanshah route. The Ottoman Bank was the main competitor in this sector, but its very limited business in Iran meant that it had problems of obtaining cover for such exchange operations. However, during the 1920s road and rail construction in Iran began to cast a shadow over the future of this transit traffic. The Iranian government sought to redirect the trade through Mohammarah. In 1930 the transit business was virtually ended by Iranian import controls and exchange regulations. This was a severe jolt for the Imperial Bank. The Baghdad bazaar was left with large stocks on its hands, and bankruptcies mounted. Between March 1930 and March 1931 the branch reduced its lending by 40% overall and its lending to Iraqi-owned businesses by 53%. Over the next couple of years business was strictly confined to first class borrowers, with surplus funds being kept in London by maintaining a large overbought position in Sterling. This caution was rewarded by a welcome absence of bad debts at the branch.

The blow to the Iranian transit trade left the Iraqi branches of the Imperial Bank casting around for business in the 1930s. By 1933 and 1934 some trade with Iran recovered, largely because of smuggling of goods. In addition, other sources of business were developed. The Bank helped to finance the rapid penetration of Japanese piece goods into the Iraqi market. By the mid-1930s it was not unusual for half of all credits opened by the Bank in a month to be for Japanese goods. The Bank also helped to finance the imports needed by British contractors engaged in various development projects undertaken in Iraq in the 1930s, such as the construction of bridges over the Tigris. And there were exceptional items in certain years, such as handling the shipping of bar silver to India in 1934 which produced half of Baghdad's profits for that year.

The Bank had little success in attracting business from the modern oil sector. The Turkish (later Iraq) Petroleum Company gave its business to the

Table 9.3. *Earnings, charges and profits at Baghdad branch 1920–45*
(£ Sterling)

Years	(1) Exchange	(2) Interest	(3) Commission	(4) Charges	(5) Profit[c]
1920–March 1924[a]	132 884	25 003	4781	88 193	63 153
1925–29[b]	75 383	16 341	6074	65 731	26 100
1930–34	49 676	36 221	6277	71 633	20 386
1935–39	32 599	74 892	9550	75 303	42 888
1940–45 (6 years)	110 014	59 384	25 144	153 220	50 643

Notes:
[a] This figure does not include data for March 1920.
[b] Data for March 1926, September 1926 and March 1927 are not available.
[c] Column 5 is basically (1) to (3) minus (4), but a number of items such as bad debt provision have been excluded from the table.

Table 9.4. *Earnings, charges and profits at Basra branch 1915–45*
(£ Sterling)

Years	(1) Exchange	(2) Interest	(3) Commission	(4) Charges	(5) Profit (or loss)[a]
1915–September 1919	110 414	41 449	7949	30 790	123 703
1920–March 1924	100 932	28 409	7612	73 051	11 326
1925–29	40 743	19 395	4772	57 165	(5323)
1930–34	21 913	12 935	1564	38 806	(2305)
1935–39	10 830	30 054	3852	37 242	8983
1940–45 (6 years)	98 686	58 181	12 365	116 692	70 606

Note: [a] Column 5 is basically columns (1) to (3) minus (4), but a number of items such as bad debt provisions and in 1943–44 profits from bullion dealings have been omitted.

Imperial Bank's rivals. In February 1926 the Imperial Bank opened a branch at Kirkuk partly in an attempt to attract some oil company accounts, as well as to provide further facilities for the RAF. However, the Eastern Bank had already established a branch in the town, and the oil company failed to make an anticipated move of its base from Tuz to Kirkuk. As a result, Kirkuk branch was left with a mixed bag of local advances and promissory notes. The branch never made a profit, and was closed in March 1929 after losing £1722. The same fate awaited the Imperial Bank's other attempt to secure some oil-related business. In 1927 Anglo–Persian Oil Company opened the

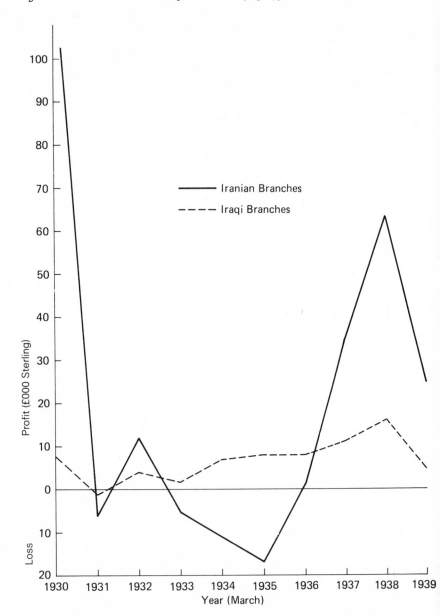

Fig. 2 Imperial Bank profits in Iraq and Iran 1930–39

Alwand refinery near Khanaqin to refine the oil from the Naft Khanna oil field in the Transferred Territories. The Imperial Bank opened a branch in the city in January 1928, but almost no business materialised and the branch was closed 15 months later after losing £798.

The profits of the Baghdad and Basra branches are summarised in five year periods in Tables 9.3 and 9.4. The pre-1939 fortunes of both branches peaked during and immediately after the First World War. Baghdad and Basra made large exchange earnings in this period, but this source of profit withered as the 1920s progressed. Interest earnings, often derived in later years from funds placed abroad, grew in Baghdad from the mid-1920s and by 1935–39 were twice as high as those from exchange. The early 1930s, the period of the collapse of the Iranian transit trade, is shown as Baghdad's least profitable period, while Basra was a loss-making operation between 1925 and 1935 (although the branch did record profits in individual years during this period). The decline in exchange business, and reduction of lending, first in response to bad debts and later to the poor condition of the date business, were the prime factors, with competition keeping margins competitive. At both branches the recovery after the mid-1930s was aided by the conclusion of the inter-bank agreements curbing competition and allowing rises in interest rates on lending.

In the absence of profit figures for the Iraqi operations of the Eastern and Ottoman Banks, it is difficult to set an objective standard to establish whether the Imperial Bank's performance in interwar Iraq was 'successful' or 'unsuccessful'. It is clear that the two Iraqi branches were doing better during much of the 1930s than the Iranian branches which numbered 24 in 1930 and 13 by 1939. Figure 2 compares the profits of Baghdad and Basra with the total profits of the Iranian branches between 1930 and 1939. In the three years between 1933 and 1935 the Iraqi branches, largely due to Baghdad, were profitable, while the Iranian branches were losing money. In all five of the ten years Baghdad and Basra either made more profits, or (as in 1931) lost less money, than all the Iranian branches of the Bank put together.

The Second World War brought an expansion of business in Iraq, as in Iran (see Chapter 11), but the Bank also had the first glimpse of problems which were to become major features of its life after the War. The outbreak of War was followed by a minor boom in Iraq, as revenues from oil exports boosted the government's efforts and officially sponsored monopolies for dates and grain helped to re-establish some prosperity in the agricultural sector. This brought good business to the Imperial Bank, although political developments cast some shadows on the situation. A section of the Iraqi army began manipulating anti-British sentiments, with suspicions about British policies in Palestine encouraging this trend. In April 1941 a government headed by Rashid Ali, who had already been Prime Minister of Iraq on two previous occasions, came to power supported by a group of army colonels. The new government launched an Iraqi bank, the Rafidain Bank, which opened in May 1941. There had been discussion for years about the establishment of a central bank, but nothing concrete had been done about it.

The creation of the Rafidain Bank was perhaps the main economic achievement of Rashid Ali's short-lived government. The British government became convinced that the Iraqi government was pro-German, and on 29 April 1941 British troops landed at Basra.[24] The Iraqi government retaliated by placing the British banks in Baghdad in the hands of a liquidator.

This sequestration was the first of a series which the Bank was to experience in the Middle East over the next 40 years. Unlike future nationalisations, however, Rashid Ali's proved only temporary. Following an Iraqi attack on the RAF air base the British Army occupied the whole of the country. By June 1941 the government had fallen, a pro-British administration was installed, and the liquidation of the foreign banks was revoked. The Rafidain Bank survived the occupation of Iraq, and during the war years, aided by the acquisition of most of the government accounts from the Eastern Bank, it began establishing a sound commercial banking business.

Meanwhile, after June 1941, the Imperial Bank's business in Iraq boomed. Basra became a large military base, and between 1941 and 1944 the British Army spent over £60 million there.[25] Wartime expenditures generated an inflationary boom, as in Iran, with the wholesale price index of 100 in 1939 rising to nearly 500 in 1946. The wartime inflation forced up the Bank's costs substantially, as shown in Tables 9.3 and 9.4, but the Bank also secured a large increase in business. The Imperial Bank acquired a considerable share of British Army business, plus the even more valuable accounts of the US Army in the region. Basra's profits were transformed and the branch earned more money between 1940 and 1945 than during the 20 years between 1920 and 1940.

The Imperial Bank, therefore, built a viable banking business in interwar Iraq, in contrast to the earlier episode in Mesopotamia in the 1890s. Although profits were small after the mid-1920s, and the Bank had not established itself as the leading bank in Iraq, it survived the dislocation of the Iranian transit trade and developed expertise in purely Iraqi trade such as the export of dates. It took the Second World War, however, to expand significantly the Bank's earnings in Iraq, and it remained to be seen when the War ended whether the branches could build on their strong wartime performance and retain profits at their new levels.

9.3 THE BANK IN BOMBAY 1919–34

Bombay, where the Imperial Bank opened its agency in June 1919, was a different world of banking altogether from Iran, or even Iraq. The city had the most active capital market in India, and a well-developed banking system. In 1919 61 banks operated in India, including 11 exchange banks – all represented in Bombay – which specialised in foreign exchange and the finance of foreign trade. Total bank deposits in India amounted to Rupees 2156.2 million (£162 million), of which the exchange banks held 34%. The exchange banks included the leading names in British Eastern banking, such as the Mercantile Bank of India, the National Bank of India, the Chartered Bank of India, Australia and China and the Hongkong Bank, as well as specialists in trade with particular countries, such as the Comptoir National D'Escompte (France) and Yokohama Specie Bank (Japan).[26]

It was in this second category of exchange banks that the Imperial Bank fitted. The branch was never intended to become a factor of importance in Indian exchange banking. Rather, the Bank was conceived as a kind of service agency for the Iranian and Iraqi branches. 'Our Bombay branch is upon a different footing from that of all other branches, for whose assistance it exists', E. M. Eldrid, the London Manager, explained in March 1932 '... We do not want the IBP to "cut a figure" in Bombay banking circles.'[27] It was easier to state this ideal than to put it into practice, and although the Bank certainly never 'cut a figure' in Bombay, the value of the branch to the other branches of the Imperial Bank in the 15 years of its existence seems to have been very limited.

The circumstances in which the Imperial Bank operated during the 1920s and early 1930s were undoubtedly troublesome for all the exchange banks, and some appreciation of India's economic history in the interwar years is necessary to put the Bank's performance in context. Although the period saw growth in India's modern industries, the country's external sector was very unstable. The 1920s saw substantial fluctuations in India's overseas trade, and in the exchange rates of its currency. The pre-War gold exchange standard in India broke down during the War, and from 1919 it proved impossible for several years to secure a stable exchange rate for the Rupee, notwithstanding, for instance, an attempt to stabilise it in 1920. The Rupee floated, indeed, until 1927. It had tumbled during 1920 and 1921, reaching a low of around 16 before rising from late 1921–22 as world demand for Indian exports rose. In 1925–26 a Royal Commission on Indian Currency and Finance met under the chairmanship of Edward Hilton-Young, who as Lord Kennet was to join the Imperial Bank's Board in 1937. This Commission examined all aspects of the Indian currency system, and among other points

Table 9.5. *Branch Balances at Bombay, 1920, 1926, 1932 (million Rupees)*

	March 1920 Balances		March 1926 Balances		March 1932 Balances	
	Debit	Credit	Debit	Credit	Debit	Credit
All branches	68.2	108.8	44.1	43.2	10.9	10.3
% Tehran	20	43	7	4.5	5	16
% Rest of Iran	43	30	39	40.5	9	5
% Iraq	37	27	54	55	86	79

Note: The Rupee–Sterling exchange rate was 8.57 in March 1920, and 13.33 in the two other years.

recommended a fixed rate of 13.33. This was implemented in 1927, but between 1929 and 1931 the collapse of prices for India's agricultural exports, and worries about the pace of Indianisation in the Government of India, exerted a strong downward pressure on the Rupee. In September 1931 the Rupee was devalued alongside Sterling against gold, a step which quite accidentally relieved the pressure on the currency by stimulating substantial gold exports from India for the rest of the decade.

India's foreign trade was buffeted by the changes in the exchange rates, as well as by other pressures. The high exchange rate in 1919 and early 1920 stimulated a huge import boom, but the subsequent slump in the Rupee caused a major crisis and imports fell sharply, not recovering their 1920 levels until 1924. This cycle of boom and slump had a particularly bad effect on Bombay's cotton textile industry, which entered a period of crisis during the 1920s, made worse by the strong Japanese competition to its products. In 1929, with the onset of the Depression and falling world agricultural prices, the value of India's foreign trade began to fall, reaching a low point in 1933–34 before a general trade recovery began in 1935.[28] It was against this unstable canvas that the Imperial Bank attempted to establish a new branch.

Bombay agency was opened in 1919 with a capital of Rupees 1 million (£75 000), and it retained this sum until 1929 when Rupees 0.8 million (£60 000) were withdrawn and given to Baghdad branch. The remainder of the capital was eventually consumed by a bad debt. The branch's most important source of funds was not capital but the balances kept at the branch by the other branches of the Imperial Bank. Table 9.5 gives the state of these balances for three selected years. This table demonstrates one of the central problems of Bombay. In the immediate period after the new branch was opened the Bank's Iranian and Iraqi branches kept large funds in Bombay for purposes of financing trade between India and Iran and Iraq. Credits exceeded debits by a big margin, and left Bombay with substantial surplus funds. By the mid-1920s this situation had changed, and, in particular, the balances of the Iranian branches fell away. This was a reflection of the steady fall in Indian trade with Iran, a particular problem faced by the Imperial Bank in addition to the general problems in Indian trade and currency outlined above. The British and Indian share of Iran's visible imports fell from 67% in 1920–2, to 46% in 1925–29 and 29% in 1930–34.[29] In 1930 Iranian government regulations controlling commerce and exchange led to a very sharp fall in Indian–Iranian trade, just as it had reduced Iraqi–Iranian trade. As a result of these factors, Bombay found an increasing proportion of its branch funds originating from Basra and Baghdad. Iraq used Indian currency, and there was a substantial trade between the two countries in piece goods and dates. The Iraqi branches were also happy to use their funds in this way when domestic lending opportunities were restricted. However, Iraq's trade with India also declined over the period, especially after Japanese piece goods began replacing Indian ones. India's share of Iraq's imports declined from 20.4% to 7.0% between 1925–32 and 1933–39. Moreover the introduction of the new Iraqi currency in 1933 removed the reason for the Iraqi branches to place funds in Bombay, and effectively spelt the end of large-scale funding for the branch from this source.

Bombay branch made little attempt to garner local deposits. In March 1920 they stood at £152 000 (Rupees 1.3 million). They edged up to £180 000 (Rupees 2.4 million) in 1926, but fell to £120 000 (Rupees 1.6 million) in 1932 and £45 000 (Rupees 600 000) in March 1934.

During the 1920s the branch acquired small amounts of deposits, mostly lodged by merchants with some Iranian or Iraqi business connections. The branch generally considered that these deposits were more trouble and expense than they were worth as it was obliged to offer rates comparable with those of other banks. In 1928 2% per annum interest was paid on current accounts above Rupees 2000 (£150), and up to 4.5% on fixed deposits. In that year it was decided to limit current accounts strictly to those which provided good business, in order to economise on staff.[30] During the early 1930s there was a sustained campaign to reduce the number of current accounts, which fell from 270 to 162 between 1931 and 1932. In place of deposits, and as branch balances declined, Bombay branch ran an overdraft with London Office (on which no interest was charged until 1929) and from the mid-1920s regularly borrowed funds on the inter-bank market.

Table 9.6 gives the earnings, charges and profits in Bombay in five-yearly periods between 1920 and 1934. The pattern of business shows marked similarities to that of the Iraqi branches. Exchange earnings peaked in the first years of the branch's existence, with 75% of exchange earnings between 1920 and 1924 being made before March 1921. The branch clearly found

Table 9.6. *Earnings, charges and profits at Bombay branch 1920–34*
(£ Sterling)

Years ending (March)	(1) Exchange	(2) Interest	(3) Commission	(4) Charges	(5) Profit or loss[a]
1920–24	205 759	19 373	6530	121 225	110 437
1925–29	21 993	33 164	1936	85 368	(27 954)
1930–34	12 856	15 709	2322	53 996	(23 311)

Note a: Column (5) is basically columns (1) to (3) minus (4), but a number of smaller items have been excluded.

opportunities for profit during the sharp exchange rate fluctuations of this period, and actually prospered during the 1920–21 slump. This was a period when other British banks, too, found ·it easy to make profits on occasion, although the fluctuating exchanges meant that results tended to be unstable. The Mercantile Bank of India's Bombay branch, for example, earned profits of nearly £100 000 in 1919, but then slumped to a small loss in the following year.[31]

   A large business was done in these opening years with other banks, such as the National Bank of India, in buying and selling Sterling. Some of the exchange earnings of this period seem to have stemmed from speculative exchange transactions, but this was a risky activity in which fingers could get burned. In March 1922 the branch made a £10 000 exchange loss (and carried a further loss over to the next year) after a Manager's exchange position 'got out of hand without his noticing that it had got so bad as it had'.[32]

   The early Bombay Managers attempted to strengthen their branch by urging that Imperial Bank should open elsewhere in India. Calcutta was looked upon with envy as India's 'leading' exchange market, and the Bank got as far as considering staff to open a branch there before the scheme was dropped in 1923.[33] Karachi was also considered for a branch during 1921 and 1922, but the idea never turned into a reality and in 1925 the Bank definitely ruled it out.[34]

   From the mid-1920s India's declining trade with Iran, and the stabilisation of the Rupee currency, reduced Bombay's exchange earnings. The branch was left with a dwindling and second-rate exchange business. 'The banks who are in a position to do a large and genuine business naturally are offered more business than others not so favourably situated', one disgruntled Bombay Manager commented in March 1925, '... Business very often is only offered to us when it has been turned down by other banks.'[35] The imposition of exchange controls in Iran in 1930 caused exchange earnings to tumble even further, quite apart from the general difficulties caused by the near collapse of the Indian currency between 1929 and 1931 and the general fall in Indian trade. The branch's plight, which would have been dire in any circumstances, was not helped by poor management within the Bank. An investigation by an Inspector in 1932 discovered that branch Managers in Iran had failed to keep Bombay informed of exchange rates in Iran, with the result that the Bombay Manager had to operate using out of date knowledge of the very market of which he was supposed to be the expert.[36]

The branch's interest earnings arose largely from putting funds out on call in the Bombay money market, and lending to other banks. In March 1920 the branch lent some Rupees 3.9 million (£455 076) in this fashion, and in the mid-1920s profits from this source helped to cushion the fall in exchange earnings. Substantial balances were also kept with the National Bank of India. Declining branch balances, however, reduced the funds Bombay had for such lending. By March 1930 the branch had only Rupees 0.8 million (£60 000) lent, and in March 1934 only 0.3 million (£22 500). The Depression of the early 1930s greatly limited lending opportunities. 'Money has mostly been little better than a drug in the market', the Bombay Manager reported in September 1933, 'often difficult to place at even very low rates.'[37]

Some Bombay managers naturally looked with envious eyes at sources of banking business other than Iraq or Iranian-related trade. There was a regular business in discounting *hundis*, or local trade bills, but this activity collapsed in 1929. There was an attempt to penetrate the lucrative Japanese cotton and piece goods trade, and an agent was appointed in 1924 in Kobe to assist this business. However, the branch found it could only attract the custom of second rate firms compared to banks that had their own branches in Kobe, and bad debts ensued. This was a problem throughout the 1920s. The Bank was unknown in Bombay, and when it ventured away from Iranian or Iraq-related trade it could only secure business the more established banks had rejected. The worst instance was a loan in 1930 of Rupees 0.4 million (£30 000) to a Saudi Arabian pearl merchant who allegedly needed funds after he was unable to get some payments from customers. The Manager had seen the loan as a promising chance to restore the Bombay branch's profitability. The merchant soon left Bombay for Saudi Arabia, leaving the branch with a bad debt. In July 1932 the Bank's travelling inspector, T. Sheahan, was despatched to Jiddah to try to recover the loan. Sheahan stayed in Jiddah until March 1933, but was unable to obtain any repayment and the debt was written off as irrecoverable.

The fall in earnings at Bombay branch was particularly unfortunate as the costs of running the branch could not be reduced proportionately. Staff and accommodation costs were higher than in Iran. The Bank's premises were leased until August 1934 at a fixed rent of Rupees 19 800 (about £1500) per annum. Moreover, the cost of European officers at the branch, and there were up to four officers allocated to the branch in the 1920s, were higher than in Iran because Europeans were expected to keep up appearances in Bombay by joining the right clubs and maintaining large households. The Bank had also made an expensive blunder in 1920 when it purchased a house for its staff, a move which not only threw up the challenge to the Bank's status in India, but was also a thoroughly ill-advised piece of business. The house cost Rupees 0.5 million (£37 000), but this price seems to have been quite excessive and recognised as such by the Bank within a year.[38] The building was sold in 1930 for about £10 500.[39]

The losses recorded by Bombay branch after 1924 did not necessarily demonstrate that it was a complete business failure. As the branch's purpose was to help the other branches, it did not seek to make a market profit on its operations with them. The branch did not charge other branches commission for the business it handled and the margins it made on the use of branch funds were regulated by Chief Office. Arguably, the branch would have fared better if Managers had been allowed to charge other branches for their services, as Bombay's losses might have looked less demoralising and there would have been fewer temptations to make unwise loans. The Bank never estimated during the 1920s how much it saved by having its own branch in Bombay, although several Bombay Managers hazarded guesses. One calculated that the branch had saved the Bank £9942 in commission charges in the half year ended March 1920,[40] but such estimates probably included an element of self-justification. When the Bank did address the subject a little more rigorously in 1932 it found few savings, although this was a low point in Iranian trade with India. In April 1932 Baghdad branch estimated that it would have cost Rupees 3372 (£253) in commission and perhaps Rupees 16 636 (£1240) in lost interest on the three previous years if it had used the Hongkong Bank in Bombay as agents rather than Bombay office.[41] This theoretical saving of about £500 per annum from the branch with which Bombay had the closest business links from the late 1920s was no strong justification for retaining a branch in India.

After 1930 there was a campaign to cut costs at the branch. The number of European staff was reduced to three and then to two. The Manager's salary was cut by £300 per annum, and local staff were reduced in number and their salaries cut. The total salary bill fell from Rupees 48 393 (£3630) in March 1929 to Rupees 30 484 (£2287) in September 1933. But earnings fell quicker than costs. In London, S. F. Rogers, on reading the branch's Report on Progress for September 1933, simply commented: 'A more convincing argument for closing this branch could hardly be found.'[42] Soon afterwards the Board made the decision to close the branch when the lease of its premises expired, and at the end of August 1934 the branch was duly closed. Lloyds Bank in Bombay were appointed the Imperial Bank's correspondents, and retained that position until the Imperial Bank, under its new name of The British Bank of the Middle East, returned to Bombay in 1954.

The Imperial Bank's second experience in India, therefore, had not been a happy one. The branch had most certainly not 'cut a figure', to use Eldrid's phrase, in Bombay. The branch had been undermined by the decline in the original reasons for its opening, as Indian trade with Iran and Iraq fell, and Iranian exchange controls and the advent of an Iraqi currency changed the terms on which the remaining trade was financed. Yet there was sufficient evidence of poor management and confusion of purpose to suggest that the Imperial Bank could have done better despite the circumstances. Lloyds Bank's Indian branches contrived to make profits in the late 1920s and early 1930s despite all the problems of the period.[43] The Mercantile Bank's Bombay branch, after losing £33 090 between 1928 and 1931, was restored to profitability thereafter.[44] Perhaps the complexity of Bombay banking was too great for men accustomed to doing business in Iran.

10

THE BANKERS 1914–45

The interwar years were a staid period sandwiched between the frenetic activity and high profits of the two World Wars. The pioneering days in Iran were over, while the pioneering era in the Arab world was yet to come. The Imperial Bank's British staff were left to run an established and, within Iran, prestigious organisation. Their lives were, on the whole, more comfortable than before 1914. Yet the Bank did not respond well to the new challenges of the period – the rise of Iranian nationalism, the competition of the Bank Melli, and the Depression – and part of the explanation for this lies with the nature of its staff.

The overall picture of the Bank's British staff in this period is of a solid, but uninspired and uninspiring group of men, supervised by an ageing Board. In the rush to find staff after the end of the First World War men were taken on – including one with only one leg – who would not have been considered before 1914. Many of the recruits do not seem to have been considered satisfactory and reports on staff were peppered with comments such as 'no use whatever' and 'another dud'.[1] More seriously, the Bank had throughout the period a shortage of men considered capable of holding senior management posts. 'We are so seriously short of senior men', S. F. Rogers observed in 1927, 'the real trouble being that so-called senior men are no good for the senior posts.'[2] The same theme was taken up by Roger's successor as London Manager, E. M. Eldrid. 'Length of service rather than outstanding merit', he wrote to E. Wilkinson in 1932, 'may have helped some Officers to the higher grade.'[3]

Two hundred and six men joined the overseas staff of the Imperial Bank between 1914 and 1945. The new recruits seem to have been all British, although the Bank's staff continued to include a number of 'Levantines', such as E. Wilkinson, who had joined before 1914. Table 10.1 gives the ages of men joining the overseas staff in this period. The table shows a shift in the age distribution of recruits. Between 1919 and 1923 28% of recruits were under

266

Table 10.1. *Age of recruits to Imperial Bank 1914–45*

Years	Under 20	21–26	Over 27	Unknown	Total
1914–18	8	7	1	—	16
1919–23	20	39	11	2	72
1924–28	33	24	2	—	59
1929–38	31	16	—	1	48
1939–45	10	1	—	—	11
Totals	102	87	14	3	206

Table 10.2. *Resignations and dismissals of recruits 1914–45*

Years staff joined	Resigned at London Office	Resigned during first three years overseas	Dismissed during first three years overseas
1914–18	5	1	1
1919–23	17	14	4
1924–28	28	5	4
1929–38	24	2	2
1939–45	2	2	1
Totals	76	24	12

20, but the majority of recruits were aged between 21 to 26, and 15% were aged over 27. Many of these older men had experience in other jobs, or the Armed Forces. After 1924 the proportion of recruits under 20 steadily rose, reaching 64% in 1929–38.

The Imperial Bank continued to experience a high turnover of staff. Table 10.2 shows the recruits between 1914 and 1945 who resigned or were dismissed, either while still in London Office, or during the period of their first three years overseas.

The table shows that staff turnover was even higher than in the pre-1914 period. Between 1914 and 1945 over a half of recruits resigned or were dismissed while in London or during their first three years in the East. The large number of resignations from London Office during the 1920s is particularly noticeable.

As before 1914 a number of factors lay behind the high staff turnover. The Bank's rules on marriage led to some resignations. Other men could not stand life in Iran. Four of the 1914–18 recruits joined the Army to fight in the First World War and did not return to the Bank. Five of the men who joined during the 1930s joined the Armed Forces in the Second World War. During the 1930s the Bank, as an economy measure, encouraged some retirements from its service, a policy which helped to reduce total overseas staff numbers from 68 in 1930 to 53 in 1934 and 43 in 1940, at which level it stayed until the end of the War.

The urgent desire to find staff after the end of the First World War led the Bank to search desperately for men. In response to A. O. Wood's pleas in July 1919 for 21 men to be sent immediately to Iran, Rogers catalogued the difficulties he faced. He had contacted the Ex-Officers Employment Bureau and interviewed three men, but none of them had wished to join the Bank. 'We have had some applications from mostly Irish Banks', Rogers continued, 'and I may have success in obtaining 3 or possibly 4 before the end of August.' However Rogers preferred Scots to Irish, if only the Bank could recruit them. 'The majority of the men from the Scottish banks go to the bigger Eastern banks', he bemoaned. 'I think they as well as ourselves prefer men from the north of the Tweed to those from Ireland.' As for former Army men, Rogers found them, 'spoilt by the excellent pay they received in the Army. One young fellow after an interview and after all the information with regard to our service was supplied to him, calmly wrote to me that the prospects of pay and promotion were not sufficiently good to induce him to leave this country.'[4] The Bank was reduced to scraping the proverbial barrel for staff. The large number of resignations from the 1919–23 cadre of recruits suggests that many inappropriate men were hired and soon left, but 'duds' remained in the Bank's service and did nothing to improve the quality of the staff.

The number of men who had to leave because of unsuitability is difficult to calculate because of the thin line between dismissal and forced resignation, but it is known that 12 of the men who joined between 1914 and 1945 were dismissed during their first three years overseas. A whole range of factors could lead to a man being dismissed or asked to resign. Some staff were dismissed because they proposed marriage to women who were considered undesirable. One man was dismissed and another asked to resign because they caught venereal disease. Drink was a regular factor in dismissals. One man had to go because he suffered 'from insomnia and as a remedy drinks large quantities of whiskey.'[5] Another disintegrated in front of the Chief Manager's eyes. 'I have never seen a man "crack" quicker than he did in the end', Wilkinson wrote in 1929, 'he simply went to pieces and was in a state of continual semi-intoxication.'[6]

Death made a further contribution to the Bank's staff turnover. Thirteen men died in service between 1914 and 1945: two men committed suicide, three died from pneumonia, two from septicaemia, one from meningitis, one from jaundice and another failed to recover from a kidney operation. One man was killed in a car accident and another in a plane crash. David Brown died in 1918 from a heart attack. Four of the deaths were in the space of six months in 1936 and 1937, the cumulative tragedies having an inevitably depressive effect on the Imperial Bank's small British staff in Iran.[7]

The Bank's salaries remained a constant source of complaint from staff. At the end of the War the starting salary for a junior on his first overseas contract was raised to £300 per annum, and in 1923 this was increased to £350. Considerable confusion was caused, however, by the method under which the salaries of more senior staff were calculated. As before 1914, branches and their Managers' salaries were graded in order of importance. In the early 1920s, for example, the two extremes (leaving aside Chief Office) were Baghdad and Bombay, whose Managers earned £1200 per annum, and Nasratabad, whose Manager earned £475. However, each man also had a 'substantive' salary which was based on his age and experience. There were always difficulties when, as happened often, a man filled a post which had a salary either higher or lower than his 'substantive' pay. Although there were conventions – such as an officer occupying a post more important than his rank drawing 50% of his 'substantive' pay and 50% of the pay of the post – an element of discretion left the way open for disputes. Moreover, the concept of 'substantive' salary was very vague. McMurray freely admitted in 1923 that he did 'not know what the substantive pay of any manager is'.[8]

As early as 1923 McMurray had urged reform of the salary structure but the Finance Committee rejected his proposals. It was not until 1930, apparently on the intitiative of one of the directors, E. A. Chettle, that the strange system in operation was finally swept away.[9] The grading of posts was abolished and replaced by one of salary grades for individuals. Managers were placed on grades with salaries rising £50 per grade from £600 to £1000 while more junior staff were on a similar, but lower scale. However, goodwill created by this reform was dissipated by the Bank's economy drive of the early 1930s. The starting salary was reduced from £350 to £300 in 1933, and was not restored to the previous level until 1936. It was increased to £400 in 1942. Promotions from one grade to another were also made more difficult in the early 1930s.[10] This economy drive, however, was fairly general in Britain in the 1930s, and affected a range of professions from bankers to school-teachers. The Imperial Bank was only doing what many other employers were doing at the time.

Further complications were caused by the rates of exchange used to pay salaries. Until 1930 salaries were paid in Iran using the Bank's adjustment rate of 55 Krans to the £1 Sterling. As the actual exchange rate was lower for much of the period, staff in Iran found this 'exchange privilege' an attractive arrangement. They remitted any savings from their salaries back to Britain at the actual exchange rate. In Iraq and India, however, staff found this payment system less favourable. Their salaries were converted first into Krans, and then into Rupees at the current exchange rate. In the process, and given the fluctuations in the Rupee in the early 1920s, staff outside Iran found they lost any 'exchange privilege'.[11] It was not until 1930 that salaries in Iraq and India were converted directly from Sterling.

In 1930 the fixed rate of 55 Krans to the £1 was abandoned. As Iranian currency depreciated against Sterling and the cost of living rose, the Bank changed the salary rate fairly frequently, attempting a compromise between the official exchange rate and the rate current in the bazaars. In February 1938, for example, the Bank decided, in the light of an official rate of 80.5 and the market rate of 150, to make the salary rate 110.[12] There were also difficulties over staff remittances. During the 1930s staff seem to have remitted an increasing proportion of their salaries, perhaps because there was little to buy in Iran. By 1938 this had reached 50% in certain cases, and was a cause of concern for the Bank for the more foreign exchange which was used for remittances, the less could be used for remitting profits.[13] In July 1938 the Board decided to limit staff remittances to 30% of their salary but this raised such a chorus of complaint that in the following October the proportion was raised to 40%, and in April 1940 to 45%.[14]

In addition to their salaries, the British staff of the Bank continued to benefit from bonuses. Between September 1916 and 1923 staff received a special War Allowance of 15% until 1918 and 25% thereafter. In addition, at the end of the War those who had been in the Bank's service in August 1914 were given a special War Bonus of three months' salary. Until 1940 British staff received an annual bonus of 10% of their salaries. Special cost of living and War Allowances were in operation again after 1943.

The only change in the Bank's Provident Fund in this period came in October 1920, when the Bank's contribution to the Fund was raised from 10% to 20% of a man's monthly salary. No pension scheme was formulated in the interwar period, but the Bank continued to award gratuities when an officer retired. These gratuities were at the discretion of the Bank, and reflected the Board's likes and assessment of a man's performance. Wood and McMurray both received £10 000 when they retired, whilst Wilkinson only received £8000.

10.2 MOTIVES, CAREERS AND TERMS OF SERVICE

As before the First World War, a variety of motives seem to have led men to join the Imperial Bank. Contact with the Middle East was one important factor. 'Haji' Evans, the 'Shaikh of Basra', had been employed by Coutts before 1914, but had served with the British Army in Cairo during the War and had fallen in love with the East. Although he returned to Coutts after the end of the War, he wanted to return to the East, and when he saw an advertisement for an Eastern bank in 1919, he applied to join. It was the Imperial Bank of Persia. J. D. Hammond, who joined in 1925, heard about the Bank from his brother, who had served with the British Army in Mesopotamia, and had travelled to that country with the wife of one of the Bank's officers.

Some men wanted to escape from the tedium of an office job in Britain, and had no connection with the Middle East. C. D. Lunn, for example, had worked for the Midland Bank for six years in Huddersfield and Leeds. After deciding he wanted to work abroad, he applied to a number of British overseas banks in India and also the Hongkong Bank, and was eventually accepted by the Imperial Bank in 1930. E. S. Jenkins – who joined the Bank in 1935 – decided in his last year of school that he wanted to work abroad. His mother was concerned, and eventually the family reached a compromise that he should apply for 'what was known as a safe job abroad ... a British bank abroad'. The bank Manager of Jenkins' father recommended three names – the Imperial Bank, the Imperial Bank of India and the Hongkong Bank – and Jenkins junior applied to the first one because it 'appealed' to him.[15]

Staff recruitment was a haphazard affair. The Bank regularly advertised for staff in *The Times* and *Daily Telegraph*, except during the early 1930s when fewer men were being taken on. The Bank's name was never mentioned, and the following advertisement which appeared in *The Times* in November 1937 was characteristic of the interwar period.

British Bank operating in the East has London vacancy for public school boy of good parentage and physique who has passed matriculation, service abroad after training. Commencing salary £100.
Write Box K1626.[16]

On occasion the Bank made direct approaches to organisations which it was hoped would yield desirable recruits. Immediately after the end of the First World War, the Bank contacted both the Ex-Officers Employment Bureau and Army Headquarters in Iraq in an attempt to recruit former British Army officers.[17] During the later 1920s the Bank approached Oxford University Appointments Board about desirable candidates for the Bank's service. And in 1943 Lord Kennet, an old Etonian, went to Eton and Marlborough to ask boys to apply to the Bank.[18] Only the approach to Oxford yielded any applicants.

Personal recommendation remained an important avenue of recruitment. Three relatives of Sir Hugh Barnes joined the Bank as juniors, and Barnes also appears as an influence in several other men's arrival in the Imperial

Table 10.3. *Previous banking experience of Imperial Bank recruits 1914-45*

Years staff joined	Total recruits	Recruits with known previous banking experience
1914–18	16	6
1919–23	72	33
1924–28	59	23
1929–38	48	12
1939–45	11	2

Bank. The godfather of F. H. Johnson, who joined the Bank in 1921, was a friend of Barnes, as was the grandfather of P. E. H. Alexander, who joined in 1934. W. A. Buchanan seems to have recommended several Scots to the Bank's service. K. R. H. Murray, for example, who joined in 1928 and was Chief Accountant in London between 1935 and 1960, had previously worked for the London office of a firm of Scottish chartered accountants, one of whose partners knew Buchanan well.

Angus Macqueen (General Manager of The British Bank of the Middle East between 1966 and 1970, and Chairman 1974–78), was introduced to the Bank by its doctor. He had left school in Scotland in 1927, and joined a Scottish bank, although intending at some stage to work abroad. One Sunday morning, on walking home after church, he found himself behind his father and another man, who turned out to be Dr Scott, the Bank's doctor.

He was an old friend of my father's and his first question was 'what are you doing, my boy.' And I told him I was working in a bank ... I admitted that ... I wanted to serve abroad in a bank, but I was too young ... He didn't mention the Imperial Bank of Persia to me but he mentioned the Hongkong and Shanghai, in which he had friends ... our talk finished by his saying if I'd write to him in a year's time he would assist in any application I might want to make. Prior to the lapse of a year suddenly by post came an application form for me to join the Imperial Bank. Dr. Scott had met two of the Directors in Edinburgh and the enquiry was made, did he know any bright young Scots men who wanted to go abroad. And so without really any delay I was asked to come down for an interview in London.[19]

Macqueen joined the Bank as a junior in May 1930.

The background of the Bank's recruits was similar to before 1914. Previous banking experience was regarded as a merit, especially in the 1920s, but the Imperial Bank never had the Hongkong Bank's almost universal rule that recruits should have had two years experience in a joint stock bank or similar practical experience. Table 10.3 lists the number of recruits to the Bank with known previous banking experience. The Bank records on previous employment are very patchy before 1925, and it seems probable that the actual proportion of recruits with banking experience was higher in the earlier periods. The Scottish banks seem to have provided many of these recruits. Between 1924 and 1928 at least 14 of the 23 'known' bankers were from Scottish banks, and six of the 12 men between 1929 and 1938. The main English banks were also represented. Harold Musker (Deputy Chief Manager 1940–46, and General Manager of The British Bank of the Middle East 1952–62), for example, came from the London County and Westminster Bank. Overseas and foreign banks also provided recruits. T. Sheahan (Chief Inspector 1935–46) had previously worked for Crédit Lyonnais before joining the Imperial Bank in 1919, and six men came from the Hongkong Bank during the 1920s.

It was after the First World War that the first university graduates joined the Bank. Eleven graduates joined between 1927 and 1934, seven from Cambridge and four from Oxford. But this source of recruits does not seem to have been a great success. Seven resigned before ever going overseas, one resigned five years after going to Iran, and another joined the Army in the Second World War and was killed. Only two, A. L. Butt from Cambridge and G. S. Goldsworthy from Oxford, served the Bank for any length of time. It seems probable that many graduates felt frustrated by the long stays in London Office, and perhaps by the mediocre quality of some senior staff above them. The Bank, for its part, did not find that universities provided the kind of men it sought. By 1935 there was a definite policy not to recruit more graduates,[20] although one further Oxford graduate was taken on in 1938 (who resigned ten months later) and one Cambridge man in 1940.

By the 1930s the majority of recruits were school leavers, usually without any previous job experience. English recruits were taken largely from minor public schools. The public school man was held to possess the character to survive in the East, the confidence to represent the Bank abroad, and to assume authority over local staff. 'We regard personality as one of our greatest assets', the Board told its Managers in 1929, ... 'We must look to our representatives in the East, of whatever grade of service, to conduct themselves in and out of office with unremitting regard to the obligations of their position.'[21]

The majority of staff were recruited, therefore, because of their social background and skills, together with sporting ability, rather than any particular educational qualification or relevant experience. In 1923, for example, a Foreign Office official recommended one 17-year-old boy at Cheltenham College to Sir Hugh Barnes, as a possible candidate for the Bank, in the following terms: 'Keen on cricket, tennis and rugger. Nearly 6 feet in height, healthy, cheerful and fairly good looking, pleasant manners, easily led, character undeveloped. Is anxious to go abroad especially if riding would be possible.' The boy, Barnes wrote back after reading the reference,

Table 10.4. *Number of years spent in London Office 1914–38*

Years staff joined	Sent directly overseas	Period in London Office under 2 years	3–4 years	5–6 years
1914–18	6	4	1	—
1919–23	35	14	6	—
1924–28	2	21	7	1
1929–38	1	9	8	6

'is quite of the type that we are glad to have in the Imperial Bank of Persia'.[22]

The Bank's preoccupations were reflected in the initial interviews the London Manager would give applicants. E. S. Jenkins remembered his interview was on the following lines:

he asked if I rowed, which I said, No I did not. He asked if I played bridge which I did; and I said Yes. He asked me why I wanted to go abroad. He asked me whether I felt that I could work with and control Persians ... as they would be the local staff. I said I thought so.[23]

Jenkins' interview was fairly typical, although it should be emphasised that the Bank sought men with good health and outgoing personalities rather than first class sportsmen. The Bank never had the same formalities as the Hongkong Bank in selecting staff. The Imperial Bank, for instance, never set its applicants a written entrance examinaton, which was normal practice in the larger bank.

Reports on new staff confirmed the kind of qualities the Bank wanted. One man was praised for being 'a refined youth, who obviously had the advantage of a good upbringing. Has the ability, education and personality to get on.' Another received credit for being 'steady, sober, conscientious, and a good all-round sportsman in every sense of the word'.[24] It was a system designed to provide the Bank with reliable, honest men who would not let the Bank down, and by and large it succeeded. It was not a system to produce high fliers or crooks.

Most recruits to the Bank served for a time in London Office, except before 1924 when many men were despatched abroad with little or no experience in London. Table 10.4 gives the number of men sent directly overseas, and the length of time recruits who joined London Office had to wait before going East. It excludes the staff who resigned in London, figures for which are given in Table 10.2 above. The 1939–45 period is excluded because so many staff joined the Armed Forces.

During the 1920s most men who joined London Office were sent abroad within two years, but in the 1930s many men were having to wait between three and six years for appointment to the overseas staff. It was a similar story in the Hongkong Bank – where average waiting time to go East increased from a few months in 1919 to four years in the 1930s – and it almost always caused frustration among juniors. In the Imperial Bank in the early 1930s there was a definite air of tension among the juniors with so few men being sent abroad. In 1931 only one junior was sent East. C. D. Lunn, who had joined the Bank in 1930, remembered the atmosphere after the sole appointee had gone to Iran:

None of us left in London could escape the bleakness of the outlook; some, myself included, felt that we were growing older with little to show for the toll of years.[25]

In London, the juniors continued to be passed from one department to another learning the ways of the Bank. 'London Office in those days was like a school', one man who was a junior in the 1930s remembered, '... There were twelve boys and five grown-ups, and four typists, and the Manager and the Assistant Manager. And the boys were given all the work to do and the grown-ups used to correct it, like at school.'[26] Honoraria were offered to juniors who passed the Institute of Bankers' exams, and London Office also organised a tutor after 1935 to provide French lessons after working hours.

Opinions on the value of the London training remained varied. The London management considered it of value and importance. 'They are put to responsible work from the time they come into the place', Rogers wrote in 1924, 'until they either get sacked for inefficiency or go to Persia.'[27] Staff in Iran, however, tended to see time spent in London as an irrelevancy. 'The general opinion here', observed one man, 'is that he learns little in London, in fact he is wasting his time in licking stamps and bill walking while with you.'[28] It was particularly curious that no instruction in Persian was given in London. One man who was a junior in the 1920s remembered the consequences:

And one thing they didn't do which they should have done of course was to have sent one to the London Oriental School of Languages to get a basic knowledge of Persian. Because you arrived there not knowing one word, and you couldn't tell when they were speaking Persian, couldn't tell the difference between Persian and French.[29]

On appointment to the overseas service, new staff would usually be sent to Chief Office in Tehran while Bombay and Baghdad, which were also large offices, were also regular destinations. However, first appointments to smaller branches were not unknown. 'Haji' Evans was sent straight to Hamadan in 1919, J. D. Hammond to Basra in 1927 and F. Wilkes to Mohammarah (Khorramshahr) in 1928. Some juniors, especially in the 1930s, were sent East with specific tasks in view. G. S. Goldsworthy, a graduate in French and German, was recruited to Chief Office's Correspondence Department in 1930 because no one except the Chief Manager could speak Continental languages. C. D. Lunn was sent to Tehran in 1932 to help with the extra work generated by the withdrawal of the Imperial Bank's note issue.

The Bank's official policy continued to stress that its staff should learn Persian once in Iran, but it seems unlikely that many of the British staff in the interwar period had much knowledge of the language. During the 1920s, the modest incentive scheme – a bonus of £50 for passing Persian examinations – did not encourage British staff to take lessons, and the Bank's *mirzas* seem to have been over-generous when they examined British officers. In 1933, however, Wilkinson tightened up the system. Examination papers were sent to an American college at Esfahan for marking. A new examination system was also introduced. This was divided into Parts 1 and 2, which officers had to take after one and two years respectively of arriving in Iran, together with an Honours examination, which was not compulsory but for which honoraria up to £75 were paid for good performances. The examinations were in both written and spoken Persian, and candidates were also obliged to read some basic works written about Persia: D. Ross, *The Persians* for Part 1, Sir Percy Sykes, *History of Persia* for Part 2 and M. Fateh, *The Economic Position of Persia* for Honours. It would seem that the main achievement of Wilkinson's new system of examination was to reveal the poor knowledge of Persian of his staff. In the November 1934 examinations there were 13 candidates, of whom ten appeared for the examination and only two passed. In 1937 it was reported, after another set of examinations, that although the candidates had an understanding of spoken Persian, they were largely unable to read it.[30]

Leave conditions became a little more generous after the First World War, when many men had to postpone their scheduled leaves. By the 1920s a six-month leave was granted after the first five years service, another leave after the next four and a half years, and thereafter a leave after every three-and-a-half years. Wilkinson attempted, but failed, to persuade the Board to accept a system of shorter but more frequent leaves.[31] In the early 1930s ten day local leaves began to be granted to staff, but in 1935 – as an economy measure – senior staff had the interval between leaves raised from three-and-a-half to four years. It was not until 1942, as wartime staff shortages became critical, that the Bank promised that as soon as practicable it would begin granting four-and-a-half month leaves every three years. Only in December 1945 did the Bank agree to pay the passages of wives on their first trip to the Middle East, on their husbands' leaves and on their retirement, plus the fares of children under eight going abroad and under ten going back to Britain.

Formal entitlement to leave did not mean that staff always received it. During the World Wars men had to remain at their posts for extended periods, and even in peace time the scheduling of a leave programme in a small bank was a difficult process and staff could find themselves staying overseas longer than their due. The 'old hands' in the Bank tended to be unsympathetic with young men complaining about the system or requesting leaves. 'My first term abroad was over 7 and a half years without leave,' S. F. Rogers reflected in 1921 after hearing of a decision by McMurray to permit a man to marry on condition he stayed in Persia for a minimum of six years, '... Mr Buchanan tells me that his first term in the Gulf was over 6 years, so that you are letting down your man very lightly in stipulating for a minimum of 6 years.'[32]

The Imperial Bank retained tight controls on when and who its staff could marry. In 1925 the minimum income requirement before an officer could marry was raised from £500 to £600, though in 1933 it was reduced to £550. The Bank's rule, however, remained flexible, and a number of exceptions were granted according to circumstances. In 1934, for example, E. S. Matheson was allowed to marry even though his income was too low, as he promised that his wife would remain in Britain until his salary had reached the required level.[33]

The Bank continued to give great attention to the suitability of prospective wives. Wives were seen, rightly, as playing a major role in the Bank community and in their husbands' careers, and senior management sought to avoid 'difficult' women becoming Bank wives. 'How women do dominate situations to be sure', S. F. Rogers observed in 1929, 'as Sir T. J. used to say, the men are all right but the women are the very devil.'[34] The Bank's desire to influence the marriages of its staff was strengthened by the consequences when marriages went wrong. Great embarrassment was caused, for example, by one couple in the early 1920s who quarrelled loudly and publicly with one another, the wife on one occasion attempting to strangle her husband and on another throwing a finger bowl in his face.

Non-British wives continued to be frowned upon. Iranians, Armenians, Russians and Germans were particularly disliked. The Bank regularly ordered men not to marry such women and moved them to other branches in an attempt to break up undesirable liaisons. One man was threatened with dismissal in 1937 for wanting to marry the daughter of a German hairdresser. Another was refused permission in 1918 to marry a Russian, Wood citing the 'sad example' of a previous British officer who had married 'the most impossible specimen of the Tartar tribe of Transcaspia'.[35] The Bank displayed particular disapproval when its officers became involved with members of the Stevens family, a powerful 'Levantine' trading house in Tabriz which eventually collapsed in the early 1930s. Nevertheless, at least five men seem to have married scions of this family, although always after a considerable struggle with the Bank. The Imperial Bank's attitude, it must be stressed, was characteristic of all British Eastern banks of the period.

A man's wife, his social manners and his personality were all influential factors in the promotion of Bank staff. A wife held to be objectionable by colleagues could lead to a man being 'tucked away' at a provincial branch rather than appointed to a senior position at Chief Office.[36] Personality clashes were also a factor in promotion decisions, and such clashes seem to have been frequent. Despite the Bank's desire to appoint men who would 'fit in', the Bank's staff were a collection of individuals rather than a harmonious club. 'In my opinion', Butters observed in 1930, 'the IBP has a wonderful staff individually. The fault is that for some reason, climate perhaps, there is a certain amount of unrest and lack of confidence in each other.'[37] The long spells of service at small, isolated branches undoubtedly encouraged an individualism in the Bank's staff which was perhaps not seen in larger organisations.

Eccentricity was not, however, a complete bar to promotion. The choice for senior positions was limited by shortages of able men, as well as the Bank's preference for making appointments in line with a man's seniority. An illustration was the case of R. S. Oakshott. Oakshott established a reputation as an excellent banker, but during the 1920s his career seemed blighted by his Russian wife and left-wing political views. 'A very capable officer with a very sound knowledge of banking and our business', read one staff report on him in 1928, 'but his eccentricity, his very pronounced views towards society and his complete disregard of his social duties debar him from promotion to one of the higher posts.'[38] Nevertheless Oakshott's ability eventually prevailed over dislike of his wife and social manners, and he held the post of Deputy Chief Manager between 1935 and 1938.

10.3 LIFE IN IRAN

The journey from London to Iran became rather more comfortable in the interwar years. During the 1920s it was still most common for men and their wives to travel through Europe by train to Baku, and then to cross the Caspian Sea by steamer, and proceed on through Iran by road. The alternative route, which was more expensive but also more comfortable and often preferred by wives going East by themselves, was the passenger ship to Bombay and on to the Gulf. In the 1930s this route was largely superseded, except for those posted to Bombay or Bushire, by a further route: this consisted of a train journey to Marseilles, taking a ship to Haifa or Beirut via Alexandria, and then the trans-desert convoy to Baghdad. If the officer was proceeding to Tehran, he would normally complete the journey by a two-day drive. The Russian route was both cheaper and quicker – taking less than a week compared to the 12-day minimum via Marseilles – and this seems to have been the route by which most juniors were despatched, especially during the Bank's economy drive of the early 1930s.

Chief Office was the largest branch of the Bank, and where many officers and their wives had their most pleasant social life. There was a variety of sports opportunities, and a full range of social activities in the large British community. A junior could expect to attend social functions at regular intervals, while older men often played bridge. F. H. Johnson remembered the distractions of Tehran social life in the mid-1920s:

In those days, young people were quite popular because all Embassies and places like that used to encourage young people to go out. There were soirées and after dinner parties. The old boys used to get down to playing bridge or poker and of course all the ladies were left and had to be entertained. They used to get the young people, the young people from the A.P.O.C. and the Bank, like myself, and of course naturally going out so much, always white tie and tails, consequently one rather forewent one's duty as far as the Persian language was concerned.[39]

Social contacts with Iranians were infrequent. Chief Managers would socialise with high-ranking officials, and Wilkinson seems to have been particularly active in this area. More junior staff, however, were unlikely to meet many Iranians socially, especially as Reza Shah's government discouraged such contacts. C. F. Warr remembered the situation in Hamadan as early as 1925:

In those days we somehow didn't mix with the Persians at all. Very polite in the office but again even in those days dealing with women was very severe and strict, and the result was that you only ever saw the male Persians and their hospitality wasn't very generous or excellent.[40]

In Iraq, however, there were more opportunities for mixing with 'locals', and certainly 'Haji' Evans and his wife seem to have mixed well in Basra.

In most of the provincial branches the social life of Bank staff was far more restricted than in Tehran. British communities in such places were small, or non-existent, and a bachelor could face loneliness or at the very least a limited social existence. C. F. Warr recalled his early evenings as a junior in Hamadan:

There were three or four women there who had regular weekly at home days to which of course you went. You had a cup of tea and a piece of cake and a biscuit, and there was great competition amongst the women as to who could produce the nicest cakes. And then we settled down to bridge. And there was always one or two tables of bridge and at eight o' clock you were told to go home.[41]

Living conditions at some of the provincial branches were also sparse. F. H. Johnson found his spell as Manager of Bandar Abbas in 1930 a distressing experience:

It's disgusting. It's filthy. The climate ... you can't believe there is such a climate. How one survived there one just doesn't know ... There was very little doing. We had this little house, and no electricity, nothing at all. In my day one had a paraffin punkah, a paraffin fan which you lighted but, of course, the heat of the fan was far worse than the wind which it was producing. Suddenly it would blow up. One slept on the roof of course. There was a well down which you sank your drinks. For drinking water, we used to obtain this when the slow mail called in once a week.[42]

After the end of the First World War the Bank built the Haft Dastgah compound, near the British Legation, to accommodate most of its British staff in Tehran. The compound consisted of eight two-storey houses, one each for senior bachelors and juniors and the remainder for married couples. The compound had a swimming pool. Some juniors, at least, found their accommodation rather basic. The bachelor quarters, G. S. Goldsworthy observed in 1930:

consist of bedroom and sitting room only, kitchen, tin bath and 'thunder-box' having to be shared with another fellow in the quarters next door. The minimum of furniture is provided, and all bed and table linen and blankets must be bought ... The crockery and cutlery provided consist of one cup and saucer, plate, knife and fork and so on. Apparently one is not expected to entertain in one's room.[43]

By the early 1930s the whole compound was showing signs of age, with the roofs regularly letting in water. Two of the houses were demolished in 1936 and 1937, including the junior barracks, and replacements were built.

The Chief Manager's house was grand, though new Chief Managers often had harsh words to say about their predecessors' tastes. 'This house', McMurray observed to S. F. Rogers in October 1919 soon after taking over from A. O. Wood, 'is an absolute disgrace for furniture. Still the same old dilapidated stuff from Rabino's time. You know the stuff with the white covers, groggy legs and stinks like a polecat in summer (rotting straw). The curtains are a joke. Wood lived in the big hall downstairs in summer and in two of the small rooms upstairs in winter. The public rooms have not a curtain of any sort.'[44] The house's external appearance, however was imposing.

Outside Tehran, the Bank owned a great deal of property by the 1920s, and it also rented accommodation. In Bombay, the Bank purchased a house for its staff in 1920, but this proved a poor investment and the building was sold at a loss in 1930 (See Chapter 9). At Basra the Bank built a Manager's house, but all the other staff were accommodated above the Bank office. In Iran, accommodation was variable. The Manager's house at Hamadan continued to please most of its occupants. The Manager's house at Ahwaz, on the other hand, suffered a series of misfortunes in the 1930s and 1940s, from warped ceilings to a plague of white ants.

The Bank's major building project in the interwar years was the construction of a new Chief Office in Tehran. McMurray had been as critical of the Chief Office building as of the furniture in the Chief Manager's house. 'The more I see of the premises here', he wrote to London in 1919, 'the more disgusted I feel. They are not at all in keeping with our position in the country ... we have the most valuable site in Tehran and it seems a pity to have such a ramshackle building which is likely to fall down of its own accord someday.'[45] No action was taken, however, and in 1924 the south wall of the building began cracking. By 1926 plans were underway to build a new office next to the old one. Excavation work begin 1927, and the foundation stone of the new building was laid by the Minister of Court, Teymurtash, in January 1930. By August 1931 all staff had been transferred to the new Chief Office.

As before 1914, sport played an important role in the life of the Imperial Bank's British staff. In Tehran team games were feasible. The Bank, for example, had annual tournaments in hockey and soccer with teams from the Legation, the Indo–European Telegraph Company and the Anglo–Persian Oil Company. Other sporting facilities were also available. In the autumn of 1932 a nine hole Golf Club opened in Tehran, which many of the Bank's British staff joined. Outside Tehran, riding, skiing, tennis and fishing were regular activities. Men who did not enjoy sport, or at least the expatriate social life which accompanied it, found it all very tedious. 'I am not horsey or doggy', one man wrote from Basra to S. F. Rogers in 1926, 'and dislike late nights, and I also dislike tennis where I cannot walk straight off the Court into a bath.'[46] Most men, however, enjoyed sport and the relaxation it gave them, especially as the Bank made a special effort to recruit people with sporting interests.

Heavy drinking was a feature of the lives of many of the British staff. Alcohol was cheap and freely available. It offered solace for those under stress or suffering from loneliness. Drinking was also a standard feature of the expatriate communities, in which the Bank's staff were expected to participate. By 1941 'Haji' Evans was suffering from a number of illnesses, including diabetes, dermatitis and prickly heat, which he blamed on the nature of his life in Basra. 'The continual worry of chasing business', he wrote to V. L. Walter, 'of entertaining people both European and local, of standing drinks at the Club, solely to curry favour and "keep in" with those from whom business emanates is beginning to tell on my health.'[47] It was not surprising that men either became ill or, as Walter described one officer in 1944, 'addicted to the club drink habit'.[48] Dismissals for excessive drinking, as in the case of one officer found wandering the streets of Basra in 1920 in a state of complete alcoholic stupefaction, were a not unusual occurrence.

Ill-health was a regular event in the lives of the Bank's staff. Nine of the 13 men who died in the Bank's service between 1914 and 1945, died from illnesses of one sort or another. The conditions of life in Iran undoubtedly not only made British staff more vulnerable to disease, but also turned comparatively minor problems into major ones. One man in 1932, for example, caught conjunctivitis, but complications set in and eventually he had to have his eye removed. Another unfortunate officer in 1921 contracted pleurisy, malaria and pneumonia at the same time. At any one time many British staff would be ill, with malaria, typhoid and pneumonia being very common. F. H. Johnson suffered from malaria in Bushire in the late 1920s:

I had malaria of course in Bushire, quite serious, quite nasty, but they're things you expect in unhealthy places. You either die or you're cured aren't you. And of course in those days they didn't have the methods of killing mosquitoes or curing malaria. All you got was a series of injections, quinine, in your bottom. My malaria used to come on every twenty-four hours. One had one day free and then it would come on again. It was really quite serious with a temperature of 104/106. I went up to 106 on one occasion. You'd soak through your sheets, mattress, pyjamas, and everything. Then you'd go quite cold.[49]

Baghdad was notorious for diseases, with many officers and their wives suffering from Baghdad boils and sand-fly fever. T. Sheahan caught the plague whilst he was serving there in 1924. Sheahan, however, survived the disease, retired as the Bank's Chief Inspector in 1946, and lived until 1983.

The Bank always retained a doctor in Tehran, sometimes sharing him with one or other of the Legation, the Anglo–Persian Oil Company and the Indo–European Telegraph Company. In the provinces the Bank would attempt to contract a British doctor. By the interwar years both staff and their families seem to have been given free consultations with the doctor, although not all treatment was free. While 'ordinary' drugs and medicines – such as quinine, castor oil and epsom salts – and innoculations were free, more expensive drugs, operations, and confinements all had to be paid for by the staff themselves. The Bank also refused to pay for the treatment of venereal disease.

Bank wives, like their husbands, were prone to illness. A number of wives became so ill that they had to be sent home. It was not infrequent for wives to live in Britain for some at least of the period their husbands were abroad. In addition, during the Second World War many wives in Iran were evacuated to India. Such separations often put great strains on both parties. One officer tried to commit suicide by drinking anti-freeze in 1942 because he could not bear a long separation from his wife.[50] Childbirth remained an anxious time, with the risk of disease for mothers and children an ever present one. O. A. Butters and his wife, for instance, lost their baby while serving in Tabriz in 1927.

Until the Second World War, when some wives worked for the British occupation forces and others for the Red Cross, it was unknown for Bank wives to work. In the smaller branches they could find themselves, therefore, almost prisoners in Bank houses, with human contact limited to their servants who often could not speak English. In some places, like Borujerd, it was unthinkable for a wife to go far from home without her husband, or at least another British male, while social contact with local women was practically impossible. Resourceful wives, such as Vera, the wife of 'Haji' Evans, in Hamadan in the mid-1920s, kept themselves sane by keeping hens, rabbits and ducks and growing a large variety of fruit and vegetables.

In towns where there were other British wives, however, days could pass pleasantly if undemandingly for a Bank wife. Vera Evans' regime in Ahwaz seems typical. By 8.00 a.m. she had supervised the housework for the day. Between 9.30 and 12.30 there would be bridge parties with other British wives. Her husband would then arrive home for lunch, which would be followed by a siesta. They would get up at 4.30 p.m., and go to the British Club in the town. In the evening, she would either hold or go to a dinner party.[51]

10.4 THE LOCAL STAFF

The local staff played an important role in the functioning of the Bank. In 1940, after the staff reductions of the 1930s, the total local staff was 424, of whom 74 were employed in Iraq and 117 in Chief Office, Tehran. Although full staff lists do not survive, it is clear that Muslim Iranians were under-represented on the Bank's staff, many of whom were Armenian, with some Jews and Indians in the south of Iran and Iraq.

This situation was to a large extent self-perpetuating, as the normal avenue of recruitment was through recommendation by an existing and trusted member of the local staff. There is evidence that several generations of the same family joined the Bank. The father of the Bank's Chief Interpreter in Tehran between 1926 and 1934, Mobasser od-Doule, had been first head *farrash* at Mashad branch, and Mobasser od-Doule himself had served there between 1898 and 1925. Another case was M. J. Bamban, an Armenian, who joined the Esfahan branch aged 16 in 1894 and retired from the same branch in 1942. His father had been one of the Bank's early agents in Julfa, while his son joined the Bank and worked in Esfahan and, later, at Chief Office.

Recruits to the Iranian staff were supposed to pass an entrance examination in English, Persian, arithmetic and writing. This test seems to have been widely taken in the 1920s, but by the early 1930s the Bank was experiencing so many difficulties in finding high calibre Iranian applicants that the examination was waived.[52] Once recruited, the Bank offered its local staff no training, and they were expected to learn the business on the job.

The Bank's most prominent local employee, Abol Hassan Ebtehaj, joined in December 1920 at the age of 21. He was among the Bank's best qualified recruits. His father was a *mostoufi*, or man of letters, who had sent his son to Paris to be educated at the age of 12. Ebtehaj had later transferred to the Syrian Protestant College in Beirut, where he began his acquisition of what became fluent English. During the War the family had suffered from the revolutionary disturbances around Rasht, where they lived, and Ebtehaj's father had been killed by the *Jangalis*. In 1920, fearing a Red Army invasion of the north, Ebtehaj and a brother left Rasht and travelled, on foot for part of the way, to Tehran. A friend already working in the Imperial Bank told him of a vacancy in the Bank. He applied, was interviewed by the Chief Interpreter, sat the entrance examination, and in December 1920 joined the Bank.

In the immediate post-War period the Imperial Bank offered a young man such as Ebtehaj security of employment which no other institution in Iran could match. The Bank's salaries, however, were not high and considerably less than those earned by the British staff. In 1924 a structured salary system was introduced, with increments for various grades, but in the early 1930s the local staff found their salaries held down and many jobs lost as the Bank attempted to reduce costs. By the mid-1930s staff turnover was growing in the Bank, and Butters laid the blame on low salary levels. 'I know', he wrote to London in October 1936, 'their salaries have fallen far behind the increase in cost of living and their grievances are very real.'[53] Almost certainly, however, ambitious or nationalistic Iranians left the Bank to join the Bank Melli or the Iranian government for reasons other than financial ones.

There were some improvements in the local staff's conditions of service in the interwar period. In 1922 a Provident Fund was established for them, the initiative coming from the Bank's branch in Bombay which discovered that practically all the other banks in that city had retirement benefit schemes of one sort or another. Under the terms of the initial scheme, the Bank and the staff each paid 5% of a man's annual salary into the Fund, which earned 5% per annum interest. The whole of the Bank's contribution was lost if the staff member left within five years. In 1927 the Bank's contribution was increased to 10% per annum, but staff had to stay with the Bank for 15 years in order to qualify for this sum. Paid leave for local staff was not introduced until 1937. In their first five years staff were entitled to ten days annual leave, and afterwards to three weeks. Local staff also received an annual New Year bonus of 2.5% of their salary, which was increased to 5% in 1936, and gratuities were sometimes given to long-serving staff who retired. When Mobasser od-Doule retired from the Bank in 1934 after 36 years' service, he was given a gratuity of 12 months' salary.

The local staff had none of the facilities of the British officers in the Bank. It was not until 1947, for example, that V. L. Walter conceived the idea that the local staff should be provided with a sports and recreational centre. His idea was apparently provoked by Anglo–Iranian's decision to construct a club house and other amenities for its local staff in Tehran.[54] A 10 000 square metre site was purchased at Behjatabad in north-west Tehran, and the sports complex was opened in 1949. However, the Bank's subsequent policy of reducing its Iranian commitments led to a decision to sell the site in 1951.

The senior posts of the Imperial Bank, like all British Eastern banks before the Second World War, remained the preserve of the British staff. The Bank's promotion policies remained firmly delineated on racial lines. Separate salary scales and terms of employment, separate lavatories and separate social lives reinforced the distinction between local and British staff. It was a distinction which many younger British officers and their more liberal minded seniors found hard to support in Reza Shah's Iran. 'The Bank's treatment of the local staff frequently comes as a shock to even the hardest minds', one British officer wrote to S. F. Rogers in 1928, 'and has discredited the IBP in the eyes of every fair-minded member of its staff.'[55] The major stumbling block, however, was the Bank's Board which by the early 1930s was out of touch with the new Iran.

The Bank's attitudes were not to the liking of Abol Hassan Ebtehaj. Intelligent, well-educated, forceful and very confident in his own ability, Ebtehaj was performing responsible duties in the Imperial Bank soon after joining it. After serving in Tehran, he was despatched to the branch at Rasht, where, through a combination of his own personality and the apparent laziness of his British Managers, he was soon keeping the general ledger and providing the second signature on bills, despite the Bank's policy that only British officers could 'sign' for the Bank. By the late 1920s he was performing an important liaison role with the Iranian government, and also being sent on special tasks, such as recovering a bad debt from a customer in Istanbul in 1929.[56]

Ebtehaj's services for the Bank brought him salary increases, but not the status he sought. Having joined the Bank on 300 Krans per annum in 1920, by 1930 he was earning 2750 Krans and by February 1936, his last salary increase, 5250 Rials. But salary increases, and Ebtehaj's *de facto* exercise of the powers of British officers, were no substitute for status and equality of opportunity. Ebtehaj deeply resented any suggestion of inferiority to the British staff, many of whom he far surpassed in terms of intellect. 'It wasn't a question of signature', Ebtehaj later recalled, 'I demanded the same status, I said I will not remain in an institution if I cannot go to the top.'[57] Ebtehaj could not stand the apparent symbols of Iranian inferiority which existed within the Bank. After the opening of the new Chief Office, he later remembered,

I went to the wash room and it was full of people who were washing before having lunch. I noticed there was a thing stuck on the door – For Europeans Only. I got so mad, so furious. I said this is an insult to my people.[58]

Wilkinson had considerable sympathy for Ebtehaj's case. In 1931 he pressed the Board to appoint Ebtehaj to the level of a European officer, and to call him Assistant to the Chief Manager.[59] The Board in London, however, refused to consider such a precedent. After repeated applications to join the European staff, Ebtehaj resigned from the Bank on 1 July 1936 and joined the Ministry of Finance. His subsequent campaign against the Imperial Bank, especially after becoming Governor of the Bank Melli in 1942, is reviewed in Part 3 of this History.

Ebtehaj's resignation from the Imperial Bank was followed by that of others who found they could increase both their status and often their salaries by working for the government or an Iranian banking institution. In October 1936, for example, the Chief Cashier in Tehran defected to the Bank Melli; the fourteenth resignation at Chief Office in six months. Moreover, the Bank found itself increasingly unable to recruit educated young Iranians to its service.

It was not, however, until 1939 that the Bank introduced a major reform which offered its local staff a significant improvement in their status. In September 1939, with the outbreak of the Second World War threatening to denude the Bank of some of its British staff, a system of 'A' and 'B' officers was introduced. Limited 'signing' powers were given to 'B' officers, with full powers reserved for 'A' officers. Walter pressed for Iranians to be made 'A' officers on the grounds that this would reassure senior Iranian staff about their status. 'The knowledge that they have such powers', Walter wrote to London in 1940, 'will enable them to feel on an equality with their contemporaries in Government Departments and the Bank Melli Iran.'[60] In 1940, therefore, Issa Abtin, by then known as the Assistant to the Chief Manager, and Ismail Dehlevi, the Bank's Iranian lawyer, were appointed 'A' officers. In addition, some 23 local staff were made 'B' officers; seven in Tehran, three in Baghdad, two in Basra and the remainder scattered around the Iranian provincial branches. In retrospect, the Bank's new policy can be seen as being at least ten years too late.

10.5 LONDON OFFICE

London Office remained very small between 1914 and 1945. The permanent staff numbered just over a dozen for most of the period, and was stable at 13, six men and seven women, between 1936 and 1945. The office contained a number of former members of the overseas staff, some of whom had 'retired' to work in London, and others who had been sent to London to keep them out of harm's way, such as one man who had had an indiscreet relationship with an Iranian girl. After George Newell's retirement in 1917 the post of London

Manager and Secretary, and the post of Sub-Manager, were always held by former overseas staff. S. F. Rogers was London Manager between 1918 and 1929, with E. M. Eldrid his Sub-Manager after 1921. In 1929 Eldrid became London Manager and F. Hale was appointed Sub-Manager. In 1935 Hale became London Manager, with F. A. Ayrton as his Deputy. Other former overseas staff in London included M. McIver, who ran the Securities Department, and A. H. Wright, who was Chief Accountant between 1928 and 1935.

The remainder of the permanent staff had been recruited directly in Britain. These included K. R. H. Murray, Chief Accountant from 1935, and W. L. Dutton, who was Head of the Bill Department. These permanent staff were, of course, supported by the fluctuating population of juniors awaiting transfer to the East, but London Office hardly represented a dynamic presence in the City of London. 'We are', S. F. Rogers observed in 1927, 'a crowd of crocks here in London.'[61]

London Office never reverted to its pre-1914 position of being an all-male preserve. Between 1914 and 1918 the Bank had hired 10 women to work in London Office, as both clerks and typists. Three women were recruited between 1919 and 1923, six between 1924 and 1928, two between 1929 and 1938, and five during the Second World War. Some of these women acquired considerable responsibility. Prominent among these was Miss M. Owen, who joined London Office in 1917 and stayed throughout the period, one of several very long-serving ladies with the Bank. In October 1940 two women, Miss Owen and Miss S. E. Beck, were, for the first time, authorised to sign cheques on behalf of the Bank.

London Office changed its location over time. In 1924 the Bank moved from its premises at 25 Abchurch Lane to 33–36 King William Street, which offered over 7000 square feet more of floor space. The Bank, as Barnes told shareholders in 1923, had become 'hopelessly overcrowded' in Abchurch Lane.[62] In 1938 there was a further move to 51 Gracechurch Street. This office was bombed in 1940, the caretaker and his wife were killed, and for some months the Office was run from the basement. Worse was to come. In 1943 the Bank's offices were commandeered by the government and the Bank was obliged to move to small and cramped premises at 11 Telegraph Street. It was not until 1948 that the Bank was allowed to move back to 51 Gracechurch Street. Volume 2 of this History will relate how it moved several more times before Head Office was relocated to Hong Kong in 1980.

Part 3

THE END IN IRAN 1939–52

11

THE SECOND WORLD WAR

11.1 THE BANK AND THE SECOND WORLD WAR

The Second World War, like its predecessor, was a profitable experience for the Imperial Bank. It seemed for a time that Iran would stay out of the conflict. Over the previous two decades Iran and the Gulf had become a backwater in international power politics, a situation which had given Reza Shah more freedom of manoeuvre than previous Iranian rulers. In 1939, as in 1914, the country declared its neutrality. 'Iran is happily at peace with all the world', Sir Henry McMahon told the Bank's annual shareholders' meeting on 16 July 1941. Just over a month later, however, British and Soviet troops invaded and occupied Iran. Reza Shah was forced to abdicate, and was eventually replaced by his eldest son.

The Allied occupation meant that there was no repetition of the chaos seen between 1914 and 1918. The Bank completely avoided the trauma of some other Eastern banks which had offices in enemy occupied territories. The Hongkong Bank had 33 of its 37 Eastern branches overrun by the Japanese. The Mercantile Bank of India lost half of its 24 branches in the East. In contrast the Imperial Bank's business was soon booming as it serviced the requirements of the Allied Forces. At the same time the Bank was substantially freed from the irksome restrictions which had nearly driven it from Iran in the 1930s. Surprisingly too, the War brought not only new profits, but also new opportunities. In 1942 the Bank opened a branch in Kuwait, followed by another one in Bahrain in 1944. However, the dramatic story of the Bank's expansion outside Iran, which was to transform the institution within a decade, is told in Volume 2 of this History. This chapter focuses on the Imperial Bank in Iran.

The Bank's Chief Manager between July 1938 and March 1948 was V. L. Walter. Born in 1891, Walter had joined the Bank in 1908 as a junior clerk in London Office, and was sent to Iran in 1911. During the First World War he resigned in order to join the Army, but rejoined the Bank in 1919. He spent the entire interwar years in Iran, and more specifically in Tehran and Esfahan. During this period he seems to have formed a very deep attachment to Iran and things Iranian, and he acquired a deserved reputation as 'one whom Persians both liked and trusted'.[1] A shy and diffident man, Walter was also perhaps the most successful of the Imperial Bank's Chief Managers between 1925 and 1952, although the fortuitous relief from Iranian government restrictions during the Allied occupation was a significant factor in his success.

The War saw the departure of the old guard on the Bank's Board. Sir Hugh Barnes died in February 1940, and W. A. Buchanan died in June 1945. V. A. Caesar Hawkins retired in September 1939, after 32 years service on the Board. The departure of the old was not matched by a surge of new faces. Only one new director was appointed during the War, R. V. Buxton in April 1940. The 57-year-old Buxton brought, however, a welcome strengthening of the Imperial Bank's contacts in the City, for he had long worked for Martins Bank Ltd, a prominent joint stock bank, and in 1940 became a director of it. Soon afterwards Martins joined Glyn, Mills and Co, Lloyds Bank and Westminster Bank as the Imperial Bank's London bankers. While the Board's size had by the end of the War shrunk to five men, both of the two most recent appointments – Lord Kennet and Buxton – had brought with them substantial banking or financial experience outside the Imperial Bank and the Middle East.

The War reversed the decline in the Imperial Bank's balance sheet which had been such a feature of the 1930s. The total balance sheet grew by 284% between 1939 and 1945. As in the First World War, the substantial expansion came in the second half of the conflict. Deposits expanded from £3 355 430 in 1939 to £9 507 949 in 1942, and then shot to £22 096 736 in 1945, a 559% increase over 1939. In contrast, the Bank's lending grew much more slowly. Bills discounted, loans and advances grew from £2 129 528 in 1939 to £4 343 763 in 1945. The upshot was a strong increase in liquidity. The ratio of advances to deposits fell from 63% in 1939 to 20% in 1945, while the ratio of cash to deposits increased from 32% to 76% over the same period. By 1945 the Bank's holding of cash amounted to £16 812 936.

When considering these balance sheet figures, it has to be borne in mind that much of the growth was a reflection of wartime inflation in both Iran and Iraq. The causes of Iran's inflation will be discussed later in this chapter, but clearly the fivefold increase in prices there during the War was an important factor behind the balance sheet growth. On the other hand the Sterling figures were reduced by a depreciation of the Rial against Sterling. The official buying rate, and hence the Bank's adjustment rate, was 80.5 Rials to

Table 11.1. *Imperial Bank's profits 1939–45* (£ Sterling)

Year end (20 March)	'Real' profits	'Real' profits after tax and superannuation payments	Movements through inner reserves			
			Investments (written down)	Transfers (to) or from profits	Bad debts recovered (or provided for)	Published net profit
1939	122 533	72 533		(8754)	11 635	92 922[a]
1940	190 785	153 785	(50 000)	8421	3073	98 437
1941	223 133	128 133	(20 000)	5442	(492)	97 440[b]
1942	167 395	83 395	—	(48 509)	924	132 828
1943	629 742	165 742	—	40 000	14 758	140 500
1944	558 828	162 238	(25 527)	—	4623	141 335
1945	395 378	244 530	–	100 000	757	145 287

Notes:
[a] This figure is before tax or dividends had been deducted, as with all net profits in this table.
[b] In 1941 £4759 was written off bank premises.

the pound in 1939. After appreciating in 1940 and 1941, it fell to 142 in 1942, and settled at 128 thereafter (see Appendix 6).

The picture of wartime growth is sustained by the expansion of shareholders' funds. The published figures grew by 11.5% between 1939 and 1945. Inner reserves, which had amounted in 1939 to £1 449 995, fell to £1 400 646 in 1942. This fall, however, was because the relaxation of exchange controls in Iran meant that reserves were no longer required against unremitted profits. By 1945 inner reserves had grown to £1 543 914. The Bank's shareholders continued to receive their usual regular dividends. In 1939 the Bank began to make dividend payments subject to tax. The 9% paid in that year was a marginal increase from the 13/- paid in the previous year, which was equivalent to 8.874% subject to tax. 9% dividend payments were made throughout the War.

Table 11.1 examines the Imperial Bank's profits, variously defined, in the interwar years. The early years of the War saw some recovery of the Bank's profits, even though £70 000 had to be written off investments in 1940 and 1941. In 1942, although 'real' profits declined, the Bank was permitted once again to remit all its profits to Britain. £48 509 was, therefore, transferred from the Exchange Reserve Account, where it had been held against unremitted profits between March 1938 to March 1941. After 1943 'real' profits rose to a new level and, even after substantial provision had been made for Excess Profits and other taxes, the Bank was able to transfer £140 000 to the Contingency Account between 1943 and 1945.

Table 11.2. *The sources of the Imperial Bank's profits 1939–45 (£ Sterling)*

Year end (20 March)	London Office	Iranian branches	Iraq branches	Kuwait	'Real profits before tax
1939	92 307	25 090	5136	—	122 533
1940	125 147	48 188	17 450	—	190 785
1941	143 346	50 736	29 050	—	223 133
1942	105 400	46 116	17 461	(1582)	167 395
1943	148 374	431 382	37 892	12 094	629 742
1944	188 836	295 954	19 706	54 332	558 828
1945	162 001	226 808	416	24 462	395 378[a]

Note:
[a] In 1945 the Bank's new branch at Bahrain returned a loss of £7 350, and £10 958 was charged against profits to pay a special living allowance to European staff who had served overseas between September 1943 and March 1945.

Table 11.2 shows that the increase in profits, especially after 1943, was closely related to the recovery of the Bank's profitability in Iran. By 1940 Iranian profits had doubled over the previous year. Indeed, profits were higher than Table 11.2 suggests because of the arrangement whereby the interest on the Bank's Sterling advances to the Iranian Exchange Control Commission was payable to London Office in Sterling. 1943 was the Bank's bumper year in Iran. It was the first year since 1930 in which profits from the Bank's Iranian branches had exceeded those of London Office. In 1944 and 1945 the Bank's profits declined from this record level, but by those years the Bank's new branch at Kuwait had begun to make a significant contribution to profits, the beginning of a trend which was to make Kuwait the Bank's largest source of profit by the 1950s.

The War, therefore, was a period of growth for the Imperial Bank, growth of its balance sheet, of shareholders' funds and of profits. But, in retrospect, the period can be seen as a respite rather than a reprieve, for by the last two years of the War opposition to the Bank's operation was again appearing. The following sections look first at the Bank's wartime recovery, before turning to the revival of pressures against it.

11.2 THE PERIOD OF NEUTRALITY 1939–41

The two years after the outbreak of War in Europe were relatively satisfactory ones for the Bank in Iran. There was no doubt that the Iranian government and probably many Iranians preferred Germany to the Allies. Close political and economic links with Germany had developed by the end of the 1930s. In 1939 Germany replaced the Soviet Union as Iran's largest trading partner, a relationship cemented by special clearing and barter arrangements. After the outbreak of war in Europe, German trade with Iran remained at a high level. Iranian exports to Germany in 1939–40 were twice the value of those in 1937–38, and in 1940–41 these were much higher again. Imports from Germany were also very substantial in 1940–41. In addition, large numbers of Germans were resident in the country. Yet Reza Shah's relationship with Germany was not completely harmonious, especially after the Nazi–Soviet Friendship Pact in September 1939,[2] and the Imperial Bank had no restrictions placed on it because it was a British institution.

Indeed the Bank's relationship with the Iranian government after the outbreak of War was smooth, especially compared to Butters' last year as Chief Manager. By March 1940 the Bank's total loans to the ECC stood at £530 475. There was only one minor upset, in December 1939, when the government announced that the Rial was henceforth to be linked to the Dollar rather than Sterling. There were fears in the Bank that this might upset its foreign exchange operations, although the only practical effect was a drop in the official Rial–Sterling exchange rate from 64.35 to 80.50. A greater worry from the Bank's viewpoint was the continued limitation on its profit remittances. In March 1940 the Iranian branches earned profits of £48 188, but the Bank was only allowed to remit £20 119 to Britain. Walter, however, comforted himself with looking on the bright side. 'Our position by means of these unremitted earnings is greatly strengthened', he wrote to London in March 1940, 'and, with the probability of a long war in front of us, we may in the uncertain future be glad to have this reserve available.'[3]

In February 1940 negotiations began for a renewal of the Bank's Sterling Agreement with the Iranian government, which was due to expire in the following September. It soon emerged that the government was aiming both to increase the facilities the Imperial Bank offered them to £1 million, and to lower the interest paid on such a sum. In return, the Bank was offered continued status as a bank authorised to deal in foreign exchange on behalf of the ECC, a certain amount of exchange (probably £60 000) to cover its remittances to Britain, and the opportunity to become one of Bank Melli's correspondents in London and Iraq.[4]

The Iranian request for further funds raised the question of the lending limit in the Bank's Concession. The Bank's lending to the government was supposed to be limited to one-third of the paid-up capital of the Bank, even though this benchmark had been regularly ignored in the past. A draft 'Appendix 6' to its Concession was prepared by the Bank in April 1940 to allow lending to be increased up to the level of the paid-up capital, or £1 million.[5] However the British Treasury, which was exercising tight exchange controls in wartime Britain, refused to sanction such a move.[6]

After the usual tortuous negotiations a new Sterling Agreement was signed on 13 October.[7] The Bank retained the status of an authorised bank but the conditions seemed even more onerous than in 1939. Article 4 obliged the Bank to grant to the Bank Melli a Sterling overdraft of up to £500 000 at an interest rate of 2.5% per annum to be paid in London. Article 6 obliged the Bank to give the ECC a Sterling overdraft of up to £200 000, again at 2.5% interest. This overdraft was not only to be a clearing settlement for the Bank's surplus sales of foreign exchange but also, if required, against promissory notes. As the Imperial Bank in the autumn of 1940 was charging 10% interest on commercial loans for 45 days, and 12% for longer periods, the 2.5% interest rate on what was effectively a £700 000 unsecured loan to the Iranian government was very far from an ideal arrangement for the Bank.

In retrospect, however, the most significant feature of the Agreement was the terms on which the Bank's foreign exchange operations were to be conducted. In those parts of its foreign exchange operations where sales and purchases balanced, the Bank was to retain as its profit 0.5% of the official buying rate, and any surplus profit was to be credited to the ECC. Article 6, however, obliged the ECC to take over the surplus of purchases over sales of foreign exchange against payment in Rials at a 'middle rate', defined as the buying rate in Rials to the US$ plus half the difference between the buying and selling rates. Surplus sales over purchases would be covered by a payment in foreign exchange by the ECC and would be taken over by the Imperial Bank against payment in Rials at the middle rate. It was these surplus sales that could be covered by the £200 000 overdraft from the Bank. This clause was to have unforeseen and lucrative consequences for the Imperial Bank following the Allied occupation of Iran.

In the meantime, however, the 1940 Agreement's provisions for the remittance of profits to Britain were meagre. The Bank was to receive in London the interest on its loans to the Iranian government. In addition, if the overdraft facilities were not used, the Bank was allowed to remit out of its Rial profits a sum not exceeding £17 500. Finally, the Bank continued to be allowed to remit its profits from foreign exchange operations such as the purchase of usance bills against exports, commission earned on credits opened outside Iran for imports of goods into the country, and interest on bills drawn outside the country. However, even these profits were not to represent a 'higher return than 5.37% per annum on the employment of foreign exchange capital employed in this way'. As a consolation, the Imperial Bank was given a 20 million Rial overdraft facility at the Bank Melli.

Over the next year, relations between the Iranian government and the Imperial Bank were generally good. In February 1941 the Bank Melli opened an account with the Imperial Bank in London. The Bank's more relaxed

23 Esfahan branch in the 1890s.

24 Shiraz branch in the 1890s.

25 The road from Bushire to Shiraz in the 1890s.

26 Omnibus for Tehran–Qum road, 1890s.

27 Imperial Bank hockey team, Tehran 1911. V. L. Walter, standing fourth from right; E. Wilkinson, standing fifth from right.

28 F. A. G. Grey, Accountant at Tabriz in 1909, on a picnic.

29 1911 Imperial Government of Persia Sterling Loan Bond.

30 Chief Office, Tehran, on occasion of Reza Shah's Coronation, 1926.

31 The new Chief Office, 1938.

32 Cashiers' Hall, Chief Office in the 1930s.

33 Laying the foundation stone of Chief Office, Tehran, 9 January 1930. On the left are E. Wilkinson (in top hat) and H. E. Teymurtash, the Minister of Court.

35 Tabriz Manager's house 1930.

38 Shiraz Manager's house, 1950.

34 Bushire Manager's house 1910.

37 Northcote House, Bombay, 1926.

36 Khorramshahr Manager's house, 1948.

39 Rasht branch in 1931.

40 Esfahan branch in 1941.

41 Basra branch before 1929.

42 Basra branch in the 1930s.

44 Sir Hugh Barnes and Colonel Sir A. Henry McMahon walking to

43 Manager Bandar Abbas (E. S. Matheson) riding to the office on the
Bank donkey, 1931.

45 Staff of Tabríz branch, 1924, O. A. Butters (Manager), sitting fourth on the left, and G. R. Wright (Accountant), third from left.

46 Chief Office Staff, 1940. Front row seated, left to right F. Williams, H. B. Sinclair, P. C. Arnott, J. F. Burton, G. S. Goldsworthy, R. H. O. N. Roe, Issa Abtin, H. Musker, V. L. Walter, T. Sheahan, Ismail Dehlavi, H. E. A. Platt, R. W. Haig, C. D. Lynn, T. Quillim, McD'...

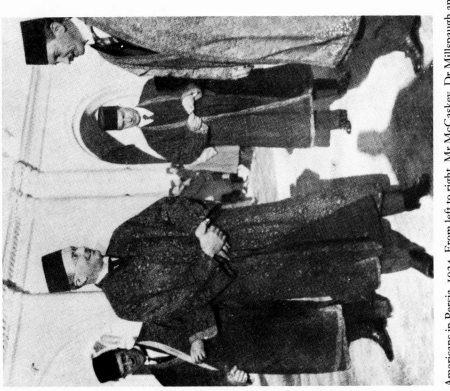

47 Americans in Persia, 1924. From left to right, Mr McCaskey, Dr Millspaugh and Colonel MacCormack, January 1924.

50 Mrs V. Evans, feeding her turkeys, Ahwaz, 1930.

49 W. R. Ward, Manager, Rasht, 1931.

52 Mr and Mrs Evans and friend, Ahwaz, 1930.

48 Mrs K. M. Ayrton, hawking in Ahwaz, 1923.

51 Basra Amateur Dramatics Society, Basra 1932.

54 Bank staff crossing the desert from Damascus to Baghdad, 1924.

55 The Nairn bus.

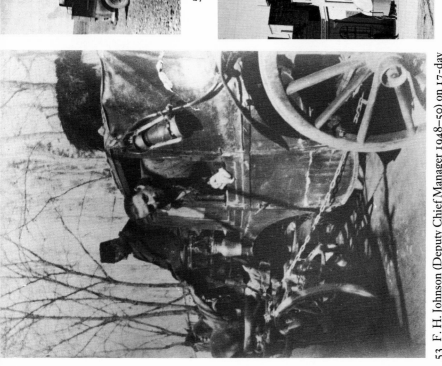

53 F. H. Johnson (Deputy Chief Manager 1948–50) on 17–day journey from Tehran to Baghdad, 1928.

56 Abol Hassan Ebtehaj and his wife, Azar, in the mid-1950s.

relationship with the Iranian government after July 1939 was matched by an improvement in its commercial business. The first year of the War in Europe saw something of a boom in Iran, as merchants and official organisations built up their stocks of essential commodities in anticipation of later shortages, while the government maintained its modernisation programme. There was a boom in credits opened abroad by the Bank, as the difficulties and risks in wartime shipping led buyers and sellers to use bankers' credits; sellers were naturally reluctant to ship goods against payment on arrival at destination. In the two months between 6 July 1939, when the Imperial Bank was allowed to resume opening credits freely, and 5 September, credits were opened to the value of over £44 000. Chief Office expanded its import credits fourfold between September 1939 and March 1940. Large credits were also opened on behalf of the government – including £90 000 against iron rails and other large amounts for steel, motor tyres and spare parts.

Other war-related opportunities for foreign exchange business were also taken. In August 1940 the Bank reopened the branch at Zahedan which had been closed in March 1939. The disruption of sea trade led to a revival of the overland route from Iran to India which passed through the town.[8] There were appeals from the local merchants, who were largely Indian, for the Imperial Bank to reopen on the grounds that the Bank Melli was providing an inadequate service, and in August the Imperial Bank obliged.[9] The new branch rapidly built up a large business financing exports of almonds, cumin and poppy seeds, and pistachio nuts, against tea imports from India.

The Bank was less interested in purely 'inland business' than in foreign exchange, for the simple reason that it could not remit the profits it earned on such business. Nevertheless, the demand for the Bank's facilities was considerable, and as funds were released from contractors' advances – which fell from 19 million Rials in March 1940 to 5 million by September of the same year – so they were employed in commercial business. In the half-year ending September 1940 the total of bills discounted by Chief Office was 54.1 million Rials, compared to 38 million Rials in the half-year ending September 1939.

By the spring and summer of 1940, however, as the situation in Europe looked increasingly bleak for Britain, the Bank began to adopt more cautious lending policies and the need for such policies was reinforced by uncertainties and disruption in the bazaars. 'Our policy must be to conserve our sterling resources and undertake no commitments that we cannot be sure of meeting or liquidating', London Office advised Walter in June 1940, '... Internal risks, including those at Chief Office, should be cleared of all but genuine short trade bills and secured short advances.'[10]

During the second half of 1940 and the beginning of 1941, the Bank paid increasing attention to maintaining liquidity. However, such caution had its compensation because the Bank found it possible to charge higher interest rates. By March 1941 most branches charged 12% per annum on their discounts and inland bills. The Bank's 20 million Rial overdraft with the Bank Melli was not used, although Walter did use its existence to maintain lending at a higher level than would otherwise have been the case.[11]

Tension grew in the spring of 1941. In May 1941 Rashid Ali fled from Baghdad to Iran after British Forces had toppled his government and occupied Iraq. Far more significantly, on 22 June 1941, Germany invaded the Soviet Union. This made the German presence in Iran a matter of immediate concern to Iran's northern neighbour. The Bank's response to the growing likelihood that Iran would become involved in the War could only be to exercise the greatest caution. 'We continue to restrict credit', Walter reported to London on 14 June 1941, 'and I fear that in Chief Office we may temporarily have reached a non-profit paying basis.'[12] By July contingency plans were being made in case the Bank had to evacuate Iran. It was hoped that damage could be limited by handing over the Bank's business to the safekeeping of the Bank Melli.[13] Meanwhile all hatches were battened down. At the end of July the Bank refused the Anglo–Iranian Oil Company's request for a 10 million Rial overdraft, as Walter did not wish to further reduce his lending to the bazaar. 'Our total inland risks in Iran', Walter explained, 'are already at a level which precludes our reducing by a further Rls 10 000 000 without weakening our standing at a time when our Bank is considered to be a potent factor in the maintenance of British influence in this country.'[14] Within a month, British and Soviet troops had invaded Iran.

11.3 INVASION AND CRISIS 1941–42

During August 1941 tension mounted in Iran. There were British and Soviet demands for the expulsion of the German community from Iran. The country became of vital strategic importance to the Allied war effort, as it offered the only alternative route to hazardous Arctic convoys by which Britain could send war supplies to Russia. On 16 August the Iranian government was warned by the Allies to remove four-fifths of all the Germans on its territory, or face the consequences. The Iranians refused to bow to this pressure and at dawn on 25 August British and Soviet troops invaded the country. There was some resistance by the Iranian Army and much panic in areas threatened by the Soviet Forces, but on 28 August the government ordered a ceasefire. The country was to be occupied for the next four years.[15]

The invasion did not come as a surprise to Walter, and it is clear that he had been privy to the British preparations. On 18 August he had telegraphed all the Bank's branches that he expected a 'crisis will develop any day now', and regular confidential warnings were issued until the day of the invasion.[16]

Prior to the Allied invasion Walter arranged for 5 million Rials to be available in Khorramshahr, and 1 million Rials in Kermanshah, ready for the use of British troops when they arrived.[17] C. F. Warr, then head of Chief Office's Foreign Exchange Department, was given the hazardous task of getting funds to the branches, although he was not informed by Walter of the ultimate purpose of his mission:

they booked me on the Tehran-Ahwaz train, a two-sleeper coupe. At the end of each coach there were two sleepers, and the rest were four and I took these two cases of notes, big suitcases, and deposited them on the rack and I was assured that as we had paid for both seats nobody else would come in. About 10 minutes or a quarter of an hour before we left the guard ... ushered in another passenger, who was a German, and who, I learnt later was specially sent down upon the eve of the Invasion by British and Russian troops to go to Bandar Shahpur and scuttle the two German merchant ships that were there. So there I was sitting in this two-seater, two bunk coupe, with six million rials on me and no defence against a Nazi. Anyway it all worked out all right and we got down there, arrived in the morning, spent the day in Ahwaz ... the Manager in Khorramshahr, F. H. Johnson, came up to meet me in Ahwaz and relieve me of my booty and he took it on and I went back to Tehran.[18]

The Allied invasion was so swift, and Iranian resistance crushed so quickly, that the Bank's British staff in Iran were only momentarily at risk. There were, however, uncomfortable moments for some. F. H. Johnson remembered the start of the British assault on Khorramshahr, where as Manager he was assisted by Angus Macqueen:

I was sleeping on the roof and woke up to an infernal din. It was a first class bombardment and I shot off my roof pretty smartly and told Angus Macqueen to do the same. Angus came over to my place and there were a few nasty pieces of metal dropping from the British guns ... And then of course the evacuation started. At about seven o'clock we saw the Persian Army and Navy retreating past the Bank house. All these chaps were going past armed with rifles etc. past our main gates, which wasn't very pleasant, so I said to Angus Macqueen, 'We'll stay inside'. And we stayed inside until about ten o'clock when suddenly appeared a British Officer and an Indian Army Officer who had come in with the Tenth Indian Division ... They didn't expect to find us alive but they found two very much alive Englishmen. I brought them into my house and we gave them breakfast. I always remember so well that we had some eggs and bacon.[19]

In Tehran there were only a few hours of tension. In the early hours of 25 August, the Bank's British staff, in accordance with a pre-arranged signal, assembled on British Legation property, either in Tehran or at Gulhak. Walter immediately asked permission to open the Bank and after some delay this was granted. He reached Chief Office at 9.30 a.m., two hours later than the normal opening time, and the Bank was immediately opened. 'This delay had occasioned some uneasiness in town', Walter later wrote, 'but our opening had a re-assuring effect.'[20] The Bank had hardly any withdrawals from depositors, and indeed between 20 August and 30 September the Bank's current account balances increased from 102.8 million Rials to 172.6 million Rials, much of which seems to have come from withdrawals from the Bank Melli.[21] Clearly many Iranians considered their funds would be safer in a British bank than in a local institution.

The Allied occupation brought rapid political change. On 16 September Reza Shah abdicated in favour of his 22-year-old son, Mohammad Reza Shah. Tehran was briefly occupied by Allied Forces. Subsequently the country divided into three zones, with Soviet troops occupying most of the north, British troops occupying most of the south, with Tehran and some other towns left unoccupied. In January 1942 Britain, the Soviet Union and Iran signed an alliance allowing the Allies the right to convey war supplies to the Soviet Union through the country, and giving them control of the transport system in order to implement this. The Allies guaranteed to withdraw their troops within six months of the War's end.[22]

The Allied occupation brought liberalisation in many fields of Iranian life. The young Shah, at least in this period, was less dictatorial than his father, and Cabinet-led government revived. By 1942 trade unions had reformed and opposition leaders were released from prison. Despite Allied censorship, the Iranian press was freer than under Reza Shah.[23] There was also seen a marked liberalisation of the previous government's economic controls, with the abolition of many trade monopolies and the relaxation of import restrictions.

After August 1941 the Iranian economy was subjected to severe dislocation. The Trans-Iranian railway was commandeered to carry supplies to the Soviet Union. At the same time, Allied military spending in Iran soared as the Allies embarked on a large-scale improvement of Iran's transport infrastructure. In December 1941 the British Army took over the management of the Trans-Iranian railway as far north as Tehran, from where responsibility passed to the Soviets. They constructed new track and imported new locomotives. Meanwhile, the British Royal Engineers and the Danish firm of Kampsax, which had supervised the construction of the Trans-Iranian railway, recruited 60 000 Iranians who widened and resurfaced about 3000 miles of north–south roads. The United Kingdom Commercial Corporation (UKCC), which had come to Iran to purchase essential commodities before the Allied intervention, organised a land transport service. It hired 1200 lorries (with their drivers), out of the Iranian total of 4000, until more were imported under Lend Lease arrangements in 1942.

Table 11.3. *Inflation in Iran 1939–45*[24]

	Wholesale prices	Cost of living
1939	100	100
June 1941	141	145
June 1942	239	254
June 1943	422	629
June 1944	513	850
March 1945	461	696

The result of Allied spending, and in particular the associated rapid expansion in money supply which will be discussed below, was inflation. There had been some inflation in the 1930s, but as Table 11.3 shows, during the War years, and especially in 1942 and 1943, the rate became very rapid.

Other Allied policies also played a role in Iran's inflationary spiral. In September 1941, for example, the Allies insisted on a devaluation of the Iranian currency from its official rate of 68.80 Rials to the pound, to a buying rate of 140 and a selling rate of 142. This made Allied purchases inside Iran much cheaper, but reduced the benefit to Iran of this spending. As prices soared and speculation became rife, a crop failure in 1942 brought famine to many areas.

For the Imperial Bank, however, the period during the Allied occupation was just like old times. As the British government's bank in Iran, the Imperial Bank found itself returned to the centre of economic decision-making. At the same time restrictions on the Bank's operations were relaxed. The controls on profit remittance, for example, were soon abandoned. In October 1941 the Bank submitted a request to the Iranian government to be allowed to remit £192 071, representing unremitted earnings, remittances to Britain by British staff in Iran (which had not been allowed since 1938), and the cost of items such as stationery and building materials which the Bank had imported.[25] In the following month the government agreed to allow the Bank the foreign exchange it required to make these remittances.[26]

The Iranian government's ability to relax its exchange controls reflected the new foreign exchange situation. Soon after the Allied occupation the Iranian government found itself increasingly short not of Sterling but of Rials, as the military required large sums of local currency to purchase their requirements. By October 1941 the ECC had insufficient local currency to cover the Imperial Bank's operations, and the Bank granted it a Rial overdraft facility at 5% per annum, reduced to 4.5% in the following month. The size of this overdraft climbed rapidly, and reached 190 million Rials by end of December 1941.

During December Walter approached the British Legation about the local currency situation, recommending that the Iranian government must be encouraged to issue more notes.[27] This was a step which the Iranians were most reluctant to take. The maximum authorised circulation of notes had been fixed at 2 billion Rials (£14 million) on 16 June 1941, and actual note circulation by the end of 1941 was around 1.8 billion Rials against which a metallic reserve of 60% in gold and silver coin or bullion was maintained. A large expansion of the note issue was seen as likely to be highly inflationary, as the volume of goods could not be expanded quickly to match it. Over the next two months, therefore, the Iranian authorities took no action. The Bank, increasingly concerned that it would be unable to advance the British authorities their immediate requirements, pressed the ECC to repay its overdraft, but in March 1942 it still stood at 170 million Rials.

In the middle of March 1942 the situation became critical. The ECC notified the Imperial Bank that the acute shortage of local currency meant that it could no longer deliver Rials to the Bank against sales of Sterling by the British government. This meant that the Imperial Bank would soon be unable to provide the local currency required by the British authorities in Iran. On 26 March Walter held long discussions at the Legation with Sir Reader Bullard, the British Minister, and the Financial Adviser to the Legation, W. A. B. Iliff. It was decided that the Iranian government would be requested to pass legislation to increase the note issue by at least 500 million Rials (or 25%) by 31 March, and to deliver 200 million Rials local currency to the Imperial Bank by 30 March. A variety of threats were proposed if these instructions were not obeyed. It was suggested, for example, that the British government could print and issue notes in Britain and distribute them in Iran. The idea of reviving the Imperial Bank's note issue was discussed, but it was discovered that the Bank had destroyed the old note plates.[28] The Bank was, however, able to provide the most serious threat to the Iranian government for Walter agreed, if something was not done about the currency question, to close the Bank to the public from noon on Monday 30th. 'I need not say I do not relish the prospect of having to take the action indicated', Walter explained to London Office, 'but I agreed as it is impossible that the Allied war effort should be hindered by the obstructive tactics of the local authorities.'[29] The ultimatum was conveyed by Sir Reader Bullard to the Iranian Prime Minister.

The government had little choice but to obey. The cessation of payments by the Imperial Bank would have caused a major financial crisis, which would have more than likely overwhelmed the Bank Melli. On 30 March the Prime Minister told Bullard that a Bill would be rushed through the Majles the following day to increase the note issue by 700 million Rials, and that as soon as the Bill was law he would repay the ECC debt to the Bank.[30] The

Legation's Financial Adviser, Iliff, had no doubt that the 'unusual expedition' shown by the Iranian government was largely a result of the threat to close the Imperial Bank, and the Bank was promised future rewards for its patriotism. Walter had expressed, Iliff minuted two months later:

> some misgivings that the fact that he had allowed the Bank to be made a willing instrument in carrying through the policy of His Majesty's Government might be 'held against' the Bank by the Persian Government. He was looking rather to the after-the-war situation. He, therefore, asked for 'extra diplomatic support'. On the authority of His Majesty's Minister I gave him the assurance that if the circumstances that he apprehended should develop, the necessary diplomatic support would be forthcoming.[31]

Unfortunately for the Bank, events after the War were to show that the 'extra diplomatic support' of British governments had a limited value.

Meanwhile, the currency crisis continued. The Iranian government clearly wanted an appreciation in the Rial's value against Sterling, and proposed to Bullard that the currency should no longer be fixed but be allowed to float. The British government was opposed to any such move, primarily because of fears that the Iranian currency would appreciate against Sterling.[32] On 1 April, the day the overdraft to the Imperial Bank was repaid, the government suddenly instructed all banks to cease making any purchases of foreign exchange. The Minister of Finance, Mr Bader, explained that he 'wished to have an opportunity of considering the position and of formulating a policy'.[33]

The Bank again came to the assistance of the British government. Walter agreed to provide an emergency Rial overdraft for British interests in Iran, including the Armed Forces, the UKCC and the Anglo–Iranian Oil Company. The overdraft was to the limit of the Bank's cash reserves. At the same time Walter agreed with the Legation that the Iranian government was to be denied any facilities, and any account holder requiring Rials had to apply to the British Legation. By May this overdraft had reached nearly 250 million Rials, on which interest of 4.5% per annum was payable.[34]

During April the Legation exercised further pressure on the Iranian government to expand the note issue. Walter was always in attendance as an adviser to British officials during the negotiations. While the British argued for an expansion of the note issue by 1.5 billion Rials the Iranians attempted to secure a higher exchange rate and the conversion into gold of at least some of their Sterling holdings. The United States government, anxious not to have any disruption to the vital supply line to the Soviet Union, urged compromise on the British.[35] The eventual outcome was a Financial Agreement between Britain and the Iranian government signed on 26 May 1942. The Iranian government undertook to ensure an adequate supply of Iranian currency 'to finance all commercial and financial transactions between the

Sterling Area on the one hand and Iran on the other'. The exchange rate was set at 128 Rials to the pound for buying, and at 130 Rials for selling (32 and 32.50 Rials to the US dollar), lower than the Iranians had wanted but still a concession by the British government. Perhaps the most significant feature of the agreement was the British government's undertaking to provide gold up to 40% of all increases in Iran's Sterling holdings. Only with such a clause could the Iranian objection that the desired expansion of the note issue was out of proportion to the Bank Melli's gold reserves be overcome. The Agreement was to last until the withdrawal of British Forces from Iran after the end of the War.[36]

The signing of this Agreement, and the expansion of the note issue agreed earlier in the year, was followed by a temporary amelioration in the currency situation. Banks were allowed again to purchase foreign exchange, and the temporary overdraft facilities with the British government were ended. At the same time the granting of a Rial overdraft to the ECC was resumed, and by the end of May this already exceeded 170 million Rials. 'So we are to some extent back where we were', the Bank's London Office reflected, 'with the difference that the increase in the Note Circulation must have eased matters, at least for the time being.'[37] In June 1942 the Iranian government felt sufficient confidence in its Sterling position to pay off the £700 000 overdraft the Bank had given to the ECC under the 1940 Agreement.

In the autumn of 1942 the currency situation became tense again. The Anglo–Iranian Financial Agreement was presented to the Majles for ratification on 11 June, but objections to it caused unanticipated delays. In January 1943 the British government agreed to convert into gold 60% of the increase in Iran's Sterling balances, and this concession finally led to the ratification of the Agreement by the Majles in June 1943. There was a similar foreign exchange agreement with the Americans, who agreed a 100% gold conversion figure.[38] As a result of these agreements, Iran's holdings of gold kept pace with the expansion of the note issue during the War, and the country also acquired a large holding of Sterling.

In August 1942, however, there were more immediate considerations. Shortages of local currency were again growing. The Imperial Bank found it possible to extract supplies of Rials from the Bank Melli only by securing the intervention of the Legation.[39] During the first week of September the Bank Melli refused to issue any local currency to the Imperial Bank unless the Majles undertook to expand the note issue, and eventually a bill for an increase of 300 million Rials was ratified.[40] In October the government, under pressure from the Allies, presented a further bill to the Majles for the expansion of the note issue by another 2 billion Rials. However, it did not press the matter strongly, probably because the government was using the opposition in the Majles to extract concessions from the British over the Financial Agreement.[41]

The British government resorted to coercion to force the Iranian hand. A British military parade was arranged in Tehran, and supplies of desperately needed wheat delayed.[42] As the supplies of local currency ran short, military preparations were made by the British Army to seize control of the Bank Melli. 'Reserve of rials held by us sufficient for two days', the Army Commander in Chief telegraphed to the War Office in London on 13 November:

... Object of plan is therefore to secure control of notes in National Bank within 48 hours of issues to us being stopped. Should this prove necessary banks will be seized by Second Northants. No opposition expected. Legation officials will then try to induce Bank officials hand over strong room keys. Failing this doors will be forced by R. E. Det. accompanying Two Northants. Strong guards will be placed on bank after forcing also guards on Imperial Bank British and American Legations.[43]

By 19 November the Iranians had succumbed to the pressures. After agreeing to a 500 million Rial note increase, the Majles ratified a bill handing their powers over the note issue to a new Bank Note Reserve Control Board. A week earlier the Majles had authorised the appointment of Dr Millspaugh as Administrator General of Finances, a move which seems to have been motivated on the Iranian side by a wish for, as one Foreign Minister put it, American advisers 'to act as a cushion between British–Soviet conflicting political interests'.[44] Millspaugh was appointed a member of the new Note Board.

The new arrangements meant that the paper currency in circulation could be expanded much more easily. By March 1945 it had reached 7.8 billion Rials, or nearly a sixfold increase since 1941.[45] The problem of finding sufficient local currency to meet Allied requirements had been solved.

11.4 THE RETURN OF MR EBTEHAJ 1943–45

On Christmas Eve 1942 Walter heard on Tehran radio that Abol Hassan Ebtehaj had been appointed Governor of the Bank Melli. Ebtehaj had worked at the Ministry of Finance after leaving the Imperial Bank in 1936, and in 1939 had been made vice-Governor of the Bank Melli. Walter had subsequently had dealings with Ebtehaj in that capacity, and Ebtehaj had been involved in the negotiations leading to the 1940 Sterling Agreement. Although the Bank's relations with Ebtehaj had always been cordial and polite, Walter was in no doubt that Ebtehaj's forceful personality and strong views would soon make themselves felt, probably at the Imperial Bank's expense. 'We hear Mr Ebtehaj', Walter wrote to London reporting his appointment to the Bank Melli, 'is already enquiring into the activities of the Exchange Commission ... I think that apart from cutting down its authority Mr Ebtehaj will endeavour to transform the Commission into an adjunct of the BMI. I feel also he may endeavour to secure for the BMI some of the foreign exchange business which now comes our way.'[46]

Walter's words were prophetic. Over the next eight years Ebtehaj was to loom over the Imperial Bank, a brilliant fireball of energy determined to restrict the British Bank's activities or, perhaps, as the Bank came to believe, drive it from Iran altogether. During the War years his freedom of manoeuvre to challenge the Bank was circumscribed. However, he formed an excellent relationship with the young Shah and this gave him a strong power base. After the abdication of Reza Shah, Ebtehaj later recalled:

> there was no central government ... The Shah was a playboy, nobody took notice of the Shah. I was appointed as Governor. He didn't know anything about it. I went to say I am the new Governor. We met for the first time and I liked him, from the first day, he liked me very much. He came to the point he'd accept anything I said'.[47]

At the centre of Ebtehaj's strategy at this time was the desire to concentrate currency, exchange and financial affairs in his hands at the Bank Melli. This meant the elimination of competing bodies within Iran, such as the ECC. It also meant a premier position for the Bank Melli in the banking system of the country. 'I consider this Bank as State Central Bank, therefore it should be a dominating factor', Ebtehaj told a meeting of the Note Reserve Control Board in June 1944, '... and not parallel or in equal position with its competing and rival institutions'.[48] To the Imperial Bank, and to his opponents in Iran, Ebtehaj's policies stemmed from an exceptional egotism. The Bank also believed Ebtehaj held a strong grudge against it for its refusal to promote him in the 1930s. To Ebtehaj, who even his detractors never denied was highly intelligent and utterly uncorruptible, it was a matter of professional competence and the need to eliminate political interference from Iranian financial affairs.[49]

During the first eight months of 1943 Ebtehaj focused his attention, as Walter had predicted, on trying to secure the abolition of the ECC and capture a share of the Imperial Bank's exchange business. Within days of Ebtehaj's appointment the Iranian government complained to the Legation about the terms on which the Bank handled, on the ECC's behalf, the British Army's exchange business.[50] It was suggested that the Army might instead place its business with the Bank Melli. This proposal did not find favour at the Legation nor with the Imperial Bank.

Yet Walter was the first to admit that Ebtehaj and the government had a strong point. The kernel of the problem was Article 6 of the 1940 Sterling Agreement and the 'uncovered' part of the ECC overdraft. On covered exchange operations the Bank received a fixed 0.5% profit. But during 1942 the Bank experienced a vast excess of purchases over sales, and this, together with the large margin between buying and selling rates, resulted in the Bank earning substantial exchange profits at the ECC's expense on uncovered operations. The surge in the Bank's profits in Iran during 1942–43 was substantially influenced by this factor.

As early as October 1942 Walter had confessed to 'feeling somewhat unhappy' about Article 6 which, he observed, had been framed when 'operations of the present magnitude and one-sided nature were not envisaged'.[51] By March 1943, after negotiations with Ebtehaj in the New Year, Walter was willing to accept a reduction on the Bank's uncovered operations from its then current 0.75% level to 0.25%, provided the government took over the exchange risk. 'I rather welcome', he wrote to London, 'the placing of our operations on a more normal footing.'[52] The greater problem, as Walter saw matters, was if Ebtehaj secured complete control over foreign exchange in Iran. 'If Mr Ebtehaj held all the sterling', Walter wrote to London in June, 'it would only be a question of time before he made difficulties in providing us with cover for our sales, or brought pressure on our Customers to purchase direct from the BMI.'[53] For some months, therefore, Walter fought a battle to preserve the independent existence of the ECC.[54]

The result was something of a draw. On 4 September 1943 a new foreign exchange agreement was signed by the Bank Melli and the Imperial Bank, replacing the 1940 agreement. The new agreement effectively reduced the substantial foreign exchange profits the Bank had been making since September 1941 and was a significant factor in the fall-off in the Bank's Iranian profits after 1943. While under the 1940 agreement all operations by the Imperial Bank and the Bank Melli had been for account for the ECC, the Bank Melli now took over the business of exchange settlement, and accepted the risk of uncovered positions. As a result Bank Melli received the greater part of the difference between the buying and selling rates. The Imperial Bank was allowed one-quarter of 1% commission on all its operations in Sterling or Dollars. The Bank Melli received the rest of the margin, or profit, on all transactions in Sterling or Dollars.[55] Thus if the Imperial Bank purchased £1 million from the British government, it received £2500 commission. As the exchange margin was 2 Rials per £ (the difference between buying and selling rates of 128 and 130), or over 1.5%, Bank Melli received approximately five-sixths of the exchange profit on all transactions in Sterling or Dollars done by the Imperial Bank, including purchases from the British government.[56] The ECC, however, was not actually abolished, retaining a rather shadowy existence over the next couple of years, nor did the Bank Melli secure the accounts of the British Army.

In 1944 Ebtehaj, energetic as ever, relieved the Imperial Bank of its business with the American Army. The American presence in Iran had grown rapidly after 1942. Dr Millspaugh arrived in Tehran at the end of 1942. The Full Powers Law in May 1943 granted him wide economic and financial powers, and most important economic posts in the Iranian government were soon filled with Americans. During 1942 American troops also arrived to assist in the transport of supplies to the Soviet Union. They took over the operation of the Trans-Iranian railway, and were soon engaged in extensive infrastructure work developing the port facilities at Khorramshahr, Bandar Abbas and Bandar Shahpur, and building roads and airports.[57]

During 1942 and 1943 the Imperial Bank handled the entire business of the American Forces in Iran. This was not a situation which Ebtehaj found satisfactory. Ebtehaj visited the American Forces' officer in charge of finance and persuaded him to give the Bank Melli some of their business. Ebtehaj later remembered:

So I said 'Would you give us a trial and if the service is not better than the Imperial Bank of Iran close your accounts.' 'Well' he said, 'All right we'll start with half of our operations with you.' And that's what they did.[58]

The Americans were clearly pleased with the Bank Melli's service, for on 12 April 1944 Walter was informed that all American Army accounts were being transferred to the Bank Melli. The official explanation was that for 'administrative reasons', the Army preferred 'to deal only with one Bank and the Bank Melli had branches in some of the centres of US Army activity' where the Imperial Bank was not established.[59]

In August 1944 Ebtehaj also paid off the ECC Rial overdraft with the Imperial Bank, depriving the Bank of a valuable source of interest.

In the meantime Ebtehaj had come into conflict with Dr Millspaugh. Millspaugh's chief achievement after arriving in Iran had been to introduce a progressive income tax bill in 1943. He also attempted to restrict profits on imports to 5%. But he found it hard to enforce such measures, and they had little practical effect. Millspaugh attempted to improve grain supplies, but his free market approach and reduction of subsidies were not well-received by poorer Iranians, nor by black marketeers. Millspaugh showed little tact in his work, and failed to appreciate the changes that had occurred in the country since he left in 1927. Perhaps the fundamental problem, though, was that while Millspaugh saw himself as engaged in a serious economic programme, even his supporters in Iran were interested mainly in the diplomatic usefulness of the American mission. During 1944 the American's relations with Iranian politicians and civil servants steadily deteriorated.[60]

In 1944 Millspaugh and Ebtehaj clashed. Such a clash was probably inevitable, as the nationalistic Ebtehaj was unlikely to respond well to instructions from an American on how to run Iran's finances. In a meeting of the Note Reserve Control Board in June 1944 Ebtehaj accused Millspaugh's Treasurer General, another American called Kenneth Le Count, of 'protecting' the Imperial Bank from his attempts to control the exchange operations. Le Count had in fact supported the Imperial Bank on several occasions, including over the need to retain an independent Exchange Commission, and this had clearly annoyed Ebtehaj. But at the meeting he also levelled wide-ranging accusations of 'fraud and dishonesty' at the American.[61] Millspaugh's request for an apology from Ebtehaj regarding these allegations, which do seem to have been unfounded, were refused. After further difficulties Millspaugh dismissed Ebtehaj from his post on 7 October for refusal to co-operate, rudeness and interference in matters outside his proper sphere of activity.[62] It was, however, a battle the American could not win. Within a few days the Iranian government had ruled that Millspaugh did not have the authority to remove the Bank Melli's Governor.[63] Ebtehaj remained at his post.

Millspaugh's power subsequently waned. In January 1945 the Majles deprived him of his economic powers, leaving to him only the financial administration. Millspaugh resigned from his post and left Iran in the following month.

Ebtehaj's defeat of Millspaugh meant that his campaign to bring Iranian banking and finance under the firm control of the Bank Melli continued with full vigour. On 15 October 1944 Walter heard that Ebtehaj had asked the Prime Minister 'for the enactment of a decree entrusting the control of foreign exchange to the BMI'.[64] The initiative was not successful, but over the next few months it was clear to all that the Imperial Bank could expect a sustained assault on its position once the War had ended. It remained to be seen if the Imperial Bank would be more successful than Millspaugh.

11.5 BANKING IN IRAN 1939–45

Table 11.4 shows the main features of the Bank's business in Iran between 1939 and 1945.[65] The most noticeable feature of the Bank's wartime business was the huge surge in deposits after 1941. The high inflation rate obviously explained much of this increase, but the Allied occupation of Iran also seems to have encouraged many depositors to place funds in the Imperial Bank. As late as June 1942 Walter reported that the Bank Melli had still not recovered from the withdrawal of confidence following the Allied entry into Iran.[66] Allied spending boosted the Imperial Bank's deposit figures and the Bank was able to increase its share of total bank deposits in Iran from 8.9% in 1939 to 22% in 1945.[67]

Table 11.4. *Imperial Bank deposits, cash and lending in Iran 1939–45* (million Rials)

Year end (20 March)	Deposits	Cash	Loans, bills and advances	Credits and guarantees	Treasury bonds
1939	178.1	75.0	110.3	54.2	—
1940	182.3	49.5	140.0	60.0	—
1941	177.7	32.9	125.0	30.3	—
1942	822.1	139.7	323.6	302.9	—
1943	1590.2	601.2	476.9	252.8	—
1944	1723.3	839.2	296.7	124.5	100
1945	1705.8	938.0	115.0	164.3	200

The Bank benefited during the middle years of the War from the relaxation of import trade controls. This is shown in the large increase in credits and guarantees in 1942. This increase largely took the form of documentary credits opened for Iranian customers to finance imports from India, the United States and elsewhere, with tea, sugar and textiles being prominent commodities. Rising prices and freer exchange conditions encouraged boom conditions in many of Iran's bazaars. 'It would scarcely be an exaggeration to say', the Manager of Tehran Bazaar office reported in September 1942, 'that importers (and the majority of our customers are directly or indirectly engaged in the import trade) have enjoyed a period of unprecedented prosperity.'[68]

The increase in the Bank's lending during 1942 and 1943 was also largely related to the booming import trade. As before the Allied occupation, however, the Bank was reluctant to expand its lending very fast. Every effort was made to restrict advances to ordinary commercial needs and to avoid any encouragement to speculators. The Bank seems to have been selective in its customers, choosing the safest and, in its view, most honest business. In March 1943 Tehran Bazaar branch reported that its lending constituted only 'a comparatively small proportion of the total banking risks'[69] in its market. Overall the Imperial Bank's share of total bank advances to the private sector seems to have fallen during the War, from 11% in 1939 to 5% in 1945.[70]

After March 1943 the Bank's lending declined. Millspaugh's regulations against speculation dampened the boom in the bazaars. There were also difficulties in the way of foreign trade in the last years of the War, although smuggling activity seems to have been extensive. By March 1945 branch Managers in such diverse cities as Hamadan, Ahwaz and Bushire were reporting dull trading conditions.[71]

The result of rapidly increasing deposits and falling advances during the last years of the War was, as Table 11.4 indicates, a large accumulation of cash. It was the size of this cash mountain which led Walter in 1944 to recommend that the Bank should invest in Iranian Government Treasury Bonds. These were first offered for sale in March 1944 by the Millspaugh administration. Walter argued that the Bonds would not only be a suitable channel for the employment of the Bank's large surplus funds but it would be politic for the Bank to invest in them as it would lay itself open to criticism if it used depositors' money simply to maintain a highly liquid position. Walter applied for 100 million Rials of Bonds, which had a six-month maturity period, as soon as they were issued. This amounted to a fifth of the total issue. The Bonds were initially not particularly well-received and the Bank could claim, with some justification that it 'had done much to popularize them with a very suspicious public'.[72] At the beginning of 1945 the Bank increased its holding of Treasury bonds to 200 million Rials.

The end of the Second World War, therefore, found the Imperial Bank in a highly liquid position. It had recovered from the low point of the 1930s and its reputation in Iran's bazaars seems to have been high. It could expect, if left to itself, to play a leading role in Iran's anticipated post-War growth. Ebtehaj, however, had other plans.

12

THE END IN IRAN

On 30 July 1952 the Bank closed for business in Iran. It did not, however, cease banking. After the end of the War the Bank's expansion in the Gulf was maintained. Branches were opened at Dubai in 1946 and Muscat in 1948. Elsewhere, the Bank opened in Lebanon in 1946, Syria in 1947 and Jordan in 1949. In 1950 two branches were opened in Saudi Arabia. The Bank's new geographical orientation was symbolised by the adoption of new names. In August 1949 the Imperial Bank of Iran was renamed The British Bank of Iran and the Middle East (BBIME), and in July 1952 it became simply The British Bank of the Middle East (BBME). The result of this remarkable transformation was that the withdrawal from Iran caused only a ripple in the Bank's balance sheet. The balance sheet total grew from £29 692 684 in 1945 to £58 786 036 in 1952. It fell to £49 811 993 in 1953, but began growing in the following year and reached £65 803 314 in 1955.

This chapter, however, is concerned not with the Bank's growth in the Arab world, but with the events which led the Bank, after 62 years, to leave Iran. The increasing importance of the non-Iranian branches allows an examination of the Bank's overall performance after 1945 to be reserved for Volume 2. Table 12.1 therefore, summarises the main features of the Bank's business in Iran between 1946 and 1952.

The Bank's post-War deposits in Iran peaked in 1947, and subsequently declined. The large fall between 1949 and 1950 is particularly striking, as is the further decline between 1950 and 1952. Loans, bills discounted and advances peaked in 1948, but fell by 28% in the following year and fluctuated at this level between 1949 and 1951. The 1952 figure showed a dramatic fall over the previous year. The ratio of loans, bills discounted and advances to deposits was low in 1946 and 1947 (12% and 15%), partly because of the Bank's obligation before 1949 to buy government Treasury Bonds, and also

Table 12.1. *Imperial Bank–BBIME deposits, cash and lending in Iran 1946–52*
(million Rials)

Year end (20 March)	Deposits	Cash	Loans, bills discounted and advances	Treasury bonds
1946	1688.6	956.1	204.9	250
1947	1863.7	796.0	279.9	245
1948	1745.7	387.6	556.7	220
1949	1541.2	628.8	398.3	174
1950	1093.4	267.9	367.8	—
1951	866.0	na	403.3	—
1952	500.7	83.4	155.3	—

Note: na = not available.

because the Bank Melli's refusal to rediscount bills and government paper meant that high cash reserves had to be maintained. However, the advances/deposits ratio reached 38% in 1948, and 46% in 1951. This represented quite a change, especially as after 1949 55% of the Bank's deposits had to be redeposited interest free with the Bank Melli.

The Bank's dwindling importance in Iranian banking is illustrated in Table 12.2, which shows its share of total bank deposits and advances between 1946 and 1952. The Imperial Bank held 21% of total bank deposits in Iran in 1946, but this proportion dwindled to reach a mere 3% in 1952. Its share of non-government bank advances peaked at 12.5% in 1948, before falling away to only 2.5% by 1952. The Bank seems to have retained a leading position in foreign exchange banking at least until 1949. Yet the change since the late 1920s, when the Imperial Bank had virtually monopolised banking in Iran, was remarkable.

The Bank's declining business was reflected in falling profits. Profits from the non-Iranian branches had become an important element in the Bank's overall profitability by the early 1950s. Table 12.3, therefore, confines itself to the Bank's profits in Iran, but the final column provides, for comparative purposes, the published profits of the Bank as a whole.

Table 12.3 shows that the Bank's Iranian business continued, after the boom years of the War, to yield profits, which were practically all remitted to Britain. In 1950, however, the Bank's business in Iran became loss-making, a trend culminating in the large loss shown for 1952. But by this period, as the Bank's overall published profit figures suggest and Volume 2 will demonstrate, there were other sources of profits and the Iranian losses could be absorbed. The Bank steadily paid a 9% dividend in each year

The end in Iran

Table 12.2. *Imperial Bank–BBIME share of total bank deposits and advances in Iran 1946–52* (million Rials)

Year end (20 March)	Total bank deposits	IBI–BBIME %	Total non-government advances[a]	IBI–BBIME %
1946	8.15	21	3.38	6
1947	9.02	21	4.31	6.5
1948	9.91	17.5	4.47	12.5
1949	10.2	15	5.28	7.5
1950	10.5	10.5	5.14	7
1951	12.37	7	5.39	7.5
1952	16.74	3	6.18	2.5

Note: [a] J. Bharier, *Economic Development in Iran 1900–70* (London, 1971), p. 243.

Table 12.3. *Imperial Bank–BBIME profits in Iran 1946–52* (£ Sterling)

Year end 20 March	Net profits (or losses) in Iran	Published profit, whole Bank
1946	181 797	134 023
1947	147 031	138 305
1948	169 297	100 344
1949	182 890	105 411
1950	(81,792)	96 949
1951	(8110)	108 089
1952	(105,140)	97 773

between 1946 and 1952, apparently impervious to the problems which beset it during the last years in Iran.

As so often with profit figures, however, they provide only a partial measure of the Bank's performance. Net profits were calculated after the deduction of charges which included a number of elements, such as provision for bad debts, new buildings and property repairs, which fluctuated from year to year. As a result the net profit figure does not provide a reliable reflection of trading performance. In the year ending March 1948, for example, charges included 28 million Rials (£218 750) for buildings, while in the following year only 2 million Rials (£15 625) was set aside. Again, in 1950 the Bank made a very large provision for bad debts and income tax, to which it became liable after the end of its Concession in 1949. The Bank privately estimated that it had made a 'profit' of £1518 rather than the loss actually registered during the year.[1]

Table 12.4. *Closing of Imperial Bank–BBIME branches in Iran 1946–52*

Branch	Date closed
Bushire	June 1949
Arak	June 1949
Tehran, Bazaar[a]	October 1949
Hamadan	March 1951
Mashad	March 1951
Rasht	September 1951
Tabriz	September 1951
Kermanshah	December 1951
Zahedan	February 1952
Esfahan	April 1952
Khorramshahr	April 1952
Shiraz	April 1952
Ahwaz	April 1952
Tehran, Chief Office	July 1952

Note: [a] Tehran Bazaar was amalgamated with Chief Office in 1949.

Despite these complexities, the view that the Bank's business was on the downturn in Iran from the late 1940s cannot be disputed. Table 12.4, which shows the elimination of the Bank's branch network in Iran, provides further evidence. The table shows that three branches were closed in 1949, with no closures in the following year. In March 1951, however, branch closures began in earnest, and by the end of July 1952 the whole branch network had disappeared.

The following three sections will examine the complex political circumstances which led to the decline of the Bank's Iranian business, and its final withdrawal from that country.

12.2 THE YEARS OF ILLUSION 1946–48

Despite the Imperial Bank's troubles in Iran in the 1930s, the lifting of many of the Reza Shah's controls and restrictions after the Allied occupation, and the high profits earned during the Second World War, seem to have calmed fears about the Bank's future, at least at Chief Manager and Board level. In 1945 V. L. Walter planned a programme of expansion in Iran, apparently with little concern for the fact that the Bank's 60-year Concession in Iran was due to expire at the beginning of 1949.

The visible strength of the Bank in Iran, in terms of bricks, mortar and apparent prestige, encouraged a belief that, whatever happened, it would continue to do business in Iran. Lord Kennet, who replaced Colonel Sir

A. Henry McMahon as Chairman of the Imperial Bank on 1 October 1945, visited Iran in 1946, and he was delighted by the high status enjoyed by the Bank. 'I was very pleasantly impressed by the position of Mr and Mrs Walter in the community', Kennet wrote, '... After the Embassy they are the Chief British residents, and exercise much influence.' Kennet was clearly convinced that such influence would not merely disappear, and he was determined that the Bank should retain its competitive position against the Bank Melli. The Bazaar Office in Tehran, he complained during his visit, was not up to the standard of the Bank's other offices, and 'must be replaced as soon as a site can be found: all the more that the BMI are building a large new Bazaar Office'.[2]

Walter's enthusiasm for Iran encouraged Kennet in his assessment of the Bank's status and future in the country. After the end of the War, Walter became an enthusiastic proponent of expanding the branch network in Iran. During Kennet's visit he suggested the Bank should reopen in Yazd and Abadan.[3] Nothing happened at that stage, primarily because the Bank was short of experienced staff, but at the end of 1947 he resumed the attack with a definite proposal to London that branches should be reopened in Yazd and Kerman. And this time he won his point. The Board authorised the opening of both branches, 'at such time as might be considered most expedient' by the Chief Manager.[4] Staff shortages, however, continued to delay the opening of the new branches, and by 1949 the political climate was no longer conducive to such a move.

Although these plans to expand the branch network were never realised, the Bank did embark on a major fixed investment programme in Iran after 1945. Between 1945 and 1950 some £500 000 was spent on property in the country. Walter appears to have been the driving force behind this investment. He argued that the building of an extension to Chief Office was 'essential if we are to retain the business and goodwill of our Customers'.[5] He was also behind the building of a large sports and recreational centre for local staff in north-west Tehran. Other substantial projects included a new home for the Deputy Chief Manager in Tehran, and a new Manager's home at Esfahan.

The enthusiasm of the Bank to expand its branch network and improve its properties in Iran could be taken as a commendable commitment to develop its banking business as well as to improve the lives of its British and local staff. In the climate of post-War Iran, however, the decisions acquire an element of the bizarre, or at least of the imprudent. 'It is fortunate indeed that the Shareholders are not aware of the employment of this £500 000 that had already been expended in the last few years', a director, Sir Geoffrey Prior, observed in July 1950, 'or it would be the subject of bitter criticism.'[6]

Prior's comment is easy to understand. Iranian nationalist and anti-foreign sentiment became increasingly strong after 1945. When the War ended, Iranian foreign policy was directed towards regaining independence by removing the Soviet and British forces of occupation. British troops finally left at the beginning of 1946, and in June Soviet troops finally went from the north.[7] But there were also many voices demanding Iran's economic independence as well. This meant developing Iran's economy and reducing the influence of foreigners over it. By late 1945 exchange controls, abolished in 1942, had been re-established, with an official policy of preserving foreign exchange reserves for expenditure on capital development. In 1949 a seven-year Development Plan was launched, entailing an expenditure of 21 million Rials. High hopes were initially held that the United States would play a leading role in funding Iran's development expenditure. But as year followed year with no American aid materialising, Iranian policy-makers had increasingly to search for internal sources of funds for their schemes.[8]

The major potential source of funds was the Anglo–Iranian Oil Company, the biggest foreign-owned company in Iran. It was an obvious target. It employed in the late 1940s some 65 000 people in Iran. It operated the world's largest refinery, at Abadan. It was a living symbol, in nationalist eyes, of the syphoning off of Iran's national wealth into foreign pockets. Oil was to emerge as the central area of conflict between Britain and Iran, and it was an area in which the Bank's destiny eventually became entwined. In December 1944 a nationalist politician, Mohammad Mosaddeq, of whom more will be heard, had introduced legislation in the Majles aimed at preventing foreign exploitation of Iranian oil. In 1946 and 1947 he led a campaign against proposed Soviet oil concessions in Iran, and during the same period he called for negotiations with Anglo–Iranian to secure 'Iran's national rights'.[9] As Iranian oil was held by post-War British governments to be of vital economic and strategic importance for Britain, the scene was set for conflict should Iranian nationalist pressure against the oil company grow.[10]

The evidence that nationalist and development aspirations were growing after 1945, and the Bank's experience in the 1930s of the directions such aspirations could take in Iran, make the Bank's optimism about its future seem unwise. But it seems even harder to understand when the special problems faced by the Imperial Bank are borne in mind. In the Bank's eyes, these problems continued to stem from one man, Abol Hassan Ebtehaj.

The Imperial Bank became more convinced than previously that Ebtehaj had a vendetta against it stemming from his complaints about the Bank before he resigned from it. 'Our difficulties come all from E.', Kennet concluded after visiting Iran in 1946.[11] He was seen as having a 'grudge' against the Bank, and of being 'jealous' of its success, of being over-emotional and incapable of rational argument. 'The Persians have a word *lars barsi* which means getting your own back, retaliation', F. H. Johnson later explained, 'and I think it was a question of *lars barsi*.'[12] This was the consensus within the Bank. 'Mr Ebtehaj', the Bank's Chief Manager explained to his British staff in August 1950, 'has been an implacable opponent of our Bank for a long time, and his hatred of our institution has not lessened with years.'[13]

In retrospect, it can be seen that the Bank's judgement was characteristic of a wider British misunderstanding of the nature and strength of Iranian nationalism. Recent research has revealed that British politicians and diplomats concerned with Iran doubted the existence of an authentic nationalist movement after 1945. Locked, at least in some respects, into a view of the country as it had been in the 1900s, they saw only irrational emotions and demagogic personalities.[14] Thus Mosaddeq, who became Prime Minister of Iran in April 1951, was regularly described by the British Ambassador of the time in his despatches to London as a 'lunatic', and characterised as being 'cunning and slippery', with 'short and bandy legs' and 'a slight reek of opium'.[15]

Ebtehaj was viewed by the Bank in much the same light and, like the Foreign Office's attitude to Mosaddeq, the view was a myopic one. There was no doubt that Ebtehaj resented his treatment in his youth by the Imperial Bank. And, like other Iranian nationalists, he disliked attitudes and pretensions which he saw as characteristic of the British Raj. 'No bank supplies housing and furniture, servants and what not', he later recalled telling the Bank. 'These are remnants of the nineteenth century, of what was done in India but we're in a different world now.'[16]

Yet Ebtehaj was never simply a man with a grudge. Widely recognised as exceptionally able and intelligent, he held strong views on the need to use the state's resources to promote economic development, and he combined these views with a professional understanding of economic and financial realities which won respect in many quarters. He was certainly never, at any time, 'anti-British'. During 1947, for example, he negotiated with the British government on the matter of the convertibility of Iran's large Sterling balances accumulated during the War. This was a matter of considerable importance to the British, as Sterling's role as a reserve currency came under increasing strain after the War, and it was regarded as vital that the Iranian balances – and the future earnings of Sterling from Anglo–Iranian Oil Company royalties – were used within the Sterling Area. In September 1947 Ebtehaj and the British government reached an agreement on this issue, which included the provision that the Iranian government would only buy goods in Dollars if they were essential and could not be purchased in Sterling. Iran was also to be compensated if Sterling was devalued, and the country's

Sterling balances were to remain convertible into Dollars. The British Treasury was on the whole relieved by the agreement, and impressed by Ebtehaj. 'He held all the cards and knew it', reported one official. 'He was obviously anxious to be friendly and to keep his country's financial affairs closely linked with us ... Ebtehaj is regarded as one of the most intelligent people in Iran. Certainly I should hope there are not many more intelligent!'[17]

Ebtehaj's policies towards the Imperial Bank rested on well-reasoned policies to promote Iran's economic development. He considered that the Bank Melli, as the central bank, had to take a leading part in regulating the economy for the purposes of development, and that it had to provide many of the resources needed for Iranian industrialisation. It was in his view quite inappropriate that a foreign bank should hold a large amount of Iranian deposits, and prevent the Bank Melli from directing such funds towards development. 'You take our deposits and don't use them', he told Kennet in 1946. 'You must recognise our right to require you to use them when we need them. We need them now.'[18] Ebtehaj suspected, indeed, that the Bank was financing its growth outside Iran with Iranian resources. He believed that the Imperial Bank had a role in Iran, but that this did not include the provision of retail banking services. 'I don't approve of a foreign bank', he later observed, 'going into a foreign country and having branch banking.'[19] The Bank should, he argued, finance foreign trade, and, as exchange regulations were administered in Tehran, there was consequently no need for branches in provincial towns. Moreover, in return for the privilege of operating in Iran, he argued that foreign banks should bring capital into the country rather than operate mainly on locally garnered deposits.

Ebtehaj's views were, over the following decades, to become the norm in many developing countries. And British overseas banks, including the Imperial Bank and its successors, adjusted their policies accordingly. In the late 1940s, however, the ideas were still novel, and beyond the experience of British bankers. They saw only policies which seemed unsound or unfair, and designed in Iran's case to ruin a bank which had done so much for the country in the past. It was not a battle between good and evil, but of mutual incomprehension.

Walter's last years as Chief Manager, before his retirement in June 1948, saw increasing tension with Ebtehaj. The conflict centred on three issues, foreign exchange, compulsory deposits with the Bank Melli, and the date on which the Bank's Concession was deemed to end. On each matter, however, the Bank either won its case or secured substantial concessions.

In September 1945 Ebtehaj suddenly gave notice to the Imperial Bank that he intended to cancel the September 1943 Foreign Exchange Agreement which had confirmed the Bank's right to deal in foreign exchange, and it was made clear that his recommendation was that no new agreement should be made.[20] Foreign exchange, he argued, must be wholly under the control of the central bank. This was by no means an exceptional claim. In Australia, for example, the commercial banks had historically held the bulk of the country's gold and foreign exchange. But in 1931 the Commonwealth Bank (the forerunner of the Reserve Bank of Australia) took responsibility for exchange rates, and in 1945 the country's reserves were formally concentrated in the central bank. Walter, however, considered that Ebtehaj's views could not possibly be supported by the Iranian government. But worries began to mount when it was learnt that Ebtehaj had forcefully argued, before an informal meeting of the Iranian Cabinet, that the Imperial Bank should not be allowed to deal in foreign exchange.[21]

The Bank resorted, as it was to do increasingly, to the British Embassy. Harold Musker, the Deputy Chief Manager between 1939 and 1947 and Acting Chief Manager while Walter was on leave, called on the Ambassador, Sir Reader Bullard, and explained the Bank's difficulties. There was a sympathetic audience. The Bank had been most helpful to official British policy in Iran during the War. Moreover, it was regarded as a major British commercial asset in Iran and, through its branch network, as a means of maintaining British influence throughout the country, a particularly important function given the intensification of the Cold War and the activities of Iran's Communist Party, the Tudeh. '[The Bank's] local representatives and the way in which it conducts its affairs, enjoy the general respect of Persians', one Foreign Office official observed in 1947, 'and provide a better illustration of the "British way of life" than many tons of pamphlets.'[22] On the other hand, Foreign Office sympathy was not always translated into the 'extra diplomatic support' which Walter had been promised during the March 1942 currency crisis. Not only was the oil company regarded as the priority, but the British government also sought, as mentioned above, to retain good relations with the Bank Melli and the Iranian government as a holder of large Sterling balances.

In October 1945, however, Sir Reader Bullard was prepared to exercise influence on the Imperial Bank's behalf. He had an audience with the Shah on 7 October and put forward the Bank's case, and he also pressed the matter with the Persian Finance Minister.[23] An uncovenanted easement for the Bank came two days later when Ebtehaj was taken to hospital with kidney trouble.[24] The combination of British diplomatic pressure and the temporary removal of Ebtehaj worked, and on 17 October, following a decision by the Iranian Cabinet, a new exchange agreement with the Bank was made. There was considerable relief within the Bank, and perhaps an over-optimistic belief that Ebtehaj could be overcome by similar means if he raised further difficulties. 'On the whole, after the experience of the last two months', Musker concluded, 'I am more confident than I was before that we shall not have too much difficulty in finding some means of carrying on our business when our concession expires.'[25]

Ebtehaj had different ideas. In February 1946 he raised with Walter the question of the Imperial Bank placing a certain percentage of its deposits, probably 40%, interest-free with the Bank Melli. He offered to reach an understanding on this with the Imperial Bank, but if this could not be arranged he threatened legislation.[26] The Imperial Bank was not unsympathetic to parts of Ebtehaj's case that some of its deposits should be re-lent to the central bank. The Bank was at the peak of its post-war cash mountain. At the end of January 1946 it held total deposits of 1600 million Rials (£12.5 million), of which 1137 million Rials (£8.9 million) was held in cash. With a ratio of cash to immediate liabilities of 72%, the Bank was not in the best position to refute the allegation that it was not employing its funds to Iran's best advantage. However, the fact that the Bank Melli was not merely the central bank but also a commercial bank in direct competition with the Imperial Bank made the proposal seem unfair. Moreover, Walter was horrified by the 40% figure, which threatened to have a radical effect on the Bank's business.

The Bank immediately appealed for Foreign Office support to resist Ebtehaj's schemes, which was forthcoming.[27] Walter, meanwhile, assembled his case against the compulsory deposit proposal. Ebtehaj, however, moved quietly but effectively to implement his intentions. On 13 July a decree was issued requiring all banks to keep with the Bank Melli, free of interest, 30% of their demand and 15% of their time deposits.[28]

The immediate implementation of the decree was delayed, primarily because of a change of government in early August as well as pressure from the British government. The Imperial Bank recognised, however, that a decree on deposits would almost certainly be implemented at some stage, and so opted for a strategy of attempting to get the level of compulsory deposits reduced, to no more than 15% of total deposits.[29] A further idea was to get the Bank's large holding of Iranian Treasury Bonds on which interest was paid, included in the compulsory deposit figure.[30]

A compromise on these lines was finally worked out during October 1946 and a new decree issued by the Council of Ministers in November. The new decree obliged all banks to deposit 15% of their demand and 6% of their time deposits with the Bank Melli, and to hold Treasury Bonds equivalent to a further 15% of demand and 6% of time deposits. In addition, banks were obliged to maintain an overbought position in foreign exchange to an amount not less than the total of deposits held against credits.[31] The Bank also agreed to place with the Bank Melli 100% of the deposits it received from customers opening credits abroad. The Bank already held the requisite number of Treasury Bonds, and had usually maintained the required overbought position in the past, so the practical impact of the November 1946 measures was not that great. Nevertheless, the statutory nature of the regulation had set a precedent which would be used in later years.

The third area of conflict between Ebtehaj and the Bank in the immediate post-War years concerned the date when the Bank's Concession was due to end. The Bank assumed that its Concession would end on 30 January 1949, 60 years from 30 January 1889 when the Shah had signed the original document. The Bank felt no worries about the end of the Concession, assuming that it would be allowed to continue operating after its expiry, and was perfectly prepared to pay Iranian income tax, the exemption from which formed the sole remaining privilege of the Concession.

Walter was, therefore, disagreeably surprised in January 1947 when he received a letter from the Minister of Finance saying that, using the lunar rather than solar calendar, the Bank's Concession was due to expire in the following April.[32] It soon transpired that Ebtehaj, having taken advice from a number of lawyers, was behind the move. The Bank's Concession had been signed at a time when the lunar calendar was used in Iran, the solar calendar being introduced by Reza Shah in the 1920s. Ebtehaj argued, therefore, that the Bank should abide by the date dictated by the old rather than the new calendar. Within a few months a press campaign on this theme was underway. 'The period of concession granted to the Imperial Bank has expired', complained one newspaper, 'yet the Bank continues its business like a Bank holding concession.'[33]

Once again the Embassy became involved in the case. The new Ambassador, Sir John Le Rougetel, considered the Iranian government had no case, and he exercised pressure to resist it. The British Embassy was also influenced by the fact that the British government would lose out on income tax and excess profits tax paid by the Bank as soon as it paid income tax in Iran. The Bank was estimated to have contributed some £1.7 million to the British Exchequer between 1940–41 and 1946–47, and there was no wish to see a premature end to such contributions.[34] After a long silence, during which the Bank had even considered offering to pay Iranian income tax immediately, in October 1947 the Iranian Cabinet ruled that the Bank's Concession was deemed to end in January 1949. Walter thought the news 'too good to be true'.[35] He was right.

12.3 THE END OF THE CONCESSION: APRIL 1948–NOVEMBER 1949

On 1 April 1948 Leslie C. Payne became Chief Manager of the Imperial Bank. Payne had been born in 1902, and joined the Bank in 1922. His first overseas appointment had been to Bombay, and he had later also served in Iraq. This experience, however, did not give Payne any vision that the Bank might have a future outside Iran. He remained Iran-centred in his views, optimistic of a great future for the Bank in the country if it could last out the influence of its implacable opponent, Ebtehaj. Yet his faith in the Bank's future in Iran was not combined with the kind of sympathy for the country that Walter had displayed. He spoke little Persian, and he was not at ease socially with Iranians. 'His knowledge of the Persian language was only moderate', F. H. Johnson later recalled, 'and consequently he could not unbend and laugh with the Persians which is so necessary.'[36]

Payne also manifested an inflexibility of attitude and approach which was somewhat inappropriate for the difficult negotiations which were to lie ahead of him. His obstinacy was to lead him into conflict with the Board, and to his early retirement from the Bank. It was particularly unfortunate that Payne's strong views were not combined with any vision of the future. 'He always struck me', C. F. Warr, who was Chief Inspector between 1946 and 1951, remembered, 'as paying far more attention to comparatively unimportant details than getting a view from above of the whole picture'.[37]

Yet the Bank's difficulties after 1948 cannot be fairly blamed entirely on Payne. Pressure on the Bank was mounting under his Chief Managership, and he had a more difficult task than Walter in containing it. His responsibilities had also expanded. In addition to the complex Iranian situation, Payne had to oversee the Bank's new and far-flung branch network in the Arab world, stretching from Muscat to Beirut. He had no experience of the new territories, and no extra assistance to help him manage them. Ebtehaj seems to have disliked Payne, and regarded him as his intellectual inferior. It was no coincidence that within a few months of his becoming Chief Manager, the Bank found itself the victim of what Payne referred to as a 'blitz'.[38]

The first assault came on the matter of foreign exchange. Ebtehaj had not relented, despite the setback at the end of 1945, from his desire to restrict the Bank's ability to deal in foreign exchange. In March 1946 a system of exchange purchase permits (*gavahinamehs*) had been introduced for certain specified commodities. When an exporter sold his goods, in addition to Rials at the official rate he received exchange certificates denominated in foreign currency. These could be sold to an importer, who needed such a certificate for the amount he wished to import, as well as to pay in Rials at the official rate. The Iranian government became a large, and sometimes the largest, purchaser of exchange certificates.

Ebtehaj attempted to achieve the cancellation of the Imperial Bank's foreign exchange authorisation when the exchange permits were introduced, on the grounds that the Bank Melli needed total control of the matter, but he had again failed to carry the Iranian government. The Bank Melli, however, was granted overall control of the purchase of foreign exchange, and the Imperial Bank was ordered to follow the Bank Melli's instructions in regard to the purchase of foreign exchange.[39] On 26 July 1948 Payne was faced with a new foreign exchange decree which further curbed the Imperial Bank's business. The system of *gavahinamehs* was extended to all permitted imports, and the Bank Melli was allocated £2 million Sterling to provide funds.[40] Ebtehaj immediately refused to make any of this sum available to the Imperial Bank to enable its customers to open credits and import goods. When Payne complained to Ebtehaj, he was told: 'The BMI belongs to the country and the exchange belongs to the BMI and I will not sell exchange to your customers, and that is final.'[41]

Payne was furious at Ebtehaj's injunction. He regarded the Bank Melli's dual role as state bank and as a commercial bank as quite unacceptable, somewhat overlooking the fact that the Imperial Bank had been in a similar position before 1928. And it seemed grossly unfair that Ebtehaj, while obdurate on the exchange question, expected the Imperial Bank to co-operate with the Bank Melli in other areas. In August, for example, the Bank was told that the Bank Melli was reducing its interest rates, and was asked, and reluctantly agreed, to do likewise. The Bank was also asked to follow the Bank Melli in demanding from its customers 30% deposits against all credits opened, a device by which Ebtehaj sought to discourage non-essential imports.

Payne's response to these measures was aggressive. 'In my opinion', he advised London in August, 'it is no use trying to appease this megalomaniac, Ebtehaj, any further and we should fight him at every step.'[42] Letters of complaint were despatched to the Bank Melli and the Ministry of Finance, with Payne making it explicit that he did not consider it appropriate that the governor of a country's central bank should be 'a man with a strong bias against ... the other Banks'.[43] Payne's stand was supported, to some extent, by the smaller Iranian banks, which also disliked Ebtehaj's controls.

In the short term, Payne won some concessions. Ebtehaj agreed to sell *gavahinamehs* to the Bank's customers for opening credits, although Payne had to give in on the question of deposits against credits.[44] On the other hand, Ebtehaj's dislike of Payne and determination to curb the Imperial Bank seem to have been fired by this clash in July and August. Payne, Lord Kennet confided to another director in September, had 'got off on the wrong leg' in his Chief Managership.[45]

In November 1948 Ebtehaj redeemed the outstanding £766 377 balance on the 1911 Loan. He disliked the hold on the Southern customs that the Loan had given the Imperial Bank. He later recalled:

Anybody in my place would have done the same. I paid that off and I considered that a great reflection on Iran. That a foreign bank should collect the revenues for a sum of six hundred thousand pounds. I paid that off.[46]

The Bank's special status in Iran was, thus, further diminished.

Over the next few months rumours began circulating in Tehran of a new draft banking law proposed by Ebtehaj. The proposed law included provisions that foreign banks were not to accept deposits exceeding the amount of capital they held in Iran; that such capital was to be in the form of foreign currency, to be sold to the Bank Melli in exchange for Rials; that no branches of foreign banks were to be allowed outside Tehran; and that the Bank Melli was to be the sole authority for issuing permits to deal in foreign exchange. The Foreign Office were immediately consulted.[47] The Governor of the Bank of England, C. F. Cobbold, met Ebtehaj in London in October in an attempt to persuade him to take a more reasonable attitude to the Imperial Bank, but the results of the discussions were, as Cobbold noted, 'wholly unsatisfactory'.[48] Meanwhile, during Ebtehaj's visit to London, Lord Kennet, not entirely tactfully, went to Iran, and lobbied a number of important personages, including the Shah, on the justice of the Bank's position.[49]

This lobbying, and Foreign Office pressure, helped to stave off for the moment Ebtehaj's draft bill, but as the end of the Bank's Concession in January 1949 approached there was a resumption of attacks on the Bank in certain quarters of the Iranian press. Kennet had no doubt that Ebtehaj was the main inspirer of these pieces in 'the venal Press in Tehran', and the British Ambassador shared this assessment.[50] Moreover, in December 1948 the Bank was asked to change its name, on the grounds that the title 'Imperial' was not appropriate for a foreign bank. In the following month the Bank came up with the new name of The British Bank of Iran and the Middle East (BBIME), and this title was adopted in August 1949 following an appropriate amendment to the Bank's Royal Charter.

Ebtehaj's pressure had a slow, corrosive effect on ministers in the Iranian government, most of whom still seem to have had no wish drastically to curb the Imperial Bank's powers. On 3 January Ebtehaj had attended a Cabinet meeting and reputedly threatened to resign unless the Bank Melli was, amongst other things, made 'the sole authority for granting permits to dealers in foreign exchange'.[51] The Cabinet did not agree, and Ebtehaj did not resign, but on 13 January the Ministry of Foreign Affairs did suggest that Payne and Ebtehaj should start direct negotiations with one another on the Bank's future. Payne had no wish to resume negotiations with the 'megalomaniac', but on 25 January the Finance Minister, Golshayan, a known supporter of the Bank, told a shocked Payne that unless the required negotiations were concluded before 30 January, the Bank would not be allowed to continue operating after the end of its Concession.[52]

The British Embassy again exercised pressure on the Bank's behalf, arguing to the Iranian government that serious negotiations could not possibly be concluded in four days. Le Rougetel, however, had by now become convinced that the Imperial Bank was too inflexible. Le Rougetel was determined to support the Bank, believing it would be disastrous for British prestige in Iran if it was forced to close, but he considered a visibly intransigent stance would bring the feared disaster rather than avert it. 'Ebtehaj's views cannot be ignored', he warned the Foreign Office, 'without creating a situation which may have a disastrous effect on our interests and prestige in this country.'[53] It seemed particularly important to handle the situation with tact for, in January 1949, public pressure against the Anglo–Iranian Oil Company was also beginning to mount. On 10 January the Iranian Prime Minister had demanded a large share of the profits of the company, whose wealth, he alleged 'did not accord with the poverty of the nation'.[54]

Ebtehaj was persuaded that he could not expect a decision by 30 January, and in return the Bank agreed to negotiate seriously with him.[55] On 31 January, the Bank was informed that its operations could continue until 19 February, and under Le Rougetel's pressure, the new deadline date was quietly shelved over the following weeks.

Payne, the Bank's London Office, the Foreign Office, the Bank of England, the Iranian government and Ebtehaj then engaged in a series of unproductive negotiations and consultations. The kernel of the immediate problem was that Payne, both because of his personality and also because he had constantly to refer matters for decision to London, was not the right man to negotiate with Ebtehaj. Both Payne and the Foreign Office came to the conclusion that one of the Bank's directors should be sent to Tehran. As a result, on 17 February 1949 Sir Kinahan Cornwallis, a former diplomat with great Middle Eastern experience, arrived in Tehran, accompanied by Harold Musker, the former Deputy Chief Manager who had joined London Office in 1947 as Sub-Manager.

Cornwallis's arrival broke the deadlock. He had the authority to be flexible in the negotiations, and he also had a new, and clearer negotiating brief. After it had been ascertained that neither the Bank of England nor the British government would support a policy of total opposition to Ebtehaj's demands,

Cornwallis had been authorised to agree that the Bank would import £1 million new capital into the country. Furthermore he argued that the Bank's properties in Iran were worth at least a further £1 million, and therefore that the Bank was in effect willing to employ £2 million capital in the country. He also offered to place 50% of the Bank's deposits with the Bank Melli. Negotiations with Ebtehaj began on 19 February. The Iranian counter-proposal was that the Imperial Bank should place 60% of its deposits with the Bank Melli, and place a further 15% in Treasury Bonds. When Cornwallis told Ebtehaj that the Bank could not possibly make a profit on the remaining 25% of its deposits, he was advised to reduce the Bank's overheads by closing all the branches outside Tehran.[56] The Bank privately calculated that if it took such a step it probably could operate profitably using the extra £1 million capital and with up to 65% of its funds deposited with the Bank Melli, but as the Bank had no intention of closing its branch network this line of thought was not followed in the negotiations.[57] There was some movement in the negotiations. Ebtehaj lowered his demands to 65% of deposits being handed over to the Bank Melli. Cornwallis raised his offer to 55%, together with a limitation of deposits to 225% of the capital employed by the Bank in the country. But there the negotiations stuck.

Cornwallis was able to use to good effect his authority and diplomatic skills, which were superior to Payne's. On 5 March he had an hour-long audience with the Shah, during which he put the Bank's case and warned that the Bank would be forced to withdraw from Iran if Ebtehaj had his way. On 7 March he had a final, private meeting with Ebtehaj during which the latter agreed to reduce the percentage of deposits to 60%, provided the Bank closed its provincial branches. Cornwallis, having made his case at the highest levels, now refused to move his negotiating position and he made clear to Ebtehaj, and to the Prime Minister whom he met on the 8th, that he planned to leave Tehran on the 9th.

It seemed for a day that all might be lost. On the 9th Kennet and the Bank's Deputy Chairman, R. V. Buxton, wrote to the British Foreign Secretary, Ernest Bevin, pleading, 'at the eleventh hour', the 'urgent need in which this British Chartered Bank stands for the help and protection of His Majesty's Government'.[58] This plea, however, was unnecessary. At a luncheon party on the same day at the British Embassy in Tehran, the Minister of Foreign Affairs told Cornwallis that he could leave the country 'with a tranquil mind'.[59] On the 10 March it was learned that a new banking decree was to be introduced, and this was approved by the Council of Ministers on 14 March.

The 14 March 1949 decree represented a major triumph for the Bank. The decree would formally acknowledge not only its right to operate after the end of the Concession, but also to operate on the terms on which Cornwallis had insisted. The decree stipulated that foreign banks could retain deposits up to 225% of their capital in Iran, and property in the country up to a value of £1 million Sterling could rank as capital.[60] For the Imperial Bank, the new decree meant that, on converting £1 million into Rials, it would have to give 55% of its total deposits to the Bank Melli. In practice, this meant that while before the decree the Bank had had 350 million Rials out of its total deposits of 1300 million at the Bank Melli or in Treasury Bonds, (on which the interest had by then fallen to only 0.5% per annum), this had to be increased to 580 million. The Bank could survive such terms, especially because, soon after the decree, its existing branch network and its authorisation to deal in foreign exchange were approved. By the end of March 1949 the Bank had transferred its £1 million capital to Iran.

Unfortunately for the Bank, the Cornwallis agreement in March was not followed by a period of peace. The Bank was persuaded, as a 'goodwill gesture', to close some of its branches and in June Bushire and Arak were closed, and by October Tehran Bazaar had merged with Chief Office. More seriously, over the next few months Ebtehaj, despite protests from the British Embassy, obstinately refused to supply the Bank's customers with *gavahi-namehs* derived from government exchange operations. By August the BBIME had outstanding applications from clients to open credits to the value of £250 000 and bills of collection on hand to a total of nearly £2 million. The repercussions on the economy were serious. Unpaid bills mounted, goods began to pile up at the customs, and the Bank's business began to contract. Between June 1948 and June 1949 the Bank's deposits fell by 33% and advances fell by 24%.[61]

While lack of access to official exchange remained the most pressing matter, there were also disputes between the Bank and Ebtehaj on other matters. The Bank pleaded that it should be allowed to treat deposits against credits opened through the Bank as public deposits, and hence part of the sum in calculating the 55% proportion which had been given to the Bank Melli. Ebtehaj maintained that the Bank's agreement in 1946 to transfer to the Bank Melli 100% of the deposits it received from customers opening credits abroad had to be maintained. The Bank also chafed at the interest rates the Bank Melli obliged it to charge. The Bank calculated for the Foreign Office that its net profit for the three months ended 20 June would have risen from its actual figure of 20 000 Rials (£156) to 4.94 million Rials (£38 600), if it had been allowed access to official exchange, to charge higher interest rates and retain a proportion of its deposits against credits.[62]

All seemed set for another bout of acrimonious conflict when the two main protagonists in Tehran, Ebtehaj and Payne, left the country, providing a breathing space for those of a more conciliatory nature. Ebtehaj's departure in August for an extended visit to the United States and Britain was particularly important, as he was still the main driving force on the Iranian side for measures against the Bank. During his visit to Washington for the annual meeting of the World Bank, the British Chancellor of the Exchequer had a 'friendly talk' with him about the BBIME during which Ebtehaj agreed to submit the whole question to arbitration by the Governor of the Bank of England.[63] When Ebtehaj came to London he met with Cobbold. While refusing to become entangled in formal arbitration, Cobbold did attempt to act as honest broker and stressed the unreasonableness of blocking BBIME's access to foreign exchange.[64] Ebtehaj was influenced little, if at all, by this advice, and, in the event, the important thing about his overseas visit was that negotiating in Tehran fell to the Minister of Finance, Golshayan. The Finance Minister was prepared to extract better terms from foreign enterprises in Iran, but he did not wish to see them leave the country. In July, in line with this strategy, he had negotiated a Supplemental Agreement with the Anglo–Iranian Oil Company, which would have doubled Iran's royalties in the short-term and increased them more in the long-term. But this agreement was never ratified, as a Mosaddeq supporter literally talked out the bill in the few days before the fifteenth Majles was dissolved.[65]

When he turned his attention to the Bank, Golshayan also had a less awkward man with whom to negotiate. Payne's absence on leave between 29 June and the end of November, left the Bank's affairs in the hands of F. H. Johnson, the Deputy Chief Manager. Johnson had negotiated concessions for the Imperial Bank in Kuwait in 1941 and Dubai in 1946, which will be discussed in Volume 2, and he again proved his negotiating ability during Payne's absence. Johnson and Golshayan, who knew each other well socially, spent four months discussing the terms of a possible settlement.

On 13 November an agreement was signed by Johnson and Golshayan. The Bank secured what it had long been seeking: access to official exchange for sale to its clients, and the resumption therefore of its foreign exchange business. The BBIME was guaranteed foreign exchange equivalent to up to £12 million. As Iranian imports were worth around £35 million per annum, the Bank was in effect offered a chance to retain a sizeable proportion of foreign trade finance.[66]

12.4 THE END: NOVEMBER 1949–JULY 1952

By the agreements of March and November 1949 the BBIME had, despite growing nationalism and Ebtehaj's desire to reduce it to a one branch bank undertaking the finance of foreign trade, won the right to continue a widely based banking business in Iran. Yet, in July 1952, the Bank closed its business. What had happened?

At the end of 1949 the Bank's Board, reflecting on the success of the Cornwallis mission, appointed Sir Geoffrey Prior as Resident Director in Tehran for one year. Prior had joined the Indian Political Service in 1923, and later served in the Gulf where he had become a friend of F. H. Johnson. He had been Political Resident in the Gulf between 1939 and 1946, and had subsequently retired. As Volume 2 of this History will explain, during his period as Political Resident in the 1940s Prior had been exceptionally helpful to the Imperial Bank when it secured permission to open in Kuwait, Bahrain and Dubai. His appointment to the Bank's Board could, therefore, be seen as a post-retirement reward for past services. However, Kennet, who appointed him, stressed the Bank's need for his skills as a diplomat. Prior, Kennet told Payne in November 1949, was to act as the Bank's 'ambassador in the Middle East . . . a diplomat and not a banker'.[67] Johnson for one had his doubts about Prior's usefulness, despite their friendship. He later recalled:

One evening we went round to the Paynes and Sir Geoffrey had arrived that night. Payne said, 'There's somebody here you know, Sir Geoffrey Prior has been appointed Resident Director', and I said 'why?'. In other words what can he do that we cannot do? He knew nothing about banking. I think he came out as a figurehead to add a little prestige to the Bank, and see whether in his position he could do anything. But I think Ebtehaj just laughed at him.[68]

Over the next year the Bank's negotiations in Tehran were handled by Prior, Payne and Johnson. Prior clearly had appropriate diplomatic skills and presence, but Johnson's doubts whether he was the right man for the job seem valid. Prior's Indian Civil Service background did not equip him with great insight into Iranian nationalism, nor did it seem to give him any special entrée to the British Embassy. 'He was a complete autocrat and he knew Persia', C. F. Warr, then Chief Inspector, later recalled, 'but better still he knew the Gulf better than Persia. He didn't speak Persian and he didn't really know anything about banking.'[69]

Prior's diplomatic talents were soon in demand. On his return to Tehran, Ebtehaj had been furious about the November agreement, and refused to recognise it.[70] The Bank Melli refused to allow BBIME any foreign exchange. And on 31 December 1949 the Council of Ministers supported Ebtehaj's demand that the Bank had to sign a new agreement with him.

By early 1950 the Bank's foreign credit business, denied access to official exchange, was grinding to a halt once again. The situation was worsened when the government introduced a new import quota arrangement. Allocation of permits for unrestricted goods was placed in the hands of the Bank Melli, which discriminated against the BBIME in issuing them. By 10 June

1950 the Bank had only received a total of 83 permits out of 1336 issued by the Bank Melli.[71] During these same months pressure was also mounting against the Anglo–Iranian Oil Company. In February 1950 the opening of the sixteenth Majles was followed by the appointment of an Oil Commission, chaired by Dr Mosaddeq. The clamour for nationalisation of the oil company grew over the following months.[72]

The Bank's business began to suffer severely. The year ending March 1950 revealed a net loss on the Bank's Iranian business of £81 792. The lack of access to official exchange had drastically curbed foreign exchange business, while the Bank's available resources were sharply diminished by the obligation to place a high proportion of its deposits, interest free, with the Bank Melli. Moreover, the Bank seemed to be in a downward spiral. Its inability to provide foreign exchange facilities for its clients resulted in substantial deposit losses. Deposits were down 29% in March 1950 over the previous year. The Bank's correspondence was full of fulminations against the 'stupid' and 'incredible' policies of Ebtehaj, and all hope was pinned on the expectation that he must, eventually, be toppled from power. 'It does not seem unreasonable to hold out as long as possible', Kennet wrote to Prior in June, 'on the chance of a turn in fortune's wheel.'[73]

Within days the wheel had turned. At the end of the month the weak Iranian government fell, and the Shah appointed the Chief of Staff of the Army, General Ali Razmara, as Prime Minister. The British government had been hoping for some years that a 'strong' government would emerge in Tehran, which could provide the political stability the British regarded as a prerequisite for future economic development. Razmara seemed to be the ideal answer.[74] He certainly seemed the answer to BBIME's prayers, for he appointed a long-time political enemy of Ebtehaj, Dr Taghi Nasr, as the Minister of Finance. Ebtehaj was dismissed as Governor of the Bank Melli on 19 July. Ebtehaj later remembered the circumstances which led to his departure from the Bank Melli:

I think it was mostly the work of the Prime Minister, the military man who thought that I would be a hindrance to him. Knowing me he thought he couldn't give me orders and he wanted somebody who would take orders from him.[75]

Ebtehaj's involvement in the BBIME's affairs finally ceased. He was appointed Ambassador to France, and in 1953 became Director of the Middle East Department of the International Monetary Fund. In the following year Ebtehaj became head of the Plan Organisation in Iran, and between 1954 and 1959 he used the country's oil revenues for large development projects for land irrigation, road improvement and bridge building. It was one of the most successful Third World economic development programmes, but Ebtehaj ran the Plan Organisation as he had run the

Bank Melli, refusing to bow to politicians and making enemies at a fast rate. He resigned in 1959, and after making a series of public protests about corruption in the Shah's government, he was held in prison in 1961 and 1962. At one stage he was offered release on a bail of $140 million, but he was subsequently freed after an international outcry. In 1960 he established a private bank, Iranians Bank, and over the following two decades this became a successful operation.

Ebtehaj's departure from the Bank Melli in 1950 seemed to have released BBIME from its long ordeal at his hands. On 29 July, when Payne and Prior met Nasr and the new Bank Melli governor, Ebrahim Zand, the Iranians agreed to implement in full the foreign exchange agreement of November 1949.[76] The Bank, it seemed, had finally come through the crisis.

Rather surprisingly, however, it was precisely at the moment when Ebtehaj had lost his influence that the Bank's Board undertook a major review of its operations in Iran, and decided to run them down. No one factor explains this shift of policy. The long conflict with Ebtehaj had had a wearying effect and raised doubts whether a viable banking business could ever be run in Iran. 'I do not consider that any legislation, however favourable, gives us any real security', Prior had advised Kennet in May 1950, 'for it can be altered at a moment's notice and a percentage or a sentence amended which might have a deadly effect.'[77] Such fears stood in contrast to the Bank's growing success in countries outside Iran, especially in Kuwait. One director, F. Hale, noted the Bank's 'appalling' profit performance in Iran since the late 1920s.[78]

The outbreak of the Korean War, and fears that the conflict between the West and the Communist world would spill over to politically unstable Iran, added a sense of urgency to the Board's reconsideration of its investments in that country. During July 1950 Musker calculated that the Bank's losses, should Iran be invaded overnight by the Soviet Union, would amount to £3 266 162.[79] In other words, as Kennet observed in a confidential memorandum to his Board, if Iran were 'to disappear behind the Iron Curtain', the Bank would 'lose an amount equivalent to the whole of our capital and reserves'.[80]

These considerations led to a Board decision, in early August 1950, to reduce its commitments in Iran. 'Our present lay-out in Persia', Kennet told Prior on 4 August, 'is such as to continue to attract Nationalist opposition.'[81] It was decided that the £1 million capital transferred to Iran under the Cornwallis agreement must be withdrawn. The Board also wished to renegotiate the obligation to place compulsory deposits with the Bank Melli. It was decided to insist that the 55% percentage should be reduced to 15%, with an equal amount in interest-bearing Iranian Treasury Bonds. And if the terms obtainable from the authorities were such as to prevent it carrying on its business except at a loss, then the Bank was determined to withdraw as soon as its business could be liquidated. 'In deciding to reduce our capital in Persia', Kennet explained to Prior at the end of August, 'it is understood that we decide also to spend no more upon new land or buildings in Persia; and as to banking business, to enter into no fresh long-term commitments, and on all accounts to keep our liabilities short and liquid.'[82]

As part of the new policy, the Board began to re-assess the whole management structure of the Bank. By August it was virtually decided to withdraw Chief Office from Iran, with London being considered the most likely place for its relocation. There was a debate on whether the Bank would appoint another Chief Manager after Payne, and in October an internal Committee on Organisation recommended instead the establishment of two Regional Managers, one for the Arab branches and one for Iran. Meanwhile, F. H. Johnson was retired some years before his time, apparently as part of the Board determination to overcome any resistance to its policy of running down the Iranian operations.

The Bank's change of heart revived the problem, long familiar in the Bank's history, of different perspectives between London and Tehran. While London was converted to a firm policy of reducing its Iranian commitments, Payne's view of the Bank remained centred on Iran. He was, therefore, unwilling to use the threat of withdrawal in negotiating with the Iranian authorities, for fear the threat might turn into a reality. Prior, despite his earlier pessimism on the Bank's future in Iran, had sympathy with the Chief Manager's view, though he retained a more realistic assessment of the Iranian political situation than Payne.

Over the following six months Payne and Prior attempted to negotiate with the Iranian authorities on the lines proposed by Board, although modified to take regard of what they saw as the realities of life in Iran. 'It is', Prior advised Kennet, 'impossible to secure rapid results in Persia.'[83] London, however, grew in impatience, and pressed for the reduction of the Bank's commitments. Part of the Gulhak site and of the Chief Office compound were put up for sale, and in November H. Musker, the London Office Sub-Manager, was sent to Tehran to assist the reductions in the Bank's overheads.

By the end of the year the Board decided they could wait no longer. On 20 December it was decided that the obligatory six months' notice of withdrawal of the Bank's £1 million capital should be given to the Iranian government on 1 January 1951. This presaged the liquidation of the Bank's Iranian business.[84] Payne, nevertheless, continued to temporise, suggesting to the Bank Melli that the BBIME would still continue to operate in Iran if the March 1949 decree which had obliged the Bank to import capital was repealed. The Board, although willing to stay in Iran if all its demands were met, were far from pleased with Payne's behaviour, and on 11 January a Board Resolution ordered him to tell the authorities that the Bank was going to liquidate its business.[85] The Board fixed 1 April as the date when there would be a public announcement of the Bank's intention to close business on 1 July.

There was an element of bluff in this stance. BBIME was not well placed to close its business by July. When C. F. Warr, the Chief Inspector, calculated in early January the Bank's situation if it ceased business on 1 July, he found that there would be insufficient funds to repay depositors.[86] Moreover, further Rial funds were needed to pay for the Bank's £1 million capital in Iran. The March 1949 decree had included an undertaking by the Bank Melli to refund capital imported by a foreign bank at the same rate that it had been converted into Rials. Sterling had subsequently been devalued later in the year. The Rial had not followed Sterling, and the new exchange rate had changed to 89.4 buying, and 90 selling. Nevertheless in April 1950 BBIME had been obliged to agree that it would still repurchase its capital from the Bank Melli at 130 Rials to the £1. 'We are completely bogged down in this country', Prior observed, 'like a stalled car in a road subject to avalanches.'[87]

At the end of January 1951, however, there were signs of a breakthrough. General Razmara's government was, as Kennet had hoped, seriously disturbed by the BBIME's threat to withdraw from Iran. The government proposed that the Bank could repatriate its £1 million capital, and still stay in business provided total deposits did not exceed one billion Rials (£11.2 million).[88] By mid-February it had been agreed that the Bank Melli would pay the BBIME £1 million in London against payment of 130 million Rials in Tehran, and that a new banking law would be introduced in a few weeks.[89] On 7 March the Bank Melli deposited with the BBIME in London £1 million on fixed deposit for one year, interest-free. In return, BBIME deposited 130 million Rials interest-free with the Bank Melli. The Bank, it should be noted, had achieved not the actual repatriation of its capital, but Sterling cover for it in London by means of the Bank Melli's deposit with it of the £1 million Sterling.

Nevertheless the morning the £1 million arrived, Kennet later recalled, 'we all felt a very great load off our minds'.[90] It was, indeed, one of the greatest strokes of luck the Bank had had in Iran for some time, for on the same day the cheque arrived in London General Razmara was assassinated by a member of a fanatical Islamic brotherhood which preached the liberation of Iran from foreign influence. Within days the political situation had become much more xenophobic. On 15 March the Majles passed a law proposing in principle the nationalisation of the oil industry. In April Dr Mosaddeq became Prime Minister, and on 1 May the Shah gave his assent to a decree nationalising the oil industry.

These political developments confirmed Kennet's view that the policy of running down the Bank's commitments in Iran should continue. 'Persia', Kennet wrote to Payne on 14 March, 'is no longer a suitable scene for the prudent long-term investment of British capital . . . our chief interests are now elsewhere than in Persia. We are thus enabled to reduce our commitments in Persia to the extent which prudence requires, without prejudicing the Bank's future prosperity.'[91] It was not a perspective which Payne shared. He indiscreetly, or perhaps deliberately, conveyed Kennet's views to the British Ambassador, now Sir Francis Shepherd. This in turn elicited Foreign Office protests to the BBIME that its withdrawal would be a serious blow to British prestige in Iran.[92]

Payne's indiscretion – for the Board wished, at least in public, to keep its options open – caused a further deterioration in his relations with London. The Board and the Chief Manager were now close to the situation which their respective predecessors had been in in 1908. As in 1908, the Board were convinced that Iran was too risky a place in which to operate. Payne, like Rabino, thought he knew better, and argued. London, as in 1908, would not countenance their Chief Manager disagreeing on such a major policy issue. 'You do not distinguish clearly enough between the occasions on which we are asking for your advice before coming to a decision', Kennet wrote to Payne on 12 April, 'and those on which, having had the benefit of your advice, we send you instructions.'[93]

The Bank's decision to continue to run down its Iranian business was a factor in Prior's departure from Iran in April 1951. His initial one-year appointment had been extended by four months. But he had clashed with Kennet over F. H. Johnson's retirement in 1950, which he had strongly opposed, and his mission to act as the Bank's ambassador in Iran had to be judged, in the last resort, as a failure. Nevertheless, there was no sign of rancour when Prior left the Bank.

Business began to be wound down. In March 1951 Mashad and Hamadan branches were closed, marking the beginning of a programme of branch closures spread over the following 15 months. In May the Bank applied to withdraw £250 000 of its capital under the agreement with the Bank Melli. This measure reduced its capital to the minimum in relation to deposits required by the March 1949 decree, in view of the decline in the deposit base. Notice for the withdrawal of a further £200 000 was given on 22 August. The run down of business continued amidst a growing crisis in British–Iranian relations. During May British troops began to be despatched to the Mediterranean, in apparent readiness for action in Iran to protect the oil company. And in July the Anglo–Iranian Oil Company closed its Abadan refinery.[94]

Payne, meanwhile, paid the price for disagreeing with the Board. During

August 1951, while on leave, he was asked to retire.[95] When he returned to Tehran to collect his belongings he made his feelings plain to C. F. Warr. 'Oh let's get this straight, Warr', he remembers Payne saying, 'I did not resign, I was sacked.'[96] Warr succeeded Payne as Acting Chief Manager. But it was made clear that neither he, nor anyone else, would be appointed Chief Manager. His task, in Kennet's words was 'to liquidate our Persian business'.[97] Meanwhile, as Volume 2 will discuss in greater detail, the Bank's administrative structure was undergoing considerable surgery. In April 1951 a Western Regional Manager was appointed, based in Beirut. In January 1952 an Eastern Regional Manager was appointed at Baghdad, with jurisdiction over the Gulf. And in June 1952 Harold Musker, who had been London Manager and Secretary since January 1951, was appointed to the new position of General Manager.

Warr was left with the melancholy task of closing down Iran. He was well engaged on this task, even though the decision to withdraw was still a closely guarded secret, when on 17 September the BBIME's authorisation to deal in foreign exchange was suddenly cancelled, without the six months' notice required by the Bank's foreign exchange agreement. BBIME had finally become directly involved in the oil crisis. Britain had retaliated against the nationalisation of Anglo–Iranian by banning the export of sugar, iron and steel to Iran, and suspending the convertibility facilities granted to Iranian Sterling balances in London. The action against BBIME was the Iranian response. In one sense, Ebtehaj's campaign against the Bank had proved a blessing in disguise, for in convincing it of the need to run down the Iranian operations, the Bank was spared much greater losses when the oil crisis erupted.

Protests from the Bank and the Foreign Office proved of no effect as relations between Britain and Iran deteriorated. The only question, for BBIME, was how long it would take to liquidate its debts and put its affairs in sufficient order to be able to close down in Iran. At the end of January 1952 the Bank announced that Chief Office, which was to be the last branch to close, was to stop transacting any fresh business on 30 July 1952.

Warr ran the business down as quickly and as competently as could have been hoped. Zahedan branch was closed in February 1952, Esfahan, Khorramshahr, Shiraz and Ahwaz followed in April. Property and office equipment were put up for sale. Chief Office was sold to the Bank Bazerghani, Iran's first private commercial bank which had been founded in 1950, for 29.6 million Rials (£331 096), although the Bank estimated the value at over 60 million Rials. BBIME was, as one Embassy official noted, 'more interested in getting it off their hands than in haggling'.[98] The March 1949 decree did not include any undertaking to allow the Bank to remit the proceeds of its property sales. Warr, therefore, applied them as provision against bad debts, leaving the Bank's profits intact for remittance.

The Bank's closure on 30 July seems to have passed almost unnoticed, except by Warr and his assistants working to wind up its affairs. It was, as one Foreign Office official had observed several months previously, 'a sad end to a fine story of British enterprise'.[99]

12.5 BANKING IN IRAN 1946–52

Despite the Bank's conflicts with the Iranian government and the Bank Melli, the difficulties in securing supplies of *gavahinamehs*, and the obligations to hand deposits over to the Bank Melli and purchase Treasury Bills, the Imperial Bank–BBIME maintained a commercial banking business until almost the end of its life in Iran. There were even signs, in the last few years, of a greater willingness to finance industrial projects, although the bulk of the Bank's business continued to be the provision of trade finance.

The complexity of Iran's foreign exchange regulations and the concentration of *gavahinameh* supply in Tehran meant that the pre-War trend towards the centralisation of foreign exchange business in the capital was continued after 1945. The Bank believed in 1948 that about 70% of all imports into Iran went first to Tehran, and were then distributed to the provinces.[100] Similarly, exports came from the provinces to Tehran, and their despatch overseas was arranged in the capital. Chief Office, therefore, concentrated on the finance of overseas trade, and it did the bulk of documentary credit and collection business. A very brisk business was undertaken after the end of the War, as imports poured into Iran, and Chief Office also had a good import business in 1947 and 1948, before the events of 1949 diminished its resources. The corollary of Chief Office's large business in foreign trade was that the provincial branches had little activity in that sector. Even the branch at the large port of Khorramshahr did almost no import business on its own account, and concentrated on the finance of local business and the forwarding of goods up-country.

The local trade financed by the branches continued, as before the War, to cover a wide spectrum of commodities. Tabriz, for example, purchased exchange against dried fruits, leather, cotton piece goods, matches, carpets and so on, while sales were against imported haberdashery and piece goods, automobile accessories, tyres, hides and rice. Mashad financed the movement of wool and the other exports of Khorassan province. Shiraz financed trade in lambskins, gum, tea and tobacco, while Rasht remained heavily committed in the rice trade. The Bank still performed an important role in several provincial towns, and the Bank's closure of branches such as Mashad and

Rasht caused considerable commercial disruption and provoked many petitions from groups of merchants against the closures.

Branches such as Arak, Hamadan and Kermanshah were engaged mostly in local bill discounting, and often the business was on a very small scale. J. L. A. Francis, who had joined the Bank in 1947 and was Manager of Hamadan between 1948 and 1950 (and later Secretary of BBME 1955–70 and 1972–79), remembered Hamadan's business as 'a great deal of drawing of bills by one set of tupenny-ha'penny merchants on another set of tupenny-ha'penny merchants ... It was all very small beer and it was the same kind of business that you'd imagine was done in the bazaar by a *sarraf*, a money-lender with a hole in the wall.'[101]

The Bank continued to lend often on an unsecured basis, F. H. Johnson remembered of his time as Deputy Chief Manager in the later 1940s:

Most things was on a man's bond, on his honour. Sometimes one did one's best to protect oneself by getting some kind of security but security was very scarce, and seldom asked for. The Persian considers his signature his bond, and very seldom lets you down.[102]

The Bank Melli, as a local bank, was a powerful competitor, and at many branches its competition had left the Imperial Bank with a much reduced business. At Khorramshahr, Francis, whose first overseas posting in the Bank was as Accountant at this branch in 1947, remembered that the Bank 'shared the business which was marginal down to poor if not very dodgy, whereas the lion's share and certainly all the good business went to the Bank Melli'.[103] The feeling that the Bank was running down made Francis, and many other young officers, relieved when they were transferred out of Iran. In his case it was to Kuwait in 1950. 'When I left Iran ... I felt that it was a turning wicket, things were getting very difficult indeed, and I was certainly hoping that I would be posted to some other place.'[104]

Yet the old Bank was still prepared to take initiatives in new areas. At Esfahan the branch had a large business with the cotton weaving and spinning mills which had grown up during Reza Shah's industrial drive. At the end of the 1940s the Bank became involved in financing a company set up to erect an electrical power station in Esfahan to service their mills. The company employed a British firm as consulting engineers on the project, and Payne agreed to finance the shipment of machinery and materials 'so that a really good example of British enterprise and industry could be installed in Iran'. The Bank, Payne told London, 'has frequently been taunted for not assisting Iranians in economic improvements', and this was one of his answers to the charge.[105]

Such projects, however, carried more risks than short-term trade finance, and in the political and economic circumstances of the period the risk was even higher. The Esfahan company ran out of funds when less than half of the power station was complete. By the beginning of 1950 the Bank was owed £400 000 by the company, and as late as 1955 it was still owed £68 000.[106] Bad debts indeed mounted in the last years of the Bank. When Musker visited Iran at the end of 1950 he estimated the total of 'locked-up' risks at Chief Office alone as at least 94.8 million Rials (£1 060 402), which he considered 'appalling'.[107]

The Bank was also troubled by dishonesty among its local staff once the intention to leave Iran became clear. Warr remembered:

As soon as we'd decided to go out of Persia there was a spate of defalcations throughout Tehran Chief Office. It was quite distressing. And it was not only ordinary clerks but one or two of the 'B' officers. They all had very good reasons in their own minds for doing it, but nevertheless it was embezzlement and it was a great disappointment one way and another.[108]

12.6 EPILOGUE

When C. F. Warr left Iran in September 1952 there were still many loose ends to be tied. In particular, £550 000 of the Bank's capital was still trapped in the country, and the Bank was owed 80 million Rials (nearly £900 000) in uncollected debts. Warr left the resolution of these affairs in the hands of J. D. Hammond, who had been acting Deputy Chief Manager since 1950, supported by another British officer, R. R. Rees, and two senior Iranians, Ismail Dehlevi – the Legal Adviser – and Taghi Azarmi, the former Assistant to the Chief Manager.

Within months, however, it had become impractical to maintain the two British officers in Iran. On 22 October diplomatic relations were severed between Britain and Iran. The Iranian government, moreover, was known to be preparing a large retrospective tax claim against the Bank. Although The British Bank of the Middle East, as BBIME was renamed on 16 July 1952, had a rival claim for damages arising from the government's unilateral decision to withdraw its foreign exchange authorisation in September 1951, there were fears that the British staff would be used as hostages for 'extorting tax claims'.[109] In December, therefore, Hammond and his colleague left Tehran, 'ostensibly for consultation in London but actually not to return'.[110]

Azarmi ran the non-operational Tehran Office over the next two years, assisted by Dehlevi, a small number of 'B' officers and supporting clerical staff. The Bank moved to a small office in a tower-block in Avenue Saadi, but the Office still cost around £18 000 per annum to maintain, including the cost of pensions to former employees. It did, however, perform a useful role in collecting debts. When Hammond left Tehran the Bank was still owed around 80 million Rials. By March 1955 this figure had been reduced by 50%.

During these years the remittance back to Britain of most of the Bank's capital was also secured. The problem on this front continued to be the Bank's undertaking to purchase its capital for the Bank Melli at 130 Rials to the £1. BBME was not prepared to convert Sterling at 90 to raise Rial funds to buy Sterling back at 130. So the strategy was maintained of using recoveries of outstanding debts to repatriate further sums of the Bank's capital, and by 1955 the Bank's capital had all been repatriated to Britain.

The third matter that occupied Tehran Office's attention in these years was tax. In January 1953, as had been feared, the Bank received a large tax claim for 37.5 million Rials (or nearly £420 000) for tax owed since 1949. The Bank considered the claim totally unjustified, but it was pressed even after the government of Dr Mosaddeq was overthrown in August 1953. In April 1954 the Bank was obliged to pay 1.7 million Rials (£19 000) for taxes owed up to March 1951, but further larger payments continued to be demanded.

C. F. Warr was sent to Tehran in March 1955 to investigate this and other matters. Warr secured a dropping of all the tax claims after paying over 4.6 million Rials (£51 454).[111] Settlement of the income tax issue cleared the way for the final closure of the Tehran Office. Warr also investigated the prospects for the return of the Bank to Iran, but found these still to be uncertain. 'For the time being', Musker told his Board in March 1955, 'we can put out of our minds any near possibility of opening a branch of our own in Persia.'[112]

Four years later BBME did in fact resume its Iranian connection. That story, however, belongs to Volume 2.

APPENDICES

The difficulties which have for a considerable time been pending between the Government of His Imperial Majesty the Shah and the Baron Julius de Reuter having now been definitely overcome, and the Concession which was granted to the aforesaid Baron Julius de Reuter, the 25th July 1872, being annulled, it has been mutually agreed upon as follows:-

Article 1
The Government of His Imperial Majesty the Shah concedes by these presents to the Baron Julius de Reuter, and his associates or representatives, the right of establishing a State Bank in the Persian Empire under the style or title of the 'Imperial Bank of Persia'.

This right is granted for a period of 60 years from the date of the signature of the present Concession by His Imperial Majesty the Shah.

The head office and the domicile of the Bank shall be at Teheran, and the Bank may establish branch offices in the other towns in Persia and abroad.

In order to develop the commerce and increase the riches of Persia, the Imperial Bank, outside any operations which appertain to a financial institution, may undertake on its own account or on account of third parties all matters financial, industrial, or commercial which it may think advantageous to this end, on the condition, however, that none of these enterprises be contrary to treaties, laws, usages, or the religion of the country, and that previous notice thereof be given to the Persian Government.

The Imperial Bank shall not enjoy the right to lend money on, or buy any lands, villages, or other real property throughout the Empire, excepting the lands necessary for the construction of a suitable establishment at Teheran, and for its branches in the provinces: the Bank is likewise forbidden to discount, or make advances on Government bills which have not been drawn on the Bank.

Article 2
The capital of the Imperial Bank shall be 100,000,000 francs (£4,000,000), and the Bank shall issue a certain number of shares in series. The Bank shall be considered to be formed as soon as the first series of 25,000,000 francs (£1,000,000), has been subscribed. The subscription shall be opened in different capitals, amongst others, Teheran, Berlin, London, Paris, St. Petersburgh, and Vienna, provided the Government in these different places permit it.

The shares shall be to bearer, but the Bank may also issue inscribed shares.

341

The Bank, whenever it thinks it advantageous, may, with the consent of the Government, add to its capital and to the number of its shares.

Article 3

The Imperial Bank shall, as State Bank, have the exclusive right of issuing notes to bearer, payable at sight. The Bank shall not issue notes above the value of 20 million francs (£800,000) without giving notice to the Persian Government. In order to promote the development of public credit, to place a limit on the circulation of silver money and increase that of gold, the Imperial Bank accepts in principle the introduction of a single standard on the basis of the gold *Toman*; during the 10 years which follow the formation of the Bank, the Government of His Imperial Majesty and the Directors of the Bank will come to an understanding as to the means and measures most favourable to attain this end. At the same time, taking into account the exigencies of the actual monetary situation, the issue of Bank notes will at first be on the basis of the silver *Kran*.

These notes shall be accepted by all the agents and employés of the Imperial Government, and they shall be legal tender for all transactions in Persia. But as soon as the Bank be unable to pay the value of one of its notes, the circulation of Bank notes shall be prohibited throughout the Empire, and the Bank shall be compelled to pay all its notes.

In order to guarantee this payment of notes, the Bank expressly binds itself to hold cover in specie equal to at least half the value of the notes in circulation for a period of two years from its commencing operations, and to at least one-third after the lapse of the said period of two years.

The difference between this reserve fund in specie and the value of the notes issued shall be covered by securities for realty or personalty belonging to the Bank, and deposited in its coffers in Persia.

The Imperial Bank shall be bound to pay its notes at sight at the place of issue; nevertheless the notes of the branch offices shall be payable also at Tehran.

The notes shall be in Persian, and no notes of a lower denomination than two *tomans* shall be issued without the authorisation of the Government. The Bank notes shall bear a mark or seal to indicate that they have been checked by the Persian Government; they shall be signed by a Director or Administrator of the Bank and by the chief cashier at their place of origin.

The Government of His Imperial Majesty the Shah binds itself not to issue any kind of paper money during the terms of this Concession, nor to authorise the creation of any other Bank or other Institution possessing a like privilege.

Article 4

The Imperial Government will not guarantee the capital of the Bank: it can, at its choice, subscribe to it or favour the subscription by Persian subjects to the extent of a fifth of the capital called up, or abstain from all participation whatsoever therein.

The Concessionnaire, his associates or representatives shall be entrusted with, and solely responsible for, the division of the capital into shares, the number and value of the Bank notes conformably to Article 3 of these presents, the organisation and administration of the Bank, the nomination of the officials and employés of the Bank, both in Persia and abroad, and the financial management of the Bank; and all profits which the Bank may make, as well as all losses it may sustain, shall be entirely on their account and at their risk.

The Government of His Imperial Majesty the Shah will for the purpose of exercising its High supervision over the Bank, appoint an Imperial High Commissary.

This High Commissary shall be entitled to take cognizance of the management of the Bank, and to see that the business of the Bank be conducted conformably to these presents. He shall by virtue of his office attend the general meetings, as well as the board meetings at Teheran, as often as he may be invited to do so. He shall check the issue of Bank notes and shall see to the strict observance of the provisions of Article 3 of these presents. He shall also be charged with the supervision of the relations of the Bank with the Imperial Treasury. He shall be debarred from interfering with the management and administration of the Bank, and his function shall impose no responsibility on the Imperial Government.

Article 5

The object of this Bank as a National Institution being the public weal and the good of the State, the Government of His Imperial Majesty the Shah shall provide the military protection which is indispensible to the safety of its head office and of its branches.

The Government shall facilitate as far as possible the acquisition of necessary lands and sites in those places where the Bank may establish its head office and branches, by mediating between the Bank and the proprietors in a manner, alike equitable, and favourable to the enterprise.

The Bank, its offices and branches shall be wholly exempt from every kind of tax and duty, as also its shares, notes, receipts, cheques, and all documents emanating from the Bank in its general business and transactions. But if the Government should introduce fiscal stamps, the Bank shall take no bill of exchange or other negotiable instrument circulating in Persia which does not bear such fiscal stamp.

Article 6

The Imperial Bank shall facilitate the payments of the Imperial Treasury in Persia and abroad, and for each service that the Government demands of the Bank, the Government and the Directors of the Bank shall determine by mutual consent the commission to be paid to the Bank.

After its formation and the payment of its capital, the Imperial Bank shall lend to the Government of His Imperial Majesty the Shah the sum of one million francs (£40,000) at the rate of 6 per cent. per annum for a period of 10 years. The interest and the repayment of capital shall, at the desire of His Imperial Majesty, be deducted from the 6 per cent. of the net profits of the Bank assured to the Government by Article 7 of these presents.

Further, the Bank, after its formation, shall always hold itself at the disposal of the Imperial Government for all loans or advances of which the Government may be in need. These advances or loans shall be made on security to be agreed upon in each case by the Persian Government and the Bank, or else they shall be considered to form part, *pro tanto*, of the reserve fund to be held by the Bank as a guarantee for the paper money. The Government shall repay these loans or advances at the expiry of the respective periods agreed upon. The whole of the interest shall be regularly paid at the end of each Persian financial year, *i.e.*, 20th March. The first of these advances, exclusive of the above mentioned million francs, shall be five million francs (£200,000) on current account, and at the rate of 8 per cent. per annum.

Article 7

At the end of each Persian financial year (20th March) the Imperial Bank shall pay to the Government of His Imperial Majesty the Shah, or credit the Government with 6 per cent. on the net profits for the year. In case the afore-mentioned 6 per cent. on the net profits do not in the year attain to a sum of 100,000 francs (£4,000), the Bank shall be bound to complete this sum, and charge such difference or whole, as general expenses, without right to deduct the same from the said shares of net profits of the ensuing year.

Article 8
The caution money (£40,000) which was deposited in the Bank of England in 1872 by the Baron Julius de Reuter, shall be handed over to the Persian Government as a guarantee for the formation of the Bank. The day after the formation of the Bank the Persian Government shall repay the said Baron Julius de Reuter the above-mentioned sum of £40,000. If the Bank be not formed within nine months from the date of the signature of these presents by His Imperial Majesty, the said caution money shall become the property of the Persian Government, and the present Concession shall be considered null and void, save in the event of a war, breaking out between any of the great Powers in Europe, or, in which Persia might find herself engaged, or in any other case of *vis major*.

Article 9
On the formation of the Imperial Bank, the first directors shall publish the statutes by which the Bank will be governed, which statutes shall be strictly in accordance with the stipulations of these present. After the formation of the Bank, the aforesaid statutes cannot be modified excepting by the decision of a general meeting of shareholders, who, in such modifications, shall always respect the provisions of these presents.

Article 10
In order to exercise and maintain the rights granted to it by these presents, the Imperial Bank shall be under the High protection of His Imperial Majesty the Shah and of his Government; and the Bank undertakes to respect the general laws of the country. In the case of a difference arising between the Persian Government and the Bank, or between the Bank and private individuals, each party shall appoint one or two arbitrators: from the decisions of such arbitrator or arbitrators there shall be no appeal. In the event of the arbitrators not agreeing, they shall appoint an umpire to give a final decision.

Article 11
The Imperial Bank being ready to incur forthwith the sacrifices necessary for developing the resources of the country by the exploitation of its natural riches, the Persian Government grants to the said Bank for the term of the present Concession, the exclusive right of working throughout the Empire the iron, copper, lead, mercury, coal, petroleum, manganese, borax, and asbestos mines which belong to the State, and which have not already been ceded to others. The Persian Government shall, as appendix to this Concession, deliver to the Baron de Reuter on the day of the signature of these presents, an official list of mines already ceded. The gold and silver mines, and mines of precious stones, belong exclusively to the State, and should the engineers of the Bank discover any such, they must immediately notify the same to the Government of His Imperial Majesty the Shah.

Excepting the necessary engineers and foremen, all the workmen engaged on the mines must be subjects of His Imperial Majesty the Shah.

The Persian Government shall assist the Bank by all the means in its power to obtain workmen at the current wage of the country.

All mines which the Bank has not commenced working within 10 years of its formation shall be deemed to have been abandoned by it, and the State may dispose of the same without consulting the Bank.

Article 12
The lands necessary for the working of these mines and for the construction of roads to the nearest and quickest means of transport shall be given gratis to the Bank, where they are on State domain; if such lands belong to private individuals, the Imperial Government shall assist the Bank by all the means in its power to treat with them on the most favourable conditions.

The material necessary for the above-mentioned works shall enter Persia without paying any duty whatsoever; and the lands and buildings of the said works shall be free from every tax and duty.

Article 13
The Persian Government shall receive annually 16 per cent. of the net profits of all mines worked by the Bank. On the expiry of the term of the present Concession, the mines, with their lands, buildings, accessory construction and plant, shall revert to the Persian Government, according to the most favourable rules and regulations generally adopted by other Powers who have stipulated in this behalf.

Article 14
In consideration of the rights granted to him by these presents, the Baron Julius de Reuter formally, emphatically, and without reserve renounces all other rights or privileges granted to him by the former Concession of the 25th of July 1872, which becomes null and void by these presents.
30 January 1889.

APPENDIX No. 1

Within 10 days of his arrival the undersigned binds himself to deliver to the Minister for Foreign Affairs in London the original of the Concession granted to the Baron Julius de Reuter the 25th July 1872. The said document will be addressed to the representative of Her Britannic Majesty at Teheran, who promises to deliver it to the Persian Government.

Done at Teheran the 30 January 1889.

George de Reuter.

APPENDIX No. 2

It is understood that the Imperial Bank shall repay the Persian Government the salary of the High Commissary who is mentioned in Article 4 of the Concession. The said salary shall be 3,000 *tomans*, which the Bank shall pay at the end of each Persian financial year, *i.e.*, 20 March.

Done at Teheran the 30 January 1889.

APPENDIX No. 3*

It is understood that the caution money of £40,000 which, according to Article 8 of the Concession is to be paid to the Persian Government, shall be paid to his Imperial

*Note. – This Appendix is done in duplicate, the other copy being signed by the Baron George de Reuter in the presence of (and his signature attested by) Her Britannic Majesty's Envoy Extraordinary and Minister Plenipotentiary to the Court of Persia.

Majesty the Shah. This sum will, as regards His Imperial Majesty, represent the loan of a million francs (£40,000) provided for in Article 6, which thus becomes paid in advance. The day after the formation of the Bank His Imperial Majesty will, by virtue of this arrangement, order the directors of the Imperial Bank to pay this sum to the Baron Julius de Reuter as repayment of the caution money, instead of receiving for his Government the said loan of one million francs mentioned in Article 6.2

This Appendix shall have the same effect as if it had been Incorporated word for word in the body of the original Concession.

4 February 1889.

APPENDIX No. 4

The following Articles shall prevail so far as they vary any provision of the original Concession and Appendices.

Article 1
The chief place of business of the Bank shall be fixed at Teheran and the original issue of all its Bank notes shall be made there only.

Article 2
The Imperial Bank shall not without the consent of the Persian Government accept Mortgages upon any lands or other real property or without such consent or discount or make advances on Government Bills not drawn on the Bank.

Article 3
The Capital of the Bank may be divided into such shares or stock as may be deemed expedient. The Bank may be constituted in accordance with the law of the Country in which the Capital or the greater part thereof shall be subscribed. The subscription may be opened in such place or places only as deemed expedient. The shares shall be nominative shares.

Article 4
The following shall be the guarantee for the repayment of the notes viz: the Bank is bound to hold a metallic reserve equal to at least one third of the amount of its notes in circulation. The metallic reserve to the extent of two thirds thereof may be in bullion. The difference between this metallic reserve and the amount of the notes in circulation shall not at any one time be more than the amount of the paid up Capital.

Article 5
The Government of His Imperial Majesty the Shah will name an Imperial High Commissary to exercise its High supervision over the Bank. The High Commissary's functions shall be as follows:- He shall have the right to attend the General Meeting of the Bank and also to attend any periodical meetings of the management at Teheran. He will bring to the notice of the Imperial Government any violation of the stipulations of the Act of Concession and he will particularly see to the fulfilment of the stipulations of Article 3 of the Act of Concession as explained by these statutes. He will facilitate all communications between the Bank and the Imperial Treasury but his function will impose no responsibility on the Imperial Government as he is not to interfere in the administration or management of the affairs of the Bank.

Article 6
The Bank shall not be required to make any advances to the Imperial Government beyond the stipulated £40,000 sterling without having approved securities for such further advances. The total amount of loans by the Bank to the Government shall not at any one time exceed one third of the then paid up Capital of the Bank.

Article 7
The first annual payment to the Government of His Imperial Majesty under Article 7 of the Concession shall be made on the 20th March which shall next ensue after the expiration of one year from the time the Bank commences Banking operations in Persia.

Article 8
In the event of the Arbitrators appointed under Article 10 of the Act of Concession being unable to agree as to the appointment of a final Umpire to settle any difference which shall arise between the Bank and any private individuals such final Umpire shall be appointed by the representative at Teheran of one of the following Governments *viz.* France, Germany, Austria and Italy. Questions arising between the Bank and private persons in the provinces may by consent of both parties be decided by a local Umpire to be appointed by the Consul or Consular representative of any of the above named powers. In the event of any difference between the Bank and the Imperial Government the Bank shall have the right to demand that an expert shall be appointed as final Umpire and that such expert shall be resident in Europe and be appointed by the Presidents of the State Banks of France, Germany, Austria and Italy or one of them. The Imperial Government undertakes to immediately put into execution such decisions as may be arrived at either by the Agreement of Arbitrators or the determination of the final Umpire.

Article 9
The Bank shall not itself carry on the Mining and other Works mentioned in Articles 11, 12 and 13 nor the industrial Undertakings mentioned in Article 1 of the Concession but the Bank may sell or cede to one or several persons all or any of the privileges rights and powers specified in such Articles such Cession or sale to take effect in accordance with the terms of the Act of Concession provided that the Bank shall name the person or persons to the Imperial Government for its approval without which approval such cession or sale shall not be valid. Should the approval of the Imperial Government be delayed or withheld without good reasons assigned the Bank may demand that the matter be referred to arbitration under Article 10 of the Act of Concession as explained by Article 8 hereof. The annual payments under Article 13 of the Act of Concession shall be made by the person or persons working the Mines. The Bank guarantees the correctness of the Accounts and the receipt by the Government of its rights set forth in Article 13. The Bank shall be at liberty to prospect and generally to test the value of all or any such mining properties and Works.

Done at Brighton the 27 July 1889.

Source: English translation of Concession enclosed in T. Holland to Sir Philip Currie, 16 July 1889, FO 60/507, Public Record Office. The Concession, including the definitive version of Article 4 whose drafting passed through several stages, is also held in BBME Archives.

APPENDIX No. 5

Having regard to the need for adapting the terms of the Concession of The Imperial Bank of Persia (Incorporated by Royal Charter in 1889) signed on the 30 January,

1889, and amended and completed by subsequent Appendices, to the new situation in Persia and to the economic possibilities which this situation presents and, consequently, for amending the said terms in respect of the matters hereafter mentioned,

The Imperial Government of Persia, herein called 'The Government,' represented by H. H. Mehdi Kouli Khan Hedayat, Minister of Finance and President of the Council of Ministers,

And the Imperial Bank of Persia, herein called 'The Bank', represented by Messrs. Sidney Frank Rogers, member of the Board of Directors, and Edward Wilkinson, Chief Manager of the Bank,

Have agreed as follows:-

Article 1

The Bank renounces the right to issue Bank Notes which was granted to it as an exclusive right by the Government.

It is agreed that The Bank remains liable for the repayment under the control of the Government's High Commissary and within a period to be agreed between The Government and The Bank, but not later than the 20th June, 1931, of the whole of the Notes issued by it.

At the expiration of the said period the Bank will pay to the Government the amount required for repayment of such of the Notes as shall not then have been presented.

Article 2

Consequent upon the preceding Article:-

(1)   The Government will relinquish the exercise of its special control through the medium of its High Commissary over the Bank as soon as the repayment of the Notes, which it has placed in circulation, has been effected by it under the control of the said High Commissary.

The post of High Commissary to the Bank shall be abolished and the payment which the Bank makes to the Government as salary of the said High Commissary shall cease to be payable.

(2)   As from the coming into force of the present appendix the Royalty amounting to 6 per cent. of the net profits of each financial year, which is payable to the Government under the terms of the Bank's Concession, shall cease to be payable.

(3)   In consideration of the renunciation by the Bank of the right to issue Bank Notes, the Government shall pay to the Bank, in London, on the 20th March, 1931, the sum of £200,000 (two hundred thousand pounds sterling) in cash.

(4)   The Government authorises the Bank to accept mortgages on immovable property of every kind, and further, in order to secure repayment of its advances, to acquire immovable property assigned as security, provided however, that such acquisition shall be only temporary and for a period not exceeding one year.

Article 3

In case any difference shall arise between the Government and the Bank, which may not be susceptible of friendly settlement, resort shall be had to Arbitration at the request of either of the two parties.

The procedure in regard to such Arbitration shall be as follows:

Each party shall, within a period not exceeding three months, appoint its own Arbitrator.

Should either party fail, during the said period, to make such appointment, the party so failing shall be deemed to accept, as sole Arbitrator, the Arbitrator appointed by the other party.

The two Arbitrators shall examine the difference and use their best endeavours to determine the same within a period not exceeding three months. In default of their having agreed upon their decision within this period of time, they shall within a further period, not exceeding one month, agree upon the appointment of a third Arbitrator who shall join the other two, and the Arbitration Tribunal thus constituted shall decide by a majority.

In default of the Arbitrators coming to an agreement, within the period above-mentioned, as to the appointment of the third Arbitrator, the party who is the more diligent shall apply to the President of the Economic and Financial Organisation of the League of Nations, to appoint the third Arbitrator. As from the appointment of the latter, the Arbitration shall proceed as above. The decision of the Arbitrators, or, as the case may be, of the Arbitration Tribunal, composed of the Arbitrators, shall be carried into effect without appeal or recourse of any kind.

In the event of any one of the persons appointed not being able to act, application shall be made to the President of the Economic and Financial Organisation of the League of Nations, to appoint a substitute for him.

Article 4

The duly authorised representatives of the Bank having declared that their signatures give legal and irrevocable force to the provisions of these presents, so far as concerns the Bank, without the Governing Body of the Bank having to submit the same for any ratification whatever, these presents shall come into force immediately upon the ratification thereof by the Majliss, which shall take place at latest on the 15th Khordad, 1309 (5th June, 1930).

These presents have been signed by:

M. K. K. Hedayat,
    President of the Council of Ministers and Minister of Finance.

Sydney Rogers,
    Member of the Board of Directors of the Bank.

Edward Wilkinson,
    Chief Manager of the Bank.

Done at Teheran, the 13th May, 1930

APPENDIX 2: THE IMPERIAL BANK OF PERSIA CHARTER OF
INCORPORATION

Victoria by the grace of God, of the United Kingdom of Great Britain and Ireland, Queen, Defender of the Faith, Empress of India, to all to whom these presents shall come, greeting:

Whereas it has been represented to Us that the persons hereafter named have obtained from His Imperial Majesty the Shah of Persia a concession dated on a day equivalent to the thirtieth day of January, in the year of our Lord one thousand eight hundred and eighty-nine, with several appendices thereto bearing subsequent dates, and additional Articles dated on a day equivalent to the twenty-seventh day of July, in the year of our Lord one thousand eight hundred and eighty-nine, and are desirous of forming a joint stock company for the purpose of establishing and carrying on a bank in Persia in pursuance of the said concession.

And whereas for the better accomplishing those objects the said persons have humbly besought Us to grant to them, and to the several other subscribers of the capital of the Company, our Royal Charter of Incorporation which We are minded to do under the conditions and subject to the restrictions and provisions hereinafter contained.

Now know Ye, that as well upon the prayer of the said persons as also of Our especial grace, certain knowledge, and mere motion, We have granted, constituted, ordained, and appointed, and by these Our presents do grant, constitute, ordain, and appoint as follows:-

1.   Our trusty and well beloved Baron Julius de Reuter, of Kensington Palace Gardens, in the County of Middlesex; Baron John Henry William Schröder, of No. 145, Leadenhall Street, in the City of London, Merchant; Reuben David Sassoon, of No. 12, Leadenhall Street, in the said City of London, Merchant; and Walpole Greenwell, of No. 21, Finch Lane, in the said City of London, Stockbroker; and such other persons and bodies politic and corporate as may become proprietors of any share or shares in the capital of the Company hereby established, and their respective executors, administrators, or assigns shall be one body politic and corporate by the name of the Imperial Bank of Persia, and by that name shall and may sue and be sued in all courts, and shall have perpetual succession with a common seal, which may be by them varied and changed at their pleasure.

2.   The Company hereby incorporated (hereafter in this Our charter referred to as 'the Company') shall be established for the purpose of carrying on for a term of thirty years, commencing from the date of this Our charter (which term is hereinafter referred to as the term of the charter), the business of a banker in Persia, but not elsewhere, save and except that they may carry on by or through agencies such financial operations as being commenced in Persia have to be continued elsewhere, or being commenced elsewhere have to be continued in Persia, subject nevertheless to such restrictions and provisions as are contained in this Our charter.

3.   It shall be lawful for the Company, during the term of the charter, to make, issue and circulate in Persia, notes payable to bearer on demand, and to re-issue the same, subject nevertheless to the provisions of the said concession, appendices and Articles, and of the laws of Persia:

Provided that –

(a)   The Company shall keep, at their principal and branch banks in Persia, a metallic reserve equal to at least one-third of the total amount of such notes issued by the principal and branch banks of the Company in Persia and in circulation; and

(b)   The difference between the metallic reserve and the amount of notes so issued and in circulation shall not at any one time exceed the amount of the capital of the Company for the time being actually paid up, after deduction of the amount which in pursuance of the deed of settlement hereinafter mentioned is to be paid for the acquisition of the said concession.

4.   The metallic reserve to the extent of two-thirds thereof may be in bullion, but, subject to that restriction, may consist of gold or silver, or partly of gold and partly of silver, and may be in the form of coin, or partly of coin and partly of bullion, and if at any time either gold or silver forms the exclusive standard in Persia, not less than three-fourths of the metallic reserve shall be the metal forming such exclusive standard.

5.   The metallic reserve shall be set apart to meet the claims of the holders of the said notes, and shall not be mortgaged or charged so as to derogate from the charge in favour of these holders, and the notes shall be a first charge on such metallic reserve in priority to the claims of other creditors.

6.   It shall be lawful for the Company during the term of the charter to carry into effect the powers conferred by the said concession, appendices and articles, so far as

they relate to banking, and further to promote companies or associations for the purpose of carrying into effect the remainder of the concession, appendices and articles, and also to do all things necessary to carry out the 9th of the said articles, but otherwise it shall not be lawful for the Company itself to undertake any business other than the business of a banker.

7.   It shall be lawful for the Company to take and hold such lands, buildings, and hereditaments in the United Kingdom as may be thought necessary or proper for the purpose of the office of the Company, not exceeding in the whole in annual value five thousand pounds, calculated at the respective times of the taking thereof, and to sell, grant, demise, exchange, convey, or dispose of the same or any of them.

And we do hereby grant unto every person and body politic, if otherwise competent, Our special licence and authority to grant, sell, alien, and convey in mortmain unto and for the use of the Company and their successors any such land, buildings and hereditaments.

8.   The Company shall be bound by and fulfil all and singular the obligations on their part contained in the said concession, appendices and articles so far as they are authorized so to do by this Our charter, and shall be at liberty, with the consent of the Commissioners of Our Treasury, to apply for and obtain from His Imperial Majesty the Shah of Persia any further concession or concessions consistent with this Our charter, and shall equally be bound by and fulfil all and singular the stipulations contained in any such concession or concessions so far as they are consistent with this Our charter.

9.   The capital of the Company shall be the sum of one million pounds sterling, divided into shares of ten pounds each, with power for the Company from time to time by special resolution to increase the capital, but so that the total capital shall never exceed four million pounds sterling.

10.   The Company shall not commence business until it has been made to appear to the satisfaction of the Commissioners of Our Treasury that the said capital of one million pounds sterling has been subscribed, and that one quarter of that sum has been actually paid up.

11.   The Company shall not, unless it has been made to appear to the satisfaction of the Commissioners of Our Treasury that one-half of the said one million pounds sterling capital has been actually paid up, carry on business for more than six months after such commencement, or issue any notes payable to bearer on demand.

12.   If the Company becomes insolvent, every proprietor for the time being of any share in the capital shall be individually liable to contribute not only such part or parts of every share held by such proprietor in the capital of the Company as has not been theretofore called for and paid up, but also such further sums of money not exceeding the full amount of the share or shares held by such proprietor in the capital of the Company, as shall be requisite and necessary to pay, satisfy and discharge the debts, engagements, and liabilities of the Company, so that each proprietor shall for the purposes aforesaid, be liable to pay and contribute, in addition to the amount of every share held by him, a further sum equal to the amount of such share or shares.

13.   Provided that if the assets of the Company, including such portion of the shares held by the proprietors as are at the time not called for and paid up, are insufficient to satisfy the claims of both the note-holders and the general creditors, the sums contributed by the proprietors in addition to the amount of their shares under the last preceding paragraph of this Our charter, shall be liable first to satisfy the claims of the note-holders before being applied towards payment of the debts of the general creditors.

14. The Company shall have a domicile in England and shall also have a board of directors in London. More than one-half of the capital at any time issued by the Company shall be issued in the United Kingdom.

15. The Company shall be regulated in accordance with a deed of settlement, the draft of which shall be approved by the Commissioners of Our Treasury before it is executed, and if the Commissions of Our Treasury certify to Us that a draft so approved is not executed within twelve months after the date of this Our charter, it shall be lawful for Us, Our heirs and successors, at any time thereafter, by writing under Our Great Seal, to declare this Our charter to be absolutely void.

16. Such deed of settlement shall provide for the bank remaining British in character, for its being regulated by a body of directors in the United Kingdom, for the majority of the directors being British subjects, for carrying out the requirements and directions of clauses 3, 4, 5, 12 and 13 of this charter, and for special resolutions being passed in like manner as special resolutions under the Companies' Act, 1862. Subject to such provisions as aforesaid being made and retained, the deed of settlement may be altered by special resolution of the Company so that it shall not be contrary to anything in this Our charter.

17. Where it is made to appear to the Commissioners of Our Treasury on the application of the Government of Persia, or the Government of any of Our possessions abroad, or by any person or body politic appearing to be interested, that there is reasonable cause to suppose that the Company is insolvent, or that the Company has suspended payments for not less than sixty days, or is being, or has been, wound up, or that the said concession has by forfeiture or otherwise determined, or that any of the provisions of this Our charter have not been complied with, the said Commissioners may require the Company to give within such time and with such particulars as may be specified in the requisition, a return of such information and particulars as may appear to Our Commissioners necessary for ascertaining whether the Company have or have not complied with the charter, and thereupon the Company shall give such return, and permit the same to be verified, both by inspection of their books and otherwise, by such person or persons as the Commissioners of Our Treasury may appoint, and if the Company fail to give such return, or to permit such verification, or give a false return, or if after such return and verification it appears to the Commissioners of Our Treasury that the Company is insolvent, or has suspended payments, or is being, or has been wound up, or that the said commission has by forfeiture or otherwise determined, or that any of the provisions of this Our charter have not been complied with, the Commissioners of Our Treasury may if they think fit certify the same to Us under their hands, or the hands of any two of them, and upon such certificate it shall be lawful for Us, Our heirs and successors, if We shall be so minded, by writing under Our Great Seal, absolutely to revoke and make void this Our charter, and everything therein contained. Provided nevertheless, that the power of revocation so hereby reserved shall not have or be construed to have the effect of preventing of barring any proceeding by *scire facias*, or otherwise according to law, to annul or repeal the said charter.

18. And We do further will and declare that on the determination of the said term of thirty years, the business so to be carried on by the said Company shall cease, so far as the same may depend upon or be carried on under or by virtue of the powers and provisions herein given and contained, unless We, Our heirs or successors, shall, by writing under Our Sign Manual, declare to the contrary, and shall authorize the continuance of the said business under the provisions of this Our Royal Charter for such term, and under such provisions and conditions as We, Our heirs or successors, shall think fit, and any term for which it is so renewed shall be construed to be part of the term of the charter.

19.   And We do, for Us, Our heirs and successors, grant and declare, that this Our charter, or the enrolment thereof, shall be in all things valid and effectual in the law according to the true intent and meaning of the same, and shall be recognised as valid and effectual by all Our courts and judges in England and elsewhere, and by the respective governors for the time being of all Our colonies, possessions, and dependencies, and all other officers, persons and bodies, politic and corporate, whom it doth, shall or may concern, and that the same shall be taken, construed, and adjudged in the most favourable and most beneficial sense for the best advantages of the said Company, as well in Our several courts of record in Our United Kingdom of Great Britain and Ireland, and in Our several colonies, possessions, and dependencies aforesaid, as elsewhere, and notwithstanding any non-recital, mis-recital, uncertainty, or imperfection therein.

IN WITNESS whereof we have caused these Our Letters to be made patent. Witness Ourself at Westminster this second day of September, in the fifty-third year of Our Reign.

By warrant under the Queen's Sign Manual,

Muir Mackenzie.

Note. The original Charter was modified by Supplementary Charters dated

17 December 1894
21 January 1920
24 July 1922
1 September 1924
24 May 1935
21 July 1936
27 November 1945
18 July 1949

which incorporated alterations in connection with movements in the level of the Bank's capital and various extensions of the period of its incorporation, even subsequent to the expiry of its concession, of the territories in which it could carry on branch banking, and of the powers of the Bank.

APPENDIX 3: *The Imperial Bank's balance sheet (selected items) 1890–1952 (£ Sterling)*

Year end (20 September)	Deposits	Bills payable	Note issue	Cash & at call	Investments	Bills discounted loans & advances	Bills receivable	Acceptances	Premises	Balance sheet total
1890	113 015	458 800	—	392 288	60 000	1 258 557	60 269		6313	1 789 427
1891	225 233	666 520	28 334	676 385	377 361	692 451	313 010		11 176	2 128 441
1892	356 120	470 533	55 451	469 497	230 294	994 561	285 538		17 214	2 081 234
1893	285 338	679 232	59 107	187 601	373 406	842 773	637 918		19 351	2 155 398
1894	269 162	510 139	95 515	184 859	135 900	1 099 561	478 535		17 407	1 920 261
1895	239 165	358 277	72 668	141 987	133 020	822 619	292 418		10 650	1 402 695
1896	225 878	883 995	82 203	201 029	129 690	1 187 101	410 891		11 309	1 940 021
1897	216 803	591 924	38 000	205 344	125 730	1 042 862	199 402		11 509	1 584 848
1898	219 677	997 017	72 763	197 966	112 680	1 501 983	210 041		12 747	2 035 416
1899	179 581	113 265	117 491	261 725	109 890	643 966	126 304		14 762	1 156 648
1900	280 758	131 332	206 422	239 120	129 262	741 716	253 705		13 814	1 377 616
1901	278 265	119 333	264 333	507 699	142 325	570 387	176 893		23 941	1 421 245
1902	282 390	133 839	330 493	605 955	142 337	552 850	196 693		22 338	1 520 174
1903	225 439	148 963	346 808	733 497	138 379	494 096	118 658		22 571	1 507 202
1904	410 519	205 658	480 721	1 032 345	164 769	570 345	99 878		30 378	1 897 674
1905	426 118	217 765	526 479	639 486	396 404	778 115	140 339		32 042	1 986 386
1906	527 460	177 586	460 911	474 506	404 553	974 583	115 560		32 709	2 001 911
1907	549 048	382 752	395 012	387 093	411 288	1 107 049	189 084		34 512	2 189 027
1908	607 937	287 302	430 435	677 017	202 795	1 168 115	116 726		37 514	2 202 167
1909	686 541	243 064	634 649	892 813	311 901	1 123 645	83 004		37 371	2 448 734
1910	746 854	419 389	683 945	776 033	354 952	1 426 956	152 294		42 878	2 753 114
1911	775 792	559 496	805 133	934 478	677 103	1 150 094	245 486		50 687	3 057 848
1912	725 010	499 386	859 065	1 340 844	677 035	723 782	209 635		53 128	3 004 425
1913	905 995	514 501	962 419	1 220 603	663 085	1 125 173	240 859		55 309	3 305 029
1914	695 368	671 804	832 012	1 088 066	631 843	1 127 669	203 128		51 834	3 102 541
1915	703 199	740 857	207 961	612 624	545 874	1 126 123	152 196		49 308	2 486 124
1916	727 838	888 753	180 002	700 830	429 201	1 202 854	275 477		42 509	2 650 871
1917	1 187 774	1 711 315	562 008	1 206 878	1 568 346	1 209 787	336 132		29 194	4 350 337
1918	1 789 369	4 337 837	667 153	1 392 389	3 518 298	1 996 275	790 620		19 165	7 716 747
1919	2 830 065	5 184 733	1 109 202	2 103 003	3 731 079	3 241 933	987 733		13 060	10 076 809
1920	3 228 336	3 378 404	670 204	3 339 575	1 535 222	1 738 789	1 591 090		55 420	8 260 996
1921	2 805 375	2 616 712	733 327	3 055 205	1 499 172	1 872 801	605 073		50 118	7 172 372

Year end (20 March)

Year											
1924	4 165 429	2 023 188	1 060 108	2 972 083	1 646 325	2 359 117	1 319 646		51 107	8 348 277
1925	3 916 722	1 654 565	1 301 146	2 675 780	1 699 029	2 316 708	1 280 675		29 788	8 001 999
1926	4 842 729	1 814 287	1 841 420	4 243 972	1 653 985	2 774 129	1 026 282		14 037	9 682 404
1927	6 483 396	2 481 275	2 154 902	4 262 264	1 987 231	4 564 976	1 506 910		37 527	12 358 908
1928	7 804 441	2 710 936	2 527 471	5 153 685	3 003 720	4 661 199	1 490 265		23 626	14 332 495
1929	6 176 015	2 203 395	3 021 884	6 186 438	2 536 787	2 404 765	1 571 097	371 172	32 808	13 103 068
1930	4 212 056	1 790 610	2 724 408	5 005 938	2 347 019	1 606 795	1 142 830	127 889	14 374	10 244 844
1931	2 895 227	1 697 244	1 681 761	3 030 435	3 306 309	1 010 265	532 154	103 937	2963	7 986 062
1932	2 555 647	1 379 834	1 413 465	2 256 089	3 354 208	846 933	514 282	80 420	8520	7 060 454
1933	2 730 969	1 551 160		1 059 772	3 545 805	869 787	450 910	150 622	7744	6 084 640
1934	3 128 793	1 655 914		1 053 273	3 467 919	1 268 583	653 617	278 159	5373	6 726 924
1935	3 065 478	2 009 720		1 278 923	3 552 066	1 222 163	694 194	620 325	2670	7 370 341
1936	3 587 911	1 827 576		1 102 424	3 259 738	2 082 757	654 581	970 266	1592	8 071 358
1937	3 539 235	1 643 817		899 602	2 844 480	2 447 445	838 219	891 497	1041	7 922 584
1938	3 740 552	1 605 191		866 212	3 056 518	2 720 367	550 655	627 361	1000	7 822 113
1939	3 355 430	1 659 603		1 070 647	3 167 940	2 129 528	512 847	853 552	1000	7 735 514
1940	4 544 830	1 738 014		928 267	2 749 548	3 420 789	1 058 608	1 149 689	1000	9 307 900
1941	4 448 313	1 757 198		926 667	2 729 728	3 612 074	818 848	629 012	1000	8 777 329
1942	9 507 949	1 812 389		3 782 045	3 926 357	4 642 246	894 325	2 490 313	1000	15 736 287
1943	16 668 336	2 651 727		9 172 409	4 618 285	6 358 137	1 146 367	2 275 617	1000	23 571 815
1944	20 233 362	3 074 219		14 226 052	4 624 590	5 389 683	1 093 746	1 318 179	1000	26 653 230
1945	22 099 736	3 767 070		16 812 936	5 853 961	4 343 763	937 902	1 743 301	1000	29 692 864
1946	23 728 923	3 664 581		12 652 737	9 645 272	6 209 068	1 012 208	4 070 076	1000	33 590 360
1947	24 663 245	2 980 517		12 341 801^a	9 547 508	8 273 659^b	1 654 879	7 023 991	1000	36 842 838
1948	23 032 799	3 359 005		10 235 148^a	7 838 736	8 228 158^b	2 287 697	3 986 268	1000	32 577 008
1949	22 297 488	4 459 600		12 498 597^a	4 826 458	9 089 332^b	2 506 546	5 384 726	1000	34 396 659
1950	26 995 960	5 005 620		17 859 055^a	2 985 349	9 702 266	3 682 204	4 601 565	75 000	38 905 439
1951	33 612 092	5 786 111		19 609 205^a	5 113 874	13 257 144	3 678 863	9 782 414	100 000	51 541 500
1952	45 765 466	3 322 983		32 645 295^a	6 054 581	9 221 043	3 478 936	7 268 181	100 000	58 768 036

Notes:

a Cash figures for these years include Statutory Deposits with the Bank Melli, these totalled £1 741 054 in 1947; £1 732 092 in 1948; £1 385 457 in 1949; £6 596 383 in 1950; £5 590 941 in 1951 and £3 080 511 in 1952.

b Bills Discounted, Loans and Advances in these years include Iranian Government Treasury Bonds totalling £1 914 063 in 1947; £1 718 750 in 1948 and £1 338 462 in 1949. It also includes Iraq Government Treasury Bills of £350 000 in 1949.

355

APPENDIX 4: *Imperial Bank published shareholders' funds 1890–1904 (£ Sterling)*

Year end (20 Sept.)	Capital	Published reserves	Profit & loss account	Total published shareholders' funds
1890	1 000 000	150 000	67 864	1 217 864
1891	1 000 000	150 000	58 354	1 208 354
1892	1 000 000	150 000	49 130	1 199 130
1893	1 000 000	100 000	31 721	1 131 721
1894	1 000 000	14 485	30 957	1 045 442
1895	650 000	42 285	40 297	732 582
1896	650 000	65 488	32 457	747 945
1897	650 000	63 495	24 626	738 121
1898	650 000	72 459	23 500	745 959
1899	650 000	72 459	23 853	746 312
1900	650 000	72 459	36 645	759 104
1901	650 000	80 000	29 314	759 314
1902	650 000	100 000	23 451	773 451
1903	650 000	100 000	35 992	785 992
1904	650 000	115 000	35 776	800 776

Imperial Bank published shareholders' funds and inner reserves 1905–52

Year end (20 Sept.)	Capital	Published reserves	Profit & loss account	Total published shareholders' funds	Inner reserves
1905	650 000	130 000	36 024	816 024	15 273
1906	650 000	150 000	35 953	835 953	9048
1907	650 000	175 000	37 215	862 215	36 051
1908	650 000	185 000	41 494	876 494	46 051
1909	650 000	185 000	49 479	884 479	48 095
1910	650 000	200 000	52 925	902 925	94 515
1911	650 000	210 000	57 426	917 426	118 117
1912	650 000	210 000	60 965	920 965	128 636
1913	650 000	210 000	62 114	922 114	127 085
1914	650 000	210 000	43 358	903 358	143 438
1915	650 000	150 000	34 108	834 108	70 369
1916	650 000	160 000	44 277	854 277	67 449
1917	650 000	190 000	49 240	889 240	92 635
1918	650 000	220 000	52 388	922 388	297 642
1919	650 000	250 000	52 809	952 809	245 084
1920	650 000	280 000	54 051	984 051	136 916
1921	650 000	310 000	56 955	1 016 955	293 777
1922	650 000	340 000	63 721	1 053 721	526 970
1923	650 000	370 000	64 644	1 084 644	714 970

Year end (20 March)

Year end	Capital	Published reserves	Profit & loss account	Total published shareholders' funds	Inner reserves
1924	650 000	390 000	59 552	1 099 552	710 197
1925	650 000	420 000	59 566	1 129 566	896 313

1926	650 000	470 000	63 968	1 183 968	755 464
1927	650 000	520 000	69 335	1 239 335	1 191 953
1928	650 000	570 000	69 646	1 289 646	1 123 464
1929	650 000	610 000	70 602	1 330 602	1 399 627
1930	650 000	650 000	89 881	1 389 881	1 508 335
1931	650 000	690 000[a]	87 893	1 427 893	1 509 991
1932	650 000	710 000[a]	91 087	1 451 087	1 214 304
1933	650 000	730 000[a]	91 889	1 471 889	1 366 234
1934	650 000	740 000[a]	94 058	1 484 058	1 434 773
1935	650 000	750 000[a]	94 818	1 494 818	1 626 523
1936	650 000	760 000[a]	95 604	1 505 604	1 558 714
1937	1 000 000	750 000	98 034	1 848 034	1 411 208
1938	1 000 000	750 000	99 008	1 849 008	1 456 686
1939	1 000 000	750 000	116 930	1 866 930	1 449 995
1940	1 000 000	760 000	115 367	1 875 367	1 468 190
1941	1 000 000	760 000	122 807	1 882 807	1 471 462
1942	1 000 000	800 000	125 635	1 925 635	1 400 646
1943	1 000 000	850 000	126 135	1 976 135	1 443 233
1944	1 000 000	900 000	127 469	2 027 469	1 443 546
1945	1 000 000	950 000	132 757	2 082 757	1 543 914
1946	1 000 000	980 000	146 780	2 126 780	1 574 817
1947	1 000 000	1 000 000	175 085	2 175 085	1 605 700
1948	1 000 000	1 050 000	115 935	2 165 935	1 626 748
1949	1 000 000	1 100 000	121 845	2 221 845	1 682 485
1950	1 000 000	1 150 000	119 294	2 269 294	1 628 045
1951	1 000 000	1 200 000	129 383	2 329 383	1 608 775
1952	1 000 000	1 250 000	129 906	2 379 906	1 090 567

Note:
[a] Between 1931 and 1936 £200 000 was shown on the balance sheet as the amount received from the Iranian government for the surrender of the note issue. In this table this sum has been added to the Bank's reserve account.

APPENDIX 5: *Imperial Bank published net profits (after tax) 1890–1952*

		Net profits (£ Sterling)
Year end (20 September)	1890	62 249
	1891	42 528
	1892	64 814
	1893	33 715
	1894	24 384
	1895	24 214
	1896	40 616
	1897	36 382
	1898	33 958
	1899	35 307
	1900	46 490
	1901	37 868

Year end (20 March)	
1902	49 138
1903	47 540
1904	49 784
1905	55 248
1906	59 930
1907	67 262
1908	55 279
1909	47 985
1910	58 447
1911	64 501
1912	53 538
1913	51 149
1914	31 244
1915	25 749
1916	50 170
1917	79 962
1918	78 149
1919	75 421
1920	76 242
1921	82 904
1922	86 766
1923	85 924
1924	49 908
1925	85 014
1926	129 402
1927	135 367
1928	135 312
1929	125 955
1930	124 279
1931	93 013
1932	88 194
1933	85 802
1934	77 169
1935	75 760
1936	75 786
1937	77 430
1938	65 974
1939	92 922[a]
1940	98 437
1941	97 440
1942	132 828
1943	140 500
1944	141 335
1945	145 287
1946	134 023
1947	138 305
1948	100 350[b]
1949	105 411
1950	96 949
1951	108 089
1952	97 773

Notes: The published net profit figure is after British income tax and deductions of payments to the Iranian government under the terms of the Concession, but before payment of dividends and transfers to published Reserve Fund.
[a] Between 1939 and 1947 tax on dividends was no longer deducted from net profits.
[b] Between 1948 and 1952 tax on dividends was again deducted from net profits.

APPENDIX 6: *Exchange rates*
(Kran–£1 Sterling before 1932; Rials–£1 Sterling thereafter)

Year end (20 September)	Average annual exchange rate[a]	Imperial Bank balance sheet rate[b]	Imperial Bank profit adjustment rate[c]
1890	35	na	
1891	34	32.5	
1892	36	38	
1893	38	42	
1894	50	49	
1895	50	52.5	
1896	50	50	
1897	51	52.5	
1898	51	50	
1899	52	50	
1900	52.5	51.5	
1901	53	53	
1902	57	56	
1903	56	54.5	
1904	61	58	
1905	61	59	
1906	55	56	
1907	49.5	50	
1908	52.5	56	
1909	54	55	
1910	54.5	55	
1911	55	54.5	
1912	56	55	
1913	55.5	55	
1914	62	60	
1915	58.5	63	
1916	39	63	
1917	29	55	25
1918	27.5	55	20
1919	25.5	55	17
1920	34	55	10
1921	51	55	18
1922	56.5	55	58.75
1923	47.5	55	46

Year end (20 March)

1924	42	55	45.5
1925	43.5	55	41.5
1926	48.5	55	42.5
1927	49	55	44.5
1928	48	55	40
1929	58	51.5	51
1930	63.5	55	59.5

Adjustment rate (official buying rate)

1931	89.5
1932	90
1933	103
1934	77
1935	66
1936	80
1937	80.5
1938	80.5
1939	80.5
1940	64.35
1941	68.80
1942	142
1943	128
1944	128
1945	128
1946	128
1947	128
1948	128
1949	128[d]
1950	89.40
1951	89.40
1952	89.40

Notes:

[a] The exchange rates given for 1890 to 1899 are not averages, but figures for particular dates at Tehran (when available) given in C. Issawi, *The Economic History of Iran 1800–1914* (Chicago, 1971), pp. 343–5. After 1900 the exchange rates are averages for the Iranian year ending in March. They are from E. B. Yaganegi, *Recent Financial and Monetary History of Persia* (New York, 1934), p. 73. 'Free' market rates fluctuated so widely after 1930 that it seems pointless to cite annual figures.

[b] The Imperial Bank's balance sheet adjustment rate is the exchange rate the Bank used to convert its Persian assets and liabilities into Sterling at each year-end. In the 1890s the Bank's branches had their own adjustment rates. The rates for 1891 to 1894 are for Mashad, as Tehran's are unknown. The rates for 1895 to 1899 are Tehran's. Exchange conversions in this book have used the Bank's adjustment rate unless otherwise stated.

[c] Between 1917 and 1930 the Bank used a different rate to convert its Persian profits into Sterling than to convert its assets and liabilities. Half-years might have different profit adjustment rates from year-ends.

[d] On 20 March 1949, the Bank adjusted the accounts at 130, the official selling

rate, for the period January to March. This was because it was temporarily oversold
in Sterling.
na = not available.

APPENDIX 7: *Imperial Bank payments to the Iranian government 1890–1935*
(£ Sterling)

Year end (20 September)	
1890	4072
1891	4000
1892	4381
1893	4000
1894	4000
1895	4000
1896	4000
1897	4000
1898	4000
1899	4000
1900	4000
1901	4000
1902	4000
1903	4000
1904	4000
1905	4000
1906	4037
1907	5452
1908	4000
1909	4000
1910	4036
1911	4424
1912	4000
1913	4000
1914	4000
1915	4000
1916	4000
1917	5104
1918	4988
1919	4814
1920	4000
1921	5292
1922	5538
1923	5484
Year end (20 March)	
1924	3186
1925	5426
1926	8260
1927	8300

1928	8637
1929	116 164
1930	17 954
1931	756
1931–34	nil
1935	30 000

Note: Between 1890 and 1928 the Imperial Bank paid the Iranian government 6% of published net profits (before tax and, of course, the government's royalties). In 1929 the Bank agreed to make the calculation on a different basis. Under this new arrangement, the Bank paid the government £28 860 in that year, together with an additional £87 304 to cover royalties which the government claimed it was owed from past years. Royalty payments ceased when the Bank stopped issuing notes in 1932, but in 1935 the Bank agreed to make a further £30 000 payment as a response to the government's claim that it had been underpaid royalties in the past.

APPENDIX 8: A NOTE ON IRANIAN NAMES AND TITLES

Some explanation of these may be useful. Until 1925 there were no surnames in Iran. Individuals often denoted their place of origin by the use of a suffix such as Esfahani or Shirazi. *Khan* was another usual suffix, sometimes awarded by the Shah as a title, but assumed as well as a sign of gentility similar to the British use of 'esquire'. Prefixes were also commonly used, to denote, for instance, that a person was directly descended from the Prophet. *Mirza* was a habitually used prefix and meant that the bearer was an educated man: it was a title used by scribes, secretaries and scholars. *Mirza* was also used as a suffix, denoting in this case that the bearer of the title was a prince. The gift (and sale) of extravagant non-hereditary titles to ministers and officials was a particular feature of the Qajar dynasty – for example Amin os-Soltan ('Trusted of the King'), Moshir od-Doule ('Counsellor of State') and Naser ol-Molk ('Helper of the Kingdom'). After the death of the holder, such titles could either be bestowed on his son or some other courtier or official. Other titles, such as Amin ol-Zarb ('Master of the Mint') or Serdar-Sepah ('Head of the Army'), described the position and function of the bearer. These were the result of government or military appointment, and although non-hereditary were in fact often held in the same family.

In 1925, the then Prime Minister, Reza Khan, abolished all military titles, and suggested the use of surnames. He himself adopted the family name of Pahlavi which had pre-Islamic origins. Ten years later, in 1935, all titles and honorifics were officially abolished by government decree, including the polite terminology of social rank.

APPENDIX 9: SHORT BIOGRAPHIES OF LEADING PERSONALITIES

AHMAD SHAH QAJAR (1897–1930). Last of the Qajar Shahs, he succeeded his father Mohammad Ali Shah in July 1909 when he was 12 years old. Until he came of age, Persia was governed by a Regent. He was crowned in Tehran in July 1914 at the age of 17, and deposed in December 1925.

AMIN OD-DOULE, MIRZA ALI KHAN (1844–1904). Served in the Persian Foreign Ministry in 1860s. Appointed Secretary to Naser od-Din Shah 1870, and Private Secretary in 1873. Head of Mint 1875–76. Minister of Posts 1876–95 and Minister of Pensions and Endowments 1881. Granted title of Amin od-Doule in

1883. Accompanied Shah on European trips 1873, 1878 and 1889. Leader of the reformist administration 1896–98, and appointed Prime Minister 1897. His Tehran palace became the Bank's Chief Office.

AMIN OS-SOLTAN, MIRZA ALI ASGHAR KHAN (1854–1907). Inherited his father's title and offices, becoming *inter alia* Minister of Court and Chief of Customs 1883. Named Sadr-e A'zam, 1888. Went with Shah to Europe 1889. Reappointed as Prime Minister 1898–1903, and granted title of Atabek-e A'zam (Lord Warden of the Realm). Negotiated British Loan of 1892 and Russian Loans of 1900 and 1901. Recalled as Prime Minister by Mohammad Ali Shah April 1907, but assassinated end of August 1907.

AYRTON, FRANK A. (1887–1951). Joined Bank's overseas staff in 1909. Served in the following Persian branches – Kermanshah, Tabriz, Shiraz, Esfahan, Kerman, Ahwaz, Tehran Bazaar and Chief Office. Appointed Deputy Manager, London Office, 1935; Manager, 1947. Retired in 1951, and died later that year.

BARNES, SIR HUGH SHAKESPEARE (1853–1940). His career in the Indian Civil Service culminated in the Lieutenant Governorship of Burma 1903–1905. He was a Member of the Council of India from 1905 to 1913. He was appointed a director of the Anglo–Persian Oil Company in 1909, and of the Imperial Bank of Persia in 1913. He remained on both Boards until his death. He was Chairman of the Bank from 1916 to 1937.

BULLARD, SIR READER WILLIAM (1885–1976). His career in the Levant Consular Service included postings in the Middle East, Balkans and Russia, and culminated in his appointment as Minister and then Ambassador in Tehran 1939–46. Author of *Britain and the Middle East* (1951) and *Camels Must Go* (1961).

BUTTERS, ORD A. (b. 1881). Joined the Bank's overseas staff in 1909 and served in the following branches – Mohammarah, Shiraz, Rasht, Nasratabad, Mashad, Tabriz and Baghdad. Served in Persia under General Sykes between 1916 and 1918. Became Chief Inspector in 1930, and acted for the Chief Manager in 1931. Appointed Chief Manager in 1934. Retired in 1939.

CLIVE, RT. HON. SIR ROBERT HENRY (1877–1948). After service as HM's Consul General in Tangier and Munich, served as British Minister to Tehran from 1926 to 1931.

CORNWALLIS, SIR KINAHAN (1883–1959). Served in the Sudan Civil Service 1906–14 and the Egyptian Civil Service 1914–24. Director, Arab Bureau Cairo 1916–20. Advisor to Ministry of Interior, Iraq Government, 1921–35. Foreign Office 1939–41. Ambassador in Baghdad 1941–45. Chairman, Middle East (Official) Committee, Foreign Office 1945–46. Director of the Bank 1945–59. Visited Iran 1949 to negotiate Bank's *modus operandi* agreement with Iranian government.

COX, MAJOR GEN. SIR PERCY Z. (1864–1937). Consul General, Bushire 1904 and Political Resident Persian Gulf 1909. Secretary, Foreign Department of the Government of India 1914. Chief Political Office Indian Expeditionary Force 'D' (Mesopotamia) 1914–18. Acting British Minister, Tehran, 1918–20. High Commissioner, Mesopotamia, 1920–23.

CURZON, GEORGE N. FIRST MARQUESS OF KEDLESTON (1859–1925). Under Secretary of State for India 1891–92. Under Secretary of State for Foreign Affairs 1895–98. Viceroy and Governor General of India 1899–1905. Lord Privy Seal 1915–16. Secretary of State for Foreign Affairs 1919–24. A director of the Persian Bank Mining Rights Corporation. Wrote *Persia and the Persian Question* (1892).

DALTON, LIONEL E. (1859–1905). Formerly with New Oriental Bank Corporation in Bushire. Joined Imperial Bank in 1890 as Manager, Bushire. Opened Shiraz branch in 1892. Appointed acting Sub-Manager, Tehran, and Inspector of Branches in 1893. Acted for Chief Manager in 1895. Took over duties as Manager, Shiraz, in 1896. Appointed Chief Inspector 1899; Sub-Manager and Chief Inspector 1901, and Deputy Chief Manager in 1903. Died in a gun accident in April 1905.

D'ARCY, WILLIAM KNOX (1848–1917). Granted oil concession by Persian government in May 1901. Formed First Exploitation Company May 1903. With Burmah Oil Company, formed Concessions Syndicate Ltd in May 1905. Director of Burmah Oil Co. 1909–17. Director of Anglo–Persian Oil Co. 1909–17.

DAVAR, ALI AKBAR (1887–1934). Prosecutor General of Persia 1911. Director of Public Education 1921. Formed Radical Party in 1925. Minister of Public Works, 1925–26. Minister of Justice and close adviser to Reza Shah 1927–33, he was assigned the task of completely reorganising the Ministry of Justice.

DURAND, RT HON. SIR H. MORTIMER (1850–1924). Foreign Secretary, Government of India 1884–94. British Minister in Tehran 1894–1900.

EBTEHAJ, ABOL HASSAN (1899–   ). Joined Imperial Bank in 1920. Worked in Exchange and Superintendent's Departments before becoming Assistant Chief Inspector. Applied for promotion to grade rank (level of European staff), but was refused. Resigned 1936. Joined Ministry of Finance. Government Inspector, Agricultural Bank, and Controller of state-owned companies 1936. Vice-Governor Bank Melli (State Bank) 1938. Chairman and Managing Director Mortgage Bank 1940. Governor Bank Melli 1942–50. Chairman Iran Delegation to Bretton Woods Conference 1944. Ambassador to France 1950–52. Adviser to Managing Director IMF 1952. Director Middle East Dept. IMF 1953. Managing Director Plan Organisation Tehran 1954–59. Chairman Economic Commission Baghdad Pact 1956. Member High Economic Council 1954–59. Founder of Iranians' Bank 1959 (private Bank associated with Citibank, New York 1968). Chairman 1959–77. Imprisoned under Shah's regime November 1961. Charges dropped, and released June 1962. Founder and Chairman, Iran American International Insurance Co. 1974–79.

ELDRID, ERNEST M. (1876–1961). Joined London Staff of Bank in 1893 as a junior; and overseas staff in 1897. Opened Kerman sub-branch 1904. Served in Shiraz, Yazd, Kerman, Mashad, Tabriz, and Rasht (during Jangali troubles). Appointed Sub-Manager London Office in 1921, and Secretary of the Bank in 1927. Manager and Secretary 1930–1935. Director of the Bank 1934–56.

EVANS, 'HAJI' HAROLD (1894–   ). Appointed to overseas staff of Imperial Bank in 1919. Acting Accountant, then Accountant Basra branch 1923–27. Manager Basra 1934–41 and 1943–46. He also served at Baghdad, Tehran, Hamadan, Borujerd, Ahwaz and Bushire. Retired in 1946.

FIRUZ MIRZA, PRINCE NOSRAT OD-DOULE (1888–1937). Eldest son of Farman Farma. Minister of Justice 1916 and 1918–19. Minister of Foreign Affairs 1919–20. Governor of Fars 1923–24. Minister of Justice 1925. Minister of Finance 1927–29.

GOLSHAYAN, A. G. Iranian Minister of Finance in the government of Mohamed Saed which came to power in November 1948. Negotiated the Supplemental Agreement of July 1949 between the Iranian government and Anglo–Iranian Oil Company, and the March 1949 Agreement between the government and the Bank.

GREENWAY, CHARLES, FIRST BARON OF STANBRIDGE EARLS (1857–1934). Joined Shaw Wallace & Co., India, 1893; partner 1897. Senior partner R. G. Shaw & Co. London. Managing Director Lloyd Scott & Co. 1910. Director

Anglo–Persian Oil 1909–34; Managing Director 1910–19. Chairman 1914–27; President 1927–34. Chairman Persian Railway Syndicate, 1919–20. Director Imperial Bank of Persia 1910–18.

GREY, RT. HON. SIR EDWARD, FIRST VISCOUNT OF FALLODON (1867–1933). Under Secretary of State for Foreign Affairs 1892–1895; Secretary of State for Foreign Affairs 1905–16.

GRIFFIN, SIR LEPEL H. (1840–1908). Joined Bengal Civil Service 1860. Chief Secretary Punjab 1871–80. Chief Political Officer Afghanistan 1880. Resident at Indore and Agent of Governor General for Central India 1881–88. Resident at Hyderabad 1888. Chairman, East India Association; Burmah Ruby Mines Ltd.; Persian Bank Mining Rights Corporation. Director Imperial Bank of Persia 1889–1908; Chairman 1898–1908.

HALE, FREDERICK (1882–1968). Joined overseas staff of Bank 1907. Served at Esfahan, Tehran Bazaar, Shiraz, Ahwaz, Kermanshah and Soltanabad. Opened Birjand branch in 1913. Appointed Deputy Chief Manager Tehran in 1925; Assistant Sub-Manager London Office 1928; Sub-Manager, London, 1930; Manager, London, 1935. Retired in 1947. Director 1947–60.

HARDINGE, RT. HON. SIR ARTHUR H. (1895–1933). HM's Commissioner and Consul General, British East African Protectorate, 1896–1900. HM's Minister, Tehran, 1900–05. Wrote *A Diplomatist in the East* (1928).

HAWKINS, V. A. CAESAR (1860–1945). A protégé of Sir Thomas Jackson (q.v.), he was Sub-Manager of the Hong Kong branch of the Hongkong Bank at the end of Jackson's Chief Managership; then appointed Chief Inspector. Resigned 1907. Director Imperial Bank of Persia 1908–39. Resident Director in Tehran for six months in 1908. Chairman of Bank's Finance Committee 1914–39.

ILIFF, SIR WILLIAM A. B. (1898–1972). Financial Counsellor at British Legation, Tehran, 1941–44. Representative of HM Treasury in Middle East 1944–48. Loan Director World Bank 1948; Assistant to President 1951; Vice-President 1956–62.

JACKSON, SIR THOMAS (1841–1915). Bank of Ireland, Belfast, 1860. Went East to join Agra Bank 1864. Entered Hongkong Bank 1866. Chief Manager Hongkong Bank 1876–1902, except for two short periods. Appointed to London Committee Hongkong Bank, 1902–15. Director of London & County, then London, County and Westminster Bank 1903–15. Director of Imperial Bank 1902; Chairman 1908–15.

JOHNSON, FRANK HARCOURT (1900–). Joined Bank's London staff 1921; overseas staff 1923. Served in following branches – Tehran, Duzdab, Bushire, Nasratabad, Esfahan, Bandar Abbas, Yazd, Pahlavi, Shiraz, Khorramshahr, Baghdad. Advocated Bank's expansion into the Arab world and the Levant. Appointed Deputy Chief Manager Tehran 1948. Acted for Chief Manager in 1949. Retired 1951.

KENNET OF THE DENE, EDWARD HILTON YOUNG, LORD (1879–1960). Member of British government Financial Missions to India 1920, Poland, 1924, Iraq 1925 and 1930. Chairman of various Commissions, including Indian Currency and Finance 1926. British representative at Hague Conference on International Finance 1922. Financial Secretary to HM's Treasury 1921–22. Minister of Health 1931–35. Chairman Foreign Transactions Advisory Committee 1937–39. Chairman Treasury Capital Issues Committee 1939–59. Director Imperial Bank, BBIME and BBME 1937–56; Chairman 1945–52 and 1953–55. Visited Iran twice, in 1946 and 1948.

KESWICK, WILLIAM (1835–1912). Director of Jardine & Co., China merchants,

and of Matheson & Co., London. Chairman, Jardine, Matheson. Member of Hong
Kong Legislative Council; Consul and Consul General. Director of Indo–China
Steam Navigation Co. Director, Hongkong Bank; Chairman 1880–81; member of
London Committee 1890. Chairman, British and Chinese Corporation. President,
China Association. Unionist MP for Epsom 1899–1912. First Chairman Imperial
Bank of Persia 1889–1899; director 1889–1912.

LANDSDOWNE, HENRY C. K. PETTY-FITZMAURICE, 5TH MARQUESS
(1845–1927). Governor-General and Viceroy of India, 1888–93. Secretary of War
1895–1900. Foreign Secretary, 1900–05. Minister Without Portfolio, 1915–16.

LASCELLES, RT. HON. SIR FRANK CAVENDISH (1841–1920). Agent and
Consul General Bulgaria 1879. HM's Minister Rumania 1886. British Minister to
Persia 1891. Ambassador to Russia 1894 and Germany 1895–1908.

LE ROUGETEL, SIR JOHN H. (1894–1975). Entered Diplomatic Service 1920.
Served in Vienna, Budapest, Ottawa, Tokyo, Peking, The Hague, Bucharest,
Moscow, Shanghai and London. Ambassador to Iran 1945–60.

LINDENBLATT, DR KURT German national; recruited from National Bank of
Bulgaria to be first Director and Manager of Persia's national bank, Bank Melli,
1928–33. Accused of permitting unsound loans and becoming involved in illegal
foreign exchange dealings, he was tried, sentenced to 18 months' imprisonment and
fined.

LORAINE, RT. HON. SIR PERCY L. (1880–1961). Third Secretary, British
Legation Tehran, 1907. British Minister to Persia 1921–26.

MCLEAN, DAVID (b. 1833). An expert in Eastern exchange and silver, he was
one of the Hongkong Bank's leading Managers; in Shanghai 1864–72 and London
1872–89. Refused the offer of Chief Managership three times. First officer of
Hongkong Bank to be elected to its London Consultative Committee, 1889–94.
Director, British and Chinese Corporation. Director Imperial Bank 1889–1903.

MACLEAN, H. W. (b. 1861). Tabriz manager of New Oriental Bank Corpor-
ation when recruited by Imperial Bank in 1890. Opened Esfahan branch 1890;
manager Tabriz branch 1893–98. Acting Chief Manager 1899, and Deputy Chief
Manager 1899–1900. Resigned 1900. Appointed by Persian government as Mint
Master 1901. Dismissed 1902 as result of Russian pressure. Conducted Economic
Survey of Persia for British Board of Trade 1903. Represented various British
commercial interests in Tehran from 1913, notably Anglo–Persian Oil, Persian
Railways Syndicate and Persian Transport Co. Attached *ex officio* to British
Legation Tehran.

MCMAHON, COL. SIR A. HENRY (1862–1949). Joined Indian Political Department 1890 after military service in the Punjab. Involved in boundary demarcations
between Baluchistan and Afghanistan 1894, 1895 and 1896, and Persia and
Afghanistan in Seistan 1903–05. Foreign Secretary to Government of India
1911–14. High Commissioner Egypt 1914–16. British Commissioner on Middle
East International Commission, 1919. Director of Imperial Bank 1917–49; Chairman 1937–45.

MCMURRAY, JAMES H. (1877–1950). Appointed to Bank's London staff 1897;
overseas staff 1900. Served at Tehran Bazaar, Nasratabad and Hamadan branches,
opening the latter in 1909. Head of Commission of Control of Expenditure which
financed Russian forces in Persia 1917–18. Awarded OBE for services 1918, and
CBE 1921. Appointed Chief Manager of Bank 1919. Resigned 1925 owing to ill
health. Elected to Board 1928. Director 1928–50. Mission to Persia 1929.

MACQUEEN, ANGUS (1910–   ). Joined Bank in 1930. Appointed to overseas
staff 1934. Served in following branches – Baghdad, Tehran, Tehran Bazaar,

Esfahan, Khorramshahr, Kermanshah, Hamadan, Shiraz, Bushire, Ahwaz, Kuwait, Aden, Beirut, Damascus and Casablanca. Appointed Deputy General Manager London in 1962; General Manager 1966–70. Director BBME 1970–78; Chairman 1974–78.

MALKAM KHAN, MIRZA (1833–1908). Son of Armenian convert to Islam. Studied in Paris 1843–52. Official Persian government translator 1852–56. Member of official missions to Istanbul and Paris 1856–57. Wrote first of a series of essays on reform 1858–59. Banished to Ottoman territory 1861. Held various diplomatic posts in Ottoman Empire in 1860s; became Ottoman citizen 1869. Recalled as advisor to Mirza Hoseyn Khan Moshir od-Doule in 1872. Persian Ambassador to England 1873–89. Dismissed 1889. Titles, rank and salary revoked 1891. Became noted *emigré* proponent of reform until 1898, when appointed Persian Minister to Rome, 1898–1908.

MARLING, SIR CHARLES M. (1862–1933). Counsellor, British Legation Tehran 1906–09; *Chargé d'Affaires* 1910; and British Minister Tehran 1915–19.

MEHDI KHAN, MOBASSER OD-DOULE (b. 1894). Entered Bank's service in Mashad, 1898, working there as clerk, Chief Clerk, and then the Bank's Agent in Nishapur. Transferred to Tehran 1926. Head of Exchange Department and then Chief Interpreter. Retired in 1934.

MILLSPAUGH, DR ARTHUR C. (1883–1955). Petroleum specialist in US State Department 1920–22; Foreign Trade Adviser 1921–22. Administrator General of Persian Finances, 1922–27, and of Iranian Finances 1943–45. Author of *The American Task in Persia* (1925), and *Americans in Persia* (1946).

MOHAMMAD ALI SHAH QAJAR (1872–1925). Valiahd (Crown Prince) during Mozaffar od-Din's reign, he succeeded his father in 1907. Was crowned as Persia's first constitutional monarch but was unsympathetic to nationalist movement, and abrogated the Constitution in 1908. Deposed by the constitutionalists in 1909. Tried to regain throne in 1911–12, with Russian help. Finally banished to Russia 1912.

MOHAMMAD REZA SHAH PAHLAVI (1920–80). Succeeded his father in 1941 at the age of 21. Proclaimed end to absolute rule, granting power to Cabinet and Majles. Forced into exile early August 1953 by the Prime Minister, Dr Mosaddeq (q.v.). Returned almost at once when Mosaddeq fell from power three days later in a royalist counter coup. Forced to leave Iran by Islamic Revolution of 1979.

MORNARD, JOSEPH J. (1865–1916). Belgian national who was appointed to Persian Customs Administration 1900. Head of Central Customs Administration 1901. Inspector General of Customs 1907; and then Administrator of Customs when Naus (q.v.) was dismissed. Came into conflict with Shuster (q.v.) 1911. Appointed Treasurer General in January 1912, after Shuster's dismissal. Responsible for first general account of government revenues and expenditure to be published, 1913. Resigned July 1914.

MOSADDEQ, DR MOHAMMAD (1876–1967). Persian Governor of Fars 1920; Minister of Finance 1921; Governor of Azerbaijan 1922 and Minister of Finance 1923. Member of Majles 1923–27. Opposed Reza Shah's accession 1925. Leader of Nationalist upsurge 1944 onwards; represented Tehran in Majles and led National Front Party. Prime Minister of Iran 1951–53. Nationalised oil industry 1951. Removed from power by coup; subsequently imprisoned December 1953–August 1956.

MOSHIR OD-DOULE, MIRZA HOSEYN KHAN (1828–1881). After studying in Paris, he was appointed Persian Consul in Bombay 1851, then Tiflis 1855–58. Minister, then Ambassador to Istanbul 1858–70. Minister of War and Commander of the Army (Sepahsalar) 1871. Appointed Prime Minister (Sadr-e Azam) 1871. Took Shah to Europe 1873. Dismissed from all posts September 1873. Reinstated as Foreign Minister December 1873. Minister of War 1874. Dismissed from all posts 1880. Had considerable reputation as a reformer; was pro-western and the chief Persian promoter of the Reuter Concession.

MOZAFFAR OD-DIN SHAH QAJAR (1853–1907). Second son of Naser od-Din Shah. Declared Valiahd (Crown Prince) 1862. Governor of Azerbaijan from 1861. Succeeded father 1896. Visited Europe twice 1901 and 1902, but England on the latter visit only. Invested with Order of the Garter in Persia 1903. Signed Constitution December 1906, agreeing to set up National Assembly and a Court of Justice.

MUSKER, HAROLD (1897–1970). Joined Bank's London staff 1920; overseas staff 1921. Served at various branches, including Bombay, Tehran, Barforush, Duzdab, Basra, Mohammarah, Shiraz and Kermanshah. Inspector's Department 1932. Appointed Chief Accountant 1938; Deputy Chief Manager 1939; Deputy Manager London 1946; Manager 1951–52. General Manager in London 1952–61. Director 1960–66.

NASER OD-DIN SHAH QAJAR (1831–1896). Became Shah in 1848. Made three visits to Europe. Granted the Imperial Bank's Concession 1889. Received by Queen Victoria at Windsor later the same year, and invested with the Order of the Garter. Assassinated in 1896.

NAUS, JOSEPH. A Sub-Manager of the Belgian Customs and Excise Administration, he was appointed Director of Persian Customs in 1898. Charged with reorganisation of Customs in March 1899. Director of Revenues and Minister of State in 1901. Took over direction of Postal Services in 1902. Named Minister of Customs and Posts 1903. Attacked in the Majles 1907, and forced to resign. At peak of his achievements, he was simultaneously Minister of Customs and Posts, Administrator of Customs, Treasurer, Head of Passports and Member of the Supreme Council of State.

NEWELL, GEORGE (1847–1929). Recruited from the London branch of the Comptoir National d'Escompte de Paris in 1889 to be Secretary of the Imperial Bank. Appointed Manager and Secretary in 1899. Retired in December 1917.

NORMAN, HERMAN C. (1872–1955). Entered Diplomatic Service 1894. Secretary of British Delegation to Paris Peace Conference 1919. British Minister to Persia 1920–21.

PAYN, THOMAS Recruited from Bombay branch of the Comptoir National d'Escompte de Paris in 1891 to open Bombay agency of Imperial Bank and Bank of China, Japan and the Straits. Opened the jointly owned Calcutta agency in 1892, becoming Chief Agent in India. Resigned 1894 to become London Manager of Bank of China and Japan.

PAYNE, LESLIE C. (1902–1973). Joined Bank's London staff 1922; overseas staff 1924. Served at various branches, including Bombay, Nasratabad, Mohammarah, Esfahan, Kermanshah, Soltanabad and Baghdad. Appointed acting Chief Accountant 1939; Chief Accountant 1940; Deputy Chief Manager 1946; Chief Manager 1948. Asked to resign in 1951.

PRIOR, SIR C. GEOFFREY (1896–1972). Indian Political Service 1923. Secretary, Persian Gulf Residency 1927. Political Agent Bahrain 1929–32. Deputy Secretary to Indian Foreign Ofice 1933. Prime Minister Alwar State 1936–38. Political Resident Persian Gulf 1939–46. Member Middle East War Council 1941–42. Represented India at Foreign Ministers' Conference 1945. Governor Baluchistan 1946. Retired 1949. Appointed Resident Director British Bank of Iran and the Middle East 1949. Resigned 1951.

RABINO, JOSEPH (1843–1919). Recruited from the Crédit Lyonnais in Egypt, 1889, to be first Chief Manager of Imperial Bank. Responsible for establishment of the Bank in Persia. Resigned from the Bank in 1908, and retired to London.

RAZMARA, GEN. ALI (1902–1951). Graduate of St Cyr, he served in Persian Cossack Brigade. As Chief of Staff of the Army, responsible for the restoration to central authority of the separatist Communist regime in Azerbaijan in 1946. Appointed Prime Minister June 1950. Committed to a programme of reforms and the rooting out of corruption. The nationalisation of the oil industry followed his assassination in March 1951.

REUTER, BARON GEORGE DE (1863–1909). Younger son of Baron Julius de Reuter. Visited Persia October 1888. Negotiated Bank Concession with Persian authorities, and was one of the signatories. One of the Bank's first directors, he was also a director of the Persian Bank Mining Rights Corporation.

REUTER, BARON PAUL JULIUS DE (1816–1899). Founded Reuters News Agency, transferring its head office to London in 1851 when the cable was laid between England and France. Became British subject 1857. Awarded Barony of Duchy of Saxe-Coburg-Gotha in 1871. Granted famous Reuter Concession, the precursor of the Imperial Bank Concession, in 1872. A founder of the Imperial Bank.

REZA SHAH PAHLAVI (1878–1944). Rose through ranks to command Persian Cossack Brigade. One of the two leaders of the 1921 Coup. Became Commander-in-Chief of the Armed Forces, and Minister of War, in successive cabinets 1921–23. Appointed Prime Minister 1923. Proclaimed Shah by special Constituent Assembly in 1925: first ruler of new Pahlavi Dynasty. Crowned 1926. Architect of programme of reform and state-led industrialisation. Abdicated in 1941.

ROGERS, SYDNEY F. (1866–1936). Appointed to Bank's overseas staff 1892. Completed liquidation of Baghdad and Basra agencies 1893–94. Served in Yazd, Shiraz, Mashad and Tabriz branches. Appointed Deputy Chief Manager Tehran 1908. Acted for Chief Manager 1909. Retired from Persia 1910. Appointed Sub-Manager London; Manager and Secretary London 1918–27; Manager 1927–30. Director 1927–36, and member of Finance Committee.

SALISBURY, ROBERT ARTHUR TALBOT GASCOYNE-CECIL, 3RD MARQUESS OF (1830–1903). Secretary of State for Foreign Affairs 1878–80, 1885–86, 1887–92, 1895–1900. Prime Minister 1885–86, 1886–92, 1895–1902.

SCHINDLER, GEN. SIR A. HOUTUM (d. 1916). Naturalised British subject of German origin who had become a General in the Shah's army. An ex-employee of both the Indo–European Telegraph Co. and Persian Telegraphic Services, he began working for Reuter in 1889. Appointed the Bank's Adviser in Tehran later the same year. Became Inspector of Branches. In nominal charge of the Bank's roads department, and from March 1890, Inspector General of Mines for the Persian Bank Mining Corporation. Dismissed from Bank's service in 1894. Contributed to Persian entry in 9th and 11th editions of *Encyclopaedia Britannica*.

SHEAHAN, TIMOTHY (1894–1983). Appointed to Bank's overseas staff 1919. Served in Basra, Baghdad, Soltanabad, Hamadan, Mohammarah, Bombay, Barforush and Kerman. Travelling Inspector 1931–34; acting Chief Inspector 1934–37; Chief Inspector 1937–46. Retired 1946.

SHEPHERD, SIR FRANCIS M. (1893–1962). Appointed to Consular Service 1920. A variety of postings culminated in his first Ambassadorial appointment to Iran in 1950–52. Subsequently HM Ambassador to Poland 1952–54. Retired 1954.

SHUSTER, W. MORGAN (1877–1960). In Cuban Customs Service 1899–1901. Collector of Customs, Manila 1901–06. Member, Philippines Commission

1906–09. Invited by Majles to be Financial Adviser and Treasurer General 1911. Dismissed January 1912 as a result of Russian pressure. Wrote *The Strangling of Persia* (1912). Adviser to Persian government on the North Persian oil concessions 1920–24.

TEYMURTASH, ABDOL HOSEYN KHAN (1888–1933). Persian Governor of Gilan 1918. Minister of Justice 1922. Governor General of Kerman 1923–24. Minister of Public Works 1924. Minister of Court and close adviser to Reza Shah 1925–32. Arrested January 1933, tried and convicted on fraud charges. Died in prison.

TOWNLEY, SIR WALTER B. (1863–1945). Third Secretary, British Legation Tehran 1889–92. HM Minister Rumania 1910–12; Persia 1912–15.

VOSUQ OD-DOULE, MIRZA HASAN KHAN (1868–1930). Persian Minister of Foreign Affairs 1911; 1913–14. Prime Minister and Minister of Foreign Affairs 1916–17 and 1918–20. Negotiated Anglo-Persian Agreement 1919. Minister of Finance 1926.

WALTER, VIVIAN L. (1891–1971). Appointed to Bank's London Staff 1908; overseas staff 1911. Resigned to join army in World War One; rejoined Bank 1919. Served mainly in Tehran and Esfahan. Appointed Acting Chief Accountant 1919. Confirmed as Chief Accountant 1923. Acted as Deputy Manager in 1929 and 1930. Manager Esfahan 1930. Appointed Deputy Chief Manager 1938; Chief Manager 1939–48. Retired 1948.

WARR, CYRIL F. (1904–   ). Appointed to Bank's London staff 1922; overseas staff 1924. Served at Abadan, Ahwaz, Hamadan, Mashad, Birjand, Kermanshah and Tehran. Appointed Travelling Inspector 1941; Chief Inspector 1946; Acting Chief Manager 1951–52. Closed Chief Office for business July 1952. Deputy General Manager London 1953–62; General Manager 1962–65; Director 1966–70.

WILKINSON, EDWARD (1879–1937). Engaged in Odessa from Crédit Lyonnais 1902. Acting Chief Accountant 1905. Resigned 1906; reappointed 1907, as Acting Chief Accountant again. Confirmed as Chief Accountant 1912. Manager Mashad branch 1913–15. Chief Accountant Tehran 1915. Acting Deputy Chief Manager 1919; confirmed 1921. Chief Manager 1925–34.

WOLFF, RT. HON. SIR HENRY DRUMMOND (1830–1908). Member of Diplomatic Service. Member of Parliament 1880–85. Founder Member of Primrose League. HM's Minister in Persia 1888–91.

WOOD, AUGUSTUS OTTIWELL (1865–1921). Recruited from New Oriental Bank Corporation, Bombay, 1893, and appointed acting Accountant Bushire. Acting Manager Bushire 1896; acting Manager Esfahan 1899; Manager Esfahan 1902. Appointed acting Chief Inspector 1906; Chief Manager 1908. Retired 1919. First ex-officer of Bank to be elected to Board, 1920.

APPENDIX 10: CHIEF MANAGERS OF THE IMPERIAL BANK 1889–1952

Joseph Rabino   *October 1889–August 1908*
Augustus O. Wood   *August 1908–September 1919*
James McMurray   *September 1919–November 1925*
Edward Wilkinson   *November 1925–October 1934*
Ord A. Butters   *October 1934–July 1939*
Vivian L. Walter   *July 1939–March 1948*
Leslie C. Payne   *March 1948–August 1951*
C. F. Warr (acting)   *August 1951–July 1952*

NOTES

NOTES TO INTRODUCTION

1 The best accounts of the nineteenth century history of these banks remain A. S. J. Baster, *The Imperial Banks* (London, 1929) and *idem*, *The International Banks* (London, 1935).

2 The most useful scholarly histories include those of the National Bank of Australasia, G. Blainey, *Gold and Paper* (Melbourne, 1958), the Australia and New Zealand Bank, S. J. Butlin, *Australia and New Zealand Bank* (London, 1961) and the Bank of London and South America, D. Joslin, *A Century of Banking in Latin America* (London, 1963). The more popular histories include the studies of the constituent banks of Standard Chartered, Sir Compton Mackenzie, *Realms of Silver: one hundred years of banking in the East* (London, 1954) and J. A. Henry, *The First Hundred Years of the Standard Bank* (London, 1963); the history of Grindlays by G. Tyson, *100 Years of Banking in Asia and Africa* (London, 1963); and the history of Barclays D.C.O. by Sir Julian Crossley and John Blandford, *The DCO Story* (London, 1975). The study of the Hongkong Bank by Maurice Collins, *Wayfoong* (London, 1965) also falls into this category. *The History of the Hongkong Bank* by Professor F. H. H. King, which is being researched concurrently with this History, will be the first in-depth scholarly study of that bank.

CHAPTER I THE FOUNDATION OF THE BANK

1 S. Bakhash, *Iran: Monarchy, Bureaucracy and Reform under the Qajars 1856–1896* (London, 1978), pp. 43–6; N. R. Keddie, *Roots of Revolution* (London, 1981), pp. 59–60.

2 J. Bharier, *Economic Development in Iran* (London, 1971), p. 20.

3 C. Issawi, (ed.) *The Economic History of Iran 1800–1914* (Chicago, 1971). This volume of annotated documents and readings is the best source on the nineteenth-century economy of Iran, and readers seeking further information on the views expressed in this text, and qualifications to those views, are recommended to

consult the Issawi volume. There is also an exhaustive study of the nineteenth-century Iranian economy by A. Seyf, 'Some Aspects of Economic Development in Iran, 1800–1906' (PhD Reading, 1982). This thesis disputes some of Issawi's views, suggesting, for instance, a much slower rate of growth for Iranian foreign trade over the century than Issawi (p. 586).

4 Issawi, *Economic History*, chapter 6. For the view of an authoritative British contemporary, see G. N. Curzon, *Persia and the Persian Question* (London, 1892), vol. 2, pp. 523–5.

5 Issawi, *Economic History*, p. 70; G. Nashat, *The Origins of Modern Reform in Iran, 1870–1880* (Chicago, 1982), p. 114.

6 Issawi, *Economic History*, chapter 8. P. W. Avery and J. B. Simmons, 'Persia on a Cross of Silver, 1880–1890', *Middle Eastern Studies* 1974.

7 N. R. Keddie, *Iran. Religion, Politics and Society* (London, 1980), p. 125.

8 There is a fine account of the Russian advance, and of British–Russian relations in Iran generally, in F. Kazemzadeh, *Russia and Britain in Persia 1864–1914* (New Haven, 1968).

9 R. L. Greaves, *Persia and the Defence of India 1884–1892* (London, 1959), p. 25.

10 *ibid*, pp. 194–5 and *passim*.

11 *ibid*, p. 141.

12 Curzon, *Persia*, vol. 1, p. 3.

13 Bakhash, *Iran*, chapter 2; Nashat, *Origins*, chapter 7.

14 Bakhash, *Iran*, p. 29.

15 Kazemzadeh, *Russia and Britain*, pp. 100–3.

16 G. Storey, *Reuter's Century* (London, 1951). Twenty years later a Royal Warrant gave de Reuter and his heirs the privileges of foreign nobility in England.

17 H. Collins, *From Pigeon Post to Wireless* (London, 1925), p. 117.

18 Curzon, *Persia*, vol. 1, p. 480.

19 Concession of H. I. M. the Shah to Baron Julius de Reuter (Translation). Enclosure in W. T. Thomson to Lord Granville, 20 May 1873, Foreign Office files (hereafter FO) 60/405, Public Record Office. See also Issawi, *Economic History*, pp. 177–84, and L. E. Frechtling, 'The Reuter Concession in Persia', *The Asiatic Review* (1938), pp. 518–33.

20 Kazemzadeh, *Russia and Britain*, p. 108.

21 Nashat, *Origins*, p. 131.

22 Bakhash, *Iran*, p. 114.

23 Collins, *From Pigeon Post*, *passim*. R. A. McDaniel, *The Shuster Mission and the Persian Constitutional Revolution* (Minneapolis, 1974), pp. 12–13.

24 Charles E. Harvey, *The Rio Tinto Company* (Penzance, 1981), pp. 6–9. A. Matheson (ed.), *Memorials of Hugh M. Matheson* (London, 1899).

25 H. Matheson to James Bullen Smith, 27 December 1872, Jardine Skinner Archives, File No. 78, Cambridge University Library.

26 H. Rawlinson to Sir John Kaye, 7 August 1872; FO 60/405.

27 de Reuter to Lord Granville, 12 September 1872, FO 60/405.

28 Foreign Office to de Reuter, 15 October 1872, FO 60/405.

29 Kazemzadeh, *Russia and Britain*, p. 110.

30 W. T. Thomson to Rt. Hon. Earl Granville, 2 December 1873, FO 60/405.

31 M. Entner, *Russo–Persian Commercial Relations 1828–1914* (Florida, 1965), pp. 18–19.

32 Kazemzadeh, *Russia and Britain*, p. 109.

33 Bakhash, *Iran*, p. 114.

34 Kazemzadeh, *Russia and Britain*, pp. 112–13.

35 *ibid*, p. 115–17. D. Wright, *The Persians Amongst the English* (London, 1985), pp. 121–35.
36 The political and economic power of the *ulama* was growing under the Qajars. See H. Algar, *Religion and State in Iran, 1785–1906: The Role of the Ulama of the Qajar Period* (Berkeley, 1969), and Keddie, *Roots of Revolution*, chapter 1 gives a short survey of Iran's religious history.
37 Bakhash, *Iran*, pp. 115–18.
38 *ibid*, pp. 119–20.
39 Collins, *From Pigeon Post*.
40 Kazemzadeh, *Russia and Britain*, pp. 123–4.
41 Collins, *From Pigeon Post*, pp. 169–70.
42 Note to Lord Tenterden from Lord Derby, May 1874, FO 60/406.
43 Kazemzadeh, *Russia and Britain*, pp. 135–43.
44 *ibid*, pp. 144–6.
45 W. T. Thomson to Foreign Office, 17 September 1874, FO 60/406.
46 De Reuter to Lord Derby, 12 November 1875, FO 60/407.
47 Collins, *From Pigeon Post*, p. 180.
48 De Reuter to Earl Granville, 24 January 1885, FO 60/476.
49 conversation between H. Rawlinson and de Reuter, 15 May 1885, FO 60/476.
50 Memorandum by Sir Julian Pauncefote, 12 August 1885, FO 60/476.
51 Greaves, *Persia*, pp. 98–9.
52 Memorandum by Sir Julian Pauncefote, 14 August 1885, FO 60/476.
53 Note by Lord Salisbury, 14 August 1885, FO 60/476.
54 Greaves, *Persia*, p. 100.
55 Entner, *Russo–Persian Commercial Relations*, p. 9. See also A. Seyf, 'Some Aspects', p. 585.
56 Kazemzadeh, *Russia and Britain*, p. 176.
57 Foreign Office to A. Nicolson, 21 February 1887, FO 60/485.
58 Kazemzadeh, *Russia and Britain*, pp. 175–6.
59 H. Algar, *Mirza Malkam Khan* (London, 1973), pp. 118–19.
60 *ibid*, p. 120.
61 For example, E. G. Browne, *The Persian Revolution of 1905–1909* (Cambridge, 1910). See also Wright, *The Persians*, pp. 152–7.
62 Bakhash, *Iran*, p. 171.
63 Greaves, *Persia*, p. 142.
64 Drummond Wolff to Marquis of Salisbury, 12 October 1889, FO 60/551.
65 Algar, *Mirza Malkam Khan*, p. 48. Kazemzadeh, *Russia and Britain*, pp. 156–8.
66 Dr Tholozon to G de Reuter, 9 April 1895, Archives of The British Bank of the Middle East (hereafter BBME), X74/2.
67 Greaves, *Persia*, p. 122.
68 Kazemzadeh, *Russia and Britain*, p. 195.
69 *ibid*, p. 202.
70 *ibid*, p. 209. M. Entner, *Russo–Persian Commercial Relations*, pp. 28–9.
71 Drummond Wolff to Lord Salisbury, 17 October 1888, FO 65/1354.
72 *ibid*.
73 Drummond Wolff to Lord Salisbury, 21 October 1888, FO 60/1354.
74 *ibid*.
75 A. S. J. Baster, *The Imperial Banks* (London, 1929), pp. 104–6, 258–9.
76 Drummond Wolff to Lord Salisbury, 14 August 1888, FO 60/493.
77 Drummond Wolff to Lord Salisbury, 8 November 1888, FO 65/1355.
78 Drummond Wolff to Lord Salisbury, 28 November 1888, FO 60/1355.

79 Drummond Wolff to Lord Salisbury, 12 December 1888, FO 60/496.
80 *ibid.*
81 Drummond Wolff to Lord Salisbury, 28 January 1889, FO 60/503.
82 Morier to Lord Salisbury, 28 May 1889, FO 65/1378.
83 De Reuter to Lord Salisbury, 21 June 1889, FO 60/506.
84 Baster, *The Imperial Banks*, pp. 266–8.
85 *ibid*, chapters 3 and 4.
86 Foreign Office to Treasury, 2 July 1889, FO 60/507.
87 Treasury to Foreign Office, 13 July 1889, FO 60/507.
88 Agreements of 3 August and 4 September 1889 between Baron Julius de Reuter, J. Henry Schröder & Co., David Sassoon & Co. and Walpole Greenwell & Co., BBME S69.
89 S. Chapman, *The Rise of Merchant Banking* (London, 1984), pp. 55–6, 60, 97, 121. The archives of J. Henry Schröder were not available when this History was being written. Schröders have now commissioned Dr Dick Roberts to write their history, but he has been unable to provide concrete evidence on the firm's links with de Reuter.
90 C. Roth, *The Sassoon Dynasty* (London, 1942); Stanley Jackson, *The Sassoons* (London, 1968).
91 Chapman, *Rise*, p. 131.
92 Roth, *Sassoon Dynasty*, pp. 132–3. Wright, *The Persians*, p. 138.
93 T. B. Brockway, 'Britain and the Persian Bubble 1888–1892', *Journal of Modern History*, XIII, 1941, pp. 40–1.
94 Chapman, *Rise*, p. 132.
95 F. H. H. King, draft History of the Hongkong and Shanghai Banking Corporation (hereafter draft History).
96 King, draft History, will deal at length with McLean's career in the Hongkong Bank.
97 Chapman, *Rise*, pp. 35, 80, 134. R. Fulford, *Glyn's 1753–1953* (London, 1953), *passim*.
98 Chapman, *Rise*, p. 29; D. Joslin, *A Century of Banking in Latin America* (London, 1963), pp. 65–6.
99 D. Wright, *The English Amongst the Persians* (London, 1977), p. 99.
100 T. A. B. Corley, *A History of the Burmah Oil Company* (London, 1983), pp. 42–44; *Times Obituary*, 11 March 1908.
101 Curzon, *Persia*, vol. 1, p. 477.
102 Drummond Wolff to FO, 8 March 1889, FO 60/503.
103 General A. Houtum Schindler to Baron Julius de Reuter, 4 February 1889, BBME S109.
104 Curzon, *Persia*, vol. 1, p. 475.
105 *The Statist*, 28 September 1889, p. 345.
106 Translation of Amin os-Soltan's telegram, 20 October 1889, BBME S110.

CHAPTER 2 SURVIVAL AGAINST THE ODDS 1889–95

1 Imperial Bank of Persia Board Minutes (hereafter BM), 7 and 15 October 1889, BBME.
2 J. Rabino, *Memories* (Cairo, 1937). Birth Certificate, General Registrar Office, London, 29 March 1843.
3 *Journal of the Institute of Bankers*, vol. VIII, pt. 1, January 1887; *Statistical Society Journal*, **47**, 1884.

4 Dr Tholozon to G. de Reuter, 9 April 1895, X74/2, BBME.
5 J. Rabino, *Memories*, p. 8.
6 D. Joslin, *A Century of Banking in Latin America* (London, 1963), pp. 22–3.
7 J. Rabino to G. Newell, 14 January 1890, X7/1, BBME.
8 Yale to Hardinge, 11 September 1897, Hardinge Papers (Cambridge University Library).
9 Rabino, *Memories*, p. 9.
10 Agreement between Imperial Bank of Persia and NOBC, 15 April 1890, S99, BBME.
11 D. Fraser, *Persia and Turkey in Revolt* (Edinburgh and London, 1910), p. 175.
12 Joslin, *Century*, p. 24.
13 BM, 9 August 1893, BBME.
14 A. P. H. Hotz to W. Keswick, 10 December 1893, X74/1, BBME.
15 S. F. Rogers to A. O. Wood, 15 April 1918, X55, BBME.
16 S. Chapman, *The Rise of Merchant Banking* (London, 1984), pp. 78–81.
17 A. S. J. Baster, *The Imperial Banks* (London, 1929), pp. 147–57.
18 'The New Oriental Bank Corporation: A Lesson in Bad Banking', *Bankers' Magazine* 1894, pp. 69–80.
19 F. H. H. King, Draft History of Hongkong Bank.
20 For a discussion of the *sarrafs* see W. M. Floor, 'The Bankers (sarraf) in Qajar Iran', in *Zeitschrift der Deutschen Morgenlandischen Gesellschaft* (1979), pp. 263–81. Many of the comments about the Imperial Bank of Persia in this article are misleading.
21 J. Rabino to H. W. Maclean, 2 March 1893, enclosed in J. Rabino to G Newell, 3 March 1893, X7/1, BBME.
22 J. Rabino to H. Drummond Wolff, 9 July 1890, enclosed in H. Drummond Wolff to Lord Salisbury, 10 July 1890, FO 60/512.
23 Correspondence between J. Rabino and G. Newell, 9 April 1891, 2 October 1891, 30 November 1891, X7/1, BBME.
24 J. Rabino to G. Newell, 18 June 1891, X7/1, BBME.
25 J. Rabino to G. Newell, 14 January 1890, X7/1, BBME.
26 J. Rabino to G. Newell, 4 May 1891, BBME.
27 BM, 21 December 1892, BBME.
28 Rabino, *Memories*, p. 11.
29 BM 17 September 1890, BBME.
30 J. Rabino, 'Banking in Persia', *Journal of the Institute of Bankers*, vol. XIII (1892), p. 35.
31 W. F. Spalding, *Eastern Exchange, Currency and Finance* (London, 1924), p. 146.
32 J. Rabino to G. Newell, 21 June 1890, X7/1, BBME.
33 J. Bharier, 'Banking and Economic Development in Iran'. *Bankers' Magazine*, 1967, p. 295.
34 C. Issawi, *Economic Development in Iran* (Chicago, 1971), pp. 36–7.
35 G. Newell to J. Rabino, 9 November 1893, attached to J. Rabino to G. Newell, 4 December 1893, X7/1, BBME.
36 J. Rabino to G. Newell, 4 December 1893, X7/1, BBME.
37 Joslin, *Century*, pp. 25, 33, 37, 67–8.
38 Chapman, *Rise*, pp. 76–7.
39 J. Rabino to G. Newell, 14 January 1890 and 25 May 1891, X7/1, BBME.
40 J. Rabino to G. Newell, 17 September 1893, X7/1, BBME.
41 J. Rabino to G. Newell, 13 October 1892, X7/1; Telegram Tehran to London, 9 August 1892, X4/1, BBME. FO 1893 Annual Series No. 1268, and 1894

Annual Series No. 1376.
42 A. P. H. Hotz to W. Keswick, 27 May 1891, X74/2; E. Sassoon to W. Keswick, 11 October 1891, X74/1, BBME.
43 J. Rabino to G. Newell, 28 November 1892, X7/1, BBME.
44 F. Kazemzadeh, *Russia and Britain in Persia 1864–1914* (New Haven, 1968), pp. 245–7. D. Wright, *The Persians Amongst the English* (London, 1985), pp. 152–66.
45 Drummond Wolff to Lord Salisbury, 20 March 1890; and 3 April 1890 enclosing the terms of the Concession signed on 8 March 1890; FO 60/553.
46 Kazemzadeh, *Russia and Britain*, p. 249.
47 G. Newell to W. Keswick, 26 August 1891, X1/1; G. Newell to Tobacco Corporation Ltd, 2 September 1891, X2/1; and J. Rabino to G. Newell, 21 September 1891, X7/1; BBME.
48 Robert A. McDaniel, *The Shuster Mission and the Persian Constitutional Revolution* (Minneapolis, 1974), pp. 42–7; Kazemzadeh, *Russia and Britain*, pp. 250–7; N. Keddie, *Religion and Rebellion in Iran: The Tobacco Protest of 1891–92* (London, 1966), pp. 83–93.
49 Keddie, *Religion and Rebellion*, p. 68–72.
50 J. Rabino to G. Newell, 4 January 1892, X7/1, BBME.
51 Kazemzadeh, *Russia and Britain*, p. 263.
52 S. Bakhash, *Iran: Monarchy, Bureaucracy and Reform under the Qajars 1856–1896* (Oxford, 1978), pp. 243–4.
53 C. Issawi, *An Economic History of the Middle East and North Africa* (London, 1982), pp. 65–8.
54 F. Lascelles to Lord Salisbury, 6 and 8 March 1892; Foreign Office Telegram to F. Lascelles, 14 March 1892; F. Lascelles to Foreign Office, 14 March 1892, FO 60/554.
55 Kazemzadeh, *Russia and Britain*, pp. 267–8.
56 Telegrams London to Tehran, 17 March 1892, and Tehran to London, 21 March 1892, X4/1, BBME.
57 F. Lascelles to Foreign Office, 18 April 1892, FO 60/555.
58 Foreign Office to Lascelles, 20 April 1892, FO 60/555.
59 BM, 27 April 1892, BBME.
60 BM, 11 May 1892, BBME.
61 F. Lascelles to Lord Salisbury, 18 May 1892, FO 60/555.
62 Memorandum from E. Barrington to P. Currie, 1 September 1892, FO 60/555.
63 McDaniel, *The Shuster Mission*, p. 47. Telegram from Rabino to London, 11 October 1892, X4/1, BBME.
64 M. Entner, *Russo–Persian Commercial Relations, 1828–1914* (Florida, 1965), pp. 32, and 39–40.
65 B. V. Anan'ich, *Rossiikoe samoderzhavie i vyvoz kapitalov* (Leningrad, 1975), p. 15.
66 *ibid*, pp. 14–15; Kazemzadeh, *Russia and Britain*, pp. 273–6.
67 J. Rabino to G. Newell, 28 December 1891, X7/1, BBME.
68 Entner, *Russo–Persian*, chapter 3.
69 R. L. Greaves, *Persia and the Defence of India 1884–1892* (London, 1959); and 'British Policy in Persia 1892–1903' part 1, in *Bulletin School of Oriental and African Studies*, XXVIII, 1965.
70 Witte's Report to the Tsar, not later than 25 March (6 April) 1894. Quoted by Anan'ich, *Rossiikoe*, p. 15.
71 *ibid*, p. 17.
72 Kazemzadeh, *Russia and Britain*, p. 274.
73 J. Rabino to G. Newell, 20 August 1894, X7/1, BBME.

74 E. Sassoon to G. Curzon, 26 March 1890; 11 April 1890; 14 May 1890; F111/71A, India Office Library (IOL).
75 Lepel Griffin to A. H. Schindler, 14 February 1891, F111/71A, IOL.
76 G. Liddell to W. Keswick, 23 February 1891, X74/2, BBME.
77 Statement of G. Liddell to Earl of Rosebery, 13 January 1894, FO 60/576.
78 Lepel Griffin to A. H. Schindler, 9 April 1891, F111/71A, IOL.
79 Lepel Griffin to G. Curzon, 28 October 1892, F111/71A, IOL.
80 Report on Visit to Persia by James Mactear, 6 September 1893, R5/3, BBME.
81 Lepel Griffin to Earl of Rosebery, 26 October 1893, FO 60/576.
82 *ibid*, and minute by P. Currie, 28 October 1893.
83 J. Rabino to G. Newell, 4 December 1893, X7/1, BBME.
84 Greaves, *Persia*, p. 180–1.
85 Committee of the Board of Directors of the Imperial Bank of Persia to consider the question of Persian roads, S26, BBME.
86 G. Newell to Sir Philip Currie, 23 November 1893, X2/1, BBME.
87 J. Rabino to G. Newell, 3 June 1890, X7/1, BBME.
88 Translation of Ahwaz Road and Transport Concession, HO 31B, BBME.
89 Hollams Sons, Coward and Hawkesley to G. Newell, 24 March 1890, X74/2, BBME.
90 Roads Committee, 14 November 1890, S26, BBME.
91 G. Newell to Foreign Office, 23 November 1893, X2/1, BBME.
92 A. Hotz to W. Keswick, 23/24 May 1891, X74/2, BBME.
93 BM, 5 August 1891, BBME.
94 W. Keswick to Chief Manager, 1 January 1892; G. Newell to Chief Manager, 18 March 1892, X1/1, BBME.
95 G. Newell to Foreign Office, 23 November 1893, X2/1, BBME.
96 W. Keswick to A. Hotz, 21 November 1892, X1/1, BBME.
97 J. Rabino to G. Newell, 16 March 1893, X7/1, BBME.
98 London Office to Chief Manager, 12 October 1893, X1/1, BBME.
99 G. de Reuter to W. Keswick, 1 January 1894, cited by Lord Rosebery to Sir Frank Lascelles, 29 January 1894, FO 248/580.
100 G. de Reuter to W. Keswick, 1 January 1894, X74/1, BBME.
101 G. de Reuter to G. Newell, 18 May 1894; R. de Gubbay to G. de Reuter, 9 June 1894, X74/1, BBME.
102 Foreign Office to India Office, 21 August 1894, No. 186, enclosing Telegram 56 of 20 August 1894 from Conyngham Greene to Foreign Office, FO 60/563.
103 Anan'ich, *Rossiikoe*, p. 16.
104 A. H. Schindler to G. Curzon, 4 February 1895, F111/62, IOL.
105 C. Issawi, *Economic Development in Iran* (Chicago, 1971), pp. 74, 120–21, 129–30.
106 Draft A. P. H. Hotz to Board, 1891, Box 32E, BBME.
107 G. Newell to Baghdad Agency, 16 September 1891, X1/1, BBME.
108 A. G. C. Grandjean to G. Newell, 25 February 1892; S. Rogers to G. Newell, 21 July 1895; X3/1, BBME.
109 A. G. C. Grandjean to G. Newell, 23 June 1892, X3/1, BBME.
110 A. G. C. Grandjean to G. Newell, 8 February 1893, X3/1, BBME.
111 British Consular Reports 1893.
112 J. Rabino to G. Newell, 25 April 1892; J. Rabino to G. Newell, 8 September 1890; X7/1, BBME.
113 G. Newell to J. Rabino, 1 February 1894, quoting a letter from J. B. Cross, 16 January 1893, X1/2, BBME.

114 Agreement between J. Rabino and Manager of Baghdad Branch of Imperial Ottoman Bank, 2 September 1893, S/107, BBME.
115 G. Newell to A. G. C. Grandjean, 4 February 1896, X1/3, BBME.
116 G. Newell to Deloitte, Dever Griffiths, 19 December 1895, X2/1, BBME.
117 P. W. Avery and J. B. Simmons, 'Persia on a Cross of Silver, 1880–1890', *Middle Eastern Studies*, 1974, pp. 261 ff.
118 Hollams Sons, Coward and Hawkesley to G. Newell, 4 December 1893, X74/1, BBME.
119 W. Keswick to T. H. Sanderson, 30 March 1894; T. H. Sanderson to W. Keswick, 11 April 1894; FO 60/563.
120 Treasury to Hollams Sons, Coward and Hawkesley, 22 August 1894, FO 60/563.
121 BM, 21 January 1891, BBME.
122 T. Payn to G. Newell, 2 June 1892, X11, BBME.
123 T. Payn to G. Newell, 1 November 1893, X11, BBME.
124 G. Newell to A. F. Simpson, 11 May 1894, X1/2, BBME.
125 Minutes of Inspection Committee, 5 and 12 November 1895, BBME.
126 Minutes of Inspection Committee, 24 April 1899, BBME.
127 BM, 20 November 1889, BBME.
128 G. Newell to T. Payn, 27 January 1893, X11, BBME.
129 G. Newell to T. Payn, 12 May 1893, X11, BBME.
130 Minutes of Inspection Committee, 4 October 1893, BBME.
131 Inspection Committee, 9 May 1894, BBME.
132 Rabino, *Memories*, p. 17.
133 A. P. H. Hotz to W. Keswick, 20 May 1891, X74/2, BBME.
134 Conyngham Greene to G. Curzon, 30 June 1894, F111/61, IOL.

CHAPTER 3 RECOVERY AND CONFLICT 1896–1908

1 Directors' Report to the 10th Ordinary General Meeting of the Imperial Bank, 18 December 1899.
2 F. H. H. King, Draft History of Hongkong Bank.
3 S. Jackson, *The Sassoons* (London, 1968), p. 97. E. Sassoon to W. Keswick, 22 December 1896, X74/2, BBME.
4 P. Griffiths, *A History of the Inchcape Group* (London, 1977), p. 71. Obituary, *The Times*, 3 November 1910.
5 T. Jackson to V. A. Caesar Hawkins, 23 March 1908, X1/14, BBME.
6 G. Newell to T. Gordon, 15 May 1896, X1/3.
7 F. Kazemzadeh, *Russia and Britain in Persia 1864–1914* (New Haven, 1968), pp. 296–301, provides a fuller account of this event.
8 J. Rabino to London Office, 1 May 1896, X4/2, BBME.
9 Telegram London Office to J. Rabino, 2 May 1896; W. Keswick to T. Sanderson, 7 May 1896, X2/1, BBME.
10 F. Kazemzadeh, *Russia and Britain*, p. 487. A more balanced interpretation of Naus, based on extensive research in Belgian archives, is given in A. Destrée, *Les Fonctionnaires Belges au Service de la Perse 1898–1915* (Liège 1976). See especially pp. 52, ff. See also M. Entner, *Russo–Persian Commercial Relations 1828–1914* (Florida, 1965), pp. 53–4.
11 J. Rabino to G. Newell, 2 April 1896, X7/2, BBME.
12 General Schindler to G. N. Curzon, 14 November 1897, Curzon papers, F111/64, India Office Library (IOL).

13 G. Newell to H. M. Durand, 4 August 1897, X2/1, BBME.
14 Contract for the Supply of Five Millions of Miscals of Silver to the Imperial Mint, enclosed in J. Rabino to G. Newell, 9 July 1896, X7/2, BBME.
15 Memorandum on Subsidiary Coinage by H. W. Maclean, enclosed with H. W. Maclean to G. Newell, 17 October 1899, X7/5, BBME.
16 Sir Lepel Griffin to T. Sanderson, 21 February 1900, X2/1, BBME.
17 M. Durand to Lord Salisbury, 29 July 1901, FO 60/601.
18 J. Rabino to G. Newell, 6 August 1896, X7/2, BBME. Destrée, *Les Fonctionnaires*, p. 39.
19 J. Rabino to G. Newell, 10 and 17 May 1897, X7/3, BBME.
20 There are accounts of the loan negotiations in Kazemzadeh, *Russia and Britain*, and R. L. Greaves, 'British Policy in Persia, 1892–1903', I and II, *Bulletin of the School of Oriental and African Studies* (1965). Neither writer was able to use the BBME archives.
21 W. Keswick to Lord Salisbury, 11 March 1898, X2/1, BBME.
22 Kazemzadeh, *Russia and Britain*, pp. 307–9.
23 FO to W. Keswick, 24 June 1898, FO 60/601.
24 B. V. Anan'ich, *Rossiikoe samoderzhavie i vyvoz Kapitalov* (Leningrad, 1975), p. 20.
25 Sir Lepel Griffin to J. Rabino, 13 February 1900, XI/6, BBME.
26 J. Rabino to G. Newell, 29 April 1900, X7/5, BBME.
27 J. Rabino to Sir Lepel Griffin, 12 March 1900, X7/5, BBME.
28 D. McLean to G. Newell, 22 October 1900, X74/3; Sir Lepel Griffin to J. Rabino, 25 October 1900, X1/7, BBME.
29 J. Rabino to G. Newell, 5 April 1900, X7/5, BBME.
30 Telegram No. 8 from A. Hardinge, 14 March 1901; Sir Lepel Griffin to Sir Thomas Sanderson, 15 March 1901, enclosing Telegram from IBP London to IBP Tehran; A. Hardinge to Lord Lansdowne 2 April 1901, and enclosures; FO 60/645.
31 Telegram No. 42 from A. Hardinge to Lord Lansdowne, 28 March 1903, FO 60/676.
32 There is a penetrating discussion of these differences in official British policy in David McLean, *Britain and Her Buffer State* (London, 1979), chapter 3.
33 Telegram No. 31, Lord Lansdowne to A. Hardinge, 28 March 1903, FO 60/676.
34 Sir Lepel Griffin to T. Sanderson, 26 July 1901, X1/8, BBME.
35 R. W. Ferrier, *The History of the British Petroleum Company* (Cambridge, 1982), vol. I, p. 40 ff.
36 Private Telegram, A. Hardinge to Lord Lansdowne, 29 September 1901, FO 60/645.
37 Telegrams from the Viceroy, Lord Curzon, 12 May and 2 October 1901, FO 60/645.
38 Greaves, 'British Policy in Persia', II, p. 298.
39 Telegram No. 116 from C. Hardinge, 6 November 1901, FO 60/645.
40 Note by Lord Lansdowne on *ibid*, and Telegram No. 54, Lord Lansdowne to A. Hardinge, 16 November 1901, FO 60/645.
41 Private telegram from Hardinge, 13 January 1903, FO 60/676.
42 A. Hardinge to Lord Lansdowne, 28 March 1903, FO 60/676.
43 Telegram No. 35, Lord Lansdowne to A. Hardinge, 3 April 1903, FO 60/676.
44 A. Hardinge to Lord Lansdowne, 3 September, 1904, FO 60/714.
45 J. Rabino to G. Newell, 3 and 20 September 1904, X7/9, BBME.
46 Kazemzadeh, *Russia and Britain*, pp. 472–4. Telegram from Viceroy, 13 April 1905, and Note on the Persian Loan by RG, 1 May 1905, FO 60/714.

380 *Notes to pp. 90–103*

47 B. G. Martin, *German–Persian Diplomatic Relations 1873–1912* (The Hague, 1959), pp. 107–20.
48 G. Newell to Foreign Office, 12 April 1905; G. Newell to Foreign Office, 26 April 1905. Sir Lepel Griffin to A. Hardinge, 15 July 1905 enclosed in Sir Lepel Griffin to T. Sanderson, 15 July 1905, X2/2, BBME.
49 Colonel Trench to Sir Lepel Griffin, 24 January 1901, HO 31B, BBME; McLean, *Britain*, p. 62.
50 L. Dalton to G. Newell, 20 December 1902, X7/7; Sir Lepel Griffin to Lord Lansdowne, 22 May 1903, X2/2, BBME.
51 Major R. L. Kennion to Secretary of Government of India in the Foreign Department, 24 August 1907, enclosed in Letter from Imperial Bank, 19 February 1908, L/P S/10/176, IOL.
52 J. Rabino to G. Newell, 13 March 1900; J. Rabino to Sir Lepel Griffin, 30 May 1900, X7/5, BBME.
53 J. Rabino to G. Newell, 1 August 1901, X7/6, BBME.
54 McLean, *Britain*, pp. 54–5, 58.
55 A. Hardinge to Foreign Office, 3 March 1904, FO 60/714: A. Hardinge to Lord Lansdowne, 23 August 1905, enclosed in J. Rabino to G. Newell, 26 August 1905, X7/10, BBME.
56 H. L. Rabino, Report, enclosed in H. W. Maclean to G. Newell, 12 August 1899, X7/5, BBME.
57 McLean, *Britain*, pp. 64–6; 'The Story of the Euphrates Company', *The Near East and India*, 24 November 1932.
58 T. Sanderson to Sir Lepel Griffin, 2 January 1902, X74/3, BBME.
59 McLean, *Britain*, p. 68.
60 McLean, *Britain*, p. 69.
61 Sir Lepel Griffin to J. Rabino, 6 March 1901, X1/7, BBME.
62 J. Rabino to Sir Lepel Griffin, 25 January 1900, X7/5, BBME.
63 Memorandum on the Exchange Business of Imperial Bank, enclosed in J. Rabino to G. Newell, 16 March 1899, X7/5, BBME.
64 V. A. Caesar Hawkins to T. Jackson, 29 July 1908, X8/5, BBME.
65 G. Newell to J. Rabino, 8 December 1898, X1/5, BBME.
66 J. Rabino to G. Newell, 21 October 1896, X7/2, BBME.
67 G. Newell to J. Rabino, 5 and 11 November 1907; and Board Note on Loans, Advances and Discounts, 25 November 1897, X1/4, BBME.
68 G. Newell to J. Rabino, 24 September 1896, X1/3, BBME.
69 J. Rabino to G. Newell, 31 January 1898, X7/4, BBME.
70 J. Rabino to G. Newell, 31 January 1898, X7/4, BBME.
71 Anan'ich, *Rossikoe*, p. 55.
72 *ibid*, p. 130.
73 Observations on Board's Reaction to Centralisation Scheme, in J. Rabino to G. Newell, 2 August 1901, X7/6, BBME.
74 J. Rabino to G. Newell, 17 and 20 October 1906, X7/11, BBME.
75 G. Newell to Sir Lepel Griffin, 8 November 1902, X7/7, BBME.
76 Memorandum enclosed in J. Rabino to G. Newell, 28 January 1905, X7/9; Sir Lepel Griffin to J. Rabino, 28 March 1906, X1/12, BBME.
77 Sir Lepel Griffin to J. Rabino, 19 February 1902, HO 31B, BBME.
78 Sir Lepel Griffin to J. Rabino, 13 December 1902, X1/9, BBME.
79 R. McDaniel, *The Shuster Mission and the Persian Consitutional Revolution* (Minneapolis, 1974), p. 54–65.
80 Sir Lepel Griffin to A. Hardinge, 1 March 1906, X2/2; FO to Sir Lepel Griffin,

3 March 1906, X74/4, BBME.
81 J. Naus to J. Rabino, 15 June 1906, X7/11, BBME.
82 Kazemzadeh, *Russia and Britain*, p. 537; McDaniel, *Shuster*, pp. 61–2.
83 J. Rabino to G. Newell, 17 July 1907, X8/1, BBME.
84 V. A. Caesar Hawkins to T. Jackson, 5 August 1908, X8/5, BBME.
85 Appendix to Finance Committee's Minutes on Persian Accounts at 20 September 1907, HO 21, BBME.
86 C. Issawi, *The Economic History of Iran 1800–1914* (Chicago, 1971), p. 43.
87 Telegrams from A. O. Wood and E. Dalton to Auditors, 7 December 1907, X7/12, BBME.
88 J. Rabino, *Memories* (Cairo, 1937), pp. 16–17.
89 J. Rabino to Sir Lepel Griffin, 3 January 1908, X7/12 BBME.
90 J. Rabino to Board, 7 March 1908 and 11 March 1908; G. Newell to J. Rabino, 2 April 1908, X8/3, BBME.
91 Martin, *German–Persian*, p. 125.
92 Caesar Hawkins to T. Jackson, 2 July 1908, X8/5, BBME.

CHAPTER 4 BANKING FOR GOVERNMENTS 1909–14

1 A. O. Wood to G. Newell, 10 April 1909, X7/13, BBME.
2 The early history of the Anglo-Persian Oil Company is told in great detail by R. W. Ferrier, *The History of the British Petroleum Company* (Cambridge, 1982), vol. I. There is a shorter discussion in Geoffrey Jones, *The State and the Emergence of the British Oil Industry* (London, 1981), chapter 5. Both books contain much information, and conflicting interpretations, of Charles Greenway. Greenway's early career with Burmah Oil can be followed in T. A. B. Corley, *A History of the Burmah Oil Company 1886–1924* (London, 1983).
3 Corley, *History*, p. 210.
4 Jones, *State*, chapter 6; Ferrier, *History*, chapter 6.
5 BM, 29 November 1911, BBME.
6 A. O. Wood to G. Newell, 15 July 1909, X7/13, BBME.
7 The account of Shuster in Persia in this paragraph and later in the chapter is, of necessity, condensed. The reader seeking more information is encouraged to consult the excellent study by Robert A. McDaniel, *The Shuster Mission and the Persian Constitutional Revolution* (Minneapolis, 1974). F. Kazemzadeh, *Russia and Britain in Persia, 1864–1914* (New Haven, 1968), chapter 9 provides a good account of the period 1910–14.
8 W. M. Shuster, *The Strangling of Persia* (London, 1912).
9 Ferrier, *History*, pp. 190–1.
10 Memorandum by H. W. Maclean, in Sir W. Townley to Sir Edward Grey, 295, 9 July 1913, Persia No. 1 (1914), Cd 7280.
11 Morgan Shuster to A. O. Wood, 10 January 1912, X7/15, BBME.
12 For the problems of the Russian Bank, see B. V. Anan'ich, *Rossiikoe Samoderzhavie i Vyvoz Kapitalov* (Leningrad, 1975), p. 185.
13 Sir Thomas Jackson to L. Mallet, 16 February 1909, X2/2, BBME.
14 Agreements enclosed in S. F. Rogers to London, 27 April 1910, and S. F. Rogers to G. Newell, 27 May 1910, X7/14, BBME.
15 Finance Committee, September 1910, BBME.
16 S. F. Rogers to G. Newell, 9 March 1910, X7/14, BBME.
17 S. F. Rogers to G. Newell, 26 March 1910; A. O. Wood to G. Newell, 8 October 1910, X7/14A, BBME.

18 A. O. Wood to G. Newell, 29 November 1911, X7/15, BBME.
19 A. O. Wood to G. Newell, 14 February 1912, X7/15, BBME.
20 D. Brown to G. Newell, 22 May 1913, X7/16, BBME.
21 L. Mallet to G. Newell, 15 July 1913, X2/3, BBME.
22 S. F. Rogers to Foreign Office, 23 July 1913, X2/3, BBME.
23 G. Newell to Foreign Office, 11 March 1914, X2/3, BBME.
24 Kazemzadeh, *Russia and Britain*, pp. 552–62; D. McLean, *Britain and Her Buffer State* (London, 1979), pp. 97–100.
25 S. Chapman, *The Rise of Merchant Banking* (London, 1984), p. 176.
26 Sir T. Jackson to L. Mallet, 19 October 1910, X2/3, BBME. D. McLean, 'International Banking and its Political Implications: The Hongkong and Shanghai Banking Corporation and the Imperial Bank of Persia, 1889–1914', in F. H. H. King (ed.), *Eastern Banking* (London, 1983), pp. 5–6.
27 G. Newell to Foreign Office, 11 November 1910, X2/3, BBME.
28 BM, 14 June 1911. Underwriting lists in T67, BBME.
29 A. O. Wood to G. Newell, 24 May 1911, X7/14A, BBME.
30 Joint note addressed to the Persian government by the British and Russian Ministers in Tehran on 18 February 1912, in Appendix 3 to C120b, Second memorandum as to Persian government loans, India Office, 27 November 1912, FO 371/1711.
31 Sir E. Grey to Sir W. Townley, 30, 6 March 1913; Sir G. Townley to Sir E. Grey, 205, 24 April 1913 and 189, 30 April 1913, Cd 7280, Persia No. 1 (1914).
32 Sir W. Townley to J. Mornard, 6 May 1913, Enclosure 3 in Sir Walter Townley to Sir Edward Grey, 236, 13 May 1913, Cd 7280, Persia No. 1 (1914).
33 A. O. Wood to G. Newell, 6 May 1911, X7/14A, BBME.
34 A. O. Wood to G. Newell, 14 June 1911, X7/14A, BBME.
35 A. O. Wood to G. Newell, 20 January 1913, X7/16, BBME.
36 Finance Committee, September 1914, BBME.
37 Report of a Commercial Survey of the East Persian Trade Route between Quetta and Mashad, 1919, by Major B. Temple, HO 21A, BBME.
38 D. Brown to Sir Walter Townley, 21 May 1913, enclosed with D. Brown to G. Newell, 22 May 1913, X7/16, BBME.
39 S. F. Rogers to G. Newell, 13 November 1909, X7/14, BBME. See also McLean, 'International Banking', pp. 11–12.
40 A. O. Wood to G. Newell, 23 November 1910, X7/14A, BBME.
41 D. Brown to G. Newell, 8 May 1913, X7/16, BBME.
42 A. O. Wood to G. Newell, 8 May 1909, X7/13, BBME.
43 G. Newell to Foreign Office, 10 June 1914, X2/3; BBME. See also McLean, *Britain*, pp. 133–6.
44 McLean, *Britain*, p. 133.
45 Sani od-Doule to A. O. Wood, 5 December 1910, X7/14A, BBME.
46 A. O. Wood to Sani od-Doule, 7 December 1910; A. O. Wood to Caesar Hawkins, 9 May 1911, X7/14A, BBME.
47 McLean, *Britain*, pp. 119–21. See McLean, pp. 111–25 for an enlightening discussion of British and Russian railway schemes in Iran.
48 Memorandum of Association of the Persian Railways Syndicate, R6/1, BBME. Lord Cowdray's business career is discussed in J. A. Spender, *Weetman Pearson, First Viscount Cowdray 1856–1927* (London, 1930), and Jones, *State*, pp. 63–77, 179–80, 190–2, 202–3, 217–8.
49 Kazemzadeh, *Russia and Britain*, pp. 674–5.
50 McLean, *Britain*, p. 115. A. O. Wood to C. Hawkins, 27 February 1911, X7/14A,

BBME. For the Baghdad railway, see C. Issawi, *An Economic History of the Middle East and North Africa* (London, 1982), pp. 56–7.

51 Sir W. Townley to Sir E. Grey, 15, 23 February, and 3 and 5 March 1913, Persia No. 1 (1914), Cd 7280.

52 J. McMurray to S. F. Rogers, 12 November 1919, X51/3, BBME.

53 A. O. Wood to G. Newell, 5 April 1911, X7/14A. Finance Committee, March 1911, BBME.

54 E. M. Eldrid to A. O. Wood, 7 May 1914; A. O. Wood to G. Newell, 21 May 1914, X7/17, BBME.

55 C. Issawi, *The Economic History of Iran* (Chicago, 1971), p. 302. McDaniel, Shuster, pp. 34–5. A. Seyf, 'Some Aspects of Economic Development in Iran, 1800–1906', (Reading PhD 1982), chapter 8.

56 BM, 29 November 1911 and 3 January 1912, BBME.

57 Finance Committee, March 1913, BBME.

58 These estimates are derived from the reports on branches in Finance Committee, September 1909. Unfortunately it is not possible to derive similar statistics for all the years in this period.

59 Report of a Commercial Survey of the East Persia Trade Route between Quetta and Mashad, 1919 by Major B. Temple, HO 21A, BBME.

60 Finance Committee, March 1914, BBME.

CHAPTER 5 THE BANKERS 1889–1914

1 Sir G. Prior to Lord Kennet, 30 April 1950, X88, BBME.

2 Comparisons with the Hongkong Bank throughout this chapter are drawn from F. H. H. King, Draft History.

3 J. Rabino to G. Newell, 15 May 1893, X7/1, BBME.

4 S. F. Rogers to G. Newell, 2 February 1910, X7/14, BBME.

5 J. Rabino to G. Newell, 11 September 1900, X7/5, BBME.

6 J. Rabino to G. Newell, 29 May 1893, X7/1, BBME.

7 G. Newell to J. Rabino, 2 August 1906, X1/13, BBME.

8 R. S. Sayers, *Lloyds Bank in the History of English Banking* (Oxford, 1957), pp. 71–2; R. Fulford, *Glyns 1753–1953* (London, 1953), pp. 169, 171; E. Green, 'Edward Holden', in D. J. Jeremy (ed.), *Dictionary of Business Biography*, vol. III (London, 1985).

9 Herbert Cave to Mr Johnson, 4 January 1911, GM's Box A, BBME.

10 S. J. Butlin, *Australia and New Zealand Bank* (London, 1961), p. 313.

11 D. Baker to G. Newell, 18 July 1892, X7/1, BBME. A rate of 40 Krans to the £ has been assumed to express the prices in Sterling.

12 G. Calver, Oral History, BBME.

13 W. Keswick to G. Newell, 30 September 1895, X74/2, BBME.

14 G. Newell to J. Rabino, 26 February 1892, X1/1, BBME.

15 Note by Sir Lepel Griffin on S. F. Rogers to J. Rabino, enclosed with J. Rabino to G. Newell, 23 November 1907, X7/12, BBME.

16 J. Rabino to G. Newell, 26 December 1892, X7/1, BBME.

17 Memorandum on Condition of Staff, enclosed in J. Rabino to London, 28 January 1905, X7/9, BBME.

18 H. Cave to Mr Johnson, 4 January 1911, GM's Box A, BBME.

19 Sir Lepel Griffin to J. Rabino, 10 July 1900, X1/7, BBME.

20 G. Newell to J. Rabino, 6 April 1905, X1/12, BBME.

21 Report by L. E. Dalton, 4 June 1903, attached to notes by G. Newell and T. E. Gordon, 2 January 1905, X7/9, BBME.

22 A. O. Wood to G. Newell, 9 July 1914, X7/17, BBME.
23 Margo Sinclair, Oral History, BBME. The men in question were H. L. G. Taylor (her father) and W. J. d'Alton.
24 Sir Lepel Griffin to J. Rabino, 3 November 1903, X1/10, BBME.
25 J. Rabino to Sir Lepel Griffin, 15 April 1901, X7/6, BBME.
26 BM, 18 September 1895, BBME.
27 T. A. B. Corley, *A History of the Burmah Oil Company* (London, 1983), p. 158.
28 G. Newell to H. O. James, 21 October 1915, X1/17, BBME.
29 A. O. Wood to G. Newell, 20 January 1913, X7/16, BBME.
30 J. Rabino to G. Newell, 21 March 1892, X7/1, BBME.
31 A. O. Wood to W. J. P. Church, 24 February 1913, X7/16, BBME.
32 G. Newell to W. H. Church (the man's father), 6 June 1913, X1/17, BBME.
33 B. Messervy to G. Newell, 31 May 1905, X7/9; BM, 28 June 1905, BBME.
34 Notes by W. F. Manson, March 1910, GM's Box A, BBME.
35 A. F. Grundy to G. Newell, 22 July 1895, X3/1C, BBME.
36 D. Baker to G. Newell, 7 February 1892, X3/1A, BBME.
37 A. Churchill to G. Newell, 22 August 1896, X3/1B, BBME.
38 D. Baker to G. Newell, 18 July 1892, X7/1, BBME.
39 H. Cave to Mr Johnson, 4 January 1911, GM's Box A, BBME.
40 *ibid.*
41 W. D. Van Lennep to G. Newell, 3 June 1891, X3/1C, BBME.
42 J. Rabino to G. Newell, 25 January 1892, X7/1, BBME.
43 A. H. Wright to A. Grundy, enclosed in J. Rabino to G. Newell, 21 December 1905, X7/10, BBME.
44 J. Rabino to G. Newell, 13 July 1907, enclosing extract of private letter of W. Wilkinson to A. Grundy, X7/12, BBME.
45 H. Cave to Mr Johnson, 15 June 1913, GM's Box A, BBME.
46 G. Newell to J. Rabino, 21 April 1904, X1/11, BBME.
47 J. Rabino to G. Newell, 29 May 1890, X7/1, BBME.
48 J. Rabino to G. Newell, 18 March 1892, X7/1, BBME.
49 J. Rabino to G. Newell, 27 May 1897, X7/3, BBME.
50 J. Rabino to G. Newell, 5 April 1905, X7/9, BBME.
51 A. O. Wood to G. Newell, 14 November 1908, X7/13, BBME.
52 R. W. Ferrier, *The History of the British Petroleum Company* (Cambridge, 1982), pp. 268–9. Sir Arnold Wilson, *South West Persia: A Political Officer's Diary 1907–1914* (London, 1941), p. 107. The man was E. B. Soane.
53 D. Wright, *The English Amongst the Persians* (London, 1977), p. 90.
54 A. Grundy to G. Newell, 17 August 1896, X3/1C, BBME.
55 Memorandum by Dr Thin, 17 October 1893, X74/1, BBME.
56 J. Rabino to G. Newell, 16 July 1904, X7/9, BBME.
57 M. Ferguson to G. Newell, 24 March 1898, X3/1C, BBME.
58 L. E. Dalton to G. Newell, 13 September 1902, X7/7, BBME.
59 D. Brown to G. Newell, 19 June 1913, X7/16, BBME.
60 H. Cave to Mr Johnson, 15 June 1913, GM's Box A, BBME.
61 D. Baker to G. Newell, 6 October 1892, X3/1A, BBME.
62 J. Rabino to G. Newell, 2 July 1904, X7/9, BBME.
63 Margo Sinclair, Oral History, BBME. The woman in question was Margo Sinclair's mother, Mrs Taylor. Margo Sinclair was born two days before the first anniversary of her sister's death.
64 M. Savage to G. Newell, 16 January 1899, X3/1C, BBME.

65 A. Nelson to G. Newell, 19 July 1904, X 74/4, BBME.
66 G. Newell to L. E. Dalton, 27 June 1892, X1/2; J. Rabino to G. Newell, 7 December 1904, X7/9; H. Cave to Mr Johnson, 4 January 1911, GM's Box A; Y35/1 *passim*; BBME.
67 Sir Lepel Griffin to H. W. Maclean, 1 June 1899, X12/1, BBME.
68 J. Rabino to G. Newell, 13 April 1899; J. Rabino to G. Newell, 26 April 1899; X7/5, BBME.
69 Memorandum by H. W. Maclean on Local Staff, approved by J. Rabino, 21 June 1900, X7/5, BBME.
70 E. M. Eldrid to G. Newell, 20 March 1906, Y35/1, BBME.
71 Sir Lepel Griffin to J. Rabino, 5 January 1907, X1/13, BBME.
72 A. H. Ebtehaj, Oral History, BBME.
73 J. Rabino to G. Newell, 9 May 1906, enclosing letter from A. S. Johannes, X7/11, BBME.
74 Note by J. Rabino on A. F. Grundy's list of recommended staff increases, attached to J. Rabino to G. Newell, 26 November 1895, X7/2, BBME.
75 J. Rabino to G. Newell, 17 March 1898, X7/4, BBME.
76 M. Ferguson to G. Newell, 14 April 1898, Y35/1, BBME.
77 Miss M. Owen's recollections, in 'Memories, Recollections and Anecdotes of British Staff in Persia and their wives', compiled by C. D. Lunn, November 1974, GM's Box A, BBME.

CHAPTER 6 THE BANK AT WAR 1914–18

1 There is an exhaustive study of British policy in Iran in this period in W. J. Olson, *Anglo–Iranian Relations during World War I* (London, 1984). There are brief accounts of Iran in the First World War in N. Keddie, *Roots of Revolution* (London, 1981) and M. E. Yapp, '1900–1921: The Last Years of the Qajar Dynasty,' in H. Amirsadeghi, *Twentieth Century Iran* (London, 1977), pp. 17–20.
2 C. Sykes, *Wassmuss: 'The German Lawrence'* (London, 1936).
3 Olson, *Anglo-Iranian Relations*, p. 66.
4 H. Nicolson, *Curzon: The Last Phase* (New York, 1939), pp. 127–8. R. K. Ramazani, *The Foreign Policy of Iran 1500–1941* (Charlottesville, 1966), p. 124.
5 Olson, *Anglo-Iranian Relations*, pp. 118–29.
6 *ibid*, pp. 143–9.
7 *ibid*, p. 149.
8 L. C. Dunsterville, *The Adventures of Dunsterforce* (London, 1921).
9 A. O. Wood to Sir W. Townley, 22 September 1914, X7/17, BBME.
10 J. McMurray to S. F. Rogers, 12 November 1919, X51/3, BBME.
11 R. W. Ferrier, *The History of the British Petroleum Company* (Cambridge, 1982), vol. I, p. 267.
12 *Statist*, 25 October 1919, p. 737.
13 Private Ledger, BBME.
14 Statement attached to A. O. Wood to G. Newell, 23 September 1916, X7/18; A. O. Wood to Sir Hugh Barnes, 20 November 1916, X7/18, BBME.
15 A. O. Wood to G. Newell, 22 March 1917, X7/18, BBME.
16 W. F. Spalding, *Eastern Exchange, Currency and Finance* (4th edition, London, 1924), pp. 330–31.
17 D. Brown to G. Newell, 28 August 1916, X7/18, BBME.
18 Sir Percy Sykes, *A History of Persia*, vol. 2 (3rd edn, London, 1958), p. 534.
19 C. M. Marling to A. O. Wood, 14 December 1916, X7/18, BBME.

20 Dunsterville, *Adventures*, p. 25.
21 *ibid*, p. 103.
22 Sir Percy Sykes, *A History of Persia*, vol. 2, p. 445.
23 Report on the robbery at Yazd branch, 17 February 1916, enclosed in H. Barnes to L. Oliphant, 31 March 1916, FO 371/2732.
24 R. Oakshott's Report on Rasht, 20 November 1917–11 August 1918, enclosed in A. O. Wood to Sir Hugh Barnes, 19 September 1918, X76, BBME.
25 G. Newell to Foreign Office, 14 January 1916, X2/4, BBME.
26 Minute by L. Oliphant, 21 March 1916; Treasury to Under Secretary of State at Foreign Office, 8 February 1916, FO 371/2732.
27 A. O. Wood to S. F. Rogers, 7 July 1919, X55, BBME.
28 A. O. Wood to S. F. Rogers, 7 November 1918, X30/2, BBME.
29 A. O. Wood to G. Newell, 29 April 1915, X7/17, BBME. Olson, *Anglo-Iranian Relations*, pp. 79–82.
30 Finance Committee, September 1915, BBME.
31 C. Marling to Foreign Office, 27 April 1915, FO 371/2427.
32 C. Marling to Sir Edward Grey, 4 May 1915, FO 371/2427.
33 A. O. Wood to S. F. Rogers, 27 January 1919, X51/2, BBME.
34 A. O. Wood to Mohtashem os-Soltaneh (Minister of Finance), 21 September 1914, X7/17, BBME.
35 A. O. Wood to Sir W. Townley, 22 September 1914, X7/17, BBME.
36 A. O. Wood to G. Newell, 3 February 1915; X7/17, BBME.
37 A. O. Wood to G. Newell, 13 January 1916, X7/17, BBME.
38 A. O. Wood to Minister of Finance, 13 January 1916, X51/1, BBME.
39 J. Bharier, *Economic Development in Iran 1900–1970* (London, 1971), p. 71 Table 4 and p. 108 Table 3.
40 A. O. Wood to G. Newell, 18 January 1917; G. Newell to Persian Minister, 10 December 1917, X26, BBME.
41 A. O. Wood to G. Newell, 18 January and 22 February 1917, X7/18, BBME.
42 S. F. Rogers to Persian Minister, 9 January 1918; Telegram from Tehran, 30 December 1917, X26, BBME.
43 S. F. Rogers to A. O. Wood, 19 December 1918, X51/2, BBME.
44 A. O. Wood to G. Newell, 10 and 27 April 1916, X7/18, BBME.
45 A. O. Wood to G. Newell, 8 July 1915, citing Telegram from London, 3 July 1915, X7/17, BBME.
46 Silver Contract, attached to A. O. Wood to G. Newell, 23 October 1916, X7/18, BBME.
47 Minute by L. Oliphant, 17 January 1916, FO 371/2732.
48 Foreign Office to Imperial Bank, 14 September 1914, FO 371/2071.
49 C. M. Marling to Sir Edward Grey, 21 June 1915, FO 371/2428. Olson, *Anglo-Iranian Relations*, pp. 57–60, 105.
50 Telegram from C. M. Marling to Sir Edward Grey, 2 October 1915, FO 371/2435; A. O. Wood to G. Newell, 6 January 1917, X7/17.
51 Olson, *Anglo-Iranian Relations*, p. 58.
52 C. M. Marling to Sir Edward Grey, 26 October 1915, FO 371/2435.
53 Olson, *Anglo-Iranian Relations*, p. 145.
54 A. O. Wood to A. H. Schindler, 18 April 1918, X55, BBME. J. M. Balfour, *Recent Happenings in Persia* (London, 1922), p. 157, gives a figure of £409 000, which has been revised upwards using Bank sources. Olson, *Anglo-Iranian Relations*, p. 59, says that the moratorium payments ceased in May 1917, but Bank sources suggest it was a month earlier.

55 Minute by Eyre Crowe, 7 November 1918, on P. Cox to A. J. Balfour, 3 November 1918, FO 371/3262.
56 Sir Percy Sykes remarks at Imperial Bank's 29th AGM, April 1919.
57 Dunsterville, *Adventures*, pp. 177–8.
58 Mr Mitra's Report, 21 November 1918, X30/2, BBME.
59 G. Newell to L. Oliphant, 26 April 1916, X2/4, BBME.
60 Telegram from Tehran, enclosed in G. Newell to L. Oliphant, 10 August 1917, X2/5, BBME.
61 A. O. Wood to G. Newell, 25 October 1917, X51/1, BBME.
62 A. O. Wood to G. Newell, 21 December 1916, X7/18, BBME.
63 A. O. Wood to G. Newell, 28 December 1916; C. Huson to A. O. Wood, 3 April 1917, X7/18; Sir Hugh Barnes to L. Abrahams, 30 January 1917, X2/5, BBME.
64 A. O. Wood to G. Newell, 28 December 1916, X7/18, BBME.
65 G. Newell to FO, 9 January 1917, X2/5; Conference held on 27 February 1917, X30/1, BBME.
66 Treasury to Imperial Bank, July 1918 (undated), X30/1, BBME.
67 S. F. Rogers to Treasury, 30 July 1918, X30/1, BBME.
68 Treasury to Imperial Bank, 12 August 1918, X30/1, BBME.
69 Minutes on Conference at the Treasury on 6 September 1918, X30/1, BBME.
70 Memorandum by Sir Hugh Barnes, September 1918 (undated, probably the 10th), X30/1, BBME.
71 Mr Mitra's Report, 21 November 1918, X30/2, BBME.
72 Bharier, *Economic Development*, pp. 104–5, 111.
73 Treasury to Imperial Bank, 12 August 1918, X30/1, BBME.
74 C. Huson to Major R. E. Holland, 31 March 1917, X7/18, BBME.
75 Chief Office Progress Reports, 1915, BBME.
76 Note by Caesar Hawkins on Shiraz Progress Report, September 1917, BBME.
77 A. O. Wood to Sir Hugh Barnes, 18 February 1917, X76, BBME.

CHAPTER 7 'LORD CURZON'S BANK OF PERSIA' 1919–28

1 J. McMurray to S. F. Rogers, 6 August 1922, X19/1, BBME.
2 A. O. Wood to Sir Hugh Barnes, 27 September 1917, X76, BBME.
3 Telegram from Sir Hugh Barnes to A. O. Wood, 28 June 1919, X4/17.
4 Telegram from A. O. Wood to E. M. Eldrid, 18 August 1919, X51/2, BBME.
5 J. McMurray to S. F. Rogers, 12 November 1919, X51/3, BBME.
6 C. F. Warr, Oral History, BBME.
7 A. H. Ebtehaj, Oral History, BBME.
8 Tehran Progress Report, September 1923, BBME.
9 Telegrams from Tehran, 30 August 1921 and 8 September 1921; Telegrams to Tehran, 7 and 15 September 1921; X4/19, BBME.
10 C. F. Warr, Oral History, BBME.
11 Memorandum by S. Armitage-Smith, 14 February 1921, reprinted in R. Butler, and J. P. T. Bury, (eds.), *Documents on British Foreign Policy 1919–1939*, 1st Series (London, 1963), vol. XIII, No. 677.
12 Treasury to Foreign Office, 6 September 1919, X30/3, BBME.
13 Treasury to Imperial Bank, 7 April 1920, X30/4, BBME.
14 Lord Curzon's Memorandum for the War Cabinet on the conclusion of the Anglo–Persian Agreement of 9 August 1919, reprinted in Butler and Bury (eds.), *Documents*, vol. IV, No. 710.
15 N. Keddie, *Roots of Revolution* (London, 1981), pp. 82–3; M. E. Yapp, '1900–21:

The Last Years of the Qajar Dynasty', in (ed.) H. Amirsadeghi, *Twentieth Century Iran* (London, 1977), pp. 20–1. See also G. Lenczowski, *Russia and the West in Iran 1918–1948* (Ithaca, 1949), and D. N. Wilber, *Riza Shah Pahlevi: The Resurrection and Reconstruction of Iran* (New York, 1975).

16 R. W. Ferrier, *The History of the British Petroleum Company* (Cambridge, 1982), pp. 358–71.
17 J. Marlowe, *Iran* (London, 1963), p. 45.
18 Note by A. O. Wood, 11 August 1919, X51/2, BBME. Yapp, '1900–21', p. 21.
19 J. McMurray to S. F. Rogers, 17 February 1920, X51/3, BBME.
20 Keddie, *Roots*, pp. 83–4.
21 Yapp, '1900–1921', p. 22; L. Oliphant to Sir Hugh Barnes, 12 January 1921, FO 371/6399.
22 Telegram from Sir Hugh Barnes to J. McMurray, 21 January 1921, FO 371/6399.
23 Wilber, *Riza Shah Pahlavi*, pp. 42–43; Keddie, *Roots*, pp. 86–7.
24 Keddie, *Roots*, pp. 86–7, and L. P. Elwell-Sutton, 'Reza Shah the Great: Founder of the Pahlavi Dynasty,' in G. Lenczowski (ed.), *Iran Under the Pahlavis* (Stanford, 1978), pp. 12–21.
25 Telegram from J. McMurray, 5 March 1921, X4/18, BBME.
26 Telegram from J. McMurray, 30 August 1921, X19/2, BBME.
27 Sir Hugh Barnes to Under Secretary of State, 6 October 1921, X19/3, BBME.
28 Sir Hugh Barnes to L. Oliphant, 28 December 1921, X19/3, BBME.
29 Telegram to Tehran, 3 December 1921; Telegram from Tehran, 3 December 1921; X19/3, BBME.
30 J. McMurray to S. F. Rogers, 15 February 1922, X19/1, BBME.
31 Telegraphic exchange between Foreign Office and Sir Percy Loraine, 4 and 8 May 1922, FO 371/7816.
32 Foreign Office to Imperial Bank, 10 and 19 June 1922, X19/3, BBME.
33 S. F. Rogers to J. S. R. Wright, 15 June 1922, X19/1; S. F. Rogers to L. Oliphant, 30 June 1922, X19/3, BBME.
34 Foreign Office to Imperial Bank, 11 September 1922, X19/3; Telegram from Tehran, 12 September 1922, X19/1, BBME.
35 S. F. Rogers to J. McMurray, 12 June 1923, X17; BBME.
36 S. F. Rogers to J. McMurray, 14 June 1923, X17, BM 13 June 1923, BBME.
37 Imperial Bank to Foreign Office, 12 and 16 May 1924, X25, BBME.
38 L. Oliphant to Imperial Bank, 18 June 1924, X25, BBME.
39 S. F Rogers to J. McMurray, 20 October 1921, X19/1, BBME.
40 Minute by L. Oliphant, 25 July 1921, FO 371/6447.
41 J. McMurray to S. F. Rogers, 15 February 1922, X19/1, BBME.
42 J. McMurray to S. F. Rogers, 6 August 1922, X19/1, BBME.
43 Marlowe, *Iran*, p. 52.
44 Wilber, *Riza Shah Pahlavi*, p. 68; A. C. Millspaugh, *The American Task in Persia*. (New York, 1925), pp. 40–1.
45 Millspaugh, *American*.
46 Tehran Progress Report, September 1923, BBME.
47 J. McMurray to S. F. Rogers, 19 February 1925, X28/2, BBME.
48 Telegram from Tehran, 4 May 1925; Telegrams to and from Tehran, 9 July 1925, X4/21, BBME.
49 E. Wilkinson to S. F. Rogers, 6 May 1926, X28/2, BBME.
50 Telegram from Tehran, 20 December 1922, X19/2, BBME.
51 Calculated from Bank data and figures for total customs receipts from J. Bharier,

Economic Development in Iran 1900–1970 (London, 1971), p. 71.
52 S. F. Rogers to E. Wilkinson, 15 July 1926, X17, BBME.
53 For alternative figures which differ slightly from the Imperial Bank's because of different dates used and certain omissions, see *Quarterly Reports* of Ministry of Finance, Tehran, 1923–28. These also give figures for loans to government, silver, alimentation and defective coin.
54 S. F. Rogers to J. McMurray, 29 November 1923, X34, BBME.
55 C. F. Warr, Oral History, BBME.
56 See, for instance, figures in Table 13.3, Ferrier, *History*, p. 617.
57 J. McMurray to C. McCaskey, Treasurer General, 17 July 1923, X34, BBME.
58 S. F. Rogers to J. McMurray, 23 October 1924, X34, BBME.
59 E. Wilkinson to S. F. Rogers, 12 November 1925, X17, BBME.
60 Chairman's Statement to Shareholders, December 1923.
61 J. McMurray to S. F. Rogers, 14 May 1924, X17, BBME.
62 *ibid.*
63 J. McMurray to London, 19 March 1925, X34, BBME.
64 *ibid.*
65 E. Wilkinson to S. F. Rogers, 23 April 1927; E. Wilkinson to S. F. Rogers, 25 June 1927, X27, BBME.
66 S. F. Rogers to E. Wilkinson, 13 July 1927, X27; Memorandum by E. R. Lingemann, Acting Secretary in Charge of Commercial Affairs, 5 October 1926, FO 371/11499.
67 E. Wilkinson to S. F. Rogers, 5 February 1927, X17, BBME.
68 BM, 13 April, 16 November and 14 December 1927; 4 January 1928, BBME.
69 E. Wilkinson to S. F. Rogers, 3 December 1927, X17, BBME.
70 J. McMurray to S. F. Rogers, 14 October 1920, X51/3, BBME; Telegram from Tehran, 14 July 1925, FO 371/10848.
71 Telegram from Tehran, 13 January 1923, X4/20. BBME.
72 Finance Committee Report on Barforush, September 1923, X29, BBME.
73 London Confidential Letter, 15 September 1927, V6, BBME.
74 BM, 13 September 1922, BBME.
75 F. H. Johnson, Oral History, BBME.
76 Memorandum by A. H. Wright, 7 November 1924, S11, BBME.
77 Chief Office Progress Report, September 1928, BBME.
78 C. F. Warr, Oral History, BBME.
79 E. Wilkinson to S. F. Rogers, 12 February 1927, V6, BBME.
80 Inspector's Report on Bushire, March 1917, X29, BBME.
81 BM, 22 December 1920, 6 September 1922, BBME.
82 Imperial Bank to Imperial Bank of Canada, 1 July 1926, X36, BBME.
83 Telegram from Tehran, 24 March 1925, X4/21; Results for year to 20 March 1926, V11, BBME.
84 C. F. Warr, Oral History, BBME.
85 *ibid.*
86 *ibid.*
87 F. H. Johnson, Oral History, BBME.
88 S. F. Rogers to E. Wilkinson, 27 July 1926, X28/2, BBME.
89 Tehran Progress Report, March 1923. BBME.
90 Tehran Progress Report, September 1925, BBME.
91 E. Wilkinson to S. F. Rogers, 20 August 1927, X27, BBME.
92 Tehran Progress Report, September 1924, BBME.
93 H. Norman to Foreign Office, 15 April 1921, FO 371/6428.

94 BM, 25 January 1922; Imperial Bank to Foreign Office, 3 September 1924; FO 371/10157.
95 Telegram from Tehran, 1 December 1925, X4/21, BBME.
96 S. F. Rogers to J. McMurray, 22 May 1924, X17, BBME.
97 E. Wilkinson to S. F. Rogers, 28 August 1926, X17, BBME.
98 E. Wilkinson to S. F. Rogers, 21 September 1926, X28/2, BBME.
99 S. F. Rogers to E. Wilkinson, 28 October 1926, X28/2, BBME.
100 E. Wilkinson to S. F. Rogers, 16 November 1926, X28/2, BBME.
101 Chairman's Statement to Shareholders, July 1927; E. Wilkinson to A. C. Millspaugh, 25 January 1927, X87, BBME.
102 Minute by L. Oliphant, 11 July 1927, FO 371/12283.

CHAPTER 8 THE BANK AND THE NEW IRAN 1928–39

1 For more general accounts of this period see A. Banani, *The Modernisation of Iran 1921–41* (Stanford, 1961); G. Lenczowski (ed.), *Iran under the Pahlavis* (Stanford, 1978); and H. Katouzian, *The Political Economy of Modern Iran 1926–1979* (London, 1981), pp. 75–137.
2 D. Joslin, *A Century of Banking in Latin America* (London, 1963), chapter 14; R. S. Sayers, *The Bank of England 1891–1944* (Cambridge, 1976), vol. 1, pp. 263–7.
3 W. J. d'Alton, to E. M. Eldrid, 30 December 1930, X89, BBME.
4 E. Wilkinson to E. M. Eldrid, 11 June 1931, X51/20, BBME.
5 Sir Hugh Barnes to E. Wilkinson, 17 January 1934; E. Wilkinson to E. M. Eldrid, 6 February 1934; E. M. Eldrid to E. Wilkinson, 28 February 1934, Box 32F, BBME.
6 D. Lunn, *The Rags of Time* (Salisbury, 1983), p. 2.
7 C. F. Warr, Oral History, BBME.
8 BM, 8 February 1939, 8 March 1939, BBME.
9 K. Bradford, Oral History, BBME.
10 Sir R. Clive to A. Henderson, 15 May 1930, FO 370/14545.
11 Sir Hilton Young, 'The Key to the Middle East', *The Listener*, 23 July 1930.
12 F. H. H. King, Draft History of the Hongkong Bank.
13 Quoted in R. W. Ferrier, *The History of the British Petroleum Company* (Cambridge, 1982), p. 607.
14 *ibid*, chapter 13; P. J. Beck, 'The Anglo–Persian Oil Dispute 1932–33,' *Journal of Contemporary History* (1975).
15 E. Wilkinson to S. F. Rogers, 7 October 1928, X51/13, BBME.
16 E. Wilkinson to S. F. Rogers, 20 May 1928, X87, BBME.
17 S. F. Rogers to E. Wilkinson, 11 June 1928, X87, BBME.
18 E. Wilkinson to S. F. Rogers, 14 July 1928, X87, BBME.
19 London Confidential Letter, 9 January 1930, Box 28A, BBME.
20 Tehran Confidential Letter, 14 July 1928, X87, BBME.
21 London Confidential Letter, 9 January 1930, Box 28A, BBME.
22 E. Wilkinson to K. Lindenblatt, 20 June 1928, X87, BBME.
23 Sir R. Clive to R. Henderson, 4 April 1930, FO 371/14544.
24 E. Wilkinson to A. H. Teymurtash, 16 December 1928, X51/13, BBME.
25 Memorandum by Sir Henry McMahon, 26 July 1929, Box 32A, BBME.
26 E. Wilkinson to A. H. Teymurtash, 16 December 1928, X51/13, BBME.
27 London Confidential Letter, 29 April 1929, S11, BBME.
28 Treasurer General to Imperial Bank of Persia, 21 May 1929, S11, BBME.

29 Memorandum by J. McMurray, 3 December 1928 enclosed in S. F. Rogers to Messrs Coward Chance & Co., 6 December 1928, Box 21A, BBME.
30 Draft letter from Sir Hugh Barnes to A. H. Teymurtash, 9 April 1929, Box 21A, BBME.
31 London Confidential Letter, 9 August 1929, Box 21A, BBME.
32 Ferrier, *History*, p. 609.
33 London Confidential Letter, 29 April 1929, Box 32F, BBME.
34 London Confidential Letter, 17 October 1929, Box 28A, BBME.
35 London Confidential Letter, 31 October 1929, Box 28A, BBME.
36 E. Wilkinson to S. F. Rogers, 9 November 1929, Box 28A, BBME.
37 BM, 23 October 1929; 15 January 1930; Report of Meeting of Finance Committee, 14 January 1930, HO Box 4, BBME.
38 Tehran Confidential Letter, 21 December 1929, Box 28A, BBME.
39 Tehran Confidential Letter, 17 December 1929, Box 28A, BBME.
40 Telegram from Tehran, 2 February 1930, X4/23, BBME.
41 Telegram from Tehran, 13 February 1930, X4/23, BBME.
42 Dr K. Lindenblatt to E. Wilkinson, 6 March 1930, S/18, BBME.
43 Memorandum by Mr Lingemann on the Exchange Situation, enclosed in Sir R. Clive to Mr A. Henderson, 20 April 1930, FO 371/14544.
44 Telegram from Tehran, 25 February 1930, X4/23, BBME.
45 E. Wilkinson to W. A. Buchanan, 15 March 1930, X62, BBME.
46 Sir R. Clive to Mr A. Henderson, 4 April 1930, FO 371/14544.
47 Interview of Mr Rogers with Minister of Court on March 31, reported by E. R. Lingemann, FO 371/14544.
48 London Confidential Letter, 16 April 1930, X62, BBME.
49 S. F. Rogers to Sir H. Barnes, 22 April 1930, FO 371/14545.
50 Minister of Finance to Imperial Bank of Persia, 13 May 1930, Box 32A, BBME.
51 Memorandum to Ministry of Finance, 21 March 1931; E. Wilkinson to H. E. S. H. Taqizadeh, Ministry of Finance, 4 April 1931, S11, BBME.
52 Tehran Report on Progress, 20 March 1932, BBME.
53 Tehran Confidential Letter, 4 May 1941, enclosing memorandum on revenue transfers; Agreement between Imperial Bank of Persia and Ministry of Finance, 2 July 1930, Box 28A, BBME.
54 E. Wilkinson to E. M. Eldrid, 15 April 1931, X91, BBME.
55 Sir H. Barnes to Sir L. Oliphant, 28 April 1931, Box 32A, BBME.
56 O. A. Butters to E. M. Eldrid, 19 August 1931, S11, BBME.
57 Tehran Confidential Letter, 2 December 1931, X87, BBME.
58 M. Rezun, 'Reza Shah's Court Minister: Teymourtash', *International Journal of Middle East Studies* (1980), vol. 12, No. 2.
59 Tehran Report on Progress, 20 September 1932, BBME.
60 Tehran Report on Progress, 20 March 1933, BBME.
61 R. B. Stobaugh, 'The Evolution of Iranian Oil Policy, 1925–1975', in Lenczowski, *Iran*, pp. 204–6.
62 Katouzian, *Political Economy*, p. 115.
63 J. Bharier, *Economic Development in Iran 1900–1970* (London, 1971), pp. 194–207.
64 W. Floor, *Industrialisation in Iran 1900–1941* (Centre for Middle Eastern and Islamic Studies, University of Durham, Occasional Papers Series No. 23, 1984).
65 Tehran Confidential Letter, 28 February 1933, Box 21C, BBME.
66 Tehran Confidential Letter, 25 March 1933, Box 21C, BBME.
67 London Confidential Letter, 7 April 1933, Box 21C, BBME.
68 London Confidential Letter, 2 August 1935, Box 28A, BBME.

69 Tehran Confidential Letter, 5 August 1935, Box 28A, BBME.
70 Summary of Conversations with General Amir Khosrovi at Bank Melli, 12–21 December 1935, Box 28A, BBME.
71 Tehran Confidential Letter, 18 February 1936, X51/33, BBME.
72 Letter to Minister of Finance, 2 March 1936; Tehran Confidential Letter 3 March 1936, X51/33, BBME.
73 Minister of Finance to Imperial Bank of Iran, 18 April 1938, Box 3, BBME.
74 London Confidential Letter, 22 December 1938, Box 3, BBME.
75 London Confidential Letter, 22 December 1938, Box 3, BBME.
76 Tehran Report on Progress, 20 December 1938, BBME.
77 Lord Kennet, Notes on the position of the Imperial Bank of Iran, 22 December 1935, Box 21, BBME.
78 Telegram from Tehran to London, 14 May 1939, Box 3, BBME.
79 Tehran Confidential Letter, 20 January 1929, enclosing Mr Barry to Chief Manager, 2 January 1929, X51/13, BBME.
80 F. H. Johnson, Oral History, BBME.
81 London Confidential Letter, 30 June 1933, Box 28, BBME.
82 Bharier, *Economic Development in Iran 1900–1970*, pp. 243 gives figures for total bank deposits and advances from 1938.
83 V. L. Walter to F. Hale, 9 March 1941, X51/42, BBME.
84 Floor, *Industrialisation*, p. 24.
85 Sir R. Clive to A. Henderson, 5 October 1929, FO 371/13800.
86 Report on Progress, 20 March 1939, BBME.
87 E. Wilkinson to E. M. Eldrid, 7 October 1930, X91, BBME.
88 Tehran Confidential Letter, 15 September 1936, X51/34, BBME.
89 F. Hale to Richard Costain Ltd, 3 June 1936, Box 32A, BBME.
90 Tehran Report on Progress, 20 September 1939, BBME.
91 Khorramshahr Report on Progress, 20 March 1939, BBME.
92 F. H. Johnson, Oral History, BBME.
93 A. Macqueen, Oral History, BBME.

CHAPTER 9 IRAQ AND INDIA 1915–45

1   For the political background of Iraq in this period, see S. H. Longrigg, *Iraq 1900–1950* (London, 1953) and E. and E. F. Penrose, *Iraq: International Relations and National Development* (London, 1978). British policy is examined in P. Sluglett, *Britain in Iraq* (London, 1976).
2   A. O. Wood to G. Newell, 11 October 1915, X7/17; G. Gardner to S. Rogers, 5 July 1926, X79, BBME.
3   H. Barnes to L. Oliphant, 19 November 1917, L/P S/11/123, India Office Library.
4   Memorandum by Chief Manager to all branches, 6 February 1906, V/8, BBME.
5   G. Newell's comments on A. O. Wood to G. Newell, 30 July 1910, X7/14, BBME.
6   A. O. Wood to G. Newell, 14 December 1916, X7/18, BBME.
7   C. Huson to S. F. Rogers, 21 July 1918, X3/12, BBME.
8   A. H. Wright to A. O. Wood, 20 July 1921, X85, BBME.
9   Memorandum enclosed with Imperial Bank of Persia to Treasury, 28 July 1921, T(Treasury Files) 160/F3537/1. Public Record Office.
10 Memorandum by S. F. Rogers, after conversation with E. C. Dalton, May 1921; File on Charter Changes, Box 21A, BBME.

11 Sir H. Barnes to L. Oliphant, 11 July 1921, FO 371/6447.
12 Imperial Bank of Persia to Treasury, 15 May 1922, T160/584/F3537/1.
13 India Office to Imperial Bank, 4 September 1922, T160/584/F3537/1.
14 Longrigg, *Iraq* and Penrose, *Iraq*.
15 C. Issawi, *An Economic History of the Middle East and North Africa* (London, 1982), p. 31.
16 M. S. Hasan, Foreign Trade in the Economic Development of Modern Iraq (Oxford D. Phil, 1958), pp. 201–2.
17 The IPC was jointly owned by the Anglo–Persian Oil Company, the Shell Group, Compagnie Française des Pétroles, and an American consortium of companies. For the early history of the Mesopotamia oil concessons and industry, see R. W. Ferrier, *The History of the British Petroleum Company* (Cambridge, 1982), vol. 1, pp. 165–75.
18 Issawi, *Economic History*, p. 199. Penrose, *Iraq*, pp. 137–44.
19 India Office to Foreign Office, 8 June 1917, enclosing correspondence between the Viceroy and Sir Percy Cox; H. Barnes to L. Oliphant, 19 November 1917 and Minutes attached; India Office to FO, 1 December 1917; FO 371/3053.
20 A. Macqueen, Oral History, BBME.
21 Basra Report on Progress, September 1923, BBME.
22 Hasan, Foreign Trade, p. 242.
23 *ibid*, pp. 252–8.
24 M. Khadduri, *Independent Iraq* (Oxford, 1951), pp. 181–90; Penrose, *Iraq*, pp. 101–3.
25 Penrose, *Iraq*, p. 150.
26 A. G. Chandavarkar, 'Money and Credit 1858–1947', *Cambridge Economic History of India* (Cambridge, 1983), vol. 2, pp. 775 and 782–3.
27 E. M. Eldrid to G. Weldon, 15 March 1932, X43, BBME.
28 The above paragraph is a very bald summary of highly complex events. For scholarly accounts of the issues raised see B. R. Tomlinson *The Political Economy of the Raj 1914–1947* (London, 1979), chapter 3; K. N. Chaudhuri, 'Foreign Trade and Balance of Payments (1757–1947)', *Cambridge Economic History of India* (Cambridge, 1983), vol. 2, chapter x; B. R. Tomlinson, 'Britain and the Indian Currency Crisis, 1930–2', *Economic History Review* (1979), vol. xxxii.
29 J. Bharier, *Economic Development in Iran 1900–1970* (London, 1971), p. 108. The figures are for imports which were subject to customs duties. The British and Indian figures do not seem to have been disaggregated before 1934.
30 S. F. Rogers to W. Cuthbert, 2 August 1928, X83, BBME.
31 Data for Mercantile Bank's profits from Hongkong Bank Group Archives, Hong Kong. I am grateful to S. W. Muirhead and Margaret Lee for researching this information.
32 E. C. Dalton to S. Rogers, 3 March 1922, X85, BBME.
33 E. C. Dalton to S. Rogers, 2 March 1923, X92, BBME.
34 S. Rogers to W. J. d'Alton, 12 February 1925, X79, BBME.
35 Bombay Report on Progress, March 1925, BBME.
36 Memorandum by A. H. Wright, 28 November 1933, V/8, BBME.
37 Bombay Report on Progress, September 1933, BBME.
38 A. H. Wright to A. O. Wood, 20 July 1921, X85, BBME.
39 BM, 3 December 1930, BBME.
40 Bombay Report on Progress, March 1920, BBME.
41 R. Oakshott to E. M. Eldrid, 6 April 1932, X43, BBME.
42 S. F. Rogers' comments on Bombay Report on Progress, September 1933, BBME.

43 J. R. Winton, *Lloyds Bank 1918–1969* (October, 1982), chapter 6, discusses Lloyds' activities in India, where Lloyds acquired a small branch network in 1923 after the purchase of Cox and Co.
44 Information on Mercantile Bank profits from Hongkong Bank Group Archives.

CHAPTER 10 THE BANKERS 1914–45

1 J. McMurray to S. F. Rogers, 1 September 1921, X51/4; E. Wilkinson to E. M. Eldrid, 21 February 1933, X51/26, BBME.
2 S. F. Rogers to E. Wilkinson, 27 September 1927, X80, BBME.
3 E. M. Eldrid to E. Wilkinson, 18 July 1932, Miscellaneous Box, BBME.
4 S. F. Rogers to A. O. Wood, 15 July 1919, X51/2, BBME.
5 Staff Report, 28 April 1921, Y2/2, BBME.
6 E. Wilkinson to S. F. Rogers, 29 September 1929, X51/15, BBME.
7 D. Lunn, *A Land Called Lost* (Salisbury, 1980), pp. 5–12.
8 J. McMurray to S. F. Rogers, 28 May 1923, X51/6, BBME.
9 J. McMurray to S. F. Rogers, 28 May 1923, X51/6; E. A. Chettle to E. M. Eldrid, 28 July 1930; Miscellaneous Box, BBME.
10 E. M. Eldrid to E. Wilkinson, 18 November 1932, X91, BBME.
11 C. Huson to A. O. Wood, 16 August 1917, X51/1; BBME.
12 BM, 16 February 1938, BBME. ·
13 V. L. Walter to F. Hale, 28 June 1938, X51/38, BBME.
14 V. L. Walter to F. Hale, 26 July 1938, X51/38; Staff Circulars 31 October 1938 and 4 April 1940, BBME.
15 E. S. Jenkins, Oral History, BBME. Interviews with H. Evans and J. D. Hammond.
16 *The Times*, 17 November 1937.
17 S. F. Rogers to A. O. Wood, 30 June 1919, X55; A. O. Wood to S. F. Rogers, 13 March 1919, X51/2; BBME.
18 Lord Kennet to F. Hale, 8 January 1943, S. G. Box 24, BBME.
19 A. Macqueen, Oral History, BBME.
20 E. M. Eldrid to C. E. D. Peters, 21 January 1935, Box 32A, BBME.
21 S. F. Rogers to M. Tagg, 12 December 1929, GM Box A, BBME.
22 L. Oliphant to Sir Hugh Barnes, 18 June 1923; Sir Hugh Barnes to L. Oliphant, 19 June 1923, Box 32A, BBME.
23 E. S. Jenkins, Oral History, BBME.
24 Baghdad Staff Report, 1 February 1930; Mashad Staff Report, 20 September 1930; Y2/4, BBME.
25 Lunn, *A Land*, p. 96.
26 Interview with G. A. Calver, 1984.
27 S. F. Rogers to R. N. Dewar-Durie, 1 January 1924, X92, BBME.
28 R. N. Dewar-Durie to S. F. Rogers, 6 December 1923, X92, BBME.
29 F. H. Johnson, Oral History, BBME.
30 R. Iliff to O. A. Butters, 4 January 1937, X51/35, BBME.
31 E. Wilkinson to E. M. Eldrid, 22 July 1930, X51/18, BBME.
32 S. F. Rogers to J. McMurray, 17 November 1921, X51/5, BBME.
33 BM, 14 March 1934, BBME.
34 S. F. Rogers to E. Wilkinson, 12 December 1929, X83, BBME. Sir T. J. was, of course, Sir Thomas Jackson.
35 A. O. Wood to S. F. Rogers, 21 May 1918, X55, BBME.
36 S. F. Rogers to E. Wilkinson, 27 September 1927, X80, BBME.

37 O. A. Butters to E. M. Eldrid, 3 December 1930, X89, BBME.
38 Staff Report, 30 September 1928, Y3, BBME.
39 F. H. Johnson, Oral History, BBME.
40 C. F. Warr, Oral History, BBME.
41 *ibid.*
42 F. H. Johnson, Oral History, BBME.
43 G. S. Goldsworthy to C. D. Lunn, 15 October 1930, GM's Box A, BBME.
44 J. McMurray to S. F. Rogers, 22 October 1919, X51/3, BBME.
45 J. McMurray to S. F. Rogers, 7 September 1919, X51/3, BBME.
46 C. A. Gardner to S. F. Rogers, 19 January 1926, X79, BBME.
47 H. Evans to V. L. Walter, 29 June 1941, Staff files, BBME.
48 V. L. Walter to F. Hale, 12 November 1944, X51/48, BBME.
49 F. H. Johnson, Oral History, BBME.
50 Dr D. S. Davies to V. L. Walter, 1 January 1942, X51/44, BBME.
51 Manuscript by Vera Evans, pp. 65–70.
52 London Confidential Letter 21 December 1933; Tehran Confidential Letter 16 January 1934, Miscellaneous Box, BBME,.
53 O. A. Butters to F. Hale, 6 October 1936, X51/34, BBME.
54 V. L. Walter to F. Hale, 30 April 1947, X51/54, BBME.
55 R. W. Hunter to S. F. Rogers, 2 May 1928, X83, BBME.
56 A. H. Ebtehaj, Oral History, BBME.
57 *ibid.*
58 *ibid.*
59 E. Wilkinson to E. M. Eldrid, 12 August 1931, X51/21, BBME.
60 V. L. Walter to F. Hale, 14 January 1940, X51/41, BBME.
61 S. F. Rogers to E. Wilkinson, 14 July 1927, X80, BBME.
62 Annual General Meeting of Imperial Bank of Persia, 22 December 1923, BBME.

CHAPTER 11 THE SECOND WORLD WAR

1 D. Lunn, *The Rags of Time* (Salisbury, 1983), p. 27.
2 R. K. Ramazani, *Iran's Foreign Policy 1941–1973* (Charlottesville, 1975), pp. 25–7.
3 Tehran Report on Progress, March 1940, BBME.
4 Tehran Confidential Letter, 26 February 1940, X51/41, BBME.
5 Draft Appendix to the Concession, April 1940. Imperial Bank to the Treasury, 19 June 1940, Box 32B, BBME.
6 Treasury to Imperial Bank, 26 July 1940, Box 32B, BBME.
7 Tehran Confidential Letter of 20 October 1940, enclosing Sterling Agreement between Bank Melli and Imperial Bank with effect from 23 September 1940, X51/42, BBME.
8 Annual Economic Report, British Consulate Mashad, enclosed with A. N. Cumberbatch to Department of Overseas Trade, 19 April 1940, FO 371/24577.
9 Tehran Confidential Letter, 8 April 1940, X51/41, enclosing letter from Consulate General Mashad, BBME.
10 London Confidential Letter, 21 June 1940, X52/16, BBME.
11 Tehran Confidential Letter, 30 March 1941, X51/43, BBME.
12 Tehran Confidential Letter, 14 June 1941, X51/43, BBME.
13 Tehran Confidential Letter, 7 July 1941, X51/43, BBME.
14 Tehran Confidential Letter, 28 July 1941, X51/43, BBME.

15 Ramazani, *Iran's Foreign Policy*, pp. 27–32; G. Lenczowski, *Russia and the West in Iran, 1918–1948* (Ithaca, 1949), pp. 167–74.
16 Copies of all Branch Telegrams despatched from 9 to 28 August, enclosed in Tehran Confidential Letter, 1 September 1941, X51/43, BBME.
17 Tehran Confidential Letter, 8 September 1941, X51/43, BBME.
18 C. F. Warr, Oral History, BBME.
19 F. H. Johnson, Oral History, BBME.
20 Tehran Confidential Letter, 1 September 1941, including diary of events from 23 to 31 August 1941, X51/43, BBME.
21 Tehran Confidential Letter, 6 October 1941, X51/43, BBME.
22 Lenczowski, *Russia and the West*, p. 175.
23 Nikki R. Keddie, *Roots of Revolution* (London, 1981), pp. 114–15.
24 R. Greaves, '1942–1976: The Reign of Muhammad Riza Shah', in (ed.) H. Amirsadeghi, *Twentieth Century Iran* (London, 1977), p. 54.
25 V. L. Walter to Minister of Finance, 28 October 1941, X51/43, BBME.
26 Tehran Confidential Letter, 10 November 1941, X51/43, BBME.
27 Memorandum sent to Commercial Secretary, British Legation, 27 December 1941, enclosed with Tehran Confidential Letter, 28 December 1941, Box 28A, BBME.
28 Telegrams from and to Sir Reader Bullard, 27 and 28 March 1942, FO 371/31403.
29 Tehran Confidential Letter, 30 March 1942, X51/44, BBME.
30 Sir Reader Bullard to Anthony Eden, 6 April 1942, FO 371/31404.
31 Report by Financial Counsellor to the British Legation on Operations on HM Government's Special Account, 6 June 1942. Also minute by N. E. Young, 26 June 1942. FO 371/31405.
32 Foreign Office to British Legation, 9 April 1942, FO 371/31403.
33 Sir Reader Bullard to Anthony Eden, 6 April 1942, FO 371/31404.
34 Report by Financial Counsellor to the British Legation Tehran on Operations on HM Government's Special Account, 6 June 1942, FO 371/31405.
35 US Embassy to Sir M. Peterson, 27 April 1942, FO 371/31404.
36 Copy of Financial Agreement between the United Kingdom and the Imperial Iranian Government, enclosed in E. Holman to Rt. Hon. Anthony Eden, 1 June 1945, FO 371/31405.
37 London Confidential Letter, 29 May 1942, Box 32B, BBME.
38 Report of the Administrator General of the Finances of Iran 20 February–21 March 1943, enclosed with Tehran Confidential Letter, 10 May 1943, X51/46, BBME.
39 Tehran Confidential Letter, 10 August 1942, X51/45, BBME.
40 Tehran Confidential Letter, 14 September 1942, X51/45, BBME.
41 Tehran Confidential Letter, 19 October 1942, X51/45, BBME.
42 P. Avery, *Modern Iran* (London, 1965), pp. 365–6.
43 C. in C. Persia and Iraq to War Office, 13 November 1942, FO 371/31407.
44 Ramazani, *Iran's Foreign Policy*, p. 82.
45 J. Bharier, *Economic Development in Iran 1900–1970* (London, 1971), p. 80.
46 Tehran Confidential Letter, 28 December 1942, X51/45, BBME.
47 A. H. Ebtehaj, Oral History, BBME.
48 Report on Meeting of the Note Reserve Control Board, June 1944, Box 3, BBME.
49 Interviews with Mr Ebtehaj in London 1984 and 1985.
50 Iranian Ministry of Foreign Affairs to HM Legation, 28 December 1942, Box 32B, BBME.

51 Tehran Confidential Letter, 12 October 1942, X51/45, BBME.
52 Tehran Confidential Letter, 8 March 1943, X51/45, BBME.
53 Tehran Confidential Letter, 7 June 1943, X51/46, BBME.
54 V. L. Walter to A. C. Millspaugh, 20 June 1943, Box 3, BBME.
55 Agreement with Bank Melli, 21 September 1943, X51/46, BBME.
56 Memorandum by V. L. Walter, 25 January 1944, Box 32B, BBME.
57 Lenczowski, *Russia and the West*, pp. 263–4, 273–4.
58 A. H. Ebtehaj, Oral History, BBME.
59 V. L. Walter to R. F. Lovee, 29 April 1944 enclosed with Tehran Confidential Letter, 30 April 1944, X51/47, BBME.
60 Ramazani, *Iran's Foreign Policy*, pp. 78–85; G. Lenczowski, *Russia and the West*, pp. 264–9.
61 Report on Meeting of the Note Reserve Control Board, June 1944, Box 3, BBME.
62 Copy of A. C. Millspaugh to A. H. Ebtehaj, 7 October 1944, enclosed with Tehran Confidential Letter, 12 October 1944, X51/48, BBME.
63 Tehran Confidential Letter, 15 October 1944, X51/48, BBME. G. Lenczowski, *Russia and the West*, pp. 268–9.
64 Tehran Confidential Letter, 15 October 1944, X51/48 BBME.
65 The figures given in Table 11.4 are not fully reconcilable with those given in the Bank's overall balance sheet. Some of the discrepancies arise because the Bank's balance sheet also included its operations in London, Iraq and the Gulf as well as Iran.
66 Tehran Confidential Letter, 1 June 1942, X51/44, BBME.
67 Total deposit figures from Bharier, *Economic Development*, p. 243.
68 Tehran Bazaar Progress Report, September 1942, BBME.
69 Tehran Bazaar Progress Report, March 1943, BBME.
70 Advances figures from Bharier, *Economic Development*, p. 243.
71 Hamadan, Ahwaz, and Bushire Progress Reports, March 1945, BBME.
72 Tehran Confidential Letter, 10 June, 1945, X51/49, BBME.

CHAPTER 12 THE END IN IRAN

1 H. Musker to Lord Kennet, 20 April 1950, S.G. Box 24, BBME.
2 Notes on the Visit to Iran and Iraq, 26 November 1946, S.G. Box 24, BBME.
3 Notes on Conversation between Lord Kennet and V. L. Walter, October 1946, S.G. Box 24, BBME.
4 BM, 14 January 1948, BBME.
5 V. L. Walter to F. Hale, 14 May 1946, X51/52, BBME.
6 G. Prior to Lord Kennet, 16 July 1950, X88, BBME.
7 G. Lenczowski, *Russia and the West in Iran* (New York, 1949); R. Ramazani, *Iran's Foreign Policy 1941–1978* (Charlottesville, 1975), S. Chubin and S. Zabih, *The Foreign Relations of Iran* (California, 1974).
8 G. Lenczowski, *The Middle East in World Affairs* (London, 4th edition, 1980), pp. 187–90.
9 Ramazani, *Iran's Foreign Policy*, p. 181. William Roger Louis, *The British Empire in the Middle East 1945–51* (Oxford, 1984), pp. 68–9.
10 Louis, *British Empire*, p. 55.
11 Note to Directors by Lord Kennet, 26 November 1946, S.G. Box 24, BBME.
12 F. H. Johnson, Oral History, BBME.
13 CM's Confidential Circular to British Staff, 29 August 1950, HO21, BBME.
14 Louis, *British Empire*, pp. 638–40.

15 *ibid*, pp. 651–3.
16 A. H. Ebtehaj, Oral History, BBME.
17 Sir W. Eady to Sir O. Sargent, 13 October 1947, FO371/62017.
18 Notes on the Visit to Iran and Iraq, 26 November 1946, S.G. 24, BBME.
19 A. H. Ebtehaj, Oral History, BBME.
20 Tehran Confidential Letter, 16 September 1945, Box 3 Misc, BBME.
21 Tehran Confidential Letter, 30 September 1945, Box 3 Misc, BBME. The Cabinet meeting was on 26 September.
22 Minute by L. F. L. Pyman, 12 September 1947, FO 371/62017.
23 Tehran Confidential Letter, 9 October 1945, Box 3 Misc, BBME.
24 Tehran Confidential Letter, 15 October 1945, Box 3 Misc, BBME.
25 Tehran Confidential Letter, 22 October 1945, Box 3 Misc, BBME.
26 V. L. Walter to F. Hale, 18 February 1946, X51/51, BBME.
27 Foreign Office to Tehran Embassy, Tel. No. 13, 1 March 1946, FO 371/52692.
28 Decree of 13 July, enclosed in Tehran to London, 30 July 1946, X51/52, BBME.
29 V. L. Walter to F. Hale, 6 August 1946, X51/52, BBME.
30 Note to Chairman, 19 September 1946, quoting telegram from V. L. Walter, 17 September, S.G. Box 24, BBME.
31 V. L. Walter to F. A. Ayrton, 30 October 1946; V. L. Walter to F. Hale, 27 November 1946, X51/53, BBME.
32 Telegram from V. L. Walter to F. Hale, 21 January 1947, Box 21C, BBME.
33 *Tehran Mosavver*, 9 May 1947. Signed by the Editor, Mr Dehghan.
34 J. Le Rougetel to Rt. Hon E. Bevin, 20 June 1947; Memorandum by N. S. Roberts, 19 June 1947, FO 371/62054; Lord Kennet to Sir Geoffrey Prior, 30 December 1949, S.G. Box 24, BBME.
35 Tehran Confidential Letter, 22 October 1947, HO21C, BBME.
36 F. H. Johnson, Oral History, BBME.
37 C. F. Warr, Oral History, BBME.
38 Tehran Confidential Letter, 25 August 1948, Box 3 Misc, BBME.
39 V. L. Walter to F. Hale, 10 June 1946, X51/52, BBME.
40 Foreign Exchange Decree, 26 July 1948, Box 89, BBME.
41 Tehran Confidential Letter, 25 August 1948, Box 3 Misc, BBME.
42 *ibid*.
43 Tehran Confidential Letter, 1 September 1948, Box 3 Misc, BBME.
44 *ibid*.
45 Lord Kennet to E. M. Eldrid, 20 September 1948, S.G. Box 24, BBME.
46 A. H. Ebtehaj, Oral History, BBME. Ebtehaj's memory that the figure was £600,000 is mistaken.
47 Minute by J. Chadwick, 31 January 1949, FO 371/75487. Minute by L. Pyman, 29 September 1949, FO 371/68758.
48 C. F. Cobbold to J. Le Rougetel, 26 October 1948, FO 371/68758.
49 J. Le Rougetel to B. A. B. Burrows, 10 November 1948; Minute by R. A. Clinton Thomas, 21 November, on J. Le Rougetel to Rt. Hon. E. Bevin, 16 November 1948; FO 371/68758.
50 Lord Kennet to B. A. B. Burrows, 23 December 1948, S.G. Box 24, BBME; J. Le Rougetel to Rt. Hon. E. Bevin, 2/3 January 1949, FO 371/75487.
51 J. Le Rougetel to Rt. Hon. E. Bevin, 5 January 1949, FO 371/75487.
52 Minute by J. E. Chadwick, 31 January 1949, FO 371/75487.
53 J. Le Rougetel to Foreign Office, 28 January 1949, FO 371/75487.
54 *Times*, 11 January 1949. And see generally, R. B. Stobaugh, 'The Evolution of

Iranian Oil Policy, 1925–75', in G. Lenczowski (ed.), *Iran under the Pahlavis* (Stanford, 1978).

55 J. Le Rougetel to Foreign Office, 29 January 1949, FO 371/75487.
56 Reports of meetings on 19/20 February 1949, S.G. Box 23, BBME.
57 F. A. Ayrton to M. R. Wright, 4 March 1949, FO 371/75488.
58 Lord Kennet and R. V. Buxton to Rt. Hon E. Bevin, 9 March 1949, S.G. Box 23, BBME.
59 Resume of Negotiations by L. C. Payne, 20 June 1949, H.O. 21C, BBME.
60 Translation of decree of 14 March 1949 enclosed in J. Le Rougetel to Rt. Hon. E. Bevin, 16 March 1949; Minute by R. A. Clinton Thomas, 14 March 1949, FO 371/75488.
61 J. Le. Rougetel to Rt. Hon. E. Bevin, 19 July and 16 August 1949, FO 371/75489.
62 *ibid*, enclosing figures prepared by BBIME.
63 Minute by A. Leavett, 28 September 1949, FO 371/75489.
64 Memorandum by C. F. Cobbold, sent by him to Sir H. Wilson Smith, 12 October 1949, enclosed with Treasury to Foreign Office, 27 October 1949, FO 371/75489.
65 G. Kirk, 'The Middle East 1945–1950' in A. Toynbee, ed., *R.I.I.A. Survey of International Affairs 1935–46* (London, 1954), p. 97; Sir Anthony Eden, *Full Circle* (London, 1960), p. 192–3.
66 Minute by A. Leavett, 18 November 1949, on J. Le Rougetel to Foreign Office, 16 November 1949; J. Le Rougetel to Rt. Hon. E. Bevin, 18 November 1949, FO 371/75489.
67 Lord Kennet to L. C. Payne, 22 November 1949, enclosed in F. A. Ayrton to L. C. Payne, 22 November 1949, X52/20, BBME.
68 F. H. Johnson, Oral History, BBME.
69 C. F. Warr, Oral History, BBME.
70 Minute by A. Leavett, 3 December 1949, on J. Le Rougetel to Foreign Office, 1 December 1949, FO 371/75489.
71 Notes on Interview with Prime Minister on 10 June, enclosed in Tehran Confidential Letter, 12 June 1950, HO21B, BBME.
72 Ramazani, *Iran's Foreign Policy*, pp. 188–89.
73 Lord Kennet to Sir Geoffrey Prior, 23 June 1950, X88, BBME.
74 Louis, *British Empire*, pp. 632–7.
75 A. H. Ebtehaj, Oral History, BBME.
76 Tehran Confidential Letter, 31 July 1950, HO 21B, BBME.
77 Sir Geoffrey Prior to Lord Kennet, 10 May 1950, X88, BBME.
78 F. Hale's Memorandum to Lord Kennet, 16 September 1950, S.G. Box 24, BBME.
79 Memorandum by H. Musker, 24 July 1950, S.G. Box 24, BBME.
80 Confidential Memorandum by Lord Kennet, 2 July 1950, S.G. Box 24, BBME.
81 Lord Kennet to Sir Geoffrey Prior, 4 August 1950, X88, BBME.
82 Lord Kennet to Sir Geoffrey Prior, 28 August 1950, X88, BBME.
83 Sir Geoffrey Prior to Lord Kennet, 17 September 1950, X88, BBME.
84 Lord Kennet to Sir Geoffrey Prior, 21 December 1950, X88, BBME.
85 BM, 11 January 1951, BBME.
86 Memorandum by C. F. Warr, 9 January 1951, attached to Sir Geoffrey Prior to Lord Kennet, 9 January 1951, X88, BBME.
87 Sir Geoffrey Prior to Lord Kennet, 9 January 1951, X88, BBME.
88 Lord Kennet to Sir Geoffrey Prior, 1 February 1951, X88, BBME.
89 Tehran Confidential Letter and enclosures, 19 February 1951, HO21B, BBME.

90 Lord Kennet to Sir Geoffrey Prior, 15 March 1951, X88, BBME.
91 Lord Kennet to L. C. Payne, 14 March 1951, S.G. Box 24, BBME.
92 Sir Francis Shepherd to R. J. Bowker, 2 April 1951, FO 371/91484; Lord Kennet to L. C. Payne, 12 April 1951, S.G. Box 24, BBME.
93 Lord Kennet to L. C. Payne, 12 April 1951, S.G. Box 24, BBME.
94 Ramazani, *Iran's Foreign Policy*, p. 205.
95 Lord Kennet to L. C. Payne, 7 August 1951, S.G. Box 24, BBME.
96 C. F. Warr, Oral History, BBME.
97 Lord Kennet to C. F. Warr, 30 August 1951, S.G. Box 24, BBME.
98 J. Fearnley to D. Logan, 27 September 1952, FO 371/98626.
99 Minute by N. D. M. Ross, 16 January 1952, FO 371/98626.
100 Tehran Bazaar Progress Report, March 1948, BBME.
101 J. L. A. Francis, Oral History, BBME.
102 F. H. Johnson, Oral History, BBME.
103 J. L. A. Francis, Oral History, BBME.
104 *ibid.*
105 Tehran Confidential Letter, 4 January 1950, Box 3 Misc, BBME.
106 *ibid*; and C. F. Warr's Report, March 1955, S13, Tehran closure file, BBME.
107 H. Musker to R. V. Buxton, 4 January 1951, S.G. Box 23, BBME.
108 C. F. Warr, Oral History, BBME.
109 R. V. Buxton to Sir James Bowker, 12 December 1952, S.G. Box 23, BBME.
110 Telegram to Tehran, 9 December 1952, HO21, BBME.
111 C. F. Warr's Report, March 1955, S13, BBME.
112 Notes for Directors, 23 March 1955, HO34, BBME.

SELECT BIBLIOGRAPHY

1. PRIMARY SOURCES

This book has drawn extensively on the Archives of The British Bank of the Middle East held by the Hongkong Bank Group. These Archives, which are currently kept by the Hongkong Bank in London, are an immensely rich source of information about the Bank and its environment, and stretch back to 1889. In addition, considerable use has been made of the Oral Histories of selected retired members of staff of the BBME. These Oral Histories, which have been transcribed and are in manuscript form, are also held in the Bank Archives. Information on the Hongkong Bank and the Mercantile Bank of India has been obtained from the Hongkong Bank Group Archives in Hong Kong.

The archives of the British government were also of fundamental importance. The BBME's almost constant contact with the British government has meant that a great deal of information about the Bank is available in the public domain. In the Public Record Office, the Foreign Office papers (series 60, 65, and 371) were the most important sources and Treasury Papers (File 160) were also utilised. In the India Office Library, the records of the Political and Secret Department (L/PS/10 and L/PS/11) and papers of Lord Curzon of Kedleston (F 111) were valuable. In addition to these manuscript sources, the printed Parliamentary Papers and Consular Reports yielded important economic and political information.

A number of private collections of papers were utilised. The most valuable for aspects of this study were the Jardine Skinner Archives and the Papers of Lord Hardinge of Penshurst, both held by the University Library, Cambridge.

Newspapers and journals yielded much information. The *Bankers' Magazine*, *Journal of the Institute of Bankers*, *The Economist*, *The Statist* and *The Times* were all consulted.

2. SECONDARY SOURCES

This bibliography is intended as a guide to the most relevant literature to the history of the BBME, in its political, economic and banking context. It does not list all the sources cited in the text, while it does list some literature which has not been cited but has been read for background information. Persian language sources for the period covered by this book were examined, but were found to yield remarkably little useful information. The few Persian sources of importance have been extensively used by several of the writers listed below, and thus have not been cited separately in this bibliography.

BOOKS AND ARTICLES

Abrahamian, E., *Iran: Between Two Revolutions* (Princeton, 1982).
Agah, M., 'Some Aspects of Economic Development of Modern Iran' (D. Phil. Oxford, 1958).
Anan'ich, B. V. *Rossikoe Samoderzhavi i Vyvoz Kapitalov* (Leningrad, 1975).
Arfa, Gen. H., *Under Five Shahs* (London, 1964).
Avery, P., *Modern Iran* (London, 1965).
Avery, P. & Simmons, J. B., 'Persia on a Cross of Silver 1880–1890', *Middle Eastern Studies*, Vol. 10 (1974).
Bakhash, S., *Iran: Monarchy, Bureaucracy & Reform under the Qajars 1856–1896* (London, 1978).
Balfour, J. M., *Recent Happenings in Persia* (Edinburgh and London, 1922).
Banani, A., *The Modernisation of Iran 1921–41* (Stanford, 1961).
'Banque des Prêts de Perse' (Tabriz, 1904) (Confidential Report).
Baster, A. S. J., *The Imperial Banks* (London, 1929).
Baster, A. S. J., *The International Banks* (London, 1935).
Beck, P. J., 'The Anglo-Persian Oil Dispute 1932–33', *Journal of Contemporary History* (1975).
Bharier, J., 'Banking & Economic Development in Iran', *Bankers' Magazine*, Vol. 204 (1967).
Bharier, J., 'Banking in Iran', *Financial Times World Banking Survey* (1967).
Bharier, J., *Economic Development in Iran 1900–1970* (London, 1971).
Blainey, G., *Gold and Paper* (Melbourne, 1958).
Bogdanov, L. F., *Persii* (St Petersburg, 1909).
Brockway, T. B., 'Britain and the Persian Bubble 1888–1892', *Journal of Modern History*, XIII, (1941).
Browne, E. G., *The Persian Revolution of 1905–1909* (Cambridge, 1910).
Butlin, S. J., *Australia and New Zealand Bank: The Bank of Australasia and the Union Bank of Australia Limited 1828–1951* (London, 1961).
Butler, R. & Bury, J. P. T., eds., *Documents on British Foreign Policy 1919–1939*, First Series, Vols IV and XIII (London, 1963).
Cain, P. J., *Economic Foundations of British Overseas Expansion 1815–1914* (London, 1980).
Calver, G. A., 'The Foundation of the Imperial Bank of Persia', (Hongkong & Shanghai Banking Corporation, 1980).
Chandavarkar, A. G., 'Money and Credit 1858–1947', *Cambridge Economic History of India*, Vol. 2 (Cambridge, 1983).
Chapman, S., *The Rise of Merchant Banking* (London, 1984).
Chaudhuri, K. N., 'Foreign Trade and Balance of Payments (1757–1947)', *Cambridge Economic History of India*, Vol. 2 (Cambridge, 1983).
Chirol, V., *The Middle Eastern Question* (London, 1903).
Chubin, S. & Zabih, S., *The Foreign Relations of Iran* (California, 1974).
Collins, H. M., *From Pigeon Post to Wireless* (London, 1925).
Collis, M., *Wayfoong, The Hongkong and Shanghai Banking Corporation* (London, 1965).
Corley, T. A. B., *A History of the Burmah Oil Company* (London, 1983).
Crossley, Sir J. & Blandford, J., *The DCO Story* (London, 1975).
Curzon, G. N., *Persia and the Persian Question* (London, 1892).
Destrée, A., *Les Fonctionnaires Belges au Service de la Perse 1898–1915* (Liège, 1976).
'Diplomaticus', 'The Imperial Bank of Persia', *Asiatic Quarterly Review* (Oct. 1899).

Dunsterville, L. C., *The Adventures of Dunsterforce* (London, 1921).
Eden, Sir A., *Full Circle* (London, 1960).
Elwell-Sutton, L. P., *Modern Iran* (London, 1941).
Elwell-Sutton, L. P., *Persian Oil: A Study in Power Politics* (London, 1955).
Elwell-Sutton, L. P., 'Reza Shah the Great: Founder of the Pahlavi Dynasty', in Lenczowski, G. (ed.), *Iran Under the Pahlavis* (Stanford, 1978).
Entner, M., *Russo–Persian Commercial Relations 1828–1914* (Florida, 1965).
Evans, V. M., 'Sixty-five Years of Retrospect' (Unpublished).
Fateh, M., *The Economic Position of Persia* (London, 1926).
Fatemi, N. S., *Diplomatic History of Persia, 1917–23* (New York, 1952).
Ferrier, R. W., 'The Development of the Iranian Oil Industry', in Amirsadeghi, H. (ed.), *Twentieth Century Iran* (London, 1977).
Ferrier, R. W., *The History of the British Petroleum Company* (Cambridge, 1982). Vol. 1.
Floor, W. M., 'The Bankers (Sarraf) in Qajar Iran', *Zeitschrift der Deutschen Morgenlandischen Gesellschaft* (1979).
Floor, W. M., *Industrialisation in Iran 1900–1941* (Centre for Middle Eastern and Islamic Studies, University of Durham, Occasional Papers Series No. 23, 1984).
Fraser, D., *Persia and Turkey in Revolt* (Edinburgh & London, 1910).
Frechtling, L. E., 'The Reuter Concession in Persia', *The Asiatic Review*, XXXIV (1938).
Fulford, R., *Glyns 1753–1953* (London, 1953).
Glukhoded, V. S., *Problemy ekonomicheskog razvitia Irana* (Moscow, 1968).
Gordon, Gen. Sir T. E., *A Varied Life* (London, 1906).
Gordon, Gen. Sir T. E., *Persia Revisited* (London, 1896).
Graves, P., *The Life of Sir Percy Cox* (London, 1942).
Greaves, R. L., 'British Policy in Persia 1892–1903', *Bulletin School of Oriental and African Studies*, XXVIII, 1 & 2 (1965).
Greaves, R. L., *Persia and the Defence of India 1884–1892* (London, 1959).
Greaves, R. L., '1942–1976, The Reign of Muhammed Riza Shah' in Amirsadeghi H. (ed.), *Twentieth Century Iran* (London, 1977).
Greaves, R. L., 'Some Aspects of the Anglo–Russian Convention & its working in Persia 1907–14' in *Bulletin School of Oriental and African Studies*, XXXI, 1 & 2 (1968).
Griffiths, P., *A History of the Inchcape Group* (London, 1977).
Griffiths, W. E., 'Iran's Foreign Policy in the Pahlavi Era', in Lenczowski, G. (ed.), *Iran Under the Pahlavis* (Stanford, 1978).
Gupta, R. N., *Iran, An Economic Study* (New Delhi, 1947).
Handbook of Mesopotamia (Admiralty Intelligence, 1918).
Hardinge, A. H., *A Diplomatist in the East* (London, 1928).
Harvey, C. E., *The Rio Tinto Company* (Penzance, 1981).
Hasan, M. S., 'Foreign Trade in the Economic Development of Modern Iraq' (D.Phil, Oxford, 1958).
Henry, J. A., *The First Hundred Years of the Standard Bank* (London, 1963).
Hilton Young, Sir E., 'The Key to the Middle East', in *The Listener* (23 July 1930).
Issawi, C., *An Economic History of the Middle East and North Africa* (London, 1982).
Issawi, C., 'De-industrialisation and Re-industrialisation in the Middle East since 1800', *International Journal of Middle East Studies*, Vol. 12 (1980).
Issawi, C. (ed.), *The Economic History of Iran 1800–1914* (Chicago, 1971).
Issawi, C., 'The Iranian Economy 1925–1973', in Lenczowski, G. (ed.), *Iran Under the Pahlavis* (Stanford, 1978).

Issawi, C., 'The Tabriz–Trabzon Trade 1830–1900: Rise & Decline of a Route', *International Journal of Middle East Studies*, 1, (1970).
Iverson, C., *Monetary Policy in Iraq* (Copenhagen, 1954).
Jackson, S., *The Sassoons* (London, 1968).
Jones, G., *The State and the Emergence of the British Oil Industry* (London, 1981).
Joslin, D., *A Century of Banking in Latin America* (London, 1963).
Katouzian, H., *The Political Economy of Modern Iran 1926–1979* (London, 1981).
Kazemzadeh, F., *Russia and Britain in Persia* (New Haven, 1968).
Keddie, N. R., *Iran: Religion, Politics and Society* (London, 1980).
Keddie, N. R., *Religion and Rebellion in Iran: The Tobacco Protest of 1891–92* (London, 1966).
Keddie, N. R., *Roots of Revolution* (London, 1981).
Keddie, N. R., 'The Origins of the Religious–Radical Alliance in Iran', *Past & Present* (1966).
Kedourie, E. & Haim, S. G. (eds.), *Towards a Modern Iran* (London, 1981).
Kent, M., *Oil and Empire, British Policy and Mesopotamian Oil 1900–1920* (London, 1976).
Khadduri, M., *Independent Iraq – A Study in Iraqi Politics 1932–1950* (London, 1960).
King, F. H. H., 'British Chartered Banking: Climax in the East' in King, F. H. H. (ed.), *Asian Policy, History and Development, Collected Essays* (Centre of Asian Studies, University of Hong Kong, 1979).
Kirk, G., 'The Middle East 1945–50', in Toynbee, A. (ed.), *R.I.I.A. Survey of International Affairs 1935–46* (London, 1954).
Knapp, W., '1921–1941: The Period of Riza Shah', in Amirsadeghi, H. (ed.), *Twentieth Century Iran* (London, 1977).
Kosogovsky, V. A., *Iz Tegeranskogo dnevnika* (Moscow, 1960).
Lambton, A. K. S., *Landlord and Peasant in Persia* (London, 1969).
Lenczowski, G., *Russia and the West in Iran 1918–1948* (Ithaca, 1949).
Lencowski, G., *The Middle East in World Affairs* (London, 1980, 4th ed.).
Lomnitskii, S., *Persiia i Persy* (St Petersburg, 1902).
Longrigg, S. H., *Iraq 1900–1950* (London, 1953).
Longrigg, S. H., *Oil in the Middle East* (London, 1968).
Louis, W. R., *The British Empire in the Middle East 1954–1951* (Oxford, 1984).
Lunn, D., *A Land Called Lost* (Salisbury, 1980).
Lunn, D., *Rags of Time* (Salisbury, 1983).
McDaniel, R. A., *The Shuster Mission and the Persian Constitutional Revolution* (Minneapolis, 1974).
Mackenzie, Sir Compton, *Realms of Silver: 100 Years of Banking in the East* (London, 1954).
McLean, D., *Britain and Her Buffer State* (London, 1979).
McLean, D., 'Finance and "Informal Empire" before the First World War', *Economic History Review*, XXIX (1976).
McLean, D., 'International Banking and its Political Implications: The Hongkong and Shanghai Banking Corporation and the Imperial Bank of Persia, 1889–1914,' King, F. H. H. (ed.), *Eastern Banking* (London, 1983).
Maclean, H. W., *Report on the Condition and Prospects of British Trade in Persia* (Board of Trade, London, 1904).
Mannanov, B., *Iz istorii Russke-iranskih otnoshenii v kontse* XIX–*nachale* XX *reka* (Tashkent, 1964).
Mansfield, P., *Middle East* (Oxford, 1980, 5th ed.).
Marlowe, J., *Iran* (London, 1963).
Marlowe, J., *The Persian Gulf in the Twentieth Century* (London, 1962).

Martin, B. G., *German–Persian Diplomatic Relations 1873–1912* (The Hague, 1959).
Matheson, A., (ed.), *Memorials of Hugh M. Matheson* (London, 1899).
Millspaugh, A. C., *Americans in Persia* (Washington, 1946).
Millspaugh, A. C., *Financial and Economic Situation 1926: Persia* (Tehran and New York, 1926).
Millspaugh, A. C., *The American Task in Persia* (New York, 1925).
Monroe, E., *Britain's Moment in the Middle East 1914–1956* (London, 1963).
Nashat, G., *The Origins of Modern Reform in Iran, 1870–1880* (Chicago, 1982).
Nicolson, H., *Curzon: The Last Phase* (New York, 1939).
Olson, W. J., *Anglo-Iranian Relations during World War I* (London, 1984).
Owen, R., *The Middle East in the World Economy 1800–1914* (London, 1981).
Penrose, E. & E. F., *Iraq: International Relations and National Development* (London, 1978).
Platt, D. C. M., *Finance Trade and Politics in British Foreign Policy 1815–1914* (Oxford, 1968).
Quarterly Reports of the Administrator General of the Finances of Persia 1923–1928 (Tehran).
Rabino, J., 'An Economist's Notes on Persia', *Journal of the Royal Statistical Society*, LXIV (1901).
Rabino, J., 'Banking in Persia', *Journal of the Institute of Bankers*, XIII (1892).
Rabino, J., *Memories 1843–1915* (Cairo, 1937).
Rabino, J., 'On a Proposed Reform of the Egyptian Currency', *Journal of the Institute of Bankers*, VIII (1887).
Rabino, J., 'Some Statistics of Egypt', *Statistical Society Journal*, 47 (1884).
Ramazani, R. K., *Iran's Foreign Policy 1941–1973* (Charlottesville, 1975).
Ramazani, R. K., *The Foreign Policy of Iran 1500–1941* (Charlottesville, 1966).
Rezun, M., 'Reza Shah's Court Minister: Teymourtash', *International Journal of Middle Eastern Studies* (1980).
Roth, C., *The Sassoon Dynasty* (London, 1942).
R.I.I.A. Surveys of International Affairs, 1952 and 1954 (London, 1955 & 1957).
Saikal, A., *The Rise and Fall of the Shah* (London, 1980).
Sayers, R. S., *Lloyds Bank in the History of English Banking* (Oxford, 1957).
Sayers, R. S., *The Bank of England 1891–1944* (Cambridge, 1976) Vol. 1.
Schindler, Gen. Sir A. H., 'Persia', in *Encyclopaedia Britannica* (1911 ed.).
Seyf, A., 'Some Aspects of Economic Development in Iran, 1800–1906' (Ph.D. Reading, 1982).
Shuster, W. Morgan, *The Strangling of Persia* (London, 1912).
Sluglett, P., *Britain in Iraq* (London, 1976).
Spalding, W. F., *Eastern Exchange, Currency & Finance* (London, 1924, 4th edn.).
Spender, J. A., *Weetman Pearson, First Viscount Cowdray 1856–1927* (London, 1930).
Stobaugh, R. B., 'Evolution of Iranian Oil Policy 1925–8' in G. Lenczowski (ed.), *Iran Under the Pahlavis* (Stanford, 1978).
Storey, G., *Reuter's Century* (London, 1951).
Sykes, C., *Wassmus: 'The German Lawrence'* (London, 1936).
Sykes, P. M., *History of Persia* (London, 1958, 3rd ed.).
Tagieva, S. A., *Natsional'no – osvoboditel'noe dvizhenie v Iranskom Azerbajane v 1917–1920* (Baku, 1956).
Ter-Gukasov, G. I., *Politicheskie i ekonomicheskie interesy Russii v Persii* (Petrograd, 1916).
'The New Oriental Bank Corporation: A Lesson in Bad Banking', *Bankers' Magazine* (1894).

'The Story of the Euphrates Company', *The Near East and India* (1932).

Thobie, J., 'Les Choix Finances de 'L'Ottomane' en Mediterranée Orientàle de 1856 à 1939', *Colloqua International: Banque Investissement dans les pays Mediterranée à l'epoque contemporaine* XIXè *et* XXè *siècles* (Marseilles, 1982).

Tomlinson, B. R., 'Britain and the Indian Currency Crisis, 1930–32', *Economic History Review* (1979).

Tomlinson, B. R., *The Political Economy of the Raj 1914–1947* (London, 1979).

Tyson, G., *100 Years of Banking in Asia and Africa* (London, 1963).

Walter, V. L., 'A Brief History of the British Bank of the Middle East in Iran', *Journal of the Iran Society* (1954).

Whigham, H. J., *The Persian Problem* (London, 1903).

Wilber, D. N., *Iran* (Princeton, 1948).

Wilber, D. N., *Iran, Past, Present and Future* (Princeton, 1967 edn).

Wilber, D. N., *Riza Shah Pahlavi: The Resurrection and Reconstruction of Iran* (New York, 1975).

Wilson, Sir A. T., *Persia* (London, 1932).

Wilson, Sir A. T., *South-West Persia: A Political Officer's Diary 1907–1914* (London, 1941).

Winton, J. R., *Lloyds Bank 1918–1969* (Oxford, 1982).

Wolff, H. D., *Rambling Recollections* (London, 1908).

Wright, D., *The English Amongst the Persians* (London, 1977).

Wright D., *The Persians Amongst the English* (London, 1985).

Yaganegi, E. B., *Recent Financial and Monetary History of Persia* (New York, 1934).

Yapp, M. E., '1900–21: The Last Years of the Qajar Dynasty', in Amirsadeghi, H. (ed.), *Twentieth Century Iran* (London, 1977).

INDEX

HONGKONG BANK GROUP HISTORY SERIES

General Editor: FRANK H H KING

Eastern Banking: essays in the history of The Hongkong and Shanghai Banking Corporation, edited by FRANK H H KING (Athlone Press).

Banking and Empire in Iran: The History of The British Bank of the Middle East, Volume 1 by GEOFFREY JONES.

Banking and Oil: The History of The British Bank of the Middle East, Volume 2 by GEOFFREY JONES.

The History of The Hongkong and Shanghai Banking Corporation: by FRANK H H KING (in preparation).

Catalogue of the papers of Sir Charles Addis, by MARGARET HARCOURT WILLIAMS, with an introduction by Roberta A Dayer, (in preparation).